MW01051772

FLIGHT INSTRUCTOR MANUAL

JEPPESEN.
Sanderson Training Products

55 Inverness Drive East, Englewood, CO 80112-5498
International Standard Book Number 0-88487-275-0
Printed in Canada

JS314530—000

Acknowledgments

This manual could not have been produced without the tireless commitment of the Guided Flight Discovery (GFD) team members listed below. Additional personnel in Jeppesen's Aviation Courseware Development department deserve special thanks for assuming responsibility for other projects so the GFD team members could focus their efforts on the creation of this text.

Project Editor
Liz Kailey

Associate Editors
Julie Boatman
Chad Pomering

Primary Writers
Eric Anderson
Jeff Cabell
Jug Eastman
Jerry Farrell
Julie Goodwin Rife
Chuck Stout
Anthony Werner
Pat Willits

Technical Support
Richard Bascobert
Marsha Beardsley
Michelle Gable
Judi Glenn
Kay Jesse
Kellie Reddick
Richard Snyder

Media Productions Manager
Rich Hahn

Lead Artist
Jay Weets

Artists
Paul Gallaway
Richard Patterson
Larry Montano
Scott Saunders

Photographers
Dave Chance
Gary Kennedy
Ramses Mellette

Welcome to Guided Flight Discovery

Guided Flight Discovery is a new concept in pilot training designed to make your professional training exciting and enjoyable. This revolutionary system is comprehensive, application-oriented, and it leads you logically through essential aeronautical knowledge areas. The program exposes you to a variety of useful, interesting information which will enhance and expand your understanding of the professional world of aviation.

While each element of the Guided Flight Discovery Pilot Training System may be used separately, the effectiveness of the materials can be maximized by using all of the individual components in a systems approach. To help you efficiently organize your studies and get the most out of your training, Guided Flight Discovery incorporates cross-references which are used to direct you to related Guided Flight Discovery study materials. The main components of the Flight Instructor Program are described below.

Flight Instructor Manual

The *Flight Instructor Manual* is your primary source for initial study and review. The text contains complete and concise explanations of the advanced concepts and ideas that every professional instructor needs to know. The subjects are organized in a logical manner to build upon previously introduced topics. Subjects are often expanded upon through the use of Discovery Insets, which are strategically placed throughout the chapters. POV Insets provide examples, from a flight instructor's point-of-view, of how learning and teaching concepts can be applied in real-world training situations. Periodically, human factors principles are presented in Human Element Insets, to help you teach your students about how their minds and bodies function in flight. Throughout the manual, concepts which directly relate to FAA test questions are highlighted by FAA Question Insets. These insets include all FAA questions that are specific to flight instruction. Questions concerning private, instrument, or commercial-level knowledge areas are covered in the *Private Pilot* and *Instrument/Commercial Manuals*. Additionally, you can evaluate your understanding of material introduced in a particular section by completing the associated review questions at the end of each section and comparing your answers to those provided in Appendix A. A more detailed explanation of the text and how to use its unique features is contained in the section entitled "Using the Manual" starting on page x.

Flight Instructor Syllabus

The *Flight Instructor Syllabus* is designed to meet or exceed the requirements of Title 14, Code of Federal Regulations (14 CFR) Part 141, for a flight instructor certification course and additional flight instructor rating courses. An applicant may enroll in the three instructor courses consecutively and become a fully qualified certificated flight instructor (CFI), with instrument and multi-engine airplane instructor privileges, at the conclusion of the training programs. An applicant who has already acquired a basic flight instructor certificate may acquire either or both of the additional instructor ratings. The Basic and Instrument Instructor Courses utilize single-engine land airplanes while the Multi-Engine Instructor Course utilizes multi-engine land airplanes with wing-mounted engines.

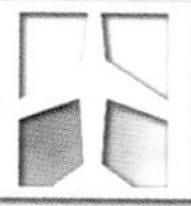

Flight School Support Materials

Flight schools which use the Guided Flight Discovery Pilot Training System may provide a variety of additional resources and instructional support materials. Guided Flight Discovery flight school support materials are designed specifically to provide you with a well-administered, quality training program. The materials help foster an environment which maximizes your potential for understanding and comprehension on your way to becoming a professional flight instructor. Some of these resources are described below.

Flight Instructor Videos

The Flight Instructor Videos are an excellent resource for use in the classroom. The dynamic videos use state-of-the-art graphics and animation, as well as dramatic aerial photography to help easily explain complex ideas.

PC-Based Aviation Training Device (PCATD)

Flight schools may also provide access to Jeppesen Sanderson's PC-based aviation training device. The FlitePro PCATD is designed specifically for instrument training and skill enhancement, and is a great tool for giving your students a head start on certain instrument maneuvers and procedures.

Flight Training Device (FTD)

A flight training device (FTD) may be incorporated by flight schools as a means to provide simulated flight training in a controlled environment. Use of the Jeppesen Ascent Trainer allows you to train your students in procedures that may be too risky or unrealistic to practice in flight.

Instructors Guide

The *Instructors Guide* is available for use by you as a flight instructor and by flight school operators. The Flight Instructor Insert for the *Instructors Guide* helps you effectively implement the Guided Flight Discovery Flight Instructor Courses.

Preface

The purpose of the *Flight Instructor Manual* is to provide you with the most complete explanations of aeronautical concepts for professional pilots. The manual features colorful illustrations, full-color photos, and a variety of innovative design techniques. The *Flight Instructor Manual* and other Guided Flight Discovery materials are closely coordinated to make learning fun and effective. To help you organize your study, the *Flight Instructor Manual* is divided into two parts:

Part I — The Journey Begins

An introduction to the fundamentals of instruction is the basis of Part I. In Chapter 1 — The Foundation of Training, you become familiar with theories of learning and how to properly communicate with your students. Teaching methods, lesson plans, and evaluation of student performance are all topics covered in Chapter 2 — The Art and Science of Teaching. Chapter 3 — Exploring Human Factors discusses the physiological and behavioral aspects of flight, and how to effectively teach aeronautical decision-making concepts to your students.

Part II — From Passion to Profession

Specialized information for the various flight instructor ratings is the focus of Part II. Chapter 4 — Becoming an Instructor covers subjects ranging from the privileges you have as an instructor to impressing a positive attitude toward flight safety upon your students. In Chapter 5 — The Basic Instructor you will gain the necessary knowledge to teach private and commercial students, in addition to providing some specialized forms of instruction. Chapter 6 — The Advanced Instructor concludes Part II by supplying the information you need to instruct instrument, multi-engine, and flight instructor applicants.

Table of Contents

APPENDICES

How the Manual Works

The Flight Instructor Manual is structured to highlight important topics and concepts and promote an effective and efficient study/review method of learning. To get the most out of your manual, as well as the entire Guided Flight Discovery Pilot Training System, you may find it beneficial to review the major design elements incorporated in this text.

PART I

Just as there are no natural-born pilots, neither are there natural-born instructors. Teaching, much like flying, is an acquired skill that must be learned and practiced unfailingly to achieve perfection. In helping your students take those first few steps on their journey into the aviation world, you will be beginning your own journey into the world of teaching. The skills you will need to effectively lead your students are different than those you have acquired in your flying career up to this point. Part I will supply you with the knowledge you need to be an effective and competent flight instructor. Beginning with *The Foundation of Training*, you are introduced to basic teaching tools and theories. Next, you will apply these concepts in *The Art and Science of Teaching*, where you delve into a variety of instructional methods. In *Exploring Human Factors*, you will gain knowledge of the behavior patterns and decision-making techniques relevant to both you and your students.

Learning Objectives

Learning objectives are provided at the beginning of each part to help you focus on important concepts.

CHAPTER 1

FOUNDATIONS OF LEARNING

Flight Instructor
Volume 1 — Fundamentals of Instruction

Cross-Reference Icon

A cross-reference icon is included at the beginning of each chapter to direct you to the corresponding video which supports and expands on introduced concepts and ideas.

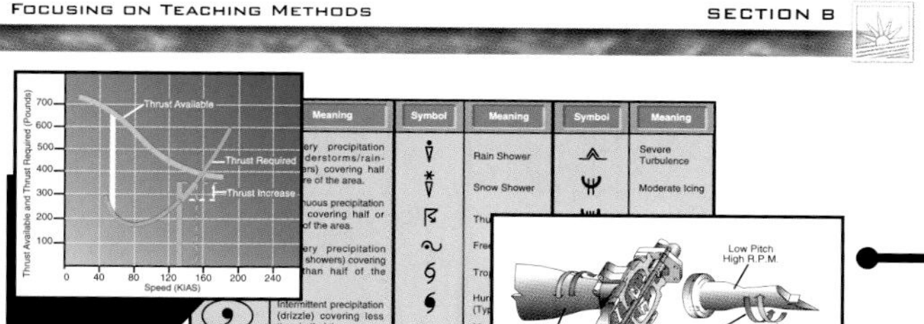

Figure 2-31. Charts, diagrams, and graphs can be used effectively to show relationships, chronological changes, distributions, components, and flow. The kind you select depends upon the type of information you want to convey, and their location and handling should be planned in advance so you can incorporate them smoothly into your presentation.

ENHANCED TRAINING MATERIALS

While you need to be familiar with all regulatory requirements applicable to the certificates and ratings you teach, you may use instructor-oriented training materials which are created to help you comply with regulations. These tools ensure you accomplish the required training, make the necessary endorsements, and use proper documentation. Whether you work as an independent instructor or you are employed by a flight school, you must make sure that each student performs a number of important tasks to specific standards. Enhanced training materials, which include these standards, can help you complete this step.

One example of these materials is a syllabus, which not only presents a course of training in a logical, building-block sequence, but has provisions for your endorsements and record keeping. Areas for logging training time can be incorporated so that the syllabus can also serve as a record for you, your students, or your school. In case your student transfers to another school or instructor, the record can be reviewed and your student's status easily assessed by the new instructor. Another example of enhanced, instructor-oriented material for pilot training is a maneuvers guide or handbook, which includes the practical test standards for each maneuver or procedure described. [Figure 2-32]

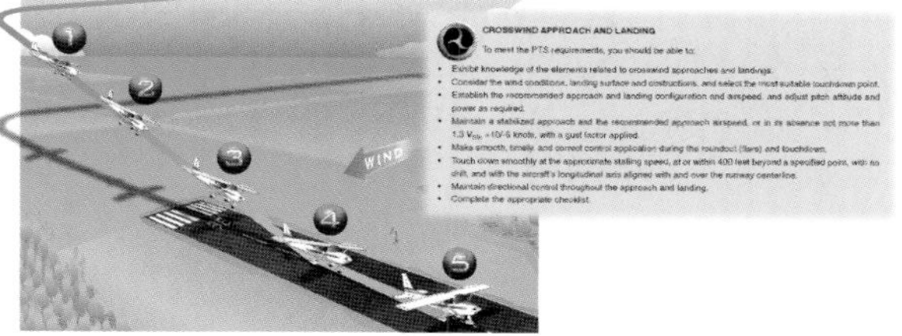

Figure 2-32. By using a maneuvers manual, your student learns from the beginning how to perform the maneuver or procedure to standard, and you need not refer to another publication to evaluate your student's progress.

Full-Color Graphics

The full-color graphics used throughout the text are carefully designed to make difficult concepts easy to understand.

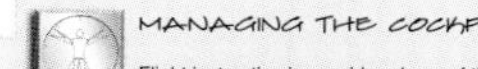

MANAGING THE COCKPIT

Flight instruction is considered one of the safest operations in general aviation. However, it takes care on the part of both the instructor and student to ensure the safety of a particular flight, especially during phases of high workload. During a period from January 1988 to December 1996, the highest concentration of instructional incidents, as reported to the ASRS (Aviation Safety Reporting System), occurred within the airport environment, including the airspace within 10 nautical miles and below 1,000 feet AGL.

The majority of flight instruction at all levels is airport-centered. During primary instruction, students focus on perfecting landings and traffic patterns, while advanced students may concentrate on instrument approaches. While landing procedures require some of the most intense focus from both the flight instructor and student, alertness to ATC transmissions and other traffic is vital as well during this phase of the flight. One common problem lies in how flight instructors must balance the desire to allow students to make and correct their own mistakes with overall flight safety and compliance with ATC directives. If flight instructors are not able to properly divide their attention between instructing their students and maintaining communication with ATC, situational awareness can be lost. This is clearly illustrated by the following ASRS report.

"We took off on (Runway) 24 instead of 30, as the tower subsequently informed us. As I reviewed the event later, with my student and in my own mind, I realized how I may have added to the uncertainty. I was busy pointing out airport markings and critiquing the flight to this point. The priority should have been communications with the tower and standard procedure."

You should not allow student errors to develop to a point where you cannot recover from them without compromising safety or violating FARs. Also, limit critiques to non-critical phases of the flight. For example, when practicing landings, you may either save critiques for a relatively low-workload portion of the traffic pattern, or taxi back between landings so you can discuss your student's performance while the airplane is stopped in a runup or ramp area. This will allow you to focus on critical communication with ATC and on other traffic, as well as keep your student from having to divide attention between listening to your critique and controlling the airplane.

student as you give practice instruction. Receiving a checkout in the right seat takes some adjustment, as the familiar cockpit temporarily becomes unfamiliar.

ORIENTATION

The cockpits of most light aircraft are designed with the single pilot in mind. If you progress to larger aircraft built for two-pilot crews, you will find more redundant systems and controls that can be easily accessed from the right seat. However, in the average training airplane, some controls are difficult to reach from the instructor's side. Normally, all of the flight instruments, the ignition switch, the primer, the electrical switches, and often the engine instruments, are located on the left side of the panel. Additionally, during your past experience, you likely became used to operating the throttle, mixture, and propeller control with your right hand, and now you must switch to using your right hand for aircraft control and your left hand to operate the power controls. Though these differences may not seem large taken separately, together they create an environment where at first you may easily lose orientation.

When you are in the right seat, your ability to accurately read the instruments on the left side of the panel diminishes. Since the instruments are offset from the center of your visual field, you must shift your eyes or move your head to see the displays. Another common problem that may be encountered is parallax resulting from the distance between an instrument's needle and the surface of the scale. Parallax is the apparent displacement of an object, if viewed first from one position, and then from another. For example, your interpretation of an airspeed, altitude, or heading when viewing the

Human Element Insets

Human Element Insets are presented in Part II to explore how the human factors aspect of flight can be taught to students. The topics, ranging from physiology to decision making, are presented with emphasis on flight-related applications.

DISCOVERING LEARNING THEORIES — SECTION A

Caution: Student Overload Imminent

Picture yourself in the practice area on the third lesson with your student. Since you have many things you need to cover, you may feel compelled to provide as much information as possible. This is quite natural, yet you might not be getting as much across as you think.

Assume you intend to introduce slow flight to your student. One way to approach this task would be to simply talk your student through the maneuver. However, your student must concentrate on aircraft control, rudder coordination, heading, altitude, airspeed, aircraft position, and collision avoidance, as well as try to listen to you. In most cases, something will be overlooked, and it might be what you are saying. A better way to introduce this maneuver and stay within your student's working memory capacity is to take the controls and demonstrate the maneuver. By relieving your student of the flying tasks, you are allowing more attention to be paid to your instruction and you are giving your student time to process the necessary information for long-term storage.

After you have demonstrated the maneuver, ask your student to talk you through it. This again helps your student process the information. Once this is done correctly, transfer the controls back to your student to perform the maneuver with as little input from you as possible. Once the maneuver is completed, take the controls again, and critique your student. As your student gains proficiency and more tasks become automatic, the need to take the controls becomes less and your student is more receptive to your instruction while flying the airplane.

CONSTRUCTIVISM

The concept of constructivism provides a unique way of thinking about how students learn. Behaviorism and cognitive theory assume all learners are the same and knowledge is simply given to students. Constructivism is based upon the idea that learners construct knowledge through the process of discovery as they experience events and actively seek to understand their environment. To employ constructivism, your role shifts from the transmitter of information to the creator of experiences. Instead of presenting material in a traditional lecture form, you guide students through the use of well-planned exercises or problems and they construct knowledge based on these experiences. [Figure 1-11]

Help your students become aware of how they learn.

Use complex learning settings that utilize realistic activities.

Allow your students to help guide their learning.

Provide an opportunity for your students to examine material from many different perspectives to gain better understanding.

Figure 1-11. There are some basic guidelines for using constructivism to enhance learning.

PERCEPTIONS AND INSIGHTS

Perceptions, which occur when meaning is given to sensations, are the basis for all learning. The sensation of hearing a landing gear warning horn has no meaning until your student can associate it with its purpose. Perceptions are often based on how people

POV Insets

POV Insets are included in each section of Part I to provide examples from a flight instructor's point of view, of how learning and teaching concepts can be applied in real-world training situations. By exploring these scenarios, you will be better able to recognize problems with your students and offer effective solutions.

Color Photographs

Color photographs are included to enhance learning and improve understanding.

CHAPTER 2 — THE ART AND SCIENCE OF TEACHING

PRESENTATION

Presentation simply means something that is presented. It could be a play, a gift, or an instructional lesson. You normally have a choice of several methods of presentation, especially during ground training sessions. An important consideration is the number of students you have. Other considerations include the type of training aids or equipment available, the subject matter, and the objectives of the training. Presentation methods include cooperative learning sessions, case studies, and computer-based multimedia programs, as well as the more traditional ways: the lecture method, the demonstration-performance method, and the guided discussion. A variety of presentation methods will be addressed in greater depth later in Section B of this chapter.

APPLICATION

Application is where your students use what you have presented. After a classroom presentation, you can ask your students to explain the new material or to perform a procedure or operation that has just been demonstrated. For example, after you have demonstrated and explained the use of the flight computer, ask your students to use the flight computer to compute groundspeed, wind correction angle, or time enroute. In most instructional situations, your explanation and demonstration activities are alternated with your students' performance efforts.

Very often you will have to interrupt your student's efforts and provide feedback in the form of corrections or further explanations and demonstrations. This is necessary because it is very important that each student perform the maneuver or operation the right way the first few times. This is when habits are established. Faulty habits are difficult to correct and must be addressed as soon as possible. You must be aware of this problem, particularly during flight instruction, since students eventually will do a lot of their practice during solo flight operations. Only after reasonable competence has been demonstrated should students be allowed to practice certain maneuvers on solo flights. Students can then practice maneuvers again and again until correct performance becomes almost automatic. However, keep in mind that periodic review and evaluation is necessary to ensure that your students have not acquired any bad habits.

Instruction for the Birds

Teaching students a complex topic such as aerodynamics, for example, is challenging, and making sure they have a good understanding of the subject is even more difficult. Now imagine the difficulty in teaching students that are not human, but avian. Animal behaviorist Irene Pepperberg is doing just that with African Grey parrots.

To 'parrot' means to simply repeat information, whether or not the information is actually understood does not matter. But Pepperberg's parrots, Griffin and Alex, are not just mimicking their teacher, they actually understand what they are saying. For example, when presented with two triangles, one yellow and one blue, and asked what is the same about them, Alex responds *"Shape."* When asked what is different he responds, *"Color!"* Pepperberg has developed several other tests to teach Alex more than 50 different objects, 5 shapes, and 7 colors in addition to the meanings of *"same"* and *"different"*—a crucial step in human intellectual development.

If you doubt that these birds do not understand the meaning of their words, consider the following example. During a recent session with the two parrots, Griffin, while trying to say *"paper,"* sputtered *"ay-uhr."* A seemingly frustrated Alex then ordered the younger bird to *"Talk clearly!"*

2-6

Discovery Insets

Discovery Insets are included throughout all sections, to expand on ideas and concepts presented in the accompanying material. The information provided in each Discovery Inset varies, but is designed to enhance your understanding of the worlds of teaching and aviation. Examples include National Transportation Safety Board investigations, aviation history, and thought-provoking questions and answers.

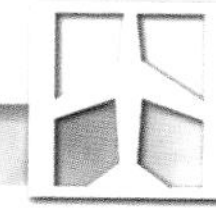

DISCOVERING LEARNING THEORIES SECTION A

RECENCY

Things most recently learned are best remembered. It is easy for students to remember a procedure immediately after you demonstrate it, but without additional review, they most likely will not recall this procedure during a subsequent lesson a week later. As illustrated earlier by the classic forgetting curve, the more time that occurs between the learning event and the attempt to recall, the greater the likelihood of forgetting. The principle of recency often determines the relative position of lectures within a course syllabus. [Figure 1-25]

The principle of recency often determines the relative position of lectures within a course syllabus.

STAGE I
FLIGHT LESSON 7
DUAL — LOCAL
RECOMMENDED SEQUENCE:
LESSON OBJECTIVES:
REVIEW:
FULL PANEL INSTRUMENT
PARTIAL PANEL INSTRUMENT
COMPLETION STANDARDS:
POSTFLIGHT DISCUSSION AND PREVIEW OF NEXT LESSON
STUDY ASSIGNMENT:

Figure 1-25. To enhance retention, key elements need to be reinforced at the end of each lesson and reviewed at the beginning of the next.

SUMMARY CHECKLIST

✓ Learning is defined as a persisting change in behavior resulting from experience with the environment, which cannot be attributed to natural growth.

✓ The theory of behaviorism is based on the study and measurement of observable behavior.

✓ Operant conditioning generally consists of three phases: cues to initiate the behavior are provided, the behavior is actually performed, and consequences associated with that performance are received.

✓ Reinforcement is a consequence that strengthens behavior. Four types of reinforcement have been identified that you can use as a flight instructor: positive reinforcement, negative reinforcement, extinction, and punishment. The use of positive reinforcement to help students learn is normally the most successful approach.

✓ The primary methods of teaching behaviors are shaping and chaining. Each time your students demonstrate the correct behavior, you provide positive reinforcement which helps shape, or develop, the correct behavior. Chaining combines behaviors students already know to assemble more complex behaviors.

✓ Cognitive theory involves mental processes, such as decision making and problem solving which are difficult to observe or measure. If your students can explain how and why they did something, you can gain valuable insight into the mental processes used.

✓ The social interaction model stresses the concept that students learn to shape their conduct after the prevailing behavior displayed in their environment.

FAA Question Insets

Information which relates directly to FAA test questions appears in tan insets. In addition to highlighting important concepts, the FAA Question Insets provide a good review tool when preparing for the Flight and Ground Instructor computerized tests. Questions specific to flight instruction are included in the Flight Instructor Manual; questions covering private, instrument, or commercial-level knowledge are covered in the Private and Instrument/Commercial Manuals.

Summary Checklists

Summary Checklists are included at the end of each section to help you identify and review the major points introduced in the section.

CHAPTER 2 THE ART AND SCIENCE OF TEACHING

✓ When you develop written tests for your students, you are usually more concerned with criterion-referenced testing than norm-referenced testing. Criterion-referenced testing measures students' performance against a standard and norm-referenced testing measure students' performance against other students.

✓ Written test questions include two general categories: the supply-type and the selection-type. Selection-type tests are typically better suited toward aviation training and evaluation, primarily because they are highly objective.

✓ Some examples of selection-type questions include true-false, multiple-choice, and matching. Multiple-choice questions are probably the most common type that you will use to evaluate students.

✓ Performance tests are good for evaluating competency with respect to an operation, a procedure, or a process. A practical test is a good example of a performance test.

✓ You should continually evaluate your CFI skills. Often you can gain insight into your own performance when you evaluate your students' performance.

KEY TERMS

Critiques	Discrimination
Evaluations	Criterion-Referenced Testing
Oral Quizzing	Norm-Referenced Testing
Written tests	Supply-Type Test Items
Reliability	Selection-Type Test Items
Validity	True-False
Objectivity	Multiple-Choice
Comprehensiveness	Matching
Usability	

QUESTIONS

1. Describe the difference between a critique and an evaluation.
2. True/False. Your critique should not contain any negative feedback because negativity compromises the principle of effect, and little learning will result.
3. Name two advantages that a written critique has over oral methods.
4. True/False. You normally evaluate your students before, during, and after a lesson.
5. What is a characteristic of an effective oral quiz question?
   A. It has a measurable answer.
   B. It should not be challenging because your student may become frustrated.
   C. It should be broad enough to evaluate a wide scope of your student's knowledge.

2-80

Key Terms

For ease of recognition and quick review, key terms are highlighted in red type when they are first introduced and defined. A list of key terms is included at the end of each section.

Questions

Questions are provided at the end of each section to help you evaluate your understanding of the concepts which were presented in the accompanying section. Several question formats are provided including completion, matching, true/false, and essay. Perforated answer sheets, which are organized by chapter, are included at the back of the text.

Passing the Torch

Courtesy of National Archives

A pilot was surrounded by beauty of earth and sky. He brushed treetops with the birds, leapt valleys and rivers, explored the cloud canyons he had gazed at as a child. Adventure lay in each puff of wind.

— Charles Lindbergh

earth and sky

The airplane is a bunch of sticks and wires and cloth, a tool for learning about the sky and about what kind of person I am when I fly. An airplane stands for freedom, for joy, for the power to understand, and to demonstrate that understanding. Those things aren't destructible.

— Richard Bach, *Nothing by Chance*

I am alive.

the lure of flying

I am alive. Up here with the song of the engine and the air whispering on my face as the sunlight and shadows play upon the banking, wheeling wings, I am completely, vibrantly alive. With the stick in my right hand, the throttle in my left, and the rudder beneath my feet, I can savor that essence from which life is made.

— Steven Coonts, *FLY! A Colorado Sunrise, a Stearman, and a Vision*

I have often said that the lure of flying is the lure of beauty. That the reason flyers fly, whether they know it or not, is the aesthetic appeal of flying.

— Amelia Earhart

Do any of these thoughts express how you feel about flying? If they do, then you understand what a truly special gift the ability to fly is. You now have the opportunity to grant this gift of joy, freedom, beauty, adventure, and power to others. As a certificated flight instructor (CFI), you hold a unique place in the world of aviation. Take a moment to stop and think, and you will realize that each one of the individuals quoted above was taught to fly by someone. These illustrious men and women had a source from which they drew their inspiration and motivation to break free of the bonds of gravity. When you become a CFI, you can be that source of inspiration and pass the torch of your passion for flight on to the next generation of aviators.

The mediocre teacher tells. The good teacher explains. The superior teacher demonstrates. The great teacher inspires.

— William A. Ward

the power to inspire

As a teacher, you possess great power. You not only have the ability to impart knowledge, you have the power to inspire, and make a student's dreams come true. From the young man who lay on the grass as a little boy, looking to the sky and longing to be a part of it, to the woman who lives for the challenges that pursuing a career in aviation provides, you hold the key to the achievement of their goals.

By teaching, you change lives outwardly and inwardly. You open up a marvelous world of adventure and discovery to your students. You are not only teaching students new skills, you are helping them grow, change, and perhaps discover something wondrous that can add new dimension to their lives. Learning to fly can increase self-confidence, spark imagination, or provide a much-needed escape from the stress of daily living. Flying may generate a newfound sense of fun in individuals overwhelmed with the nine-to-five routine, or a feeling of accomplishment in people who have always doubted their own abilities to achieve success. Hangar flying sessions, where talk of engines and airports blends with ruminations on perfect landings and spectacular sunsets, yield lasting friendships among pilots. Rewards garnered through pilot training create a ripple effect as they travel outward to touch parents, friends, spouses, or children.

Whether outwardly or inwardly, whether in space or time, the farther we penetrate the unknown, the vaster and more marvelous it becomes.

— Charles Lindbergh

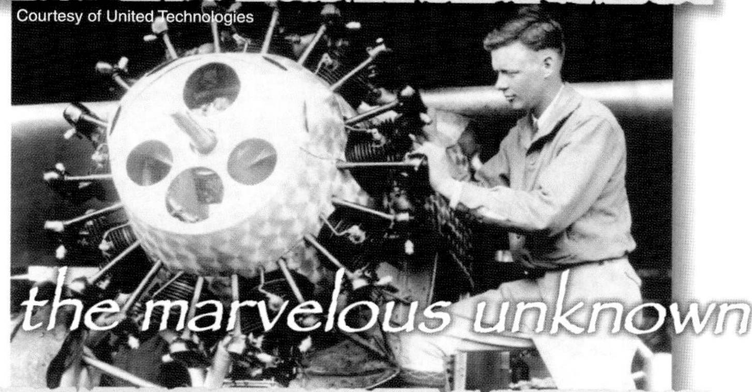

My father had been opposed to my flying from the first and had never flown himself. However, he had agreed to go up with me at the first opportunity, and one afternoon he climbed into the cockpit and we flew over the Redwood Falls together. From that day on I never heard a word against my flying, and he never missed a chance to ride in a plane.

— Charles Lindbergh

As your students leave the nest to pursue their own aviation paths, the treasure of learning follows them. Regardless of what direction you take in your flying career, as a CFI you have a far-reaching impact not only on the future of flight, but on events outside the world of aviation. Teaching someone to fly is like creating a spark that ignites a chain reaction. The motivation and training you provide may compel a student to pursue a career as an airline pilot, enabling hundreds of passengers daily to reunite with loved ones or to reach destinations essential to their jobs. The student you train today may be saving lives tomorrow as an air ambulance pilot. Your students may realize dreams to fight fires from the cockpits of slurry bombers, deliver medical supplies and doctors to remote areas, or carry world leaders to critical meetings. One of your students may go on to defend our nation as a fighter pilot, command the space shuttle, or be the first person to set foot on another planet.

The great bird will take its first flight . . . filling the world with amazement and all records with its fame, and it will bring eternal glory to the nest where it was born.

— Leonardo da Vinci

Learning is a treasure that will follow its owner everywhere.

— Chinese Proverb

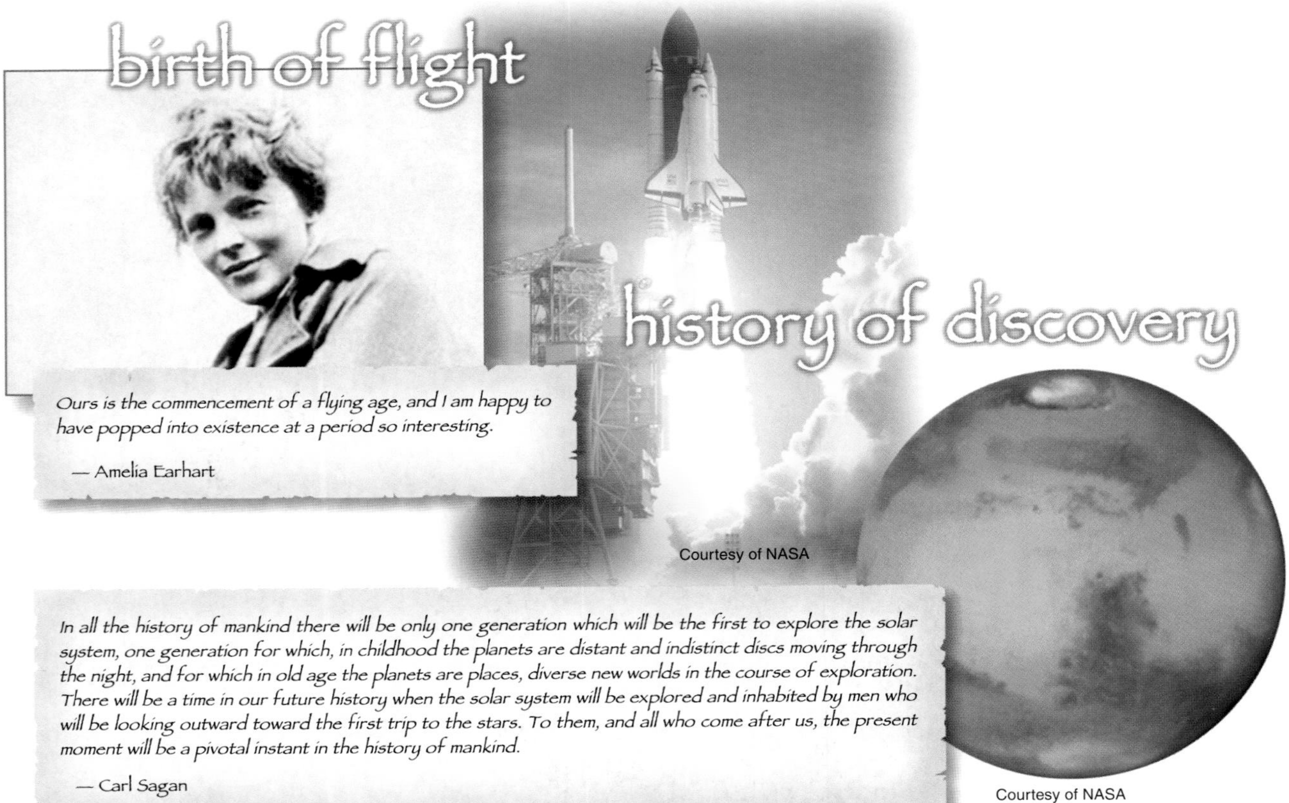

birth of flight

history of discovery

Ours is the commencement of a flying age, and I am happy to have popped into existence at a period so interesting.

— Amelia Earhart

Courtesy of NASA

In all the history of mankind there will be only one generation which will be the first to explore the solar system, one generation for which, in childhood the planets are distant and indistinct discs moving through the night, and for which in old age the planets are places, diverse new worlds in the course of exploration. There will be a time in our future history when the solar system will be explored and inhabited by men who will be looking outward toward the first trip to the stars. To them, and all who come after us, the present moment will be a pivotal instant in the history of mankind.

— Carl Sagan

Courtesy of NASA

In just the last one hundred years, humans have witnessed both the birth of flight and the genesis of travel to other worlds. Aviation has been, and always will be, an integral part of the unique history of discovery that human beings share. Our dream of flying among the stars began with our dream to break the bonds of earth's gravity and fly among the birds. From the Wright Flyer to the moon landing, from the space shuttle to the exploration of Mars, aviation is the cornerstone of our unrelenting drive to expand our horizons and explore. As a flight instructor, you can be more than just an observer as these pivotal events in history continue to unfold.

Pilots take no special joy in walking. Pilots like flying.

— Neil Armstrong

Courtesy of NASA

keys to the future

The first men to break free of earth's atmosphere had demonstrated their unique abilities in aircraft cockpits long before proving their skills in space. Most of them had an interest in aviation from an early age: Neil Armstrong had a student pilot's certificate before he had a driver's license. When you introduce young people to the accomplishments of such great aviators as the Wright Brothers, Charles Lindbergh, Amelia Earhart, John Glenn, and Neil Armstrong, they can become excited about the prospect of following in these pioneers' footsteps. Students who take an interest in flight today will be the trail-blazers of the aerospace industry tomorrow. As you help your students explore systems, weather, aerodynamics, and maneuvers, you are not only preparing them to

become pilots, you are laying a foundation of knowledge about science and technology — the keys to our future.

Being an integral part of the future of aviation is not the only reward you receive as a flight instructor. As you face the daily challenges of teaching, you may be surprised to find out how much you discover about flying. By observing your students' errors, analyzing their techniques, and evaluating their judgment and decision making, you learn volumes about your own strengths and weaknesses as a pilot. At the same time you develop creative ways to guide your students to proficiency, you are generating new techniques to polish your own piloting skills. When you prepare for lessons and research student questions, you expand your own knowledge base. Your ability to communicate effectively and relate to other people improves, and you realize a great sense of satisfaction when your students accomplish goals, from first solos to passing practical tests. You also form enduring bonds with students and fellow instructors. And you gain the flight time and experience necessary to accomplish your career goals, if you decide to move beyond instructing to pursue another aviation profession.

Flight instructing allows you to turn your passion for aviation into a profession that can keep you flying every day. What better office window exists than the windscreen of an airplane? You will find that instructing provides you with experiences that epitomize the very reasons you earned your pilot's certificate in the first place. Since each student is different and every flight unique, instructing combines challenge and adventure to produce a compelling occupation. Sharing the cockpit with individuals ranging from high school students and surgeons to actors and artists enables you to get to know students from diverse backgrounds who are equipped with a variety of abilities. You may find yourself providing a flight review to an experienced airline pilot, or helping an aerial applicator become familiar with mountain flying. Operating a wide range of airplanes and adding new skills, such as the ability to teach aerobatics, may be in your future. Instrument and multi-engine instructor ratings afford you an even greater opportunity to expand your teaching horizons. And, you will have stories that last a lifetime to impart to your friends, children, and grandchildren.

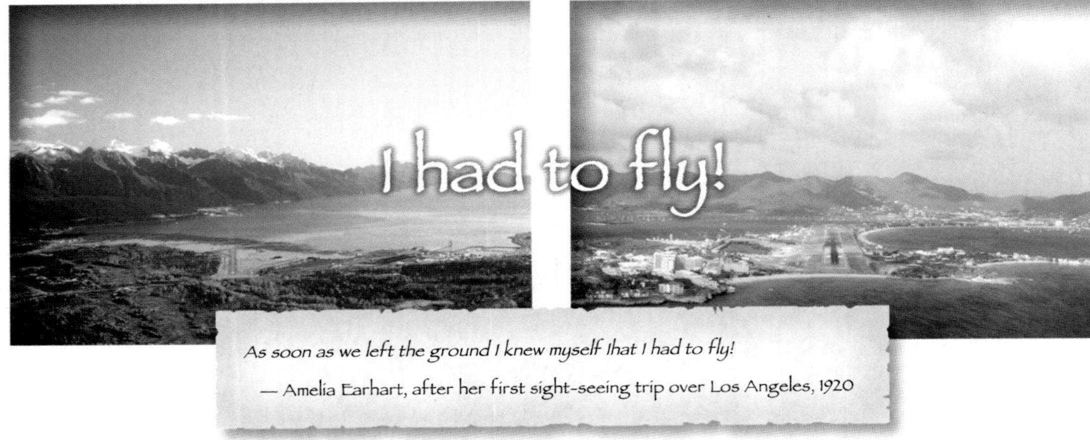

As soon as we left the ground I knew myself that I had to fly!

— Amelia Earhart, after her first sight-seeing trip over Los Angeles, 1920

Each time you lift off the runway with a new student seated beside you, bound for an adventure in the sky, you have the chance to pass on the same sense of excitement that Amelia Earhart felt on her first flight. In doing so, you are able to experience that thrill anew. This is the beauty of flight instructing, for through your students you are able to know the joy of discovering flight once again.

I've had a ball.

— Chuck Yeager, describing his 30-year Air Force career

You will too.

PART I
The Journey Begins

There's no such thing as a natural-born pilot.

— Chuck Yeager

Part I

Just as there are no natural-born pilots, neither are there natural-born instructors. Teaching, much like flying, is an acquired skill that must be learned and practiced unfailingly to achieve perfection. In helping your students take those first few steps on their journey into the aviation world, you will be beginning your own journey into the world of teaching. The skills you will need to effectively lead your students are different than those you have acquired in your flying career up to this point. Part I will supply you with the knowledge you need to be an effective and competent flight instructor. Beginning with *The Foundation of Training*, you are introduced to basic teaching tools and theories. Next, you will apply these concepts in *The Art and Science of Teaching*, where you delve into a variety of instructional methods. In *Exploring Human Factors*, you will gain knowledge of the behavior patterns and decision-making techniques relevant to both you and your students.

CHAPTER 1

FOUNDATIONS OF LEARNING

Flight Instructor
Volume 1 — Fundamentals of Instruction

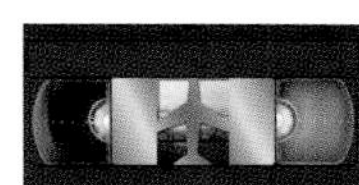

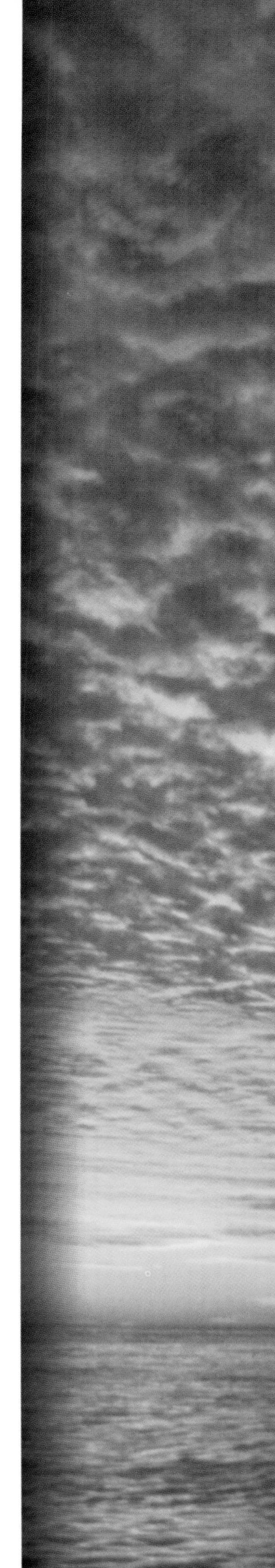

SECTION A

DISCOVERING LEARNING THEORIES

One's mind, once stretched by a new idea, never regains its original dimensions.
— Oliver Wendell Holmes

Learning stretches the mind, sparks the imagination, and opens the door to endless possibilities. The joy of learning is universal and timeless. One of the wonderful things about flying is that no matter how many hours you accumulate and how much experience you amass, you are always learning. Each flight is unique and presents an occasion to discover something new, not just about the airplane or the flight environment, but about yourself as well. As a flight instructor, you are fortunate to have the opportunity to guide individuals through one of the most exciting legs of the aviation journey: their flight training. Along the way you may be surprised to discover that as you help your students gain new abilities, you will learn more about flying than you may have thought possible.

While you may be an excellent pilot, before you embark on this voyage into the world of flight instruction, you will need to acquire new skills and knowledge to excel as a teacher. Would you walk up to a strange airplane in which you had no experience, jump in, and attempt to fly it without knowing anything about it? Of course not. As a pilot, you realize you need to know how to operate the airplane within its limitations. In fact, before you act as pilot in command of an airplane, you normally study the pilot's operating handbook and obtain an extensive aircraft checkout to become thoroughly familiar with the airplane's operating procedures, equipment, and systems. As a flight instructor, it is equally important to be thoroughly familiar with your student's learning systems. Certain basic learning principles apply to everyone, yet each student is an individual with specific learning strengths and weaknesses. Developing a complete understanding of basic learning theories will help you become an effective and successful flight instructor.

LEARNING DEFINED

Learning is defined as a persisting change in behavior resulting from experience with the environment, which cannot be attributed to natural growth. Behaviors affected by learning include physical abilities, thinking skills, and attitudes. Humans possess a powerful and unique capability and capacity for learning. Beginning at birth and occurring throughout a lifetime, learning is not limited to formal settings under the direction of a teacher, but is a constant process. Learning can be a major undertaking, such as acquiring the skills to fly, or can be a very minor task, such as discovering the quickest way to the airport.

Learning is a change in behavior as a result of experience.

The change in behavior associated with learning continues after the initial learning experience has ended and can last a lifetime. For example, a child who touches a hot stove learns not to touch it again. A person who learns to fly is changing behavior as a result of experiences encountered during flight training. As a flight instructor, you are

responsible for creating the experiences that give a student the ability to fly an airplane.

BEHAVIORISM

The theory of **behaviorism** is based on the study and measurement of observable behavior. The theory assumes three things. First, all humans learn in the same manner. Second, humans will respond to their environment in predictable ways. Third, behaviors can be learned. [Figure 1-1]

Early psychologists found that behavior can be shaped or modified by changing the stimulus accompanying that behavior. While there were several pioneers who broke ground in the development of behavioral psychology, B.F. Skinner was the most influential individual. Skinner's work led to a better understanding of the laws that govern learning. He identified two classes of behavior, operant and respondent. Operant behavior is initiated voluntarily by the individual. Turning on a fuel pump, reading a checklist, or initiating a go-around are examples of operant behavior. Respondent behavior is done involuntarily in response to a stimulus. Sneezing, flinching in response to a loud noise, and blinking the eyes when looking at a bright light are examples of respondent behavior. Operant behavior is the target of learning and therefore the most important to you as a flight instructor.

Operant conditioning, or the development of certain behaviors, generally consists of three phases: cues to

Figure 1-1. Flying an airplane requires many types of behaviors. During flight training, students exhibit behaviors that range from preflighting the airplane to making a go/no-go decision regarding a proposed flight. These are behaviors that can be observed and measured.

Classical Conditioning and Drooling Dogs

A famous experiment performed by Ivan Pavlov was one of the key elements in the formation of behaviorism. Through the process known as classical conditioning, Pavlov trained a dog to salivate at the sound of a bell. Pavlov, who was a physiologist and not a psychologist, was involved in a study of digestive juices when he discovered that dogs that had been used repeatedly in his experiments began to salivate before food was presented. This caused him to think some stimulus other than food was the cause of the salivation.

To test this theory, Pavlov strapped a dog into a harness and showed it food while ringing a bell. After a while, the dog associated the ringing of the bell with food and began to salivate upon hearing the bell, even if the food was not present. In this case, food was an unconditioned stimulus that produced the unconditioned response of salivation. The bell was considered a conditioned stimulus resulting in salivation as a conditioned response. The outcome was the discovery that responses can be modified to react to new stimuli.

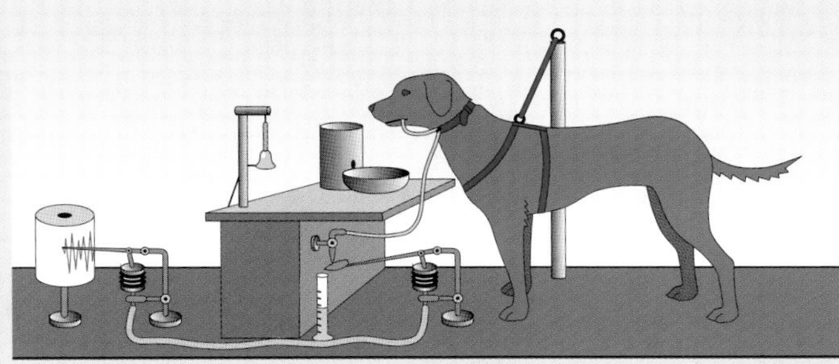

initiate the behavior are provided, the behavior is actually performed, and consequences associated with that performance are received. Cues that the student should perform certain behaviors may be in the form of verbal and nonverbal signals from you, written instructions, checklists, or the timing and sequencing of procedures or other events. When students receive the proper cues, they attempt to perform the specific behaviors to gain a desired consequence, or reward.

It is important for you to understand how students interpret your actions as consequences of their behavior. If praise is offered immediately after maneuvers have been performed correctly, students can clearly see the relationship between their behavior and your response so they are conditioned to repeat the proper procedures. However, if you are having a bad day and appear to be annoyed, your students may make erroneous assumptions about the consequences of their behavior. You may inadvertently condition your students not to repeat an appropriate behavior. The fact that your reaction was unintentional or even misinterpreted does not matter.

Reinforcement is a consequence that strengthens behavior. Four types of reinforcement have been identified that you can use as a flight instructor: positive reinforcement, negative reinforcement, extinction, and punishment. [Figure 1-2]

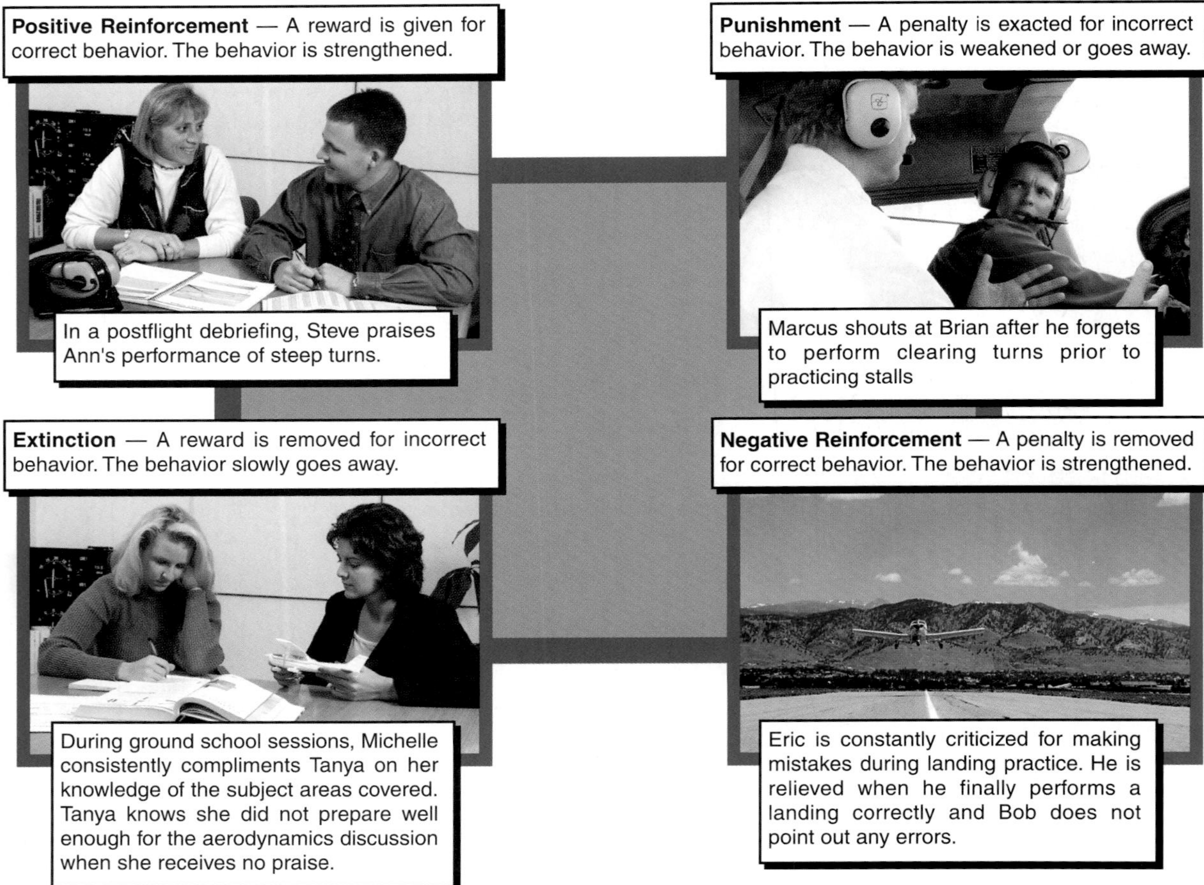

Figure 1-2. The use of positive reinforcement to help students learn is normally the most successful approach.

When students exhibit the desired behavior, whether it is performing a maneuver correctly, or making the right decision in a weather situation, positive feedback or reinforcement from you is very effective in helping them learn. Punishment should only be used as a last resort. Its success can often be short-lived and the use of punishment can generate feelings of anxiety, fear, and anger in students. Negative reinforcement can be an effective motivator only in certain situations. For example, to avoid or remove the

annoying sound of a warning horn, a student will be compelled to extend the landing gear. It may be difficult to use extinction in flight training situations since often times, for safety reasons, you cannot ignore undesired behavior, such as a student consistently missing items on a before takeoff checklist.

The primary methods of teaching behaviors are shaping and chaining. **Shaping** involves the use of carefully designed stimuli and the correct reinforcers for appropriate behavior. As the instructor, you decide what behavior you want your students to perform. Each time your students demonstrate the correct behavior, you provide positive reinforcement which helps shape, or develop, this behavior. **Chaining** combines behaviors students already know to assemble more complex behaviors. [Figure 1-3]

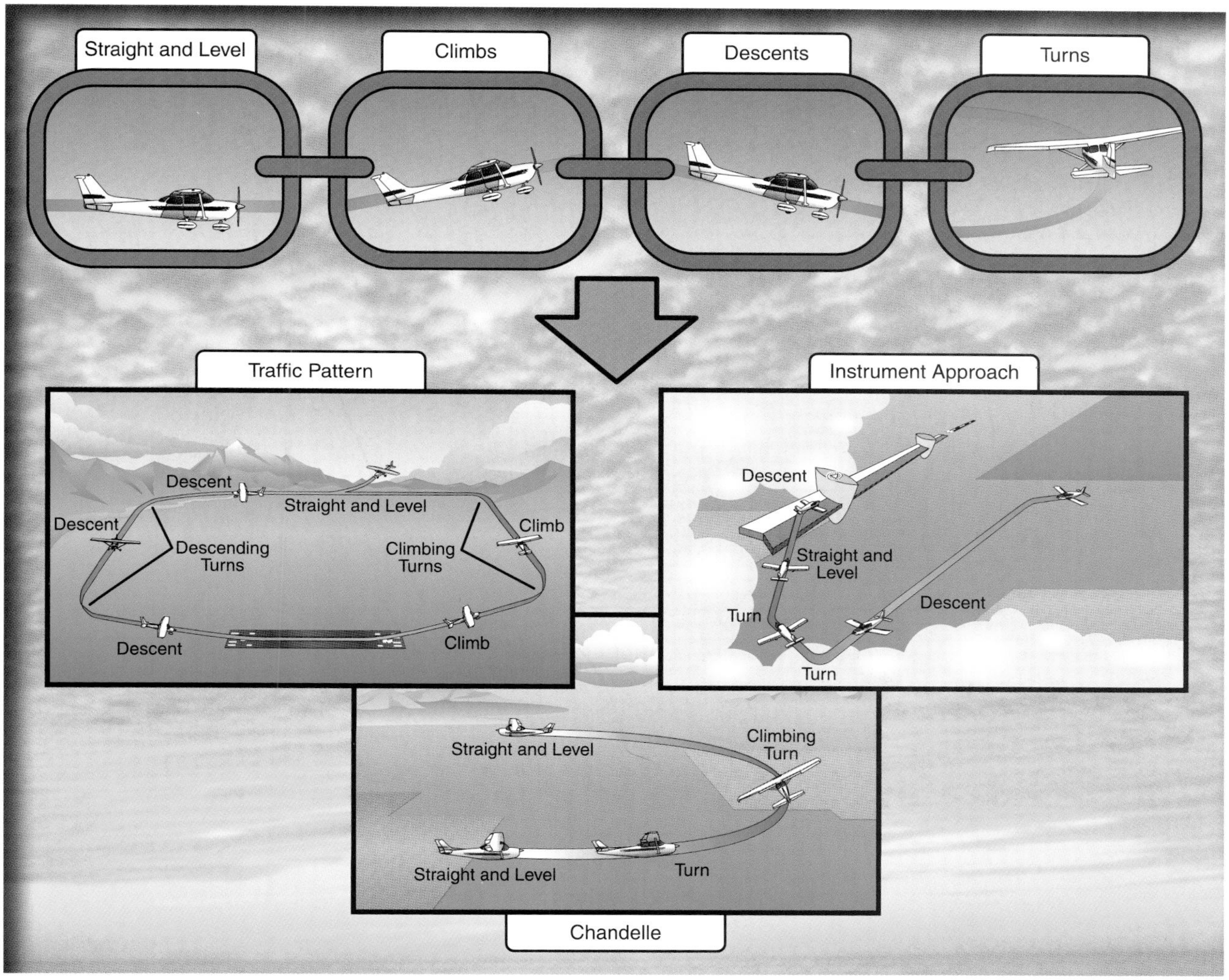

Figure 1-3. You first teach students to fly basic maneuvers by the shaping process. From these simple building blocks, other flight procedures can be accomplished though the chaining process.

COGNITIVE THEORY

Learning is not just a change in outward behavior, but involves changes in thinking, feeling, or understanding. Unlike behaviorism, **cognitive theory** involves mental processes, such as decision making and problem solving which are difficult, if not impossible, to observe or measure. You may find it very challenging to design tests or other evaluation tools to determine if learning has taken place. However, if your students can explain how and why they did something, you can gain valuable insight into the mental processes used. While there are several branches of cognitive theory, the social interaction model and the cognitive information processing model are two primary areas of focus.

Why Did You Do That?

Understanding cognitive theory means recognizing that, many times, the only way to determine why a student behaves in a particular way is to ask. For example, assume you are preparing a student for solo flight and have repeatedly discussed and simulated the procedures to be performed if an engine failure occurs after takeoff. Your student has always identified the correct actions of lowering the nose to maintain glidespeed and preparing to land in a field straight ahead. As the solo nears, you simulate the engine failure again and this time your student reacts incorrectly. When asked what action she should take, she indicates that she would attempt to turn back to the runway.

Why would she respond in this manner? She may have been distracted by something else going on in the traffic pattern and spoke too quickly or she may be nervous about the upcoming solo flight. It's possible the circumstances under which you initiated the simulation were slightly different this time and she thought another action was more appropriate, or maybe she was confused by some information from another source which conflicted with the procedures she had been taught. The only way to know why she made this mistake, and to take the proper action to ensure that the error is not repeated, is to ask her to explain what she was thinking.

SOCIAL INTERACTION

The **social interaction** model stresses the concept that students learn to shape their conduct after the prevailing behavior displayed in their environment. For example, if you have a relaxed, confident attitude in the airplane, students are less likely to be anxious and agitated during flight lessons. In addition, when people work together, attitudes and problem-solving skills can be gleaned from other members of the group. For this reason, you must carefully choose the composition of groups when gathering students together to work on exercises.

COGNITIVE INFORMATION PROCESSING

The **cognitive information processing** model describes how information is gathered, processed, and stored by the brain in much the same way it is by a computer. As scientists were designing computer models, it occurred to them that the brain might work in a similar fashion. While a computer gets input from the keyboard or other devices, the brain gets input from the senses. Just as a computer processes the data in the central processing unit, the brain processes data in working memory. Finally, while the computer stores the data to a storage disk, the brain stores data in long-term memory. [Figure 1-4]

COGNITIVE INFORMATION PROCESSING

The body's **sensory organs** receive incoming information.

The **sensory register** filters out irrelevant information in under 1 second by the process of attending.

The **working memory** codes information for storage in less than 1 minute by the process of conscious thought.

The **long-term memory** can store information for a lifetime and performs the reconstruction process.

Figure 1-4. As a flight instructor, you need to understand how students take in information, process it, and store it for later use. The cognitive information processing model describes this progression.

SENSORY REGISTER

Information coming from the body's sensory organs is received and sorted by the brain's **sensory register** via a process known as attending. The amount of information that your senses detect and send to the brain far exceeds the capacity of conscious thought. The sensory register acts as a filter that separates the important information from the unimportant information. For instance, while you are reading this, you are aware of the words and pictures on this page. However, your body is also aware of the chair in which you are sitting, the color of the room, the texture of your clothes, and any background sounds. Yet, since this information is not relevant to the task at hand, your sensory register is discarding it so you can concentrate on what you are reading. You might be aware of these sensations now because they were just mentioned, but soon you will not pay attention to them again. The sensory register can be trained to seek certain information that has been predetermined to be important. Red lights on the instrument panel are an example of this. When a red light comes on, you may not know immediately what it means, but you do know it is signaling that your attention is required. [Figure 1-5]

The sensory register is paying attention to the on-going radio transmissions while you are thinking about something else.

The sensory register detects a radio call for your airplane and alerts the working memory. You become aware of the transmission, your brain processes the information, and you respond to ATC.

Figure 1-5. You can detect your airplane's call sign while working on other tasks in the cockpit because your sensory register filters out much of the radio chatter but alerts you when your call sign is transmitted.

The ability to sort through the enormous amount of sensory input to concentrate on important information while ignoring the rest is called selective attention. If, in the process of concentrating on a new maneuver, your student does not hear an instruction from you, selective attention is being exercised. The ear detected your words, but what you said was never processed by your student's brain. Sometimes you need to reduce the workload prior to communicating an idea so your student has the capability to absorb the new information. This is especially true with a student beginning training or a student exploring complex new tasks. In addition, a good preflight briefing can prepare your student's sensory register to detect key elements of the lesson when they occur and send them to the working memory for processing.

If your student can perform routine tasks, such as trimming the airplane or scanning the instruments, you can begin to introduce more complex maneuvers. When a maneuver or procedure is learned to the point that it becomes a habit, then the sensory register monitors the activity while letting the student think about the new information being presented. This level of performance is called automaticity. [Figure 1-6]

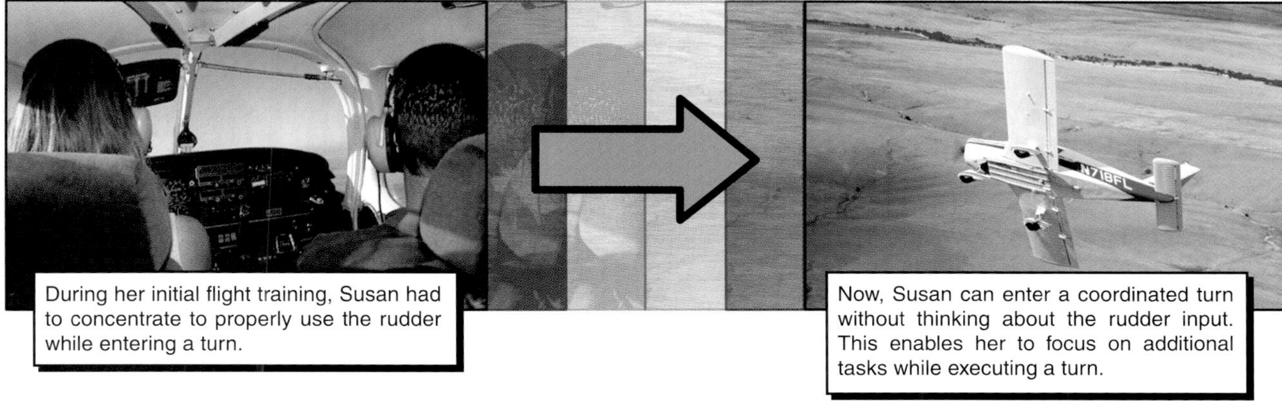

During her initial flight training, Susan had to concentrate to properly use the rudder while entering a turn.

Now, Susan can enter a coordinated turn without thinking about the rudder input. This enables her to focus on additional tasks while executing a turn.

Figure 1-6. A student is performing with automaticity when rolling into a turn without consciously thinking about rudder pressure or back pressure on the elevator.

Pattern recognition is a key component of the sensory register. Pattern recognition occurs when new input is recognized because it matches or is similar to something already known. To provide a foundation for further processing, incoming information must be analyzed and familiar patterns identified. [Figure 1-7]

Figure 1-7. To identify a stimulus, the brain may use previously stored information about the features of a class of objects or events.

The interpretation of the flight instruments by the pattern of the needles is one example of the use of pattern recognition in the cockpit. As an instructor, you should be aware of the errors that can occur in this process. For example, assume you requested a level-off at 5,000 feet MSL and your student stops climbing at 4,000 feet MSL Your student may recognize that the large needle on the altimeter indicates that the airplane is level at a thousand-foot increment, but may not be reading the exact altitude.

WORKING MEMORY

Working memory, also known as short-term memory, is the part of the cognitive information processing system where conscious thought takes place. In working memory, information is processed and sent to long-term memory for storage. Information is also retrieved from long-term memory and sent back to working memory. When information enters working memory, it takes between 5 to 10 seconds for the data to be processed and moved to long-term memory. If this process is interrupted or prevented, the item the student is trying to remember can be lost in about 20 seconds. The primary types of interference that disrupt this process are proactive and retroactive. Proactive interference occurs when something learned just prior to the presentation of material prevents the proper processing of the new material. Retroactive interference occurs when the new information is presented too quickly and disrupts processing of the previous material. To prevent these types of interference from occurring, you must allow a period of time for the student to finish processing the subject matter just presented before moving on to the next item.

Working memory processes two primary types of information: visual and auditory. Visual information is processed separately and does not interfere with auditory information. This means that pictures can enhance a verbal presentation without causing confusion. However, two visual or two auditory inputs will interfere with each other and prevent the processing of both. [Figure 1-8]

To provide the most effective instruction, you must be aware of working memory's capacity. Students can think of approximately 5 to 9 items at any given time. This is far less than the information detected by the senses. Until they can perform routine tasks,

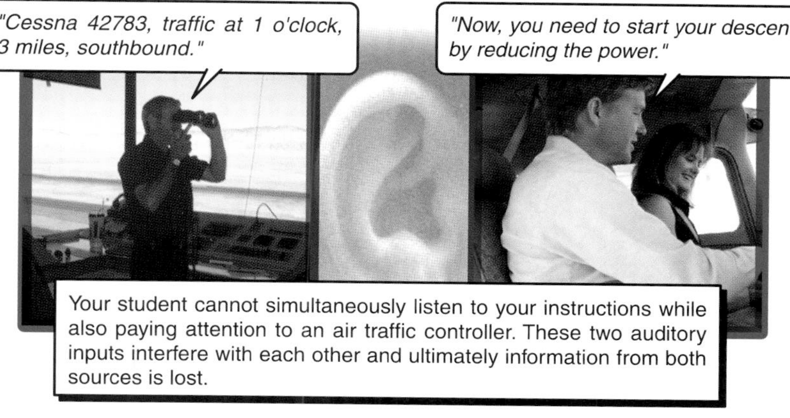

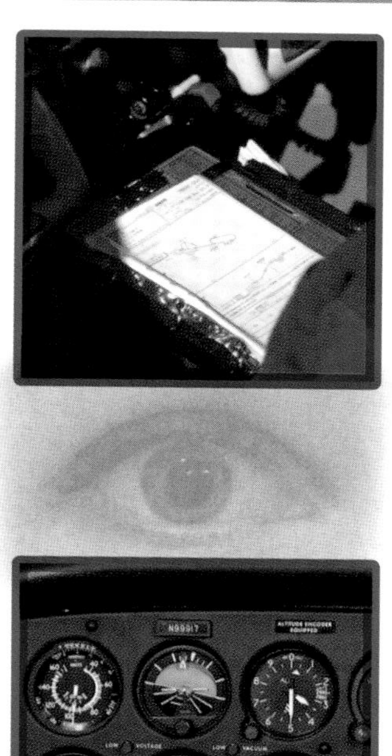

Figure 1-8. Effective lessons use visual and verbal information to complement each other. Overloading students with simultaneous inputs of visual or verbal information causes interference and reduces retention.

such as holding altitude or scanning for traffic, students can be easily overloaded when you attempt to instruct them. The more information presented, the quicker the items are forgotten. When you need to teach important information to your students, especially during the early stages of training, you should take control of the airplane so they can concentrate on your instructions and properly process the material. [Figure 1-9]

Working memory transfers information to long-term memory by two processes: rehearsing and coding. An example of rehearsing is a student repeating numbers, such as aircraft speeds, over and over while preparing for an aircraft checkout. Although rehearsal will

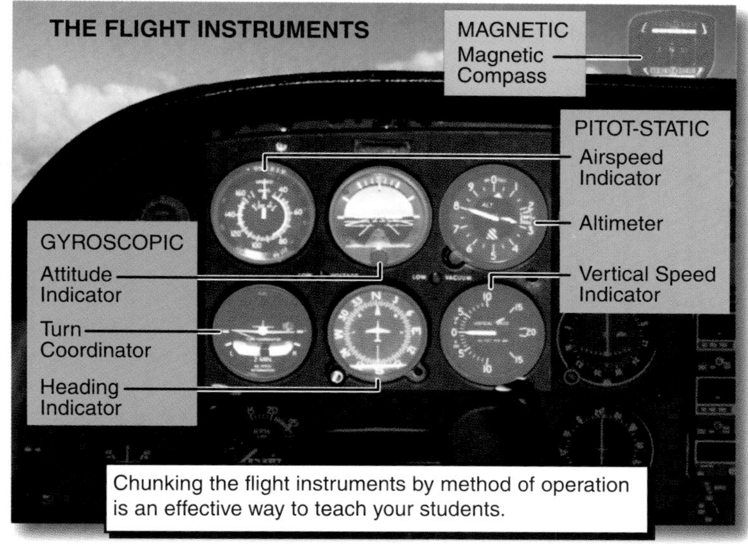

Figure 1-9. Chunking is an effective way to manage the capacity limits of working memory.

help fix the numbers in the student's long-term memory, coding is normally a more effective way of processing information. Coding is the process of relating incoming information to concepts and ideas already in memory. For example, if the approach speed of the aircraft used for the checkout is the same as another familiar aircraft, it will be easier for the student's working memory to process this information. [Figure 1-10]

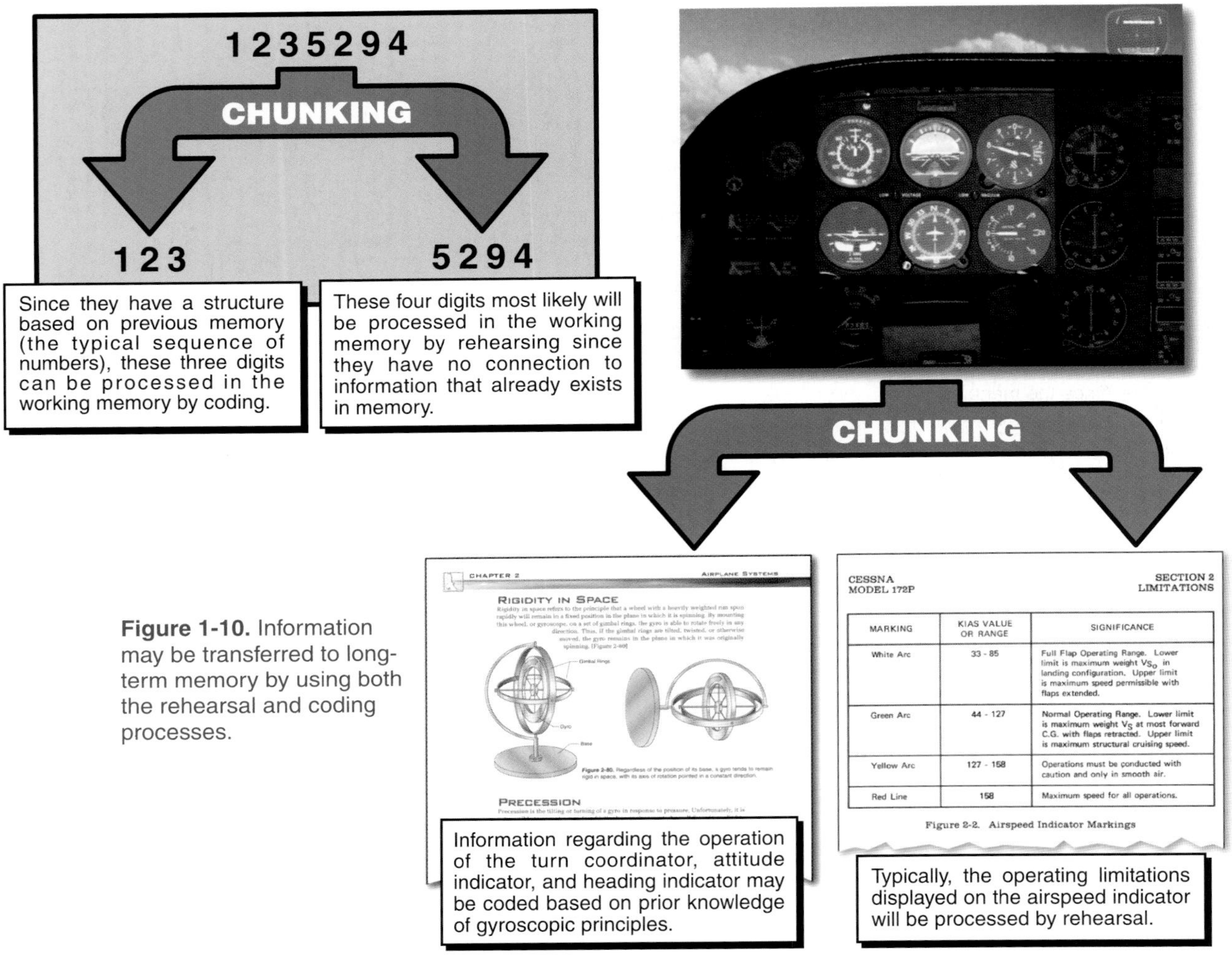

1235294

CHUNKING

123

5294

Since they have a structure based on previous memory (the typical sequence of numbers), these three digits can be processed in the working memory by coding.

These four digits most likely will be processed in the working memory by rehearsing since they have no connection to information that already exists in memory.

CHUNKING

CHAPTER 2 AIRPLANE SYSTEMS

RIGIDITY IN SPACE

PRECESSION

Information regarding the operation of the turn coordinator, attitude indicator, and heading indicator may be coded based on prior knowledge of gyroscopic principles.

CESSNA
MODEL 172P

SECTION 2
LIMITATIONS

MARKING	KIAS VALUE OR RANGE	SIGNIFICANCE
White Arc	33 - 85	Full Flap Operating Range. Lower limit is maximum weight V_{S_0} in landing configuration. Upper limit is maximum speed permissible with flaps extended.
Green Arc	44 - 127	Normal Operating Range. Lower limit is maximum weight V_S at most forward C.G. with flaps retracted. Upper limit is maximum structural cruising speed.
Yellow Arc	127 - 158	Operations must be conducted with caution and only in smooth air.
Red Line	158	Maximum speed for all operations.

Figure 2-2. Airspeed Indicator Markings

Typically, the operating limitations displayed on the airspeed indicator will be processed by rehearsal.

Figure 1-10. Information may be transferred to long-term memory by using both the rehearsal and coding processes.

In addition to coding information using similar material contained in existing memory, items that typically require rehearsal for processing can be coded using mnemonics. A mnemonic is a symbolic device or cue used to help remember information. Examples of mnemonics in aviation are memory aids, such as the I'M SAFE checklist which enables you to evaluate your fitness for flight or ARROW which is used to recall required aircraft documents.

LONG-TERM MEMORY

The final component of the cognitive information processing system is **long-term memory**, which is used for long-term storage of items and can have a duration of a lifetime. Information comes from working memory in the form of codes that are placed in the brain. It is very important for you to understand that memory is a reconstruction of an experience and is not an exact recall. When people remember an experience, the memory codes needed are retrieved from the various brain cells and put together to form the memory. Memories are susceptible to alteration over time, personal biases and perceptions, as well as individual motivations. In some cases, memories can be created and believed as if they were real, even though they are not.

Caution: Student Overload Imminent

Picture yourself in the practice area on the third lesson with your student. Since you have many things you need to cover, you may feel compelled to provide as much information as possible. This is quite natural, yet you might not be getting as much across as you think.

Assume you intend to introduce slow flight to your student. One way to approach this task would be to simply talk your student through the maneuver. However, your student must concentrate on aircraft control, rudder coordination, heading, altitude, airspeed, aircraft position, and collision avoidance, as well as try to listen to you. In most cases, something will be overlooked, and it might be what you are saying. A better way to introduce this maneuver and stay within your student's working memory capacity is to take the controls and demonstrate the maneuver. By relieving your student of the flying tasks, you are allowing more attention to be paid to your instruction and you are giving your student time to process the necessary information for long-term storage.

After you have demonstrated the maneuver, ask your student to talk you through it. This again helps your student process the information. Once this is done correctly, transfer the controls back to your student to perform the maneuver with as little input from you as possible. Once the maneuver is completed, take the controls again, and critique your student. As your student gains proficiency and more tasks become automatic, the need to take the controls becomes less and your student is more receptive to your instruction while flying the airplane.

CONSTRUCTIVISM

The concept of **constructivism** provides a unique way of thinking about how students learn. Behaviorism and cognitive theory assume all learners are the same and knowledge is simply given to students. Constructivism is based upon the idea that learners construct knowledge through the process of discovery as they experience events and actively seek to understand their environment. To employ constructivism, your role shifts from the transmitter of information to the creator of experiences. Instead of presenting material in a traditional lecture form, you guide students through the use of well-planned exercises or problems and they construct knowledge based on these experiences. [Figure 1-11]

Figure 1-11. There are some basic guidelines for using constructivism to enhance learning.

PERCEPTIONS AND INSIGHTS

Perceptions, which occur when meaning is given to sensations, are the basis for all learning. The sensation of hearing a landing gear warning horn has no meaning until your student can associate it with its purpose. Perceptions are often based on how people

Cross-Country to the Limits

You ask your student to plan a VFR cross-country based on specific conditions that you provide. You present a situation in which the airplane will be overweight if full fuel is added. In addition, the amount of fuel that can be added will not allow the airplane to reach its destination without a fuel stop. The student must solve several problems to effectively plan this flight. How much fuel can the airplane carry with the current load? Is it enough to reach the destination? Is it better to try to reduce the payload or to plan a fuel stop? How would reducing the payload and increasing the fuel affect the airplane's CG? Are there any airports along the route which can serve as good fuel stops? How would loading the airplane to maximum takeoff weight affect performance considering the proposed flight conditions?

By working through an exercise such as this one, your student will be able to construct knowledge about concepts such as effective problem solving, flight planning, weight and balance calculations, and aircraft performance. Since there are many different options available in this situation, you also will gain an understanding of your student's thought processes by discussing the conclusions that have been reached.

expect things to be. If you do not take great care to guide them, your students may develop incorrect perceptions and will not fully grasp what you are attempting to teach. For example, assume you are providing a complex airplane checkout to a student who has no experience with retractable landing gear systems. After you repeatedly simulate engine failures in the practice area, your student expects that when the power is reduced, a horn will sound. When returning to the airport, the student decreases power to slow the airplane for landing and neglects to lower the landing gear. The warning horn has no effect since the student perceives it to be associated with the reduction in power. [Figure 1-12]

Perceptions, which occur when meaning is given to sensations, are the basis for all learning.

The basic need to maintain and enhance the organized self affects all of a person's perceptions.

Insights are the mental grouping of perceptions into meaningful wholes. Leading students to insights is one of your primary responsibilities as an instructor. By carefully designing your lessons, you can provide opportunities for your students to gain insights and throughout each lesson, you can point out relationships between various perceptions as they occur to guide your students to the proper insights. For example, when students are learning how to recognize an approaching stall, they observe the high pitch attitude of the airplane, hear the sound of the stall warning horn, and feel a slight buffeting. The student may correctly perceive that these sensations are all signs of an impending stall. You also can point out how each of these elements relates to the angle of attack of the wing, providing your students with insight into what causes a stall. Students can gain insights without your intervention, but sometimes these insights may be false or misleading. For example, a student might associate the perceptions of the approaching stall solely with a reduction in airspeed and not necessarily with the increase in angle of attack of the wing.

As the number of perceptions increase, opportunities for a student to gain insights increase. Discussions on the ground, demonstrations with models, and practicing straight-ahead and turning stalls in a variety of configurations are all experiences which provide additional perceptions and help a student formulate insights into stalls. These many anchor points for developing and relating insights provide a better foundation for long-term retention. In addition, helping a student acquire and

Self-concept has great influence on the total perceptual process. You may foster the development of insights by helping your student acquire and maintain a favorable self-concept.

Fear or the element of threat will narrow the student's perceptual field.

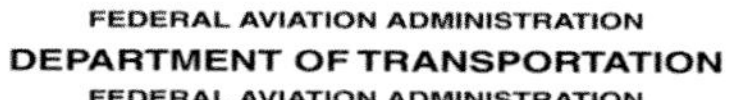

FEDERAL AVIATION ADMINISTRATION
DEPARTMENT OF TRANSPORTATION
FEDERAL AVIATION ADMINISTRATION

STATEMENT OF DEMONSTRATED ABILITY

This form cannot be used in lieu of a medical certificate; it should be attached to your medical certificate.

AIRMAN'S NAME AND ADDRESS

John T. Doe
12345 E. Nowhere St.
Somewhere, IA 54321

Physical Organism — A person who has limited abilities with one or more senses will perceive differently than someone who does not. For example, a student who has limitations regarding the perception of color is normally required to have a special medical authorization to act as pilot in command.

Basic Needs — A person's fundamental need is to maintain and enhance the organized self. Essentials such as food, clothing, and shelter maintain the physical self, while sights, sounds, and feelings become part of the psychological self. Students have barriers that block those things which may threaten either the physical or psychological self.

Self-Concept — A student's self-image has a great influence on the perceptual process. For example, if a student's flying experiences support a positive self-image, learning is enhanced and the student tends to remain receptive to subsequent training. Experiences leading to a negative self-concept can inhibit learning and cause a student to reject additional instruction.

Goals and Values — To assist you in predicting how they will interpret experiences and instructions, it is important to understand the precise kinds of goals, beliefs, and values which students hold. Poor performance during an important lesson may be more devastating to a student who has long dreamed of a flying career than it is for a student who regards flying as a hobby.

Time and Opportunity — Time to experience the learning event and the opportunity to build upon prior knowledge is important in formulating the proper perceptions. A student may be able to stall an airplane on the first attempt regardless of previous experiences. However, in order to develop an accurate perception of stalls and stall recovery, the time to practice and relate the new sensations associated with these procedures to past experiences in the normal flight regime is essential.

Element of Threat — Fear can narrow the perceptual field by causing attention to be limited to the threat and not to be focused on the material in the lesson. If the fear of being involved in an accident is overwhelming, a student may perceive landing practice as dangerous and may not be able to focus on improving performance.

Figure 1-12. You need to take into account all of the factors that can affect a student's ability to formulate the correct perceptions.

Mental groupings of perceptions into meaningful wholes are called insights. One way you can provide insights to your students is by teaching the relationships as they occur in a safe environment.

maintain a favorable self-concept and providing a non-threatening and comfortable learning environment can enhance the creation of insights. If you are uneasy about performing stalls or give your students the impression that this maneuver is too challenging to master, your students will most likely be uncomfortable practicing stall procedures and will have a difficult time forming the proper insights.

FORGETTING AND RETENTION

Understanding the theories of **forgetting** and **retention** is very useful in enhancing the teaching process. In order for learned material to be retained, it must have been properly processed and stored in long-term memory. There are several reasons that material cannot be remembered. The information may have never been learned in the first place or the student may have lost the ability to retrieve it due to disuse over a period of time. In addition, interference and repression can cause material to be forgotten.

FORGETTING

Material that was never successfully processed into long-term memory by working memory, cannot be remembered. If the information does not exist in the student's brain, it cannot be retrieved. The breakdown of neural pathways between the various cells where memories are stored is another reason that things are forgotten. In other words, routes to the location of the memories in the brain are forgotten. When preparing for a test or a checkride, students study or practice until they are at the point where the information is easily remembered. If after completing an exam, they do not use the material for a while, the pathways in the brain are forgotten. If they were to review and resume practice, then the pathways should return. The memories were not lost, but the internal road signs to the location of those memories were lost. To overcome this phenomenon, you should have your students use the learned information as soon as possible after they are exposed to it. [Figure 1-13]

The difficulty in recalling facts after a number of years is known as disuse.

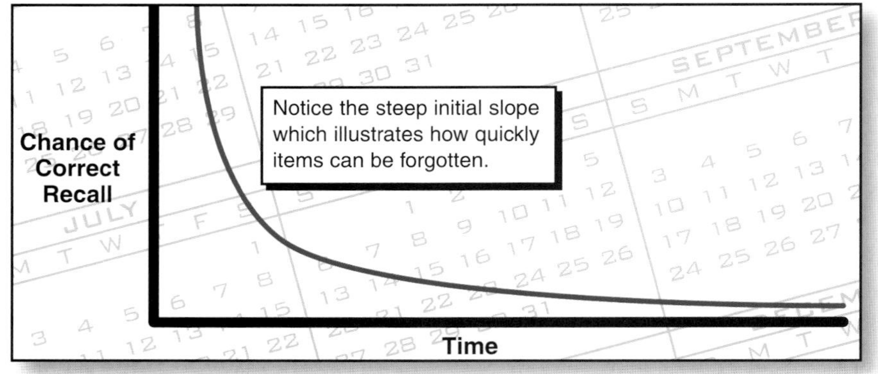

Figure 1-13. The effect of disuse over a period of time is illustrated by the classic forgetting curve. The more time that passes between the learning event and the attempted retrieval, the more likely it is that the student will forget.

Interference occurs when something is forgotten because a certain experience has overshadowed it, or when the learning of similar things has intervened. Interference can arise from competing material learned either before or after the information that the student wishes to remember. Similar material seems to interfere with memory more than dissimilar material. For example, a student receiving checkouts in two different airplanes during the same time period may confuse speeds or the operation of systems. Also, new material that is not fully learned or understood is more likely to be subject to interference. This is

Interference occurs when the learning of one thing overshadows the learning of another.

Submerging unpleasant memories into the subconscious is known as repression.

why it is so important to ensure students have sufficient time and opportunity to gain the proper meaning of concepts before moving on to new subject areas.

The concept of **repression** stems from the work of Sigmund Freud. Experiences that are unpleasant or produce anxiety may be buried into the subconscious part of the mind and cannot be recalled. This forgetting is not intentional, but is part of the individual's self-defense mechanisms to prevent undue stress. This type of forgetting is not common in flight training, but may occur in some cases.

RETENTION

To foster retention, you must ensure you create conditions that allow you to present material thoroughly and help students gain its full meaning. This type of learning is called deep learning and it involves principles and concepts anchored to knowledge that your students already have. In contrast, surface, or rote, learning is shallow without much concern for understanding and meaning. [Figure 1-14]

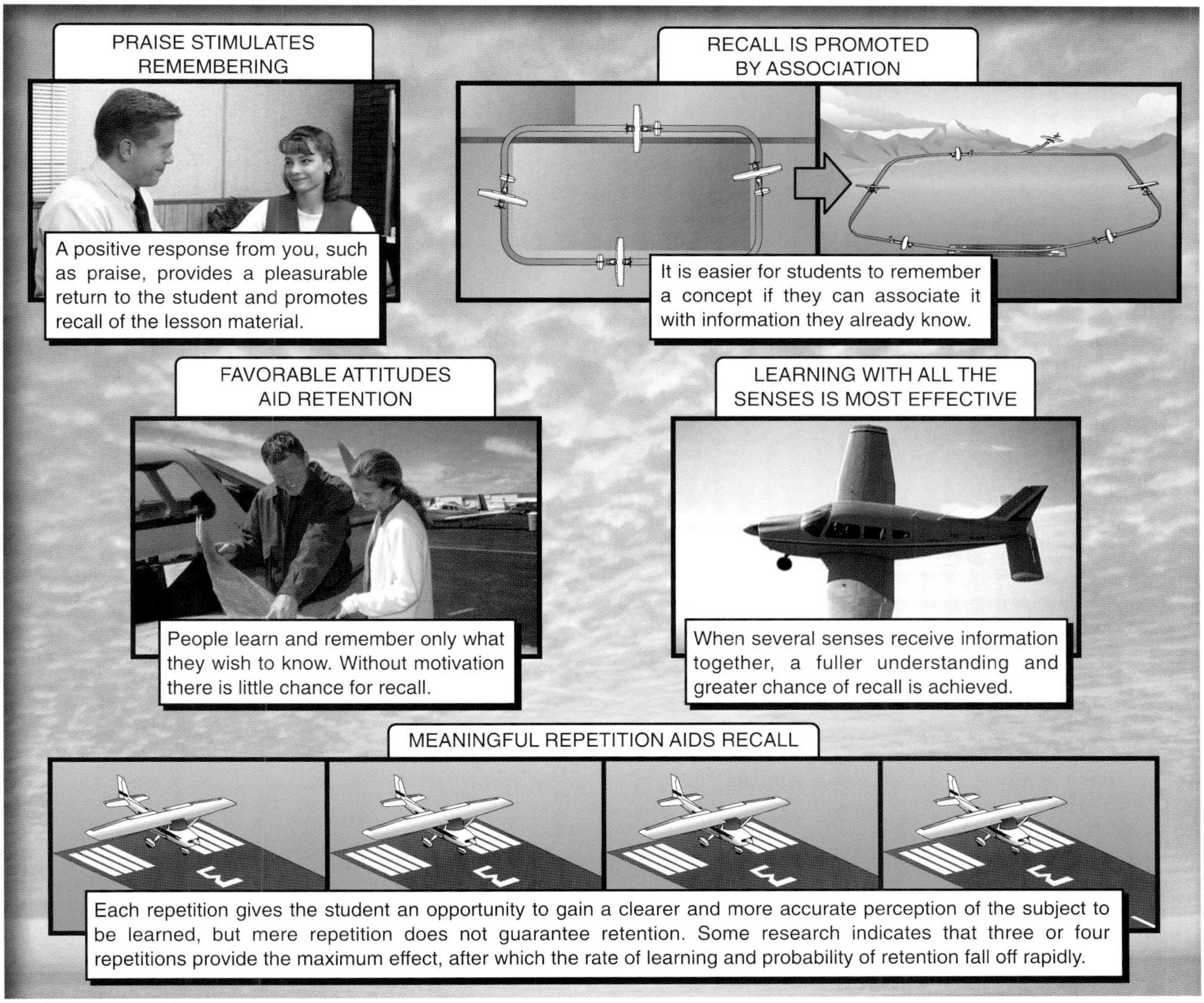

PRAISE STIMULATES REMEMBERING

A positive response from you, such as praise, provides a pleasurable return to the student and promotes recall of the lesson material.

RECALL IS PROMOTED BY ASSOCIATION

It is easier for students to remember a concept if they can associate it with information they already know.

FAVORABLE ATTITUDES AID RETENTION

People learn and remember only what they wish to know. Without motivation there is little chance for recall.

LEARNING WITH ALL THE SENSES IS MOST EFFECTIVE

When several senses receive information together, a fuller understanding and greater chance of recall is achieved.

MEANINGFUL REPETITION AIDS RECALL

Each repetition gives the student an opportunity to gain a clearer and more accurate perception of the subject to be learned, but mere repetition does not guarantee retention. Some research indicates that three or four repetitions provide the maximum effect, after which the rate of learning and probability of retention fall off rapidly.

Figure 1-14. These five principles can promote deep learning and enhance your student's retention of course material.

A positive response from you, such as praise, provides a pleasurable return to the student and promotes recall of the lesson material.

Studies on learning in classroom settings provide insight into how students pay attention and their chances of retention of material during the traditional lecture. Since students are disregarding whatever was on their minds when they arrived and are beginning to focus on the lesson, their attention levels and retention rates actually increase during the first 5 minutes or so of a class. After the next 10 to 15 minutes, attention levels decrease continually until the last 5 to 10 minutes when the students refocus their attention to the lesson. Students retain a significant amount of material from the first 10 to 15 minutes and the last 5 to 10 minutes of class. In the middle of a traditional hour-long lecture, less than 50% of the class is paying attention at any one given time. Students passively listening to a lecture have roughly a 5% retention rate over a 24-hour period. This rate is not high considering the amount of time spent lecturing. Students more actively engaged in the learning process have a much higher retention rate. Teaching methods which promote better retention will be discussed in Chapter 2. [Figure 1-15]

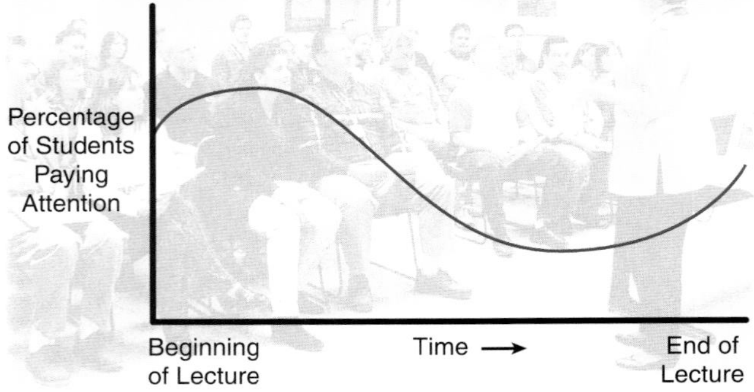

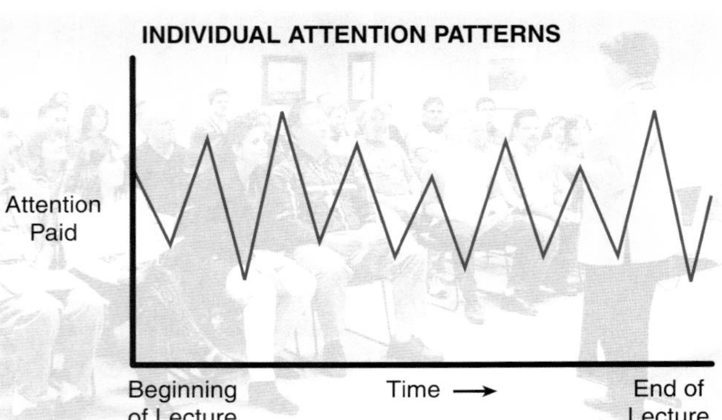

Figure 1-15. The overall percentage of students paying attention in a classroom initially rises, then falls to below 50% until just before the class ends. Individuals pay attention at various levels throughout the lesson.

CHARACTERISTICS OF LEARNING

Over the years, several distinct characteristics of learning have become the standard. A good understanding of these basic characteristics will help you develop and deliver effective instruction.

LEARNING IS PURPOSEFUL

As individuals, students will see things from their own perspectives. The motivations of each student are different and unique, yet are key components to the learning process. Motivations may be subtle and difficult to identify. Past experiences and backgrounds, as well as future goals can affect readiness to learn and influence student tactics and strategies during the learning process. For example, a student who has spent time as a passenger in small aircraft and is planning to pursue a flying career may welcome the opportunity to expand activities beyond traditional lessons. However, a student with no previous aviation experience who wants to obtain a pilot's certificate solely for recreational flying may only want to learn the minimum required to pass the practical test.

Motivations may be subtle and difficult to identify.

Normally, the most effective way for you to provide motivation is by promising rewards. This positive motivation may involve financial gain, achievement of a favorable self-image, personal comfort or security, or group approval. For example, you may point out that if your student prepares well for each lesson, less time will be spent on review so money can be saved. You can help improve your student's self-image by offering praise after a maneuver is preformed correctly, and you can make the student aware of how learning a procedure enhances flight safety. In addition, the approval of friends, family and other pilots can be a positive motivator during pilot training. Since negative motivation can cause students to react with fear and anxiety, reproofs or threats should be avoided with all but the most overconfident and impulsive students.

Since negative motivation can cause students to react with fear and anxiety, reproofs or threats should be avoided with all but the most overconfident and impulsive students.

Normally, the most effective way for you to provide positive motivation is by promising rewards. Motivation is tangible if students believe their efforts will be rewarded in a definite manner.

Since students desire a tangible return for their efforts, rewards must be constantly apparent during instruction. If they understand that a task will be useful in preparing for future activities, students will be more willing to pursue learning it. Individual goals vary and can range from short-term objectives measured in hours or days to long-term ambitions measured in years or a lifetime. It is important that you try to understand student needs and attitudes so you can design activities to help students reach their goals. If you can relate what you are teaching to a student's goal, then you will attach a stronger purpose to the learning and increase motivation. [Figure 1-16]

Figure 1-16. If you know your student is planning to buy an airplane and travel extensively after completing training, you can design lessons that focus on cross-country flight planning for long trips in a variety of areas in the country.

LEARNING IS A RESULT OF EXPERIENCE

Learning cannot take place unless the student personally experiences something. You cannot learn for your students, they must do it for themselves. You are simply the facilitator that guides students through the learning experiences you create. If an experience challenges students, as well as requires involvement with feelings, thoughts, memory of past experiences, and physical activity, it is more effective than a learning experience in which all students have to do is commit something to memory. Learning of a physical skill requires actual experience in performing that skill. The same is true for mental

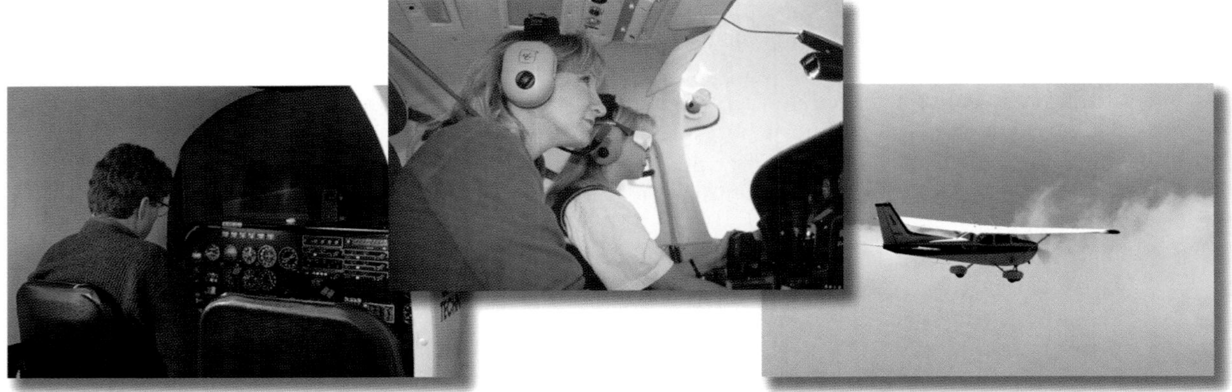

Figure 1-17. While all learning is a result of experience, it takes place in different forms and in varying degrees of depth. No two people have the same experiences during flight training.

skills. For example, if you want to teach sound judgment and decision making, then you must let students make decisions and see the results. [Figure 1-17]

LEARNING IS MULTIFACETED

Learning involves more than just memorizing facts and performing maneuvers. Learning, to be truly effective, engages a student's mind, body, and feelings. To ignore these aspects of learning means to underestimate the potential you have for providing the best instruction possible. Learning has been classified into several types: verbal, conceptual, perceptual, motor, problem solving, and emotional. [Figure 1-18]

Figure 1-18. In most learning situations, the more complex the learning exercise, the more you need to involve many types of learning at the same time.

While learning the subject at hand, students may be gaining other knowledge as well. For example, depending on what they experience, students may develop good or bad attitudes about aviation or they may learn skills which can be used in other aspects of their lives such as effective communication, organizational abilities, and assertiveness. This type of learning is sometimes referred to as incidental, but it may have a great impact on the total development of the student.

The learning process may include verbal, conceptual, and problem solving elements.

Incidental learning occurs when students learn things in addition to the material covered in the lesson.

LEARNING IS AN ACTIVE PROCESS

Students do not soak up knowledge like a sponge absorbs water. Presenting information to students does not guarantee it will be remembered and you cannot assume that students can apply what they know because they can quote a correct answer verbatim. All research on retention points to active learning as a means of increasing retention. To be an active process, learning must involve reading, writing, discussing, thinking, and doing. [Figure 1-19]

Figure 1-19. Classrooms in which the most learning takes place usually promote student participation and response to the lesson material. Strategies for creating active learning environments will be presented in Chapter 2.

PRINCIPLES OF LEARNING

Since the turn of the century, psychologists have discovered several consistent principles that can be applied to most learning situations. These **principles of learning**, sometimes called laws of learning, provide insight into effective learning and can provide a foundation for basic instructional techniques. These principles are derived from the work of E. L. Thorndike, who first proposed the principles of effect, exercise, and readiness. Three later principles were added: primacy, recency, and intensity.

READINESS

Students learn better when they are ready and they do not learn well if they see no reason for the lesson. **Readiness** implies a certain degree of single-mindedness and eagerness. You can help students get ready to learn by showing them the relevance of each lesson toward their objectives and by ensuring they understand how the total course of training will help them reach their overall goals. [Figure 1-20]

Figure 1-20. Knowing the aspirations of your students will enable you to tailor your training to individual needs and to provide the proper motivation.

The principle of readiness suggests that individuals will make more progress if they have a clear objective.

There are several factors that you will not be able to influence when it comes to student readiness. Students who are fatigued, suffering from personal problems, or are otherwise distracted by situations outside of the training environment may lack the necessary desire to learn on a particular day or even for an extended period of time. For example, a student may not be able to prepare properly for lessons due to additional workload caused by a change in jobs. In this case, you may consider postponing further training until the student is established in the new position and is ready to focus on flying again.

EXERCISE

Things are remembered best when they are repeated often. The principle of **exercise** is the basis for drill and practice. The mind can rarely retain, evaluate, and apply new concepts or experiences after a single exposure. While you need to provide opportunities for meaningful practice, students should only practice as much as needed and avoid unnecessary repetition. For example, learning to land an airplane is a complex and demanding task. Students can easily become fatigued and eventually performance will deteriorate to the point where learning ceases if too many landing attempts are done at once. [Figure 1-21]

The principle of exercise states that things most often repeated are best remembered.

Providing opportunities for a student to practice and then directing this process toward a goal is the basis of the principle of exercise.

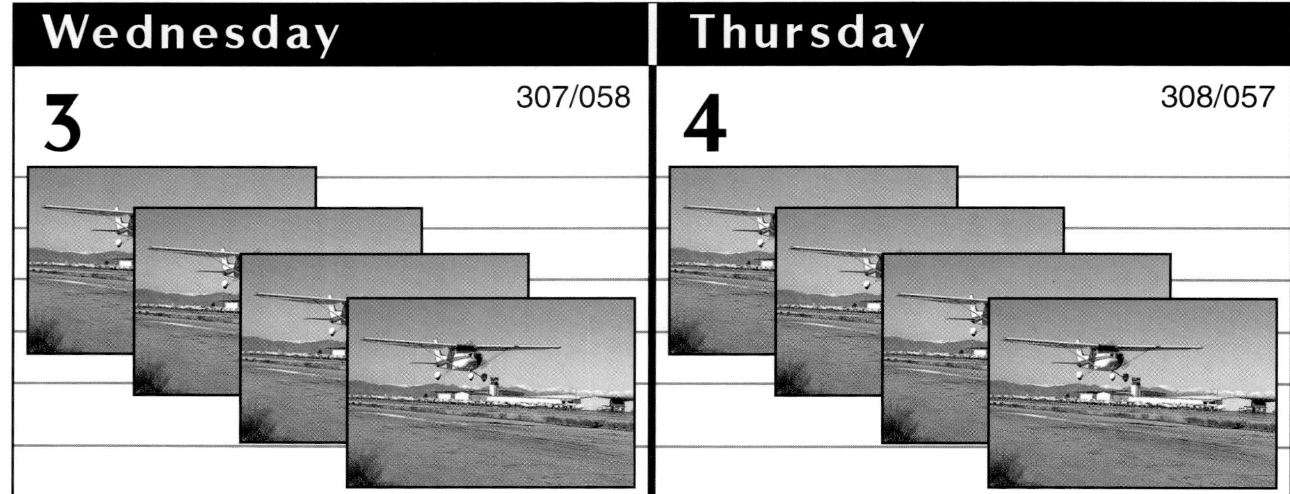

Figure 1-21. Learning may be enhanced by performing two lessons which include four landings in each rather than one lesson with eight landings.

EFFECT

The principle of **effect** is based upon the emotional reaction of the student and states that learning is strengthened when it is associated with a pleasant experience. This principle was a major topic of Thorndike's research and is one of the basic premises for the concept of behaviorism. Keep in mind that you do not need to be negative in order to create a negative learning situation. For example, if you attempt to teach landings during the first flight, the student is likely to feel inadequate, confused, and frustrated. The feeling of accomplishment is a powerful tool and with a little forethought, each lesson can be filled with new tasks that can be easily achieved by your students. Stressing how complex or dangerous some operation or maneuver is can make learning difficult and may cause

students to be apprehensive or hesitant. You need to impress upon students that challenging tasks can be mastered and are well within their capabilities. [Figure 1-22]

The principle of effect is based upon the emotional reaction of the student.

Figure 1-22. Students should have a feeling of satisfaction and accomplishment after completing a lesson. When you are debriefing students at the end of each flight, emphasize the positive aspects of the lesson, as well as those areas needing improvement.

Can Stress Sharpen Your Memory?

Although it may seem to be a confusing contradiction, stress can both hinder and help memory. Everyday stressors such as managing finances, and dealing with pressures at work or school can adversely affect memory. However, experiencing the stress associated with a physical crisis, such as being pursued by an animal or being the victim of a crime actually sharpens memory. When faced with stress, the adrenal glands secrete steroid hormones called glucocorticoids which are necessary for survival during a short sprint away from an immediate danger. However, studies have indicated that too much of these hormones released during a long-term stressful situation can actually damage neurons in the hippocampus, the structure in the brain which plays an essential role in forming and retrieving memories.

INTENSITY

Vivid and dramatic learning experiences are the ones that students tend to remember best. The term **intensity** implies students learn more from doing the real thing than from a substitute. Your students will normally gain a greater understanding of maneuvers through practice in the airplane than they will by examining these procedures on the ground. However, with today's technology, vivid and active learning experiences can be brought into the classroom to more closely simulate situations that may occur in flight. In addition, by using your imagination you can create lessons filled with discussions, activities, and scenarios which have direct application to the flight environment. [Figure 1-23]

The principle of intensity states that students will learn more from the real thing than from a substitute.

Figure 1-23. Using videos, flight training devices, and computer-based training programs, as well as presenting problem-solving exercises and realistic scenarios can increase the intensity of your teaching and promote long-term student retention.

PRIMACY

The principle of **primacy** states that things learned first often create strong and unshakable impressions. This means you need to ensure you are teaching material correctly the first time. The effort it takes to unlearn and relearn far exceeds that required to learn the right information initially. To effectively lay the foundation for further instruction, first experiences should be positive and meaningful, as well as correct. [Figure 1-24]

The principle of primacy states that something learned first creates a strong impression.

Figure 1-24. It is very hard to break students of the habit of steering with the yoke while taxiing if they were allowed to do this during initial training.

RECENCY

The principle of recency often determines the relative position of lectures within a course syllabus.

Things most recently learned are best remembered. It is easy for students to remember a procedure immediately after you demonstrate it, but without additional review, they most likely will not recall this procedure during a subsequent lesson a week later. As illustrated earlier by the classic forgetting curve, the more time that occurs between the learning event and the attempt to recall, the greater the likelihood of forgetting. The principle of **recency** often determines the relative position of lectures within a course syllabus. [Figure 1-25]

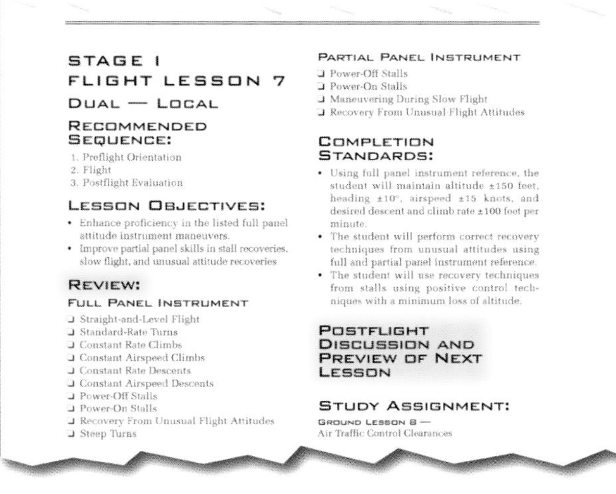

STAGE I
FLIGHT LESSON 7
DUAL — LOCAL

RECOMMENDED SEQUENCE:
1. Preflight Orientation
2. Flight
3. Postflight Evaluation

LESSON OBJECTIVES:
- Enhance proficiency in the listed full panel attitude instrument maneuvers.
- Improve partial panel skills in stall recoveries, slow flight, and unusual attitude recoveries

REVIEW:
FULL PANEL INSTRUMENT
- ❑ Straight-and-Level Flight
- ❑ Standard-Rate Turns
- ❑ Constant Rate Climbs
- ❑ Constant Airspeed Climbs
- ❑ Constant Rate Descents
- ❑ Constant Airspeed Descents
- ❑ Power-Off Stalls
- ❑ Power-On Stalls
- ❑ Recovery From Unusual Flight Attitudes
- ❑ Steep Turns

PARTIAL PANEL INSTRUMENT
- ❑ Power-Off Stalls
- ❑ Power-On Stalls
- ❑ Maneuvering During Slow Flight
- ❑ Recovery From Unusual Flight Attitudes

COMPLETION STANDARDS:
- Using full panel instrument reference, the student will maintain altitude ±150 feet, heading ±10°, airspeed ±15 knots, and desired descent and climb rate ±100 feet per minute.
- The student will perform correct recovery techniques from unusual attitudes using full and partial panel instrument reference.
- The student will use recovery techniques from stalls using positive control techniques with a minimum loss of altitude.

POSTFLIGHT DISCUSSION AND PREVIEW OF NEXT LESSON

STUDY ASSIGNMENT:
GROUND LESSON 8 —
Air Traffic Control Clearances

Figure 1-25. To enhance retention, key elements need to be reinforced at the end of each lesson and reviewed at the beginning of the next.

SUMMARY CHECKLIST

✓ Learning is defined as a persisting change in behavior resulting from experience with the environment, which cannot be attributed to natural growth.

✓ The theory of behaviorism is based on the study and measurement of observable behavior.

✓ Operant conditioning generally consists of three phases: cues to initiate the behavior are provided, the behavior is actually performed, and consequences associated with that performance are received.

✓ Reinforcement is a consequence that strengthens behavior. Four types of reinforcement have been identified that you can use as a flight instructor: positive reinforcement, negative reinforcement, extinction, and punishment. The use of positive reinforcement to help students learn is normally the most successful approach.

✓ The primary methods of teaching behaviors are shaping and chaining. Each time your students demonstrate the correct behavior, you provide positive reinforcement which helps shape, or develop, the correct behavior. Chaining combines behaviors students already know to assemble more complex behaviors.

✓ Cognitive theory involves mental processes, such as decision making and problem solving which are difficult to observe or measure. If your students can explain how and why they did something, you can gain valuable insight into the mental processes used.

✓ The social interaction model stresses the concept that students learn to shape their conduct after the prevailing behavior displayed in their environment.

- ✓ The cognitive information processing model describes how information is gathered, processed, and stored by the brain in much the same way it is by a computer.
- ✓ Information coming from the body's sensory organs is received and sorted by the brain's sensory register via a process known as attending. The sensory register acts as a filter that separates the important information from the unimportant information.
- ✓ When a maneuver or procedure is learned to the point that it becomes a habit, then the sensory register monitors the activity while letting the student think about the new information being presented. This level of performance is called automaticity.
- ✓ Pattern recognition occurs when new input is recognized because it matches or is similar to something already known.
- ✓ Working memory is the part of the cognitive information processing system where information is processed and sent to long-term memory for storage.
- ✓ To prevent interference from occurring, you must allow a period of time for the student to finish processing subject matter just presented before moving on to the next item.
- ✓ Working memory transfers information to long-term memory by two processes: rehearsing and coding. Coding is the process of relating incoming information to concepts and ideas already in memory.
- ✓ A mnemonic is a symbolic device or cue used to help remember information. Examples of mnemonics in aviation are memory aids, such as the I'M SAFE checklist or ARROW which is used to recall required aircraft documents.
- ✓ Long-term memory is used for long-term storage of items in the brain and can have a duration of a lifetime.
- ✓ Constructivism is based upon the idea that learners construct knowledge through the process of discovery as they experience events and actively seek to understand their environment.
- ✓ Perceptions, which occur when meaning is given to sensations, are the basis for all learning. You need to take into account all of the factors that can affect a student's ability to formulate the correct perceptions.
- ✓ Insights are the mental grouping of perceptions into meaningful wholes. Leading students to insights is one of your primary responsibilities as an instructor.
- ✓ There are several reasons that material cannot be remembered. The information may have never been learned in the first place or the student may have lost the ability to retrieve it due to disuse over a period of time. In addition, interference, and repression can cause material to be forgotten.
- ✓ Interference occurs when something is forgotten because a certain experience has overshadowed it, or when the learning of similar things has intervened.
- ✓ Submerging unpleasant memories into the subconscious is known as repression.
- ✓ Past experiences and backgrounds as well as future goals can affect readiness to learn and influence student tactics and strategies during the learning process.
- ✓ You must create appropriate learning experiences for your students. The more students are involved in their learning experiences, the more likelihood of long-term retention of the material.

- ✓ Learning has been classified into several types: verbal, conceptual, perceptual, motor, problem solving, and emotional. In most learning situations, the more complex the learning exercise, the more you need to involve many types of learning at the same time.
- ✓ Incidental learning occurs when students learn things in addition to the material covered in the lesson.
- ✓ The principle of readiness suggests that individuals will make more progress if they have a clear objective.
- ✓ The principle of exercise states that things most often repeated are best remembered.
- ✓ The principle of effect is based upon the emotional reaction of the student.
- ✓ Vivid and dramatic learning experiences are the ones that students tend to remember best. The principle of intensity implies students learn more from doing the real thing than from a substitute.
- ✓ The principle of primacy states that something learned first creates a strong impression.
- ✓ Things most recently learned are best remembered. The principle of recency determines the relative position of lectures within a course syllabus.

KEY TERMS

Learning

Behaviorism

Operant Conditioning

Reinforcement

Shaping

Chaining

Cognitive Theory

Social Interaction

Cognitive Information Processing

Sensory Register

Working Memory

Long-Term Memory

Constructivism

Perceptions

Insights

Forgetting

Retention

Interference

Repression

Characteristics of Learning

Principles of Learning

Readiness

Exercise

Effect

Intensity

Primacy

Recency

QUESTIONS

1. Define learning.

2. Give an example of each type of reinforcement that can be used with students. Identify which type is normally the most effective in helping students learn.

3. True/False. Cognitive theory involves mental processes, such as decision making and problem solving which are difficult to observe or measure.

4. Provide an example of a situation in which a student is performing at the level of automaticity.

5. Working memory transfers information to long-term memory by rehearsing and coding. Explain the difference between these two processes.

6. What learning theory is based upon the idea that learners build knowledge through the process of discovery as they experience events and actively seek to understand their environment?

   A. Behaviorism

   B. Constructivism

   C. Cognitive Theory

7. List at least four elements that can affect a student's perceptions.

8. Describe at least two reasons why students may forget material.

9. True/False. Incidental learning occurs when students learn things in addition to the material covered in the lesson.

Match the following statements to the principles of learning which they represent.

10. Kristen found that she learned more by practicing simulated emergency procedures in the airplane with her instructor than reading about them in a textbook.	A. Readiness
11. After a review of the ILS approach procedures during a preflight briefing, it was easy to for Pat to fly the approach during the lesson.	B. Primacy
12. Laurie was excited about learning ground reference maneuvers since her instructor explained that these procedures would help her prepare to fly the traffic pattern.	C. Recency
13. The students had fun during a class session in which they played roles as flight crewmembers to practice crew coordination and decision making.	D. Effect

14. After practicing the chandelle four times, Chad felt very comfortable with the maneuver and was able to remember the procedures during the next lesson.

E. Intensity

15. Jeff always remembered the importance of using a checklist during his preflight since it was one of the first things that his instructor emphasized during his first lesson.

F. Exercise

SECTION B
EXPLORING LEARNING STYLES AND DOMAINS

As an instructor, you need to consider that each of your students is an individual, and each of them learns in a unique way. Learning style is a concept that can play an important role in improving instruction and student success. It is concerned with student preferences and orientation at several levels. For example, a student's information processing technique, personality, social interaction tendencies, and the instructional methods used are all significant factors that apply to how individual students learn. [Figure 1-26]

Figure1-26. Understanding learning styles gives you insight into designing effective instruction. Students vary in their preferences for learning environments and teaching methods.

In addition to how students learn, the four levels of learning and the learning domains consider what is to be learned. For example, is it knowledge only, a change in attitude, a physical skill, or a combination of knowledge and skill?

LEARNING STYLES

Learning styles are a combination of behaviors and processes students use to absorb and retain new information or skills. All students learn differently, and training programs should be sensitive to these differences.

RIGHT BRAIN/LEFT BRAIN

The right brain/left brain theory is based on the concept that each hemisphere of the brain processes information differently. [Figure 1-27] Students with **right-brain** dominance are characterized as being spatially oriented, creative, intuitive, and emotional. They may be very good with art or music and can easily put together the big picture. Those with **left-brain** dominance are more verbal, analytical, and objective. Students who are left-brain dominant may be very good in math, language, or at analyzing details. However, the separate hemispheres of the brain do not function independently. For example, the right hemisphere may recognize a face, while the left associates a name to go with the face.

LEFT BRAIN
- Verbal
- Analytical
- Objective

RIGHT BRAIN
- Creative
- Intuitive
- Emotional

Figure 1-27. The left hemisphere of the brain tends to specialize in linear information processing by identifying and isolating individual parts of a whole. It is characterized by focus on logic and reasoning. The right hemisphere specializes in processing visual information and consolidating parts into meaningful wholes.

REFLECTIVE/IMPULSIVE

You may have noticed that some people stop and consider many factors before taking action while others act without much thought. A **reflective** student considers all possibilities or alternatives before making a decision while an **impulsive** student makes a quick assessment and then decides. These traits have some significant implications when teaching. For example, in testing situations, reflective students may spend too much time considering their answers to the point they cannot finish exams in time or they may change answers from right to wrong. Impulsive students may not read each question or all of the answer choices entirely. As a result, they tend to select the first choice that appears correct.

Encourage students who take a long time to make a decision to look at the question and answers, choose, and move on. The majority of the time their initial choices are correct. In most cases, when students change their selection, they change the right answer to a wrong one. Advise students who are too quick to answer to slow down, read the entire

Reflecting on Impulsive Emergencies

A good way to tell if students are reflective or impulsive is by observing their actions while practicing simulated engine failures during cruise flight. A reflective student may have trouble selecting an appropriate emergency landing field, especially if there are several to choose from. An impulsive student may choose the first field available and overlook a more suitable one.

When instructing reflective students, stress the fact that while they are doing the correct thing by considering all their options, a timely decision needs to be made, especially in an emergency situation. On the other hand, impulsive students need to be made aware of the fact that the first choice may not always be the best one. Point out that, especially during an engine failure at cruising altitude, there is enough time to consider the alternatives and make a sound decision.

question and each of the possible answers, choose, and move on. Simply making your students aware of these tendencies may be enough to help improve their performance during testing situations.

HOLIST/SERIALIST

The holist/serialist theory focuses on two ways students process information. For example, **holists** use a top-down strategy to process information while **serialists** prefer a bottom-up method. Serialists prefer to start at the beginning and examine material in order. Each piece of information is linked to others to eventually create an overall picture. In many cases, theory is learned separately from the practical applications. Holists, on the other hand, prefer to start with the overall concept, then determine how each piece of information fits that concept. They typically make considerable use of analogies when seeking meaning and understanding. Holistic students like to study several parts of the lesson simultaneously and seek to understand both theory and practical applications at the same time. [Figure 1-28]

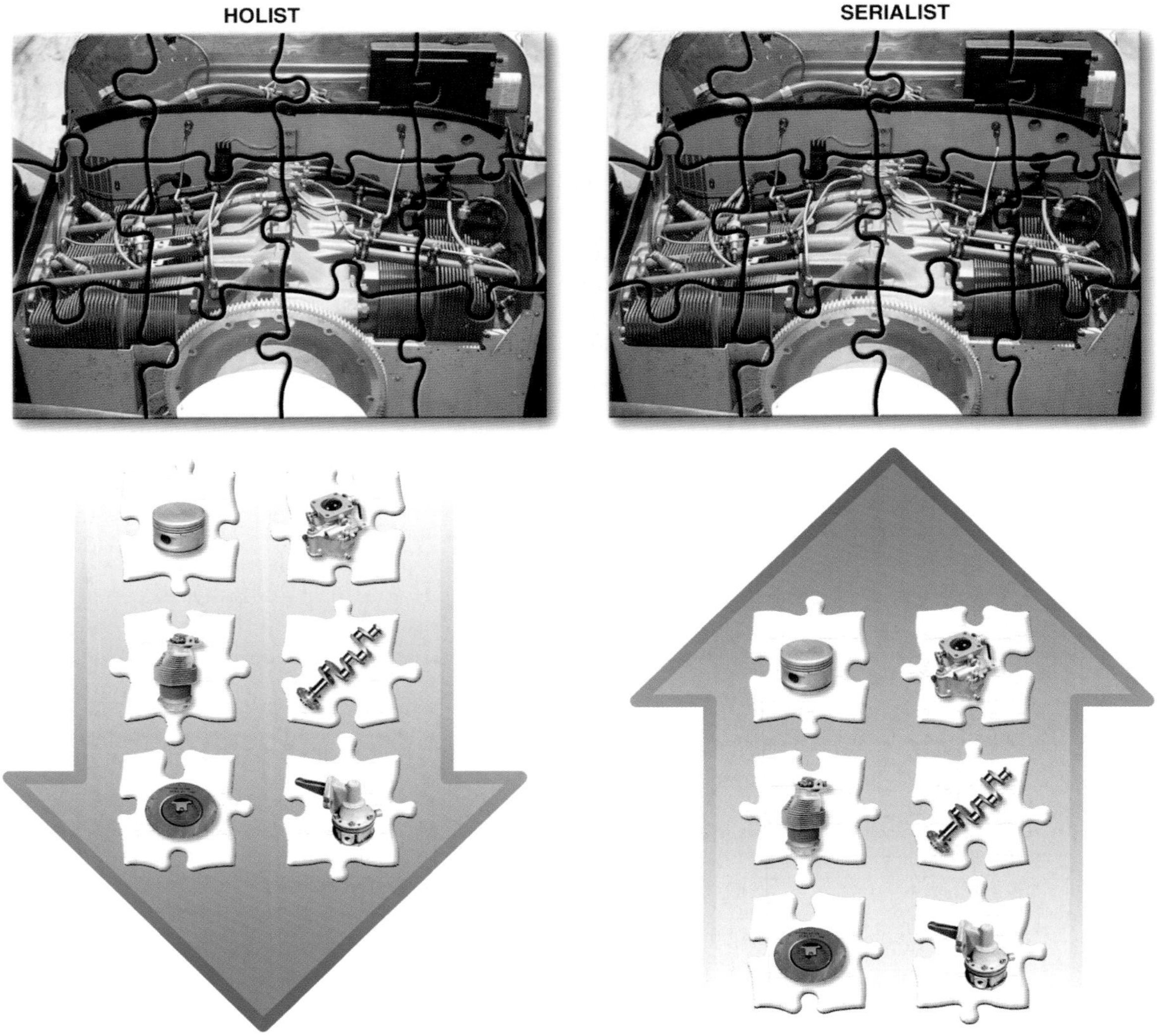

Figure 1-28. Holists tend to focus on the overall engine first and then examine the individual components. Serialists start with the components and piece them together to understand the whole engine.

AUDITORY/VISUAL/KINESTHETIC

These learning styles are based upon the dominant sense involved in the learning process: auditory, visual, or kinesthetic. Some students learn primarily by listening, others by watching, and the rest by doing. This means you must incorporate all three types of

Figure 1-29. With a little planning, you can create activities that accommodate all three learning styles.

activities in lessons, especially if you are teaching more than one student at a time, to accommodate the learning styles of each student. [Figure 1-29]

AUDITORY

Auditory learners acquire knowledge best by listening. They may need to talk about a topic to hear their thoughts. Students who are auditory learners are typically independent, competitive, goal oriented, and learn well by analyzing and conceptualizing information. Memorizing information is one of their main strengths. Since auditory learners are similar to serialists, it works well to present material to them in a logical sequence and link each new bit of information to knowledge they already possess. Make sure your students have time to think about and discuss the material so it can be thoroughly processed.

Since they are comfortable with conventional teaching methods, auditory learners tend to achieve higher grades in traditional settings than those with other learning styles. Auditory learners normally do well in settings where material is presented and reviewed orally. Asking students to repeat or restate material in their own words also enhances their learning. [Figure 1-30]

Figure 1-30. Lectures, guided discussions, or any group activity in which students discuss information with each other are all effective methods to teach auditory learners.

VISUAL

Students who learn best with their sense of sight are **visual learners**. Sharing many characteristics with holists, visual learners are conceptual and global in their learning preferences. They prefer to absorb the big picture first, then break the information down into individual parts. When teaching visual learners, you need to ensure they have a clear understanding of the overall objective and where the lesson is heading. They have a tendency to depend upon you for much of the learning rather than on textbooks.

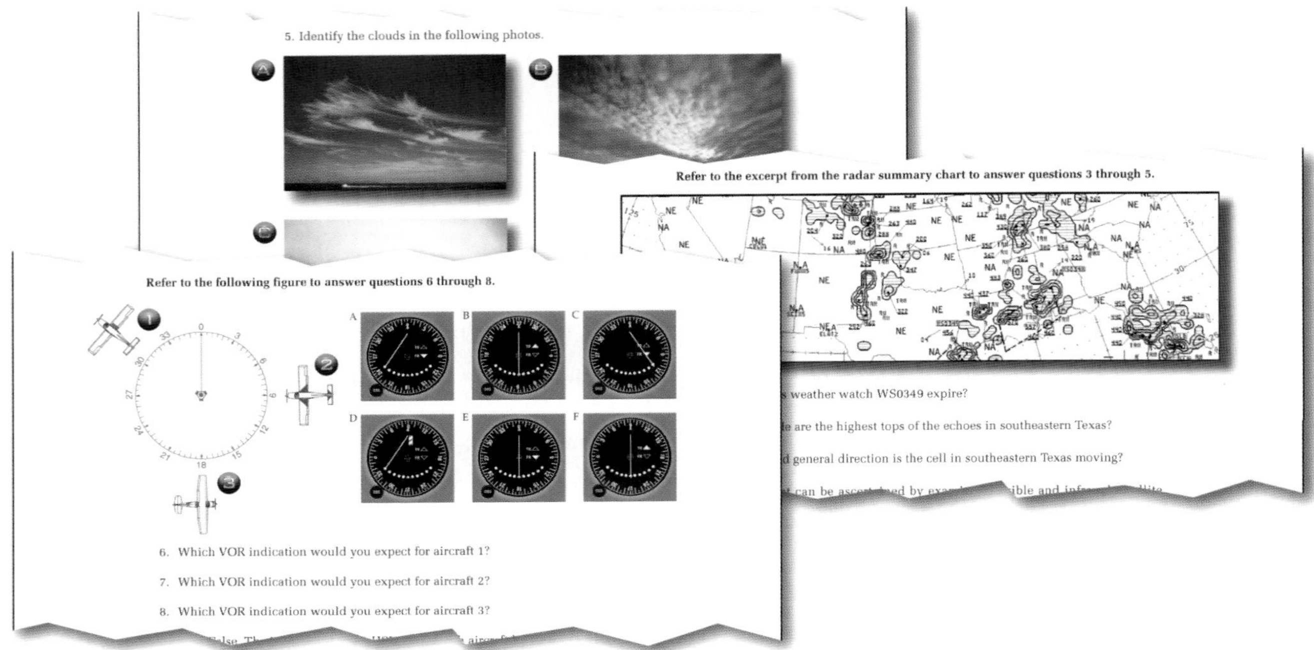

Figure 1-31. Be aware that when evaluating the performance of visual learners, traditional multiple choice exams typically do not effectively measure success. Open-ended tests usually result in more accurate assessments of achievement.

Since visual learners are typically at a disadvantage in traditional, formal settings, you may need to use alternative methods to instruct these students. For example, group activities in informal settings and role playing scenarios may be effective. Photos, diagrams, schematics, demonstrations, and other visually stimulating material such as video and computer-based instructional programs can be good tools for teaching visual learners. [Figure 1-31]

KINESTHETIC

Kinesthetic learners prefer to be doing something and primarily absorb information through the actual hands-on experience. While these types of learners may feel at home in the cockpit, they may be overlooked in the typical classroom setting. Since kinesthetic learners need to be creative and active, they do not do well sitting quietly at a desk or table.

When teaching students who are kinesthetic learners, you need to provide them with as many concrete learning activities at possible. Demonstrations, simulations, and other learning experiences, such as computer-based programs that actively engage students are good tools for teaching kinesthetic learners. For example, when discussing airplane powerplants, allow these students to actually see and touch an engine and its parts. The fact that flight training requires a hands-on practical application of skills favors kinesthetic learners. However, kinesthetic learners typically do not perform as well as auditory and visual learners on traditional written tests. To accurately assess the learning of these students, you must use nontraditional evaluation methods. Rather than administering a multiple-choice test, you should ask for demonstrations of tasks. [Figure 1-32]

Figure 1-32. Kinesthetic learners ascertain more from performing a preflight inspection than studying a checklist.

What Works Best for You?

You have been on three or four training flights with your student, Chad, and you are having a difficult time determining his learning style. One way to find out would be to simply ask, *"What works best for you?"*

For example, after discussing S-turns with Chad on the ground and demonstrating them with a model, you then perform them in the airplane. After the flight, ask Chad if the discussion before the flight helped him understand the maneuver any better. Whatever the response, you will get an idea as to what style of learning is working the best. If it did not help, you will know not to spend as much time discussing maneuvers, and to concentrate more on practical experience in the airplane. On the other hand, if Chad did gain something from the discussion, continue using this method in future lessons.

DOMAINS OF LEARNING

Levels of learning may be classified in any number of ways. Four basic levels of learning have traditionally been included in aviation instructor training: rote, understanding, application, and correlation. Rote learning is the simple memorization of factual information, without understanding or being able to apply what has been learned. Understanding is the ability to explain the how and why of those facts. Application is the act of putting those facts and understanding into practical use. Correlation is associating what has been learned, understood, and applied with previous or subsequent learning. The correlation level should be the objective of all aviation instruction. An example of the correlation level of learning is when a student uses knowledge and skills about the pitch and power relationship in slow flight and applies it to flying a final approach in the traffic pattern.

An FAA examiner giving a student a simulated engine failure without providing any instructions or guidance is an example of testing at the application level. Most instructors stop teaching when reaching the application level.

The level of learning that is concerned with facts, such as aircraft speeds, is rote learning.

When a student is required to explain something, such as how maximum certificated weight affects maneuvering speed, the understanding level of learning is being tested.

In addition to the four basic levels of learning, psychologists have developed three **domains of learning**: cognitive, psychomotor and affective. These domains represent what is to be gained during the learning process, either knowledge, skills or attitudes. Each domain is divided into levels that identify the educational objectives that have been met when

The cognitive domain involves learning and utilizing information from many sources.

The skills needed to control the airplane are part of the psychomotor domain.

Developing attitudes to make safe decisions involves the affective domain.

Figure 1-33. The three domains of learning are found throughout flight training.

students are able to perform specific tasks. An understanding of these domains can enable you to effectively construct lesson plans that target specific learning and accurately measure student performance. [Figure 1-33]

COGNITIVE DOMAIN

The **cognitive domain** is the category of learning concerned with knowledge and thought processes. Dr. Benjamin Bloom's hierarchical taxonomy for the cognitive domain includes six educational objective levels, each of which develops a foundation for the next. During pilot training, educational objectives in the cognitive domain refer to knowledge which may be gained as the result of attending a ground school, reading about airspace classifications, listening to a preflight briefing, reviewing meteorological reports and forecasts, or participating in computer-based training. [Figure 1-34]

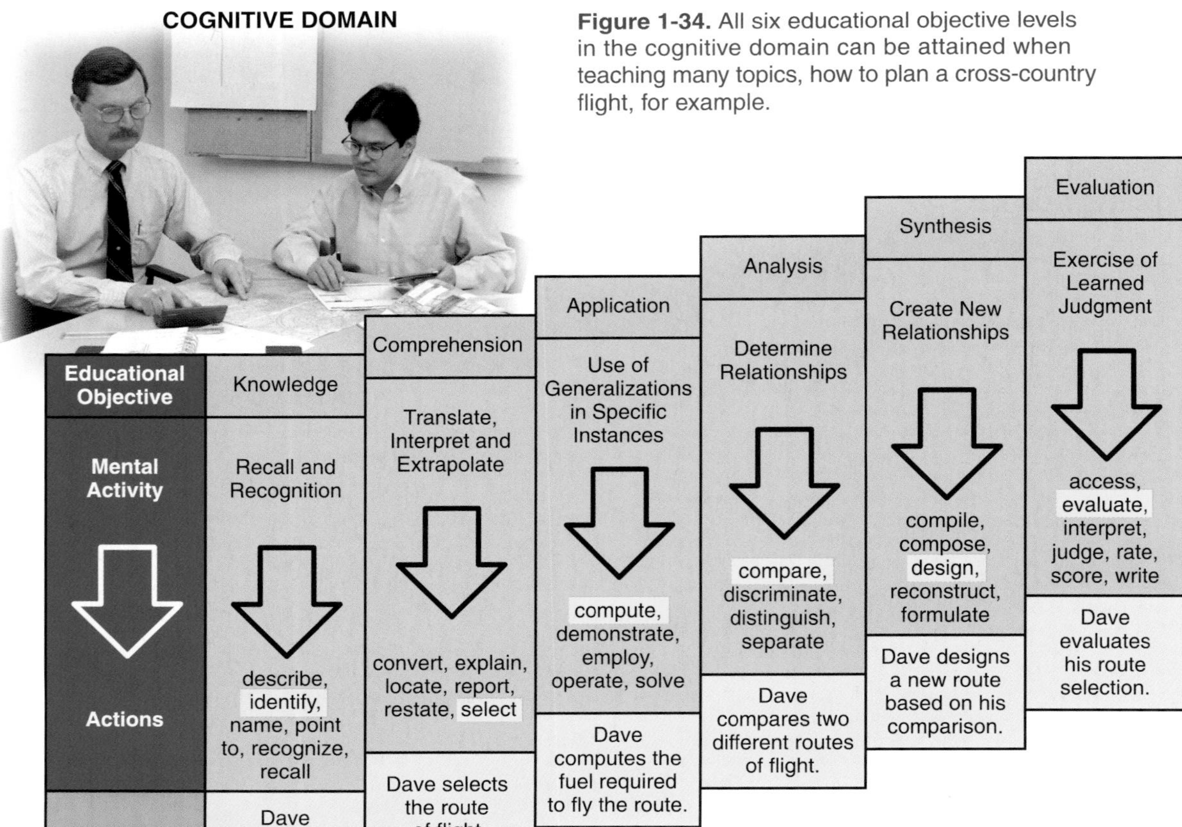

Figure 1-34. All six educational objective levels in the cognitive domain can be attained when teaching many topics, how to plan a cross-country flight, for example.

PSYCHOMOTOR DOMAIN

Since learning to fly an airplane requires the development of fine and exact physical skills, your understanding of the **psychomotor domain** is essential to effective flight instructing. Typical activities involving these skills include learning to preflight an airplane, performing a landing, flying an instrument approach procedure, and programming a GPS receiver. As physical tasks and aircraft equipment become more complex, the requirement for integration of cognitive and psychomotor skills increases. The levels of learning with respect to psychomotor skills are outlined in figure 1-35.

PSYCHOMOTOR DOMAIN

Educational Objective	Perception	Set	Guided Response	Mechanism	Complex Overt Response	Adaption	Origination
Skill Level	Awareness of Sensory Stimulus	Relates Cues/ Knows	Performs as Demonstrated	Performs Simple Acts Well	Skillful Performance of Complex Acts	Modifies for Special Problems	New Movement Patterns/ Creativity
Actions	choose, detect, identify, isolate, compare	begin, move, react, respond, start, select	assemble, build, calibrate, fix, grind, mend	same as at lower level except with greater proficiency	same as at lower level except more highly coordinated	adapt, alter, change, rearrange, reorganize, revise	combine, compose, construct, design, originate
Example	Julie detects a 30° change in the desired heading.	Julie moves the controls to correct for the change.	Julie calibrates the correction required to regain the original course.	With practice, Julie becomes more proficient at maintaining headings.	Julie becomes more efficient at coordinating all of her flying duties.	Julie alters her instrument scan to pay close attention to the heading indicator.	Julie designs an instrument scan to avoid heading deviations.

Figure 1-35. Lessons that specifically target each level in E. J. Simpson's hierarchical taxonomy for the psychomotor domain give students the skills and abilities needed to become safe and effective pilots.

Learning psychomotor skills takes time and practice and involves more than just using muscles. Students need to learn the sequence or procedure, recognize if the skill is being performed correctly and determine the corrective action they must take if it is not. There are several aspects of learning psychomotor skills that you need to keep in mind.

DESIRE TO LEARN

If you ask your students to think back to when they learned to perform certain skills, they might be surprised at how much more readily they learned skills that appealed to their own needs. Where the desire to learn or improve was missing, little progress was made. To improve their performance, your students must not only recognize mistakes, but also make an effort to correct them. A student who lacks the desire to improve is not likely to make the effort and consequently will continue to practice errors. By relating the lesson objective to your students' intentions and needs you will build on their natural enthusiasm.

PATTERNS TO FOLLOW

When learning a psychomotor skill, students need clear step-by-step examples to understand what is required to perform the procedure. Imagine how difficult it would be ask your students to perform S-turns without ever demonstrating one. Having a model to follow permits students to get a clear picture of each step in a sequence so they understand what is required and how to do it. [Figure 1-36]

The best way to prepare your student to perform a task is to provide a clear, step-by-step example.

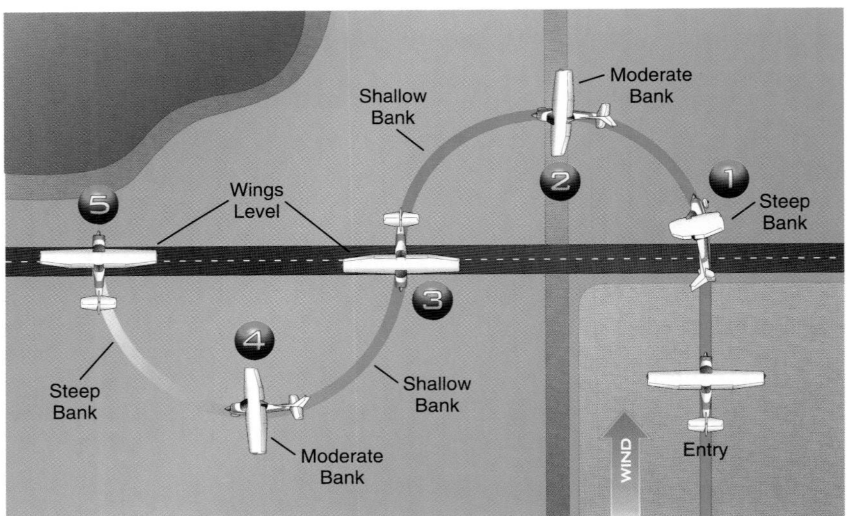

Figure 1-36. Breaking down a maneuver into individual steps makes it easier to absorb the information.

PERFORM THE SKILL

Simply demonstrating a procedure or maneuver is not enough; your students need to practice to become knowledgeable. As your students gain proficiency in a skill, verbal instructions from you have more meaning. Whereas a long, detailed explanation is confusing before students begin practicing a new maneuver, specific comments are more meaningful and useful after the skill has been partially mastered. For example, first introducing your students to stalls by giving them a detailed, extensive explanation makes learning difficult. Starting with a simple explanation and demonstrating the maneuver in the airplane is more effective.

KNOWLEDGE OF RESULTS

There are simple skills where your students will be able to discover their own errors, and there are complex skills where they will need help from you to determine their mistakes. Students may know something is wrong, but may not know how to correct it. In any case, students rely on your feedback to make them aware of their progress. By giving them feedback as soon as possible after a lesson, you improve their chances of learning from their mistakes and correcting them. A good way to make students aware of their progress is to repeat a demonstration or example and show them the standards their performance must ultimately meet.

PROGRESS FOLLOWS A PATTERN

When a student is learning something new, performance typically improves rapidly at first. However, after a while, progress slows. This **learning plateau** can be due to a variety of reasons. [Figure 1-37] For example, your student may have

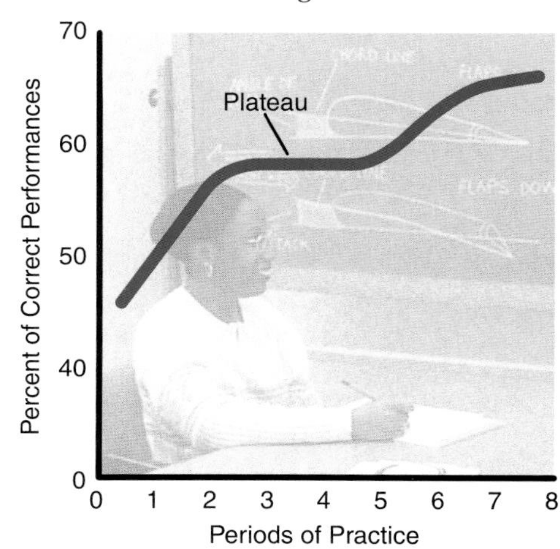

Figure 1-37. Students normally experience a temporary learning plateau at some point in their training.

reached capability limits, may misunderstand some aspect of the task, or might simply be consolidating new skills. Your student could be experiencing a lack of motivation or a different teaching method may be necessary to increase progress.

A plateau, or leveling-off, in your student's learning curve is normal and temporary.

It is normal to expect learning to slow or even regress when new or more complex tasks are introduced. As skills are practiced and students gain experience, the learning curve will eventually show an increase. You can expect to encounter learning plateaus at certain points in the training program, such as during the introduction of takeoffs and landings. Initially, students have difficulty flying the airplane, talking on the radio, following traffic, performing pre-landing checks, and remembering to correct for wind drift. It may seem that your students suddenly cannot hold altitude, airspeed, or headings as before. The most likely reasons are the increased workload and the division of attention required to do so many tasks simultaneously. Yet, each time they practice the traffic pattern, students develop more coordination, learn to manage their workload, and gain confidence. At some point, it seems that everything falls into place and progress resumes. The main thing to remember is a learning plateau is normal and does not mean learning has ceased.

While individual student learning curves are unique, they share one common characteristic in that most students eventually achieve success. Be careful about making early evaluations of a particular student's chances of accomplishment. Before you suggest that your student cannot succeed, you should try various methods and techniques. [Figure 1-38]

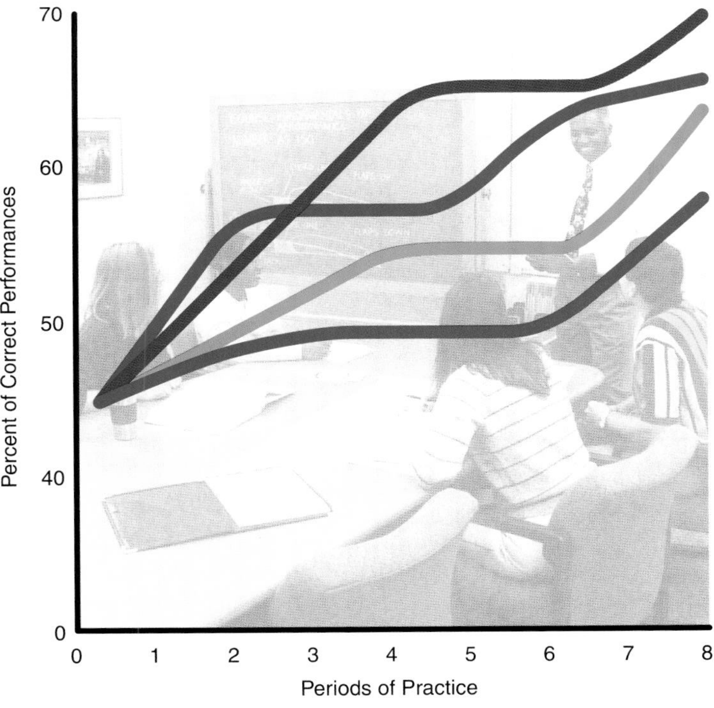

Figure 1-38. Individuals learn at different rates as shown by the different learning curves.

AFFECTIVE DOMAIN

D. R. Krathwohl's hierarchical taxonomy for the **affective domain** focuses on feelings, attitudes, personal beliefs, and values. These factors affect the choices students make. Safety, judgment, and decision-making are the primary areas of flight training concerned with the affective domain. Measuring educational objectives in this domain is not easy. For example, how do you evaluate a positive attitude toward flight safety? [Figure 1-39]

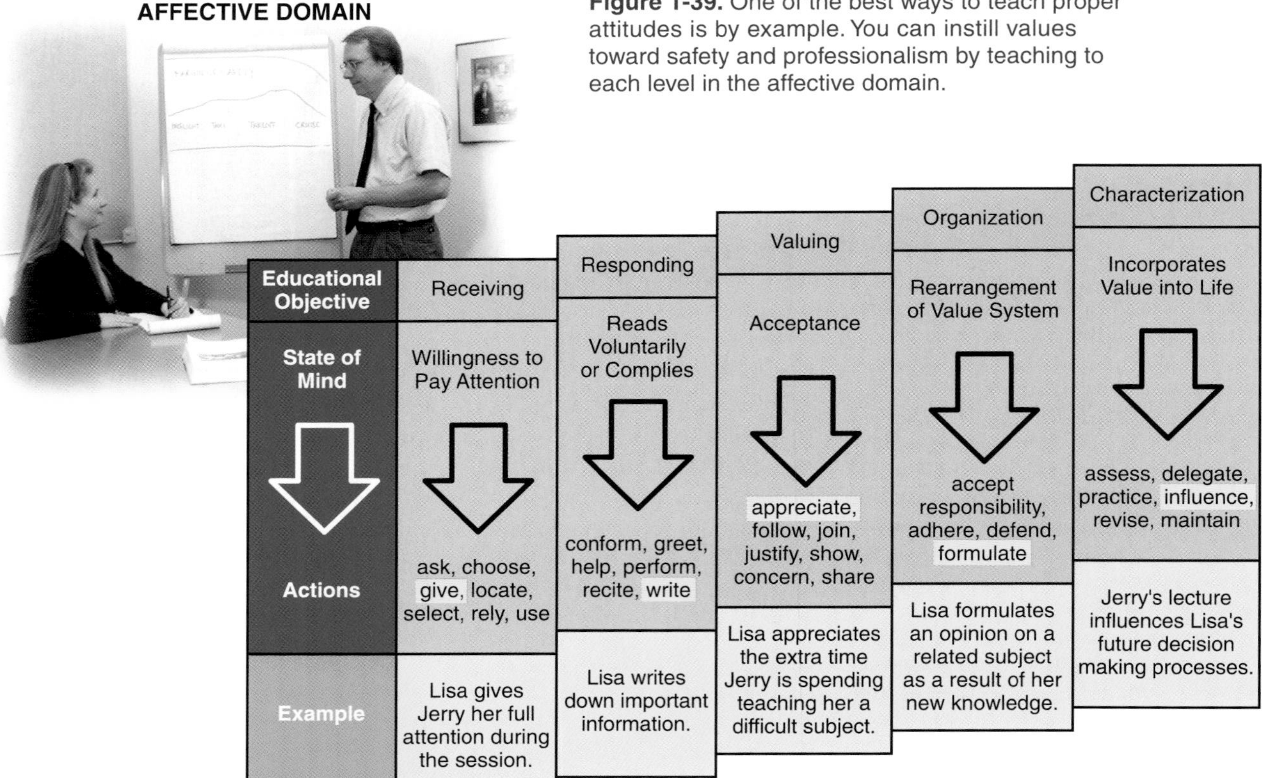

Figure 1-39. One of the best ways to teach proper attitudes is by example. You can instill values toward safety and professionalism by teaching to each level in the affective domain.

TRANSFER OF LEARNING

Since students interpret new things in terms of what they already know, some degree of transfer is involved in all learning. During a learning experience, knowledge or skills they have gained in the past may aid students, and a **positive transfer of learning** occurs. On the other hand, it is sometimes apparent that previous learning interferes with student understanding of the current task, and a **negative transfer of learning** takes place. [Figure 1-40]

Figure 1-40. A negative transfer of learning occurs when the learning of one skill interferes with the learning of another. For example, learning to drive a car can be a hindrance when learning to taxi an airplane.

The concept of transfer of learning may explain why students of apparently equal ability have differing success in certain areas. Negative transfer may hinder the learning of some; positive transfer may help others. This points to a need to know a student's past experience and what has already been learned. In lesson and syllabus development, you should plan for transfer by organizing course materials in a meaningful sequence. Each phase should help your student learn what is to follow.

A negative transfer of learning occurs when the performance of a maneuver interferes with the learning of another maneuver.

A positive transfer of learning occurs when the performance of one maneuver helps your student to perform a different maneuver.

SUMMARY CHECKLIST

- ✓ Learning styles are a combination of behaviors and processes students use to absorb and retain new information or skills.
- ✓ The right brain/left brain theory is based on the concept that each hemisphere of the brain processes information differently.
- ✓ Students with right-brain dominance are characterized as being spatially oriented, creative, intuitive, and emotional.
- ✓ Students with left-brain dominance are verbal, analytical, and objective.
- ✓ A reflective student considers all possibilities or alternatives before making a decision while an impulsive student makes a quick assessment and then decides.
- ✓ The holist/serialist theory focuses on two ways students process information. Holists use a top-down strategy to process information while serialists prefer a bottom-up method.
- ✓ Auditory learners acquire knowledge best by listening.
- ✓ Students who are auditory learners are typically independent, competitive, goal oriented, and learn well by analyzing and conceptualizing information.
- ✓ When teaching visual learners, you need to ensure they have a clear understanding of the overall objective and where the lesson is heading.
- ✓ Kinesthetic learners prefer to be doing something and primarily absorb information through the actual hands-on experience.
- ✓ Demonstrations, simulations, and other learning experiences, such as computer-based programs that actively engage students are good tools for teaching kinesthetic learners.
- ✓ Four basic levels of learning have traditionally been included in aviation instructor training: rote, understanding, application, and correlation.
- ✓ Rote learning is the simple memorization of factual information, without understanding or being able to apply what has been learned.

- ✓ Understanding is the ability to explain the how and why of those facts.
- ✓ Application is the act of putting those facts and understanding into practical use.
- ✓ Correlation is associating what has been learned, understood, and applied with previous or subsequent learning.
- ✓ In addition to the four basic levels of learning, psychologists have developed three learning domains: cognitive, psychomotor and affective.
- ✓ The cognitive domain is the category of learning concerned with knowledge and thought processes.
- ✓ Since learning to fly an airplane requires the development of fine and exact physical skills, your understanding of the psychomotor domain is essential to effective flight instructing.
- ✓ By relating the lesson objective to your student's intentions and needs you will build on their natural enthusiasm.
- ✓ When learning a psychomotor skill, students need clear step-by-step examples to understand what is required to perform the procedure.
- ✓ A good way to make students aware of their progress is to repeat a demonstration or example and show them the standards their performance must ultimately meet.
- ✓ When a student is learning something new, performance typically improves rapidly at first, then begins to slow. This is known as a learning plateau.
- ✓ D. R. Krathwohl's hierarchical taxonomy for the affective domain focuses on feelings, attitudes, personal beliefs, and values.
- ✓ Since students interpret new things in terms of what they already know, some degree of transfer is involved in all learning.

KEY TERMS

Learning Styles

Right-brain

Left-brain

Reflective

Impulsive

Holists

Serialists

Auditory Learners

Visual Learners

Kinesthetic Learners

Domains of Learning

Cognitive Domain

Psychomotor Domain

Learning Plateau

Affective Domain

Positive Transfer of Learning

Negative Transfer of Learning

QUESTIONS

1. Give three examples of learning styles.

2. True/False. Students with right-brain dominance are typically very good in math, language, and analyzing details.

3. What type of student considers all the possibilities before making a decision?

   A. Holist
   B. Impulsive
   C. Reflective

4. Describe how serialists approach learning.

5. What type of student primarily absorbs information through hands-on experiences?

   A. Visual
   B. Auditory
   C. Kinesthetic

6. List and define the three learning domains.

7. True/False. You should give students feedback as soon as possible following a lesson.

8. What type of transfer of learning occurs when previous learning interferes with the understanding of a new task?

   A. Lateral
   B. Positive
   C. Negative

SECTION C
EXCHANGING IDEAS

When you teach, you introduce new concepts and present pertinent information, as well as explain and demonstrate procedures. An exchange of ideas, or communication, takes place when your students provide feedback on your instruction, express their thoughts, and perform tasks based on your directions. Communicating effectively with your students is key to your success as an instructor. A clear and complete understanding of the communication process is necessary to help your students reach their goals.

THE COMMUNICATION PROCESS

The **communication process** consists of three basic elements: the source, the symbols used to communicate the message, and the receiver. In addition, feedback is essential if effective communication is to take place. [Figure 1-41]

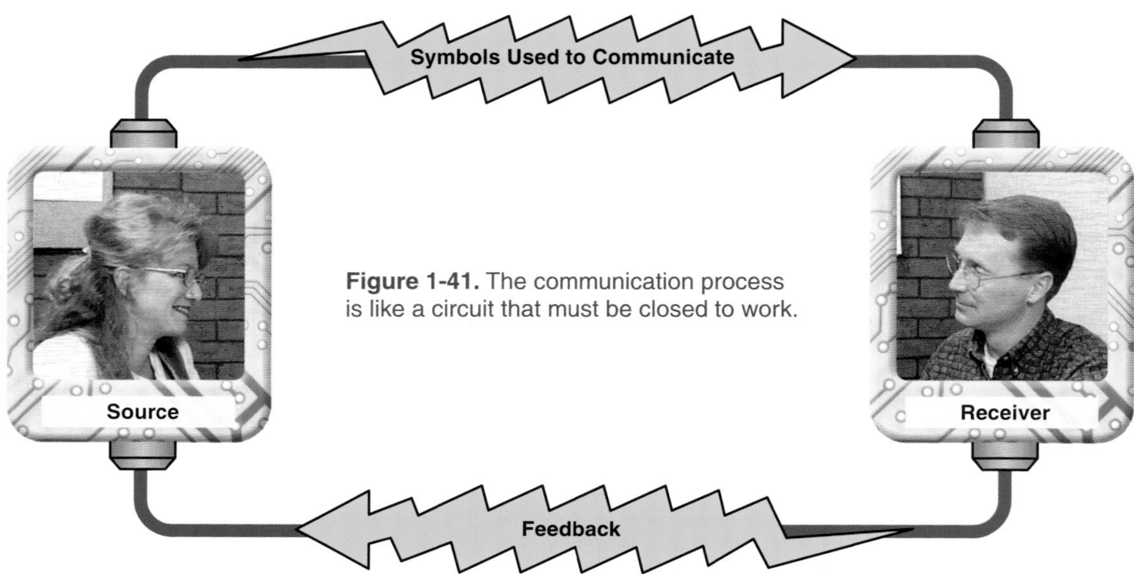

Figure 1-41. The communication process is like a circuit that must be closed to work.

SOURCE

The **source** of communication is the person or other media that is sending the message. When you instruct someone, you are the source of the information. If the material you want communicated is contained in a textbook, manual, or computer program, then that reference is the source of the communication. Whatever you choose as the source, you need to consider three basic factors. First, you should use language that is meaningful to your listeners. Second, you need to remember that you can consciously and subconsciously reveal your attitudes to your students. Third, you must ensure the message you are trying to communicate is accurate, stimulating, and up to date.

The ability to use language appropriately to convey ideas is key to effective communication. By evaluating the background of your students, you can determine the vocabulary which will have meaning for them. For example, use of unfamiliar aviation terminology impedes communication with students who are just beginning flight training. However, using technical aviation language is appropriate if you address a group of flight instructors. You may lose credibility with more advanced students if your vocabulary is oversimplified.

To communicate effectively, you must reveal a positive attitude while delivering your message.

In order to be a successful communicator, you must speak from a background of up-to-date and stimulating material.

You can easily convey your attitudes to your students by the words you use and the mannerisms you display. Always project a positive attitude toward your students and the subject you are teaching. Your reaction to a question, the tone in your voice when discussing a subject, and your outward enthusiasm, all send messages about your attitude. If you are enthusiastic about teaching, then your students will have a more positive attitude toward the subject. If you are somewhat ambivalent about the topic, then your students will generally have less interest or place less importance on it. [Figure 1-42]

Figure 1-42. You can keep your student's interest and maintain your credibility by ensuring your material is accurate, current, and relevant to the training goal. To hold your student's attention, you must develop creative ways to keep your presentations, on even the most difficult topics, entertaining and engaging.

SYMBOLS

Your message is transmitted by the **symbols** you chose. These symbols can be words, sounds, pictures, expressions, or any number of printed or computer-based resources. Most often, communicators select the channels of hearing and seeing to convey information.

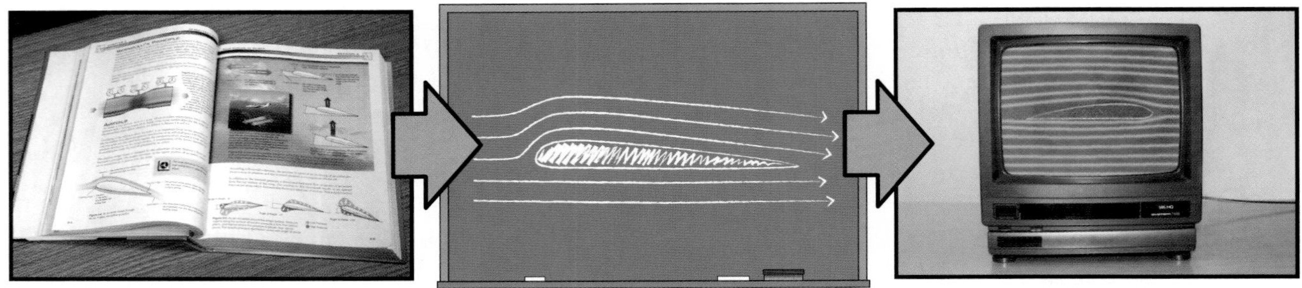

Figure 1-43. Effectively communicating new ideas and concepts to your students may require you to use many types of symbols together, such as a variety of audiovisual aids.

For developing motor skills, the sense of touch is added as the student practices the skill. The most successful communicators use a variety of symbols to transmit their ideas. [Figure 1-43]

You can effectively gain and retain your student's attention by using a variety of audiovisual aids.

For your message to be meaningful to your students, you must be certain they understand the symbols you are using. For example, if you use aviation acronyms, slang, and abbreviations with students who are unfamiliar with these symbols, effective communication is compromised. If you do not define aviation terms when teaching, your students will not fully understand the information you are trying to convey. Students may assign incorrect meanings to terms and receive a different message than you intended. [Figure 1-44]

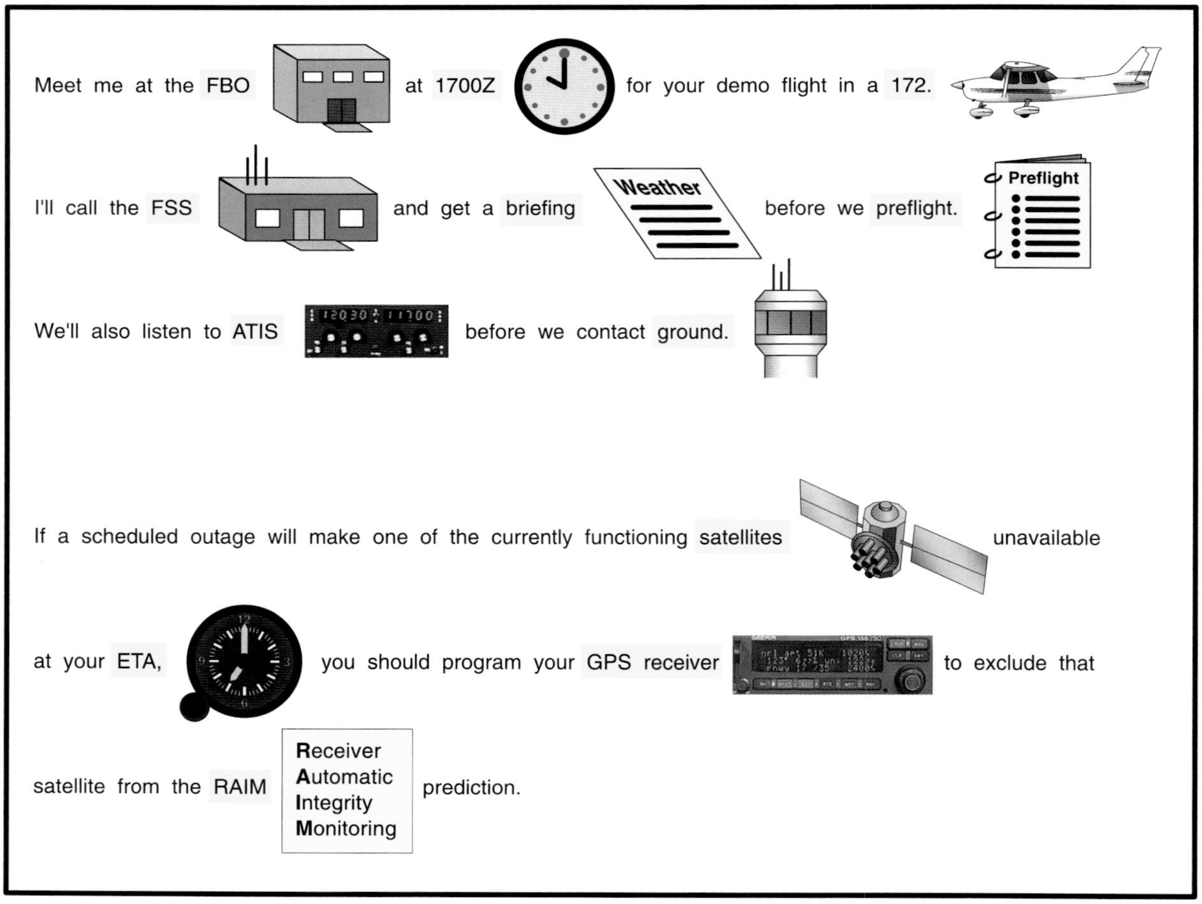

Meet me at the FBO at 1700Z for your demo flight in a 172.

I'll call the FSS and get a briefing (Weather) before we preflight. (Preflight)

We'll also listen to ATIS before we contact ground.

If a scheduled outage will make one of the currently functioning satellites unavailable at your ETA, you should program your GPS receiver to exclude that satellite from the RAIM (Receiver Automatic Integrity Monitoring) prediction.

Figure 1-44. Put yourself in a student's place. How well would you have understood these statements prior to learning the technical language of aviation?

Seeing is Believing

Communication Scenario:

Kyle (CFI): *"Can't you see that you're not on the centerline?"*

Laurie (Student): *"No, I can't see."*

Translation:

Kyle (CFI): *"Don't you understand that the airplane is not aligned with the runway centerline?"*

Laurie (Student): *"I can't see the centerline or the runway from this position. All I can see is the panel."*

The conclusion which can be drawn from this scenario is that Laurie is sitting too low in the airplane. The confusion occurs from a misunderstanding of the word **see**. Experts estimate that over 14,000 meanings exist for the 500 most commonly used words in the English language. This can make it difficult to determine what a person means by a given word without knowing its particular connotation to the speaker.

RECEIVER

The **receiver** is the listener, reader, or student. Your students are the receivers of your message when you instruct. To select the most effective means of communicating with your students, you need to understand their backgrounds, motivations, attitudes, and abilities. Age, gender, and cultural differences all affect the communication process. While you should be aware that student backgrounds and experiences vary, do not make assumptions based on this knowledge that can hinder effective communication. For example, the fact that a student is a college graduate does not guarantee rapid advancement in aviation training. A student's education will certainly affect your style of presentation, but that style should be based on the evaluation of the student's knowledge of the aviation subject being taught. You should remember that some people and cultures are sensitive to certain words and mannerisms. The more you know about your students, the better you can communicate with them.

Failure of your students to listen effectively can destroy the communication process. Active listening involves more than just physically hearing a message. Your students must interpret and evaluate the information received and then respond. Remember that learning is defined as a change in behavior as a result of experience. If the behavior of your students changes as you intended, then effective communication has taken place. Monitoring student **feedback** is another way to gauge whether your students are receiving the correct message. If your students do not provide feedback, then it is your responsibility

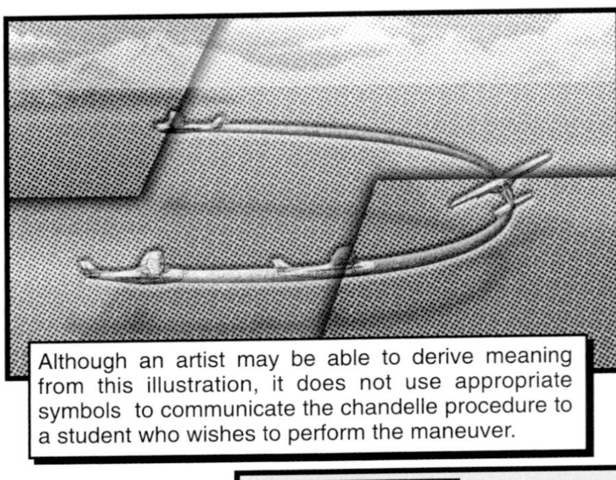

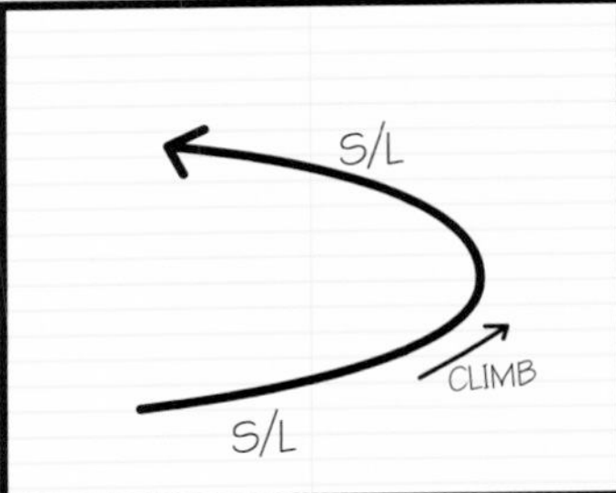

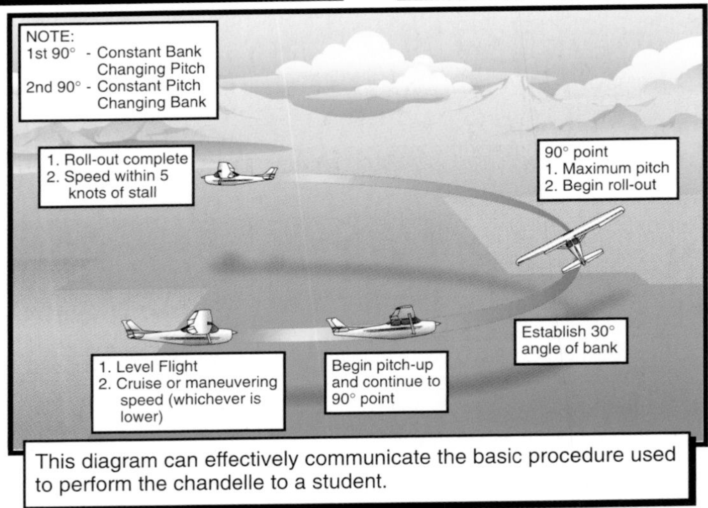

Figure 1-45. Although the use of illustrations can be an effective means of communication, you must select symbols which are appropriate to the message you want to convey to the student. Student feedback may prompt you to reevaluate your choice of symbology.

to ask for it. Based on the feedback you receive, you may need to modify the symbols you are using to optimize communication. [Figure 1-45]

Feedback normally takes the form of clarification, paraphrase, or summarization. Clarifying responses often begin with simple statements or open-ended questions. For example, your student may ask, *"Would you please clarify that?"* or *"I don't understand what you mean."* Paraphrasing is restating your message in the student's own words. This way you and your student can check the accuracy of what has been heard. Normally, a paraphrasing response begins with a phrase such as this, *"As I understand you . . ."* or *"In other words . . ."* Finally, summarizing responses, which sum up the main ideas you have expressed, are especially appropriate for lengthy ground school sessions. Your student may begin a summarizing response like this, *"Everything we have discussed so far . . ."*

The effectiveness of communication is measured by the similarity between the idea transmitted and the idea received. Truly effective communication has taken place when the receivers understand and change behaviors accordingly.

This discussion has focused on you, the instructor, as the source of information presented to the receiver, your student. However, when you listen to student feedback, you take on the role of the receiver who then may have to provide feedback to clarify your student's message. In order for you to become an effective teacher, you must also become an effective listener. It is important to hear what your students are actually saying, as well as listen to their

Stalling Around

Communication Scenario:

Kristen (CFI): *"Are you ready to practice stalls today?"*

Jim (Student): *"Well, I read the material you assigned."* Jim is distracted and fidgety.

Translation:

Kristen (CFI): *"Do you feel comfortable with the procedures for setting up and recovering from a stall? Do you understand how stalls occur and what we will be doing during the lesson?"*

Jim (Student): *'I don't understand some of the assignment and I am nervous about practicing stalls."*

Jim is anxious about practicing stalls but is uncomfortable telling this to Kristen. By observing Jim's body language, Kristen could have sensed Jim's hesitation. In response to Jim's acknowledgement that he read the material, Kristen might have provided the following feedback to more accurately determine Jim's feelings: *"In other words, you understand the material and feel comfortable with performing stalls?"*

message. Messages are only partly apparent in the words themselves. For example, you should note verbal and nonverbal cues such as your student's tone of voice or body language. You can also use your own knowledge of the student's past actions to interpret meaning.

BARRIERS TO EFFECTIVE COMMUNICATION

The complexity of language can lead to misunderstandings and a breakdown of communication. There are four **barriers to effective communication**: lack of common experience, confusion between the symbol and the symbolized object, abstractions, and interference.

LACK OF COMMON EXPERIENCE

A **lack of common experience** between the communicator and the receiver is probably the greatest single barrier to effective communication. Many people seem to believe that words transport meanings from speaker to listener in the same way an airplane carries cargo from one location to another. Words, however, rarely carry precisely the same meaning from the mind of the instructor to the mind of the student. Words by themselves have no meaning. They are merely verbal symbols. Throughout our entire lives, from formal schooling to everyday occurrences, experiences have enabled us to continually derive meaning from our language. We attach meaning to words just as we attach meaning to traffic signs or markings on instruments and placards. However, in many cases, the meaning we assign a word is not accurate.

It is absolutely essential you make certain your students understand exactly what you mean, especially regarding words that can have multiple meanings. Within a specific culture, common meanings are established for various symbols. For example, a red light means stop, caution, or warning. A green light means go, or that everything is normal. This symbology is fairly universal, even in the aviation environment. Yet, less universal symbols mean different things to people who live in different regions, or who have unique cultures and backgrounds. The same is true for people who have different occupations, especially those working in technical fields. This is the primary reason for the standardization efforts in airport signage, the standards promulgated by the International Civil Aviation Organization (ICAO), and even the radio phraseology standards in the AIM.

Teaching, by its very nature, means there is a lack of common experience between you and your student. This simple fact puts a great deal of the responsibility for effective communication on you. Your student's understanding of the meaning of words needs to be the same as your understanding. As you introduce technical language, you should define new terms and be certain your student grasps the correct meaning of your vocabulary, as well as that used by ATC and other persons within the field of aviation. [Figure 1-46]

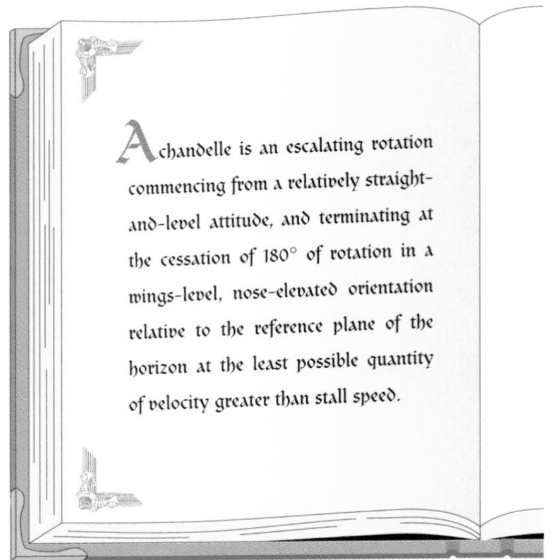

Figure 1-46. The terminology used in this description of a chandelle is not commonly used by pilots when discussing a maneuver. If you find this paragraph difficult to understand, imagine how confusing aeronautical terminology and radio phraseology must be for the beginning student.

Probably the greatest barrier to effective communication is a lack of a common experience level between you and the student. Both the communicator and the listener must have some experience with the concepts or objects to which the words refer.

CONFUSION BETWEEN THE SYMBOL AND THE SYMBOLIZED OBJECT

The fact that words and other symbols do not always carry the same meaning can lead to **confusion between the symbol and the symbolized object**. A common example is the term *"takeoff power."* To some, it might mean to advance the throttle to the power setting required for takeoff, and to others it might mean to retard the throttle to idle. Another example of this confusion is when students ask if they should turn the airplane to the left and you acknowledge with the term *"right."* Students might interpret this response to mean the intention to turn left is correct, but others might interpret it to mean they should turn right instead. Acknowledging the question with the term *"correct"* instead of *"right"* will eliminate this sort of confusion. [Figure 1-47]

Figure 1-47. The words comprising this description do not accurately represent the items they symbolize. For example, the word bank is used by this instructor to symbolize turn. While performing the chandelle, a turn of 180° is necessary, not a 180° bank.

Seventy What?

Communication Scenario:

Lorraine (Student): *"What speed should I fly on final?"*

Derek (CFI): *"Seventy."*

The airspeed indicator is calibrated in both knots and MPH. The student interprets the final approach speed as 70 MPH, and the CFI meant 70 knots. What implications does this misunderstanding present? How might a situation like this be avoided?

OVERUSE OF ABSTRACTIONS

Abstractions are general terms that do not carry specific meanings. Concrete terms, or words, have exact and definite meanings that students can relate to their experience and knowledge base, leaving little room for misunderstanding. The word aircraft is an abstract term, as it means any vehicle designed to fly. If you refer to an aircraft during a discussion, your students would not have a clear idea as to what you mean. However, if you mention a Boeing 747-400, then every student who knows what a Boeing 747-400 looks like would have a specific mental image of the aircraft to which you are referring. Another example of using abstractions is asking your students to *"throttle back."* This terminology does not specifically describe what you mean or how much to retard the throttle. However, if you tell your students to *"reduce the power setting by 200 r.p.m.,"* then they would know exactly what action to take. [Figure 1-48]

To perform a chandelle, you must use proper control inputs to begin the maneuver and initiate corrective action if errors are made throughout the maneuver. At the completion of the chandelle, the airplane will be in a suitable configuration if the appropriate procedure was followed.

Figure 1-48. The abstract words used in this description of the chandelle would not generate a specific mental image in the mind of your student.

The danger with using abstractions is they do not evoke in the student's mind the specific items of experience you intend.

Abstractions should be avoided as much as possible, especially when you are trying to teach specific information. However, there are times when the use of abstractions is appropriate, such as during discussions of aerodynamics or airplane performance, since these general concepts can be applied universally to all airplanes. After providing a foundation using abstractions, you must connect basic concepts to concrete examples which your students can apply to their current situation. [Figure 1-49]

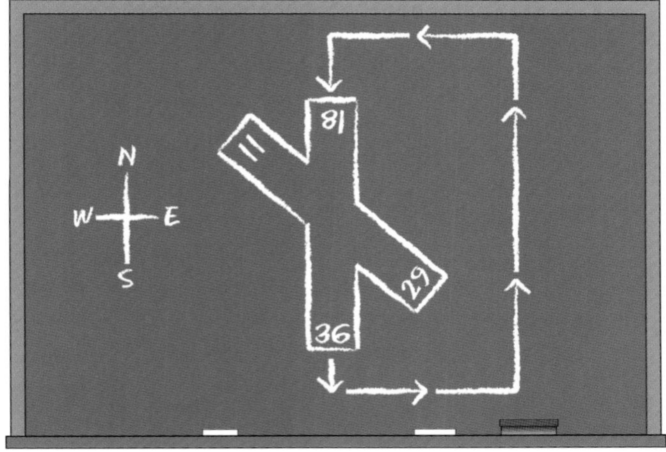

Figure 1-49. A good example of an effective use of abstractions is when teaching airport layouts and traffic patterns. It is impossible to describe every airport that your students may encounter. First, basic runway nomenclature and airport layouts, as well as traffic pattern procedures, are taught using generic airports. Next, diagrams of specific airports can be used during training to allow students to relate these abstract concepts to something they have experienced, thereby providing specific meaning.

INTERFERENCE

As an instructor, you can control most barriers to effective communication. However, **interference** is made up of physiological, environmental, and psychological factors that are beyond your direct control. You need to be aware of the effects that these factors have on the communication process.

Physiological interference results from any biological problem, such as hearing loss, loss of visual acuity, injury, or illness, that impedes the reception of the communication symbols. When students are not feeling well, they cannot concentrate on the message being sent. You need to be aware of the well-being of your students and be ready to adapt to any situation that may arise, including postponing the intended lesson until such time as the student is ready to resume training. You may be able to reduce physiological interference in certain situations. For example, some students may need to sit on a cushion to properly see over the glare shield. You can help students feel more comfortable by reassuring them that this situation is normal and by pointing out the positive aspects of increased visibility and enhanced safety.

Environmental interference is caused by external factors, such as the noise level in the airplane, radio transmissions, or conflicting traffic that distracts your student. Using headsets with an intercom or earplugs can reduce the interference caused by excessive noise. While headsets can increase the clarity of radio transmissions and exchanges between you and your student, some types are not effective at reducing noise, so you may need to use them in combination with earplugs. [Figure 1-50]

Figure 1-50. Headsets and an intercom system can reduce environmental interference and make effective communication easier.

Psychological interference results from how you and your student feel during the communication process. For example, if either of you are not fully attentive or committed to the lesson, the communication process will suffer. Psychological interference can also occur due to a lack of motivation on your part or on the part of your student, emotional problems, or simply a poor student/instructor relationship. Fear or mistrust between you and your student can essentially shut down effective communication. If you sense that this is occurring, talk with your student and try to determine the source of the problem. In some cases, you may need to suggest that your student fly with another instructor.

DEVELOPING COMMUNICATION SKILLS

Just like other skills, **communication skills** need to be developed, practiced, and continually improved upon. The ability to communicate effectively as an instructor begins with an understanding of the communication process and is enhanced by experience and training.

INSTRUCTIONAL COMMUNICATION

Instructional communication is unique since most of the information typically flows in one direction. While it is true that two-way communication exists during instruction, normally you are the primary communicator, and your students are the primary receivers. Since you should have considerable knowledge of the subject you are teaching, you can employ examples from your experiences to illustrate your points. Your insights provide valuable additions to the information contained in training materials and can help your students readily understand how theory is put into practice. [Figure 1-51]

"One Saturday, I was scheduled to give a mountain checkout. We were planning to leave first thing in the morning and return by noon. When we got a weather briefing, Flight Service told us that the weather should be great all morning but by late afternoon, a front was supposed to move through. Ceilings were going to go down with deteriorating visibility and there was a chance for rain turning to snow later on."

"Since the front was not supposed to arrive until after our flight, my student still felt pretty good about going. But, knowing how unpredictable the weather in the mountains can be at times, and how few options we had if the conditions did deteriorate during the flight, I made the decision to postpone the checkout."

"Two other CFIs at the club decided to fly to one of the same airports on our proposed route that morning. Their intention was to eat brunch and then return before the frontal passage."

"Well, the front came through earlier than originally forecast and they were stuck in the mountains. Fortunately they made the right decision not to attempt to fly back, so they had to leave the plane at the airport and rent a car to return home. The weather stayed bad for over a week and they had to pay for the time the plane was sitting there until the conditions improved enough to fly out of the mountains."

Figure 1-51. If you are teaching a lesson on weather hazards, you can talk about your previous experiences regarding weather-related decisions. By discussing various situations, your thought processes, and how you chose to handle specific instances involving questionable weather conditions, you can increase your student's understanding and interest.

Instructional communication not only focuses on facts, but also on how and why things should be done. It is very easy to concentrate your instruction on student achievement of the lower levels of learning since knowledge of facts and figures is easy to measure. Accurately determining if your students have achieved higher-level learning is more difficult, requiring a great deal of thought and planning. You cannot gauge the effectiveness of instructional communication until you are sure your students have a clear understanding of what you have told them. You need to have some method of accurately evaluating student comprehension and ability to apply knowledge of the subject. Written tests, oral quizzing, and observing student performance of a task are some evaluation techniques which are discussed in Chapter 2.

PRACTICING COMMUNICATION

During your initial training, acting as a flight instructor is a good way to practice instructional communication. With your instructor playing the role of a student, you should practice both in-flight lessons, as well as ground instruction to gain skills in both settings. You must find communication techniques that fit your personality and that you are comfortable using. Be careful not to simply mimic teaching methods used during your training, but employ the best techniques from all of your previous instructors. As you gain experience as an instructor, you will continue to refine instructional communication skills and to explore and develop new ones.

EFFECTIVE LISTENING

Effective **listening** skills also need to be developed and practiced. Hearing your students talk and listening to what they are saying are two different things. To master the art of listening, you must develop an attitude of wanting to listen. [Figure 1-52]

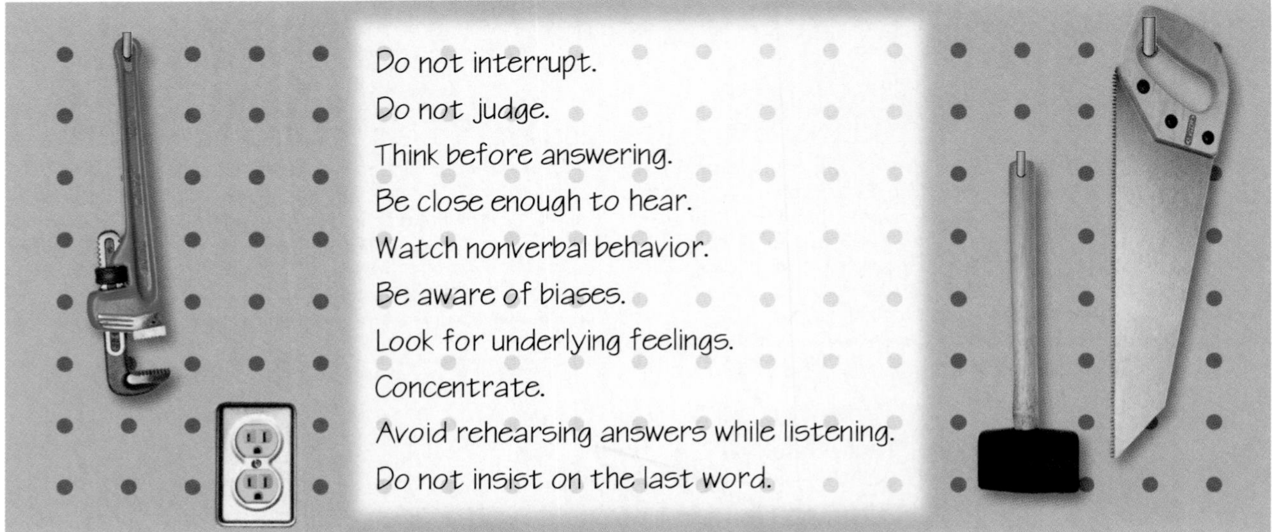

Figure 1-52. Instructors can use a variety of techniques, or tools, to become better listeners.

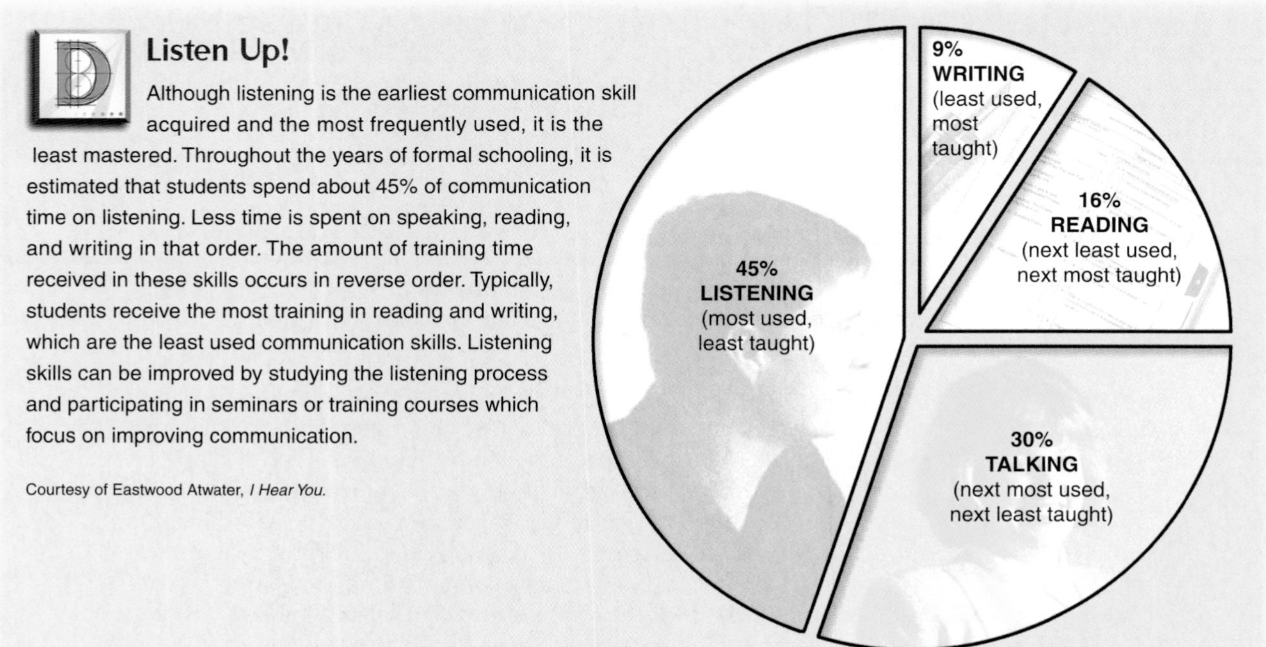

Listen Up!

Although listening is the earliest communication skill acquired and the most frequently used, it is the least mastered. Throughout the years of formal schooling, it is estimated that students spend about 45% of communication time on listening. Less time is spent on speaking, reading, and writing in that order. The amount of training time received in these skills occurs in reverse order. Typically, students receive the most training in reading and writing, which are the least used communication skills. Listening skills can be improved by studying the listening process and participating in seminars or training courses which focus on improving communication.

Courtesy of Eastwood Atwater, *I Hear You.*

There are several things you can do to teach your students how to become better listeners. First, students must be ready to listen. They must have time to clear their thoughts and focus on you. If they do not have this time to get ready to listen, they most likely will miss what you are saying. For example, at the beginning of a lecture, summarize the topics of discussion, and then give your students a moment to prepare to listen.

Emotions play a large role in determining how well your students listen. You must encourage your students to listen to understand, not refute. An example of a student listening to refute is one who continually challenges your knowledge of a particular subject, resulting in very little retention of information. Students also have difficulty listening when they are not emotionally calm. If the thought of performing stalls makes your students nervous, it will be difficult for them to listen when you are discussing this subject. If you sense your students are anxious, you can take the time to provide a more detailed explanation with an emphasis on safety issues which may cause concern.

To help your students grasp the overall topic of discussion, have them focus on capturing the main ideas by emphasizing the primary objectives of the lesson. Too often, students try to concentrate on various facts and miss the big picture. For example, a student who is preoccupied with memorizing specific data on an instrument approach chart, may not understand the basic approach procedures being described.

Make sure your students guard against daydreaming during a lesson. Most students can listen much faster than you can talk, which leaves room for their minds to wander rather than concentrate on the lesson. By frequently requesting feedback or posing questions, you can help keep your students from daydreaming. Encouraging the development of good note-taking habits is another way to improve student listening skills. If your students have been away from formal learning environments for some time, they may need to be reminded to take notes during ground school sessions. [Figure 1-53]

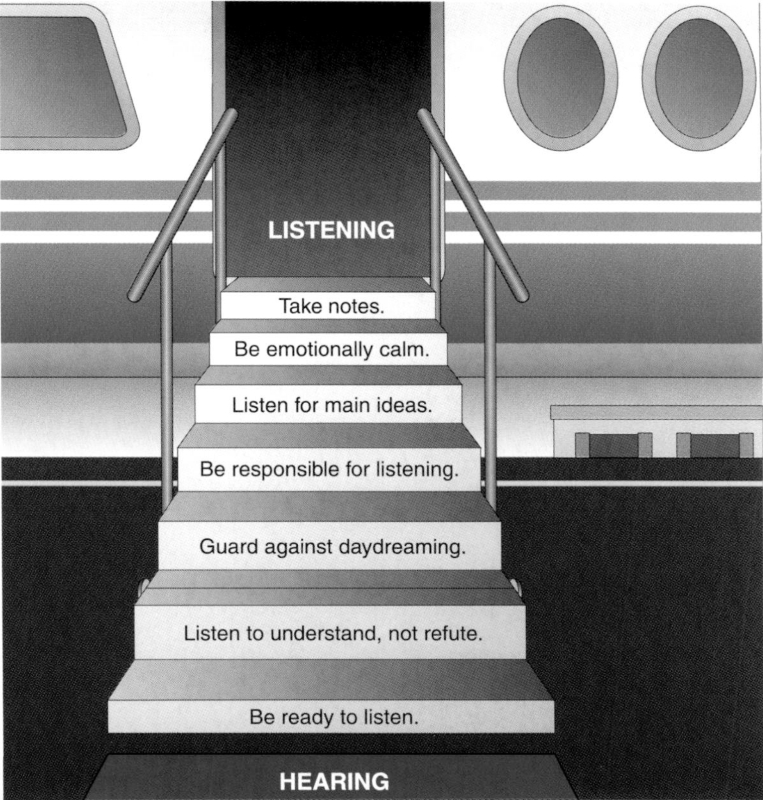

Figure 1-53. By following these steps, students can become better listeners and thereby more effective learners.

SUMMARY CHECKLIST

- ✓ The communication process consists of three basic elements: the source, the symbols used to communicate the message, and the receiver.
- ✓ The ability to use language appropriately to convey ideas is key to effective communication. By evaluating the background of your students, you can determine the vocabulary which will have meaning for them.
- ✓ You must reveal a positive attitude if you are to communicate effectively.
- ✓ In order to be a successful communicator, you must speak from a background of up-to-date and stimulating material.
- ✓ Your message is transmitted by the symbols you chose, such as words, sounds, pictures, expressions, or any number of printed or computer-based resources.
- ✓ You can effectively gain and retain your student's attention by using a variety of audiovisual aids.
- ✓ To select the most effective means of communicating with your students, you need to understand their backgrounds, motivations, attitudes, and abilities.
- ✓ Monitoring student feedback is one way to gauge whether your students are receiving the correct message. If your students do not provide feedback, then it is your responsibility to ask for it.
- ✓ A lack of common experience between the communicator and the receiver is probably the greatest single barrier to effective communication.
- ✓ The fact that words and other symbols do not always carry the same meaning can lead to confusion between the symbol and the symbolized object.
- ✓ Abstractions are general terms that do not carry specific meanings. The danger with using abstractions is they do not evoke in the student's mind the specific items of experience you intend.
- ✓ Interference is a barrier to effective communication made up of physiological, environmental, and psychological factors that are beyond your direct control.
- ✓ Instructional communication is unique since most of the information typically flows in one direction. During your initial training, you should practice instructional communication both in flight and on the ground, with your instructor playing the role of a student.
- ✓ Effective listening skills also need to be developed and practiced by you and your students.

KEY TERMS

Communication Process

Source

Symbols

Receiver

Feedback

Barriers to Effective Communication

Lack of Common Experience

Confusion Between the Symbol and the Symbolized Object

Abstractions

Interference

Communication Skills

Instructional Communication

Listening

QUESTIONS

1. Name the three basic elements that comprise the communication process.

2. True/False. As long as you use appropriate symbols to convey your message, your attitude is not a factor in ensuring effective communication.

3. Why is it important to monitor student feedback?

4. List the four barriers to effective communication.

5. Select the true statement regarding the use of abstractions.

   A. You should never use abstractions when communicating with students.
   B. Abstract terms generate specific mental images in the mind of a student.
   C. Abstractions should be avoided as much as possible when you are trying to teach specific information.

6. Select the true statement regarding interference as a barrier to effective communication.

   A. Your student's physical well being is not important when considering interference.
   B. Environmental interference can be reduced through the use of an intercom and headsets.
   C. Ensuring that your student can see over the glare shield is a way to reduce psychological interference.

7. True/False. When teaching, you should avoid using examples from your experiences, and concentrate solely on the material contained in the textbook.

8. Select the true statement regarding communication skills.

   A. You should mimic the teaching methods that were used during your training.
   B. As you gain teaching experience, your communication skills tend to deteriorate.
   C. During your initial training, role playing as a CFI is a good way to practice your communication skills.

9. Select the true statement regarding effective listening.

   A. Have your students concentrate on the specific details, rather than the main ideas.
   B. Unlike effective communication skills, effective listening skills do not need to be developed and practiced.
   C. At the beginning of a lecture, it may be helpful to summarize the topics of discussion, and then give your students a moment to prepare to listen.

CHAPTER 2

THE ART AND SCIENCE OF TEACHING

Flight Instructor
Volume 1 — Fundamentals of Instruction

SECTION A
INTRODUCING THE TEACHING PROCESS

Preparation

By learning you will teach; by teaching you will learn.
— Latin Proverb

Presentation

Since learning is defined as a change of behavior as a result of experience, **teaching** may be described as the systematic and deliberate creation of practical instructional events (experiences) which are conducive to learning. The key to effective teaching is a sound understanding of the principles of learning. As a flight instructor, you must creatively use these principles to develop realistic experiences that maximize learning. This is a complicated task. It involves much more than a simple process of transferring your knowledge or skill to your students. You not only need to know how students learn, but you also need to master a variety of teaching methods and techniques. In addition, you usually have to do this within the constraints imposed by the environment in which the instruction is given.

Application

The principles of learning, which were covered in Chapter 1, are not easily separated into a definite number of steps. Sometimes, learning occurs almost instantaneously, and at other times it is acquired only after long, patient study and practice. The teaching process, on the other hand, can be divided into a reasonable number of steps. [Figure 2-1]

Review and Evaluation

The proper sequence that an instructor should use in the teaching process is preparation, presentation, application, and review and evaluation.

Figure 2-1. Although there is a diversity of opinion among educational psychologists, close examination of various lists of steps in the teaching process reveals that most include four basic steps — preparation, presentation, application, and review and evaluation.

PREPARATION

To be a successful instructor, you must be properly prepared for each lesson or instructional period. **Preparation** entails an understanding of what you need to teach, developing an effective lesson plan, and ensuring that you are current on the subject matter or procedures to be taught. You also should make certain that all appropriate equipment, materials, and supplies needed for the lesson are readily available and in good condition. As a general rule, the quality of instruction that you provide will be directly related to the effectiveness of your preparation.

One of the first priorities for any lesson is to establish well-defined objectives. Statements of objectives should be specific, measurable, and attainable within the allotted time. In addition, standards, conditions, and evaluation procedures must be considered. These subjects are discussed in detail later in this chapter.

When defining the objectives, you should refer to appropriate publications. FAR Part 61 contains FAA certification requirements for pilot certificates and ratings. The FARs are identified by a specific number (Aeronautics and Space Title 14) within the larger group of rules contained in the Code of Federal Regulations (CFR). You also need to understand the requirements outlined in the applicable practical test standards (PTS). Along with the regulations and PTS, you may use a commercially prepared syllabus that provides a summary or outline of a course of training. [Figure 2-2]

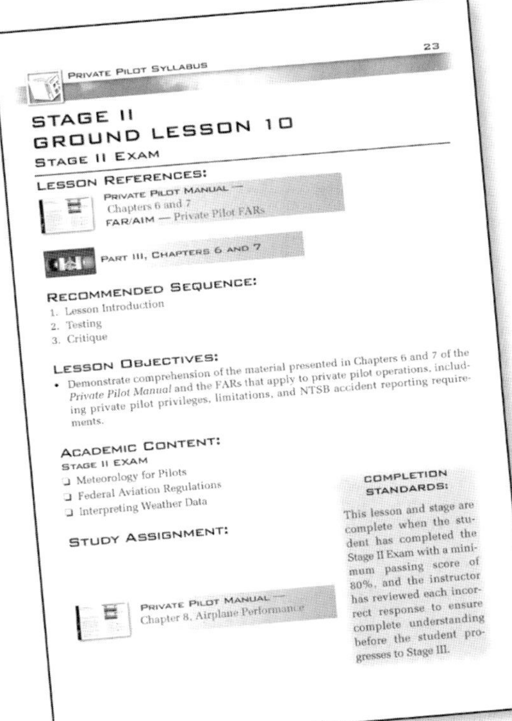

PRIVATE PILOT SYLLABUS 23

STAGE II
GROUND LESSON 10
STAGE II EXAM

LESSON REFERENCES:
PRIVATE PILOT MANUAL — Chapters 6 and 7
FAR/AIM — Private Pilot FARs

PART III, CHAPTERS 6 AND 7

RECOMMENDED SEQUENCE:
1. Lesson Introduction
2. Testing
3. Critique

LESSON OBJECTIVES:
- Demonstrate comprehension of the material presented in Chapters 6 and 7 of the *Private Pilot Manual* and the FARs that apply to private pilot operations, including private pilot privileges, limitations, and NTSB accident reporting requirements.

ACADEMIC CONTENT:
STAGE II EXAM
- ❑ Meteorology for Pilots
- ❑ Federal Aviation Regulations
- ❑ Interpreting Weather Data

STUDY ASSIGNMENT:
PRIVATE PILOT MANUAL — Chapter 8, Airplane Performance

COMPLETION STANDARDS:
This lesson and stage are complete when the student has completed the Stage II Exam with a minimum passing score of 80%, and the instructor has reviewed each incorrect response to ensure complete understanding before the student progresses to Stage III.

Figure 2-2. A syllabus helps you organize an overall instructional plan that includes a step-by-step progression and a logical lesson sequence from beginning to end. This facilitates a building block concept which allows you, as well as your students, to clearly see what is required along the way.

PERFORMANCE-BASED OBJECTIVES

One good way to write lesson plans is to begin by formulating **performance-based objectives**. You can use the objectives listed in the syllabus or the appropriate PTS as the starting point. These objectives are very helpful in delineating exactly what and how tasks need to be accomplished during each lesson. Once you have written the performance-based objectives, much of the work of writing a final lesson plan is completed. Section C in this chapter discusses lesson plans in depth and provides examples of a variety of acceptable formats.

You can use performance-based objectives to set measurable, reasonable standards that describe the desired performance of your students. These objectives provide a way of stating what performance level is required of your students before they are allowed to progress to the next stage of instruction. Again, objectives must be clear, measurable, and repeatable. In other words, they must mean the same thing to any knowledgeable

Figure 2-3. Performance-based objectives are made up of a description of the skill or behavior, conditions, and criteria. Each part is required and must be stated in a way that will leave every reader with the same picture of the objective, how it will be performed, and to what level of performance.

ELEMENTS OF PERFORMANCE-BASED OBJECTIVES

Descriptions of the Skill or Behavior—Desired outcome of training stated in concrete terms that can be measured.

Conditions—The framework under which the skill or behavior will be demonstrated.

Criteria—The standard which will be used to measure the accomplishment of the objective.

reader. The objectives must be written. If they are not written, with time, they become subject to the fallibility of recall, interpretation, or loss of specificity. [Figure 2-3]

DESCRIPTION OF THE SKILL OR BEHAVIOR

The **description of the skill or behavior** explains the desired outcome of the instruction. It actually is a learned capability, which may be defined as knowledge, a skill, or an attitude. The description should be in concrete terms that can be measured. Terms such as "knowledge of . . ." and "awareness of . . ." cannot be measured very well and are examples of the types of verbiage which should be avoided. Phrases like "able to select from a list of . . ." or "able to repeat the steps to . . ." are better because they can be measured. Furthermore, the skill or behavior described should be logical and within the overall instructional plan.

CONDITIONS

Conditions are necessary to specifically explain the rules under which a skill or behavior is demonstrated. Information such as equipment, tools, reference material, and limiting parameters should be included. Sometimes while writing the objective, you will notice a problem. This might be your student saying, *"But, what if . . . ?"* This is a good indication that the original version was confusing. If it is confusing to one student, it will be confusing to others and should be corrected. [Figure 2-4]

Figure 2-4. If a desired objective is to navigate from point A to point B, it is not specific enough for all students to do it in the same way. Inserting conditions narrows the objective.

CRITERIA

Criteria refers to a list of standards which measure the accomplishment of the objective and should be stated so that there is no question whether the objective has been met. The conditions and criteria may change slightly during the development of objectives, and you should refine them as necessary. As noted earlier, the PTS already have many of the elements needed to formulate performance-based objectives. In most cases, the objective is listed along with sufficient conditions to describe the scope of the objective. The PTS also have specific criteria or standards you can use to grade performance; however, the criteria may not always be specific enough for a particular lesson. You should feel free to write performance-based objectives to fit the desired outcome of the lesson. Figure 2-5, for instance, depicts a well-defined lesson objective from the task, Pilotage and Dead Reckoning, in the *Private Pilot Practical Test Standards.*

Figure 2-5. The criteria may include that navigation from A to B should be accomplished within 5 minutes of the pre-planned flight time and that enroute altitude be maintained within 200 feet.

OTHER USES OF PERFORMANCE-BASED OBJECTIVES

The use of performance-based objectives expands the conventional idea of an objective to include conditions and criteria. This expansion opens the way for the performance-based objective to be used to fill in many of the blanks on the lesson plan. For example, having formulated the conditions under which your student will accomplish the objective, you have already done most of the work toward determining the elements of the lesson and the schedule of events. The equipment necessary, as well as instructor/student actions anticipated during the lesson, have also been identified. By listing the criteria for the performance-based objectives, you have established the completion standards normally included as part of the lesson plan.

Use of performance-based objectives also provides your student with a better understanding of the big picture, including knowledge of exactly what is expected. This overview can alleviate a significant source of frustration on the part of your student.

Performance-based objectives apply to all three domains of learning: cognitive (knowledge), affective (attitudes, beliefs, values), and psychomotor (physical skills). In addition, since each domain includes several educational objective levels, performance-based objectives may easily be adapted to a specific performance level of knowledge or skill. In most cases, pilot training programs focus on the application level of learning or higher.

PRESENTATION

Presentation simply means something that is presented. It could be a play, a gift, or an instructional lesson. You normally have a choice of several methods of presentation, especially during ground training sessions. An important consideration is the number of students you have. Other considerations include the type of training aids or equipment available, the subject matter, and the objectives of the training. Presentation methods include cooperative learning sessions, case studies, and computer-based multimedia programs, as well as the more traditional ways: the lecture method, the demonstration-performance method, and the guided discussion. A variety of presentation methods will be addressed in greater depth later in Section B of this chapter.

APPLICATION

Application is where your students use what you have presented. After a classroom presentation, you can ask your students to explain the new material or to perform a procedure or operation that has just been demonstrated. For example, after you have demonstrated and explained the use of the flight computer, ask your students to use the flight computer to compute groundspeed, wind correction angle, or time enroute. In most instructional situations, your explanation and demonstration activities are alternated with your students' performance efforts.

Very often you will have to interrupt your student's efforts and provide feedback in the form of corrections or further explanations and demonstrations. This is necessary because it is very important that each student perform the maneuver or operation the right way the first few times. This is when habits are established. Faulty habits are difficult to correct and must be addressed as soon as possible. You must be aware of this problem, particularly during flight instruction, since students eventually will do a lot of their practice during solo flight operations. Only after reasonable competence has been demonstrated should students be allowed to practice certain maneuvers on solo flights. Students can then practice maneuvers again and again until correct performance becomes almost automatic. However, keep in mind that periodic review and evaluation is necessary to ensure that your students have not acquired any bad habits.

Instruction for the Birds

Teaching students a complex topic such as aerodynamics, for example, is challenging, and making sure they have a good understanding of the subject is even more difficult. Now imagine the difficulty in teaching students that are not human, but avian. Animal behaviorist Irene Pepperberg is doing just that with African Grey parrots.

To 'parrot' means to simply repeat information, whether or not the information is actually understood does not matter. But Pepperberg's parrots, Griffin and Alex, are not just mimicking their teacher, they actually understand what they are saying. For example, when presented with two triangles, one yellow and one blue, and asked what is the same about them, Alex responds *"Shape."* When asked what is different he responds, *"Color!"* Pepperberg has developed several other tests to teach Alex more than 50 different objects, 5 shapes, and 7 colors in addition to the meanings of *"same"* and *"different"*—a crucial step in human intellectual development.

If you doubt that these birds do not understand the meaning of their words, consider the following example. During a recent session with the two parrots, Griffin, while trying to say *"paper,"* sputtered *"ay-uhr."* A seemingly frustrated Alex then ordered the younger bird to *"Talk clearly!"*

REVIEW AND EVALUATION

Before the end of an instructional period, you should review what has been covered during the lesson and require your students to demonstrate how well the lesson objectives have been met. Evaluation is an integral part of each classroom or flight lesson. It not only tells you how well your students are progressing, it also gives you a good indication of how effective you have been in teaching the lesson.

Your evaluation may be informal and recorded only for your own use in planning the next lesson for your students, or it may be formal. Most likely, the evaluation will be formal and the results recorded to certify your students' progress in the course. Methods of integrating training syllabi and record keeping will be introduced later in this chapter.

In either case, your students should be made aware of their progress. Any advances and deficiencies should be noted at the conclusion of the lesson. Failure to make your students aware of their progress, or lack of it, may create a barrier that could impede further instruction. [Figure 2-6]

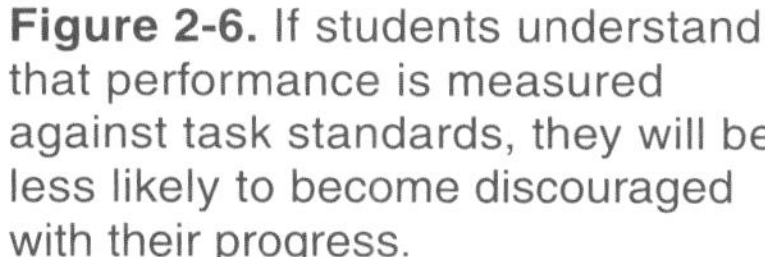

Figure 2-6. If students understand that performance is measured against task standards, they will be less likely to become discouraged with their progress.

In aviation training programs, you should remember that it often is difficult for students to get a clear picture of their progress. Students in flight training seldom have a chance to compare their performance with other students. However, they are in a competitive situation with an unseen competitor — competency — and they are normally able to weigh their performance only against yours. Your feedback must adequately compare their performance to the completion standards of the lesson plan so your students really know how they are doing. Otherwise, your students may become discouraged when their only visible competition, you, are doing well and they are not.

In addition to a review of knowledge and skills learned during the instruction period just completed, each lesson should include a selective **review and evaluation** of things previously learned. If the evaluation reveals a deficiency in knowledge or performance, it must be corrected before new material is presented.

If deficiencies or faults not associated with the present lesson are revealed, they should be carefully noted and pointed out to your students. Corrective measures that are practicable within the limitations of the current lesson should be taken immediately. Remedial actions, which are beyond the scope of the immediate lesson, must be included in future lessons in order to minimize unsafe practices or other discrepancies.

Evaluation of student performance and accomplishments during a lesson should be based on objectives and goals established in the lesson plan.

The evaluation of student performance and accomplishment during a lesson should be based on the objectives and goals that were established in your lesson plan. Review and evaluation procedures allow you and your students to have a valid picture of where they stand in respect to the established standard. Review and evaluation in every lesson provides opportunities for both positive feedback and correction of faults.

SUMMARY CHECKLIST

- ✓ Teaching may be described as the systematic and deliberate creation of practical instructional events (experiences) that are conducive to learning.
- ✓ Effective teaching is based upon a sound understanding of the principles of learning. You also must be well prepared and be able to use a variety of teaching methods and techniques.
- ✓ The basic steps and the proper sequence in the teaching process are preparation, presentation, application, and review and evaluation.
- ✓ As a general rule, the quality of instruction that you provide is directly related to the effectiveness of your preparation.
- ✓ One of the first priorities in preparation for any lesson is to establish well-defined objectives. The objectives should be specific, measurable, and attainable within the allotted lesson time.
- ✓ Performance-based objectives are used to set measurable, reasonable standards that describe the desired performance of your students. These objectives provide a way of stating what performance level is expected of your students before they are allowed to progress to the next stage of training.
- ✓ Performance-based objectives consist of three main parts: a description of the desired skill or behavior, conditions, and criteria. The description of the skill or behavior should be specific and measurable.
- ✓ The conditions stated in performance-based objectives explain the rules under which the skill or behavior is demonstrated.
- ✓ The criteria in performance-based objectives list the standard by which students will be measured. Examples of criteria are: maintains appropriate airspeed ±10 knots, altitude ±200 feet, and heading within 10°.
- ✓ Listing criteria in performance-based objectives helps you establish completion standards which are normally included in a lesson plan.
- ✓ Three of the traditional presentation methods in the teaching process are the lecture method, the demonstration-performance method, and the guided discussion.
- ✓ The application step in the teaching process involves student performance of what you have explained or demonstrated.
- ✓ Review and evaluation should be accomplished before the end of every instructional period.
- ✓ Evaluation provides you with a gauge of your students' progress as well as your own effectiveness as a teacher.

- ✓ Selective review and evaluation of knowledge and skills learned previously should be included in every lesson. If the evaluation reveals a deficiency, it must be corrected before new material is presented.

- ✓ The evaluation of your students' performance and accomplishment during a lesson should be based on the objectives and goals which were established in your lesson plan.

KEY TERMS

Teaching

Preparation

Performance-Based Objectives

Description of the Skill or Behavior

Conditions

Criteria

Presentation

Application

Review and Evaluation

QUESTIONS

1. What is the key to effective teaching?

   A. Experience
   B. Knowledge of the subject matter
   C. An understanding of the principles of learning

2. What are the four basic steps in the teaching process?

3. What should your first priority be during development of a lesson plan?

   A. Determine the objectives
   B. Determine the lesson content
   C. Determine the completion standards

4. What are the three parts of performance-based objectives?

5. True/False. Performance-based objectives provide a way of stating what performance level is expected of a student before that student is allowed to progress to the next stage of training.

6. Write a performance-based objective for a lesson on basic attitude instrument flight. Assume the student is in the final stages of preparing for the practical test.

7. True/False. During the application step in the teaching process, you should try to avoid interrupting student responses or demonstrations.

8. When should review and evaluation occur during an instructional period?

   A. Before the end
   B. At the mid-point
   C. At the beginning

SECTION B

FOCUSING ON TEACHING METHODS

If you think back to one hundred years ago, the average classroom was a far different place than it is today. Students sat at hard wooden desks, focused forward at the teacher's lecture. In present-day schools, students work in groups, go on field trips, and cooperate on projects that make learning an active, hands-on process. We know more now about how people learn, and you can apply this knowledge to the flight training you provide. If you have several different teaching methods in your repertoire, you more easily adapt to various instructional situations. Your students can only benefit. [Figure 2-7]

Figure 2-7. Just as classrooms have changed over the years, so may you update your teaching methods to reflect new ideas and technologies.

ORGANIZING MATERIAL

Materials for individual lessons must be organized so there is a logical progression toward a desired goal. Usually for your students, this goal will be a certificate or rating. To help you create a plan of action, you can use a **syllabus**, which incorporates a description of each lesson, including objectives and completion standards. Section C in this chapter contains more information on the requirements for an aviation training syllabus, and the building-block concept of curriculum development.

Although some schools and independent instructors may develop their own syllabi, many use commercially developed syllabi that have been selected for use in their aviation training programs. If you use a commercial syllabus, then you are only responsible for organizing the material within each lesson plan. The traditional way of building a lesson plan is to compose an introduction, provide development, and summarize with a conclusion.

INTRODUCTION

The **introduction** sets the stage for the rest of the lesson by relating the coverage of the material to the entire course. The effort you put into leading off your subject will be

rewarded in an increased sense of motivation and understanding in your student. The introduction itself is typically composed of three elements: attention, motivation, and an overview of what is to be covered.

The introduction relates the coverage of the material to the entire course, and it should follow the proper sequence: attention, motivation, overview.

ATTENTION

The purpose of the **attention** element is to help your students gain interest in the lesson. You could accomplish this by telling a story, making an unusual statement, asking a question, or telling a joke. Though any of these may be appropriate, given the circumstances, the method which you use needs to relate to the subject and establish a background for developing the desired learning outcomes. If you tell a story or joke that does not apply to the focus of the lesson, you risk distracting your students, when your main goal is to gain everyone's attention and concentrate on the subject.

MOTIVATION

The goal of the **motivation** element is to offer your students specific reasons why the lesson content is important to know, understand, apply, and perform. For example, you may discuss an incident in which the information provided in the lesson content was not properly used. [Figure 2-8] Some students may be motivated simply by a reminder of an upcoming test on the material, though emphasizing this point should be your last resort. More importantly, the goal should relate specifically to each student and instill a desire to know the information.

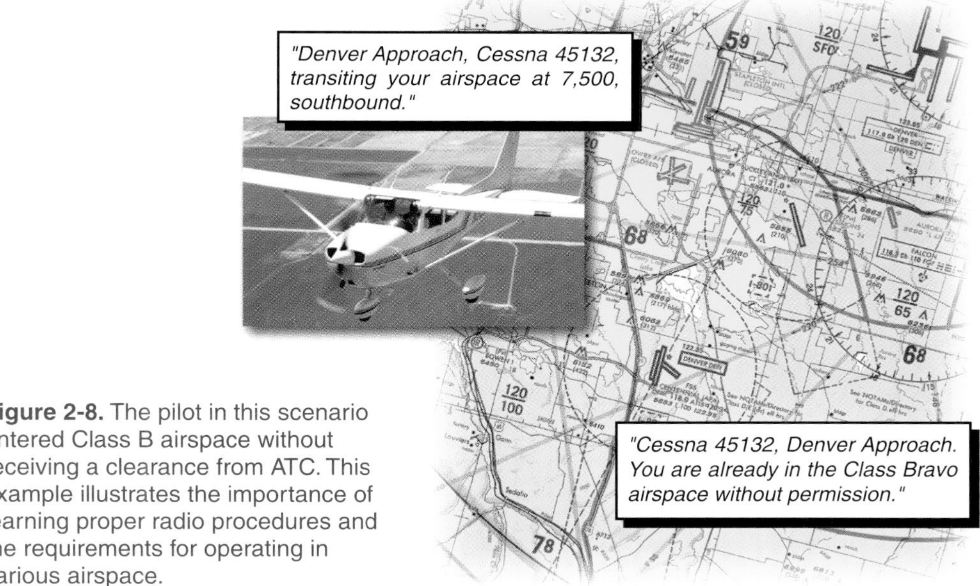

Figure 2-8. The pilot in this scenario entered Class B airspace without receiving a clearance from ATC. This example illustrates the importance of learning proper radio procedures and the requirements for operating in various airspace.

OVERVIEW

The introduction to every lesson should include an **overview** of the subjects you will cover during the period. A concise presentation of the objective and key ideas, supplemented with appropriate visual aids, gives your students a clear picture of what is to come. Avoid apologizing for the length and/or difficult content, as this may dampen your students' enthusiasm for the lesson.

DEVELOPMENT

The **development** is the main body of the lesson and contains a detailed look at the subject matter. To help your students achieve the desired learning objectives, you must organize

When teaching from the known to the unknown, you are building on your student's previous experiences and knowledge.

the information in such a way as to show the relationship from one main point to another. You normally emphasize the primary relationships by developing the main points in one of several ways. [Figure 2-9]

Figure 2-9. Developing your material in a structured way speeds up the process and makes it easier for you to follow a logical progression.

You may find it helpful to outline your presentations so that you are clear on the main and subordinate points before beginning the lesson. Each point should be arranged so there is a logical progression from one to the next with transitions that help keep your students oriented and aware of the lesson flow. This technique also permits effective sorting or categorizing chunks of information in the working or short-term memory. This level of lesson organization takes work on your part, but students need these logical connections in order to remember what they have learned and put it to use. Conversely, poorly organized information is virtually useless to students, since they will have trouble understanding and recalling the material.

The method of arranging lesson material from simple to complex, past to present, and known to unknown, shows the relationships of the main points to the lesson.

CONCLUSION

An effective **conclusion** reiterates the main points of the lesson and relates them to the objective. When you review these points at the end of the session, you reinforce key ideas and aid your students in retaining the information. You should avoid introducing new ideas in the conclusion, because they may confuse your students.

SELECTING TEACHING METHODS

Since each teaching situation is unique, the setting and purpose of the lesson determines which teaching method is used: lecture, cooperative learning, guided discussion, demonstration-performance, telling-and-doing technique, integrated method of instruction, computer-based training, or a combination of these.

LECTURE METHOD

The **lecture method** is the most widely used form of presentation, and you should understand the advantages and limitations of the format. Lectures are typically used to introduce new material, summarize ideas, show relationships between theory and practice, and reemphasize main points within a course of study. You can use the lecture method in

many different settings, as well as combine it with other methods to give added direction and focus to the presentation.

In the teaching process, the lecture method is suitable for presenting new material, summarizing ideas, and for showing relationships between theory and practice. The lecture method uses time economically, as well.

You may choose from several types of lectures, such as the **illustrated talk**, where you can use a number of visual aids to convey ideas to your students. During a **briefing**, you may remind your students of several key points without elaboration on the material. In a **formal lecture**, your purpose is to inform, persuade, or entertain without eliciting interaction by your listeners. When you give a **teaching lecture**, your presentation should be developed in such a way as to encourage some student participation.

TEACHING LECTURE

You may favor the teaching lecture, since it allows for participation by your students. When developing a teaching lecture, you should determine the method you will use to organize the material, considering the class size and the depth of the presentation. Keep in mind that the success of the lecture is contingent upon your ability to communicate effectively, and providing too much detail can be as bad or worse than incomplete coverage of the main points. Then, your first step in preparing a lecture is to establish the objective and desired outcome. To determine the effectiveness of the lecture, you must develop a keen perception for subtle responses from the class, such as facial expressions, note-taking, and the general interest level in the topic you are discussing.

The first step in preparing a lecture is to establish the objective and desired outcome.

You must develop a keen perception for your students' subtle responses and be able to interpret them in order to successfully deliver a teaching lecture.

PREPARING THE TEACHING LECTURE

Careful preparation is the key to successful performance when delivering a lecture, and it should begin well before class. [Figure 2-10] In each step of the presentation, you should support every point to be covered with examples, comparisons, statistics, or anecdotes. In fact, your students may not believe or understand each point you make without evidence from experts, or having the idea contrasted with more familiar situations. Using your personal experience can also help you build a strong presentation, evoking more interest from your students and opening the door to questions that aid learning.

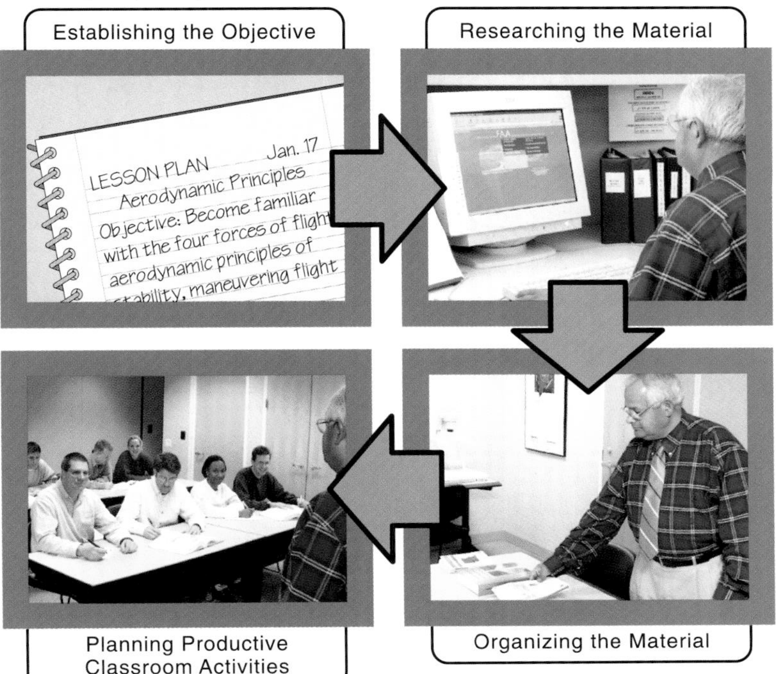

Figure 2-10. Researching the material may include going to the Internet to round out your knowledge of the topic.

After organizing and writing your lesson plan, you should rehearse the lecture to build your self-confidence. Also, if you can, have another knowledgeable person, preferably another instructor, sit in on your dry run to critique your lecture and delivery. A critic may help you judge the adequacy and validity of your supporting materials and instructional aids, as well as the content of your presentation.

USING SUITABLE LANGUAGE

During a teaching lecture, you should use simple words and phrases, such as those you would find in a newspaper, so you are easily understood. You may find that slang and colloquialisms, if used appropriately, help to keep your students interested. However, using substandard English, with grammatical errors and vulgar terms, makes you appear less intelligent and shows disrespect toward your students.

Use of vulgarisms and errors in grammar detract from your dignity and reflect upon your perception of your students' intelligence.

If your subject of discussion includes technical terms, you need to define each one as it is used so all your students are clear on the meaning. As you prepare your lecture, make sure you can define each concept in specific terms. If you cannot, you probably need to research the topic further. This is a good way to discover the gaps in your own training and work to fill them. [Figure 2-11]

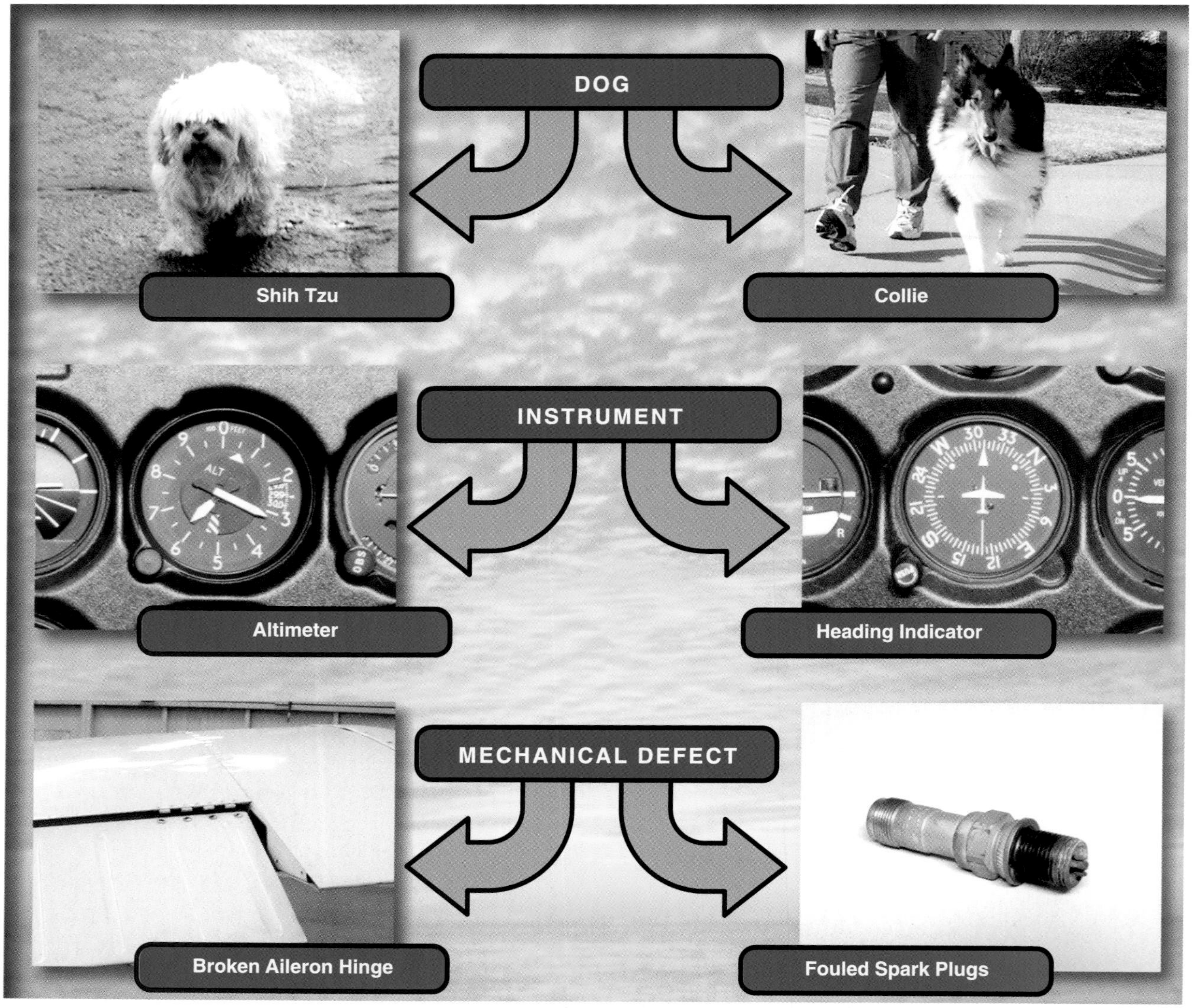

Figure 2-11. Whenever possible, use specific words rather than general ones. As an example, if you use the words, "*a leak in the fuel line*," it tells your student more than if you use the broad term, "*mechanical defect.*"

Another way to add life to your lectures is to vary your tone of voice and the pace at which you speak. Also, use sentences of differing lengths, because consistently using short ones results in a choppy style. On the other hand, unless long sentences are carefully constructed, they are difficult to follow and your students may easily lose track of where you are within a train of thought. Normally, you can avoid wordy sentences if you lecture from notes rather than reading straight from text, since most people do not use long sentences in normal speech.

DELIVERY STYLES

You may include several styles of delivery in your lectures. [Figure 2-12] The teaching lecture works best if you deliver it in an extemporaneous manner, as mentioned previously. Speak from a mental or written outline and avoid reading the material or memorizing the exact words. Since the words you use to express ideas are spontaneous, the lecture feels more personalized and less formal. Since you talk directly to your students, you can observe their actions more readily, and adjust your presentation based on their responses. For example, if your planned coverage of a particular concept leaves your students looking puzzled, you can elaborate until their reactions change to understanding, or you can ask questions to determine exactly where the source of confusion lies before proceeding.

Figure 2-12. Depending on the circumstances, a lecture is delivered in one of four ways.

USE OF NOTES

If you are well-prepared for your lecture, or you have given the presentation before, you may be able to deliver it effectively without notes. However, when the subject you are covering is complex, you may find an outline or index cards help you ensure accuracy, ease any fear you have of forgetting the material, and keep you on track if you tend to ramble. Use notes sparingly and in an unobtrusive manner, but there is no need to hide them from your students. For example, you can place an outline where it is easy to refer to, or use index cards if you walk around the room as you lecture.

LECTURE STYLES

You may conduct your lectures either in a formal or informal manner, depending on your audience. A teaching lecture is typically considered an **informal lecture**, as it lends itself to active student participation. If your students feel they are able to participate, and the atmosphere is friendly and relaxed, learning is enhanced. Because of this effect, you should normally use an informal style, and reserve a formal lecture for a more conservative atmosphere.

The distinguishing characteristic of an informal lecture is the student's participation.

You can include your students in an informal lecture by asking questions. You may need to elicit questions from specific students, especially in larger classes, so be prepared to call on people throughout the room. You can also use questions to determine the experience levels and backgrounds of your students so that you can both tailor the presentation to their needs, and encourage them to add to the lecture according to their experience. However, keep in mind it remains your responsibility to plan, develop, and present the majority of each lesson, so you should not let individual students take over large portions of the class period.

An instructor can inspire active student participation during lectures through the use of questions.

Advantages and Disadvantages of the Lecture Method

Lectures possess a number of advantages. First, a lecture is often the most convenient way to address a large group. The format may also be useful when the information you want to present is difficult for your students to acquire on their own, or if they do not have time to research the material. A lecture may supplement another teaching method, perhaps serving as an introduction to a demonstration. In a lecture, you are able to present a number of ideas in a short period of time, and you can organize your facts logically. A lecture is also a tool for bringing a common frame of reference to students of diverse backgrounds.

However, the lecture method does have several drawbacks. All too often, the rigid setting inhibits student participation, and your students may be compelled to sit back and let you do all the work. Since learning is an active process, your students cannot try to passively absorb the material and expect to remember it. Also, the lecture method is not ideal for certain learning outcomes, like the development of motor skills which require hands-on practice. It is harder to judge your students' understanding of the subject and their progress during a lecture, and you risk presenting more information in a class period than your students can digest.

Since you may find it difficult to hold all of your students' attention for an entire class period, you need considerable skill in speaking to make the most of the lecture method. If you can include some form of participation within your lecture, you increase the amount of information your students retain. One form of active learning that has been successfully incorporated into the classroom setting is cooperative learning.

Cooperative Learning Method

Cooperative, or group learning is a teaching method in which you organize students into small groups so that they can work together to maximize both their own and each other's learning. A number of research studies in diverse school settings, and across a wide range of subject areas, indicate that greater academic achievement is possible by incorporating this strategy. For example, students who have been involved in cooperative learning tend to have higher test scores, higher self esteem, improved social skills, and greater comprehension of the subjects they are studying. The most significant characteristic of the **cooperative learning method** is that it continually requires your students to actively participate in the learning process.

Conditions

Although there are many advantages to cooperative learning, it needs to be implemented correctly in order to succeed. Each activity your students engage in is known as a **group task**, which may emphasize academic achievement, cognitive abilities, or physical skills. In order for the group task to be effective, you must describe in clear terms what specific knowledge or abilities your students need to acquire.

You should organize small groups of approximately 3 to 6 students so that they are mixed, considering academic abilities, ethnic backgrounds, race, and gender. Your students

should not be allowed to form their own groups based on friendship or cliques. The main advantages with mixed groups are that students tend to interact and achieve in ways that are rarely found with other instructional strategies. They also tend to become tolerant of diverse viewpoints, consider the thoughts and feelings of others, and seek more support and clarification of varying opinions.

Before your students begin working together, you need to provide a clear explanation of exactly what they must accomplish, in what order, and with what materials, as well as describe any exercises they need to finish before the end of the group task. In order for the effort to be effective, your students need to value the objectives of the lesson and believe that everyone in the group needs to master the information and/or skill. If you construct a situation where your students determine their own objectives, each person in the group must accept them. When you structure the group task in this way, your students believe that they need to work together to complete the required exercise. To accomplish this, you need to set up the task so that all are rewarded for a good effort, or receive a poor grade for failing to complete the task correctly. By the same token, all your students need to feel that they have an equal chance of learning the content and/or skill, and earn the rewards for success, regardless of the group they are in. [Figure 2-13]

Figure 2-13. You may divide your class into groups and have them assemble the planning for an air race. Design group tasks so that everyone's participation is required in order to complete the exercise successfully.

Each student and group needs to be provided with enough time to learn the targeted information and/or skill. If time is limited, the benefits of having your students perform the group tasks will be limited as well. In fact, research shows that cooperative learning benefits are greatest when students are able to work in the same mixed groups for several weeks.

SOCIAL SKILLS

When instructing by the cooperative learning method, you need to make sure the room or space you are in allows your students to cluster so they can easily converse and complete any written activities as a group. Also, you may need to provide your students with a brief refresher on the social skills they need to employ: leadership, trust-building, conflict management, constructive criticism, compromise, negotiation, and clarification. You may find that assigning each student a specific role in the group aids you in ensuring these skills are used. For example, designating one student in each group to serve as leader may solve conflict at a later point.

DEBRIEF ON GROUP EFFORTS

Your students should spend some time after the group tasks have been completed to consider how well they were able to work together to meet the required objectives. They should reflect on how they helped each other understand the content, how they used the resources and task procedures, how they employed social skills to enable individual and group success, and how they might improve in the future in each of these areas.

GUIDED DISCUSSION METHOD

In any group learning situation, you rely on your students to provide ideas, experiences, and opinions, and this is especially true when you are leading a **guided discussion**. This method is particularly useful during classroom instruction and during pre- and postflight briefings after your students have gained some knowledge and experience with the topic presented. In essence, the guided discussion is the opposite of the lecture, as you try to draw out what your students know rather than tell them directly. The more your students participate and add to the discussion, the more effective the learning environment. All members of the group should be involved in the process, and you should pay particular attention to those students who do not join in naturally. You need to treat everyone fairly, encourage questions, model patience and tact, and respond to each student's input. If you notice any sarcasm or ridicule, diffuse it by asking one of the students a question, or changing topics altogether. You are the facilitator in this setting, and your goal is to encourage discussion among your students.

USE OF QUESTIONS

In a guided discussion, learning is achieved through your skillful use of questions. Questions can be categorized by function and by characteristics. You often use a question to open a topic for discussion, known as a **lead-off question**. After the discussion develops, you may use a **follow-up question** because you want students to explain a concept more thoroughly, or you need to bring the discussion back to a point from which it has wandered.

In a guided discussion, learning is produced through the skillful use of questions. An overhead question should be used to begin a guided discussion with a group of students. A lead-off question on the subject of torque may be, *"How does torque affect an airplane?"* Lead-off questions typically begin with how or why.

Questions are also characterized by how they are structured, and to whom they are directed. An **overhead question** is posed to the entire group to stimulate thought and response from every student, and is a good choice for a lead-off question. A **rhetorical question** is similar to an overhead question, because it also inspires group thought. The difference between the two is that you provide the answer to a rhetorical question, as it basically answers itself. Therefore, this type of question is used more in a lecture, but it can also be used to connect ideas or review a concept. If you would like a response from a particular student, you may ask a **direct question**. A **reverse question** is used to redirect a student's question rather than giving an immediate response. If you want to pose a student's question to the entire group, this is called a **relay question**. [Figure 2-14]

QUESTION TYPE	SAMPLE QUESTION
Overhead Question	*"Why is a piston engine a good choice for a small general aviation aircraft?"*
Rhetorical Question	*"Is an airplane going to fly very long without fuel?"*
Direct Question	*"Steve, what is the function of the carburetor in a piston engine?"*
Reverse Question	*"Instructor, why does ice form in the carburetor?"* *"Well, what happens to the air inside of a carburetor?"*
Relay Question	*"Anyone — why would climbing to a higher altitude decrease engine performance?"*

Figure 2-14. These are examples of various questions you may use in a guided discussion.

You may take questions for granted, because you use them so often in the course of teaching. However, their effective use may result in a higher level of student learning than any other technique you employ. In general, you should ask open-ended questions that require your students to grasp concepts, explain similarities and differences, and to infer cause-and-effect relationships. [Figure 2-15]

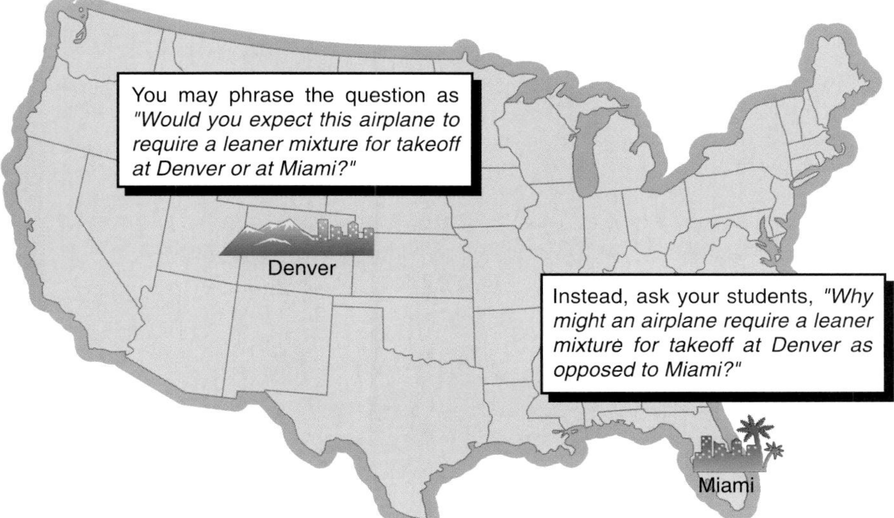

Figure 2-15. Your students could answer the first question simply by saying *"Denver."* The longer explanation required for the second question may prompt a discussion of leaning procedures, density altitude, and carburetors.

No More Bad Questions

As an instructor you may often encourage questions by assuring students that any question they ask will be valid. However, this theory does not apply to questions you ask of your students. There are indeed bad questions.

For example: consider the questions, *"What did you think of that last maneuver?"* or *"How does an airplane fly?"*

The first question is vague and may confuse your students into giving an answer that does not correspond with what you are asking. The second question is not specific enough to elicit the responses you are looking for. Better questions would be, *"Did you feel you understood my explanation of the maneuver?"* or *"Describe one theory used to explain the creation of lift."*

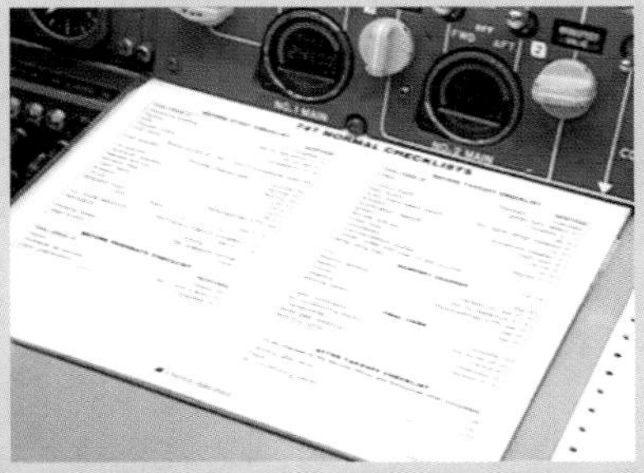

Another example of a bad question would be, *"Is the ignition switch a 'go-switch'?"*

A trick question such as this one only tests whether the student read the material provided on a particular technique, as opposed to a procedure, such as calling certain switches in the cockpit *"go"* or *"fix-it"* switches. If the student had not read the company material, even if he knew that airplane thoroughly, he would answer incorrectly.

Asking trick questions is unprofessional and may put your students off-balance, never trusting you to ask them a straight question. To avoid asking trick questions, make sure that your students have the required background information to answer your questions, and use terms they understand. For instance, avoid asking an inexperienced pilot questions concerning exceptions to obscure FARs, and stick to topics they need to know first.

PLANNING A GUIDED DISCUSSION

Planning a guided discussion follows essentially the same steps as planning the use of other teaching methods, such as lectures or cooperative learning sessions. Some suggestions for building productive guided discussions are shown in figure 2-16.

- Select a topic your students have the background to talk about intelligently. This may require more planning on your part to provide your students with advance assignments to give them the background they require.
- Establish a specific lesson objective with desired learning outcomes. Your students will develop an understanding of the subject by sharing knowledge and experiences through the discussion. Therefore, the objective is normally stated so it is appropriate to the understanding level of learning, and the desired learning outcomes should follow from the objective to build your students' comprehension to an even higher level.
- Conduct adequate research to become familiar with the topic. Look for ideas about the best way to tailor the lesson for a particular group of students. Prepare the pre-discussion assignment while you collect information and designate reading material that would be appropriate for your students to review.
- Organize the main and subordinate points of the lesson in a logical sequence. A guided discussion consists of three main parts — introduction, discussion, and conclusion. The introduction contains attention, motivation, and overview elements. During the discussion, ensure the main points build logically from the beginning and are in line with the objective. The conclusion includes a summary, remotivation, and closure.
- Plan at least one lead-off question for each desired learning outcome, or topic. The goal is to stimulate discussion, so avoid questions that require only short answers, such as yes or no, but instead create ones that begin with how or why.

Figure 2-16. A guided discussion requires detailed planning in order to be a success.

STUDENT PREPARATION

To help your students prepare for an upcoming discussion, encourage each student to take responsibility for contributing as well as benefiting from the discussion, and make the lesson objective and desired learning outcomes clear from the time the assignment is made. In cases where you do not have time to give your students a pre-discussion assignment, you should take the time at the beginning of the class period to provide an overview of the topic to be discussed.

GUIDING A DISCUSSION

You develop the techniques used to guide a discussion through practice and experience. As you gain skill in following the discussion closely, you learn where to intervene with questions to redirect the group's focus. You can establish a basic framework that helps you to successfully conduct the session, consisting of an introduction, discussion, and conclusion.

Unless students have some knowledge to exchange with each other, they cannot reach the desired learning outcomes through a guided discussion.

INTRODUCTION

A guided discussion is introduced in the same way you would introduce a lecture, including an attention element, a motivation element, and an overview of the key points. To create a relaxed, informal atmosphere, your introduction may contain anecdotes, a funny story, or an unusual question, rather than facts or statistics. This environment allows your students to understand they can ask questions freely about various aspects of the topic and moreover, feel compelled to contribute. You need to encourage this by making the students believe that their ideas and active participation are valued from the beginning.

DISCUSSION

You begin the body of the discussion by asking one of the lead-off questions you have prepared. After asking a question, be patient, since your students need the opportunity

to consider the question before answering. The more challenging the question, the more time may be required for students to react. In fact, they may not understand the question, and if you see puzzled expressions, you may need to rephrase the question.

Once the discussion has begun, you should listen carefully to the ideas, experiences, and examples contributed by your students. During your preparation, you probably listed some of the anticipated responses that would indicate whether or not your students grasp the information. [Figure 2-17]

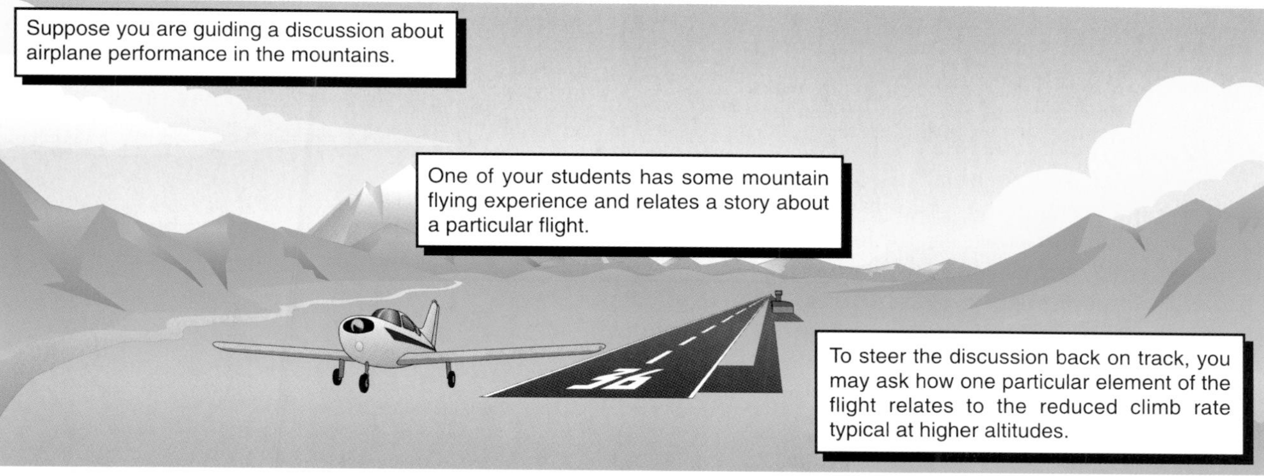

Figure 2-17. As the discussion proceeds, you may find it necessary to alter the direction, to stimulate your students to explore a particular point in greater depth, or to give more detail to a certain topic. By using follow-up questions, you should be able to steer the students toward understanding the subject.

After your students have fully discussed ideas that support each part of the lesson, you should restate them in an **interim summary**. This helps you gain the greatest value from the guided discussion method. An interim summary can be made immediately after each topic's learning outcome is completed to bring ideas together, create an efficient transition to the next topic, divert the discussion to another member of the group, or keep your students on track. This pulls together ideas developed by the group and shows how they relate and support the topic. You may skip an interim summary after the last topic when it feels more natural to begin your conclusion.

When it appears students have discussed the ideas presented during a guided discussion, one of the most valuable tools an instructor can use is an interim summary.

CONCLUSION

During the conclusion, your goal is to tie together the various points discussed, showing the relationships between the facts presented and how your students may use these facts in practical applications. Your conclusion should be succinct, but complete. If the discussion reveals that certain areas are not well understood by some of your students, you should clarify this material, or plan to cover it again. [Figure 2-18]

Figure 2-18. When concluding a discussion of frontal systems, you might point out how a recent system created hazardous weather in your area, changing over the course of several days as the front passed.

DEMONSTRATION-PERFORMANCE METHOD

The **demonstration-performance method** is based on the principle that students learn by doing. Your students learned to walk by walking, and they will learn how to fly an aircraft by performing flight maneuvers. Some mental skills, such as learning a foreign language, are also best accomplished by practice, and skills requiring the use of tools, machines, and other equipment are also well-suited to this instructional method. The essential steps in the demonstration-performance method are explanation, demonstration, student performance, instructor supervision, and evaluation.

The demonstration-performance method is well-suited for teaching a skill such as cross-country planning.

The essential steps in the demonstration-performance method are explanation, demonstration, student performance, instructor supervision, and evaluation.

In order to take advantage of this method, you need to recognize the importance of student performance in the learning process. In the beginning of a lesson including demonstration and performance, you must identify the most important learning outcomes. Then, explain and illustrate the steps involved in performing the skill being taught. Allow your students time to practice each step, so they can increase their capability. [Figure 2-19]

Figure 2-19. Problems involving the use of flight computers are well-suited to the demonstration-performance method.

EXPLANATION PHASE

The explanations you give must be clear, pertinent to the objectives of the particular lesson, and based on the known experience level of your students. At the least, you must convey to your students the exact steps they need to perform the skill and the result they should expect. Before you move past this phase, encourage your students to ask questions if they need clarification on any of the steps in the procedure.

DEMONSTRATION PHASE

Next, you need to show your students the precise steps necessary to perform the skill. Keep your demonstration as streamlined as possible, since any extraneous information may detract from the clarity of your presentation. Also, try to use the same verbiage that you used previously to describe the skill so that your students may follow the procedure more easily. Any deviations you make should be explained immediately to help your students stay focused.

Could You Run That By Me Again?

Not all demonstrations turn out the way the flight instructor has planned. Consider the following scenarios and what went wrong during each one.

Jack just got his CFI certificate, and he is proud of how well he can execute the commercial maneuvers. Jim, his commercial student, is also an experienced pilot, but he is growing frustrated with Jack because he feels like he never gets to fly.

One good demonstration is all a sharp student is likely to need. Even if Jim was not able to perform the maneuver to Jack's standards the first time, Jack still needs to let Jim try instead of giving him repeated demonstrations. Remember you can help your students learn more by letting them make small mistakes and have the chance to correct them once they have seen you demonstrate the maneuver.

Adam is not really sure how to explain lazy eights to his student, Susan. Since the maneuver came naturally to him, he has not developed the tools to impart his knowledge to Susan, for whom the maneuver is not so easy. In addition, he does not have a thorough understanding of important facets of the maneuver, so he rushes through a skimpy explanation in hopes that Susan will "just get it."

If Adam has gaps in his knowledge, he will not be able to hide them for very long. Instead of giving Susan an incomplete explanation, he should seek help from a more experienced CFI on how to teach lazy eights in a way that Susan is more likely to understand.

It has been a while since Ellen has trained a primary student, so she does not realize that introducing several maneuvers during Linda's first lesson may only confuse her new student. After turns to headings, slow flight, power-off stalls and a rectangular course, Linda's head is swimming and she feels discouraged, as though she could never understand all she needs to know to pilot an airplane.

Instead of introducing so many new elements at once, Ellen should let her enthusiasm for flying show by giving Linda time to absorb a simple flight in the local area. During the first couple of lessons, your students are adapting to sights, sounds, and feelings they may have never experienced before. This information alone provides enough material for your students to process without adding more complex tasks to their workload.

During his demonstration of slow flight, John forgets to pull on the carburetor heat before he reduces the power. He realizes his mistake well into the maneuver, and he surreptitiously turns it on while his student, Shannon, is looking at nearby traffic.

John should repeat his demonstration of the maneuver, pointing out his mistake in not using carburetor heat at the appropriate time. If he does not mention the omission, Shannon may not include this important step when she performs the maneuver. If she does notice his mistake, but he fails to call it to her attention, she may lose confidence in his ability to give her adequate flight instruction.

STUDENT PERFORMANCE/ INSTRUCTOR SUPERVISION PHASE

The student performance phase includes practice of the physical or mental task just explained and demonstrated, performed under your supervision. To learn skills, your students must repeatedly practice, and you need to allow enough time for your students to do so during the lesson period. During this phase, your students learn to follow correct

Figure 2-20. During flight training, you should have your student try a maneuver immediately after you demonstrate it, and you may offer coaching as necessary.

In the demonstration-performance method, the student performance and instructor supervision phases are performed concurrently. The last step is the evaluation phase.

procedures to reach established standards. It is important they have the opportunity to perform the skill as soon as possible after the demonstration. Prior to ending the performance phase, you should ensure that everyone is allowed to complete the task independently at least once before moving on. [Figure 2-20]

EVALUATION PHASE

During this phase, while your students perform the skill, you note how well it has been learned and whether further practice is required. From this evaluation, you can also determine the effectiveness of your presentation.

TELLING-AND-DOING TECHNIQUE

The telling-and-doing technique follows the demonstration-performance method guidelines, and consists of several steps. In addition to preparation, the steps are: instructor tells—instructor does; student tells—instructor does; student tells—student does; student does—instructor evaluates.

You can apply the demonstration-performance method to flight instruction through the telling-and-doing technique. This technique is particularly suited to teaching physical skills, so you may find it valuable when giving instruction on flight maneuvers and procedures. It follows the four steps of the demonstration-performance method, with the exception of the first step. When using the telling-and-doing technique, your first step is preparation, as it is critical to giving safe and effective flight instruction. [Figure 2-21]

STEP	DEMONSTRATION-PERFORMANCE METHOD	TELLING-AND-DOING TECHNIQUE
1	(Preparation Prior to the Lesson)	Preparation
2	Explanation	Presentation: Instructor Tells — Instructor Does
3	Demonstration	Presentation: Student Tells — Instructor Does
4	Student Performance — Instructor Supervision	Application: Student Tells — Student Does
5	Evaluation	Review and Evaluation: Student Does — Instructor Evaluates

Figure 2-21. This comparison of the steps in the teaching process, the demonstration-performance method, and the telling-and-doing technique shows the similarities as well as some differences. The main difference in the telling-and-doing technique is the transition between the second and third step: the student tells-instructor does phase.

PREPARATION

The preparation step is accomplished prior to each flight lesson, where you discuss lesson objectives and completion standards with your students in thorough preflight briefings. Your students need to know not only what will be learned, but how the lesson will proceed and how an evaluation will be made. You should also cover appropriate safety procedures during this phase.

PRESENTATION

Presentation or **instructor tells—instructor does** is the second step in this teaching process, when you demonstrate the procedure or maneuver carefully, describing the process as you go along. When you demonstrate flight maneuvers, you should explain the required power settings, aircraft attitudes, and any other pertinent factors that apply. Only during this phase do your students play a passive role. You should show them exactly how they are expected to perform the maneuver, and if you deviate from the standard, point it out and discuss the differences.

Most physical skills lend themselves to a sequential pattern where you can explain the skill in the same step-by-step order normally used to perform it. When the skill you are teaching relates to maneuvers or procedures your students are already familiar with, you can use the known-to-unknown development strategy, such as going from a rectangular course to a traffic pattern. If you are teaching more than one skill at the same time, the simple-to-complex development strategy works well. By starting with the simplest skill, your students gain confidence and are less likely to become frustrated when faced with more complex skills. [Figure 2-22]

Once you have demonstrated and explained a task, you should have your students tell you how to perform the task while you go through the motions. This is referred to as the **student tells—instructor does** step, and your students benefit from this in two ways.

Lead the rollout by approximately one-half the number of degrees of the angle of bank. Use coordinated rudder and aileron pressure as you roll out. Simultaneously begin releasing back pressure so all control forces are neutralized when the airplane reaches wings-level flight.

Leading the rollout by one-half the bank angle is a good rule of thumb for initial training, but keep in mind that the required amount of lead really depends upon the type of turn, turn rate, and rollout rate.

Ailerons control the roll rate as well as the angle of bank. When you reach the desired angle of bank, neutralize the ailerons and trim, as appropriate.

Use outside visual references and monitor the flight instruments.

After clearing the area, add a little power, turn the airplane in the desired direction, and add a slight amount of back pressure on the yoke to maintain altitude. Maintain coordinated flight by applying rudder in the direction of the turn.

Figure 2-22. You may present a level turn to a student by following these steps.

First, by freeing them from the need to concentrate on the performance of the maneuver, you allow your students to organize their thoughts regarding the steps involved and the techniques they need to use. In the process of explaining the maneuver as you perform it, your students begin translating their perceptions into insights. Mental habits form with the repetition of instruction they have previously received. Second, with your students doing the talking, you are able to evaluate their understanding of the factors involved in the performance of the maneuver. They need to understand the proper sequence and be aware of any safety precautions. If a misunderstanding exists, it can be corrected before they become absorbed in controlling the airplane.

APPLICATION

Application or the **student tells—student does** is the step in the process where learning takes place and habits are formed. If you have adequately prepared your students, and presented the maneuver to them properly, meaningful learning begins to occur. You need to remain alert during your students' practice so you can detect any errors in technique and prevent the formation of poor habits.

Verbally expressing what they are thinking helps students focus their concentration on the task to be accomplished and makes it easy for you to determine whether an error is induced by a misconception or by a simple lack of motor ability. As a result, your students are not only learning to do something, but they are also learning a self-teaching process that is highly effective in developing a skill.

The exact procedures you should use during student practice depend on factors such as your student's proficiency level, the type of maneuver, and the stage of training. You must exercise good judgment to decide how much control to use. With potentially hazardous or difficult maneuvers, you should be alert and ready to assume control of the airplane at any time, especially during your student's first attempt. Conversely, if your student is progressing normally, you can avoid unnecessary interruptions or too much assistance. [Figure 2-23]

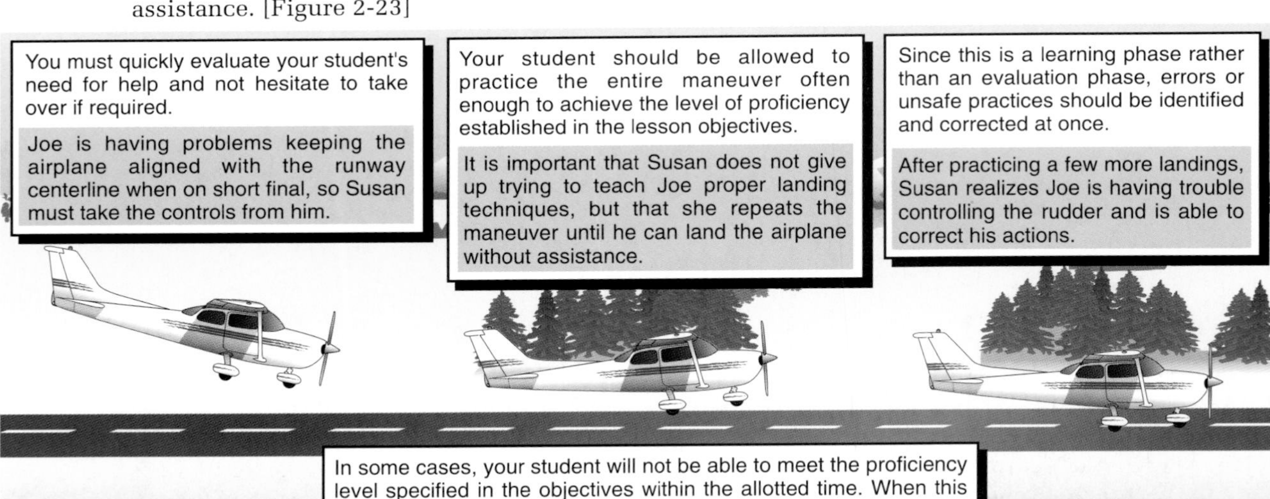

Figure 2-23. A typical test of how much control is needed often occurs during your student's first few attempts to land the airplane.

REVIEW AND EVALUATION

During the fourth step of the teaching process, review and evaluation, or the **student does—instructor evaluates**, you review what you have covered during the flight and determine to what extent your student has met the objectives outlined during the preflight discussion, or preparation phase. Since your student is no longer required to talk through the maneuver during this step, you should be satisfied that your student is well-prepared and understands the task before starting.

At the conclusion of the evaluation phase, record your student's performance and give a summary of the progress made toward the objectives. Regardless of how well a skill is taught, some of your students may experience failure. Since success is a motivating factor, you should point out the results of this phase in a positive light. When discussing areas that need improvement, offer concrete suggestions that your student can put to use. If possible, avoid ending the evaluation on a negative note.

INTEGRATED METHOD OF FLIGHT INSTRUCTION

The **integrated method of flight instruction** is instruction during which students are taught to perform maneuvers both by outside visual references and by reference to the flight instruments. For this method to be fully effective, you should instruct your students to use instrument as well as outside visual references from the time each maneuver is introduced. No distinction in the operation of the flight controls is made, no matter which references are used. The main goal of this instruction is to form solid habit patterns during initial training that will help your students achieve a more precise and competent overall skill level.

The main objective of integrated flight instruction is the formation of firm habit patterns for observing and relying upon the flight instruments.

An acceptable procedure when using the integrated method of flight instruction is to include in the student's first instruction on the function of flight controls the instrument indication to be expected, as well as the outside references used in attitude control.

ADDED PILOT COMPETENCY

Students trained using the integrated method of flight instruction typically perform all flight maneuvers and operations with added precision, not just those which require reference to flight instruments. When trained with integrated instruction, students display great ability to monitor power settings and desired headings, altitudes, and airspeeds. As your students develop the habit of checking their own performance by reference to the instruments, they will often make corrections without prompting. Landings also improve as students maintain more precise airspeed control. When this skill is combined with better cross-country navigation and coordination of flight controls, the result is greater overall pilot competency.

Since the airplane's performance depends on how closely the flight and engine instruments are monitored, and how precisely heading, airspeed, and altitude are controlled, the integrated method teaches students to operate the airplane with a high degree of efficiency. This occurs especially in high-performance aircraft that are more sensitive to being flown with the correct airspeeds and proper power settings.

One of the more obvious benefits of this method of instruction is the ability of the student to maintain controlled flight for limited periods of time if outside visual references are lost. While much of your instructional time is spent teaching students how to avoid such occurrences, incidents like these happen, and by equipping them with basic instrument skills from the beginning, you give your students the tools with which to escape from these situations.

PROCEDURES

Introducing your student to integrated flight instruction begins with the first lesson. When you show the flight controls to your student, you can point out how each flight attitude, from climb to descent, is reflected on the instruments. Most students will naturally accept the fact that the manipulation of the flight controls is identical, regardless of which references are used to determine the attitude of the airplane. To fully achieve the

Figure 2-24. Since students are accustomed to instrument flight from the beginning, they rapidly develop the ability to maneuver the airplane just as well by outside visual references as by using the instruments.

demonstrated benefits of this kind of training, the use of visual and instrument references must be constantly integrated throughout the training. [Figure 2-24]

PRECAUTIONS

You must be sure that your students develop the habit of looking for other air traffic at all times, from the start of their training. In earlier stages of training, your students may find it easier to perform flight maneuvers by reference to the instruments than by outside references. This fact may lead them to concentrate most of their attention on the instruments, when they should be primarily using outside references. This may cause considerable difficulty later in training while maneuvering by reference to ground objects, and it obviously limits vigilance for other traffic. You should carefully observe your students' performance of maneuvers during the early stages of integrated flight instruction to ensure that this tendency does not develop. Also, you should make it clear that the use of instruments is being taught to prepare your students to accurately monitor their own and their aircraft's performance, and not solely for flight into instrument meteorological conditions.

During integrated flight instruction, the instructor must be sure the student develops the habit of looking for other traffic.

FORMING INSTRUMENT SKILL

By reviewing accident and incident statistics with your students, such as those presented in the *AOPA/Aviation Safety Foundation Nall Report*, you can establish that pilots with instrument ratings have better safety records than pilots with similar flight time and no formal instrument training. If your students begin their training by learning to continuously monitor airplane performance using the instruments, they will become safer, more efficient pilots and transition to instrument flight more readily. The benefit to your students includes the ability to safely handle accidental flight into instrument meteorological conditions or low visibility, added margins of safety during night flight, and a firm foundation for future instrument training.

COMPUTER-BASED TRAINING METHOD

Many innovative training technologies are widely available to flight instructors, such as **computer-based training (CBT)**, also referred to as **computer-based instruction (CBI)**. The personal computer has revolutionized how education and training are conducted in all types of learning programs, and flight training is no exception. CBT may combine video, graphics, and interactivity to explore a particular topic or test your student's knowledge of various subjects. For example, many major aircraft manufacturers develop CBT programs to teach systems and maintenance procedures in the field. End users of the aircraft, such

as airlines, can purchase the CBT materials to accomplish both initial and recurrent training of their employees. One of the major advantages of CBT is that a student can progress at a rate that is comfortable and may be able to access the program whenever it is convenient, rather than having to wait for an instructor.

Since aviation training is wide-ranging and dynamic, entrusting an entire course to a computer program is not practical, so during **computer-assisted instruction (CAI)**, the computer is used as a tool in combination with another form of instruction. Even airline simulator programs require extensive tailoring and real-time interaction with a human instructor to provide individual feedback and personal attention.

With CBT, your role changes along with that of your students, as they become more involved in their own learning. In this situation, CBT should still be considered as an additional instructional aid to improve traditional classroom instruction. You still need to maintain complete control over the learning environment to ensure that lesson objectives are being achieved. You may also have access to a computer laboratory, often referred to as a learning or training center, which is configured into separate study areas for each of your students. In this case, you need to establish procedures to make sure the required training is accomplished, since you must certify your students' competency at the end of the course.

A number of advantages are attributed to CBT. Well-designed programs allow your students to feel as though they are in control of what they are learning and how fast they learn the material. They can explore areas that interest them and discover more about a subject on their own. Disadvantages include a potential lack of peer interaction and personal feedback. You may feel less in control of the learning situation, and it may be difficult for you to find quality CBT programs for certain subject areas.

PCATDs AND FTDs

From small flight schools to the airlines to the military, flight simulation devices are available for a wide variety of training applications. Fixed-base operators (FBOs) who offer instrument training may provide instruction in **personal computer-based aviation training devices (PCATDs)** or **flight training devices (FTDs)** for credit toward the portion of the time a pilot needs for an instrument rating. Similarly, military pilots use simulators to prepare for flying aircraft that have no two-seat training versions. Major airlines have sophisticated **flight simulators** which are so realistic that transitioning pilots may meet all qualifications to act as crewmembers by receiving all type-specific aircraft time in the simulator alone. [Figure 2-25]

The PCATD consists of a visual display of aircraft instruments together with switches and knobs that emulate the controls on an aircraft. These controls must be realistic enough so their purpose and operation is obvious, but they do not need to reflect a specific aircraft type.

A flight simulator is an FAA-approved full-size replica of a specific type of aircraft cockpit, with a motion system that simulates the forces felt during actual flight. A flight simulator includes a visual system with at least a 45-degree horizontal and 30-degree vertical field of view.

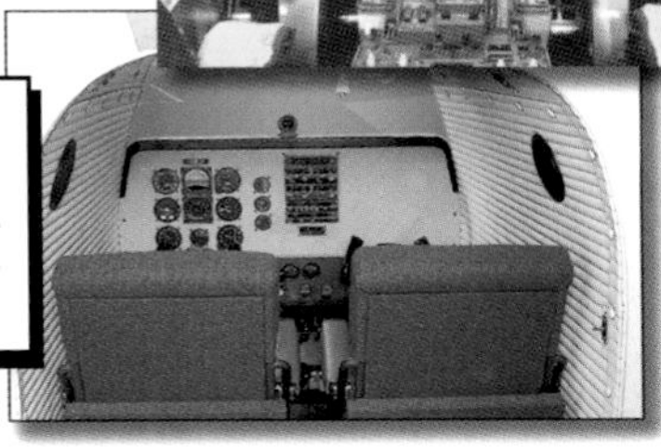

A flight training device (FTD) is an FAA-approved device like a flight simulator, with full-size instruments, equipment panels, and aircraft controls. It does not have to replicate a specific model of aircraft, but should replicate at least a set of actual aircraft. An enclosed cockpit, as well as motion and visual systems are permissible, but not required.

Figure 2-25. The relatively low cost of PCATDs allows smaller flight schools to invest in them for training.

TEST PREPARATION

Other common examples of CBT include the computer versions of test preparation materials used to study for the FAA knowledge exams. These programs typically allow your students to select their own tests, complete the questions, obtain a score, and review the questions they missed. Some of the more advanced test preparation software offer reference materials within or alongside each program, such as a FAR/AIM or textbook excerpts.

CBT APPLICATIONS

Some CBT applications guide students through a series of interactive frames where the presentation may vary with their responses. If students wish to learn more about a particular subject, they may do so by clicking the mouse on certain areas of the screen. This allows each student to focus on specific material, without having to wade through extraneous information. [Figure 2-26]

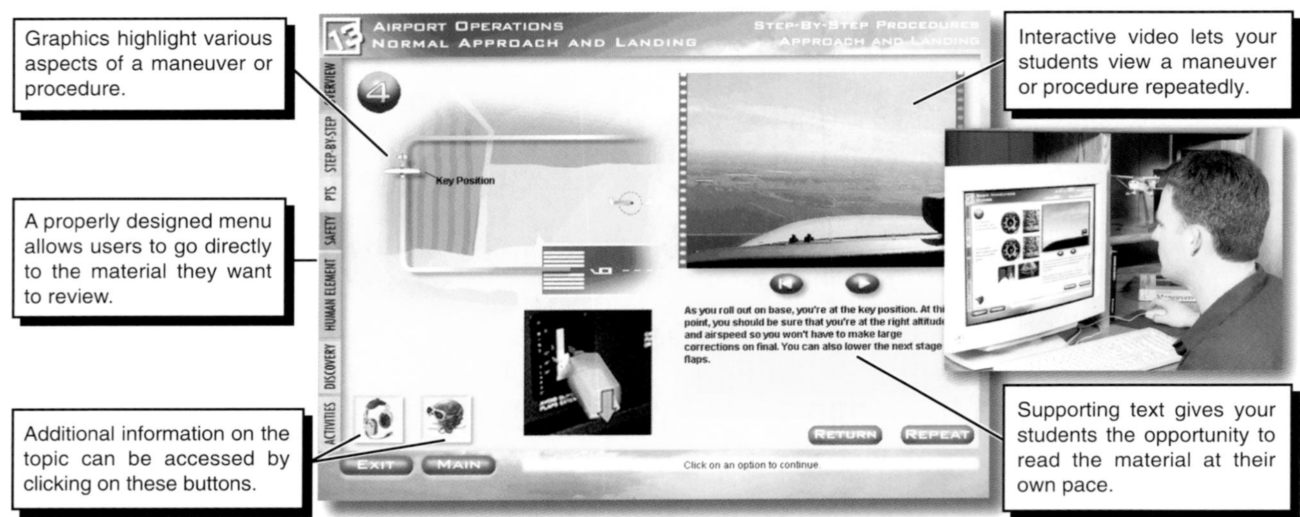

Figure 2-26. CBT often incorporates several design elements to help your student learn a particular subject. A major advantage of CBT over other forms of instructional aids is that the computer responds differently, depending on your student's input.

The computer can be a valuable resource for you to use in the formation of almost any lesson plan. One example of the possible applications for the computer in your training syllabus is to provide a program that allows your students to review procedures at their own pace while you are involved in hands-on training with other students. In this case, the CBT serves as another reference, like a textbook, and your students are able to study subjects repeatedly until they understand.

LIMITATIONS

While computers provide many advantages, they also have limitations, and improper, or excessive use of CBT should be avoided. For example, you should not rely exclusively on a CBT program to teach your students the ground instruction required to perform traffic pattern operations and landings, since there are so many variables to these flight maneuvers that cannot be covered by a single program. By the same token, you must be actively involved when your students use CBT, and this may include supervision, questions, quizzes, or guided discussions on the material covered. You must continue to monitor your students to ensure they stay on track with a training syllabus. At times, you may feel like CBT requires you to provide more one-on-one instruction than in a traditional classroom setting, but the programs may relay many concepts that typically require reinforcement. You have more time, in fact, to give specific instruction to each

Figure 2-27. In this classroom setting, several students are using a CBT program to review approach and landing procedures. Notice how the instructor is able to address individual questions as the rest of the students progress through the material.

student once you are freed from having to repeat basic information already covered by the CBT. [Figure 2-27]

USING INSTRUCTIONAL AIDS

Instructional aids differ from training media, in that **training media** typically include any physical means by which an instructional message is communicated to your students. Examples of these are your voice, printed text, video cassettes, computer programs, PCATDs, flight training devices, or flight simulators. Conversely, instructional aids are devices that assist you in the teaching process. These aids are not self-supporting, such as a video program that offers a full treatment of a particular subject. Instead they supplement or reinforce your presentation. Carefully selected charts, graphs, pictures, or other well-organized visual aids are examples of items that help your students understand and retain pertinent information.

REASONS FOR USE OF INSTRUCTIONAL AIDS

In addition to helping your students remember important information, instructional aids have other advantages. If you use them properly, they help you gain and hold your students' attention. Using both audio and visual aids to support a topic can be very effective, since your students use two important senses to absorb the material. In fact, you may want to consider that you are selling an idea, much as you might sell a product or service. Though you should keep your aids from becoming gimmicks, some pizzazz can make your presentation far more interesting to your students.

Visual aids can be used to emphasize the key points in a lesson.

One of your major goals when giving any instruction is for your students to retain as much knowledge of the subject as possible, particularly the key points. Numerous studies have attempted to determine how well instructional aids serve this purpose, and the

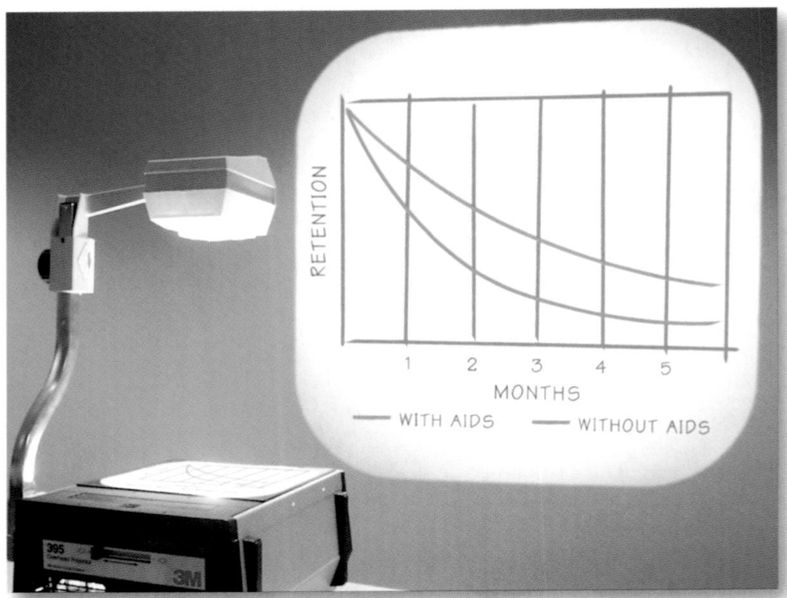

Figure 2-28. Studies show measurable improvement in student retention of information occurs when instructional aids are used in conjunction with a presentation.

results are mixed. The more modest indications show a 10 to 15% increase in retention, while more optimistic indications show as much as an 80% increase. [Figure 2-28]

As technical terminology continues to expand in everyday usage, and the backgrounds of your students become more culturally diverse, instructional aids can help convey ideas which may be difficult to explain by speech alone. Another reason for instructional aids is to clarify relationships between material objects and abstract concepts, such as the connection between the production of lift and the shape of an airfoil. When these connections are presented visually, they are often easier for your students to understand. For example, symbols, graphs, and diagrams can also show relationships of time, location, size, frequency, and value. You may be asked to teach increasing amounts in shorter periods of time, and instructional aids can assist you in doing this. For example, instead of using many words to describe a sound, object, or function, you can play a recording of the sound, show a picture of the object, or present a diagram of the function.

Guidelines For Use of Instructional Aids

The first step in determining if and when instructional aids are necessary is to clearly establish the lesson objective and be sure of what you would like to communicate. When planning a lesson, select instructional aids to support the key points. Aids are often appropriate when long segments of technical description are necessary, when a point is complex or you have difficulty putting it into words, when you find yourself forming a visual image of the subject, or for subjects where you have found students are commonly puzzled by a simplified explanation.

Aids should be straightforward and compatible with the learning outcomes you have established. If you need to explain an elaborate piece of equipment, detailed mockups or schematics may be required, but less complex equipment lends itself more to basic shapes or figures. Since you most likely will use these aids in conjunction with your oral presentation, words on these aids should be kept to a minimum. In fact, you may be able to incorporate symbols or slogans to replace

Instructional aids used in the teaching process should not be used as a crutch by the instructor.

Instructional aids used in the teaching process should be compatible with the learning outcomes to be achieved. The first step in determining if and when instructional aids are necessary is to clearly establish the lesson objective, being certain what must be communicated.

wordy phrases. Above all, avoid using the aids as a crutch. If you do not know the material you are covering, this will be evident by your lack of ability to expand upon the information presented in the aid.

Instructional aids should appeal to your students and be based on sound principles of instructional design, which will be explored further in the next section. They must have meaning for your students, lead to the desired behavioral or learning objectives, and provide appropriate reinforcement. Aids that involve learning of a physical skill need to guide your students toward mastery of a skill or task specified in the objective. When you find it practical, they should also encourage student participation.

The aids you select have no value unless your students can see or hear them clearly. If you plan to play a sound recording, check it for correct volume and quality in the classroom or environment you are using. By the same token, all lettering and illustrations on visual aids must be large enough to be seen easily by all your students regardless of where they sit. If you test the equipment you are using prior to class, you may avoid embarrassment and loss of valuable instruction time. [Figure 2-29]

Figure 2-29. If you follow these guidelines for incorporating instructional aids in your presentations, your students may show improved retention of the information you cover.

In practice, the choice of instructional aids depends on several factors. Availability, feasibility, or cost may restrict the variety and quality of aids you are able to incorporate in your presentations. Also, you need to consider the number of students in your class and the existing facilities. In some schools, the designers of the curriculum determine the use of any instructional aids, and you may have limited control over their use in this situation. On the other hand, if you work independently, you may be able to choose your own aids, but you may not have the resources to afford all the materials you would like to use. In this case, you must improvise to incorporate enough quality instructional aids to round out your presentations.

TYPES OF INSTRUCTIONAL AIDS

Some of the most common and economical aids are chalk or marker boards, and supplemental print materials, including charts, diagrams, and graphs. Other aids, which are usually more expensive, are projected materials, video, and computer-based programs, as well as models, mockups, or cut-aways.

CHALK OR MARKER BOARD

The chalk or marker board is probably the tool you will use most often as an instructor, because of its versatility and effectiveness. For example, you may use boards for joint student-instructor activities. To make the best use of classroom time, you should organize and practice writing your initial subject presentation on the board in advance. [Figure 2-30]

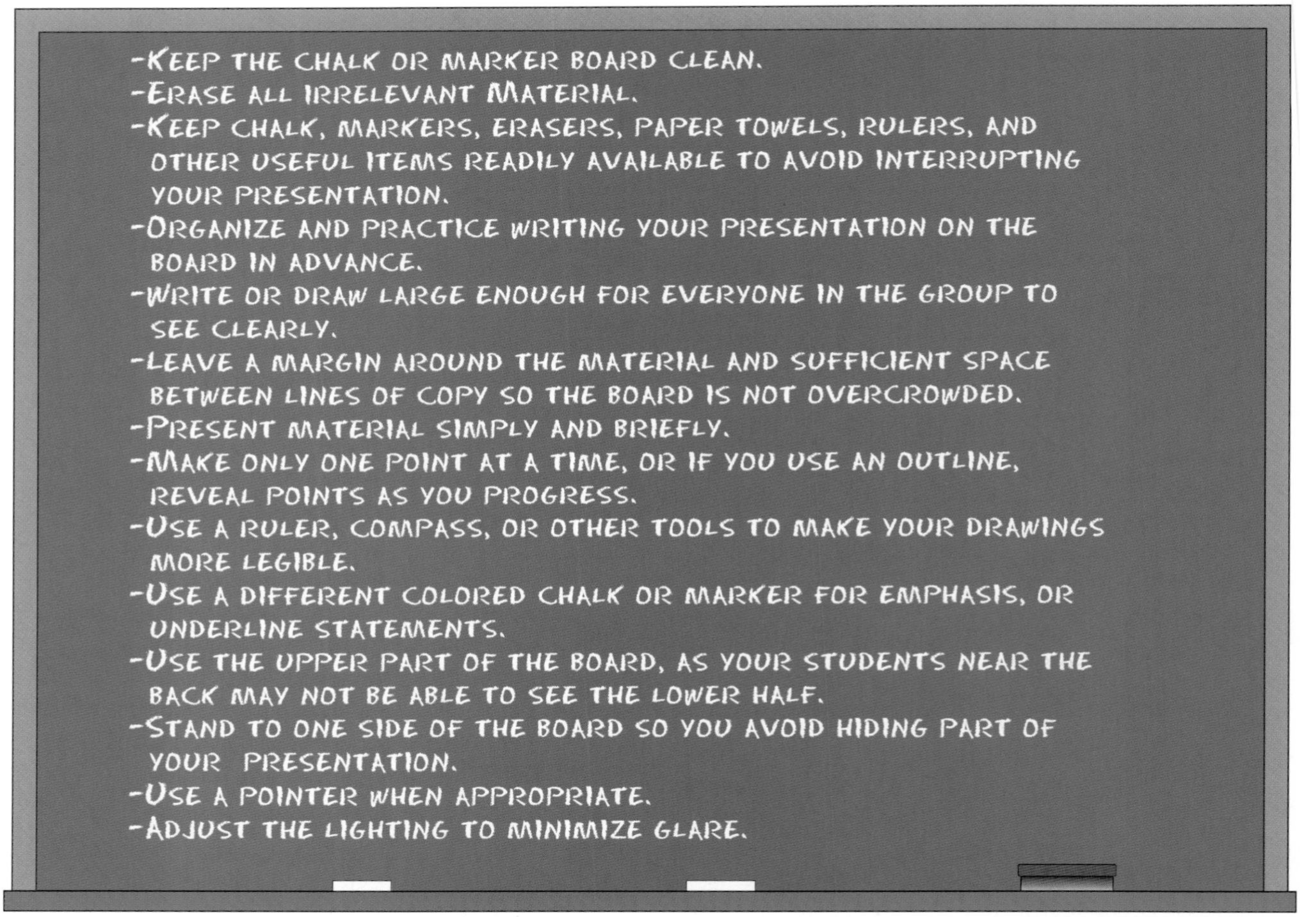

-KEEP THE CHALK OR MARKER BOARD CLEAN.
-ERASE ALL IRRELEVANT MATERIAL.
-KEEP CHALK, MARKERS, ERASERS, PAPER TOWELS, RULERS, AND OTHER USEFUL ITEMS READILY AVAILABLE TO AVOID INTERRUPTING YOUR PRESENTATION.
-ORGANIZE AND PRACTICE WRITING YOUR PRESENTATION ON THE BOARD IN ADVANCE.
-WRITE OR DRAW LARGE ENOUGH FOR EVERYONE IN THE GROUP TO SEE CLEARLY.
-LEAVE A MARGIN AROUND THE MATERIAL AND SUFFICIENT SPACE BETWEEN LINES OF COPY SO THE BOARD IS NOT OVERCROWDED.
-PRESENT MATERIAL SIMPLY AND BRIEFLY.
-MAKE ONLY ONE POINT AT A TIME, OR IF YOU USE AN OUTLINE, REVEAL POINTS AS YOU PROGRESS.
-USE A RULER, COMPASS, OR OTHER TOOLS TO MAKE YOUR DRAWINGS MORE LEGIBLE.
-USE A DIFFERENT COLORED CHALK OR MARKER FOR EMPHASIS, OR UNDERLINE STATEMENTS.
-USE THE UPPER PART OF THE BOARD, AS YOUR STUDENTS NEAR THE BACK MAY NOT BE ABLE TO SEE THE LOWER HALF.
-STAND TO ONE SIDE OF THE BOARD SO YOU AVOID HIDING PART OF YOUR PRESENTATION.
-USE A POINTER WHEN APPROPRIATE.
-ADJUST THE LIGHTING TO MINIMIZE GLARE.

Figure 2-30. Here are some guidelines for you to follow when using a chalk or marker board in the classroom. Though the principles may seem basic, most instructors forget at least one in the course of giving instruction.

SUPPLEMENTAL PRINT MATERIAL

A number of print items may be considered instructional aids, such as study guides, exercise books, course outlines, and syllabi. Well-designed course outlines are especially useful because they list key points and help your students take notes more effectively during a lecture. Print media, including photographs, charts, diagrams, graphs, and other materials can be valuable instructional aids since they provide visual images that can enhance recall. You may consider leaving some of these items posted on bulletin boards in the classroom for repeated reference, as well as in briefing rooms to help your students review important ideas prior to flight. In many cases, this type of supplemental material may be reproduced on transparencies or in computer graphic files that may be projected on a screen. [Figure 2-31]

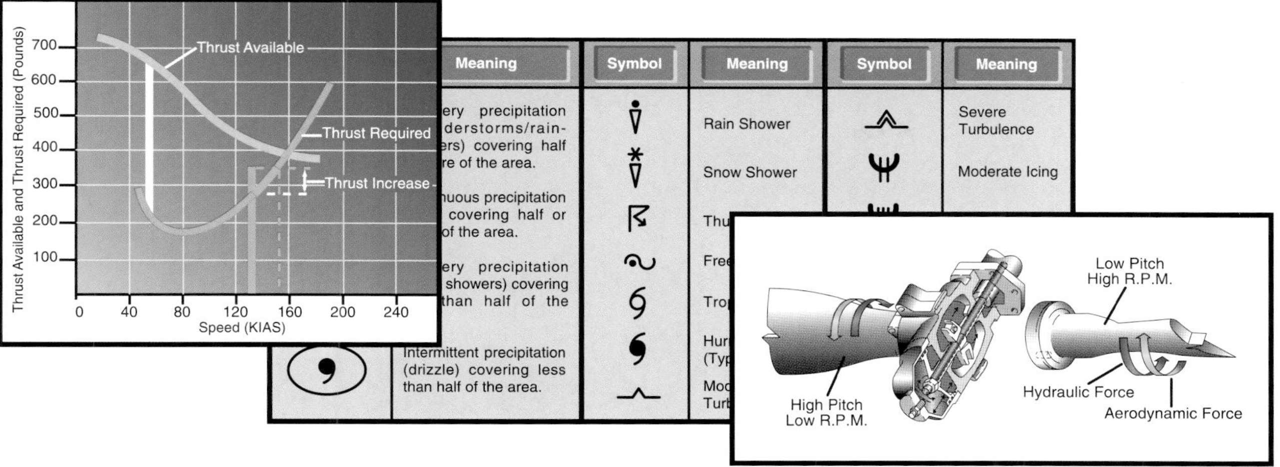

Figure 2-31. Charts, diagrams, and graphs can be used effectively to show relationships, chronological changes, distributions, components, and flow. The kind you select depends upon the type of information you want to convey, and their location and handling should be planned in advance so you can incorporate them smoothly into your presentation.

ENHANCED TRAINING MATERIALS

While you need to be familiar with all regulatory requirements applicable to the certificates and ratings you teach, you may use instructor-oriented training materials which are created to help you comply with regulations. These tools ensure you accomplish the required training, make the necessary endorsements, and use proper documentation. Whether you work as an independent instructor or you are employed by a flight school, you must make sure that each student performs a number of important tasks to specific standards. **Enhanced training materials**, which include these standards, can help you complete this step.

One example of these materials is a syllabus, which not only presents a course of training in a logical, building-block sequence, but has provisions for your endorsements and record keeping. Areas for logging training time can be incorporated so that the syllabus can also serve as a record for you, your students, or your school. In case your student transfers to another school or instructor, the record can be reviewed and your student's status easily assessed by the new instructor. Another example of enhanced, instructor-oriented material for pilot training is a maneuvers guide or handbook, which includes the practical test standards for each maneuver or procedure described. [Figure 2-32]

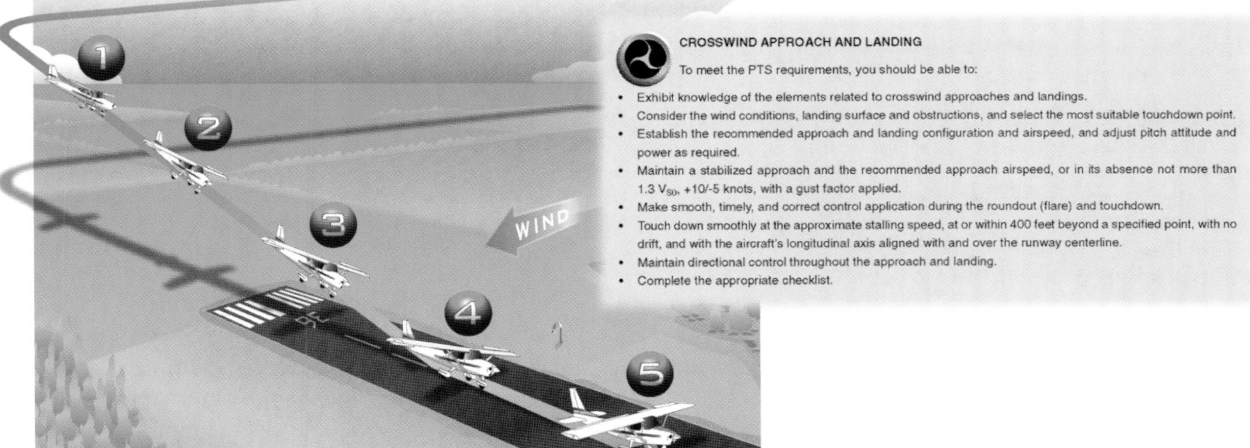

Figure 2-32. By using a maneuvers manual, your student learns from the beginning how to perform the maneuver or procedure to standard, and you need not refer to another publication to evaluate your student's progress.

Computer-based training may also be used to help you keep track of student progress and for record-keeping. As training becomes more detailed and complex to follow increased regulation, the materials you use to ensure your students are adequately prepared and properly endorsed will become more sophisticated as well.

PROJECTED MATERIAL

Traditionally, projected instructional aids have included motion pictures, filmstrips, slides, overhead transparencies, and specialized equipment such as rear-screen and opaque projectors. However, the use of motion pictures and filmstrips for training has declined, mostly due to the availability of more user-friendly media such as video. Most importantly, the content of the media must be current and adequately support the lesson.

From Filmstrips to the Future

In 1968, Sanderson Films was sold to Times Mirror and merged with Jeppesen a few years later. Paul Sanderson's involvement in aviation began in the 1940s when he was an instructor in the Navy's Aircraft Instrument and Link Trainer school. He later worked as a civilian aviation instructor and eventually headed the Link Trainer Department at the Embry Riddle School of Aviation (now Embry Riddle Aeronautical University). In 1956, Paul started his own aviation ground school program. As his program expanded, Paul wanted to ensure that students received high quality, consistent instruction regardless of who was teaching the class. He created classroom training aids by recording himself during lectures using his state-of-the-art, reel-to-reel tapes. These audio recordings were combined with slides and filmstrips to form complete classroom presentations. He also developed illustrated, preprinted notes for use by the students. The materials quickly made the Sanderson courses a tremendous success.

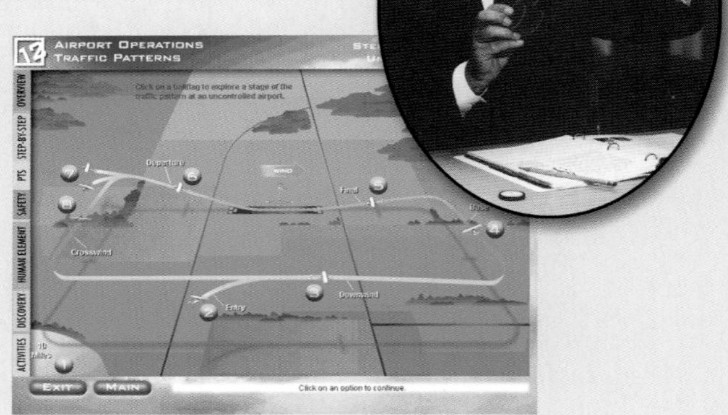

Paul's love of aviation, and his quest to share knowledge with those less fortunate, inspired him to give away many courses to prisons, military personnel, and schools for the disadvantaged. In addition, he worked closely with educational organizations, eventually creating textbooks for the aviation education market. After the sale of his company, Paul remained actively involved with Jeppesen Sanderson's Aviation Courseware Development Team for over 20 years. Not only has he provided insight, but also helped to exchange ideas and offer encouragement.

Use of projected materials requires planning and practice. [Figure 2-33] During a classroom session, you need to provide your students with an overview of the media before you show it, and after the presentation, you should allow time for questions and a summary of key points.

Bob forgot to reset the video tape from the last class, so his students need to wait while he cues the tape.

Sarah's overhead transparencies are out of order, so she gets lost during the middle of her lecture on systems.

The bulb in John's projector is slowly burning out, so halfway through class his students can no longer see the slides. He did not pack an extra bulb.

Figure 2-33. You should set up and adjust the equipment and lighting before the class period and preview the presentation.

Aside from a chalk or marker board, the overhead transparency remains one of the more convenient and cost-effective instructional aids. With acetate or plastic, you can construct your own inexpensive transparencies or copies, or you may purchase commercially prepared ones. You can write on a blank transparency as the session progresses, much as you would write on a chalk or marker board. Additional transparencies can be overlaid onto the original to show development or buildup of an event or diagram. You may also cut overlays into shapes and move them about in relation to the base transparency to display dial indications or fit several parts of a component together so relative motion can be simulated.

The overhead projector should be placed at the front of the room, allowing you to continue to make eye contact with your students. As with any projection equipment, ensure that the projector does not interfere with any of your student's line of sight. The projector usually works best on a table or low stand, and the projection angle should be adjusted to reduce or eliminate image distortion. Although it is simple to operate and requires little maintenance, you may find it bulky to handle and store, and the cooling fan may be noisy.

The opaque projector reflects light from the surface of a picture or three-dimensional object onto a regular projection screen. A postage stamp, typed material, or textbook illustrations are just some examples of the wide variety of items which may be projected, and since the material does not require special preparation, the cost is very low. [Figure 2-34]

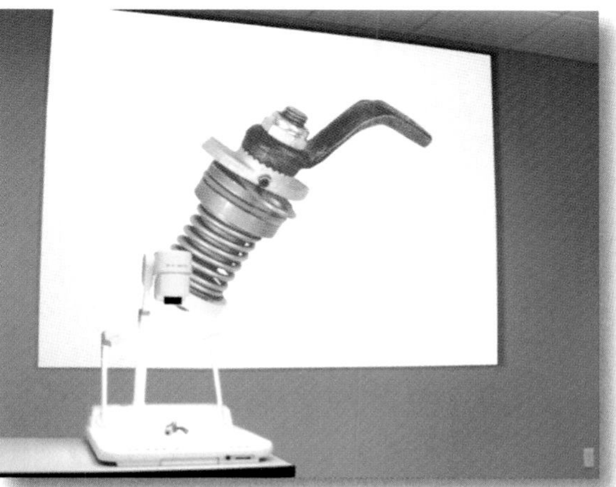

Figure 2-34. The height of usable objects is limited to the space between the top of the lowered projection plate and the body of the projector. The area of the picture or object is limited to approximately 10 inches by 10 inches.

VIDEO

Video has become one of the most popular forms of instructional aids, and there are two basic types of video to consider. **Passive video** refers to segments of video which are simply watched by your students, whereas **interactive video**, normally found on a CD-ROM or other digital media, allows your students to make choices and determine what direction the video is going to take. Passive video provides a presentation beyond what you could normally put together for your students, in many cases using special effects, and advanced graphics and animation techniques to create a lively and compelling treatment of a subject. [Figure 2-35]

Perhaps the greatest advantage to the video format is that it is familiar to your students and tends to be well-received. Video also is convenient for instruction since you have the capability to stop, freeze, rewind, and replay the video as necessary. The cost of video equipment is somewhat higher than that of other instructional aids, but still remains economical for most schools. In addition, the television and video cassette recorder can be used for other purposes outside of the classroom.

Figure 2-35. Commercially produced videos may be passive or interactive, and they are available for many aviation topics.

You should be aware of certain disadvantages with the video format. Your students may be accustomed to dramatic, action-packed video that is designed solely to entertain, and, consequently, they may find instructional videos dry and unexciting. At the same time, they are used to watching video in a passive way, without trying to absorb and retain what they are seeing and hearing. These two factors can diminish the instructional value of the videos you choose to present.

To make the most of your video presentations, you need to follow some basic guidelines. The video selection is not designed to replace you, and some prior planning allows you to determine main points and concepts you may wish to stress either during the video or in a summary. You should also prepare your students to watch the video by advising them of important ideas and segments to look for, and possibly, what may be incorrect. You need to be available to summarize the presentation and answer any questions your students may have.

Interactive video on compact discs (CDs) refers broadly to software that responds to choices and commands given by the user. For example, one student may be able to select a feature that plays additional video on a specific topic, while another student would be able to skip ahead if more information on the subject was not necessary.

Interactive video solves one of the main problems of passive video, since it increases student involvement in the learning process. Well-designed interactive video, when properly used, is highly effective as an instructional aid, since your students essentially receive a learning experience tailored to suit their needs.

In the Comfort of Your Own Home

Distance learning, also referred to as distance education, is another trend that takes advantage of interactive video. This type of learning involves the use of print or electronic media to deliver instruction when you and your students are at different locations. It may also be defined as a system and process that connects your students with resources for learning. As sources that provide access to information increase, the possibilities for distance learning expand.

Currently, a number of commercial providers have developed web-based training (WBT) courses for pilots to use for various applications. From CFI renewal to test question data bases, the variety of products available online continues to grow.

Many universities also offer classes online through virtual synchronous classrooms (V/SC). The students connect by logging on to live video of an instructor during class time, and they can discuss class topics in dedicated chat rooms on their own time. These classes are especially popular with adult learners who wish to upgrade their education but are unable to leave their jobs or hometowns due to other commitments.

Computer-Based Multimedia

Computer-based **multimedia** is simply a combination of more than one instructional media, and often includes several forms: audio, text, graphics, and video normally shown on personal computers. Information access is simplified, and sophisticated data bases can organize vast amounts of information which can be quickly sorted, searched, and cross-indexed. Computer-based training (CBT) makes use of this capability to increase student interest and learning.

Although computers are often used individually, you may also have access to equipment that can project images from a computer screen. This allows you to use a computer in conjunction with specially-designed software to create presentations using full-color graphics, photos, and simple animation for an entire class.

MODELS, MOCKUPS, AND CUT-AWAYS

There are times when you may want to refer to a more realistic representation of the topic you are discussing in class by using a model, mockup, or cut-away. Models, or copies of real objects, are typically more practical for use in the classroom than actual items because they are generally more lightweight and easier to manipulate. The scale model represents an exact reproduction of the original, while simplified models do not show all of the detail. Some models are solid and show only the outline of the object they portray, while others have moving parts. Still others, known as **cut-aways**, are built in sections and can be taken apart to reveal the internal structure. Whenever possible, the various parts should be labeled or colored to highlight relationships or key terms.

Even if a model is not entirely realistic, you can still effectively use it to explain the operating principles of the equipment it symbolizes. Models are especially adaptable to small group discussions. If you can find a model that works like the original object, or if it can be taken apart and reassembled, your students can see how each part works in relation to other parts and can better understand the mechanical principles involved. A **mockup** is a three-dimensional or specialized type of working model used for study, training or testing in place of the real object, which may be too costly or dangerous, or which may be impossible to obtain. [Figure 2-36]

Figure 2-36. The mockup may emphasize or highlight elements for learning and eliminate nonessential ones to simplify training.

TEST PREPARATION MATERIAL

There is an array of print, video, and software products designed by commercial publishers to help your students prepare for FAA exams. Test preparation materials are very effective in making your students ready for an exam, although these materials may not provide the total information necessary for your students to become safe and competent pilots. Some products are fairly basic, while others provide reference tools and additional options that make a more complete testing package. If the products are well-developed, they relieve you from having to directly supervise your students as they study for their exams and allow you to focus on the application of concepts. [Figure 2-37]

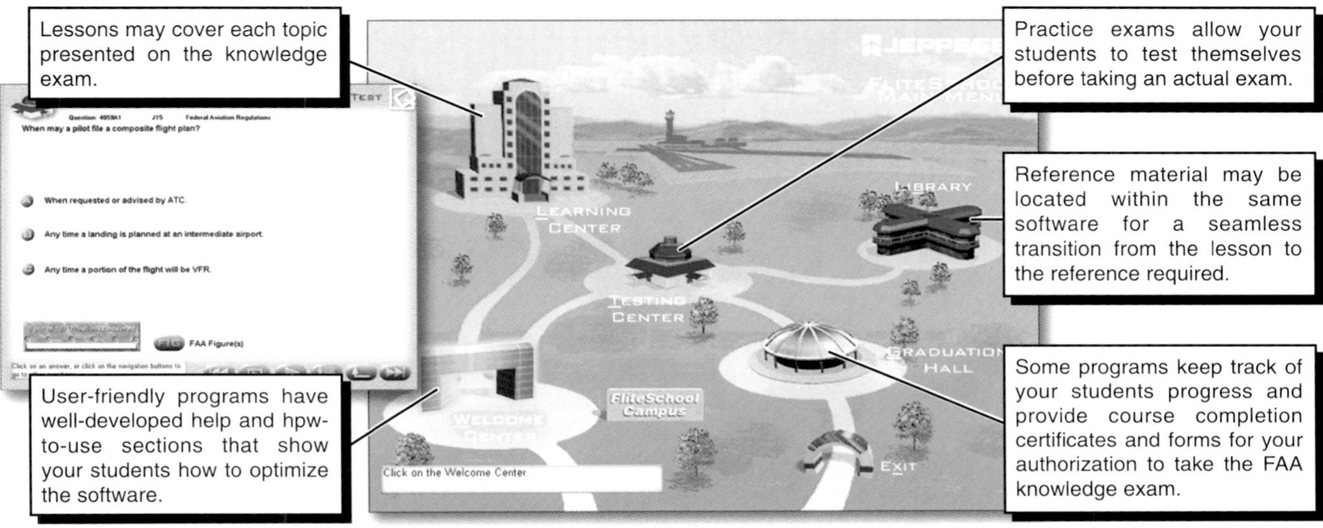

Figure 2-37. CBT and test preparation may include testing functions, reference materials, and critiques to aid your students.

FUTURE DEVELOPMENTS

In aviation training, the increased use of computer technology, such as CBT, simulation, and virtual reality will no doubt continue to expand. Emerging computer technology includes improved voice-recognition software and miniature electro-optical devices. Voice-recognition technology lets computers accept spoken rather than keyed input and is already used in such everyday applications as car phones. Miniature electro-optical devices are also entering the training arena. With this equipment, information is projected electronically on sunglass-style eyepieces which are connected to a lightweight, belt-mounted computer. This computer-aided information would be particularly useful for aviation maintenance activities, allowing the technician's eyes to easily move back and forth from stored technical data to the actual hardware while diagnosing and correcting a maintenance problem.

Trends in training indicate a shift from the typical classroom to more extensive use of a lab-type environment with computer work or study stations. This is part of the training or learning center concept in which your students may become more actively involved and responsible for their own education. In these centers, students may have access to simulation devices, computer networks, and multimedia programs. Another part of this concept includes increased use of group or cooperative learning techniques, cable or closed-circuit television, and the Internet or private intranets. Aviation-related learning centers are currently associated with colleges, universities, and research centers, and these entities, along with the major airlines, have used similar facilities for a number of years. Further growth in this type of training is likely.

One other type of computer-based technology is virtual reality. **Virtual reality (VR)** creates a sensory experience that allows the user to believe and barely distinguish a computer-generated experience from a real one. VR uses graphics with animation systems and sounds to reproduce electronic versions of real-life experience. Despite enormous potential, VR, in its current stage, has drawbacks, notably the fact it is still fairly expensive. [Figure 2-38]

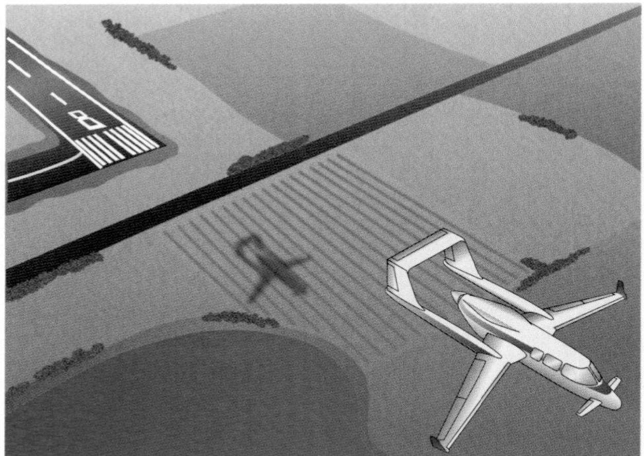

Figure 2-38. Much of the current technology used to train pilots will eventually become obsolete, and new, more complex technology will replace the old, such as in this vision of an aircraft of the future.

The implications of ongoing technological advancement in aviation training are clear. You will be challenged to stay up to date with current developments that apply to the curriculum you teach and to adopt those that are the most effective, depending on cost. Since many of the new advancements will be based on computer technology that is already in place, if you have computer experience, you are likely to be in higher demand as an instructor.

As training technology progresses, you must remember your main teaching goals and be selectively receptive to new possibilities. Information on computer networks, the

Internet, and electronic bulletin boards is generally posted by commercial providers, as well as national, state, and community government agencies. There is no guarantee that all of the information is current or accurate, so you must use your best judgment to sift through all that is available to you. [Figure 2-39]

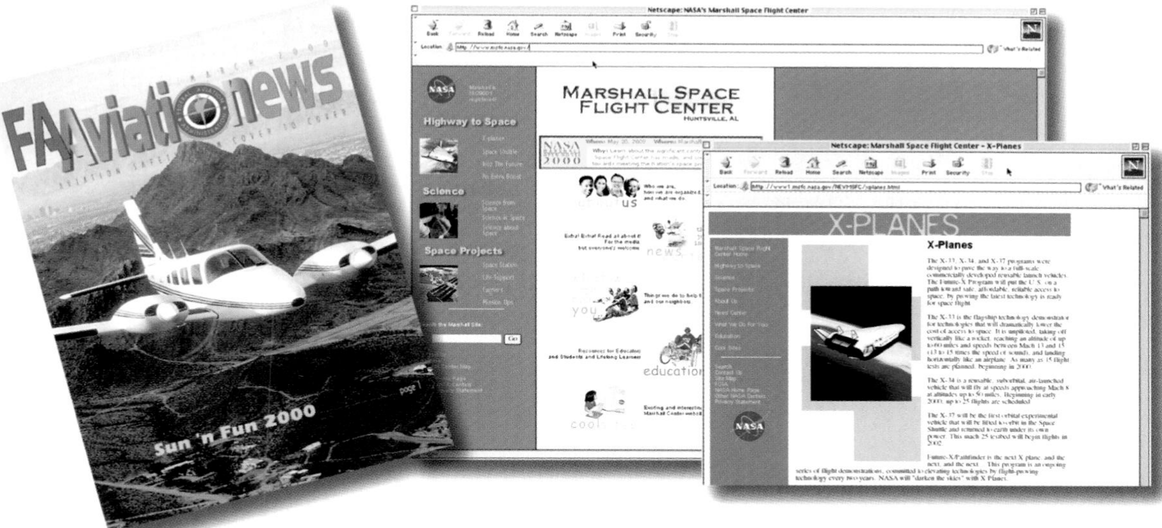

Figure 2-39. By studying professional journals to keep up with the latest training technologies, exploring the Internet, and using your imagination, you can find creative ways to teach almost any subject.

OBSTACLES TO LEARNING

Even if your students show up for a lesson on time with the required reading complete, there may still be occasions when they are simply not ready to learn for a variety of reasons that can be difficult to pinpoint. In the course of giving instruction, you may encounter certain obstacles that concern your students' attitudes, physical condition, and psychological make-up.

UNFAIR TREATMENT

Students who believe their instruction is inadequate, or their efforts are not fairly considered and evaluated, do not learn well, and their motivation suffers no matter how determined they are to learn to fly. Motivation also declines when students believe you are making unreasonable demands for performance and progress. To stimulate learning, you should strive to assign lesson objectives and completion standards that are challenging but your students consider obtainable. [Figure 2-40]

PROCEDURE	REASONABLE GOALS FOR STUDENT PILOTS	UNREASONABLE GOALS FOR STUDENT PILOTS
Normal Approach and Landing	Land +/- 300 feet of desired point.	Land on the runway numbers every time.
Steep Turns	Maintain altitude +/- 100 feet.	Maintain altitude +/- 10 feet.
Power-Off Stalls	Minimize altitude loss.	Maintain altitude with no loss.
Cross-Country Flight	Cross checkpoints within 1 n.m. of course.	Cross directly over all checkpoints.

Figure 2-40. If you assign impossible or unreasonable goals to your students, they may become discouraged, put forth less effort, and learn more slowly.

IMPATIENCE

Impatience can be a greater deterrent to learning than most people realize. Your students may wish to make their first solo or cross-country flight before you feel they are ready. Impatient students fail to understand the need for thorough preliminary training and are more focused on the desired outcome than on the path to achieving it. When mastering any complex skill, you must perfect the basics if you wish to perform the end result competently and safely. You can mitigate any impatience displayed by your students by presenting the necessary primary training one step at a time, with precisely stated goals along the way. The elements mastered with each procedure should be clearly identified as you progress to the next step.

Impatience is a greater deterrent to learning pilot skills than most people realize.

Impatience may be the result of instruction that is paced too slowly for a student who learns quickly. It is just as important for you to move a student onto the next step once mastery has been achieved as it is to complete each step before the next one is undertaken. Your students lose interest quickly when you repeat operations excessively that have already been learned adequately.

Students who grow impatient when learning basic elements of a task are those who should have the preliminary training presented one step at a time, with clearly stated goals for each step.

EMOTIONAL UPSET

If your students are worried or upset, they are not able to fully benefit from your instruction. Worry or distraction may be the result of concerns your students have about progress in the training course, or may stem from circumstances outside the training environment. Significant emotional upsets may be due to personal problems, psychiatric disturbances, or a dislike of the training program or the instructor.

You need to tailor your instruction to the interest and enthusiasm your students bring with them, but also divert their attention from their personal worries and troubles to the tasks at hand. You may find this challenging, but it must be accomplished if learning is to continue at a normal rate. You can generally prevent anxiety and emotional upset that are the result of flight training by ensuring your students understand the objectives of each step during their training, and that they know at the completion of each lesson exactly how well they have progressed and what deficiencies they need to correct.

PHYSICAL DISCOMFORT

Any physical discomfort that your students experience greatly diminishes the rate of learning during both classroom instruction and flight training. This is true no matter how diligently they apply themselves to learning the material. Temperature extremes, poor ventilation, inadequate lighting, or noise can distract students. Illnesses, motion sickness, and fatigue can also degrade performance. You should continue flight instruction only as long as your student remains alert, receptive, and performs to a level consistent with experience.

APATHY DUE TO INADEQUATE INSTRUCTION

Your students may become apathetic if they feel you prepare inadequately for lesson periods, or if the instruction you give is less than sincere, is insufficient, or contradicts what they have learned in the past. Even inexperienced students realize when you have

Figure 2-41. If you are well-prepared for your lessons, you will earn the respect of your students.

You give complete coverage of the lesson material and encourage questions.

You emphasize the correct ideas and stay on the subject.

You avoid repeating concepts unnecessarily.

You earn your student's confidence with every flight.

Students quickly become apathetic when they recognize that the instructor is not adequately prepared.

failed to prepare for a lesson, and this may immediately destroy their interest. [Figure 2-41]

An unsatisfactory presentation can result from distracting mannerisms, poor personal hygiene, or apparent irritation with your students. Your students may lose interest if your instruction is overly explicit and beneath their level, or so complicated that it is difficult to understand. You must teach specifically to the level of each student, which requires you to adjust your presentation or technique. For example, when giving instruction on how to preflight an airplane, you would present the information differently for a student who is already a skilled aviation maintenance technician than for a student with no previous aeronautical experience. The inspection remains the same, but the content that would prove meaningful to each student would change substantially.

ANXIETY

If your students experience anxiety, their perceptive ability becomes limited and they may not develop the proper insights. Your students need to feel comfortable and confident in you as an instructor if effective learning is to occur. Providing this atmosphere is one of your most important tasks. Once your students successively accomplish the goals you set for them, and they see that nothing extreme or alarming happens as a result, they will feel more and more at ease. [Figure 2-42]

Anxiety may affect students by limiting their ability to learn from perceptions.

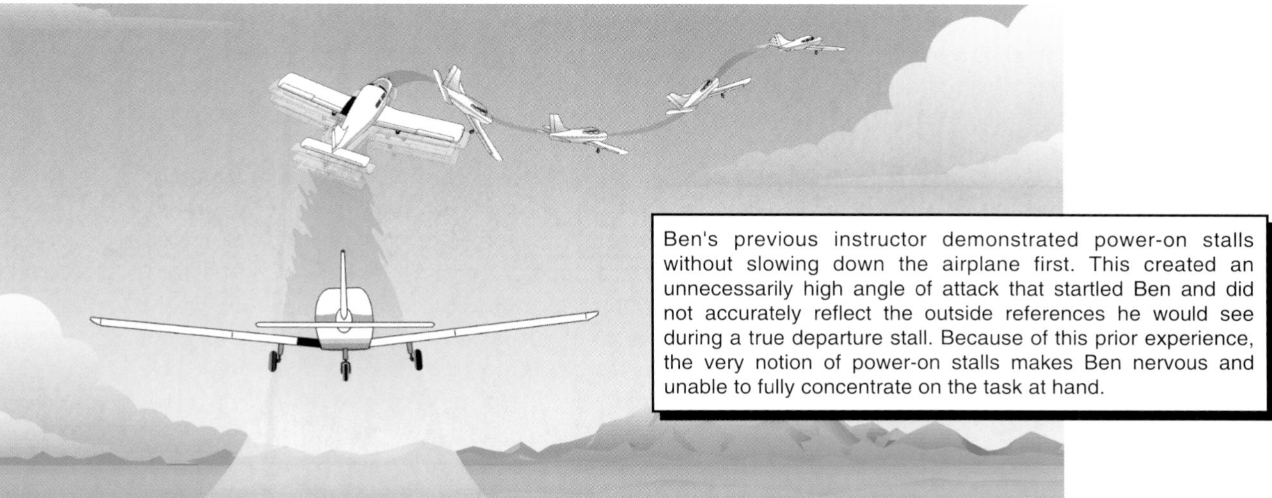

Figure 2-42. One source of anxiety in your students may be in a previous experience with another instructor that left them apprehensive of a particular maneuver.

SUMMARY CHECKLIST

- ✓ The traditional way of building a lesson plan is to compose an introduction, provide development, and summarize with a conclusion. The method of arranging lesson material from the simple to complex, past to present, and known to unknown, is one that shows the relationships of the main points to the lesson.
- ✓ Lectures are typically used to introduce new material, summarize ideas, show relationships between theory and practice, and reemphasize main points within a course of study. You may favor the teaching lecture, because it allows for participation by your students.
- ✓ You must develop a keen perception for your students' subtle responses and be able to interpret them in order to successfully deliver a teaching lecture.
- ✓ Cooperative or group learning is a teaching method in which you organize students into small groups so that they can work together to maximize both their own and each other's learning. Each activity your students engage in is known as a group task, which may emphasize academic achievement, cognitive abilities, or physical skills.
- ✓ In a guided discussion you rely on your students to provide ideas, experiences, and opinions, and you strive to draw out what your students know rather than tell them directly. This method is particularly useful during classroom instruction and during pre- and postflight briefings, after your students have gained some knowledge and experience with the topic presented.
- ✓ Unless students have some knowledge to exchange with each other, they cannot reach the desired learning outcomes through a guided discussion.
- ✓ In a guided discussion, learning is achieved through your skillful use of questions. As your students have fully discussed ideas that support each part of the lesson, you should restate them in an interim summary.
- ✓ The essential steps in the demonstration-performance method are explanation, demonstration, student performance, instructor supervision, and evaluation.
- ✓ You can apply the demonstration-performance method to flight instruction through the telling-and-doing technique, which is particularly suited to teaching physical skills. It follows the four steps of the demonstration-performance method, with the exception of the first step.
- ✓ The integrated method of flight instruction is instruction during which students are taught to perform maneuvers both by outside visual references and by reference to the flight instruments.
- ✓ In earlier stages of training, your students may find it easier to perform flight maneuvers by reference to the instruments than by outside references. This may lead them to concentrate most of their attention on the instruments, when they should be using primarily outside references.
- ✓ Computer-based training (CBT) and computer-based instruction (CBI) include PCATDs, flight training devices, flight simulators, and test preparation and training applications. CBT may combine video, graphics, and interactivity to explore a particular topic or test your student's knowledge of various subjects.

- ✓ Instructional aids used in the teaching process should be compatible with the learning outcomes to be achieved. The first step in determining if and where instructional aids are necessary is to clearly establish the lesson objective, being certain what must be communicated.
- ✓ Examples of training media include your voice, printed text, video cassettes, computer programs, flight training devices, or flight simulators. Instructional aids are devices, such as charts, graphs, pictures, or other well-organized visual aids, that help your students understand and retain pertinent information.
- ✓ As training becomes more detailed and complex to follow increased regulation, enhanced training materials you use to ensure your students are adequately prepared and properly endorsed will become more sophisticated as well.
- ✓ Passive video refers to segments of video which are simply watched by your students, whereas interactive video, normally found on a CD-ROM or other digital media, allows your students to make choices and determine what direction the video is going to take.
- ✓ Computer-based multimedia includes audio, text, graphics, and video normally shown on personal computers.
- ✓ You will be challenged to stay up to date with current developments in instructional aids that apply to the curriculum you teach and to adopt those that are the most effective, depending on cost.
- ✓ You may encounter certain obstacles that concern your students' attitudes, physical condition, and psychological make-up, including unfair treatment, impatience, emotional upset, physical discomfort, apathy and anxiety. Impatience, for example, is a greater deterrent to learning pilot skills than most people realize.
- ✓ Anxiety may affect a student by limiting the student's ability to learn from perceptions, and students quickly become apathetic if they recognize that you are not adequately prepared.

KEY TERMS

Syllabus

Introduction

Attention

Motivation

Overview

Development

Conclusion

Lecture Method

Illustrated Talk

Briefing

Formal Lecture

Teaching Lecture

Informal Lecture

Cooperative Learning Method

Group Task

Guided Discussion Method

Lead-Off Question

Follow-Up Question

Overhead Question

Rhetorical Question

Direct Question

Reverse Question

Relay Question

Interim Summary

Demonstration-Performance Method

Telling-and-Doing Technique

Instructor Tells—Instructor Does

Student Tells—Instructor Does

Student Tells—Student Does

Student Does—Instructor Evaluates

Integrated Method of Flight Instruction

Computer-Based Training (CBT)

Computer-Based Instruction (CBI)

Computer-Assisted Instruction (CAI)

Personal Computer-Based Aviation Training Devices (PCATDs)

Flight Training Devices (FTDs)

Flight Simulators

Training Media

Enhanced Training Materials

Passive Video

Interactive Video

Multimedia

Cut-Away

Mockup

Virtual Reality (VR)

QUESTIONS

1. Select the method of development most useful for relating the history of a particular subject.

   A. Past to present
   B. Simple to complex
   C. Known to unknown

2. True/False. An overhead question redirects a student's question to the group as a whole.

3. Describe a situation where using the demonstration-performance method makes more sense than delivering a lecture.

4. Explain how the telling-and-doing technique differs from the demonstration-performance method.

5. Select the item that defines the integrated method of flight instruction.

   A. The development of a student's instrument flying skills for use in IFR conditions
   B. The use of a view-limiting device to accentuate the role of the instruments during night instruction
   C. Flight instruction during which students are taught to perform flight maneuvers both by outside visual references and by reference to the flight instruments, from the first introduction of a maneuver

6. Describe the benefits of integrated flight instruction for a student transitioning to a high-performance airplane.

7. Select the answer which best describes how test preparation CBT can aid your students.

   A. The material gives students the answers to the exam.
   B. CBT provides a means for students to take the actual exam from home.
   C. Good test preparation materials allow students to select their own tests, complete the questions, obtain a score, and review the questions they missed.

8. True/False. A video cassette is a type of training media.

9. Select the type of object best portrayed by a model in the classroom.

   A. Airplane
   B. Sectional chart
   C. Attitude indicator

10. Describe how a student's impatience can be an obstacle to learning.

11. What is one trait you can avoid to keep your students from becoming apathetic?

    A. Using technical terms
    B. Showing up for a lesson without having prepared
    C. Incorporating several maneuvers into your lesson plans

12. What elements would you incorporate into a lesson on stalls that would serve to lessen a student's anxiety about the maneuver.

SECTION C
DESIGNING EFFECTIVE LESSONS

You may begin instructing students in one of many flight environments, from a large flight school or university to a small FBO at a local airport. In fact, you may first instruct in the same place in which you are training now. No matter what the situation, you quickly learn how important it is to have an underlying structure for the lessons you give. Detailed planning, whether through building your own tailored course or using lesson plans created by commercial sources, is critical for meeting the basic requirements for flight and ground instruction to complete a certificate or rating.

COURSE OF TRAINING

In education, a **course of training** may be defined as a complete series of studies leading to attainment of a specific goal. The goal might be a certificate of completion, graduation, or even an academic degree. For example, after completing a specific course of both ground and flight training, a student normally achieves the goal of obtaining a pilot certificate or rating. A course of training also may be limited to something like the additional instruction required for operating high-performance airplanes.

Other terms that are closely associated with a course of training include curriculum, syllabus, and training course outline. In many cases, these terms are used interchangeably, but there are differences. A **curriculum** may be defined as a set of courses in an area of specialization offered by an educational institution. A curriculum for a pilot school usually includes courses for the various pilot certificates and ratings. A **syllabus** is a summary or outline of a course of study. In aviation, the term **training syllabus** is commonly used to describe a step-by-step progression of learning with provisions for regular evaluations at prescribed stages. The syllabus defines the unit of training, states by objective what the student is expected to accomplish, shows an organized plan for instruction, and dictates the evaluation process. Finally, a **training course outline (TCO)** within a curriculum establishes the content of a particular course. The outline normally includes statements of objectives, descriptions of teaching aids, definitions of evaluating criteria, and indications of desired outcomes.

OBJECTIVES AND STANDARDS

Determining the overall objectives and standards is the first step in planning any instructional activity. In doing so, you should take into consideration the levels of learning in

OBJECTIVE
The student will obtain the knowledge, skill, and aeronautical experience necessary to meet the requirements for a private pilot certificate with an airplane category rating and a single-engine land class rating.

COMPLETION STANDARD
The student must demonstrate through written exams, a flight test, and appropriate records that the knowledge, skill, and experience requirements necessary to obtain a private pilot certificate with an airplane category rating and a single-engine land class rating have been met.

Figure 2-43. Before you begin any instruction, you must determine the necessary objectives and standards.

each of the three learning domains-cognitive, psychomotor, and affective. Typically, aviation training aspires to the application level of learning or higher. [Figure 2-43]

In planning any instructional activity, the first consideration should be to determine the overall objectives and standards.

Standards include a description of the desired knowledge, behavior, or skill stated in specific terms, along with conditions and criteria. Comprehensive examples of the desired learning outcomes, or behaviors, should be included in the standards. During pilot training, your students normally must perform to well-defined standards to meet the training objectives.

You can find general standards which apply to aviation training courses in various publications. For example, eligibility, knowledge, proficiency, and experience requirements are stipulated in the FARs, and performance standards are published in the applicable practical test standards (PTS). It should be noted, though, that the PTS are limited to the most critical job tasks, and they do not represent an entire training syllabus.

A broad objective of any pilot training course is to ensure that your students are competent to operate specific aircraft types under certain conditions, such as VFR. The established criteria used to determine whether training has been adequate for the issuance of pilot certificates are the passing of knowledge and practical tests. However, you should not limit your objectives to meeting only the published requirements for certification. As a successful instructor you will teach your students not only how, but also why and when. Ultimately, this leads to sound judgment and decision-making skills.

BLOCKS OF LEARNING

After you have established the overall training goal, your next step is to identify the **blocks of learning** which constitute the necessary parts of the total objective. Just as in building a pyramid, some blocks are embedded in the structure and never appear on the surface, but each is an integral and necessary part of the construction. Stated another way, the various blocks are not isolated, but essential parts of the whole. When you identify the blocks of learning for the proposed training activity, you must examine each carefully to see what is truly necessary. Extraneous blocks of instruction are

In planning instructional activity, the second step is to identify blocks of learning which constitute the necessary parts of the total objective. The use of the building block concept of instruction provides a way to ensure proper habits and correct techniques during training.

expensive frills, especially in flight training, and they delay the completion of the final objective.

Identifying the blocks of learning early is essential when you plan to teach a complex task. In this way, your students can master the segments or blocks individually and learn proper relationships. Then, you can progressively combine these blocks with other related segments until their sum meets the overall training objectives.

Extraneous blocks of instruction during a course of training detract from the completion of the final objective.

Development and assembly of blocks of learning in their proper relationship will allow the student to master the segments of the overall pilot performance requirements individually, and then combine these with other related segments.

PRIVATE PILOT — PRESOLO TRAINING

The blocks of learning identified during the planning and management of a training activity should be fairly consistent in scope. They should represent units of learning which can be measured and evaluated and not simply describe a sequence of instructional sessions. For example, the flight training of a private pilot might be divided into the following major blocks: achievement of the knowledge and skills necessary for solo, solo cross-country flight, and obtaining a private pilot certificate. [Figure 2-44]

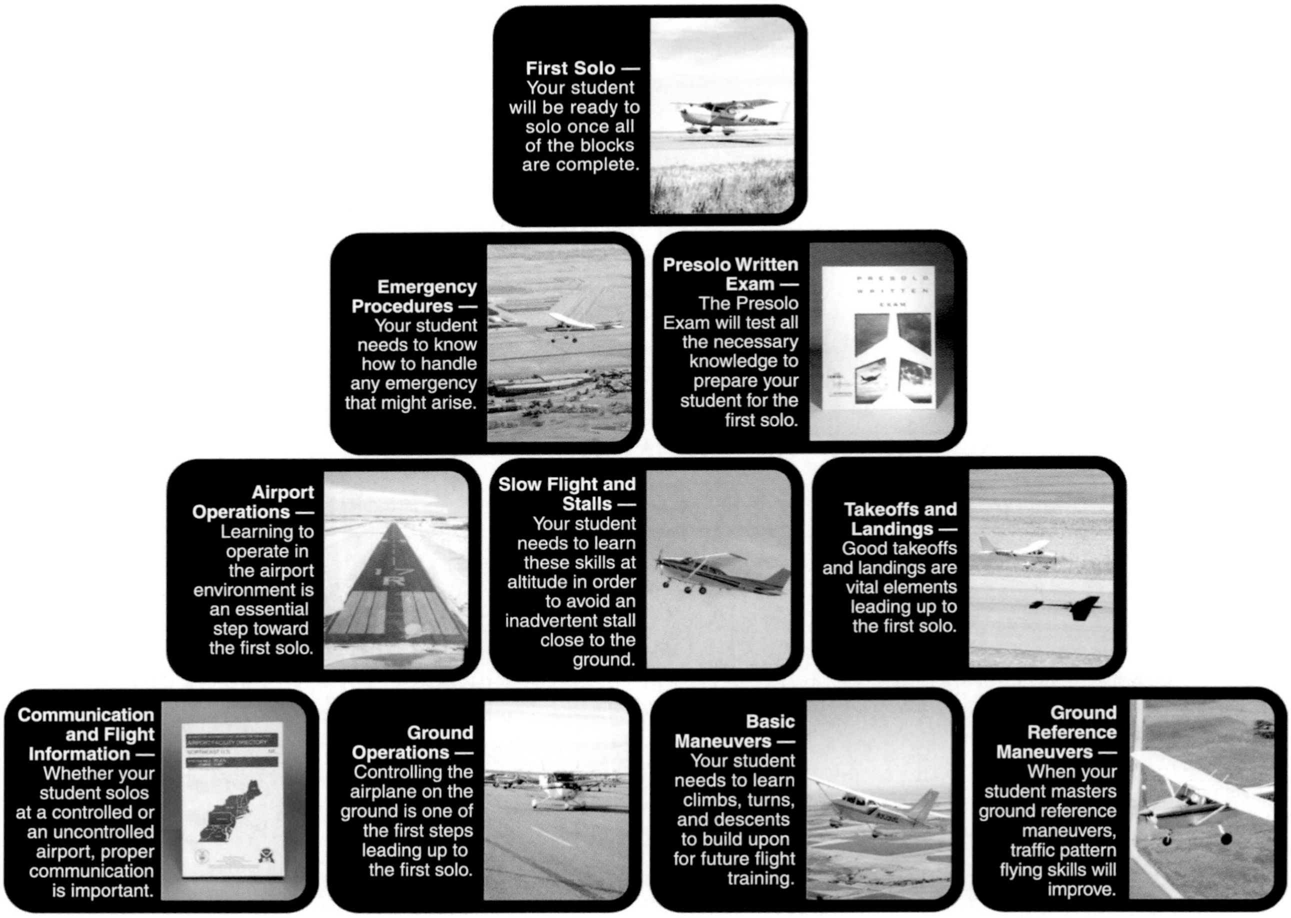

First Solo — Your student will be ready to solo once all of the blocks are complete.

Emergency Procedures — Your student needs to know how to handle any emergency that might arise.

Presolo Written Exam — The Presolo Exam will test all the necessary knowledge to prepare your student for the first solo.

Airport Operations — Learning to operate in the airport environment is an essential step toward the first solo.

Slow Flight and Stalls — Your student needs to learn these skills at altitude in order to avoid an inadvertent stall close to the ground.

Takeoffs and Landings — Good takeoffs and landings are vital elements leading up to the first solo.

Communication and Flight Information — Whether your student solos at a controlled or an uncontrolled airport, proper communication is important.

Ground Operations — Controlling the airplane on the ground is one of the first steps leading up to the first solo.

Basic Maneuvers — Your student needs to learn climbs, turns, and descents to build upon for future flight training.

Ground Reference Maneuvers — When your student masters ground reference maneuvers, traffic pattern flying skills will improve.

Figure 2-44. The presolo stage, or phase, of training is comprised of several basic building blocks. These blocks of learning, which should include coordinated ground and flight training, lead up to the first solo.

Use of the building block approach provides your students with a boost in self-confidence, which normally occurs each time a block is completed. Otherwise, an overall goal, such as earning a private pilot certificate, may seem unobtainable. If the larger blocks are broken down into smaller blocks of instruction, each on its own is more manageable.

The knowledge and skills necessary for the first solo, for example, typically begin with a basic instruction block that familiarizes your student with the airplane, including preflight procedures, ground operations, and an introduction to flight operations. The successive blocks of learning are developed in turn to produce effective lesson plans for each period of instruction. In practice, the possibilities for a breakdown and categorization of training objectives is infinite. For practical planning, you can test the size for a minimum block of learning by asking yourself whether it: contains sufficient information to provide a challenge for the student, promises a reasonable return in accomplishment for the training effort necessary, and provides a measurable objective.

As these blocks of learning are completed and your student's performance of each is confirmed to be at an acceptable level, the related blocks are combined to form larger segments of the total training objective. For example, proficiency in airspeed management, maneuvering by ground references, inflight maneuvering, and radio communication can be combined to demonstrate your student's ability to safely fly a traffic pattern at an airport with a control tower. In this manner, small blocks of learning, along with a properly coordinated training syllabus, make it possible for you to direct each period of instruction.

BUILDING BLOCKS TO VOR APPROACHES

To further illustrate the importance of blocks of learning in a course of training, consider the sequence for learning how to fly a VOR instrument approach procedure. In this example, the various learning blocks must be mastered before your student is ready for instruction in VOR approaches. A reasonably proficient instrument student at this stage of training should consistently be able to maintain altitude ± 100 feet, airspeed ± 10 knots, and heading ± 10 degrees. These are PTS criteria for many of the basic instrument maneuvers.

Can a Computer Learn?

While computers are extremely successful at storing large quantities of data, they have not shown the same talent for learning new information. However, the benefits of a computer that can learn are substantial. Instead of having to create a specialized program that allows a computer to perform a particular task, a programmer can simply provide training examples to the machine, which would then learn the task on its own. For example, a self-learning credit card approval system would use historical data about good and bad customers to estimate the risk of new applicants by determining the relationship between matched pairs of personal information and credit behavior.

A	2	p	0
9	8	1	?
b	A	H	x
!	g	I	R

One difficulty lies in any deficiency in the training data. To counteract this, the concept of hints can be applied. In this case, if you wanted a computer to recognize airplanes, simply showing it pictures of airplanes, along with objects that are not airplanes, would not supply the computer with enough information. You know that if you change the scale on the picture, or shift the object's position or orientation, an airplane remains an airplane, but the computer cannot understand this change without a hint from the programmer. You may need to offer additional examples to help prompt the computer to grasp the change. Can you tell what characteristic distinguishes the characters in the blue boxes from those in the orange boxes?

Turn the page for the answer.

Can a Computer Learn? (Continued)

Computers can face similar puzzles. Providing a hint, such as showing the computer an axis, makes it apparent that the characters in the orange boxes lack the mirror image symmetry displayed by the characters in the blue boxes.

Concept derived from "Machines That Learn From Hints" by Yaser S. Abu-Mostafa, Scientific American, April 1995, Volume 272, Number 4

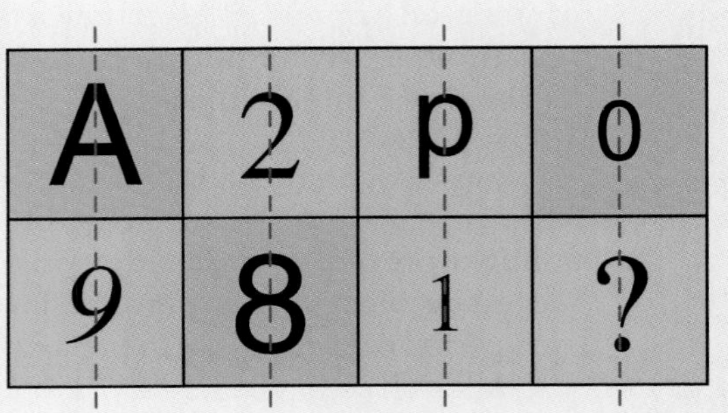

Does this mean your student has the required proficiency in basic altitude, airspeed, and heading control to fly a VOR approach? Probably not. Since the training is for an activity that will leave little time to concentrate on the basics, your student must have sufficient competence in altitude, airspeed, and heading control to make corrections automatically without consciously thinking about the process.

Next, there are a number of basic maneuvers and patterns that combine climbs, descents, turns, and airspeed transitions. Since these fundamental exercises are important elements in building your students' proficiency, they must be mastered before approach training begins. It should be apparent that basic attitude instrument flying is the first and most important building block in any instrument training program. Consider some of the other blocks of learning that are essential before instrument approaches can be introduced. For example, once students demonstrate the ability to maintain altitude, airspeed, and heading within reasonable parameters, you can introduce basic radio navigation and communication procedures. You can use simulated ATC communication and clearances to build a foundation for more advanced phases of instrument training. When your students can understand, copy, and read back a simulated clearance while controlling the aircraft during a basic navigation exercise, you can introduce other new tasks. [Figure 2-45]

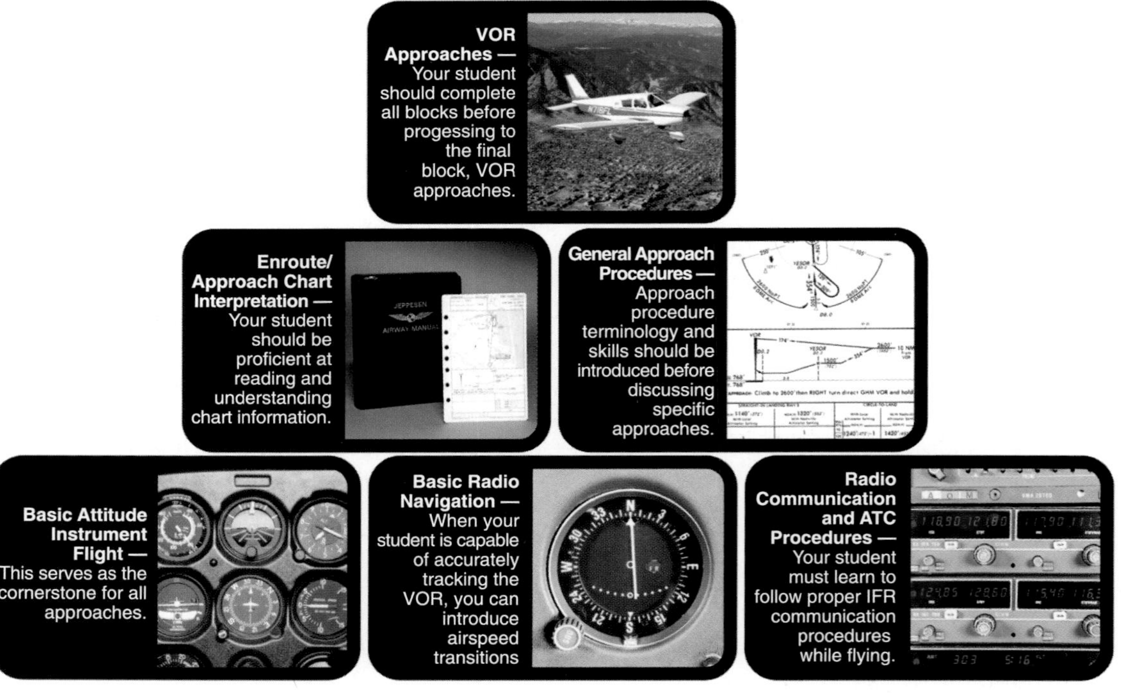

Figure 2-45. By establishing each objective and making sure each completion standard is met, it will be quite clear when your student is ready to go onto the next level. It is important to keep in mind that the blocks of learning are not isolated subjects, but all are interrelated.

If you follow the building block concept throughout the course of training, your student will be well prepared for the final block. The basic knowledge and skills will have been assimilated, and the overall plan for this segment of training will be successful. However, without careful attention to full completion of each block of learning along the way, your student will have difficulty with this last block of learning, and the overall effectiveness of the training will be compromised.

TRAINING SYLLABUS

There are a number of valid reasons why you should use a training syllabus. As technology advances, training requirements become more demanding. While an approved syllabus is mandatory for FAR Part 141 schools, it is essential you use a syllabus for instruction under FAR Part 61 as well since the regulations are quite specific about the type and duration of training. These factors, along with the continuing growth of aviation, add to the complexity of pilot education and certification. You need a practical guide to help make sure training is accomplished in a logical sequence and that all requirements are completed and properly documented. A well-organized, comprehensive syllabus can fulfill these needs.

SYLLABUS FORMAT AND CONTENT

While the format and organization may vary, a syllabus always should be an abstract or digest of the course training. It should contain blocks of learning to be completed in the most efficient order. Since a syllabus is intended to be a summary of a course of training, it should be fairly brief, yet comprehensive enough to cover essential information. This information is usually presented in an outline format with lesson-by-lesson coverage. Some syllabi include tables to show recommended training time for each lesson, as well as the overall minimum time requirements. [Figure 2-46]

Each lesson in a training syllabus should include at least the three main elements: objectives, content, and completion standards.

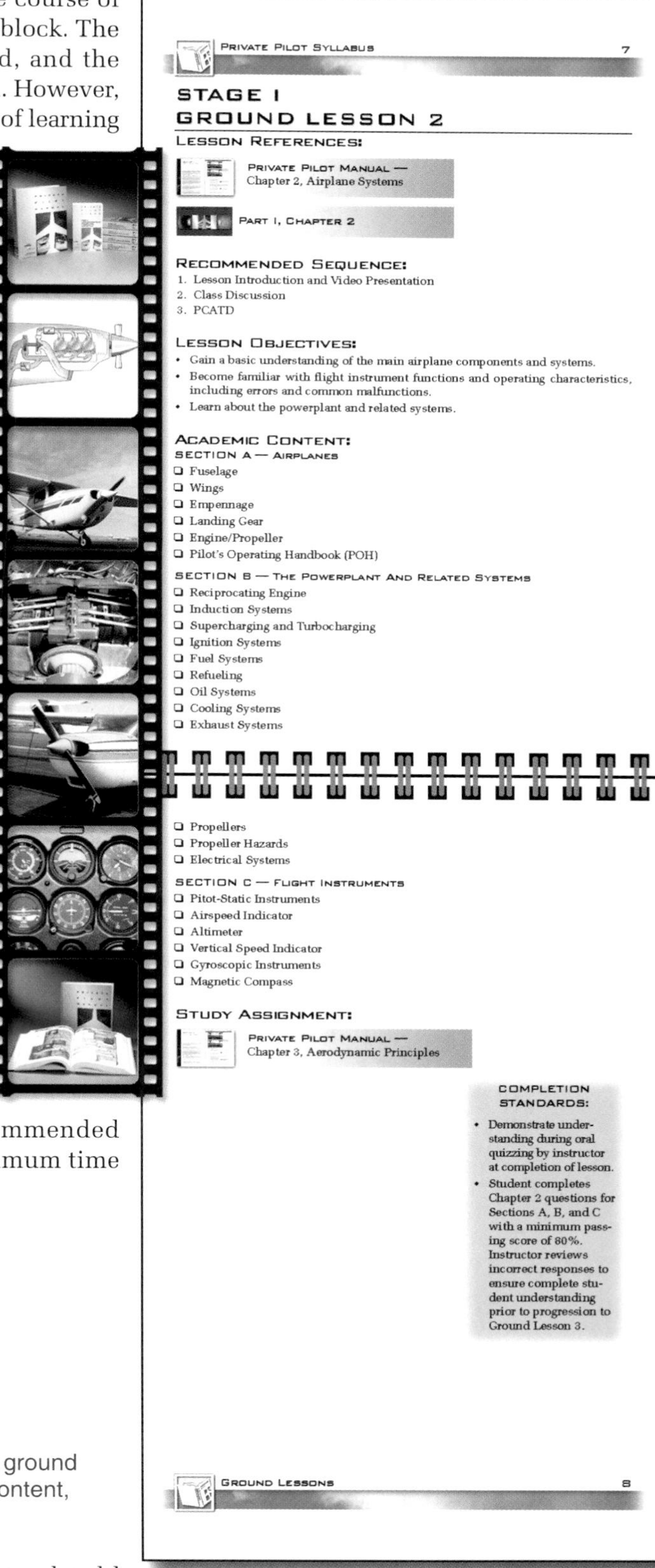

PRIVATE PILOT SYLLABUS 7

STAGE I
GROUND LESSON 2

LESSON REFERENCES:

PRIVATE PILOT MANUAL — Chapter 2, Airplane Systems

PART I, CHAPTER 2

RECOMMENDED SEQUENCE:
1. Lesson Introduction and Video Presentation
2. Class Discussion
3. PCATD

LESSON OBJECTIVES:
- Gain a basic understanding of the main airplane components and systems.
- Become familiar with flight instrument functions and operating characteristics, including errors and common malfunctions.
- Learn about the powerplant and related systems.

ACADEMIC CONTENT:

SECTION A — AIRPLANES
- ❑ Fuselage
- ❑ Wings
- ❑ Empennage
- ❑ Landing Gear
- ❑ Engine/Propeller
- ❑ Pilot's Operating Handbook (POH)

SECTION B — THE POWERPLANT AND RELATED SYSTEMS
- ❑ Reciprocating Engine
- ❑ Induction Systems
- ❑ Supercharging and Turbocharging
- ❑ Ignition Systems
- ❑ Fuel Systems
- ❑ Refueling
- ❑ Oil Systems
- ❑ Cooling Systems
- ❑ Exhaust Systems
- ❑ Propellers
- ❑ Propeller Hazards
- ❑ Electrical Systems

SECTION C — FLIGHT INSTRUMENTS
- ❑ Pitot-Static Instruments
- ❑ Airspeed Indicator
- ❑ Altimeter
- ❑ Vertical Speed Indicator
- ❑ Gyroscopic Instruments
- ❑ Magnetic Compass

STUDY ASSIGNMENT:

PRIVATE PILOT MANUAL — Chapter 3, Aerodynamic Principles

COMPLETION STANDARDS:
- Demonstrate understanding during oral quizzing by instructor at completion of lesson.
- Student completes Chapter 2 questions for Sections A, B, and C with a minimum passing score of 80%. Instructor reviews incorrect responses to ensure complete student understanding prior to progression to Ground Lesson 3.

GROUND LESSONS 8

Figure 2-46. This excerpt of a ground lesson shows a unit of ground instruction. The lesson includes three key parts: objectives, content, and completion standards.

While you may develop your own training syllabi, you should consider using well-designed commercial products. Syllabi developed for Part 141 schools contain details such as enrollment prerequisites, planned completion times, and descriptions of stage checks to measure student accomplishments for each segment of training.

Since effective training relies on organized blocks of learning, all syllabi should stress well-defined objectives and standards for each lesson. Appropriate objectives and standards should be established for the overall course, the separate ground and flight segments, and for each stage of training. Other details may be added to a syllabus such as an explanation of how to use it, and descriptions of pertinent training and reference materials, including textbooks, video, CD-ROMs, exams, briefings, and instructional guides.

How to Use a Training Syllabus

Any practical training syllabus must be flexible and should be used primarily as a guide. When necessary, you can and should alter the order of training to suit the progress of your student and the demands of special circumstances. For example, the sequence of lessons often will require some alteration or repetition to fit individual students with previous experience or different rates of learning. The syllabus also should be flexible enough so you can adapt it to weather variations, aircraft availability, and scheduling changes without disrupting the teaching process or completely suspending training.

In departing from the order prescribed by the syllabus, however, it is your responsibility to consider how the relationships of the blocks of learning are affected. You may want to skip to a different part of the syllabus when the conduct of a scheduled lesson is impossible, rather than proceeding to the next block, which may be predicated completely on skills to be developed during the lesson which is being postponed.

When it is impossible to conduct a scheduled lesson, it is preferable to conduct another lesson that is not dependent on skills to be developed during the postponed lesson.

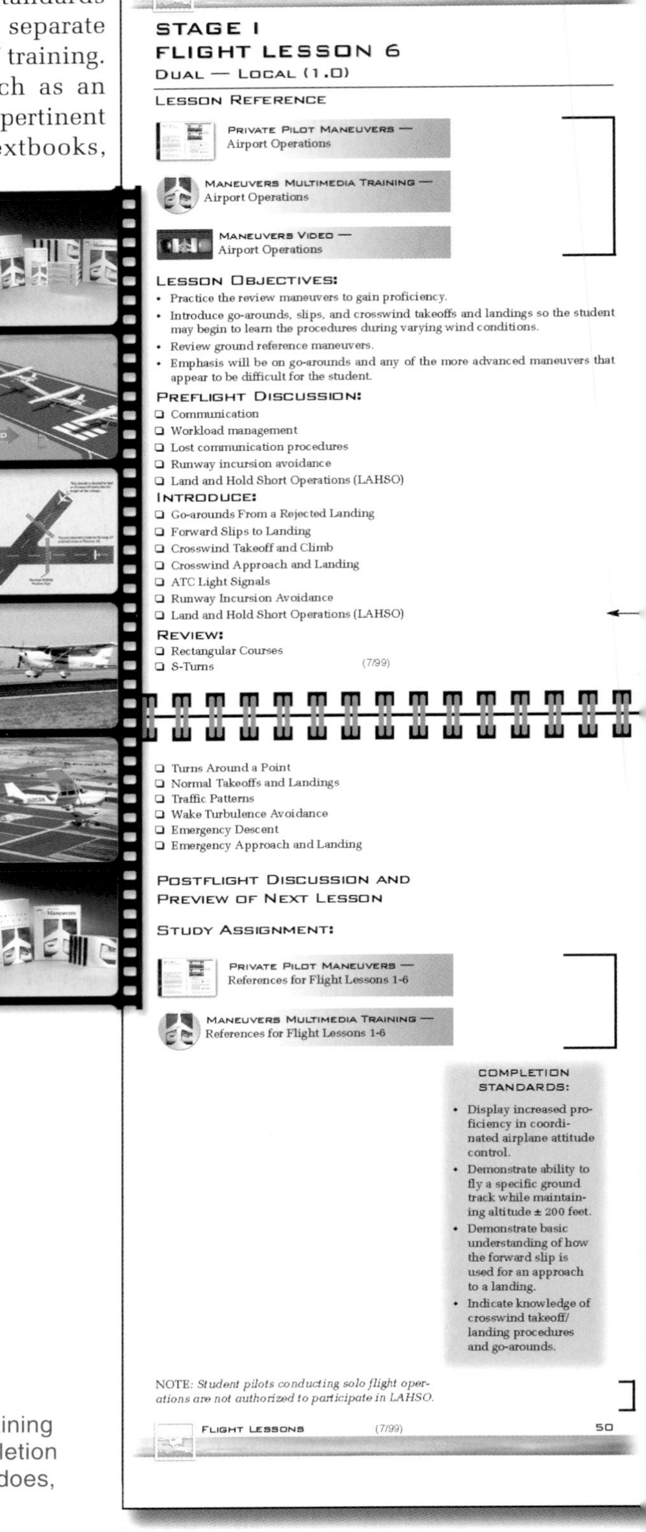

PRIVATE PILOT SYLLABUS 49

STAGE I
FLIGHT LESSON 6
DUAL — LOCAL (1.0)

LESSON REFERENCE

PRIVATE PILOT MANEUVERS — Airport Operations

MANEUVERS MULTIMEDIA TRAINING — Airport Operations

MANEUVERS VIDEO — Airport Operations

LESSON OBJECTIVES:
- Practice the review maneuvers to gain proficiency.
- Introduce go-arounds, slips, and crosswind takeoffs and landings so the student may begin to learn the procedures during varying wind conditions.
- Review ground reference maneuvers.
- Emphasis will be on go-arounds and any of the more advanced maneuvers that appear to be difficult for the student.

PREFLIGHT DISCUSSION:
- ❑ Communication
- ❑ Workload management
- ❑ Lost communication procedures
- ❑ Runway incursion avoidance
- ❑ Land and Hold Short Operations (LAHSO)

INTRODUCE:
- ❑ Go-arounds From a Rejected Landing
- ❑ Forward Slips to Landing
- ❑ Crosswind Takeoff and Climb
- ❑ Crosswind Approach and Landing
- ❑ ATC Light Signals
- ❑ Runway Incursion Avoidance
- ❑ Land and Hold Short Operations (LAHSO)

REVIEW:
- ❑ Rectangular Courses
- ❑ S-Turns

(7/99)

- ❑ Turns Around a Point
- ❑ Normal Takeoffs and Landings
- ❑ Traffic Patterns
- ❑ Wake Turbulence Avoidance
- ❑ Emergency Descent
- ❑ Emergency Approach and Landing

POSTFLIGHT DISCUSSION AND PREVIEW OF NEXT LESSON

STUDY ASSIGNMENT:

PRIVATE PILOT MANEUVERS — References for Flight Lessons 1-6

MANEUVERS MULTIMEDIA TRAINING — References for Flight Lessons 1-6

COMPLETION STANDARDS:
- Display increased proficiency in coordinated airplane attitude control.
- Demonstrate ability to fly a specific ground track while maintaining altitude ± 200 feet.
- Demonstrate basic understanding of how the forward slip is used for an approach to a landing.
- Indicate knowledge of crosswind takeoff/landing procedures and go-arounds.

NOTE: *Student pilots conducting solo flight operations are not authorized to participate in LAHSO.*

FLIGHT LESSONS (7/99) 50

Figure 2-47. A flight training lesson, like a ground training lesson, should include objectives, content, and completion standards. More than one objective could, and often does, apply to a single flight lesson.

Each training course provided by a Part 141 school should be conducted in accordance with a training syllabus specifically approved by the Federal Aviation Administration (FAA). At Part 141 schools, the syllabus is a key part of the training course outline. The instructional

facilities, airport, aircraft, and instructor personnel must be able to support the course of training specified in the syllabus. Compliance with the approved syllabus is a condition for graduation from such courses. Therefore, both you and your student should have a copy of the approved syllabus and refer to it throughout the course of training. However, as previously mentioned, you should not adhere to a syllabus so stringently that it becomes inflexible or unchangeable.

Ground training lessons normally concentrate on the cognitive domain of learning. For example, a typical lesson might include several knowledge areas, such as airports, airspace, and aeronautical charts. Flight training lessons usually focus on the psychomotor domain. Performing a chandelle or landing in a crosswind, for example, both require physical skills. The affective domain, covering areas such as safety, aeronautical decision making, and judgment are pertinent to both ground and flight training lessons. By stressing these subjects, you can favorably influence your student's attitudes, beliefs, and values. [Figure 2-47]

A syllabus should include special emphasis items that have been determined to be cause factors in aircraft accidents or incidents. For example, you should emphasize collision and wake turbulence avoidance procedures throughout your student's flight training. Lesson descriptions also may include recommended class times, reference or study materials, the sequence of training, and the study assignment for the next lesson. [Figure 2-48]

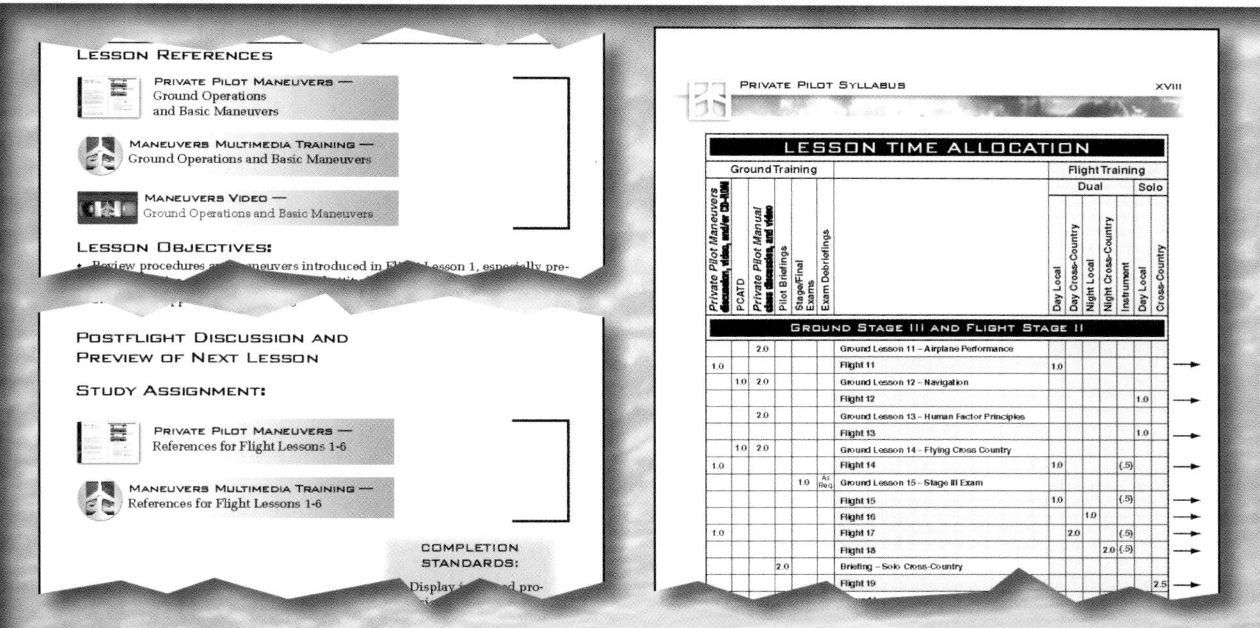

LESSON REFERENCES

PRIVATE PILOT MANEUVERS — Ground Operations and Basic Maneuvers

MANEUVERS MULTIMEDIA TRAINING — Ground Operations and Basic Maneuvers

MANEUVERS VIDEO — Ground Operations and Basic Maneuvers

LESSON OBJECTIVES:

POSTFLIGHT DISCUSSION AND PREVIEW OF NEXT LESSON

STUDY ASSIGNMENT:

PRIVATE PILOT MANEUVERS — References for Flight Lessons 1-6

MANEUVERS MULTIMEDIA TRAINING — References for Flight Lessons 1-6

COMPLETION STANDARDS:

PRIVATE PILOT SYLLABUS XVIII

LESSON TIME ALLOCATION

Ground Training							Flight Training						
							Dual					Solo	
Private Pilot Maneuvers discussion, video, and/or CD-ROM	PCATD	Private Pilot Manual class discussion, and video	Pilot Briefings	Stage/Final Exams	Exam Debriefings		Day Local	Day Cross-Country	Night Local	Night Cross-Country	Instrument	Day Local	Cross-Country
GROUND STAGE III AND FLIGHT STAGE II													
		2.0				Ground Lesson 11 – Airplane Performance							
1.0						Flight 11	1.0						
	1.0	2.0				Ground Lesson 12 – Navigation							
						Flight 12						1.0	
		2.0				Ground Lesson 13 – Human Factor Principles							
						Flight 13						1.0	
	1.0	2.0				Ground Lesson 14 – Flying Cross Country							
1.0						Flight 14	1.0				(.5)		
				1.0	As Req.	Ground Lesson 15 – Stage III Exam							
						Flight 15	1.0				(.5)		
						Flight 16			1.0				
1.0						Flight 17		2.0			(.5)		
						Flight 18				2.0	(.5)		
			2.0			Briefing – Solo Cross-Country							
						Flight 19							2.5

Figure 2-48. Information in the form of references and study assignments may be added to individual ground or flight lessons when it is necessary. Time allocation tables might also be included in a syllabus.

While a syllabus is designed to provide a road map showing how to accomplish the overall objective of a course of training, it may be useful for other purposes. As already mentioned, it can be used as a checklist to ensure that required training has successfully been completed, making it an effective tool for record keeping. Enhanced syllabi are specifically designed for record keeping, and you may find them helpful if you instruct independently.

This record keeping function is usually facilitated by boxes or blank spaces adjacent to the knowledge areas, procedures, or maneuvers in a ground or flight lesson. Most syllabi introduce specific procedures or maneuvers in one flight lesson and review them in subsequent lessons. Some syllabi also include provisions for grading student performance and recording both ground and flight training time. Accurate record keeping is necessary to keep both you and your student informed on the status of training. These records also serve as basis for endorsements and recommendations for knowledge and practical tests.

Another benefit of using a syllabus is that it helps you in the development of lesson plans. A well-constructed syllabus already contains much of the essential information that is required in a lesson plan, including objectives, content, and completion standards.

LESSON PLANS

A **lesson plan** is an organized outline for a single instructional period. It is a necessary guide that tells you what to do, in what order to do it, and what method to use in teaching the lesson. You should prepare lesson plans for each training period and ensure they show specific knowledge and/or skills you wish to teach.

A lesson plan should be put into writing, as a mental outline is not adequate. Another instructor should be able to take your lesson plan and be able to conduct the same instruction. When you put it into writing, you can analyze the lesson for adequacy and completeness. Lesson plans ensure that each of your students receives the best possible instruction under the existing conditions, and help you keep a constant check on your own performance, in addition to that of your students. [Figure 2-49]

A properly constructed lesson plan should provide an outline for the teaching method to be used in a single instructional period.

A well-thought-out lesson plan provides you with a way to check your instructional activity, as well as the performance of your students.

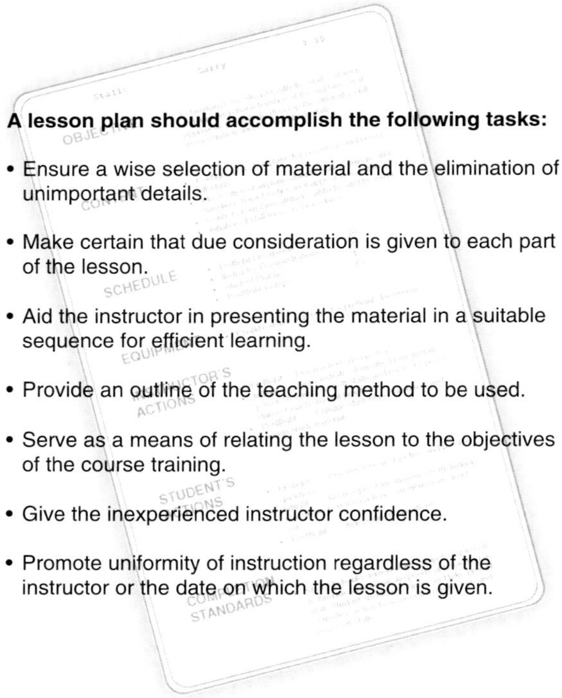

A lesson plan should accomplish the following tasks:

- Ensure a wise selection of material and the elimination of unimportant details.
- Make certain that due consideration is given to each part of the lesson.
- Aid the instructor in presenting the material in a suitable sequence for efficient learning.
- Provide an outline of the teaching method to be used.
- Serve as a means of relating the lesson to the objectives of the course training.
- Give the inexperienced instructor confidence.
- Promote uniformity of instruction regardless of the instructor or the date on which the lesson is given.

Figure 2-49. The development of lesson plans signifies, in effect, that you have taught the lessons to yourself prior to attempting to teach the lessons to students.

CHARACTERISTICS OF A WELL-PLANNED LESSON

While developing lesson plans requires time and energy, you will find that teaching is easier and more effective if you are well prepared. Planning a ground or flight lesson

usually includes several steps. After you establish the lesson objective, you must research the subject, determine the method of instruction, and identify a useful lesson-planning format. Other steps, such as deciding how to organize the lesson and selecting suitable support material, also must be accomplished. You should organize explanations and demonstrations to help your students achieve the desired learning outcome. The final steps include assembling training aids and writing the lesson plan outline. One technique for writing the lesson plan outline is to prepare the beginning and ending first. Then, complete the outline and revise as required. [Figure 2-50]

A well-planned lesson exhibits the following characteristics:

Unity—All teaching procedures and objectives should be stated in terms of desired student learning outcomes. An example of an objective from a lesson on stalls might be to familiarize the student with the warnings and handling characteristics of the airplane as it approaches a stall.

Content—Each lesson should contain new material. However, the new facts, principles, procedures, or skills should be related to previous lessons. For example, you might plan to review the procedures used to fly a rectangular course before introducing the traffic pattern to your student.

Scope—A person can master only a few principles or skills at a time, depending on the complexity. In most cases, teaching slow flight, stalls, steep turns, and emergency procedures in one lesson will be overwhelming to your student. On the other hand, devoting an entire lesson to only slow flight will probably be inefficient.

Practicality—Lesson plans conducted in an airplane or ground trainer will differ from those conducted in a classroom. Also, the kinds and quantities of instructional aids available have a great influence on lesson planning and instructional procedures. For example, you may want to integrate computer-based training into your lessons, but may not have the equipment necessary to do so.

Flexibility—Although a lesson plan provides an outline sequence for the training to be conducted, a standardized lesson plan may not be effective for all students. For example, your outline of content may include blank spaces for additional material, if required.

Relation to Course of Training—Each lesson should be planned and taught so that its relation to the course objectives are clear to each student. For example, a lesson on short-field takeoffs and landings should cover both the certification and safety objectives of the course of training.

Instructional Steps—Every lesson when adequately developed, falls logically into the four steps of the teaching process—preparation, presentation, application, and review and evaluation.

Figure 2-50. A lesson plan should be a working document that can and should be revised as needed.

A well-designed lesson plan should include new material that is related to the previous lesson.

When developing a lesson, you should organize explanations and demonstrations to help your students achieve the desired learning outcome.

LESSON DURATION AND ORGANIZATION

In planning for student performance, one of your primary considerations is the length of time devoted to practice. A beginning student reaches a point where additional practice is not only unproductive, but may even be harmful since errors increase and motivation declines. As your student gains experience, longer periods of practice make sense to reinforce properly learned techniques.

Depending on the nature of the skill you are teaching you may want to divide the lesson into several practice sessions. Learning to plan a cross-country flight, for example, requires several skills, which you normally need to teach during many sessions. When you teach a less complex lesson, you may be able to cover all the information in one practice period. For example, while teaching a student to fly S-turns requires practice, the initial skill can typically be taught in one training session.

One of the main considerations in planning for student performance during a flight lesson is the length of the practice session.

Closely related to the length of the lesson is the problem of student fatigue. You should consider fatigue when assessing your student's substandard performance early in a lesson, or when performance has deteriorated near the end of a lesson. [Figure 2-51] The amount of training that can be absorbed by one student without incurring debilitating fatigue does not necessarily indicate the capacity of another student. Fatigue which results from training operations may be either physical or mental, or both. It is not necessarily a function of physical health or mental acuity. Generally speaking, complex operations tend to induce fatigue more rapidly than simpler procedures do, regardless of the physical effort involved. You should continue flight instruction only as long as your student is alert, receptive to instruction, and is performing at a level consistent with experience.

Fatigue is the primary consideration in determining the length and frequency of flight instruction periods.

Figure 2-51. Once fatigue occurs as a result of concentration on a learning task, you should give your student a break. As an alternative, you can review other maneuvers, which may involve different elements and objectives.

THE POSITIVE APPROACH

One of your goals when creating a lesson plan is to make learning an enjoyable experience. You can maintain a high level of motivation in your students by emphasizing the positive and by making each lesson a pleasurable experience. This does not mean that you must make things easy for your students or sacrifice standards of performance. Your students will experience satisfaction from doing a good job or from successfully meeting the challenge of a difficult task.

You can most effectively maintain a high level of motivation in your students by making each lesson a pleasurable experience.

A normal flight to a nearby airport and return is a good example of the positive approach for a student's first flight lesson.

The positive approach is an effective instructional technique. An example is to point out the pleasurable features of aviation before the unpleasant possibilities are discussed.

HOW TO USE A LESSON PLAN

There are several key points to remember when you build and execute your lesson plans.

Be familiar with the lesson plan. You should study each step of the plan and be thoroughly familiar with as much information related to the subject as possible. You may need to review training material prior to teaching a particular subject area.

Use the lesson plan as a guide. A lesson plan ensures that pertinent materials are at hand and that you accomplish the presentation with order and unity. Having a plan prevents you from getting off track, omitting essential points, or introducing irrelevant material.

Is Learning to Fly a Good Idea?

Consider how the following scenarios for first lessons might impress a new student pilot without previous experience in aviation. Should your lesson consist of:

- an exhaustive indoctrination in preflight procedures with emphasis on the extreme precautions which must be taken since mechanical failures in flight are often disastrous?
- instruction in the extreme care which must be taken in taxiing an airplane, because if you go too fast, it's likely to get away from you?
- a series of stalls, since this is how many people lose their lives in airplanes?
- a series of simulated forced landings, because one should always be prepared to cope with an engine failure?

These are new experiences that might make your student wonder whether learning to fly is a good idea. The stall series may even cause your student to become airsick. In contrast, consider a flight lesson in which the preflight inspection is presented to familiarize your student with the airplane and its components, and the lesson consists of a perfectly normal flight to a nearby airport. Following the flight, you can call your student's attention to the ease with which the trip was made in comparison with other modes of transportation, and the fact that no critical incidents were encountered or expected.

Make sure your students understand the objectives. When students are able to see the benefits or purpose of the lesson, they will be motivated to learn. Not knowing the objective of the lesson often leads to confusion, disinterest, and uneasiness, and students will be less motivated.

When students are unable to see the benefits or purpose of a lesson, they will be less motivated. If you keep your students well informed about the lesson objectives and completion standards, you minimize their feelings of insecurity.

Do not accept substandard performance. You must continuously evaluate the performance of your students. Accepting lower standards to please your students may actually degrade your student-instructor relationship. Although there may be exceptions, students normally do not resent reasonable standards that are fairly and consistently applied. More importantly, uncorrected deficiencies may result in hazardous inadequacies in your students' performance. [Figure 2-52]

Flight instructors fail to provide competent instruction when they permit students to partially learn an important item of knowledge or skill.

Figure 2-52. The desire to maintain pleasant personal relationships with your students must not cause you to accept a slow rate of learning or substandard performance.

Adapt the lesson plan to the class or student. During a period of ground or flight instruction, you may find that the procedures outlined in your lesson plan are not leading to the desired results. In this situation, you should change the approach. There is no certain way of predicting the reactions of different students. An approach that has been successful with one student may not be successful with another. A lesson plan should be appropriate to the background, flight experience, and ability of your student. [Figure 2-53]

The use of a standard lesson plan may not be effective for students requiring a different approach.

Bill is a presolo student and has recently changed flight schools. After talking with Bill and reviewing his logbook, Alex decides they should practice flying traffic patterns for their first lesson together.

After struggling through three circuits around the pattern, Alex decides to change the lesson and go to the practice area to brush up on ground reference maneuvers.

Figure 2-53. You may have to modify the lesson plan considerably during the flight, due to deficiencies in your student's knowledge or poor mastery of elements essential to the effective completion of the lesson. In some cases, you may have to abandon the entire lesson.

Revise the lesson plan periodically. After you have prepared a lesson plan for a training period, systematic and continuous revision is usually necessary. This is true for a number of reasons, including availability of instructional aids, revision of regulations, new manuals and textbooks, and changes in technology.

LESSON PLAN FORMATS

The format and style of a lesson plan depends on several factors. The subject matter has a lot to do with how you present a lesson and what teaching method you use. Individual lesson plans may be quite simple for one-on-one training, or they may be elaborate and complicated for large, structured classroom lessons. Preferably, each lesson should have somewhat limited objectives that are achievable within a reasonable period of time. This principle applies to both ground and flight training.

Commercially developed lesson plans also are acceptable for most training situations, including your use as a flight instructor applicant during your practical test. However, you should recognize that even well-designed preprinted lesson plans may need to be modified. Therefore, you should use creativity when adapting these lesson plans for specific students or training circumstances. [Figure 2-54]

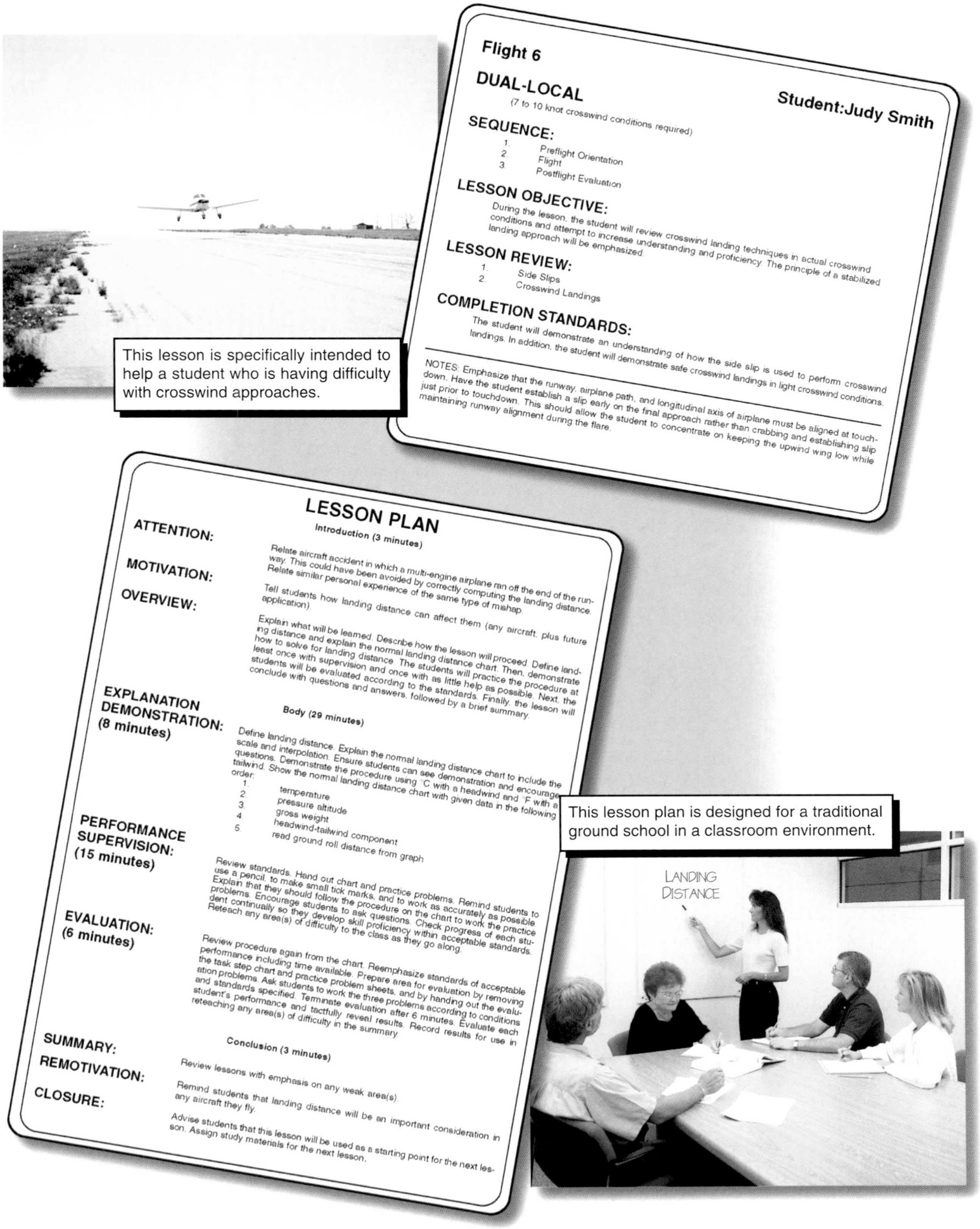

Flight 6

DUAL-LOCAL **Student:Judy Smith**

(7 to 10 knot crosswind conditions required)

SEQUENCE:

1. Preflight Orientation
2. Flight
3. Postflight Evaluation

LESSON OBJECTIVE:

During the lesson, the student will review crosswind landing techniques in actual crosswind conditions and attempt to increase understanding and proficiency. The principle of a stabilized landing approach will be emphasized.

LESSON REVIEW:

1. Side Slips
2. Crosswind Landings

COMPLETION STANDARDS:

The student will demonstrate an understanding of how the side slip is used to perform crosswind landings. In addition, the student will demonstrate safe crosswind landings in light crosswind conditions.

NOTES: Emphasize that the runway, airplane path, and longitudinal axis of airplane must be aligned at touchdown. Have the student establish a slip early on the final approach rather than crabbing and establishing slip just prior to touchdown. This should allow the student to concentrate on keeping the upwind wing low while maintaining runway alignment during the flare.

This lesson is specifically intended to help a student who is having difficulty with crosswind approaches.

LESSON PLAN

Introduction (3 minutes)

ATTENTION: Relate aircraft accident in which a multi-engine airplane ran off the end of the runway. This could have been avoided by correctly computing the landing distance. Relate similar personal experience of the same type of mishap.

MOTIVATION: Tell students how landing distance can affect them (any aircraft, plus future application).

OVERVIEW: Explain what will be learned. Describe how the lesson will proceed. Define landing distance and explain the normal landing distance chart. Then, demonstrate how to solve for landing distance. The students will practice the procedure at least once with supervision and once with as little help as possible. Next, the students will be evaluated according to the standards. Finally, the lesson will conclude with questions and answers, followed by a brief summary.

Body (29 minutes)

EXPLANATION DEMONSTRATION: (8 minutes) Define landing distance. Explain the normal landing distance chart to include the scale and interpolation. Ensure students can see demonstration and encourage questions. Demonstrate the procedure using °C with a headwind and °F with a tailwind. Show the normal landing distance chart with given data in the following order:

1. temperature
2. pressure altitude
3. gross weight
4. headwind-tailwind component
5. read ground roll distance from graph

PERFORMANCE SUPERVISION: (15 minutes) Review standards. Hand out chart and practice problems. Remind students to use a pencil, to make small tick marks, and to work as accurately as possible. Explain that they should follow the procedure on the chart to work the practice problems. Encourage students to ask questions. Check progress of each student continually so they develop skill proficiency within acceptable standards. Reteach any area(s) of difficulty to the class as they go along.

EVALUATION: (6 minutes) Review procedure again from the chart. Reemphasize standards of acceptable performance including time available. Prepare area for evaluation by removing the task step chart and practice problem sheets, and by handing out the evaluation problems. Ask students to work the three problems according to conditions and standards specified. Terminate evaluation after 6 minutes. Evaluate each student's performance and tactfully reveal results. Record results for use in reteaching any area(s) of difficulty in the summary.

Conclusion (3 minutes)

SUMMARY: Review lessons with emphasis on any weak area(s).

REMOTIVATION: Remind students that landing distance will be an important consideration in any aircraft they fly.

CLOSURE: Advise students that this lesson will be used as a starting point for the next lesson. Assign study materials for the next lesson.

This lesson plan is designed for a traditional ground school in a classroom environment.

Figure 2-54. The format of lesson plans can vary as long as objectives, content to support the objectives, and completion standards are included.

GROUND LESSON 8 — PCATD

OBJECTIVE

- Review of VOR concepts, intercepts, and tracking.

EMPHASIS

- Situational awareness; requires pilot constantly asking: Where am I? Where am I going? What am I going to do next?
- VOR utilization

SET-UP

- Choose an unfamiliar environment in which to fly (from the database map).
- Set airplane location off of a line between 2 NAVAID(s) about 40 miles apart (save as file for future use); configuration can be cruise flight or normal maneuvering flight regime.
- Utilize cockpit instrument check to set frequencies.
- Review terminology: bearing vs. radial, tracking inbound vs. outbound.

EXERCISES and MANEUVERS

- Determine position by orientation of TO/FROM and CDI centering; have student identify position on chart (paper) before looking at map screen, verify on map screen; discuss errors.
- Re-position airplane on the map screen, determine and note changes in CDI centering.
- Fly direct to selected NAVAID(s).
- Intercept a dictated radial:
  - Tune/identify NAVAID(s).
  - Determine location with respect to bearing by turning to the heading of course dictated; note on which side of airplane is desired course.
  - Determine intercept angle and turn to intercept heading.
  - Demonstrate bracketing techniques.

COMPLETION STANDARDS

- Correctly determine location and orientation TO/FROM NAVAID(s).
- Correctly determine appropriate intercept angle and heading.
- Recognize that the ability to track is heavily dependent on accurate maintenance of heading.
- Demonstrate ability to visualize position.

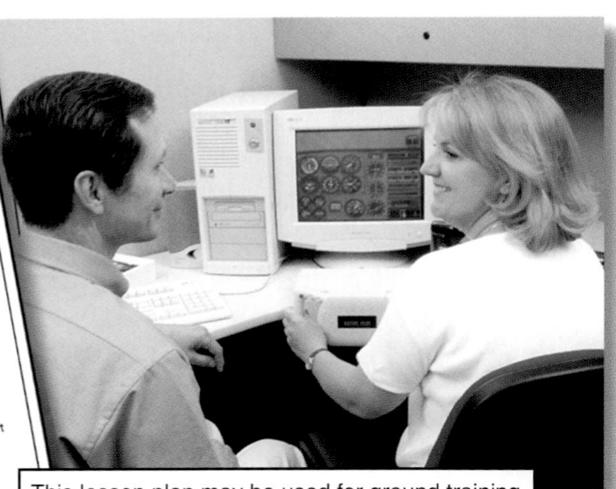

This lesson plan may be used for ground training in a personal computer-based aviation training device (PCATD) or a flight training device (FTD).

MULTI-ENGINE TRANSITION — LESSON THREE

OBJECTIVE: To complete the Baron systems instruction, review procedures for abnormal situations, including systems failures, and further review multi-engine aerodynamics and concepts. In addition, complete IFR proficiency in the ground trainer, and develop the pilot's skill and comfort operating the Baron in a variety of situations.

ELEMENTS:

- ground instruction
  - → systems
    - electrical
    - landing gear
  - → procedures
    - systems failures
    - other abnormal and emergency checklists
  - → multi-engine considerations / aerodynamics
    - zero sideslip
    - drag effects
- flight training device or flight simulator
  - → any further training needed on IFR skills
  - → utilize to practice engine failure after takeoff and single-engine go-around procedures
- flight
  - → engine failure on ground
  - → V_{MC} demo
  - → drag demo
  - → engine failure in cruise, descent
  - → systems failures including manual gear extension
  - → IFR procedures / single-engine approaches

COMPLETION STANDARDS: The lesson is complete when the student demonstrates understanding of all Baron systems and emergency procedures, and demonstrates a level of proficiency, as judged by the instructor, to transition from the instrument ground trainer to the airplane.

FURTHER STUDY: Baron POH (Section 3, Section 7)

This is a specialized flight training lesson plan for multi-engine transition.

SUMMARY CHECKLIST

✓ A course of training may be defined as a complete set of studies leading to attainment of a specific goal.

✓ In planning any instructional activity, the first consideration should be to determine the overall objectives and standards.

✓ The second step in instructional activity is to identify blocks of learning which constitute the necessary parts of the total objective.

✓ Extraneous blocks of instruction during a course of training detract from the completion of the final objective.

✓ Blocks of learning in their proper relationship allow students to master segments of the overall pilot performance requirements individually and then combine these with related segments.

✓ As flight training becomes more complex, the need for a well-organized, comprehensive training syllabus increases.

✓ Each lesson in a training syllabus should contain at least three main elements: objectives, content, and completion standards.

✓ Any practical syllabus must be flexible, and should be used primarily as a guide When necessary, the order of training can and should be altered to suit the needs of individual students or special circumstances such as weather variations, aircraft availability, and scheduling changes.

✓ A well-constructed lesson plan should provide an outline for the teaching method to be used for a single instructional period.

✓ Lesson plans, when properly designed, provide a way to check your own instructional performance, as well as that of your students.

✓ A well-thought-out lesson plan should include new material that is related to the previous lesson.

✓ An important consideration in planning a flight lesson is the length of the practice session.

✓ An example of the positive approach technique in flight training is to point out the enjoyable features before discussing any unpleasant possibilities.

✓ When students are unable to see the benefits or purpose of a lesson, they will be less motivated.

✓ When you keep your students well informed about the lesson objectives and completion standards, you minimize their feelings of insecurity.

✓ Flight instructors fail to provide adequate instruction when they permit students to partially learn an important piece of knowledge or skill.

✓ It is important to recognize that you may need to use creativity to develop lesson plans for specific students or circumstances.

✓ The use of a standard lesson plan may not be effective for students requiring a different approach.

KEY TERMS

Course of Training

Curriculum

Training Syllabus

Training Course Outline (TCO)

Blocks of Learning

Lesson Plan

QUESTIONS

1. Define a course of training and state an example of one that can be found in the aviation environment.

2. What is the desired level of learning for pilot training?

   A. Knowledge level
   B. Application level
   C. Application level or higher

3. Select the true statement regarding a training syllabus.

   A. It is designed for a phase or stage of training.
   B. It is a step-by-step building block progression of learning with review and evaluation at prescribed stages.
   C. It is a compilation of courses in an area of specialization offered by an educational institution such as a flight school.

4. What is the first step in any organized training activity?

   A. Determine the objectives and standards.
   B. Identify the blocks of learning which constitute the necessary parts of the total objective.
   C. Divide the blocks of learning into segments which are consistent in scope and can easily be evaluated.

5. A syllabus lesson should contain what elements?

6. True/False. As a general rule, you should not adhere to a syllabus so stringently that it becomes inflexible.

7. True/False. All syllabi should include enrollment prerequisites, planned completion times, and a description of check and tests.

8. True/False. As an independent instructor, you are required to use a syllabus for your flight training activities.

9. What is a lesson plan?

   A. A detailed outline for a course of training
   B. A well-defined outline for a block of learning
   C. An organized outline for a single instructional period

10. Select the true statement regarding a lesson plan.

    A. It should be limited to one main objective.
    B. It should include new material that is related to the previous lesson.
    C. The completion standards should be equal to those published in the applicable PTS.

11. On a separate sheet of paper, create a lesson plan for an instructional period during which you are to introduce slow flight to a primary student.

SECTION D
EVALUATING PERFORMANCE

The ability to properly critique and evaluate student performance is one of the most crucial skills you must have as an instructor. Your students will naturally look to you for guidance and encouragement as they attempt to complete their training. It is your responsibility to keep them informed of their progress through objective evaluation and criticism.

To enhance your student's acceptance of further instruction, you should keep them informed of the progress they have made.

CRITIQUE VERSUS EVALUATION

A critique is a step in the learning process, and an evaluation is part of the overall grading process. **Critiques** should be used to summarize and complete a lesson, as well as to prepare your student for the next lesson. **Evaluations** measure demonstrated performance against a criteria or standard, such as a grade of at least 70% to pass a written test. [Figure 2-55]

A critique is a step in the learning process, not the grading process.

CRITIQUE

EVALUATION

Figure 2-55. Critiques are informal appraisals of student performance, designed to quickly convey feedback to your students. Formal evaluations are typically in the form of written tests, oral quizzing, or check flights, and are used to measure performance and document whether the course objectives have been met.

CRITIQUES

Critiques are designed to provide your students with constructive feedback that they can use to improve future performance. If your students view critiques negatively, they will be unlikely to accept your suggestions for improvement, and little progress will result. For critiques to be as effective as possible, they should be conducted immediately after the lesson. [Figure 2-56]

When you critique your student, it should be conducted immediately after your student's performance.

Telling your students that their work is unsatisfactory with no explanation, would most likely result in your students becoming frustrated.

Figure 2-56. Critiques can be used as a reteaching tool for those areas noted as deficient during the lesson. For example, if your student is having difficulty with landings, explain why the landings were poor, and review the topics that need improvement. By explaining why the performance was substandard, you reduce the risk of your student becoming frustrated.

CHARACTERISTICS OF AN EFFECTIVE CRITIQUE

Effective critiques typically share certain characteristics, and provide students with encouragement and direction. Your critique should be factual and aligned with the completion standards of the lesson.

Your critique should provide direction and guidance.

OBJECTIVE

Your critique should always be objective, and focus on your student's performance, and not reflect personal opinions, biases, and dislikes. Be careful not to over-identify or sympathize with your student, which is known as halo error. For example, if you think your student looks like a pilot, or has personality traits similar to yours, your tendency may be to overlook some mistakes and errors, thereby reducing your objectivity.

Your critique of your student's performance should be constructive and objective.

FLEXIBLE

You should consider your student's entire performance and the context in which it was accomplished. For example, unusual conditions, such as high winds or an unfamiliar airport, need to be taken into account when you critique your student. People have good days and bad days, and your student is no exception. Better students can sometimes perform below their ability, and weaker students can perform up to standards. Your student's mood should also be taken into consideration. For example, it can be counterproductive to belabor minor errors when a student is already upset with the poor performance. [Figure 2-57]

Your critique should be flexible enough to satisfy the requirements of the moment.

Angela is a perfectionist and a very competent student, but today her ground reference maneuvers were not flawless, due to strong surface winds. Kelly, Angela's instructor, realizes that Angela is upset and therefore decides not to dwell on ground reference maneuvers during the critique.

Figure 2-57. You need to be aware of unique circumstances, and keep your critique flexible enough to accommodate different situations.

ACCEPTABLE

Before your students are able to receive criticism, they must accept you, and have confidence in you as an instructor. Your credentials, demeanor, competence, and authority all serve to build this acceptance.

Before your students willingly accept your critique, they must first accept you as an instructor.

COMPREHENSIVE

Your critique does not necessarily have to be lengthy to be comprehensive. Concentrate on covering both the good and bad points of the lesson. To keep your critique from getting too drawn out, try not to dwell on errors. Once your students understand their mistakes, move on to the next point.

CONSTRUCTIVE

Your critique should provide constructive criticism. Praise students for the things they did well and point out how they can use those abilities to improve weak areas. When discussing errors, you should always provide corrective actions that your students can use to improve their performance.

ORGANIZED

Almost any format for your critique is acceptable, as long as it is organized in some logical manner that is acceptable to both you and your student. A good technique is to start with something positive, cover the weak areas, and then end with something positive. This

Figure 2-58. One effective critiquing technique is to follow the sequence of events that occurred during the lesson. You can highlight areas where some problems occurred or where your student excelled.

During the preflight inspection, Chris did a great job of using the checklist.

While practicing steep turns, Chris lost 150 feet of altitude.

Chris performed his postflight duties very well.

helps promote the principle of effect, which states that learning is strengthened by a pleasant or satisfying feeling. [Figure 2-58]

THOUGHTFUL

During your critique, you need to be thoughtful of your student's feelings, especially with respect to self-esteem, recognition, and approval from others. To avoid belittling the dignity of your student, you may need to perform the critique in private.

SPECIFIC

You need to be specific during your critique, because using generalizations is of little value to your student. For example, if you say, *"Your landings were unsatisfactory."* your student has no clear idea of how to improve. However, if you say, *"You were holding 75 knots on final, but you should be at 65 knots."* your student knows exactly what needs to be corrected. When you conclude your critique, your student should have no doubts about what went well, what problems occurred, and how to correct the problems.

METHODS OF CRITIQUING

You may use several effective methods of critiquing. For example, to add interest and variety to the critiquing process, your students may review their own performance while you guide the discussion. Some of these methods are suitable for critiquing individual students while others are more appropriate to a classroom situation. Whichever method you choose, bear in mind that it is always your responsibility to ensure the critique is fair and accurate.

INSTRUCTOR/STUDENT CRITIQUE

The instructor/student method requires you to lead a group discussion in which members of the class are invited to offer criticism. For example, individual students in your ground school class could plan a cross-country flight, and then compare results in an open discussion/critique. Be aware that you need to control the critique carefully to prevent it from deteriorating into a free-for-all.

STUDENT-LED CRITIQUE

With this method, you ask one of your students to lead the critique. You can specify the framework of the critique, or leave it to the discretion of the student leader. Because of the inexperience of the participants, student-led critiques may not be as efficient as those that you lead, but they can stimulate interest and promote effective learning among students.

SMALL GROUP CRITIQUE

This method requires you to break the class into small groups, and assign each group a topic to critique. Then the groups present their findings to the class. For example, you could present the groups with several different accident reports and ask them determine the cause of the mishaps. This method can effectively teach your students how to work within groups to complete a task.

INDIVIDUAL STUDENT CRITIQUE BY ANOTHER STUDENT

This method calls for one of your students to critique the performance of a fellow student. For example, if you have two students that are training partners, you could have them critique each other. As with any critique, you must maintain control over the process.

SELF-CRITIQUE

The self-critique requires your students to review their own performance, and often this method can be an effective way to expose deficiencies. You must maintain control over the critique, and make allowances for your students' relative inexperience. Leave time at the end of the critique to add any of your final thoughts, and also be sure you and your students agree on what has been discussed regarding the performance during the lesson. [Figure 2-59]

Figure 2-59. Your students can gain valuable insights into their performance by critiquing themselves, while you provide a framework and guide the critique.

WRITTEN CRITIQUE

Written critiques have certain advantages over oral methods. You can devote more time to the critique and organize your thoughts more clearly, plus your students can keep the written critique and use it as a reference. However, written techniques will probably take longer to compose versus oral critiques.

EVALUATING YOUR STUDENTS

The purpose of an evaluation is to measure how well your students have learned the material in the course. You normally evaluate your students before, during, and after a

lesson, based on objectives and goals established in your lesson plan. If you find that your students are turning in faulty performances because they are overconfident, or if you have students that assume correcting errors is unimportant, you should increase the standard of performance for each lesson. [Figure 2-60]

Evaluating your student's learning should be an integral part of each lesson.

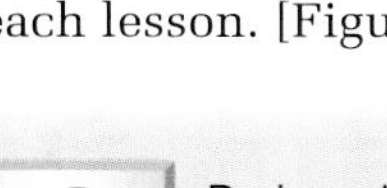

During a lesson, you should evaluate your student's performance and accomplishment based on goals and objectives you establish in lesson plans.

You should increase the standard of performance for each lesson if you have students who are turning in faulty performances due to overconfidence, or if you have students who assume correcting errors is unimportant.

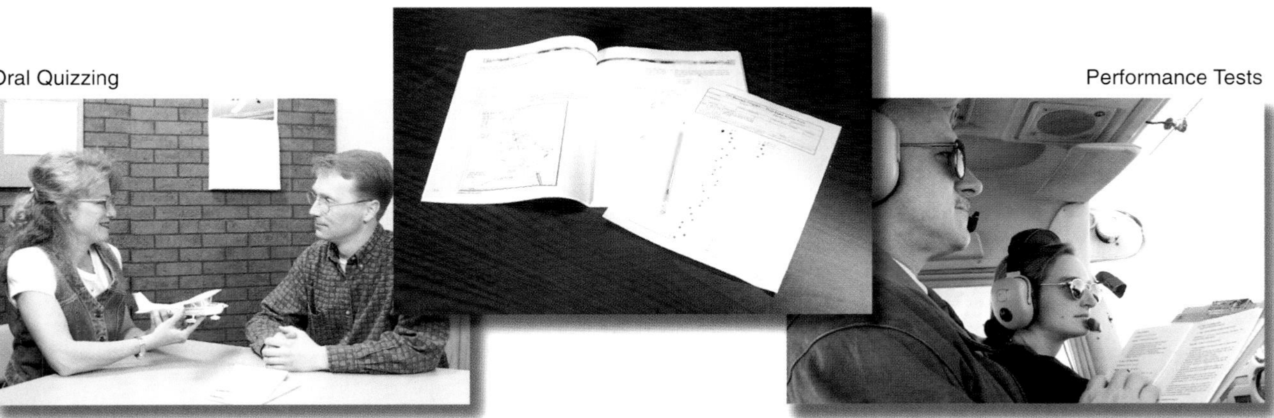

Figure 2-60. An evaluation may consist of oral quizzing, or it may be a planned event, such as a written test, or a practical test.

More Checkrides?

Once you obtain your flight instructor certificate, you may think you are done with checkrides and evaluations for a while, but do not get too complacent. You may choose to go on and get your instrument instructor and multi-engine instructor ratings, or you may have aspirations to fly for an airline someday.

When you fly for an airline, evaluations will become part of your job. Typically, at least once a year, your skills will be tested in a simulator where you may have to deal with a multitude of emergencies, from engine fires to electrical system failures. You may also get a surprise flight check, administered by the FAA. So, if you want to fly professionally, get used to being evaluated!

ORAL QUIZZING

Oral quizzing is the most common means of evaluating your student's knowledge. Questions generally may be divided into two broad categories —fact questions and thought-provoking questions. Fact questions test the lower levels of the cognitive domain and are usually concerned with who, what, where, and when. Thought-provoking questions test the upper levels of the cognitive domain and are usually concerned with how and why. For example, a fact question would be: *"Where is the elevator located?"* Conversely, a thought-provoking question could be phrased as follows: *"When the elevator is deflected, how does the airplane react?"* [Figure 2-61]

The use of proper oral quizzing during a lesson tends to promote active student participation.

Proper oral quizzing can identify points that need more emphasis and reveal the effectiveness of your training procedures.

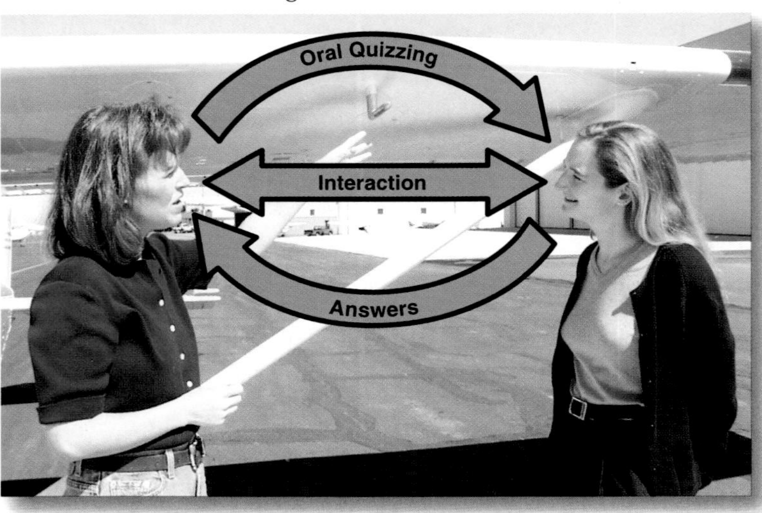

Figure 2-61. Proper oral quizzing can be a valuable learning tool for your students. Oral quizzing allows you to emphasize important points, promote your student's participation, identify your effectiveness as an instructor, and recognize areas where your student needs improvement.

CHARACTERISTICS OF EFFECTIVE QUESTIONS

You need to prepare if you are going to effectively quiz your students. One technique is to include questions in your lesson plan. Preplanned questions should be flexible enough to allow for spontaneous follow-up questions, based on the answers you receive. Effective questions center on one topic and have specific answers. Also, be sure your questions are brief, concise, and challenge your student's current level of knowledge. Remember to use good English and appropriate terminology. The use of slang or other inappropriate language has no place in effective oral quizzing.

During oral quizzing, your questions should be brief, concise, and call for specific answers that you readily evaluate.

To be effective in oral quizzing during the conduct of a lesson, a question should be difficult for that stage of training.

QUESTIONS TO AVOID

You should avoid asking questions that do not have a measurable answer. For instance, *"What is your opinion on the future of general aviation?"* would be a poor question for an oral quiz. Also, avoid questions like, *"Do you understand?"* or, *"Do you have any questions?"* The responses to these questions tell you very little about the knowledge level of your students. Students may tell you they understand when they really do not, and the fact they have no questions, also does not imply comprehension. In most cases, these questions provide no evidence of comprehension of the subject under discussion.

PUZZLE

What is the first action you should take if you are in a conventional-gear airplane with a weak right brake swerving left in a right crosswind during a full-flap, power-on wheel landing?

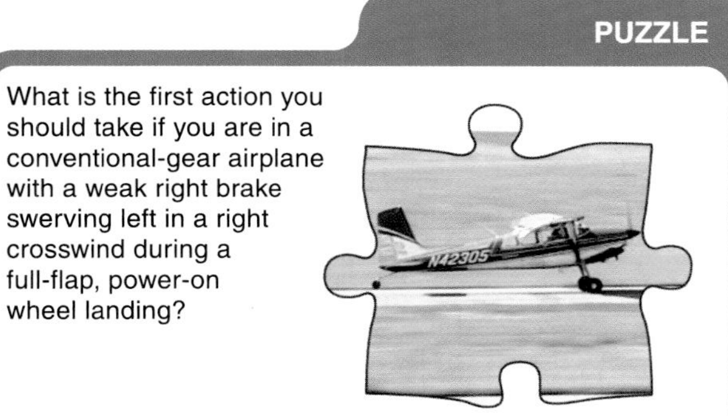

BEWILDERMENT

In reading the altimeter—you know you set a sensitive altimeter for the nearest station pressure—if you take temperature into account, as when flying from a cold airmass through a warm front, what precaution should you take when in a mountainous area?

OVERSIZED

HOW DOES AN AIRPLANE WORK?

TRICK

CFI: *"What should you do if you are on a VFR flight plan at FL210 in an airplane that is not RNAV equipped, and ATC advises you to expect direct routing to your destination?"*
Student: *"Advise ATC that I am not RNAV equipped."*
CFI: *"Wrong! You need to be on an IFR flight plan at FL210. Gotcha!"*

TOSS-UP

In an emergency, should you squawk 7700 or pick a landing spot?

Pick Landing Spot

Squawk 7700

IRRELEVANT

At what point should your airspeed be the lowest during a lazy eight?

Figure 2-62. Avoid questions like these because they will only confuse and frustrate your students.

Also, avoid trick questions because they may cause your students to feel as though they are engaged in a battle of wits with you. Finally, avoid asking questions that are irrelevant. The teaching process must be an orderly procedure of building one block of learning upon another in logical progression, until a desired goal is reached. Diversions, which introduce unrelated facts and thoughts, will only obscure this orderly process and slow your student's progress. Answers to unrelated questions are not helpful in evaluating your student's knowledge of the subject at hand. [Figure 2-62]

ANSWERING QUESTIONS FROM STUDENTS

When you answer questions from your students, you need to consider a few key points. Make sure you understand the question before you attempt to give an answer. You should display genuine interest in your students' questions, and make your answers as direct and accurate as possible. Through feedback, you can ensure your students' questions have been answered completely. Because people have different learning styles, some students may ask you questions that do not seem appropriate to the course material

Your students' confidence tends to be destroyed if you bluff whenever in doubt about some point.

It is important that you clearly understand your student's question, before you attempt an answer.

Of course you need a clearance to fly in Class C airspace. They have radar so you need a clearance. However, in the outer ring you just need a special squawk code to fly through that. And if you are landing at the primary airport, then you need GPS.

If you try to bluff or cover up, your students will be quick to sense it. This tends to destroy your student's confidence in you.

I don't know for sure if a mode C transponder is required in Class D airspace. Let's look it up to be sure.

Tell your students you will find the answer, and provide it to them later. Many times you and your students can research the answer together, creating a valuable learning experience.

being covered. Even though some questions might seem odd, make sure you answer them to your students' satisfaction. [Figure 2-63]

Figure 2-63. Should you encounter a question you cannot answer, freely admit that you do not know.

WRITTEN TESTS

Written tests are often used as evaluation devices. They include computerized tests as well as paper and pencil tests, and are often referred to as knowledge tests. A test is a set of questions, problems, or exercises (known as items) used to determine whether your students have a particular knowledge or skill. Test items measure a single objective, and call for a single response. Taking a test can be as simple as stating the correct answer to a true/false question or as complex as completing an airman knowledge written test. [Figure 2-64]

A person who the Administrator finds has cheated or committed an unauthorized act while taking an FAA knowledge test may not take another knowledge test within one year, and that person may have any of their certificates or ratings suspended or revoked.

To design effective tests, you should have an understanding of the characteristics they share; reliability, validity, usability, objectivity, comprehensiveness, and discrimination. See figure 2-65.

Be sure to stress the gravity of cheating on an FAA knowledge test to your students. If the Administrator finds a person has cheated or committed any unauthorized act while taking a knowledge test, that person is prohibited from taking an FAA knowledge test for one year. Also, that person may be subject to having any certificate or rating suspended or revoked.

TEST CHARACTERISTICS

Reliability is the degree to which test results are consistent with repeated measurements. For example, if a group of students took the same test a second time, they very likely would rank in the same order, although scores might improve slightly because of knowledge gained. The reliability of a test is equally important whether students are evaluated against each other or against a norm or standard.

Validity is the extent to which your test measures what it is supposed to measure. In other words, you must ensure that your test measures the learning objectives and nothing else.

Objectivity does not reflect the biases of the person grading the test. Selection-type tests are easy to grade objectively.

Comprehensiveness is the degree to which your test measures the overall course objectives. For example, a comprehensive airspace exam should cover many facets, such as VFR cloud clearance requirements, dimensions, entry requirements, and charting symbology.

Usability refers to the functionality of your tests. To make your test user friendly and facilitate grading, make sure the print and graphics are clear, and use concise language in both the test and the directions.

Discrimination is the degree to which your test measures small differences between your students' achievement levels. Your test must have a high degree of discrimination to distinguish the slight difference between students who are both high and low in achievement of the course objectives.

Figure 2-64. Effective tests usually share these characteristics.

So, You Wanna be a Parachute Rigger Master?

You will need to take a test. The FAA offers 68 knowledge tests, ranging from Aircraft Dispatcher to Parachute Rigger Master. In 1998, the FAA administered a total of over 129,000 knowledge tests. Some of the airplane knowledge tests breakdown as follows:

Average Test Scores:

Private Pilot Airplane 85%

Instrument Rating Airplane 85%

Commercial Pilot Airplane 89%

CFI Airplane 86%

CFI Instrument Airplane 89%

1998 FAA Airplane Knowledge Tests Given

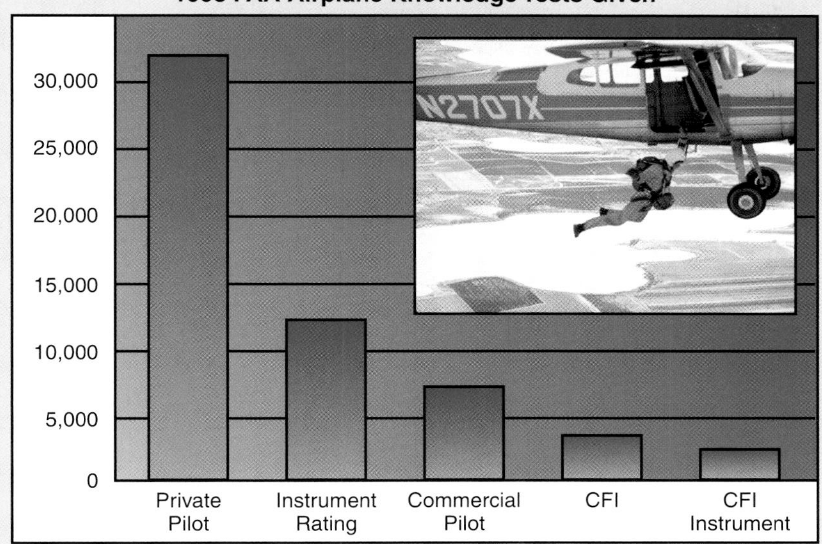

WRITTEN TEST DEVELOPMENT

When testing your students, you are usually concerned more with **criterion-referenced testing** than **norm-referenced testing**. Criterion-referenced testing evaluates student performance against a carefully written, measurable, standard or criterion; and norm-referenced testing measures your students' performance against other students. The FAA airman knowledge and practical tests are all criterion referenced, because it is necessary to measure performance against a high standard of proficiency, not other students.

You construct tests to evaluate progress toward standards that will eventually be measured at the conclusion of the training. Since tests are an integral part of the instructional process, it is important for you to be well-informed about recommended testing procedures. When developing written, criterion-referenced tests, it can be helpful to follow a four-step process. The process tends to follow a general-to-specific pattern. [Figure 2-65]

TEST DEVELOPMENT

General

Determine Level of Learning Objective
For example, at the analysis level of the cognitive domain, the objective for an instrument exam might be stated as *"Identify and describe the components and functionality of the instrument landing system (ILS)."*

List Indicators/Samples of Desired Behavior
For instance, your students should be able to successfully name the components of the ILS, such as the LOC, GS, OM, MM, IM, and approach lighting systems. They should be able to identify which components provide guidance information (LOC and GS), which provide range information (OM, MM, IM), and which provide visual information (approach lighting).

Establish Criterion Objectives
For example, the criterion objective for the previously mentioned instrument exam might be, *"Each student will demonstrate comprehension of the ILS by completing an exam with a grade of at least 70%."*

Develop Criterion-Referenced Test Items
Returning to the ILS exam, you would develop comprehensive questions that covered topics such as properly naming the components of the ILS, the function of each component, and how all these components work together to provide a precision approach. Depending on the stage of student training, you probably would limit the questions to aeronautical knowledge, rather than practical application of skills.

Specific

Figure 2-65. Following this four-step development process will help you identify the objective of your test and what questions to include in order to effectively determine your student's comprehension level.

WRITTEN TEST QUESTIONS

Written questions include two general categories, the supply-type and the selection-type. **Supply-type test items** require your students to furnish a response, and **selection-type test items** require your students to select from two or more alternatives.

SUPPLY-TYPE

This type of question may be useful when you cannot develop a selection-type problem that will properly measure your students' comprehension level. Supply-type questions are valuable in measuring your students' generalized understanding of a subject. For example, it could be very difficult to develop selection-type questions for a broad topic such as, aviation and its impact on the world economy.

The main disadvantage of supply-type test items is they cannot be graded uniformly. The same supply-type test graded by different instructors would probably be given different scores.

The main disadvantage of supply-type questions is that they are subjective. The same test graded by several instructors could easily result in different scores, or you may even grade the same test differently, depending on your mood, or the time of day. Another disadvantage of supply-type tests is the significant amount of time required for your students to complete it, and the time required for you to grade it.

SELECTION-TYPE

Selection-type tests are typically better suited toward aviation training and evaluation for several reasons. Unlike supply-type tests, selection-type tests are highly objective. For example, a selection-type test would always receive the same score, regardless of who grades it. Selection-type tests also make it possible to objectively compare your students' performance with one another, or with students in another class. Since selection-type tests typically take less time to complete, you can test more areas of knowledge than if you were using supply-type questions. Some examples of selection-type questions include true-false, multiple-choice, and matching.

One of the main advantages of selection-type test items over supply-type test items is that they can be graded objectively, regardless of the student or the grader.

True-false questions are well suited to testing your students' knowledge of facts and details. The biggest disadvantage with true-false questions is the fact that there are only two choices, so your students can guess, and still have a 50/50 chance of selecting the right answer. When you construct true-false questions, there are several principles that should be followed. [Figure 2-66]

True-false test items create the greatest probability of guessing.

A **multiple-choice** question is probably the most common type you will use to evaluate students. You may use this type of test question to determine students' achievement, ranging from acquisition of facts to understanding, reasoning, and your students' ability to apply what they have learned. Multiple-choice questions consist of two parts: the stem, which includes the question, statement, or problem, and a list of alternatives or responses. Incorrect answers are called distractors. [Figure 2-67]

One of the major difficulties encountered in the construction of multiple-choice test items is inventing distractors that will be attractive to students lacking knowledge or understanding.

Multiple-choice test items that are intended to measure achievement at a higher level of learning, should have some or all of the alternatives as acceptable, and one that is clearly better than the others. Also, you should try to keep the length of the alternatives similar.

- Include only one idea in each statement.
  True/False — The NTSB requires immediate notification after an accident has occurred.
- Use original statements rather than verbatim text.
  True/False — You can transition Class C airspace without receiving a specific clearance.
- If negatives must be used, underline or otherwise emphasize the negative.
  True/False — You cannot spin an airplane that is not stalled.
- Statements should be entirely true or entirely false.
  True/False — Often students can transition into high-performance airplanes with about five hours of instruction, but sometimes it takes some students longer.
- Avoid the unnecessary use of negatives. They tend to confuse your students.
  True/False — You should not continue the landing approach if you cannot determine if you are cleared to land or not cleared to land.
- Avoid involved statements. Keep wording and sentence structure as simple as possible. Make statements both definite and clear.
  True/False — Traffic advisories, but not resolution advisories, are provided by the traffic alert and collision and avoidance system II.
- Avoid the use of ambiguous words and terms (some, any, generally, most times, etc.)
  True/False — Generally helicopter pilots are better at transitioning to airplanes than glider pilots.
- Whenever possible, use terms which mean the same thing to all students.
  True/False — Most little aircraft use a 4-stroke powerplant to provide thrust through a horizontally mounted airfoil.
- Avoid absolutes (all, every, only, no, never, etc.) These words are known as determiners and provide clues to the correct answer. Since unequivocally true or false statements are rare, statements containing absolutes are usually false.
  True/False — The only time you can declare an emergency is when you have an engine failure due to fuel contamination.
- If a statement is controversial (sources have differing information), the source of the statement should be listed.
  True/False — Pitch controls airspeed and power controls altitude.
- Avoid patterns in the sequence of correct responses because students can often identify the patterns.
- Make statements brief and about the same length. You may unconsciously make true statements longer than false ones. Students are quick to take advantage of this tendency.

Figure 2-66. By applying these principles, you can increase the validity of your true-false questions. The principles are followed by examples of true-false questions that either do or do not meet the criteria for good questions.

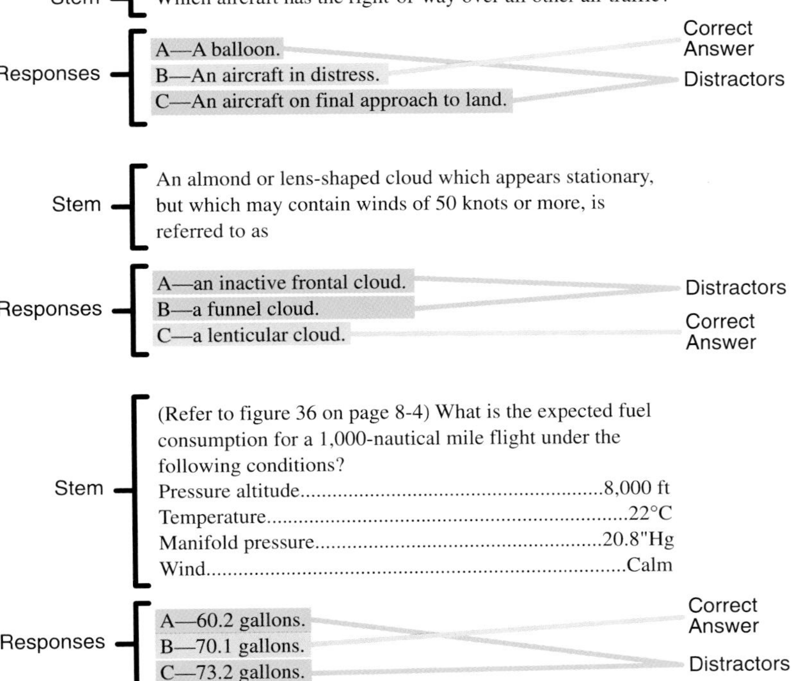

Figure 2-67. A multiple-choice stem may take several forms. For example it may be a direct question, an incomplete sentence followed by several possible phrases, or a problem based on a graph or diagram. The correct response and the distractors follow the stem.

When you design the stem of a multiple-choice question, there are some general principles that should be followed. The stem should clearly present the central problem or idea, and contain only material relevant to its solution. Generally, try to avoid using *"a"* or *"an"* at the end of the stem, because they may give away the correct answer. Be sure that every alternative fits grammatically with the stem. Also, it is generally best to avoid the use of absolutes, such as *"always"* or *"without exception"*, when writing the stem. Using these principles will help to ensure that the test item is valid.

You should formulate the distractors carefully, simply being incorrect should not be the only criteria. Some effective distractors that can be used are a common misconception, a true statement that does not satisfy the requirements of the problem, or a statement that is either too broad or too narrow for the question. To be effective, multiple-choice questions must include plausible distractors, as well as the most correct answer.

Of the selection-type tests, the matching type reduces the probability of guessing correct responses.

Matching tests are particularly good for measuring your student's ability to recognize relationships and to make associations between terms, parts, words, and phrases. Some of the principles you should follow for matching tests are: use language your students can understand, test only essential information, and give specific and complete instructions.

PERFORMANCE TESTS

Performance tests are good for evaluating competency with respect to an operation, a procedure, or a process. Throughout your students' training, their abilities will be evaluated with performance tests, such as stage exams and the practical test for their pilot certificate. Your job is to prepare students for performance tests by giving them instructions, evaluating their performance, and finally determining if they meet the performance criteria for a particular test.

A performance-type test is desirable for evaluating training that involves an operation, procedure, or process.

The performance criteria for practical tests are published in the Practical Test Standards (PTS). The purpose of the PTS is to outline the standards by which FAA inspectors and designated pilot examiners conduct tests for ratings and certificates. The objective of the PTS is to ensure the certification of pilots at a high level of performance and proficiency, consistent with safety. Similarly, most training syllabi contain performance standards for stage checks.

EVALUATING YOUR OWN PERFORMANCE

Often you can gain insight into your own performance when you evaluate your students' performance. Your proficiency as a CFI is directly related to how well your students progress through their training. By monitoring items like your students' feedback and training records, you might be able to pick up certain trends. For example, if the majority of your students are having trouble with power-on stalls, then you may want to re-evaluate the way you teach this maneuver. You can also simply ask your students, *"Is there anything I could do to help you understand?"* Many times students will have valuable feedback that you can use to enhance your teaching ability.

Another useful tool you can use to rate yourself is your students' performance during stage exams or practical tests. How your students do during a performance test is typically a direct reflection on how well you have prepared them, or in other words, what kind of job you have done as a CFI. Feedback from an examiner or another flight instructor that has flown with your students can provide you with some excellent self-evaluation tools.

Flight Review Blues

As a CFI, you could be faced with a situation where you have to evaluate a pilot who has much more experience than you. Consider the following scenario where a new CFI, Lisa, is giving the ground portion of a flight review to a retired airline Captain, Ed, who just bought a Cessna 182-RG to use for personal travel.

Lisa (CFI) *"Let's take a look at some VFR cloud clearance minimums. . . "*

Ed (Pilot) *"I don't plan on flying VFR. Just move on to something different."*

Lisa (CFI) *"I feel you should at least be familiar with cloud clearance minimums, even though you don't think you'll fly VFR."*

Ed (Pilot) *"I told you, I'm flying IFR! I've got 20,000 hours of heavy jet time, and I don't need to know all that VFR garbage!"*

Lisa (CFI) *"Well, maybe you're right. I'm sorry. Let's move on to some performance charts for your Skylane RG."*

In this scenario, Lisa was intimidated by Ed's experience level. Lisa lost control of the lesson, and gave in to Ed's demands, even though she felt that it was important for Ed to be familiar with VFR cloud clearance requirements.

Remember that you are the CFI, and you must be satisfied before you endorse someone's logbook. If worse comes to worse, and your student refuses to cooperate, you may want to consider ending the lesson, and recommend your student work with another CFI.

SUMMARY CHECKLIST

- ✓ The ability to properly critique and evaluate your students' performance is one of the most crucial skills you must have as an instructor.
- ✓ A critique is a step in the learning process, and an evaluation is a part of the overall grading process.
- ✓ Critiques are designed to provide your students with constructive feedback that they can use to improve future performance.
- ✓ The purpose of an evaluation is to measure how well your students have learned the material in the course. An evaluation may consist of oral quizzing, or it may be a planned event, such as a written test, or a practical test.
- ✓ Oral quizzing is the most common method of evaluating your students' knowledge.
- ✓ If your students ask you a question that you cannot answer, freely admit that you do not know. Never try to cover up the fact that you are unsure of the answer.
- ✓ Effective written tests usually share certain characteristics: reliability, validity, usability, objectivity, comprehensiveness, and discrimination.

- ✓ When you develop written tests for your students, you are usually more concerned with criterion-referenced testing than norm-referenced testing. Criterion-referenced testing measures students' performance against a standard and norm-referenced testing measure students' performance against other students.
- ✓ Written test questions include two general categories: the supply-type and the selection-type. Selection-type tests are typically better suited toward aviation training and evaluation, primarily because they are highly objective.
- ✓ Some examples of selection-type questions include true-false, multiple-choice, and matching. Multiple-choice questions are probably the most common type that you will use to evaluate students.
- ✓ Performance tests are good for evaluating competency with respect to an operation, a procedure, or a process. A practical test is a good example of a performance test.
- ✓ You should continually evaluate your CFI skills. Often you can gain insight into your own performance when you evaluate your students' performance.

KEY TERMS

Critiques

Evaluations

Oral Quizzing

Written tests

Reliability

Validity

Objectivity

Comprehensiveness

Usability

Discrimination

Criterion-Referenced Testing

Norm-Referenced Testing

Supply-Type Test Items

Selection-Type Test Items

True-False

Multiple-Choice

Matching

QUESTIONS

1. Describe the difference between a critique and an evaluation.
2. True/False. Your critique should not contain any negative feedback because negativity compromises the principle of effect, and little learning will result.
3. Name two advantages that a written critique has over oral methods.
4. True/False. You normally evaluate your students before, during, and after a lesson.
5. What is a characteristic of an effective oral quiz question?

   A. It has a measurable answer.
   B. It should not be challenging because your student may become frustrated.
   C. It should be broad enough to evaluate a wide scope of your student's knowledge.

6. What should you do if you cannot answer your student's question?

   A, Give your best guess, with the disclaimer that it may not be right.
   B. Admit that you do not know, but you will find the answer and provide it later.
   C. Give an answer, because your student will lose confidence in your ability if you divulge that you do not know.

7. True/False. A written test displays validity if it measures what it is supposed to measure.

8. Name one advantage selection-type tests have over supply-type tests.

9. True/False. Performance tests are good for evaluating competency with respect to an operation, a procedure, or a process.

10. How would you fix the following multiple choice question?

    What do all pilots do every time they have an emergency?

    A. They squawk 7700.
    B. They advise ATC.
    C. All of the above.

CHAPTER 3

EXPLORING HUMAN FACTORS

Flight Instructor
Volume 1 — Fundamentals of Instruction

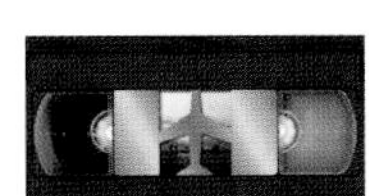

SECTION A
UNDERSTANDING HUMAN BEHAVIOR

Do you remember what compelled you to learn to fly? Was it a childhood dream you had from the first time you saw an airplane in the sky? Did you admire a relative or family friend who was a pilot? Did you think learning to fly would earn you respect and admiration? No matter what your reason for learning to fly, the fact is that there was an impetus that led you to this point in your flying career. As you prepare to be a flight instructor, it is important to realize that all of your students will have some source of motivation that drives them to sign up for that first flight lesson. Your job as an instructor is to provide an environment that assists your students in feeling compelled to learn. To do so, it is important that you have a fundamental understanding of why students act the way they do.

INFLUENCING HUMAN BEHAVIOR

The relationships you have with your students directly impact how much they learn. Since your students see you as an authority, you have the ability to influence their behavior. Every student is unique and should be looked upon as an untapped resource. All students have a desire to achieve some goal. Motivating factors may be the recognition and acceptance of one's peers, success itself, a grade, or accomplishing a lifelong dream. You need to assist your students in achieving their goals by directing their actions and modifying their behavior. Without your active intervention, students may become passive and resistant to learning.

It is important that you do not make quick assumptions about your students' abilities. Students who at first glance appear to be lazy, uncooperative, indifferent, or antagonistic may become conscientious pilots with the right guidance from you. Most students have

Work is as natural as play and rest

Work may be a source of satisfaction and performed voluntarily.

When work is a form of punishment, most people try to avoid it.

Most people exercise self-direction and control in the pursuit of goals.

A person's commitment to a particular goal relates directly to the reward associated with the achievement of that goal, most significantly—ego gratification.

Under proper conditions, the average person learns to seek responsibility. Shirking responsibility and lack of ambition are not inherent in human nature, but are usually consequences of experience.

Devoting a high degree of imagination, ingenuity, and creativity to solving common problems comes naturally to many people.

Under the conditions of modern life, the average person's intellect is only partially used.

Figure 3-1. Some generalizations concerning motivation and human nature, typically applied to industrial management, can also be used to your advantage.

the ability to learn, and you can help make the most of their potential by understanding how basic human drives and needs affect the training process. [Figure 3-1]

HUMAN NEEDS

It is critical that all of your students' basic human needs are satisfied prior to engaging in pilot training. In 1938, psychologist Henry A. Murray published a catalog of human needs and during the 1950s, Abraham Maslow organized Murray's findings according to their level of importance. Commonly referred to as **Maslow's hierarchy of human needs**, they are often depicted as a pyramid, increasing in complexity toward the pinnacle. [Figure 3-2]

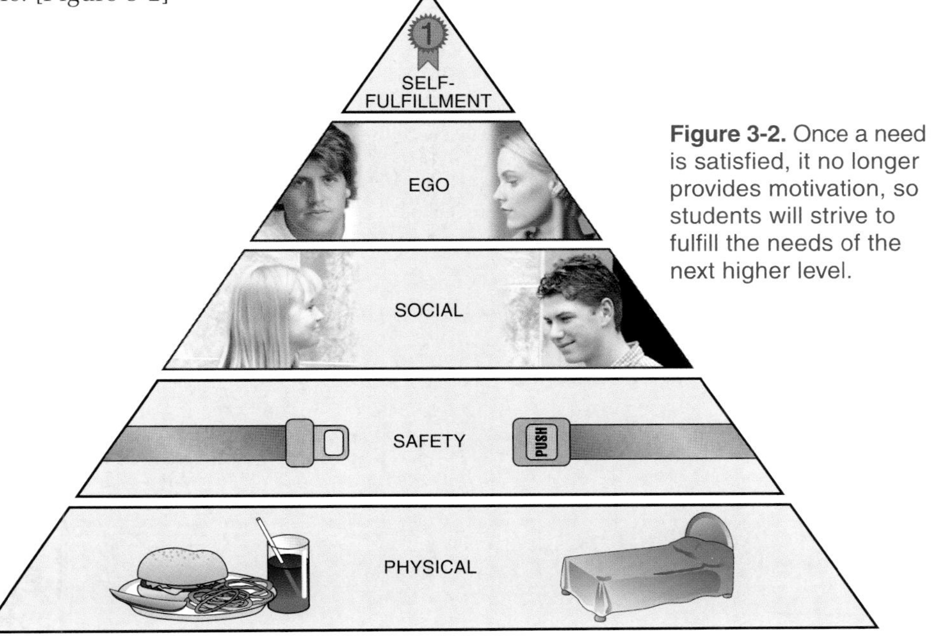

Figure 3-2. Once a need is satisfied, it no longer provides motivation, so students will strive to fulfill the needs of the next higher level.

PHYSICAL

At the bottom of the pyramid is the broadest, most elementary category—the **physical needs**. These needs encompass the necessities for survival, which include food, rest, exercise, and protection from the elements. Until these requirements are satisfied, your students cannot fully concentrate on learning, self-expression, or any other tasks. You should monitor your students' behavior to make sure that their physical needs have been met. [Figure 3-3]

Before students can concentrate on learning, their physical needs must be satisfied.

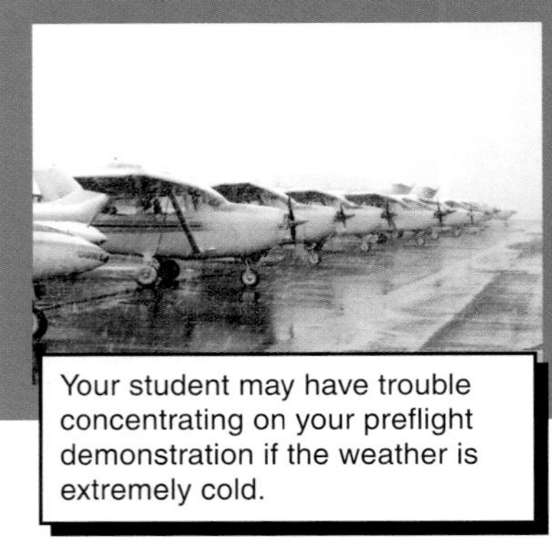

Your student may have trouble concentrating on your preflight demonstration if the weather is extremely cold.

Performance may suffer during an early morning flight if your student has not had a good night's sleep.

A lesson scheduled over the lunch hour may not be productive if your student is hungry.

Figure 3-3. It is difficult for students to perform well when they are hungry or tired.

SAFETY

The next level of Maslow's hierarchy, known as the **safety needs**, includes protection against danger, threats, and deprivation. Sometimes referred to as the security needs, they directly relate to flying. Since safety is a major concern among your students, during the initial stages of training you should avoid accentuating the dangers of flying. In addition, you should emphasize to your students that throughout their training they will be taught procedures and gain skills which will enable them to cope with nearly every hazardous situation that could occur in flight.

No News is Good News

How often have you heard a news report documenting the journey of a little airplane which took off, flew through the air, and landed safely at its destination? Many people's only knowledge of flight comes from newspaper headlines that report each aircraft accident in detail while statistics confirming the safety of flight are not deemed as newsworthy. Consequently, many students may begin flight training with an exaggerated fear for their safety.

Often, our judgment is affected by the ease with which events can be recalled rather than by an analysis of the frequency with which particular situations occur. Vivid and unusual events reported by the media are most often remembered. We seldom notice non-occurrences in the news, such as the absence of aircraft accidents. In this way, the media can cause us to formulate false perceptions of the risk involved in certain activities and actually influence us to engage in more hazardous pursuits. For example, per mile traveled, flying is much safer than driving. However, not only can media coverage of airplane catastrophes affect a prospective student's feeling toward pilot training, it can actually steer people onto the more dangerous roadways.

SOCIAL

After physical and safety needs are met, it becomes possible for students to satisfy their **social needs**. These are the needs to belong and to associate, as well as to give and receive friendship and love. Since students are usually out of their normal surroundings during flight training, their desire for association and belonging is more pronounced.

After your students are physically comfortable and have no fear for their safety, their social needs become the prime influence on their behavior.

EGO

One type of **egoistic need** relates to your students' self esteem and is directly linked to their self-confidence, independence, achievement, competence, and knowledge. Another type relates to your students' reputation, such as status, recognition, appreciation, and respect of associates. [Figure 3-4]

Figure 3-4. The egoistic need may be the main reason for a student's interest in aviation.

SELF-FULFILLMENT

Self-fulfillment needs occupy the highest level of Maslow's pyramid. They include realizing one's own potential for continued development, and for being creative in the broadest sense. Maslow included various cognitive and aesthetic goals in this echelon. Your student's self-fulfillment should offer the greatest challenge for you. [Figure 3-5]

Your student's self-fulfillment needs offer the greatest challenge to you as an instructor.

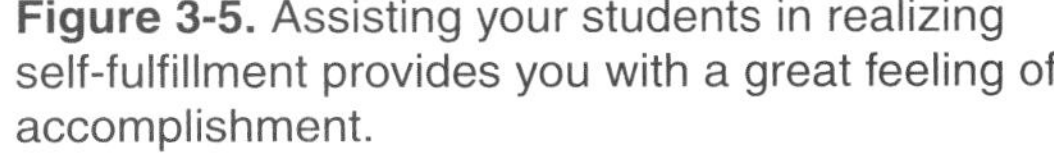

Figure 3-5. Assisting your students in realizing self-fulfillment provides you with a great feeling of accomplishment.

DEFENSE MECHANISMS

Students use **defense mechanisms** to alleviate feelings of failure and guilt, as well as to protect their sense of personal worth or adequacy. Introduced by Freud in the 1890s, these psychological security systems are subconscious, almost automatic, ego-protecting reactions to unpleasant situations.

COMPENSATION

Students who use **compensation** as a method of psychological defense often attempt to disguise the presence of a weak or undesirable quality by emphasizing a more positive one. They may lower the scope of their goals in order to avoid the chance of failure in pursuit of more difficult goals. Students who regard themselves as unskilled pilots may accentuate their winning personalities to compensate for their lack of flying ability.

PROJECTION

Projection is used by students to relegate blame for their own shortcomings, mistakes, and transgressions to others or to attribute their motives, desires, characteristics, and impulses to other people. The athlete who fails to make the team may feel sure the coach was unfair, and the tennis player who examines the racket after a missed shot is projecting blame. When students say the teacher gives them too much homework so they are not able to study for the exam, they are projecting.

RATIONALIZATION

If students cannot accept the real reasons for their behavior, they may use **rationalization**. This device permits them to substitute excuses for reasons; moreover, they can make those excuses plausible and acceptable to themselves. Rationalization is a subconscious technique for justifying actions that otherwise would be unacceptable. When true rationalization takes place, individuals sincerely believe in their excuses.

When your students cannot accept the real reasons for their behavior and use excuses to justify inadequate performance, it is an indication of the defense mechanism known as rationalization.

DENIAL OF REALITY

Occasionally students may ignore or refuse to acknowledge disagreeable realities. They may turn away from unpleasant sights, refuse to discuss unpopular topics, or reject criticism. One example of **denial of reality** in everyday life can be seen in people who become so involved with work that they ignore marital, child-rearing, or other personal problems.

REACTION FORMATION

Sometimes students protect themselves from dangerous desires by not only repressing them, but by actually developing conscious attitudes and behavior patterns that are just the opposite. This defense mechanism is known as **reaction formation**. A student may develop a who-cares-what-other-people-think attitude to cover up feelings of loneliness and a hunger for acceptance.

FLIGHT

Students may seek relief from frustrating situations by taking **flight**, physically or mentally. To take flight physically, students may develop symptoms or ailments that give them acceptable excuses for avoiding lessons. More frequent than physical flights are mental flights, or daydreaming. Mental flight provides a simple escape from problems. If students get sufficient satisfaction from daydreaming, they may stop trying to achieve their goals altogether. When carried to

When students engage in daydreaming, they display the defense mechanism known as flight. Students will use this mechanism when they want to escape from frustrating situations.

Flight from Flight

- Laurie phones you to cancel yet another lesson due to illness.
- Jim stopped scheduling flights while he *"finishes up an important project at work."* He promised to return to his training in two weeks, yet it has been over a month and you have not heard from him.
- Karen does not show up for scheduled lessons or is so late that often there is not enough time left during the lesson period to fly.
- When weather conditions are poor, you normally conduct ground school sessions. Jeff consistently ignores marginal weather reports he has received during briefings and tries to convince you conditions are ideal for flying.

Each of these students is taking flight, but unfortunately not in an airplane. If your student is avoiding training, you need to launch an investigation to determine the reasons for this exodus from the sky. Think back to previous lessons. Were there any upsetting experiences during a flight, or is your student beginning to have difficulty with a particular area of instruction? You may be able to prompt your student to return to training by providing encouragement, alleviating a fear, or promising to spend extra time on a difficult subject area.

- During your last lesson, you informed Laurie that on the next flight, you most likely would authorize her to solo for the first time. She is anxious about flying solo and is embarrassed to admit her fears to you.
- Jim is used to excelling at most of his pursuits, however his training in a multi-engine airplane has taken longer than he expected. When he began instruction, he was very clear about many hours he anticipated spending to gain his rating.
- Karen experienced motion sickness during a previous lesson while practicing attitude instrument flight.
- While Jeff is skilled in the airplane, he is apprehensive about ground school. During previous sessions, you have noticed that he had trouble understanding the material.

Now that you have discovered the reasons for the flight of these students, what could you do to help encourage them to overcome their concerns and continue to pursue training?

extremes, the world of desire and the world of reality can become so confused that the dreamer cannot distinguish one from the other. This is referred to as fantasy.

AGGRESSION

Anger is a normal, universal human emotion and everyone gets angry occasionally. Angry people may shout, swear, slam a door, or give in to the heat of emotions in a number of ways, displaying **aggression** against something or somebody. After a cooling-off period, they may see their actions as childish. In a classroom or airplane such extreme behavior is relatively infrequent, partly because students are taught to repress their emotions. Because of safety concerns or social structures, student aggressiveness may be expressed in subtle ways. They may ask irrelevant questions, refuse to participate in the class activities, or disrupt the group. If students cannot deal directly with the cause of their frustration, they may vent their aggressiveness on a neutral object or person not related to the problem.

When students display the defense mechanism called aggression, they may refuse to participate in class activities or ask irrelevant questions.

RESIGNATION

While instructing, you may encounter students who become frustrated as a result of their perceived lack of ability or understanding. This frustration can cause them to lose interest and accept defeat, no longer believing it is worthwhile or even possible to go on. The most obvious cause for this form of **resignation** takes place when, after completing an early phase of a course without grasping the fundamentals, students become more bewildered during the advanced phases. If your students allow themselves to fall into this cycle, without additional help from you, learning is negligible, although they may go through the motions of participating. The negative self-concept reflected by this defense mechanism likely contributes to failure to remain receptive to new experiences, and it creates a tendency for students to reject additional training. [Figure 3-6]

A negative self-concept is the factor which contributes most to a student's failure to remain receptive to new experiences, and which creates a tendency to reject additional training.

When students become bewildered and lost in the advanced phase of training after completing the early phase without grasping the fundamentals, they may exhibit the defense mechanism of resignation.

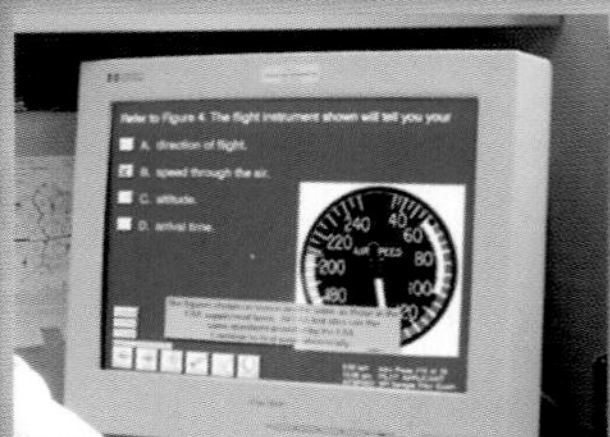

Compensation — Jack recently received his private pilot certificate but still lacks confidence in his flying ability. He often asks his instructor Steve to fly with him. Steve notices that Jack lacks coordination and is inconsistent in his judgment. Knowing that his flying is less than ideal, Jack often tells jokes and funny stories while flying with Steve to compensate for his poor skills.

Projection — Terry enrolled in a ground school, for which her father paid. After attending the school once a week for two months, she takes the FAA knowledge test and fails. Instead of facing the fact that she did not study, Terry blames her father for suggesting she attend the class on Friday nights after busy work weeks.

Denial of Reality — Harry is a private pilot preparing for his commercial check ride. Tom, his instructor, suggests he fly solo to practice landings. During a flight, Harry incorrectly enters the pattern and repeatedly cuts in front of other traffic. Tom is alerted to Harry's dangerous performance, and asks Harry if he has an explanation for his actions. Harry angrily denies having done anything wrong and storms away from the flight school.

Rationalization — Although the flight school at which Julie trains has several airplanes to choose from, she insists on flying the same one during every lesson. When she arrives at the airport, her instructor informs her that, due to a scheduling error, her favorite airplane is not available. During her lesson, Julie blames all or her mistakes on the airplane.

Reaction Formation — During a solo flight, Mike, a student pilot, ground loops an airplane. After receiving constructive criticism from his friends who are pilots, he thinks to himself, *"I'm a good pilot. They don't know what they're talking about. Who needs friends like them?"*

Flight — Instrument training is very difficult for Jane, so to avoid having to face her fear of failure, she often calls her instructor to cancel her flight lessons. She feigns an illness or exaggerates the weather forecast to make the conditions sound more ominous than they really are.

Resignation — Eric is a new student pilot who has no previous flight experience. After several lessons, Eric gets so frustrated with his inability to control the airplane that he quits flight training.

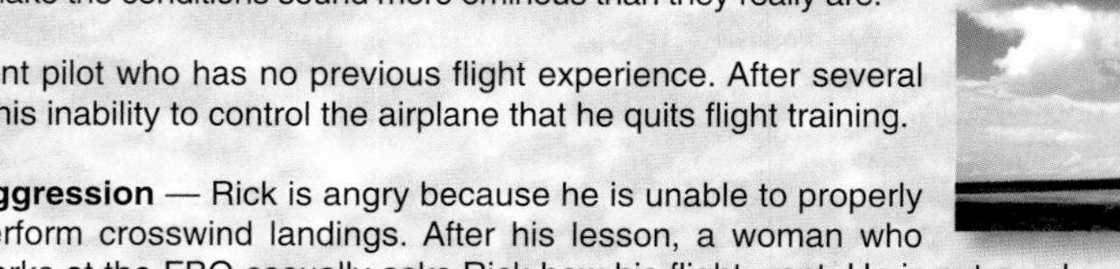

Aggression — Rick is angry because he is unable to properly perform crosswind landings. After his lesson, a woman who works at the FBO casually asks Rick how his flight went. He is extremely rude to her and snaps, *"Why don't you mind your own business?"*

Figure 3-6. If you learn to recognize defense mechanisms in the training environment, you can begin to address student frustrations.

Although defense mechanisms can serve a useful purpose, they can also be a hindrance because they involve self-deception and distortion of reality. Defense mechanisms do not solve problems. They only alleviate symptoms, not causes. Operating on a subconscious level, defense mechanisms are not subject to normal conscious checks and controls. If

you realize that your student is using a defense mechanism, try to identify the cause of the problem and then work to restore your student's motivation and self-confidence.

Although defense mechanisms can serve a useful purpose, they can also be a hindrance because they involve self-deception and distortion of reality.

It may be difficult for you to identify excessive reliance on defense mechanisms by a student; however, there are factors that can alert you to potential problems. A personal crisis or other stressful event, such as a death in the family, a divorce, or even a failing grade on an important test may trigger harmful defensive reactions. Physical symptoms such as a change in personality, angry outbursts, depression, or a general lack of interest may point to a problem. Drug or alcohol abuse also may become apparent. Less obvious indications may include social withdrawal, preoccupation with certain ideas, or an inability to concentrate. In severe cases involving the possibility of deep psychological problems, you should recommend that your student talk with a mental health professional.

PRACTICAL PSYCHOLOGY FOR FLIGHT INSTRUCTORS

While you may not be an accomplished psychologist, there are a number of factors which can assist you in analyzing student behavior and recognizing problems before and during each lesson. You also must be able to evaluate student personalities to effectively use appropriate instruction techniques.

ANXIETY

Defined as a state of mental uneasiness arising from fear, **anxiety** results from the apprehension for anything, real or imagined, which threatens the person experiencing it. Anxiety can have a powerful effect on your students' actions and ability to learn from perceptions. More visible in some students than others, it is often a significant psychological factor affecting flight instruction. Flying is a potentially threatening experience for those who are not accustomed to being off the ground. Student responses to anxiety vary extensively, ranging from a reluctance to act, to the impulse to do something even if it is wrong. Some students affected by anxiety react appropriately and more rapidly than they would in the absence of threat. Others may freeze and be incapable of doing anything to correct the situation causing their anxiety. At times, students may do things without rational thought or reason.

One way you can counteract student anxiety is by reinforcing the enjoyment to be gained from flying. You also need to treat your student's fear as a normal reaction, rather than ignoring it. Keep in mind that anxiety for student pilots usually is associated with certain types of flight operations and maneuvers. You should introduce these maneuvers with care, so your students know what to expect, and what their reactions should be. When introducing stalls, for example, you should first review the aerodynamic principles and explain how stalls affect flight characteristics. Then, carefully describe the sensations to be expected, as well as the recovery procedures. [Figure 3-7]

Figure 3-7. Choosing a calm, clear day to take a new student on a short introductory flight is one way of minimizing any anxieties that exist about learning to fly.

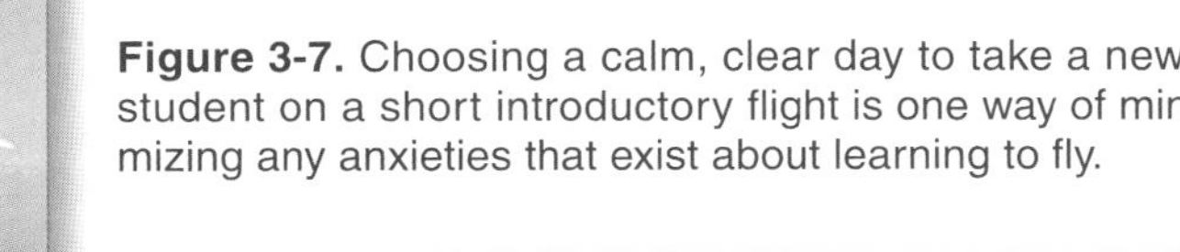

You can counteract anxiety in your students by treating their fears as normal reactions.

Student anxieties can be minimized throughout training by emphasizing the benefits and pleasurable experiences that can be derived from flying, rather than by continuously citing any serious consequences. You can explain to your students that safe flying practices are conducive to satisfying, efficient, uninterrupted operations and are not necessary only to prevent catastrophe.

NORMAL REACTIONS TO STRESS

When a threat is recognized or imagined, the brain alerts the body. The adrenal gland activates hormones, which prepare the body to meet the threat, or to retreat from it. Often called the fight-or-flight syndrome, the body prepares itself to react to an event perceived as threatening. During this period, the heart rate quickens, blood vessels constrict to divert blood to the organs that need it, and numerous other physiological changes take place.

When under stress, normal individuals usually react by responding rapidly and exactly, often automatically, within the limits of their experience and training.

When experiencing a stressful situation, average individuals begin to respond rapidly and exactly, within the limits of their experience and training. Many responses are automatic, which points out the need for proper training in emergency operations prior to an actual emergency. It is critical when encountering a stressful situation that your student has been taught to think rationally, act rapidly, and remain extremely sensitive to the environment.

ABNORMAL REACTIONS TO STRESS

For some people, reaction to stress does not produce actions that are regarded as normal. With these individuals, reactions to anxiety or stress may be inadequate or completely absent. Their responses may be random, illogical, or they may do more than is called for by the situation. During flight instruction, you are normally the only one who can observe students when they are under pressure. Therefore, you are in a position to differentiate between safe and unsafe pilot actions. You also may be able to detect potential psychological problems. [Figure 3-8]

Inappropriate laughter or singing, or extreme overcooperation are indications that a student is reacting abnormally to stress.

Figure 3-8. These student reactions are indicative of abnormal reactions to stress. None of them provide an absolute indication, but the presence of any of them under conditions of stress is reason for careful evaluation.

PSYCHOLOGICALLY ABNORMAL STUDENTS

After careful consideration of all available evidence, if you believe a student may be suffering from a serious psychological abnormality, you have a legal responsibility to refrain from approving that student for solo operations. You also must ensure that this student does not continue flight training or become certificated as a pilot. [Figure 3-9]

When you suspect your student may have a disqualifying psychological defect, arrangements should be made for another instructor, who is not acquainted with your student, to conduct an evaluation flight. After the flight, you should confer with the instructor to determine whether further investigation or action is justified.

A discussion should be held with a local aviation medical examiner (AME), preferably the one who issued the student's medical certificate, to obtain advice and to decide on the possibility of further examination of the student.

You should initiate an informal discussion with the local Flight Standards District Office (FSDO) to suggest that your student may be able to meet the skill standards, but may be psychologically unstable. Take action as soon as you have reason to question your student's mental fitness. Do not wait until your student is preparing to solo.

Figure 3-9. Although this may seem like a difficult task, there are steps you can take to help confirm the psychological makeup of your student. This enables you to effectively respond to students who are determined to be unbalanced.

If, after consultation with an unbiased instructor, your local Flight Standards District Office (FSDO), and an aviation medical examiner, you believe that your student suffers a serious psychological deficiency, you should not authorize or recommend your student to fly solo or take a practical test. Refer your student to a mental health professional.

SUMMARY CHECKLIST

✓ You can help make the most of your students' potential by understanding how basic human drives and needs affect the training process.

✓ Maslow's hierarchy of human needs is often depicted as a pyramid, increasing in complexity toward the pinnacle.

✓ Physical needs encompass the necessities for survival, which include food, rest, exercise, and protection from the elements.

✓ Safety needs include protection against danger, threats, and deprivation and they relate directly to flying.

✓ Social needs include the desire to belong and to associate, as well as to give and receive friendship and love.

- ✓ One type of egoistic need relates to your students' self esteem and is directly linked to their self-confidence, independence, achievement, competence, and knowledge. Another type relates to your students' reputation, such as status, recognition, appreciation, and respect of associates.
- ✓ Self-fulfillment needs occupy the highest level of Maslow's pyramid. They include realizing one's own potential for continued development, and for being creative in the broadest sense.
- ✓ Students use defense mechanisms to alleviate feelings of failure, and guilt, as well as to protect their sense of personal worth or adequacy.
- ✓ Students who use compensation as a method of psychological defense often attempt to disguise the presence of a weak or undesirable quality by emphasizing a more positive one.
- ✓ Projection is used by students to relegate blame for their own shortcomings, mistakes, and transgressions to others or to attribute their motives, desires, characteristics, and impulses to other people.
- ✓ If students cannot accept the real reasons for their behavior, they may rationalize, which allows them to substitute excuses for reasons and make those excuses plausible and acceptable to themselves.
- ✓ When students ignore or refuse to acknowledge disagreeable realities, they are denying reality.
- ✓ When students exhibit reaction formation, they are protecting themselves from dangerous desires by not only repressing them, but by actually developing conscious attitudes and behavior patterns that are just the opposite.
- ✓ Students may seek relief from frustrating situations by taking flight, physically or mentally. When students engage in daydreaming, they display this defense mechanism.
- ✓ When students display the defense mechanism called aggression, they may refuse to participate in class activities or ask irrelevant questions.
- ✓ Resignation can take place when, after completing an early phase of a course without grasping the fundamentals, students become more bewildered during the advanced phases. This frustration can cause them to lose interest and accept defeat, no longer believing it is worthwhile or even possible to go on.
- ✓ Although defense mechanisms can serve a useful purpose, they can also be a hindrance because they involve self-deception and distortion of reality.
- ✓ Defined as a state of mental uneasiness arising from fear, anxiety results from the apprehension for anything, real or imagined, which threatens the person experiencing it.
- ✓ You can counteract anxiety in your students by treating their fears as a normal reaction.
- ✓ When under stress, normal individuals usually react by responding rapidly and exactly, often automatically, within the limits of their experience and training.
- ✓ Inappropriate laughter or singing, or extreme overcooperation are indications that your student is reacting abnormally to stress.
- ✓ If, after consultation with an unbiased instructor, your local Flight Standards District Office (FSDO), and an aviation medical examiner, you believe that your student suffers a serious psychological deficiency, you should not authorize or recommend your student to fly solo or take a practical test.

KEY TERMS

Maslow's Hierarchy of Human Needs	Projection
Physical Needs	Rationalization
Safety Needs	Denial of Reality
Social Needs	Reaction Formation
Egoistic Needs	Flight
Self-Fulfillment Needs	Aggression
Defense Mechanisms	Resignation
Compensation	Anxiety

QUESTIONS

1. Describe each level of Maslow's hierarchy of needs.
2. True/False. Once a need is satisfied, it no longer provides motivation, so students will strive to fulfill the needs of the next higher level.

Match the following defense mechanisms (items 3 through 10) to the appropriate examples of student behavior (items A through H).

3. Projection	A. Asking irrelevant questions and refusing to participate in class activities
4. Compensation	B. Losing interest and accepting defeat
5. Denial of reality	C. Disguising an undesirable quality by emphasizing a more positive one
6. Reaction formation	D. Blaming others for their own shortcomings and mistakes
7. Rationalization	E. Substituting excuses for the real reasons for their behavior
8. Aggression	F. Developing attitudes opposite to their actual desires
9. Flight	G. Refusing to accept disagreeable realities
10. Resignation	H. Developing aliments and daydreaming

11. Provide a specific example of a student who may be exhibiting the defense mechanism of flight.
12. Name a way you can counteract student anxiety about flying.

SECTION B
MAKING DECISIONS

John has natural flying ability. He successfully masters flight maneuvers with ease and is comfortable in a wide variety of situations encountered during training. His instruction has proceeded quickly and he performs procedures correctly with only a minimum amount of guidance from you, his instructor. You feel confident he will be able to pass his private pilot practical test without difficulty.

Sarah has a strong desire to learn, but flying does not come naturally to her. She has taken more hours of flight time than the average student to complete her training, and as a result she has required a high level of attention from you. She feels uncomfortable in some flying situations and has openly communicated her concerns to you. While you feel she is competent to pass her practical test, she most likely will need frequent refresher training to maintain her piloting skills and her confidence level.

Which of these students is more likely to be involved in an incident or accident? While John may possess superior piloting skills, this does not necessarily mean that he is a safer pilot than Sarah. Not long after passing his private pilot practical test, John was involved in an incident. [Figure 3-10]

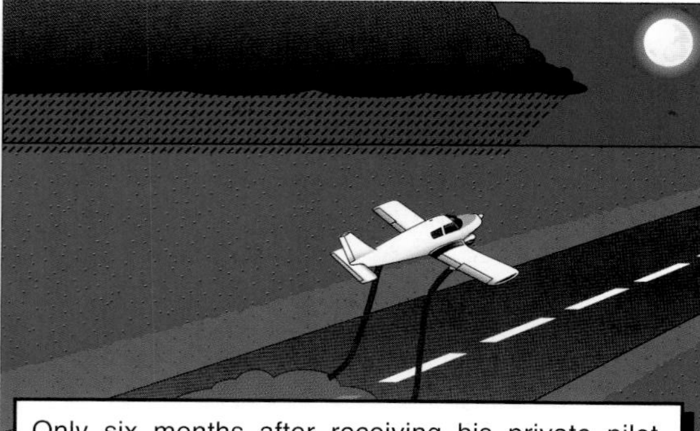

Figure 3-10. The safety of your students relies heavily on their ability to make effective decisions.

Since flying came easily to John, he became overconfident in his abilities. While he is capable of executing the proper procedures, he lacks decision-making skills. He does not possess good judgment nor recognize his limitations. While Sarah may not display the same piloting abilities as John, she does make effective decisions. She recognizes her limitations and avoids situations that require skills she does not have, as well as frequently enlists help from an instructor when she has questions about a maneuver or procedure.

As an instructor, is there something you could have done to prevent John's incident? You can never know for sure but you may be able to increase the safety of your students by providing instruction in aeronautical decision making with the same effort you apply to teaching other aspects of flying.

EXPLORING AERONAUTICAL DECISION MAKING

Aeronautical decision making (ADM) is a systematic approach to the mental process used by aircraft pilots to consistently determine the best course of action in response to a given set of circumstances. As an instructor, you must not only posses the ability to make effective decisions during flight training situations, you must be able to convey ADM principles to your students that apply to their level of experience. Beginning with their very first flight lesson, you must emphasize to your students that there is more to pilot training than acquiring technical knowledge and gaining proficiency in aircraft control. Understanding how their mind and body functions when they fly is as important as knowing the operation of the airplane's systems and equipment. For while tremendous changes in technology continue to be made to improve flight safety, one factor remains the same; the human factor. It is estimated that approximately 75% of all aviation accidents are human factors related. [Figure 3-11]

The first airplane fatality was Lieutenant Thomas Etholen Selfridge, a passenger killed in a crash of a Wright airplane at Fort Myer, Virginia, on September 17, 1908. Pilot Orville Wright survived the crash.

Courtesy of National Archives

You should teach aeronautical decision making to students beginning with the first lesson.

Figure 3-11. In the early years of aviation, the majority of accidents were the result of mechanical difficulties or weather conditions which were so severe the pilot's skills were not sufficient to cope. While aviation's safety record has steadily improved as technology has progressed, accidents still occur.

Teaching students to make sound decisions is key to preventing accidents. Traditional pilot instruction has emphasized flying skills, knowledge of the aircraft, and familiarity with regulations. ADM training focuses on the decision-making process and the factors which affect a pilot's ability to make effective choices. Not only does poor judgment lead

Faulty Construction vs. Faulty Turns

A 1911 report listed the four leading causes of airplane accidents:

1. faults of construction
2. mistakes of the pilot
3. state of the weather, and
4. fault of the public, or special or unknown factors.

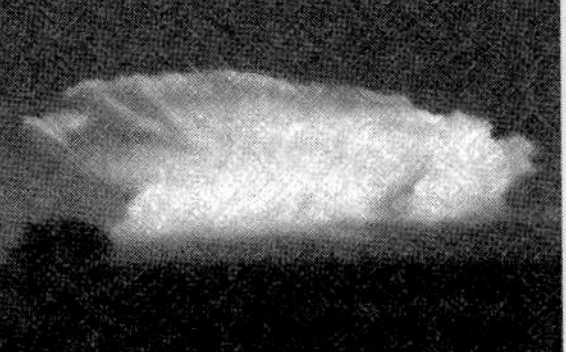

The report covered 47 accidents and 3 fatalities in 1909, and 101 accidents and 28 fatalities in 1910. Almost half of the accidents and more than half of the deaths were due to construction problems. Faulty turns were the leading pilot errors. The public cause of accidents involved the *"imprudences of spectators,"* according to the *Scientific American* summary of the French-prepared report.

to a majority of accidents, studies have shown there is a strong link between errors in decision making and the severity of accidents. Simple problems with skills may produce minor injuries and damage, while faulty decision making often results in accidents with serious injuries and fatalities.

Your students may have heard the term **pilot error** used to describe the causes of many accidents, but this term can be misleading. Pilot error means an action or decision made by the pilot was the cause of, or contributing factor which led to an accident. However, the phrase **human factors related** more aptly describes these accidents since it usually is not a single decision which leads to an accident, but a chain of events triggered by a number of factors. The **poor judgment chain**, sometimes referred to as the error chain, is a term used to describe this principle of contributing factors in a human factors related accident. It is critical that students understand this concept since breaking one link in the chain normally is all that is necessary to change the outcome of the sequence of events. One of the best ways to explain this idea to students is to discuss a specific situation which led to an aircraft accident or incident. Figure 3-12 provides an example of the type of scenario which can be presented to students to illustrate the poor judgment chain. By discussing the events that led to this incident, you can help students understand how a series of judgmental errors contributed to the final outcome of this flight.

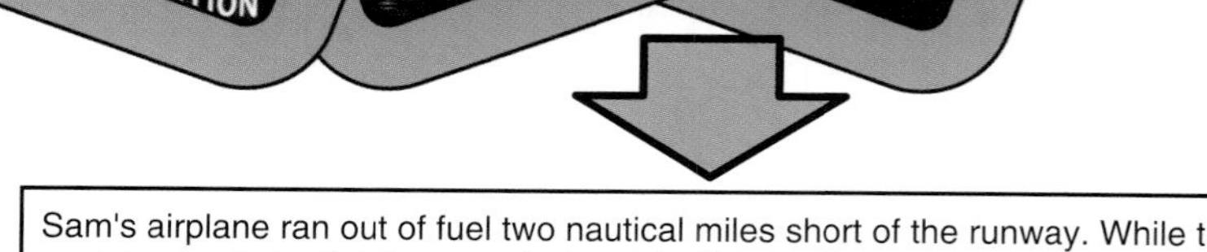

Figure 3-12. On numerous occasions during the flight, the pilot could have made effective decisions which may have prevented this incident. However, as the chain of events unfolded, each poor decision left him with fewer and fewer options.

APPLYING ADM TO INSTRUCTION

Just as you would prepare to present a technical subject, you must formulate and implement a plan to teach ADM concepts to students. Since many students learn about decision making by example, at a minimum you can ensure that you exercise good judgment during training situations and explain to your students the reasons behind your choices. While this method may generate some student decision-making skills, an organized and well-developed program of human factors training normally yields greater results.

DISCOVERING THE HISTORY OF ADM TRAINING

The idea that organized instruction is necessary to effectively address human factors and pilot judgment concepts was initially conceived by the airline industry. In response to accidents caused by pilot error, the airlines implemented extensive ADM training programs known as **crew resource management (CRM)**. [Figure 3-13] These programs focus on the effective use of all available resources including human resources, hardware, and information. Although the CRM concept originated through the airlines to improve decision making in the cockpit, CRM principles, such as workload management, situational awareness, communication, the leadership role of the captain, and crewmember coordination have direct application to the general aviation cockpit. [Figure 3-14]

1972, Eastern, L-1011, Miami — The aircraft descended into the Everglades while the crew was distracted trying to resolve a landing gear problem which turned out to be a burned-out bulb.

1977, Pan American and KLM, both B-747s, Tenerife, Canary Islands — During the takeoff roll, the KLM airplane collided with the Pan American 747 due to a mix-up in communication.

1978, United, DC-8, Portland — The aircraft ran out of fuel and crashed short of the runway due to confusion among the crew about the status of the landing gear, and a breakdown in cockpit communication about the fuel state.

1982, Air Florida, B-737, Washington National — The aircraft crashed shortly after takeoff due to airframe and engine icing. The co-pilot expressed concern about the flight situation prior to, and during, the takeoff roll.

Figure 3-13. These four accidents were the prime motivators which led the airline industry to implement human factors training.

CREW RESOURCE MANAGEMENT (CRM)

CRM "...refers to the effective use of ALL available resources; human resources, hardware, and information." Human resources "...includes all other groups routinely working with the cockpit crew (or pilot) who are involved in decisions that are required to operate a flight safely. These groups include, but are not limited to: dispatchers, cabin crewmembers, maintenance personnel, and air traffic controllers." CRM is not a single TASK, it is a set of skill competencies that must be evident in all TASKS in this PTS as applied to either single pilot or a crew operation.

Figure 3-14. You should point out to students that displaying CRM skills is an important part of any practical test. A description of CRM can be found in the practical test standards publications.

Figure 3-15. To explain the decision-making process, you can introduce the following steps with the accompanying scenario that places the student in the position of making a decision about a typical flight situation.

1 **Recognize a Change** — You notice a change has occurred or an expected change did not occur.

While on a cross-country flight, you become aware of increasing cumulonimbus clouds forming along your route.

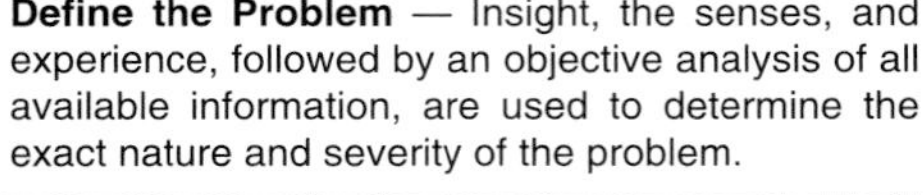

2 **Define the Problem** — Insight, the senses, and experience, followed by an objective analysis of all available information, are used to determine the exact nature and severity of the problem.

Since the weather briefing you received prior to the flight forecast clear skies, you contact Flight Watch to obtain an update. An amended forecast indicates a chance of thunderstorms ahead toward your destination. While the radar report does not display any echoes yet, PIREPs in the area indicate increasingly turbulent conditions. Your observations of the vertical development of the clouds alert you to how quickly these storms are developing. Based on your experience, you believe it will be difficult to continue to your destination without encountering at least some of the conditions caused by the changing weather.

3 **Choose a Course of Action** — You must evaluate the need to react to the problem and determine the actions that may be taken to resolve the situation in the time available. Before you decide on a response the expected outcome of each possible action must be considered and the risks assessed.

You consider the hazards associated with thunderstorms and your ability to cope with severe weather if you continue to your destination. You also consider your fuel burn if you turn around and land at a nearby airport that you have passed along your route or divert off course. After studying the chart, you conclude that you will have plenty of fuel to reach an airport located behind your position. A Flight Watch briefer informs you that the conditions are good at this airport and there are fueling services available. You decide that the best course of action is to land there and wait until the weather clears to continue to your destination.

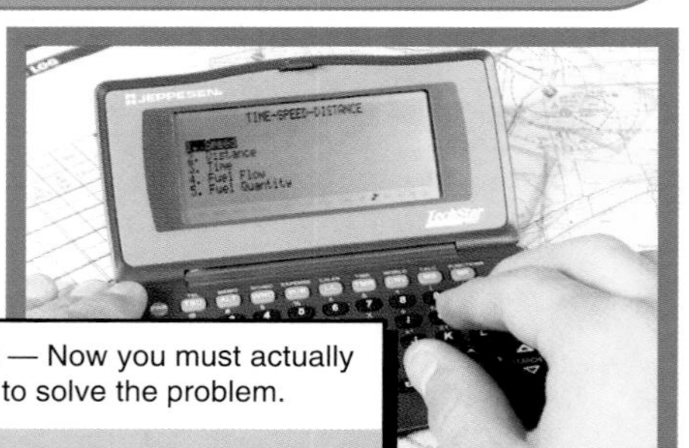

4 **Implement the Decision** — Now you must actually take the necessary steps to solve the problem.

To implement your decision, you plot the course changes, and calculate a new estimated time of arrival and fuel burn, as well as contact the nearest flight service station to amend your flight plan.

5 **Evaluate the Outcome** — Although a decision may be reached and a course of action implemented, the decision-making process is not complete. It is important to think ahead and determine how the decision could affect other phases of the flight. As the flight progresses, you must continue to evaluate the outcome of the decision to ensure that it is producing the desired result.

As you proceed to the nearest airport, you continue to monitor the weather conditions and aircraft performance to ensure that no additional steps need to be taken to guarantee the safety of the flight.

Crew resource management training has proven extremely successful in reducing accidents, and airlines typically introduce CRM concepts during initial indoctrination of new hires. You can learn from this example when conducting ADM training. In the past, some students were introduced to ADM concepts toward the completion of their training or not at all. It is important that these concepts are incorporated throughout the entire training course for all levels of students; private, instrument, commercial, multi-engine, CFI, and ATP.

EXPLAINING THE DECISION-MAKING PROCESS

People make choices every day, but how often do they think about what is involved to reach decisions? An understanding of the **decision-making process** provides your students with a foundation for developing ADM skills. Traditionally, pilots have been well trained to react to emergencies, but are not as prepared to make decisions which require a more reflective response. Some situations, such as an engine failure, require immediate action using established procedures with little time for detailed analysis. However, during most flights, there is time to examine any changes which occur, gather information, and assess risk before reaching a decision. When you present aeronautical decision making to students, it is essential to discuss how the steps in the process apply to an actual flight situation. [Figure 3-15]

PROBLEM DEFINITION

You should emphasize to students the importance of correctly defining the problem during the decision making process. For example, failure of a indicator light to illuminate could indicate that the landing gear is not down and locked in place or it could mean the bulb is burned out. The necessary actions in each of these circumstances would be significantly different. An inaccurate assessment of the situation can actually create additional difficulties. For this reason, once an initial assumption is made regarding the problem, other sources must be used to verify that the conclusion is correct. [Figure 3-16]

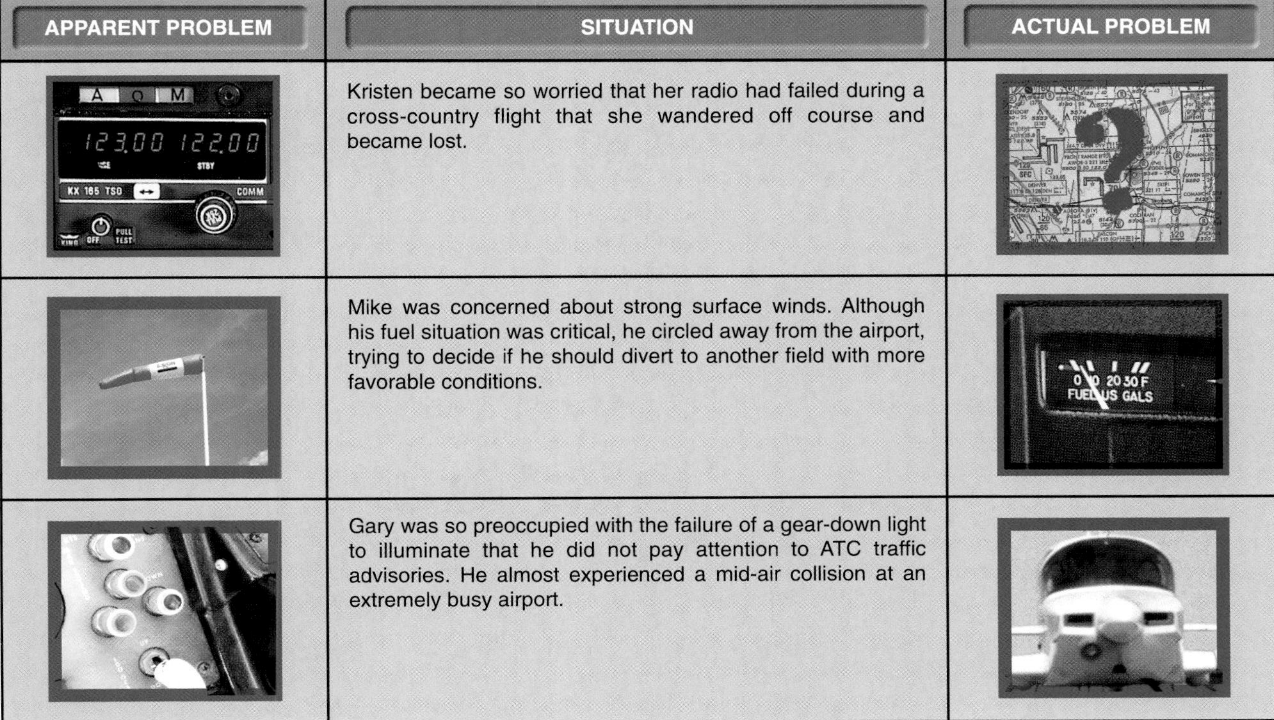

APPARENT PROBLEM	SITUATION	ACTUAL PROBLEM
	Kristen became so worried that her radio had failed during a cross-country flight that she wandered off course and became lost.	
	Mike was concerned about strong surface winds. Although his fuel situation was critical, he circled away from the airport, trying to decide if he should divert to another field with more favorable conditions.	
	Gary was so preoccupied with the failure of a gear-down light to illuminate that he did not pay attention to ATC traffic advisories. He almost experienced a mid-air collision at an extremely busy airport.	

Figure 3-16. Fixating on a problem that does not exist can divert attention from important tasks. By presenting specific examples of this type of occurrence, you can impress upon your students that failure to maintain an awareness of the circumstances regarding the flight can *become* the problem.

ASSESSING RISK

One skill your students need to learn to make effective decisions is how to assess risk. When your students are faced with making a decision regarding a flight, you can ask them to evaluate the status of the four **risk elements** — the pilot in command, the aircraft, the environment, and the operation. [Figure 3-17]

Pilot — Your fitness to fly must be evaluated including competency in the airplane, currency, and flight experience.

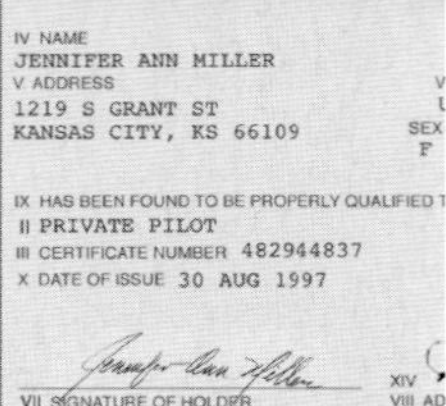

You are a noninstrument-rated private pilot with approximately 200 total hours of flight time, the majority of which is in this airplane, including only 10 hours of night flying experience. You grabbed a quick bite to eat as you drove to the airport, after working all day.

Aircraft — The airplane's performance, limitations, equipment, and airworthiness must be determined.

The airplane is in good condition and has received all the required inspections, However, it is equipped with only basic navigation equipment and does not have an autopilot.

Environment — Factors, such as weather, airport conditions, and the availability of air traffic control services must be examined.

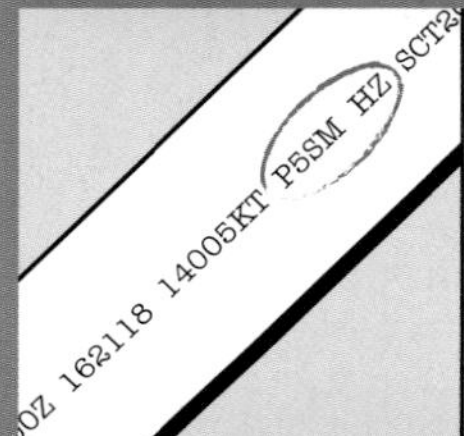

It is dusk and a portion of your flight will occur over water. Although the weather is clear, visibility is forecast to be 5 miles in haze.

Operation — The purpose of the flight is a factor which influences your decision on undertaking or continuing the flight.

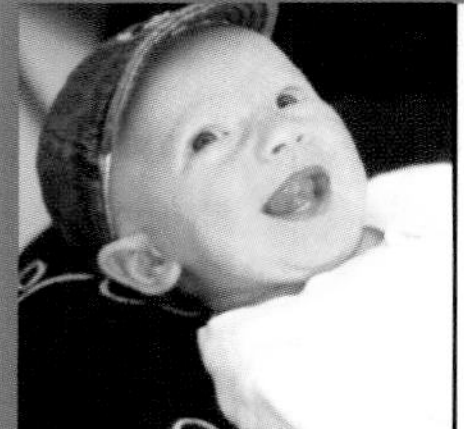

You are leaving on a Friday to attend a family celebration for your sister's new baby the next day.

Situation — To maintain situational awareness, an accurate perception must be attained of how the pilot, aircraft, environment, and operation combine to affect the flight.

While you have experience in the airplane, lack of extensive night flying and instrument time may limit your abilities in this situation. Taking off after a long week at work with little opportunity to rest and eat well can cause fatigue which can adversely affect your judgment. While the airplane is not lacking any necessary equipment, advanced navigation systems and an autopilot would reduce your workload. If the forecast weather conditions materialize, the lack of a clear horizon over water and the reduced visibility could make you very susceptible to spatial disorientation. Your desire to attend the family event could influence you to take chances or make a poor decision about continuing the flight if you have difficulties enroute.

Figure 3-17. Provide your students with a scenario and ask them to evaluate the risk elements to reach a go/no go decision. You can point out the factors they should consider to achieve an accurate perception of the flight situation. In this case, postponing the flight is a good decision.

Reviewing accident and incident research with your students can help develop their ability to more effectively assess risk. Delving into accident statistics can provide details that can increase student understanding of the risks involved with specific flying situations. For example, the majority of accident sequences begin during phases of flight that take up relatively little flight time but contain the highest number of critical tasks and the highest task complexity. Studies also indicate the types of flight activities that are most likely to result in the most serious accidents. [Figure 3-18]

Takeoff/initial climb accidents frequently are due to the pilot's lack of awareness of the effects of density altitude on aircraft performance or other improper takeoff planning resulting in loss of control or stalls during, or shortly after takeoff.

The majority of weather-related accidents occur after attempted VFR flight into IFR conditions. According to one yearly report, in multi-engine airplanes, 16.2% of fatal accidents were weather-related. For single-engine retractable gear airplanes, the figure was 47.2%. Darkness increases the likelihood of having a weather-related accident.

ACCIDENT CAUSES
PILOT-RELATED ACCIDENTS

	All Accidents	Fatal Accidents
Preflight/Taxi	4.2% (52)	1.9% (4)
Takeoff/Climb	21.2% (262)	14.2% (35)
Fuel Management	6.2% (77)	3.2% (8)
Weather	5.3% (65)	21.9% (54)
Other Cruise	2.4% (29)	6.9% (17)
Descent	1.5% (19)	0.8% (2)
Approach	7.8% (96)	14.2% (35)
Go-Around	3.0% (37)	2.8% (7)
Maneuvering	10.9% (135)	25.5% (63)
Landing	35.8% (441)	2.4% (6)
Other	1.6% (20)	6.5% (16)

Percent (0–40)

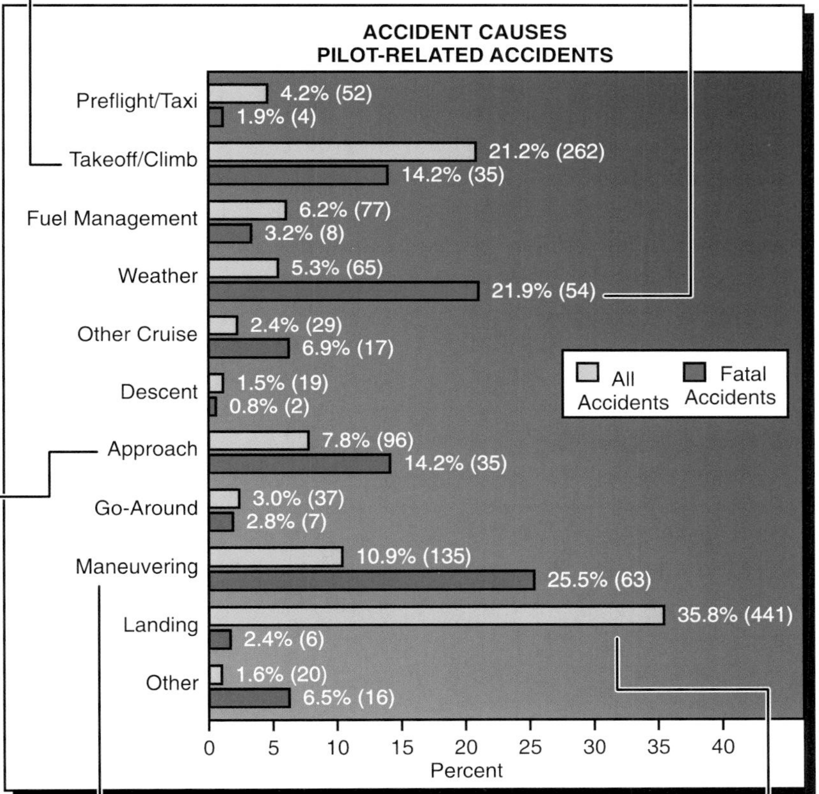

Fatal accidents that occur during approach often happen at night or in IFR conditions.

Maneuvering flight is one of the largest single producers of fatal accidents and many of these accidents are attributed to maneuvering during low, slow flight, often during buzzing or unauthorized aerobatics.

Although takeoff and landing account for less than 5% of a typical cross-country, the majority of accidents occur during these phases of flight. However, most of these accidents are not fatal.

Figure 3-18. Each year, the AOPA Air Safety Foundation publishes the Nall report which provides a detailed review of general aviation accidents compiled from NTSB data from the previous year. You can use this type of information to teach your students about risk.

Risky Business

Your new role as an instructor will present you with some unique factors that you have not had to consider previously when making go/no go decisions. Consider the scenario outlined here and evaluate the four risk elements.

Pilot — This is your fifth instructing flight of the day. You grabbed a quick lunch from the vending machines between flights.

Aircraft — You will be flying a Cessna 152 for this lesson.

Environment — Field elevation at the airport is 5,000 feet and the temperature is close to 90°F. There is a forecast for scattered thunderstorms and you can see some cumulonimbus clouds building to the west, although currently it is clear at the airport.

Operation — The scheduled lesson is to practice landings with your student. This will be her second session with a focus on landings.

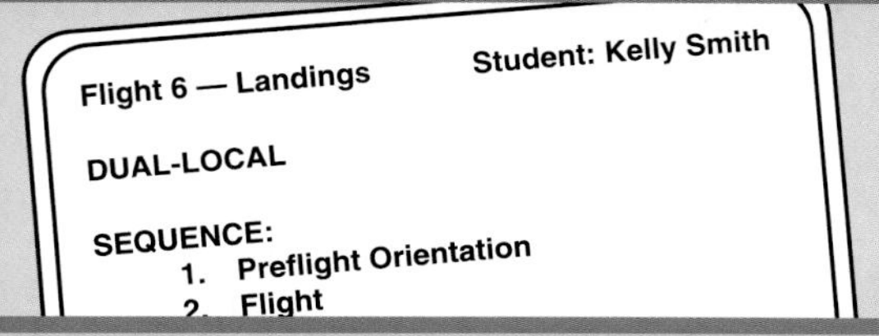
Flight 6 — Landings Student: Kelly Smith

DUAL-LOCAL

SEQUENCE:
1. Preflight Orientation
2. Flight

Situation — After considering each element, you determine that it is best to reschedule this lesson. You are fatigued and devoting the amount of attention needed to a complex lesson will be difficult. The high density altitude will significantly affect the performance of the C-152, and the heat also will be uncomfortable for both you and your student, creating an unfavorable learning environment. The building thunderstorms are also a factor. Even if they do not materialize over the airport, strong winds and turbulence generated by their development may increase the lesson's difficulty. You decide to conduct a ground lesson which covers these factors and helps your student learn about decision making.

CREATING ADM LESSONS

Since providing instruction in judgment and effective decision making is a unique part of pilot training, the methods you use to teach ADM concepts differ from those used to present other subjects. While you prepare specific lesson plans to introduce and review each flight procedure and knowledge area, ADM applies to every lesson. During both flight and ground lessons, you must be prepared to address ADM concepts as they relate to particular operations and procedures, as well as conduct specific lessons that focus on decision making and the role of human factors in aviation. [Figure 3-19]

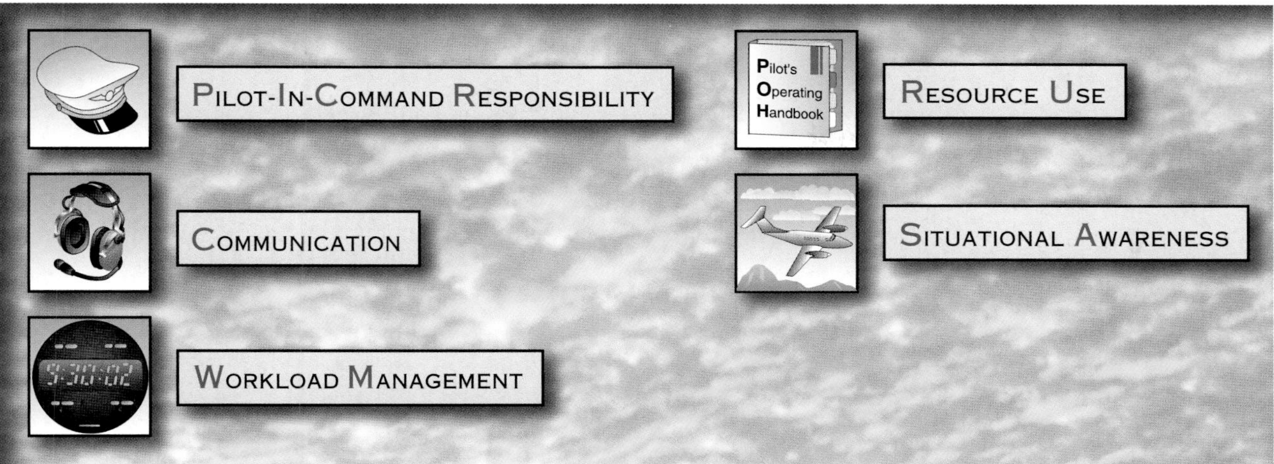

Figure 3-19. To help you teach effectively, you can organize the factors which influence aeronautical decision making into five elements.

Reviewing information from the National Transportation Safety Board (NTSB) and NASA's Aviation Safety Reporting System (ASRS) is an excellent way to help your students understand the elements which influence decision making and the consequences of poor judgment. The NTSB maintains a database of accident synopses and compiles accident statistics. ASRS reports describe situations that pilots felt compromised aviation safety. The ASRS investigates the causes underlying a reported event, and incorporates each report into a database which provides information for research regarding aviation safety and human factors. Each report is held in strict confidence and the FAA cannot use ASRS information in enforcement actions against those who submit reports. The ASRS publication *Callback* includes excerpts from ASRS reports with supporting commentaries, summaries of ASRS research studies, and related safety information.

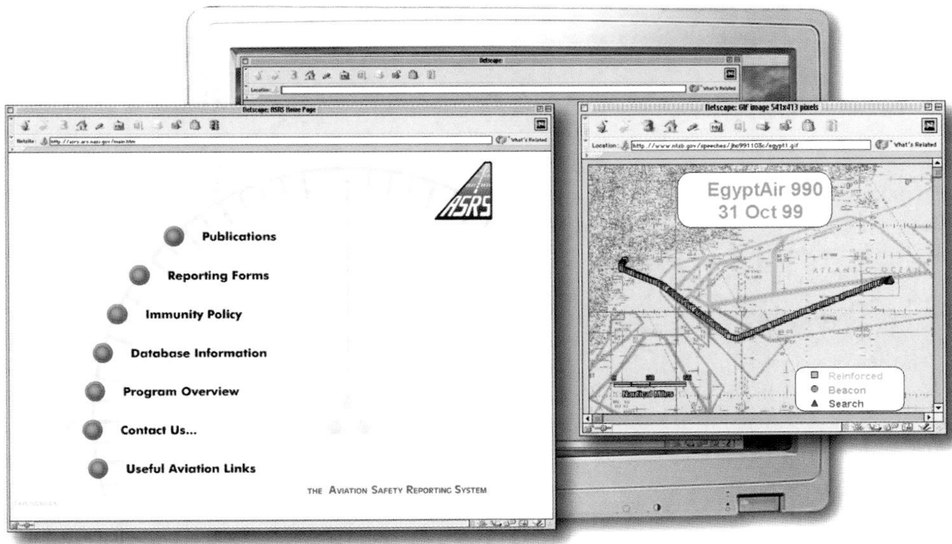

Figure 3-20. Both the NTSB and ASRS maintain extensive databases on the Internet.

Be cautious when presenting accident and incident reports to students. While many experienced pilots are interested in understanding the causes of accidents and talking about the actions that could have been taken to avoid mishaps, this type of discussion may be alarming to students who are beginning pilot training. Emphasize the overall safety of flight to your students and how most accidents can be prevented with the type of training that you are providing.

FACTORS AFFECTING DECISION MAKING

It is important that you point out to your students that being familiar with the decision-making process does not ensure that they will have the good judgment to be safe pilots. The ability to make effective decisions as pilot in command depends on a number of factors. Some circumstances, such as the time available to make a decision, may be beyond their control. However, your students can learn to recognize the factors which can be managed, and learn skills to improve decision-making ability and judgment.

UNDERSTANDING PILOT-IN-COMMAND RESPONSIBILITY

Your students should be taught from the beginning of training that the pilot in command (PIC) of an aircraft is directly responsible for, and is the final authority as to, the operation of that aircraft. While instructing, you normally are the final authority and bear the primary responsibility for the safety of the flight. For this reason, it is important you have a solid understanding of your role as pilot in command at the same time you prepare each student to effectively manage **pilot-in-command responsibility**. [Figure 3-21]

OPERATION	PERCENT OF FLYING (1997)	PERCENT OF TOTAL ACCIDENTS (1998)	PERCENT OF FATAL ACCIDENTS (1998)
Personal	43.5	68.8	72.1
Instructional	22.0	13.4	5.6
Aerial Application	6.5	6.6	1.8
Business	13.2	2.8	4.1
Positioning	*	1.7	2.9
Ferry	*	1.3	2.3
Public Use	1.8	0.8	1.5
Other Work Use	0.6	0.7	0.9
Aerial Observation	4.7	0.5	1.5
Executive/Corporate	5.0	0.2	0.0
Other/Unknown	2.9	3.4	7.3

* Included in "Other/Unknown"

Figure 3-21. The number of instructional mishaps is very small while personal flying accounts for a large proportion of general aviation accidents. These statistics illustrate the need for flight instructors to better prepare their students to assume the responsibilities of acting as PIC.

PERFORMING SELF-ASSESSMENT

Performance during a flight is affected by many factors, such as health, recency of experience, knowledge, skill level, and attitude. Explain to your students how to properly evaluate their condition to fly and reinforce the concept of self-assessment by setting an example for them. If students observe you flying when you are ill, fatigued, or have limited experience in an airplane, they most likely will emulate your behavior when they make decisions about their fitness to fly.

You can introduce the **I'm Safe Checklist** to students as a guideline to prompt them to think about their fitness for flight before taking the controls of an airplane. Students may be uncomfortable admitting they do not feel well enough to fly so you should pay close attention to signs that they may not be fit for a lesson. You may suggest rescheduling a flight or in some cases, substituting a ground lesson. To help students determine if they are prepared for a particular flight, encourage them to create **personal checklists** which state limitations based on such factors as experience, currency, and comfort level in certain flight conditions. Specifying when refresher training should be accomplished, designating weather minimums which may be higher than those listed in the FARs, and setting limitations regarding the amount of crosswind for takeoffs and landings are examples of elements which your students may include in a personal checklist. [Figure 3-22]

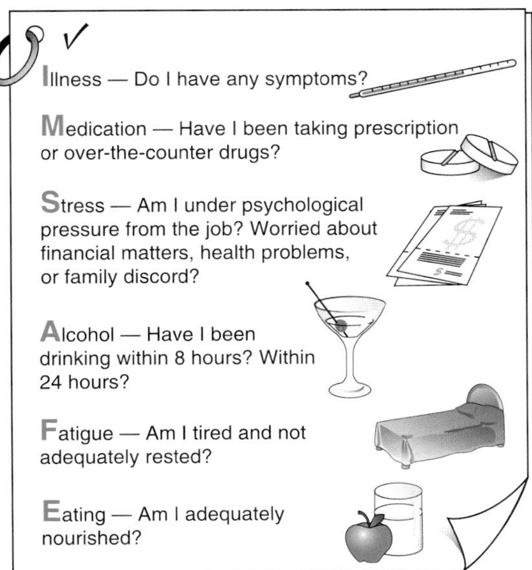

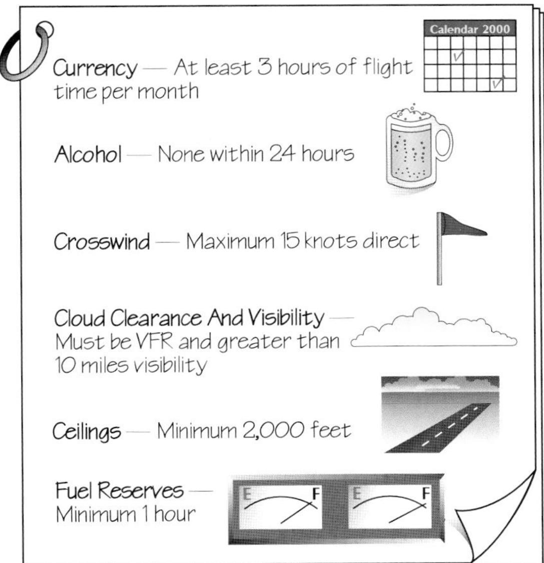

Figure 3-22. During preflight briefings, include a quick review of self-assessment checklists to reinforce the importance of fitness for flight.

RECOGNIZING HAZARDOUS ATTITUDES

Students must understand that being fit to fly depends on more than just their physical condition and recency of experience. For example, their attitudes affect the quality of their decisions. Studies have identified five **hazardous attitudes** which can interfere with a pilot's ability to make sound decisions and exercise authority properly. [Figure 3-23]

Anti-authority — Students with this attitude may resent having you tell them what to do, or they regard rules and procedures as unnecessary.

Your new student, Jim, is the president of a large company. He is not used to taking directions and resents your suggestions that he spend more time studying before lessons.

Impulsivity — Students that feel the need to do something — anything — immediately are exhibiting this attitude. They do not stop to consider the best alternative, but do the first thing which comes to mind.

During simulated engine failure practice, Jennie normally tries to restart the engine before obtaining best glide speed or looking for a suitable landing site.

Invulnerability — Some students may believe that accidents happen to others, but never to them. Students with this attitude are more likely to take chances and increase risk.

Your instrument student, Mike, is resistant to canceling lessons due to poor weather conditions. He believes that icing indicated by PIREPs will not affect his flights.

Macho — By taking risks, these students attempt to prove they are better than anyone else. While this pattern is thought to be a male characteristic, women are equally susceptible.

You overhear Cindy, a pilot in your commercial ground school class, bragging to other students about the amount of crosswind she can handle during landing.

Resignation — Students with this attitude do not see themselves as making a great deal of difference in what happens to them. When things go well, they think, *"That's good luck."* When things go badly, they attribute it to bad luck or feel that someone else is responsible. They leave the action to others — for better or worse.

Amy typically attributes her poor performance during lessons to "a bad day" and does not put any effort into correcting her mistakes.

Figure 3-23. You must be alert during training to signs that your students are exhibiting attitudes which could adversely affect their judgment.

Hazardous attitudes can lead to poor decision making and actions which involve unnecessary risk. Teach students to examine their decisions carefully to ensure their choices have not been influenced by hazardous attitudes and familiarize them with positive alternatives, referred to as antidotes, to counteract these attitudes. The most effective way to introduce your students to hazardous attitudes is to provide them with practical examples from flight situations. [Figure 3-24] Remember you can also be influenced by hazardous attitudes in instructing situations. For example, if you allow your student to exceed maneuvering speed during stall recovery because *"the aircraft can handle a lot more than the maneuvering speed,"* you are displaying an antiauthority reaction.

You can be influenced by hazardous attitudes in instructing situations. For example, if you allow your student to exceed maneuvering speed during stall recovery because *"the aircraft can handle a lot more than the maneuvering speed,"* you are displaying an antiauthority reaction.

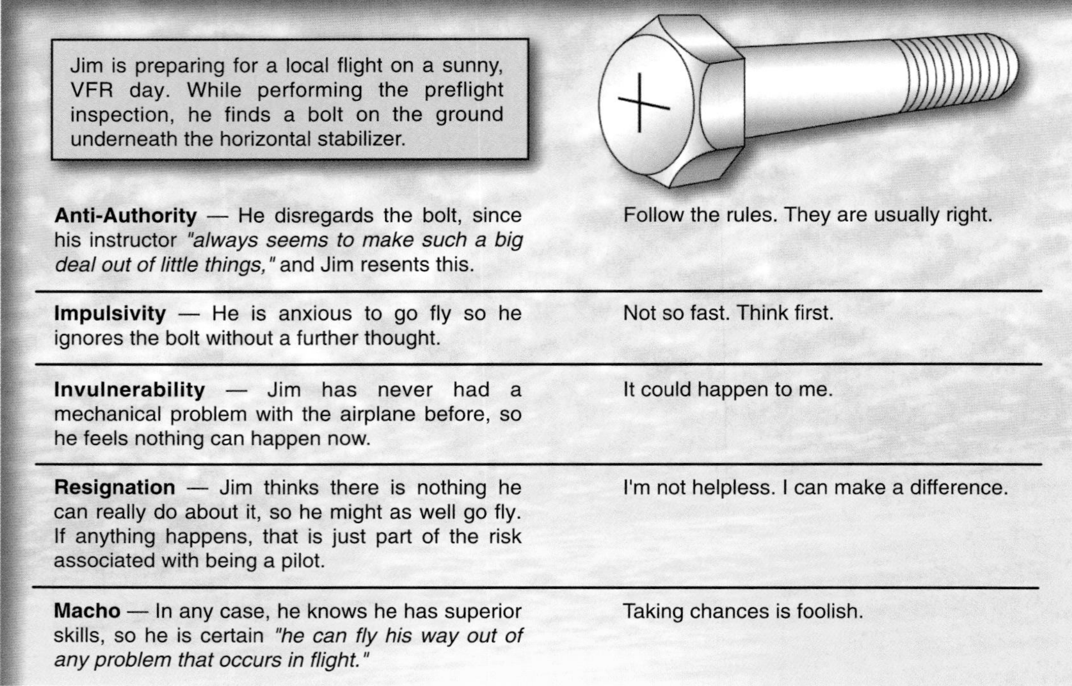

Figure 3-24. Students can be asked to identify hazardous attitudes and the corresponding antidotes when presented with flight scenarios.

FORMING INTERPERSONAL RELATIONSHIPS

Since your students most likely will carry passengers and may frequently fly with other pilots, it is important they learn how to form productive relationships with each person on board the airplane. Students pursuing private pilot certificates have no experience with passengers so you need to emphasize that as PIC, they are responsible for the safety and comfort of the individuals they are transporting. Prepare your students to explain the operation of the doors, seats, seatbelts, and oxygen equipment, if applicable, as well as to encourage passengers to speak up if at any time they experience discomfort or anxiety. You may ask students to practice briefing you as they would a passenger or encourage them to bring a friend or family member along on a dual training flight so they can become accustomed to having someone else on board.

While flying with other pilots presents an opportunity for a reduction in workload that enhances flight safety, it also presents possibilities for misunderstandings that can lead to serious problems. You need to emphasize that prior to a flight with another pilot, your students should discuss how responsibilities will be divided and what is expected from each crewmember. If it is not clear as to who will be performing certain tasks, a critical item may be overlooked or an issue may arise regarding who is in control. [Figure 3-25]

PILOT-IN-COMMAND RESPONSIBILITY

Report

"This was a training flight where I, the pilot flying, was getting checked out in a new aircraft . . . by another CFI. While I was doing the flying, the pilot not flying was handling all the electronics. We were both looking for other traffic and making radio calls. Unable to get a response from UNICOM, we decided to land on Runway 22 . . . On taxi back there was a fair amount of chatter on the UNICOM and the pilot not flying turned the volume down on the radio. We performed our before takeoff check and looked for traffic on final, base, and downwind for Runway 22. We did not turn the volume up on the radio (some takeoff check) nor did we announce our departure. While on the takeoff roll, the pilot not flying suddenly grabbed the controls, only to release them again allowing me to continue the takeoff, but pointed out [another aircraft] on short final for Runway 10! We were well past the intersection prior to his touchdown, but this was just a little too close."

Analysis

This ASRS report clearly illustrates the need for crew coordination and communication to be established prior to a flight when two pilots are involved. In the final portion of this report, the CFI states his conclusions regarding the cause of the incident.

"There were a number of factors leading up to this incident . . . Probably the most important factor, I feel, was the delineation of who was actually PIC and who was to do what. Though I was the 'sole manipulator of the controls' I assumed the role of student and expected/relied on the other CFI to assume all responsibility . . . I feel, that when two CFIs are flying together the responsibilities have to be spelled out so that there are no assumptions, second guessing, missed items/procedures and missed traffic."

Figure 3-25. Not only should you teach your students the importance of establishing open communication with another pilot in the cockpit, you must ensure that you do the same during training flights.

When Babies Fly

As an instructor, you have a responsibility to teach your students about *their* responsibility toward the safety and comfort of their passengers. When those passengers are adults, it is relatively easy to ensure they understand the operation of the seats and seatbelts, and that they are comfortable voicing any concerns, but what about when babies fly . . .

You may have students who intend to carry infants or small children in the airplane. You can provide your students with information to help them make effective decisions about ensuring the safety of children in flight.

In 1979, an FAA task force was convened to evaluate child restraint devices and systems used aboard aircraft. Through the years, numerous reports have been presented to Congress, concerning the safety of small children during flight. In 1997, the White House Commission on Aviation Safety and Security issued a final report to the President which included a recommendation on the use of child restraint systems (CRS) during flight. The report suggested that the FAA revise its regulations, requiring that all occupants of an aircraft be restrained during takeoff, landing, and during turbulent conditions, including infants and small children within a weight and height limitation.

The report also suggested that the children who met the specific requirements be restrained in a CRS. The CRS must conform to all applicable motor vehicle safety standards, and therefore the seat must contain either one or two of the following labels:

Any seat manufactured to U.S. standards between January 1, 1981 and February 25, 1985, must bear a label stating "THIS CHILD RESTRAINT SYSTEM CONFORMS TO ALL APPLICABLE FEDERAL MOTOR VEHICLE SAFETY STANDARDS."

Any seat manufactured on or after February 26, 1985, must display not only the label listed above, but the following as well: "THIS RESTRAINT IS CERTIFIED FOR USE IN MOTOR VEHICLES AND AIRCRAFT."

You can direct your students to FAR 91.107 for details on transporting small children. In addition, remind your students that a child can be a distraction and recommend that another adult who is responsible for the child always accompany them on flights. Managing workload in the cockpit is challenging enough without having to contend with a fussy baby in the rear seat.

To Be PIC or Not to Be PIC — That is the Question

Consider the consequences if you do not establish some guidelines with another pilot before takeoff. You are providing instrument instruction to Gary in his own airplane. He has considerably more flight time in this make and model than you. If an emergency situation occurs in VFR conditions, who will fly the airplane?

Your student, Ben, is pursuing a multi-engine rating. He has already learned the procedures for coping with engine failure after takeoff and has successfully managed several simulated engine-out situations. Have you established who will take control of the airplane in the event of an actual engine failure?

You are flying with another instructor, Audrea, on a cross-country for personal reasons. Each of you will fly a leg of the trip. You assume this means that during your leg, you are responsible for every aspect of the flight, including navigation and radio procedures. Audrea, who has crew experience, assumes that during her portion of the flight she will manipulate the controls while you perform other cockpit duties. What problems can arise from this misunderstanding?

PROMOTING COMMUNICATION

In Chapter 1, you learned about the importance of **communication** during instruction. Those same principles must be taught to your students so they can effectively exchange ideas in the flight environment. In an emergency situation, the ability to clearly convey information to ATC or another crewmember becomes crucial. However, students must understand that in order to plan and execute even a routine flight, they must have the skills to communicate with a wide variety of individuals. [Figure 3-26] As students gain experience and pursue additional training as pilots, the ability to communicate becomes even more critical. Instrument students must learn how to present information to and receive detailed clearances from ATC and commercial students must be taught crew coordination skills and how to convey information to passengers.

Figure 3-26. Teach your students appropriate procedures for communicating during specific operations, such as obtaining weather information from FSS briefers, requesting services from FBO line personnel, coordinating with a crewmember, and contacting ATC.

COMMUNICATING WITH ATC

Since it is a form of communication that is most likely unfamiliar, pilot/controller communication presents unique challenges to beginning students. No matter how simple and automatic the exchange of information between pilot and ATC may seem, studies have shown that there is rarely a single flight leg flown where a communication error does not occur. [Figure 3-27] To help your students prevent a breakdown in communication, teach them to use correct radio procedures, read back clearances, and when in doubt, verify instructions with ATC. Do not let your students assume controller silence after a readback is verification of their transmission. Direct them to ask the controller for a verbal confirmation. Ensure they are alert for similar call signs and that they use their call sign to acknowledge transmissions, not a double click of the mike or *"roger."*

READBACK/HEARBACK ERROR	
Controller: *"Continue holding short, Runway 35."*	Pilot: *"Position and hold, Runway 35."* Controller does not recognize pilot's error.

ALPHA-NUMERIC ERROR	
Controller: *"Turn right heading 090."*	Pilot hears: *"Turn right heading 190."*

SIMILAR CALL SIGNS	
Controller: *"Cessna 241, you're following traffic turning final. Cleared to land, Runway 27."*	Pilot: *"Roger, 421, cleared to land Runway 27."*

EXPECTATION	
Controller: *"After takeoff make left traffic for Runway 17 Left."*	Pilot hears: *"After takeoff make right traffic for Runway 17 Right."* These are the instructions the pilot usually receives and expects to hear.

VAGUE INSTRUCTIONS	
Controller: *"Maintain 2-0-0"* *(200 knots)*	Pilot believes the controller means FL200.

INAPPROPRIATE USE OF PHRASEOLOGY	
Controller: *"Verify you can make Alpha 7."*	Pilot: *"Roger."* The term roger should not be used to answer a question requiring a yes or no answer.

Figure 3-27. Your students may not be aware of the types of errors that can occur during communication with ATC unless you provide them with specific examples.

COMMUNICATING WITH CREWMEMBERS

Students who are pursuing aviation as a career and even those who anticipate flying extensively with other pilots will benefit from learning about techniques used by flight crewmembers to improve cockpit coordination. For example, when using checklists, you may introduce and practice the challenge-response method with students. Read checklist items out loud while your student completes the tasks and repeats the instructions verbally and then exchange these roles for a subsequent lesson. This process directly involves both pilots in performing essential procedures to reduce the chance that a mistake or omission will occur.

When two pilots are in the cockpit, both should be included in critical decisions when possible, not just in emergencies but also in routine practices such as programming electronic equipment and setting autopilot functions. You can emphasize this concept to students by instructing them to verify out loud when they change headings and altitudes, select new courses on navigation equipment, and enter radio frequencies. Another exercise in crew coordination is to practice departure and approach briefings with your instrument students. For example, before takeoff, ask your students to describe the proposed departure routing, either given by ATC or through published procedures. Not only does this practice improve communication skills, it reinforces the instrument procedures and allows you to verify that your students understand clearances.

A significant number of accidents have occurred when professional flight crews were engaged in unnecessary dialogue and overlooked important procedures or checklist items, such as setting the flaps properly for takeoff and extending the landing gear. To help prevent these types of accidents, the FAA issued FAR 121.542 and FAR 135.100. Commonly referred to as the **sterile cockpit** rule, these FARs specifically prohibit crewmember performance of nonessential duties or activities while the aircraft is involved in taxi, takeoff, landing, and all other flight operations conducted below 10,000 feet MSL, except for cruise flight. Exercising this rule can increase the safety of training flights as well. Conversation with students or critiques performed at inopportune times can lead to missed instructions from ATC, overlooked checklist items, or hazardous distractions from essential procedures. [Figure 3-28]

COMMUNICATION

Figure 3-28. These ASRS reports illustrate how circumstances specific to the training environment can lead to communication mishaps.

Report

This ASRS report illustrates how vague statements made by both the CFI and student can result in confusion and problems with aircraft control. *"Instructor said . . .'Uh, you can have control if you, uh want it.' I probably replied 'OK' rather than the usual 'I have control.' I began to pull the nose up slowly when I thought I felt my instructor push forward on the wheel [and] relaxed. . . Nosewheel touched down first and we bounced. . . fortunately we walked away. . . with an undamaged aircraft. 'Wishy washy' coms played a major role in this."*

Analysis

In this situation, the exchange of flight controls was not communicated effectively. The CFI did not provide the student with clear instructions and the student was not assertive enough to question the CFI's actions.

Report

"We started flying using headsets, with the radios being monitored through the headsets. After the first landing the student stated he would prefer to continue without the headsets as he didn't feel comfortable wearing them. I said OK. We got involved in doing touch and goes and I failed to notice that we had not heard from the Tower during this time. When I did notice that the speaker button was not in the proper position, I made contact with the Tower. They [Tower] terminated the flight and I was instructed to call the Tower."

Analysis

While equipment malfunctions can be barriers to effective communication, in this case, a pilot-induced headset problem led to a communication mishap with ATC. A complete lack of situational awareness occurred when the instructor and student became so focused on the lesson they failed to realize they were not receiving any transmissions from the control tower.

DESCRIBING RESOURCE USE

To make informed decisions during flight operations, students must be made aware of the resources found both inside and outside the cockpit. **Resource use** is an essential part of ADM training. Since useful tools and sources of information may not always be readily apparent, it is important to teach your students how to recognize appropriate resources. [Figure 3-29]

If your engine fails immediately after takeoff, there is not time to contact ATC prior to taking action.

If you become lost on a cross-country flight, contacting ATC for assistance can be an effective use of this resource.

Figure 3-29. Resources must not only be identified, but students must develop the skills to evaluate whether they have the time to use a particular resource and the impact its use will have upon the safety of flight. Provide your students with practical examples to illustrate this point.

IDENTIFYING INTERNAL RESOURCES

Internal resources are found in the cockpit during flight. By teaching, you help provide your students with some of their most valuable resources; ingenuity, knowledge, and skills. Encourage students in all areas of training to enhance their internal resources by improving their capabilities. This can be accomplished by frequently reviewing flight information publications, such as the FARs and the AIM, as well as by pursuing additional training.

A thorough understanding of all the equipment and systems in the aircraft is necessary for students to fully utilize all their resources. For example, advanced navigation and autopilot systems are valuable resources, but if students do not know how to use this equipment, or if they rely on it so much that they become complacent, it can be a detriment to safe flight rather than an asset. [Figure 3-30]

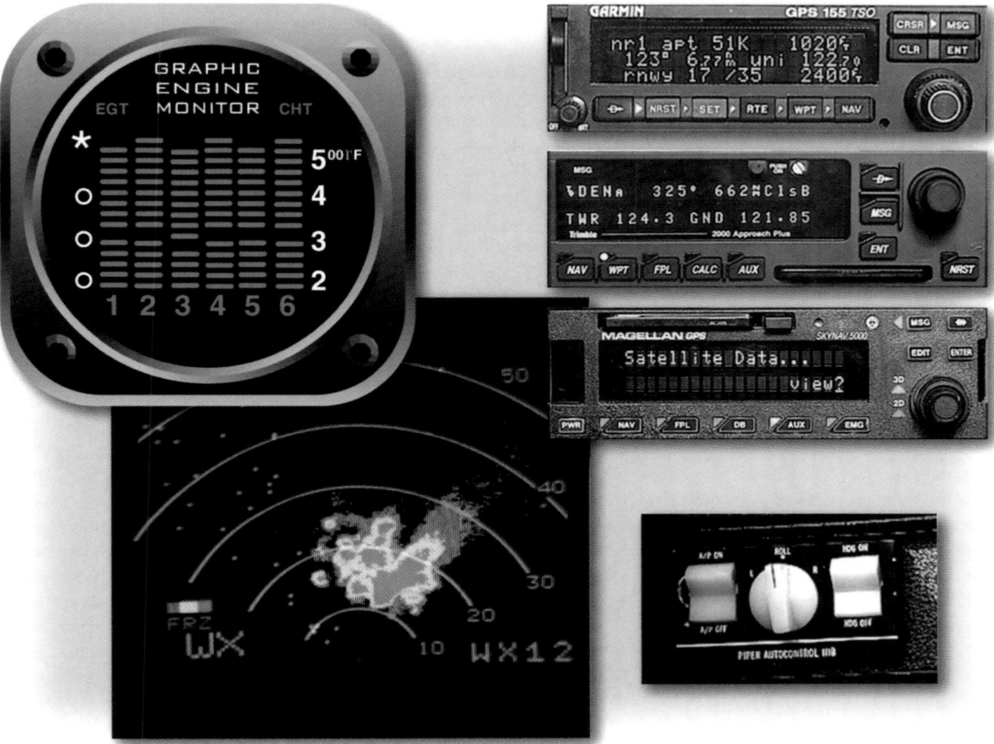

Figure 3-30. To ensure that your students understand the operation of the equipment in their training airplane, you must first be familiar with all the components of each airplane in which you instruct.

While you may consider checklist use routine, beginning students may be unfamiliar with the concept of checklists. You must point out that these lists are essential cockpit resources for verifying that the aircraft instruments and systems are checked, set, and operating properly, as well as making certain the proper procedures are performed if there is a system malfunction or in-flight emergency. In addition, you should ensure your students gain experience using the pilot's operating handbook (POH) and know how to readily access information from this important resource. Other valuable cockpit resources include current aeronautical charts, and publications, such as the *Airport/Facility Directory*.

It should be pointed out to students that passengers also can be a valuable resource. Passengers can help watch for traffic and may be able to provide information in an irregular situation, especially if they are familiar with flying. A strange smell or sound may alert a passenger to a potential problem. Students must be taught to brief passengers before the flight to make sure that they are comfortable voicing any concerns.

Resource Reluctance

You may encounter situations where students are reluctant to or do not know how to use internal resources effectively.

"I have the procedures memorized. People will think I don't know what I'm doing if I use the checklist," your student, Carl announces during the runup.

Remind students who are averse to using checklists that pilots at all levels of experience refer to checklists and that the more advanced the aircraft is, the more crucial this resource becomes.

During a flight review you ask Chad where he obtained the fuel burn figure and true airspeed he is using for cross-country performance calculations. *"This is the number the guy told me when I bought the airplane."*

Review the use of the POH with pilots who are pursuing additional ratings or who enlist your services for flight reviews and instrument competency checks.

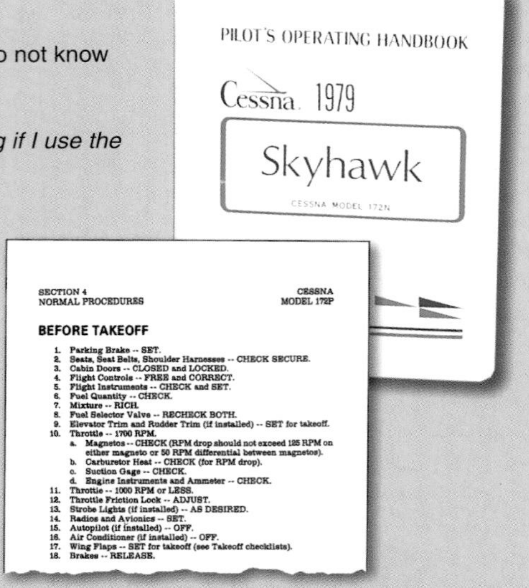

SECTION 4 NORMAL PROCEDURES — CESSNA MODEL 172P

BEFORE TAKEOFF

1. Parking Brake -- SET.
2. Seats, Seat Belts, Shoulder Harnesses -- CHECK SECURE.
3. Cabin Doors -- CLOSED and LOCKED.
4. Flight Controls -- FREE and CORRECT.
5. Flight Instruments -- CHECK and SET.
6. Fuel Quantity -- CHECK.
7. Mixture -- RICH.
8. Fuel Selector Valve -- RECHECK BOTH.
9. Elevator Trim and Rudder Trim (if installed) -- SET for takeoff.
10. Throttle -- 1700 RPM.
    a. Magnetos -- CHECK (RPM drop should not exceed 125 RPM on either magneto or 50 RPM differential between magnetos).
    b. Carburetor Heat -- CHECK (for RPM drop).
    c. Suction Gage -- CHECK.
    d. Engine Instruments and Ammeter -- CHECK.
11. Throttle -- 1000 RPM or LESS.
12. Throttle Friction Lock -- ADJUST.
13. Strobe Lights (if installed) -- AS DESIRED.
14. Radios and Avionics -- SET.
15. Autopilot (if installed) -- OFF.
16. Air Conditioner (if installed) -- OFF.
17. Wing Flaps -- SET for takeoff (see Takeoff checklists).
18. Brakes -- RELEASE.

RECOGNIZING EXTERNAL RESOURCES

The services provided by air traffic controllers and flight service specialists are possibly the greatest **external resources** during flight and can be invaluable in enabling your students to make informed in-flight decisions. Point out to your students that ATC can help decrease their workload by providing traffic advisories, radar vectors, and aid in emergency situations. Flight service stations can provide updates on weather, answer questions about airport conditions, and may offer direction-finding assistance. [Figure 3-31]

1. During her solo cross-country flight, Amy observed increasing clouds and decreasing visibility ahead along her route. She contacted Flight Watch for an update on the weather.

2. After making a decision to divert to a nearby airport, she spoke to an FSS briefer to verify airport approach control frequency information and to amend her flight plan.

3. Amy contacted approach control at her new destination and received radar vectors to the airport.

4. She enlisted the help of ground control to provide her with a progressive taxi to the FBO at the unfamiliar airport.

Figure 3-31. As you instruct, ask yourself if your students understand how to use external resources well enough to take actions similar to this student.

Since radio communication may be intimidating to beginning students or to those who normally operate from small uncontrolled airports, they may be reluctant to request assistance in flight. Provide your students with opportunities to practice using services, such as flight following and Flight Watch. If students are exposed to ATC as much as possible during training, they will feel confident asking controllers to clarify instructions and be better equipped to use this resource for assistance in unusual circumstances or emergencies. If they do not have the chance to practice in the actual flight environment, certain computer-based training programs, videos, audio tapes, and flight training devices can aid students in learning complicated radio procedures. [Figure 3-32]

Figure 3-32. Students may not be as intimidated by ATC if they understand that controllers have a desire to assist them, as this ASRS report clearly illustrates.

Report

"I got a call from ABC Approach . . . about a small aircraft trapped on top of an overcast with only about 45 minutes of fuel remaining. The pilot thought he was 40 n.m. northeast of ABC VOR, but Approach couldn't find him on their radar. The Center Controller expanded the range all the way out . . . and discovered the aircraft about 40 miles west of XYZ [more that 100 n.m. south of ABC VOR-Ed.] Being familiar with that aircraft, I realized that this pilot was in danger of losing his life. The pilot did not have enough fuel to go to an airport with good weather, committing him to land at XYZ. I told Approach to ask the pilot if he had a working autopilot on board . . . to turn it on so he could reduce his workload in keeping the aircraft right side up while in the clouds . . . Later, we found out that the pilot had broken out of the overcast and was proceeding safely to XYZ."

Analysis

This Center controller was able to aid a non-instrument rated pilot in a serious predicament. You can provide your students with examples, such as this, which illustrate the assistance that ATC may be able to provide in unusual circumstances. Students should not hesitate to ask for help if they are concerned about a situation.

You can ask your students to create a resource list as they progress through each phase of training and learn more about the flight environment. For example, when student pilots first perform a preflight inspection, identify the checklist as a resource. As they learn radio procedures, ATC can be added to the inventory. You may ask advanced students to provide you with a list of resources at the beginning of their training and then identify any they have missed. As students add to the list they will constantly be reminded of the many resources they have available to them. [Figure 3-33]

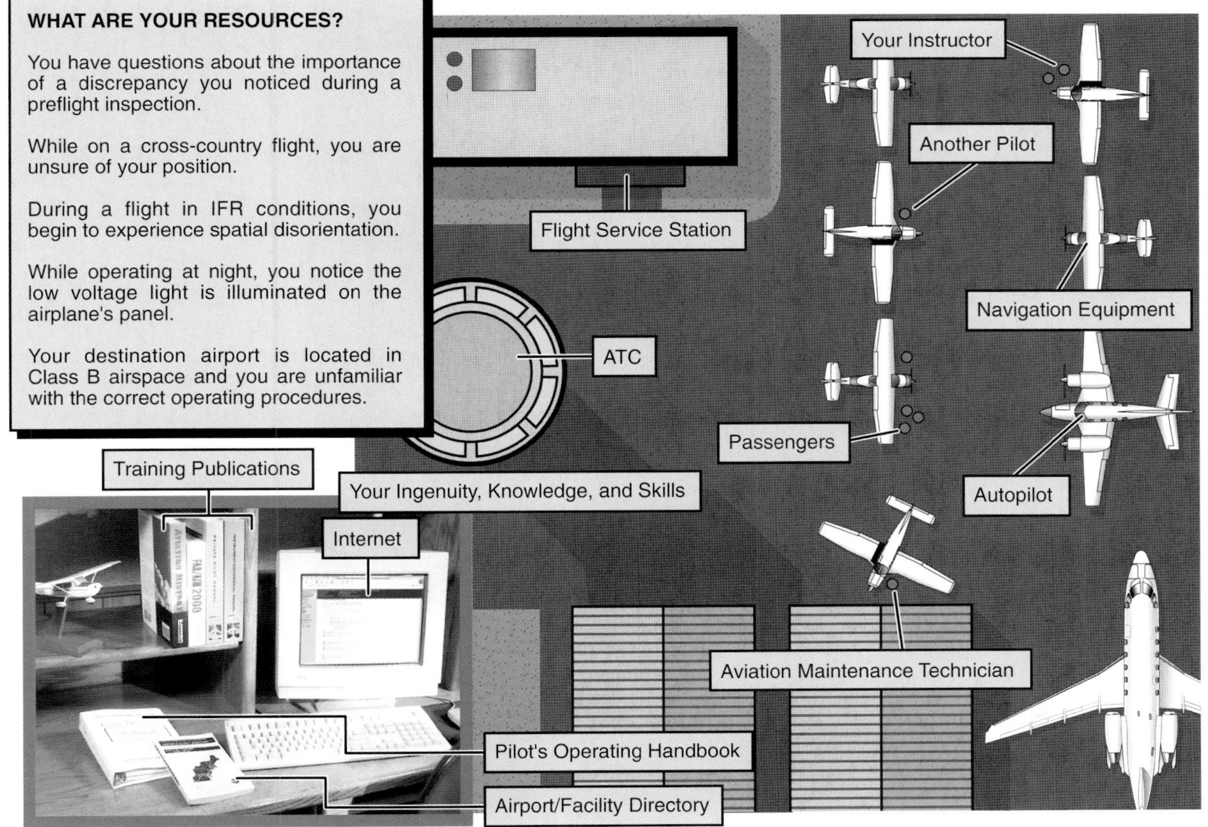

Figure 3-33. One method you can use to help students identify resources that may be valuable in specific situations is to create an activity. Students can complete an exercise similar to this one as an assignment, with your assistance, or within a group in a classroom environment.

WORKLOAD MANAGEMENT

Effective **workload management** ensures that essential operations are accomplished by planning, prioritizing, and sequencing tasks to avoid work overload. One of your primary goals when teaching your students to manage workload is to help them learn to recognize future workload requirements and prepare for high workload periods during times of low workload. [Figure 3-34] For example, during cruise, you can ask your students to explain the actions that need to be taken as they approach the airport. Students should be able to describe the procedures for traffic pattern entry and landing preparation. Reviewing the appropriate chart and setting radio frequencies well before nearing the airport reduces workload. In addition, students should listen to ATIS, ASOS, or AWOS, if available, and then monitor the tower frequency or CTAF to get a good idea of the traffic conditions to expect. Checklists should be performed well in advance so there is time to focus on traffic and ATC instructions.

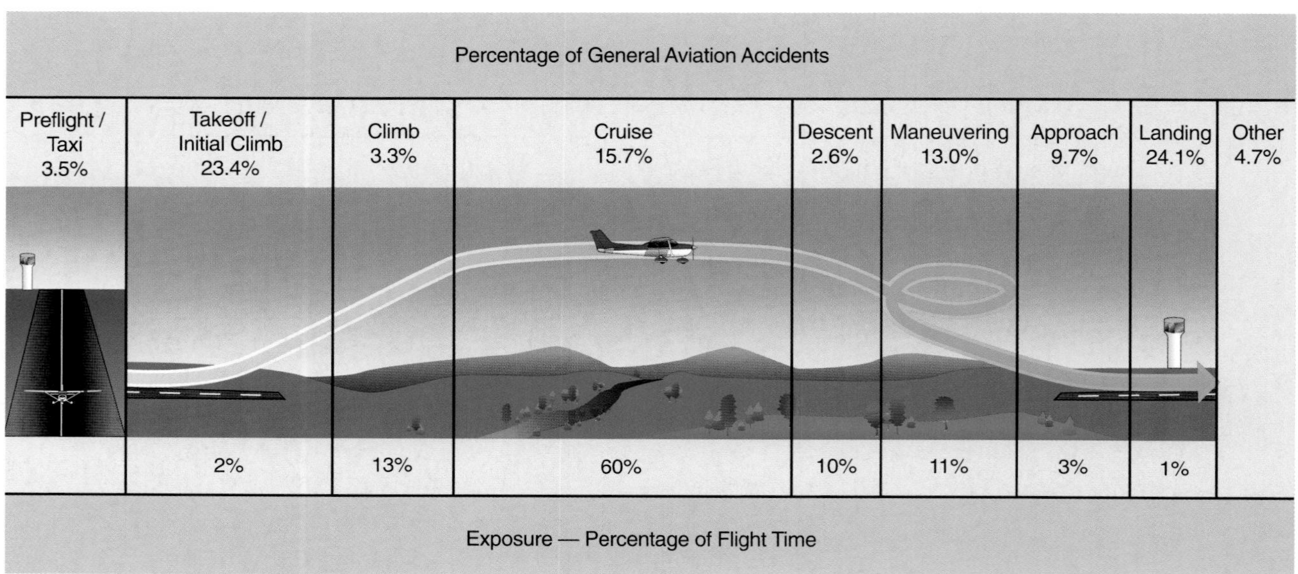

Figure 3-34. By exploring statistics with your students, they will discover that most accidents occur during periods of high workload when the chance for error is the greatest.

It is especially important for instrument students to be thinking of the actions that need to be taken as they near their destination. After they have reviewed the approach chart, you can ask them to state the approach minimums, explain the missed approach procedure, and ensure they have set and identified the appropriate navigation and communication frequencies. The briefing strip printed on approach charts can help them easily locate the essential chart information. Since operating in actual IFR conditions can be very demanding, recommend your students fly with another instrument-rated pilot to help them manage workload after their training is completed. When students training for commercial certificates or multi-engine ratings find it difficult to manage the workload of transitioning to a more complex airplane, the use of checklists can prove invaluable.

To manage workload, students must be taught to how to prioritize items. For example, during a go-around, adding power, gaining airspeed, and properly configuring the airplane are priorities. Informing the tower of the balked landing should be accomplished only after these tasks are completed. Students must understand that priorities change as the situation changes. If fuel quantity is lower than expected on a cross-country flight, the priority can shift from making a scheduled arrival time at the destination, to locating a nearby airport to refuel. In an emergency situation, the first priority is to fly the airplane and maintain a safe airspeed. [Figure 3-35]

Communication — Discussion among the crew or radio transmissions

Head-Down Work — Reviewing aeronautical charts, approach plates, programming navigation equipment, or using a flight computer

Searching for Traffic — Looking for aircraft called out by ATC, TCAD, or TCAS

Responding to Abnormal Situations — Recognizing cockpit warning indicators, identifying problems, and implementing procedures

Figure 3-35. Distractions during flights can cause attention to shift and priorities to be misplaced. Alert your students to the types of distractions that may prevent them from effectively managing their workload.

DEALING WITH DISTRACTIONS

To help students manage workload and avoid distractions, teach them to perform the majority of head-down tasks, such as reviewing charts or navigation logs during low workload periods. Set an example for your students by scheduling tasks to minimize conflicts, especially during critical phases of flight. For instance, inbound from the final approach fix on an ILS approach is not a good time to critique your student's radio procedures.

If students must perform multiple tasks at the same time, ensure their attention is not focused on one item too long to the exclusion of others. Point out interruptions when they occur, ask students what they were doing prior to the interruption, and help them identify actions which allow them to return to the original task. For example, if your students are performing the before landing checklist when ATC issues a traffic advisory, ensure they take note of the last item completed, locate the traffic, acknowledge the transmission, and promptly return to the checklist.

COPING WITH WORK OVERLOAD

Students may have trouble recognizing when they are experiencing a work overload situation. You may notice that the first effect of high workload is your students begin to work faster. As workload increases, their attention cannot be devoted to many tasks at one time, and they may begin to focus on one item. When they become task saturated, there is no awareness of inputs from various sources so decisions may be made on incomplete information, and the possibility of error increases. [Figure 3-36]

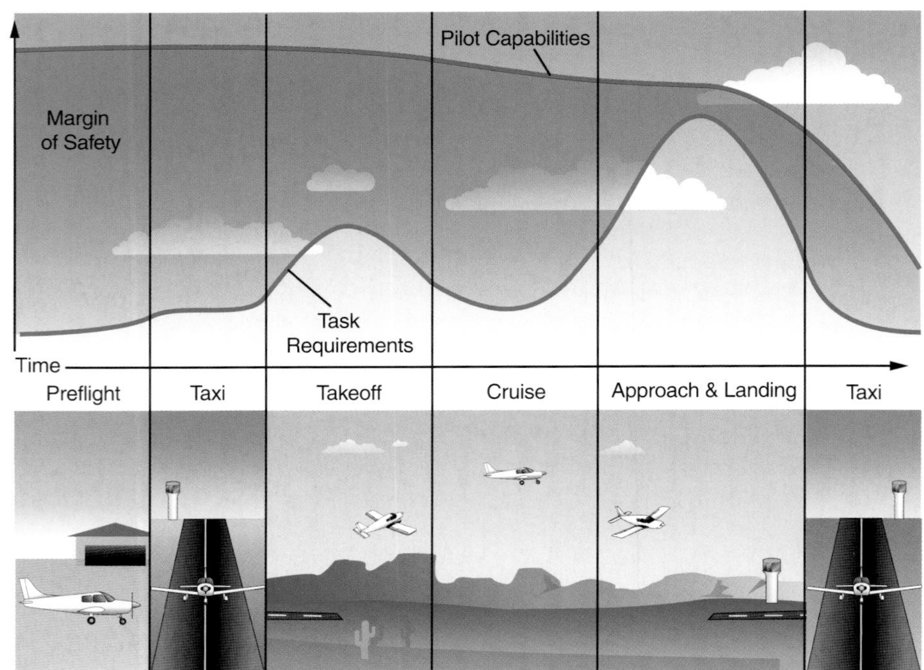

Figure 3-36. Accidents often occur when flying task requirements exceed pilot capabilities. The difference between these two factors is called the margin of safety. You can use a diagram such as this one to illustrate to your students that the margin of safety is minimal during the approach and landing. At this point, an emergency or distraction could overtax pilot capabilities, causing an accident.

To help your students recognize a work overload situation, gradually increase workload during a lesson and monitor your students' management of tasks. If you notice your students becoming focused on one item and disregarding other important tasks, suggest they stop, think, slow down, and prioritize. It is important that you point out options that may be available to decrease workload. For example, tasks, such as locating an item on a chart or setting a radio frequency, may be delegated to another pilot or passenger, an aircraft autopilot may be used, or ATC may be enlisted to provide assistance, such as radar vectors. [Figure 3-37]

WORKLOAD MANAGEMENT

Figure 3-37. In addition to teaching workload management concepts to your students, you must be prepared to manage the additional workload that accompanies instructing.

Report

"We were on a training flight and receiving traffic advisories from approach control. The student was having difficulty with aircraft control during maneuvers, so I was talking to the student for longer than normal. Aircraft may have flown into Class B airspace. My attention was drawn inside the aircraft by the student's performance."

Analysis

In this situation, tasks were not effectively prioritized. Preoccupation with critiquing the student impaired the instructor's ability to manage workload which resulted in a loss of situational awareness.

MAINTAINING SITUATIONAL AWARENESS

Since students may confuse situational awareness with knowing their position during flight, you may need to explain this concept to them. **Situational awareness** is the accurate perception of the operational and environmental factors which affect the aircraft, pilot, and passengers during a specific period of time. To maintain situational awareness, your students must understand the relative significance of these factors and their future impact on the flight. Some of the elements inside the airplane which they must consider

are the status of the aircraft systems, pilot, and passengers. In addition, an awareness of the environmental conditions of the flight, such as spatial orientation of the airplane, and its relationship to terrain, traffic, weather, and airspace must be maintained.

If you have successfully taught your students about their responsibility as PIC, the skills to communicate effectively in the flight environment, how to identify and utilize resources, and methods to efficiently manage workload, you have provided them with the tools to maintain situational awareness. For example, an accurate perception of fitness for flight can be achieved through self-assessment and recognition of hazardous attitudes, establishing a productive relationship with ATC can be accomplished by effective resource use, and an ability to cope with distractions can be obtained through workload management skills.

When your students are situationally aware, they have an overview of the total operation and are not fixated on one perceived significant factor. Your students are not maintaining situational awareness if they divert too much attention away from operations, such as controlling the airplane or scanning for traffic, when they must perform another task. [Figure 3-38]

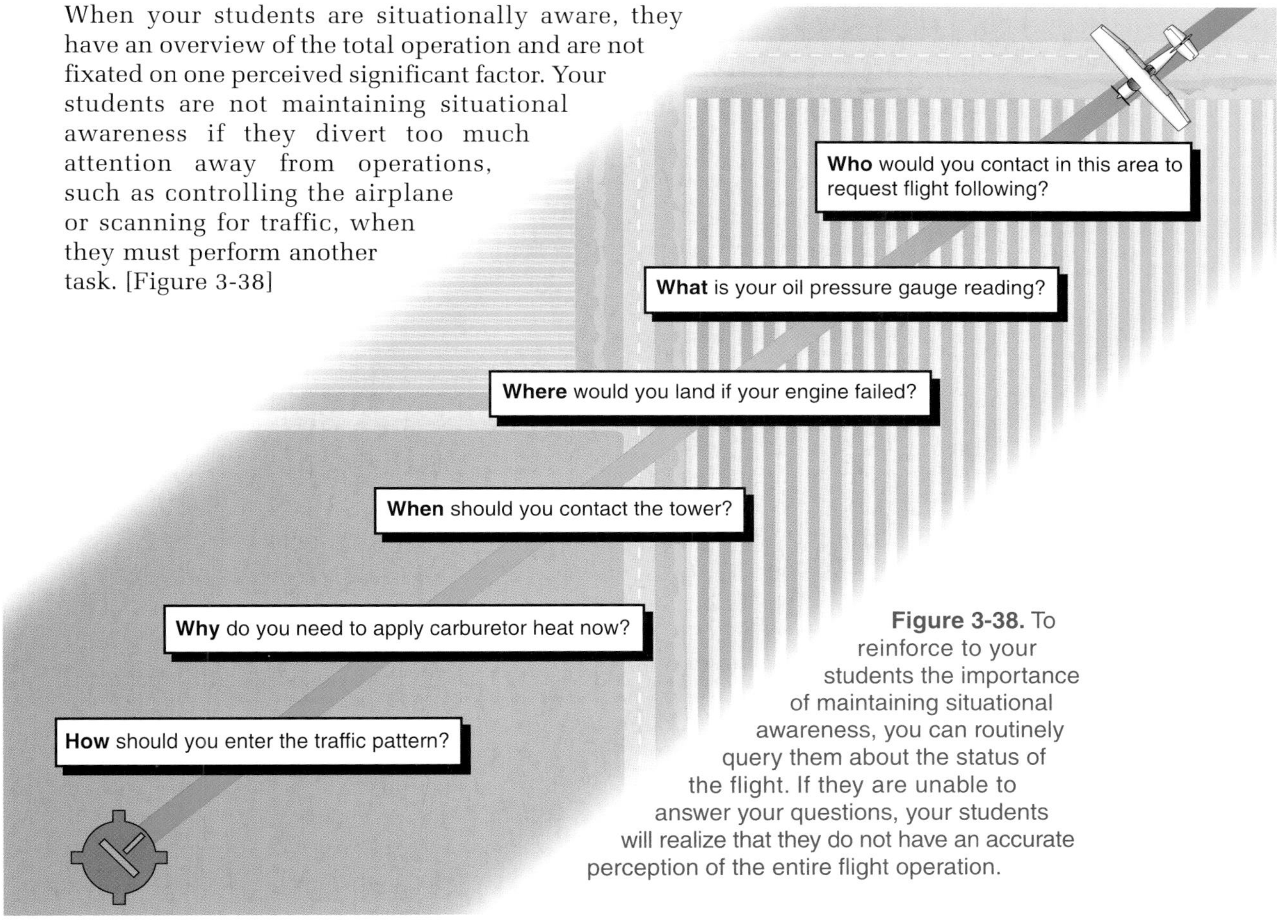

Figure 3-38. To reinforce to your students the importance of maintaining situational awareness, you can routinely query them about the status of the flight. If they are unable to answer your questions, your students will realize that they do not have an accurate perception of the entire flight operation.

RECOGNIZING OBSTACLES TO MAINTAINING SITUATIONAL AWARENESS

Fatigue, stress, and work overload can cause a loss of situational awareness. In addition, a contributing factor in many accidents is a distraction which diverts the pilot's attention from monitoring the instruments or scanning outside the aircraft. Many cockpit distractions begin as a minor problem, such as a gauge which is not reading correctly, but result in accidents as focus is shifted to the perceived problem and the pilot neglects to properly control the aircraft. To evaluate your students' ability to handle distractions, attempt to focus their attention on an imaginary problem with the communication or navigation equipment and observe if they can still maintain an overall awareness of the flight.

Complacency presents another obstacle to maintaining situational awareness. When activities become routine, your students may have a tendency to relax and not put as much effort into performance. You should be especially alert to complacency in students with significant flight experience operating well-equipped airplanes. For example, advanced students who often fly lengthy trips may be accustomed to using the autopilot regularly. While cockpit automation can help reduce workload, use of this equipment can lead to complacency if your students assume the autopilot is functioning properly and do not crosscheck the instruments or the aircraft's position frequently. If the autopilot fails, they may not be mentally prepared to fly the airplane manually. Students may need your help to recognize when they are complacent, since they perceive the operation to be progressing smoothly. [Figure 3-39]

SITUATIONAL AWARENESS

Figure 3-39. NTSB accident reports can help you illustrate the consequences of losing situational awareness.

Report

This was the first day on duty in the southern region operation for both pilots. They had never flown together. During the flight, the flight crew lost awareness of their airplane's position, erroneously believed that the flight was receiving radar services from ATC, and commenced the approach from an excessive altitude and at a cruise airspeed without accomplishing the published procedure specified on the approach chart. The crew believed that the airplane was south of the airport, and turned toward the north to execute the ILS Runway 5 approach. In actuality, the airplane has intercepted the back course localizer signal, and the airplane continued in a controlled descent until it impacted terrain.

The NTSB determined that the probable causes of this accident included the assignment of an inadequately prepared captain with a relatively inexperienced first officer and the failure of the flight crew to use approved instrument flight procedures. These conditions resulted in a loss of situational awareness and terrain clearance. Contributing factors were inadequate crew coordination and a role reversal on the part of the captain and first officer.

Analysis

This NTSB accident report can be use to illustrate to your students how the combination of many factors can lead to loss of situational awareness resulting in a controlled flight into terrain. A failure of PIC responsibility occurred, as well as inadequate communication within the cockpit and with ATC. In addition, resources, such as the instrument charts and navigation equipment, were not used properly and the busy workload of the approach phase of flight was not managed effectively.

UNDERSTANDING CONTROLLED FLIGHT INTO TERRAIN

One of the more tragic consequences of a loss of situational awareness is **controlled flight into terrain (CFIT)**. The implementation of extensive training programs and the installation of ground proximity warning systems (GPWS) have successfully reduced commercial aircraft CFIT-related accidents. However, these types of accidents are more prevalent in general aviation due to lower technology levels in the cockpit and lack of formal CFIT training. Teach your students to increase their positional awareness by paying particular attention to their location relative to terrain, and the minimum altitudes provided on aeronautical charts.

Figure 3-40. There are several techniques you can use to help your students avoid CFIT accidents.

IDENTIFYING OPERATIONAL PITFALLS

The desire to complete a flight as planned, please passengers, meet schedules, and demonstrate that they have the right stuff, can have an adverse effect on safety by causing pilots to overestimate their piloting skills under stressful conditions. As you have gained experience, you most likely have become aware of a number of classic behavioral traps into which pilots have been known to fall. [Figure 3-41] Since these **operational pitfalls** may not be as familiar to your students, describe the hazardous situations that may occur as they relate to each phase of training. For example, you may address scud running when discussing VFR weather minimums with a student engaged in private pilot training or explain the duck-under syndrome when introducing an instrument student to the procedures used to fly approaches.

OPERATIONAL PITFALLS

Mind Set — A pilot displays mind set through an inability to recognize and cope with changes in a given situation.

Scud Running — This occurs when a pilot tries to maintain visual contact with the terrain at low altitudes while instrument conditions exist.

Continuing Visual Flight Rules (VFR) into Instrument Conditions — Spatial disorientation or collision with ground/obstacles may occur when a pilot continues VFR into instrument conditions. This can be even more dangerous if the pilot is not instrument-rated or current.

Operating Without Adequate Fuel Reserves — Ignoring minimum fuel reserve requirements is generally the result of overconfidence, lack of flight planning, or disregarding applicable regulations.

Flying Outside the Envelope — The assumed high performance capability of a particular aircraft may cause a mistaken belief that it can meet the demands imposed by a pilot's overestimated flying skills.

Commercial students may be especially prone to these pitfalls.

Neglect of Flight Planning, Preflight Inspections, and Checklists — A pilot may rely on short- and long-term memory, regular flying skills, and familiar routes instead of established procedures and published checklists. This can be particularly true of experienced pilots.

Getting Behind the Aircraft — This pitfall can be caused by allowing events or the situation to control pilot actions. A constant state of surprise at what happens next may be exhibited when the pilot is getting behind the aircraft. A commercial student's transition to a more advanced airplane can have this result.

Peer Pressure — Poor decision making may be based upon an emotional response to peers rather than evaluating a situation objectively. Commercial pilots may feel particularly pressured by the demands of passengers.

Get-There-Itis — This disposition impairs pilot judgment through a fixation on the original goal or destination, combined with a disregard for any alternative course of action. Pressure to meet a schedule may impose additional strain on a commercial pilot.

	STRAIGHT-IN LANDING RWY 1					CIRCLE-TO-LAND	
	ILS DA(H) 489'(200')		LOC (GS out) MDA(H) 780'(491')			Not Authorized East of Rwy 1-19	
	FULL	RAIL or ALS out		RAIL out	ALS out	Max Kts	MDA(H)
A	RVR 24 or 1/2	RVR 40 or 3/4	RVR 24 or 1/2	RVR 40 or 3/4	RVR 50 or 1	90	860'(563')-1
B						120	880'(583')-1
C			RVR 40 or 3/4	RVR 60 or 1 1/4		140	880'(583')-1 1/2
D			RVR 50 or 1	1 1/2		165	940'(643')-2

Gnd speed-Kts		70	90	100	120	140	160
GS	3.00°	377	484	538	646	754	861
LOM to MAP	4.5	3:51	3:00	2:42	2:15	1:56	1:41

AMEND 23

CHANGES: See other side.

Alert your instrument students to these potential hazards.

Duck-Under Syndrome — A pilot may tempted to make it into an airport by descending below minimums during an approach. There may be a belief that there is a built-in margin of error in every approach procedure, or a pilot may not want to admit that the landing cannot be completed and a missed approach must be initiated.

Descent Below the Minimum Enroute Altitude — The duck-under syndrome, as mentioned above, can also occur during the enroute portion of an IFR flight.

Figure 3-41. Have you ever been tempted by or known someone who has fallen prey to one of these tendencies? If so, do not be reluctant to relate this experience to your students. By helping them realize that most pilots are vulnerable to operational pitfalls, you may prevent your students from succumbing to these same traps.

EVALUATING STUDENT DECISION MAKING

To assess your students' performance on a technical level, you determine whether maneuvers are performed accurately and that procedures are conducted in the right order. Evaluating your students' ability to apply ADM concepts can be more challenging. How did your students arrive at a particular decision? What resources were used? Was risk assessed accurately when a go/no-go decision was made? Did your students maintain situational awareness in the traffic pattern? Was workload managed effectively during a cross-country? How do your students handle stress and fatigue? You do not have to observe your students during actual emergencies or present them with complex situations to determine whether they can make effective decisions. [Figure 3-42]

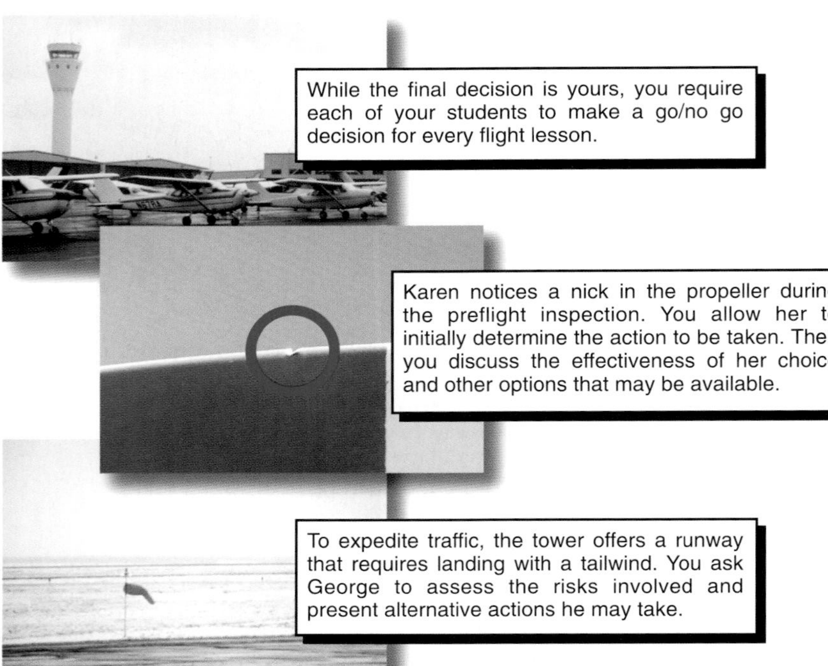

Figure 3-42. By allowing students to make decisions about typical issues that arise throughout the course of training, you can continually evaluate their decision-making ability and offer suggestions for improvement, if needed.

To ensure that your students consider aeronautical decision making concepts during each lesson, you can include ADM elements in your lesson objectives and critique your students on their application of these principles. One of your objectives for a lesson on traffic pattern operations may be to familiarize your students with workload management principles. Begin by discussing workload management principles during the preflight briefing. While in flight, your students practice techniques for effectively managing tasks, such as prioritizing procedures during a go-around, using checklists, and coping with distractions. During the postflight briefing, you critique your students' ability to avoid work overload in the traffic pattern and offer suggestions to improve workload management skills. At this time, you may present your students with a scenario, ASRS, or NTSB report which illustrates successful or faulty management of tasks during a flight.

In addition to assessing your students' judgment skills as they practice maneuvers and procedures, you can create lessons which are specifically designed to test whether students are applying ADM skills. Planning flight lessons in which you present simulated emergencies, a heavy workload, or other operational problems can be valuable in evaluating your students' application of ADM concepts. During these flights, performance can be measured on how effectively your students managed workload, or handled stress. While debriefing your students after the lessons, you can suggest ways that problems may have been solved more successfully, how tasks might have been prioritized differently, or other resources which could have been used to improve the situation.

TEACHING AVIATION PHYSIOLOGY

Since the performance and limitations of the body in flight affect judgment and the ability to make effective decisions, **aviation physiology** is an important part of ADM and human factors training. Generally speaking, most healthy people do not experience any physical difficulties as a result of flying. However, you may encounter students who have physiological problems ranging from discomfort in the ears during climbs and descents to motion sickness. You need to ensure students engaged in all levels of training are aware of the physiological factors which may affect them in flight so they will know how to recognize the onset of any symptoms in themselves and their passengers.

Regardless of the certificate or rating your students are seeking, physiology will be part of the curriculum. Some subjects are of particular importance to specific training regimens. For example, since your instrument students are wearing a view-limiting device in flight, they may likely experience vestibular disorientation at some point during training. In addition, while you should discuss the many types of hypoxia with all your students, you may need to specifically emphasize the dangers of hypoxic hypoxia to students training for a commercial certificate, since they may be flying complex airplanes capable of operating at high altitudes. While you will plan particular ground lessons to explore aviation physiology topics, such as vision, respiration, and the vestibular system, there are some areas of physiology you will need to discuss with your students early in their course of training. Factors such as motion sickness, changing air pressure, and alcohol use can affect your students' ability to perform during flight lessons and, in some cases, these topics may need to be addressed during the first flight.

MOTION SICKNESS

When the brain receives conflicting messages about the state of the body it can cause **motion sickness**, or airsickness. Anxiety and stress, which some students may feel as they begin flight training, can contribute to the nausea, dizziness, paleness, sweating, or vomiting they may experience with motion sickness. You should address this issue with beginning students and be prepared with airsickness bags in the cockpit. However, placing too much emphasis on the subject can actually increase both student anxiety and the risk of motion sickness occurring. Many students experience motion sickness during initial flights, but it generally goes away within the first 10 lessons. This fact is important to point out to students who may feel they cannot continue flight training due to their susceptibility to airsickness. In addition, it is important to remind your students that experiencing motion sickness does not reflect on their ability as a pilot. [Figure 3-43]

If your students are experiencing motion sickness have them avoid unnecessary head movements and keep their eyes focused on a point outside the aircraft.

Since Rob often becomes airsick in turbulent conditions, Kevin decides to shorten the lessons on days when the air is rough until Rob becomes more comfortable.

Although some medications can prevent airsickness in passengers, they are not recommended for use while flying since they can cause drowsiness.

John decides to take a friend on a sightseeing flight. Unfortunately it is a hot summer day and his passenger starts to experience motion sickness. To alleviate the symptoms, John opens the air vents and has her focus on some traffic outside the airplane.

Figure 3-43. You should ask your students if they are prone to motion sickness since there are techniques which you can teach them to overcome this problem. Even if your students do not experience motion sickness, you should discuss some preventive techniques in the event they need to assist passengers in the future.

Unconscious Landing

You may relate a situation such as the following incident to introduce the dangers of carbon monoxide poisoning to your students.

Although the pilot departed alone from his home airport, he would take no part in landing his high-performance single-engine airplane. It was a clear, sunny day as he cruised at 5,500 feet, enroute to Topeka, Kansas. The pilot had just switched fuel tanks and set his navigation system for his destination when he lost consciousness.

The airplane, trimmed for cruise flight and on autopilot, flew a perfectly straight course over Kansas until it ran out of fuel and glided to a landing in a field. When the pilot awoke, he was disoriented and had a severe headache. Fortunately, he was able to get out of the airplane and journey to a nearby farmhouse where he was taken by ambulance to a local hospital. The cause of the accident was determined to be a cracked manifold that allowed carbon monoxide to seep into the cabin through the heater, causing the pilot to become hypoxic.

Since carbon monoxide is an odorless gas and its presence in the cockpit may be difficult to detect, it is a good idea to inform your students about the use of carbon monoxide detectors. It is also important your students are aware of the various types of hypoxia — hypoxic, stagnant, histotoxic, and, in this case, hypemic. Typically, hypoxia is thought of as a condition that occurs at high altitudes, but it can happen any time the tissues in the body do not receive enough oxygen.

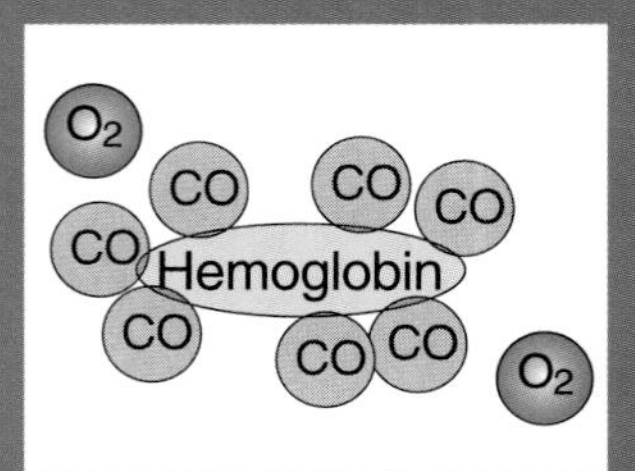

Animals at Altitude

Dr. Paul Bert, a Professor of Physiology at Paris began evaluating the effects of altitude on human physiology during the second half of the 19th century. His research began with observations of the demise of small animals in glass jars exhausted of their atmosphere. From these experiments he concluded that death occurred when the partial pressure of oxygen fell below 35 mm. Hg., regardless of the proportion of oxygen in the atmosphere. It may seem to be conventional thinking today but this recognition that the partial pressure of oxygen is vital to survival was a major landmark in the investigation of hypoxia.

Bert subsequently built the world's first man-sized decompression chamber which, although primitive by today's standards, was capable of an altitude equivalent of 36,000 feet above sea level. In this chamber he continued to experiment on animals as well as himself. In February 1874, he spent over an hour at 16,000 feet noting the effects of hypoxia and their relief by breathing an oxygen rich air mixture he had previously prepared.

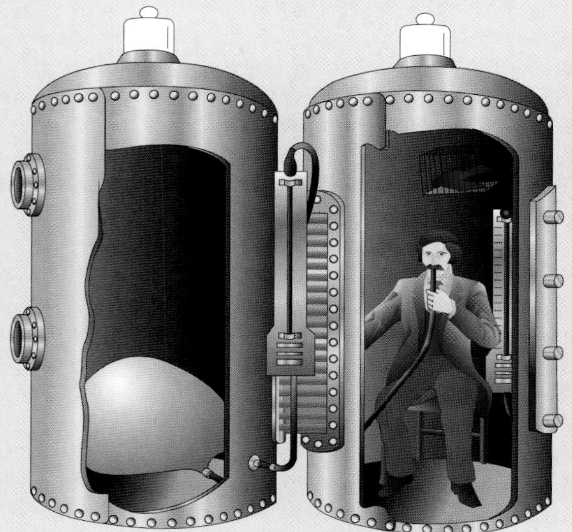

HYPOXIA

Typically students do not experience **hypoxia** during most types of training flights since maneuvers and procedures are performed at relatively low altitudes. However, you should be alert for symptoms of hypoxia, such as decreased reaction time, impaired judgment, euphoria, or drowsiness, in some students due to their physical condition. For example, students who smoke, are anemic, or have recently given blood may be particularly susceptible to hypoxia at lower altitudes than you may normally expect. In addition, carbon monoxide poisoning, which causes hypemic hypoxia, can occur at any altitude.

Since symptoms of hypoxia can range from headaches and visual impairment to euphoria and numbness, and can vary among people, suggest your students take a flight in an altitude chamber. This experience is an excellent way for your students to learn their specific reaction to hypoxia in a safe, controlled environment. An altitude chamber employs a vacuum pump to remove gas/pressure from the chamber to simulate the corresponding pressure of a particular altitude. While inside the chamber, your students will have the chance to experience their personal symptoms of hypoxia, so they will know what to look for should they suspect hypoxia in the future. The FAA began altitude chamber flights for pilots in 1962 and provides this opportunity through aviation physiology training conducted at the FAA Civil Aeromedical Institute (CAMI) and at many military facilities across the United States. [Figure 3-44]

Figure 3-44. The typical profile for an altitude chamber flight allows your students to experience hypoxia as well as a rapid decompression at 25,000 feet.

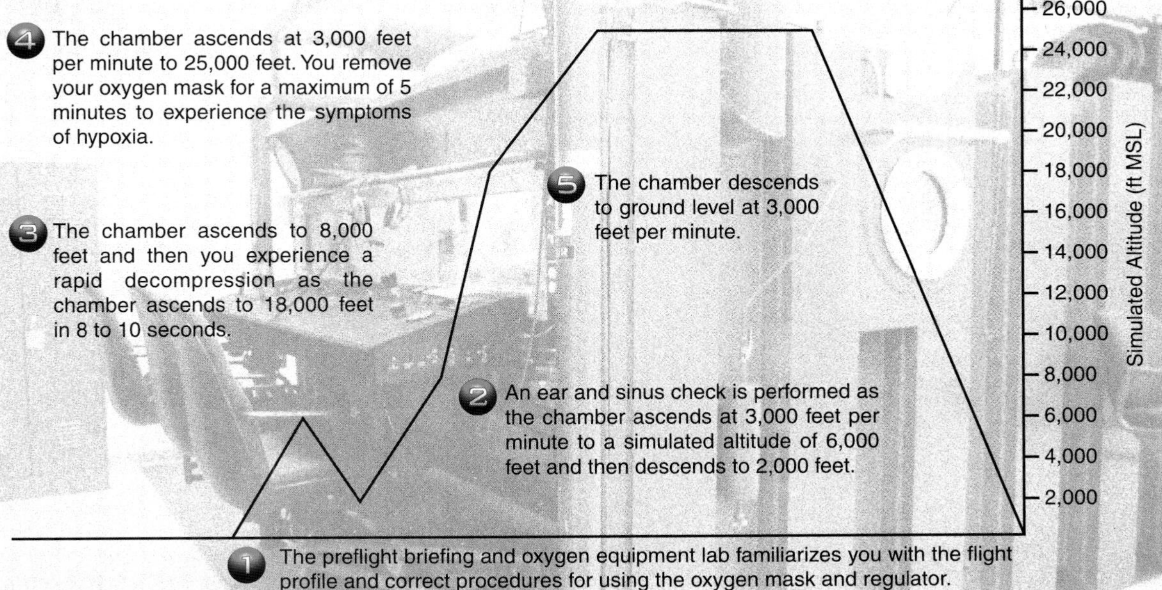

Official U.S. Air Force Photo Carter P. Luna Physiology Training Center at Peterson Air Force Base

PRESSURE EFFECTS

Be sure to familiarize your students with the effects changing pressure will have on their bodies during flight. As the airplane climbs and descends, variations in atmospheric pressure affect many parts of the body. As outside air pressure changes, air trapped in the ears, teeth, sinus cavities, and gastrointestinal tract can cause pain and discomfort.

EAR AND SINUS BLOCK

It is a good idea to discuss the effects of ear and sinus block with your students as they begin training so they will know that it is best not to fly when they are experiencing a cold or sinus congestion. Explain to your students that ear pain is normally the result of a difference between air pressure in the middle ear and outside air pressure. When the air pressure in the middle ear is equal to the pressure in the ear canal, there is no blocked feeling or pain. [Figure 3-45]

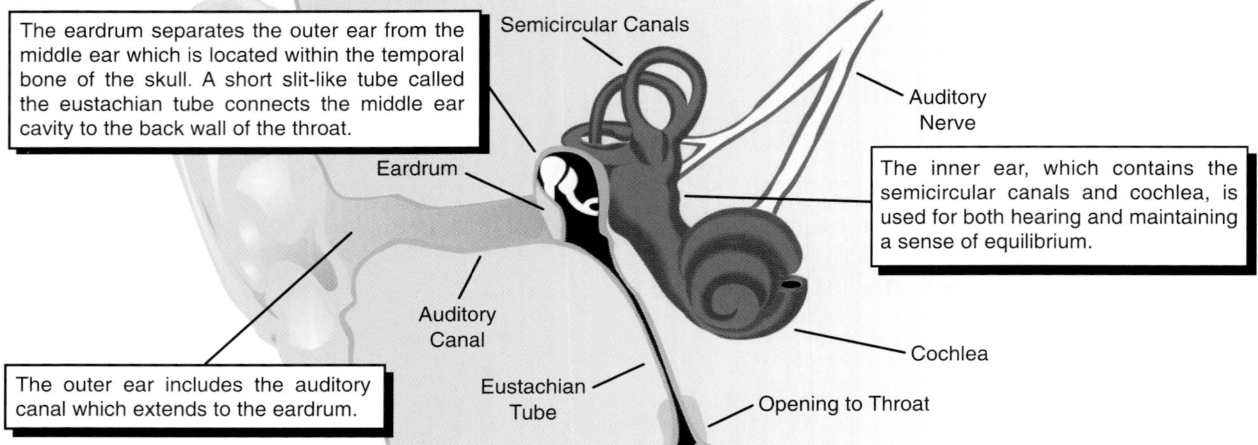

Figure 3-45. By discussing the three sections of the ear with your students, they will gain a better understanding of what causes an ear or sinus block.

During an ascent, the pressure in the auditory canal decreases and usually the higher pressure in the middle ear will open the eustachian tube to equalize the pressure. If the tube does not open, your students may feel a fullness in the ear, notice a slight hearing loss and experience discomfort since the eardrum is distended and cannot vibrate as freely. During a descent, the outside air pressure in the auditory canal will become higher than the pressure in the middle ear. This situation is harder to correct, since the eustachian tube opens more easily to let positive pressure out than it does to allow air back into the middle ear. If your students experience ear pain while flying, a slow descent rate can help prevent or reduce the severity of ear problems and the eustachian tube can sometimes be opened by yawning, swallowing, or chewing. In addition, holding the nose and mouth shut and forcibly exhaling can equalize the pressure. This procedure, which is called the **Valsalva maneuver**, forces air up the eustachian tube into the middle ear.

TOOTHACHE

Expansion of trapped air in the cavities caused by imperfect fillings, damaged root canals, and dental abscesses can produce pain at altitude. If your students experience a toothache while flying, a descent to a lower altitude may bring relief, but you should recommend that they visit a dentist for examination and treatment.

GASTROINTESTINAL PAIN

Most of the gas in the gastrointestinal tract is swallowed air, and the rest is caused by the digestion process. As altitude increases, this gas expands and can cause abdominal pain. Explain to your students that they are less likely to have this problem if they maintain good eating habits and avoid foods which produce excess gas prior to flying.

SCUBA DIVING

The reduction of atmospheric pressure which accompanies flying can produce physical problems for scuba divers. You should ask your students if they engage in this activity and alert them to the potential difficulties that can occur if they carry passengers who scuba dive. Decompression sickness, more commonly referred to as "the bends", occurs when nitrogen absorbed during a scuba dive comes out of solution and forms bubbles in the tissues and bloodstream. You may explain this phenomena by using the example of uncapping a bottle of soda. This condition is very serious and can produce extreme pain, paralysis, and, if severe enough, death. Although your students may finish a dive well within the no-decompression limits, the reduced atmospheric pressure of flying can cause the onset of decompression sickness. [Figure 3-46]

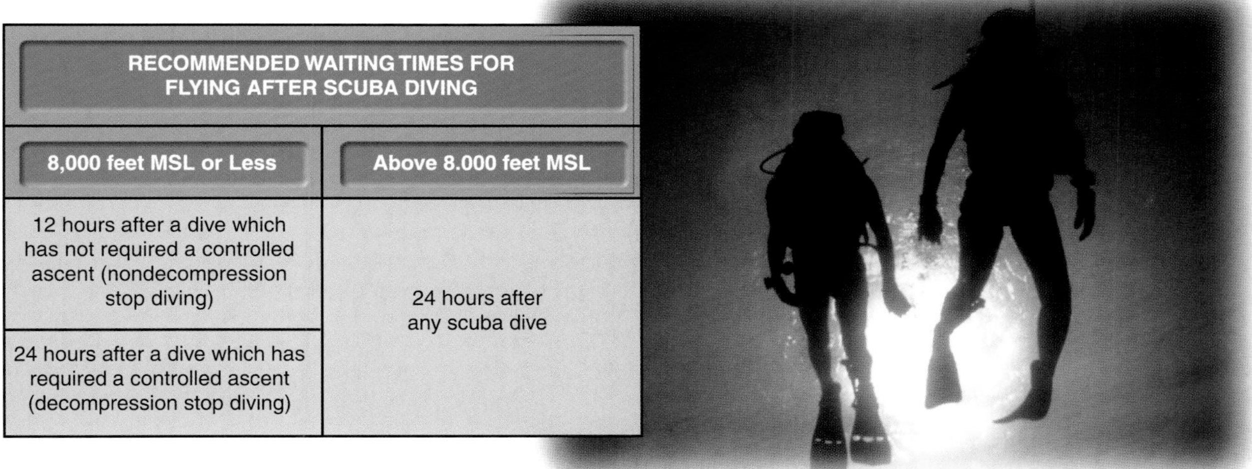

RECOMMENDED WAITING TIMES FOR FLYING AFTER SCUBA DIVING	
8,000 feet MSL or Less	**Above 8.000 feet MSL**
12 hours after a dive which has not required a controlled ascent (nondecompression stop diving)	24 hours after any scuba dive
24 hours after a dive which has required a controlled ascent (decompression stop diving)	

Figure 3-46. If your students plan to fly after scuba diving, it is important that they allow enough time for the body to rid itself of excess nitrogen absorbed during diving.

STRESS

You may want to point out to your students that a hot summer afternoon flight after a full day's work is not the best time to operate an airplane since the amount of **stress** they may be experiencing can negatively impact their performance. Your students cannot avoid stress completely and a limited amount of stress is good since it keeps them alert and prevents complacency. However, the effects of stress are cumulative and if not coped with adequately, they will eventually result in an unbearable burden. Performance will generally increase and peak with the onset of stress, and then begin to fall off rapidly as stress levels exceed your students' ability to cope. [Figure 3-47]

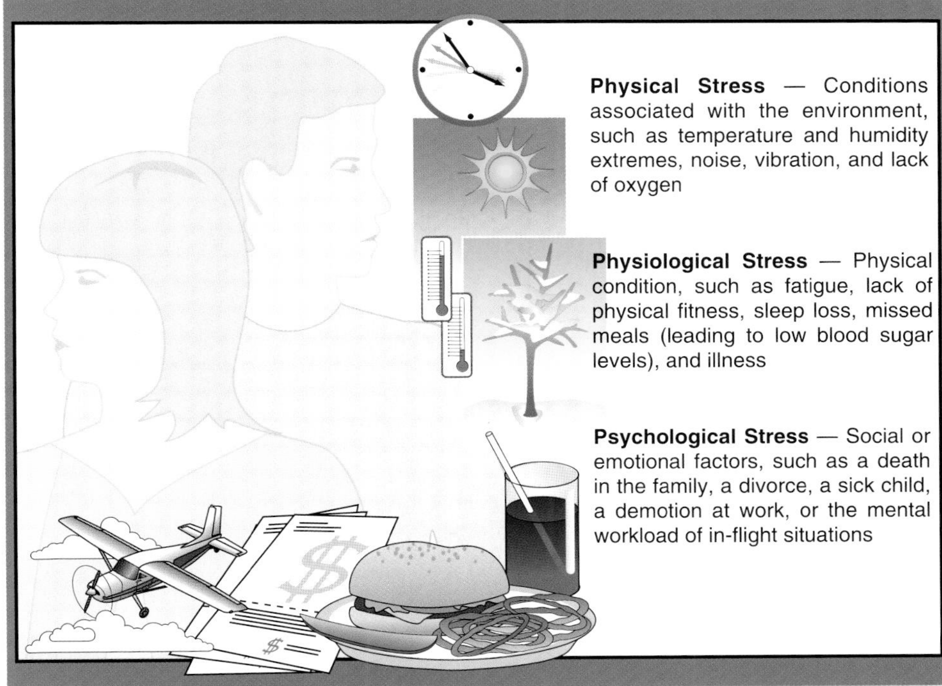

Figure 3-47. Factors which can increase your students' stress levels during flight can be placed in three categories; physical, physiological, and psychological.

One way of exploring the subject of stress with students is to recognize when stress is affecting their performance. If your students seem distracted, or have a particularly difficult time accomplishing the tasks of the lesson, you can ask them how they are feeling. Are they uncomfortable or tired? Is there stress in another aspect of their life that may be causing a distraction? This may prompt your students to evaluate how these factors affect their performance and judgment. You also should try to determine if there are aspects of pilot training that are causing excessive amounts of stress for your students. For example, if your students consistently make decisions not to fly, although weather briefings indicate favorable conditions, it may be due to apprehension regarding the lesson content. Stalls, landings, or an impending solo may cause concern for your students. By explaining a specific maneuver in greater detail or offering some additional encouragement, you may be able to alleviate some of the students' stress.

To help students manage the accumulation of life stresses and prevent stress overload, you can recommend several techniques. For example, including relaxation time in a busy schedule and maintaining a program of physical fitness can help reduce stress levels. Learning to manage time more effectively can help your students avoid heavy pressures imposed by getting behind schedule and not meeting deadlines. While these pressures may exist in the workplace, students may also experience the same type of stress regarding their flight training schedule. You can advise students to take assessments of themselves to determine their capabilities and limitations and then set realistic goals. In addition, avoiding stressful situations and encounters can help students cope with stress.

FATIGUE

Some of the effects of **fatigue** include degradation of attention and concentration, impaired coordination, and decreased ability to communicate. These factors can seriously influence your students' ability to make effective decisions. If your students become fatigued in the cockpit, no amount of training or experience can overcome the detrimental

Biological Clock

Many living organisms, including humans, possess biological clocks that count off 24-hour intervals in their lives. This internal clock effects the way we function and why we perform certain tasks better during particular times of the day.

Time	
1:00 a.m.	Pregnant women are most likely to go into labor.
2:00 a.m.	Growth hormone levels are highest.
4:00 a.m.	Asthma attacks are most likely ot occur.
6:00 a.m.	Blood pressure and heart rate begin to rise.
	Stress hormone cortisol levels increase.
7:00 a.m.	Hay fever symptoms are worst.
8:00 a.m.	Risk of heart attack and stroke is highest.
	Symptoms of rheumatoid arthritis are worst.
Noon	Hemoglobin level in the blood is at its peak.
3:00 p.m.	Grip strength, respiratory rate, and reflex sensitivity are highest.
4:00 p.m.	Body temperature, pulse rate and blood pressure peak.
6:00 p.m.	Urinary flow is highest.
9:00 p.m.	Pain threshold is lowest.
11:00 p.m.	Allergic responses are most likely.

effects. Getting adequate rest is the only way to prevent fatigue from occurring. You should emphasize to your students that they should avoid flying when they have not had a full night's rest, when they have been working excessive hours, or have had an especially exhausting or stressful day.

NOISE

Cockpit noise can contribute to fatigue, stress, and even airsickness. The understanding of speech also can be severely impeded by cockpit noise which can impair communication between you and your students as well as radio exchanges with ATC. To help alleviate these problems, the use of earplugs or headsets, while not absolutely necessary, is extremely beneficial, especially during flight instruction.

DRUGS, ALCOHOL, AND PERFORMANCE

Illness and disease also can affect your students' performance, as can the drugs which are meant to fight these illnesses. There are two things your students should consider before flying while using a drug. First, what is the condition they are treating, and second, what are the side effects of the drug used to treat the condition? Some conditions are serious enough to prohibit flying, even if the illness is being treated successfully with drugs. Instruct your students to inform their physicians they are pilots and ask about the side effects of prescription medication.

PAIN KILLERS

A question your students may ask you is, *"Can I fly if I am taking aspirin or Tylenol?"* The answer to this question is typically *"Yes."* Pain killers can be grouped into two broad classes: analgesics and anesthetics. Analgesics, such as aspirin and codeine, are drugs which decrease pain. The majority of the drugs which contain acetylsalicylic acid (Aspirin), acetaminophen (Tylenol), and ibuprofen (Advil) have few side effects when taken in the correct dosage. Although some people are allergic to certain analgesics or may suffer from stomach irritation, flying usually is not restricted when taking these drugs. [Figure 3-48]

Susan has had a stressful day at work and decides to take a couple of aspirin to alleviate her headache before her training flight at 6:00.

After discussing her situation with her instructor, she decides to postpone the flight until she is less fatigued.

Figure 3-48. It may be prudent to determine the reason your students are taking pain killers. For example, If they are taking aspirin because of a stressful day at work, they are still legal to fly, but taking the controls of an airplane may be a poor decision.

ALCOHOL

Ethyl alcohol is the most widely used and abused drug. You should familiarize your students with the regulations contained in FAR Parts 61 and 91 which apply to drug and alcohol violations and testing requirements, including motor vehicle offenses involving alcohol. Any violation or refusal to submit to an alcohol test may result in the denial of an application for a pilot certificate. Although the regulations are quite specific, it is a good idea to teach your students to be more conservative than the FARs. Most pilots allow a minimum of 12 hours to pass after the last drink before flying; commercial airlines generally require their pilots to wait 24 hours.

FITNESS FOR FLIGHT

From the beginning of training, teach your students to ask themselves several key questions to determine their physical suitability for flight. If I have an illness, does the condition present a hazard to safe flight? If I am taking a drug for an illness and it wears off during a flight, will it cause an unsafe condition? Can the drug which I am taking produce any side effect which would influence my motor, perceptual, or psychological condition? Am I fatigued? Am I experiencing excessive stress from work or home? If the answer to any of these questions is *"Yes"* or *"I don't know,"* they may not be fit to operate an aircraft. Students should understand that the FARs prohibit them from acting as pilot in command if they have a known medical deficiency which would make them unable to meet the qualifications of a current medical certificate. If your students are not sure of their physical suitability for flight, advise them to consult an aviation medical examiner.

SUMMARY CHECKLIST

✓ Aeronautical decision making is a systematic approach to the mental process used by aircraft pilots to consistently determine the best course of action in response to a given set of circumstances.

✓ It is estimated that approximately 75% of all aviation accidents are human factors related.

✓ One of the best ways to explain the poor judgment chain to students is to discuss a specific situation which led to an aircraft accident of incident.

✓ Just as you would prepare to present a technical subject, you must formulate and implement a plan to teach ADM concepts to students.

✓ Crew resource management (CRM) programs focus on the effective use of all available resources including human resources, hardware, and information.

✓ CRM principles have direct application to the general aviation cockpit and must be demonstrated on practical tests.

✓ To explain the steps in the decision-making process, you can introduce a scenario that places the student in the position of making a decision about a typical flight situation.

✓ You should emphasize to students the importance of *correctly* defining the problem during the decision making process. An inaccurate assessment of the situation can actually *become* the problem.

✓ When your students are faced with making a decision regarding a flight, you can ask them to evaluate the status of the four risk elements — the pilot in command, the aircraft, the environment, and the operation.

✓ Reviewing accident and incident research with your students can help develop their ability to more effectively assess risk.

- ✓ During both flight and ground lessons, you must be prepared to address ADM concepts as they apply to particular operations and procedures, as well as conduct specific lessons that focus on decision making and the role of human factors in aviation.

- ✓ Reviewing information from the National Transportation Safety Board (NTSB) and NASA's Aviation Safety Reporting System (ASRS) is an excellent way to help your students understand the elements which influence decision making and the consequences of poor judgment.

- ✓ To help you teach effectively, you can organize the factors which influence aeronautical decision making into five elements — pilot-in-command responsibility, communication, resource use, workload management, and situational awareness.

- ✓ You can introduce the I'm Safe Checklist to students as a guideline to prompt them to think about their fitness for flight before taking the controls of an airplane.

- ✓ To help students determine if they are prepared for a particular flight, encourage them to create personal checklists which state limitations based on such factors as experience, currency, and comfort level in certain flight conditions.

- ✓ Teach students to examine their decisions carefully to ensure their choices have not been influenced by hazardous attitudes and familiarize them with positive alternatives, referred to as antidotes, to counteract these attitudes.

- ✓ You need to emphasize that prior to a flight with another pilot, your students should discuss how responsibilities will be divided and what is expected from each crewmember.

- ✓ To help your students prevent a breakdown in communication, teach them to use correct radio procedures, read back clearances, verify instructions with ATC, be alert for similar call signs, and use their call sign to acknowledge transmissions, not a double click of the mike or *"roger."*

- ✓ Students who are pursuing aviation as a career and even those who anticipate flying extensively with other pilots will benefit from learning about techniques used by flight crewmembers to improve cockpit coordination.

- ✓ To make informed decisions during flight operations, students must learn to identify internal and external resources and evaluate whether they have the time to use a particular resource and the impact its use will have upon the safety of flight.

- ✓ Effective workload management ensures that essential operations are accomplished by planning, prioritizing, and sequencing tasks to avoid work overload.

- ✓ One of your primary goals when teaching your students to manage workload is to help them learn to recognize future workload requirements and prepare for high workload periods during times of low workload.

- ✓ Accidents often occur when flying task requirements exceed pilot capabilities. The difference between these two factors is called the margin of safety.

- ✓ Situational awareness is the accurate perception of the operational and environmental factors which affect the aircraft, pilot, and passengers during a specific period of time.

- ✓ If you have successfully taught your students about their responsibility as PIC, the skills to communicate effectively in the flight environment, how to identify and utilize resources, and methods to efficiently manage workload, you have provided them with the tools to maintain situational awareness.

- ✓ Fatigue, stress, distractions, complacency and work overload are some of the factors which can cause a loss of situational awareness.

- ✓ One of the more tragic consequences of a loss of situational awareness is controlled flight into terrain (CFIT). There are several techniques you can teach your students to help them avoid CFIT accidents in the future.

- ✓ Since operational pitfalls, such as scud running and the duck-under syndrome may not be familiar to your students, describe the hazardous situations that may occur as they relate to each phase of training.

- ✓ By allowing students to make decisions about typical issues that arise throughout the course of training, you can continually evaluate their decision-making ability and offer suggestions for improvement, if needed.

- ✓ To ensure that your students consider aeronautical decision making concepts during each lesson, you can include ADM elements in your lesson objectives and critique your students on their application of these principles. You can also create lessons which are specifically designed to test whether students are applying ADM skills.

- ✓ Since the performance and limitations of the body in flight affect judgment and the ability to make effective decisions, aviation physiology is an important part of ADM and human factors training.

- ✓ Many students experience motion sickness during initial flights, but it generally goes away within the first 10 lessons.

- ✓ A flight in an altitude chamber is an excellent way for your students to learn their specific reaction to hypoxia in a safe, controlled environment.

- ✓ Be sure to familiarize your students with the effects changing pressure will have on their bodies during flight. As outside air pressure changes, air trapped in the ears, teeth, sinus cavities, and gastrointestinal tract can cause your students pain and discomfort.

- ✓ Factors which can increase your students' stress levels during flight can be placed in three categories; physical, physiological, and psychological.

- ✓ Since fatigue can degrade attention and concentration, impair coordination, and decrease the ability to communicate, it can seriously influence your students' ability to make effective decisions.

- ✓ You should familiarize your students with the regulations contained in FAR Parts 61 and 91 which apply to drug and alcohol violations and testing requirements, including motor vehicle offenses involving alcohol.

KEY TERMS

Aeronautical Decision Making (ADM)

Pilot Error

Human Factors Related

Poor Judgment Chain

Crew Resource Management (CRM)

Decision-Making Process

Risk Elements

National Transportation Safety Board (NTSB)

Aviation Safety Reporting System (ASRS)

Pilot-In-Command Responsibility

I'm Safe Checklist

Personal Checklists

Hazardous Attitudes

Communication

Sterile Cockpit

Resource Use

Internal Resources

External Resources

Workload Management

Situational Awareness

Controlled Flight Into Terrain (CFIT)

Operational Pitfalls

Aviation Physiology

Motion Sickness

Hypoxia

Valsalva Maneuver

Stress

Fatigue

Alcohol

QUESTIONS

1. When should you introduce aeronautical decision making to students?
2. Describe an effective method for familiarizing your students with the poor judgment chain.
3. True/False. Since CRM is designed for airline flight crews, your students do not need to understand this concept.
4. Explain the steps in the decision making process.
5. Name the four risk elements which must be evaluated to reach a go/no go decision.
6. Select the true statement regarding the use of accident and incident research.

   A. The NTSB does not provide public access to accident reports.
   B. Reviewing NTSB and ASRS reports with students is not prudent since it may frighten them.
   C. Discussing accident statistics and research can help your students assess risk and understand elements which influence decision making.

7. State three items that can be included in a personal checklist.

8. Provide an example that illustrates how a student may display an attitude of resignation during a flight lesson.

9. Explain the sterile cockpit rule.

10. List at least five internal or external resources which can assist students in decision making.

11. State at least two methods students can use to effectively manage workload during flight.

12. True/False. The margin of safety is greatest during takeoff and landing.

13. Which of the following are obstacles to maintaining situational awareness.

    A. Complacency
    B. Failure of the autopilot
    C. Internal resources

14. Name an operational pitfall that an instrument student may fall prey to.

15. Describe how you could incorporate the concept of situational awareness into a lesson on traffic pattern procedures.

16. Which of the following are methods you can use to help students combat motion sickness.

    A. Suggest they focus on items inside the cockpit.
    B. Recommend they take medication to prevent airsickness.
    C. Advise they focus on objects outside the airplane and open the air vents.

PART II
FROM PASSION TO PROFESSION

The way I see it, you can either work for a living or you can fly airplanes. Me, I'd rather fly.

— Len Morgan

PART II

Although it may not seem like work at times, leading prospective aviators down the path toward a pilot certificate or rating provides you the opportunity to turn your passion for aviation into your profession. Up to this point in your flight training, you have been the receiver of information. When you obtain your flight instructor certificate, you become a conveyor of knowledge. By combining your newly acquired understanding of teaching with your aeronautical expertise, Part II explores creative ways to guide your students on their own aviation journeys. To begin, *Becoming an Instructor* places you in the right seat of the airplane and develops your professional image in addition to outlining your privileges as an instructor and covering important safety issues. Next, *The Basic Instructor* presents practical examples of how to impart information and teach the necessary skills for private and commercial students to reach their goals. In addition, you will examine methods for preparing future flight instructors and furnishing specialized types of instruction, such as flight reviews and aircraft transitions. If you choose to progress beyond your initial flight instructor certificate, *The Advanced Instructor* outlines techniques for providing effective instruction to students pursuing instrument and multi-engine ratings.

CHAPTER 4

BECOMING AN INSTRUCTOR

Flight Instructor
Volume 2 — Becoming an Instructor

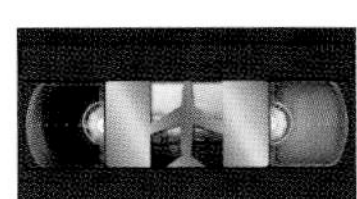

SECTION A

TRANSITIONING TO THE RIGHT SEAT

You may have been in the right seat of an airplane before, perhaps while acting as a co-pilot or as a safety pilot for a friend working on an instrument rating. As a flight instructor, you fly from the right seat, of course, but your duties are much different than those of second in command. You not only need to control the airplane from the right seat, but you must act as an authority in the cockpit to keep the flight safe and guide your student through the learning process. [Figure 4-1]

Figure 4-1. The view from the right seat will change your perspective on flying. Many instructors believe they did not truly learn to fly until they started teaching others.

THE RIGHT SEAT

When you begin your training for your initial flight instructor certificate, you first need to become accustomed to operating the airplane from the right seat. Your instructor introduces you to flight from this side of the cockpit by pointing out changes in orientation, then coaches you while you gain proficiency by performing maneuvers, and plays the

MANAGING THE COCKPIT

Flight instruction is considered one of the safest operations in general aviation. However, it takes care on the part of both the instructor and student to ensure the safety of a particular flight, especially during phases of high workload. During a period from January 1988 to December 1996, the highest concentration of instructional incidents, as reported to the ASRS (Aviation Safety Reporting System), occurred within the airport environment, including the airspace within 10 nautical miles and below 1,000 feet AGL.

The majority of flight instruction at all levels is airport-centered. During primary instruction, students focus on perfecting landings and traffic patterns, while advanced students may concentrate on instrument approaches. While landing procedures require some of the most intense focus from both the flight instructor and student, alertness to ATC transmissions and other traffic is vital as well during this phase of the flight. One common problem lies in how flight instructors must balance the desire to allow students to make and correct their own mistakes with overall flight safety and compliance with ATC directives. If flight instructors are not able to properly divide their attention between instructing their students and maintaining communication with ATC, situational awareness can be lost. This is clearly illustrated by the following ASRS report.

"We took off on [Runway] 24 instead of 30, as the tower subsequently informed us. As I reviewed the event later, with my student and in my own mind, I realized how I may have added to the uncertainty. I was busy pointing out airport markings and critiquing the flight to this point. The priority should have been communications with the tower and standard procedure."

You should not allow student errors to develop to a point where you cannot recover from them without compromising safety or violating FARs. Also, limit critiques to non-critical phases of the flight. For example, when practicing landings, you may either save critiques for a relatively low-workload portion of the traffic pattern, or taxi back between landings so you can discuss your student's performance while the airplane is stopped in a runup or ramp area. This will allow you to focus on critical communication with ATC and on other traffic, as well as keep your student from having to divide attention between listening to your critique and controlling the airplane.

student as you give practice instruction. Receiving a checkout in the right seat takes some adjustment, as the familiar cockpit temporarily becomes unfamiliar.

ORIENTATION

The cockpits of most light aircraft are designed with the single pilot in mind. If you progress to larger aircraft built for two-pilot crews, you will find more redundant systems and controls that can be easily accessed from the right seat. However, in the average training airplane, some controls are difficult to reach from the instructor's side. Normally, all of the flight instruments, the ignition switch, the primer, the electrical switches, and often the engine instruments, are located on the left side of the panel. Additionally, during your past experience, you likely became used to operating the throttle, mixture, and propeller control with your right hand, and now you must switch to using your right hand for aircraft control and your left hand to operate the power controls. Though these differences may not seem large taken separately, together they create an environment where at first you may easily lose orientation.

When you are in the right seat, your ability to accurately read the instruments on the left side of the panel diminishes. Since the instruments are offset from the center of your visual field, you must shift your eyes or move your head to see the displays. Another common problem that may be encountered is **parallax** resulting from the distance between an instrument's needle and the surface of the scale. Parallax is the apparent displacement of an object, if viewed first from one position, and then from another. For example, your interpretation of an airspeed, altitude, or heading when viewing the

Figure 4-2. Flying from the right seat requires you to adapt to a less than ideal situation for controlling the airplane. These adaptations may range from having to lean over to start the engine to more significant changes in how you interpret the instruments.

instruments from an angle in the right seat, may differ from the information shown on the instrument displays when seen from straight ahead in the left seat. [Figure 4-2]

PROFICIENCY

Once you have become accustomed to flying the airplane from the right seat, you need to develop proficiency in the maneuvers included in the private and commercial training curricula, as well as basic attitude instrument flight. This normally requires three to five hours of instruction and additional solo practice. As you rehearse these maneuvers, keep in mind that you are not only refining your skills for the practical test, but you are also gaining insight into how you will demonstrate these maneuvers to your students. To set the best example, you need to perform each maneuver with precision and professionalism.

In order to master flying from the right seat, you need to develop similar reliance on visual cues as you did when you were first starting to learn how to maneuver the airplane. This can provide you with insight into how students develop these same visual cues during initial flight training. A logbook endorsement to fly from the right seat is not required, but it provides confirmation that this training was given, and your instructor feels you are competent. You will probably have the opportunity to practice solo, and you can use this time to hone your skills in areas where you need the most practice. [Figure 4-3]

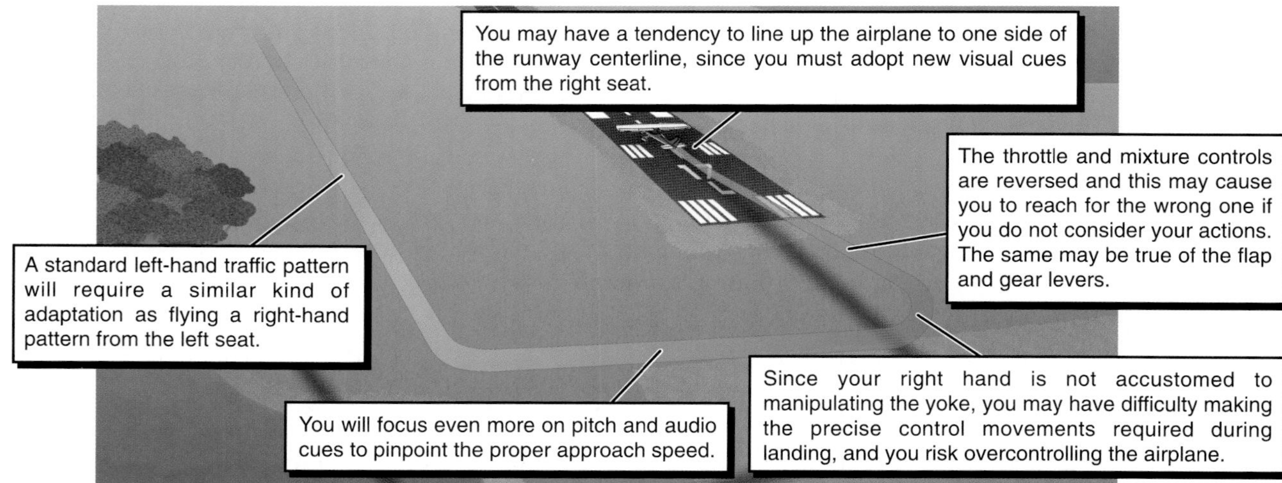

Figure 4-3. During flight instructor training, takeoffs and landings become a primary focus, since they tend to accentuate the change in visual perspective between the left and right seat. In addition, student practice in these maneuvers is some of the most challenging, because you must precisely control the airplane, and teach your student to do so, in close proximity to the ground.

In the future, when you give flight instruction, be aware that your students should not expect you to be superhuman. If you make a mistake, or perform a maneuver that does not meet the practical test standards, do not attempt to hide the error. Instead, use the situation as a learning device by pointing out the cause of your error and how you can improve your performance. Then, repeat the demonstration, this time taking care to do it properly.

PRACTICE INSTRUCTION

As you master flying from the right seat and review the materials which you will need to present to a private or commercial student, you will be introduced to **practice instruction**. Your instructor will require you to develop lesson plans for ground and flight instruction sessions. On the ground, you will be asked to explain certain concepts as you would to a student. Your instructor may pose typical student questions and offer suggestions as to how to convey information more effectively. During flight lessons, your instructor will imitate a typical student pilot whose proficiency level is appropriate to the stage of training assigned. Once you have explained and demonstrated a maneuver, your instructor will play the role of a student and perform this maneuver while making various errors. You will then be required to correct and critique this performance.

As you progress and gain proficiency in leading these sessions, your instructor may have you work with students currently pursuing their private or commercial certificates. In some cases, you may be asked to lead a classroom session of a ground school. Arrangements may also be made for you to observe dual instruction, where you sit in the back seat of an airplane while a CFI gives an actual lesson. [Figure 4-4]

Figure 4-4. When you observe a student as part of your instruction, each person involved needs to be especially vigilant about the division of duties in the cockpit. A thorough preflight briefing should ensure that everyone is clear on their responsibilities.

Keep in mind that until you have your flight instructor certificate, you may not log any practice instruction as dual given, nor can you sign a student's logbook. However, you gain insight into instruction through the questions asked by these students and the critique your instructor gives you after each lesson.

During this time, you begin developing your own character as a flight instructor. You may notice how the techniques of previous instructors have influenced your style. You may also begin to reflect on times in the past when an instructor may not have taught effectively and work to change these methods in your own teaching.

POSITIVE EXCHANGE OF FLIGHT CONTROLS

Through the course of giving flight instruction, there are many times when you need to exchange control of the airplane with your student. For example, after you demonstrate

Figure 4-5. Review the procedure for exchanging the flight controls with each student.

a maneuver, you need to pass control of the airplane so your student can attempt the maneuver. When you do so, the FAA recommends a three-step procedure to ensure that it is clear who has control of the airplane at all times. [Figure 4-5]

When you pass the controls, you should continue to fly until your student acknowledges the exchange by saying, *"I have the flight controls."* You should also check visually to establish that your student has taken control of the airplane. If you need to assume control of the airplane, you will take the controls and state, *"I have the flight controls,"* visually checking to verify your student has released the yoke. You need to ensure your student clearly understands the procedures for exchanging the flight controls before you start the airplane, so you avoid confusion and a potentially hazardous situation.

USE OF DISTRACTIONS

As you give flight instruction, you will need to prepare your students for times during flight when they could be distracted from controlling the airplane by various events or situations. Numerous studies have determined that accidents often occur when the pilot becomes distracted during critical phases of flight, and, in addition, National Transportation Safety Board statistics reveal that most stall/spin accidents occurred when the pilot's attention was diverted from the primary task of flying the aircraft. Stall/spin-related accidents in particular have accounted for about 25% of the total general aviation fatal accidents. Therefore, the emphasis on realistic distractions in training is focused on stall/spin awareness. Common **distractions** that precipitate this type of accident include engine failure; preoccupation inside or outside the cockpit while changing power, configuration, or trim; maneuvering to avoid other traffic; or clearing hazardous obstacles during takeoff and climb. You should have your students divide their attention between the distracting task and maintaining control of the aircraft. [Figure 4-6]

During training flights, an instructor should interject realistic distractions to determine if students can maintain aircraft control while their attention is diverted.

GIVING EFFICIENT INSTRUCTION

While you are flying with a student, you are making use of two normally limited resources: time and money. You must balance a student's possible desire to complete a certificate in either a limited amount of time or by spending a limited amount of money

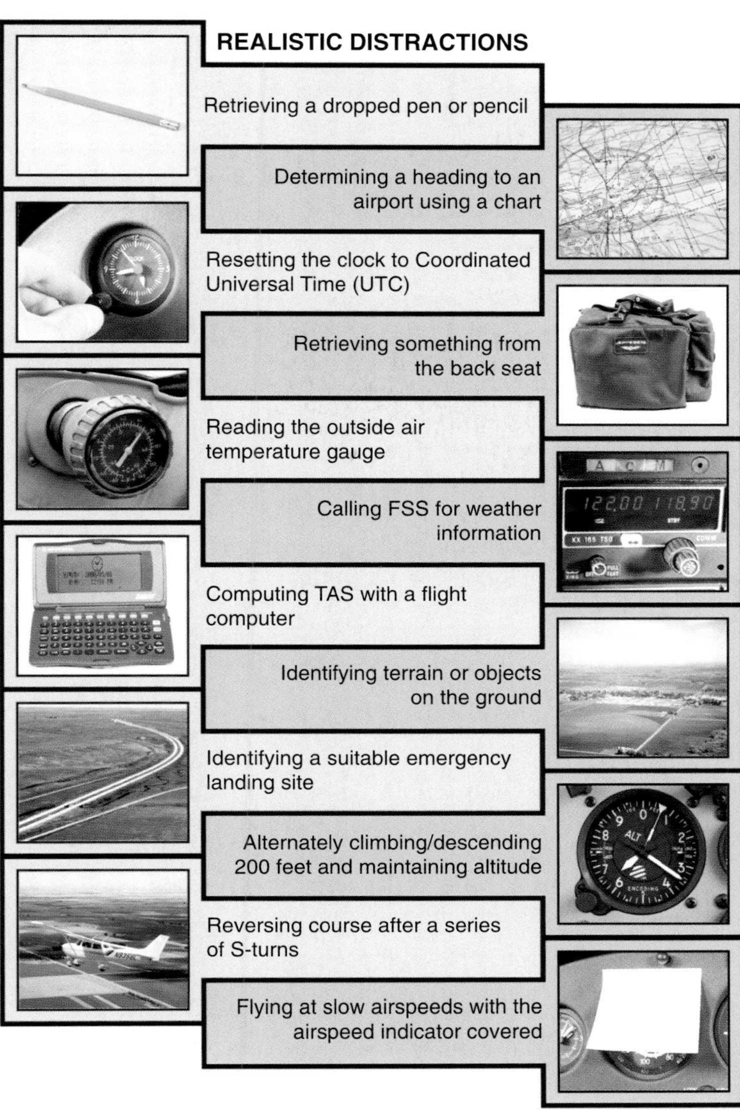

Figure 4-6. These are examples of distractions that can be used to test your students during the course of flight training.

with your desire to provide a complete course of training. In order to do this, you must plan your instructional sessions wisely and learn to take advantage of any chance to accomplish the most opportune tasks with each flight.

In order to do this, you need to assess many different factors before you begin a lesson. Are you using the optimum aircraft for the operations planned for that day? Is the equipment in the airplane working correctly for what you need to accomplish? What are the current conditions, and what weather is forecast to occur during your flight? Can you fly to another airport to eliminate distractions so you can focus on a particular task? For example, if you operate from an airport where the wind is generally straight down one runway, you may want to find a relatively quiet airport with multiple runways where you can easily practice crosswind takeoffs and landings. It may be well worth the time you spend traveling.

INSURANCE AND LIABILITY

Now that you are teaching someone else to fly, you take on more responsibility than you ever had as a private pilot. Whether you work for an FBO, flight school, or give freelance instruction, you need to be aware of how this responsibility presents new issues in the case of an accident or incident. Airplanes are typically more expensive than automobiles, and the financial consequences of aviation accidents can easily exceed a flight instructor's resources. For this reason, it is recommended that you carry some form of insurance, whether it is part of your employer's insurance coverage, your own personal policy, or both.

If you work for an FBO or flight school, you likely will be covered during most operations by your employer's insurance policy. However, because of the wide variety of policies available, you should familiarize yourself with your employer's specific policy before you determine whether you are insured in every flight operation you perform. You may not be covered when flying with a student in an aircraft not owned or leased by the flight school. In this case, you will need to check the policy for the student's airplane to see if you are insured.

If you give freelance flight instruction, or if you fly in several student-owned aircraft, you may wish to purchase some form of **non-owner liability coverage**. This policy will insure you up to prescribed amounts against claims arising from bodily injury or damage you may have caused to others or their property while using an aircraft you do not own. A separate policy will cover any damage to the aircraft itself, known as **aircraft damage liability coverage**, and it works much like the collision insurance you carry on your car. The **deductible** is the amount the policyholder is responsible for in the event of a **claim**, arising from an incident or accident. Technically, the owner's policy should cover any damages to the airplane itself after the deductible is exceeded. However, aircraft insurance is not like automobile insurance, in that the owner's policy may cover any person driving their car, regardless of who may be specifically named on the policy. In fact, many insurance providers reserve the right to **subrogate**, which means they will pursue action against a third party determined to be responsible for the accident, and attempt to recover damages from them over the amount of the deductible. As a flight instructor, it is very possible that you could be held liable for damages incurred if the accident takes place with you in the airplane, regardless of the owner's experience and/or ratings. Therefore, you must be familiar with the policies covering all aircraft you fly, and as a safety net, you should consider carrying your own insurance. [Figure 4-7]

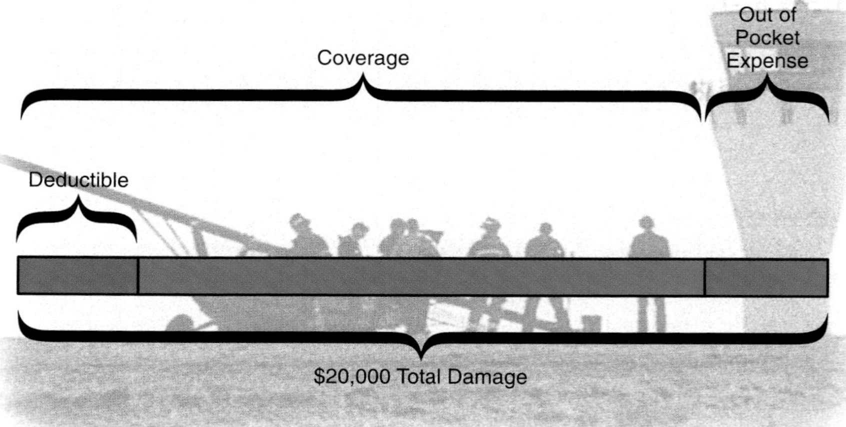

Figure 4-7. If you were involved in an accident that did $20,000 worth of damage to an airplane owned by a student, the financial responsibility borne by each person or company involved may be similar to the breakdown shown here.

Also, you may want to inform your students about their liability exposure in those operations during which they rent an airplane or fly with a friend. Just as they would ensure an airplane is airworthy for flight, so should they make certain that they are covered in case an accident occurs.

SUMMARY CHECKLIST

✓ Your instructor introduces you to flight from the right side of the cockpit by pointing out changes in orientation, then coaches you while you gain proficiency through practicing maneuvers, and plays the student as you give practice instruction.

✓ In the average training airplane, some controls are difficult to reach from the instructor's side. Normally, all of the flight instruments, the ignition switch, the primer, the electrical switches, and often the engine instruments, are located on the left side of the panel.

✓ Parallax is the apparent displacement of an object, if viewed first from one position, and then from another.

✓ As you master flying from the right seat and review the materials you will need to present to a private or commercial student, your instructor will introduce you to practice instruction.

✓ When you pass control of the airplane, the FAA recommends a three-step procedure, known as the positive exchange of flight controls, to ensure that it is clear who has control of the airplane at all times.

✓ You will need to prepare your students for times during flight when they could be distracted from controlling the airplane by various events or situations.

✓ Common distractions that precipitate stall/spin accidents include engine failure; preoccupation inside or outside the cockpit while changing power, configuration, or trim; maneuvering to avoid other traffic; or clearing hazardous obstacles during takeoff and climb.

✓ In order to give efficient instruction, you must plan your lessons wisely, and learn to take advantage of any chance to accomplish opportune tasks with each flight.

✓ As a flight instructor, you take on more responsibility than you had as a private pilot, and it is recommended that you carry some form of insurance, whether it is part of your employer's insurance coverage, your own personal policy, or both.

KEY TERMS

Parallax

Practice Instruction

Distractions

Non-Owner Liability Coverage

Aircraft Damage Liability Coverage

Deductible

Claim

Subrogate

QUESTIONS

1. True/False. Parallax refers to the problem of seeing two displays instead of one when viewed from the right seat.

2. Which maneuvers accentuate the change in visual perspective most during the transition to the right seat?

    A. Takeoffs and landings
    B. Steep turns and climbs
    C. Ground reference maneuvers

3. List variations of practice instruction that your instructor may have you demonstrate during your training.

4. Describe some common distractions that you can employ during flight instruction.

5. For what portion of an insurance claim is the policyholder typically responsible?

    A. None
    B. The total amount of the claim
    C. Only the amount of the deductible

SECTION B
TEACHING FLIGHT SAFETY

Aviation in itself is not inherently dangerous. But to an even greater degree than the sea, it is terribly unforgiving of any carelessness, incapacity or neglect.

— Original author unknown; dates back to a World War II advisory.

Flight safety is directly linked to the pilot's ability to exercise good judgment and make effective decisions. Each flight or ground lesson you conduct provides an opportunity for you to teach these skills. Often, you must present your students with aeronautical decision-making situations unique to the operations that apply to the certificate or rating for which they are training. [Figure 4-8] However, there are some safety factors that affect every type of operation, and you must be prepared to address these issues with each student you instruct.

Figure 4-8. Private, commercial, instrument, multi-engine, and flight instructor training each have unique safety issues which you must address with your students.

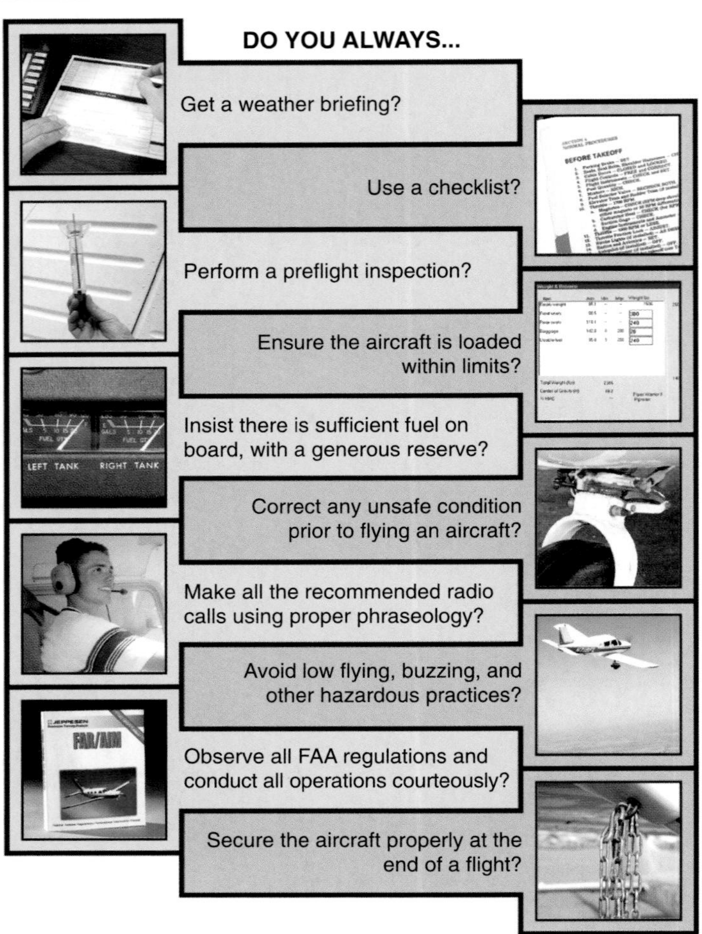

Figure 4-9. Since you are an important role model for your students, it is essential that you consistently emphasize safety by example.

As a flight instructor, it is your responsibility to be a strong flight safety advocate. You are the person your students most likely will emulate. If your students observe you violating accepted safety procedures, their opinions regarding the importance of these practices will be affected. [Figure 4-9]

PREFLIGHT CONSIDERATIONS

Teaching judgment begins well before you take off. Make sure your students obtain a weather briefing before each flight, and then quiz them about the briefing to ensure they understand how any reported hazards affect the proposed lesson. While you want your students to exercise conservative judgment, you do not want them to avoid making decisions. When students cancel a flight every time marginal conditions are forecast nearby, they may not be considering all of their options. [Figure 4-10]

Should a flight lesson prove inadvisable, you can still make this a valuable learning situation. You can observe the weather with your student, possibly from the control tower. Notice how clouds build and move, how winds shift with frontal passage, or how ceilings form and visibility decreases. Obtain the current PIREPS and give your students opportunities to gain experience interpreting this information.

In addition to making decisions about weather conditions, another preflight consideration involves an analysis of the fuel situation. In the course of normal flight training, your students may not think much about fuel since to conduct a one-hour lesson, they often take off with full fuel, more than a 4-hour supply in a typical training airplane. To help students become more aware of fuel quantity issues, ask them to compute a required landing time for each flight. [Figure 4-11] If the flight does not go as planned, your students have already determined at what time it should be terminated. Knowing your fuel situation before you take off is only part of preventing fuel problems. Fuel starvation and fuel exhaustion will be discussed later in this section.

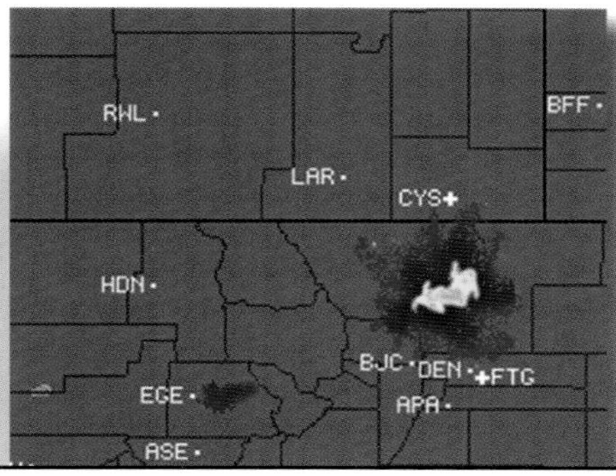

1 After receiving a briefing that forecasts thunderstorms with occasional moderate to severe turbulence and wind shear over the area, your student, Susan, calls to cancel her lesson.

2 While postponing the flight is certainly a safe choice, you ask Susan about the conditions shown on radar. She says flight service is reporting strong echoes 30 miles north of the airport moving east, as well as isolated weak echoes 40 miles to the west. There has been no change in the strength or significant movement of these echoes in the last hour.

```
TAF
KAPA 1620492 17007KT P6SM FEW100 PROB40 18015G20KT 3SM
TSRW BKN25
```

3 You ask Susan about the current conditions at the airport and about the terminal aerodrome forecast (TAF). The latest METAR indicates the sky is clear with light winds out of the south. The TAF indicates these conditions will continue with a chance of strong gusty winds in thunderstorms and rain showers during the next several hours.

4 You suggest meeting at the airport to ascertain whether the lesson is feasible. When Susan arrives, you both observe the weather and consider the proposed flight. You planned to practice landings without leaving the traffic pattern. She suggests proceeding with the flight lesson with the stipulation that you land immediately if there is any sign of cumulonimbus building within 20 miles of the airport. You agree that Susan's plan is reasonable and provides an option if adverse weather materializes close to the airport.

Figure 4-10. Weather briefings that contain potentially adverse conditions provide great opportunities to teach your students sound go/no-go decision skills.

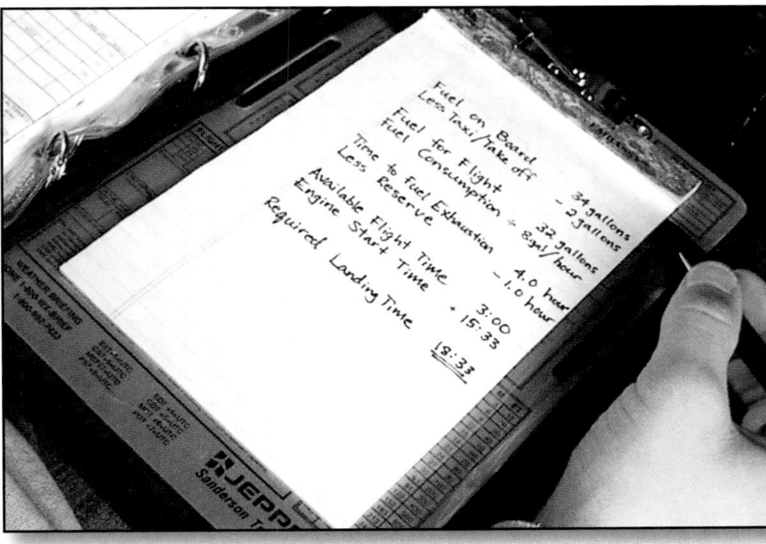

Figure 4-11. After verifying the amount of fuel on board during the preflight inspection, students can calculate the flying time less the required reserve, and add this to the engine-start time. Although the FAA requires only a 30-minute reserve for day VFR flight, the AOPA Air Safety Foundation recommends a minimum one-hour reserve for both VFR and IFR operations.

GROUND OPERATIONS

While ground operations typically elude many of the dangers of airborne operations, there are hazards your students must consider. If students are complacent, ground operations may become more dangerous than necessary.

CHECKLIST USE

It is essential to teach effective **checklist use** beginning with the first flight. If this habit is not instilled early, your students are unlikely to practice it later. Start by ensuring your students use a checklist for the preflight inspection. If the training aircraft does not have a preflight checklist on board, then use the POH, and make a copy of the appropriate pages for future use. Once your students become skilled at performing the preflight inspection, they can inspect the airplane using a flow pattern, but they should always verify they have completed each item by referring to the checklist.

Consider having your students write their own checklists based on the POH. Since the manufacturer's checklist may not be organized for a flow pattern inspection, a modified checklist may work better. [Figure 4-12] You may even give your students computer disks with checklists they can customize. Avoid including extraneous items, or the checklist will slow your students down and they will be tempted not to use it. However, make sure each student's checklist covers all the items on the manufacturer's checklist before authorizing use of the modified one.

Before Takeoff

1. Controls
   a) Parking Brake - SET.
   b) Ailerons, Elevator, Rudder - CHECK FREEDOM AND DIRECTION OF MOVEMENT.
   c) Flaps - CHECK SET AT ZERO OR 20° FOR TAKEOFF.
2. Instruments
   a) Attitude Indicator - SET.
   b) Altimeter - SET.
   c) Directional Gyro - SET.
   d) Heading Bug - SET FOR DEPARTURE COURSE.
   e) Vertical Speed Indicator - NOTE READING.
   f) Radios - SET.
   g) Autopilot - OFF, BACKCOURSE SENSING OFF.
3. Gas
   a) Fuel Selector Valve - BOTH.
   b) Mixture - RICH.
   c) Primer - LOCKED.
   d) Auxiliary Fuel Pump - CHECK FOR RISE IN PRESSURE.
4. Attitude
   a) Elevator and Rudder Trim - CHECK.
5. Runup
   a) Throttle - 1700 RPM.
   b) Magnetos - CHECK MAXIMUM 175 RPM DROP, 50 RPM DIFFERENCE.
   c) Carburetor Heat - CHECK FOR RPM DROP.
   d) Propeller - CYCLE.
   e) Engine Instruments and Ammeter - CHECK.
   f) Suction Gage - CHECK.
   g) Throttle - IDLE.
   h) Throttle Friction Lock - ADJUST.
6. Safety
   a) Doors and Windows - SECURE.
   b) Seatbelts - SECURE.
   c) Traffic - CHECK. USE RADIO AS APPROPRIATE.

Figure 4-12. Your student may wish to employ the use of acronyms or flow patterns to organize checklists.

PROPELLER HAZARDS

Every year, people are seriously injured or killed by walking into aircraft propellers. Excluding runway incursion accidents, this is one of the few causes of fatalities during ground operations. One of the reasons a propeller is so hazardous is that it becomes nearly invisible when it is rotating. Teach your students to stop the engine prior to allowing passengers to board or disembark. [Figure 4-13] During preflight, they should treat a propeller as hazardous, assuming the engine could start unexpectedly. Ensure your students verify the ignition is off before examining the propeller and remind them

BE AWARE OF THE PROP OVER THERE

Maintaining situational awareness on the ground is as important as it is during flight. While your students may be used to operating near aircraft similar to the training airplane they are flying, they may not be as familiar with propeller hazards associated with other types of aircraft. For example, you can point out that when near helicopters, they should pay particular attention to the area near the tail rotor.

In addition, float planes taxiing up to dock present unique hazards. Inexperienced persons trying to help the airplane dock are in great danger. If your students operate a floatplane, whenever possible, they should stop the engine(s) prior to reaching the dock and coast in.

Another case where your students need to maintain an awareness of their surroundings is when walking around large aircraft. Any airplane with wing-mounted engines that is large enough to allow a person to walk under the wings can be a threat, especially if your students are not used to walking beneath them.

Figure 4-13. If your student will continue a flight lesson solo, you can set a good example by ensuring the engine is shut down when you disembark the airplane.

that, even with this precaution, the engine could start if the propeller is turned and there is a broken magneto ground wire.

Prior to engine start, your students should look for people or objects around the airplane, especially near the propeller and in the path of propeller blast. Teach them to yell, *"Clear"* before engaging the starter, and to turn on the anti-collision lights, and, if the flight is at night, the position lights. Discourage students from running the engine for extended periods in a crowded ramp area. They can listen to ATIS and perform other tasks prior to engine start, and promptly taxi from the ramp area once the propeller is moving. They should attend to any remaining checklist items after the airplane is stopped in the runup area. Your students should be prepared for an emergency engine shutdown if anyone ventures close to the aircraft while the engine is running.

TAXIING

While the traditional guideline to taxi no faster than a brisk walk is sound advice for most operations, you should teach your students to use common sense. For example, in a tight ramp area it may be wise to taxi much more slowly, or to shut down the engine

Clear the Turbine!

A Boeing 727 captain submitted the following NASA ASRS report.

Arriving at the gate, could not get aircraft to accept external power (auxiliary power unit inoperative). Left #1 engine running while off-loading passengers, while still trying to get aircraft to accept external power (beacon on). Lead flight attendant came running up aisle saying to shut down the engine, that somebody had been sucked inside. Shut down engine. Went to back of aircraft and talked to caterer after he had been removed from intake. He said he did not know the engine was running. #1 engine received foreign object damage (FOD).

NASA called the pilot back. Amazingly, the caterer did survive being sucked into the engine and only received a few broken ribs. The airline revised its procedures as a result of this incident, to ensure all ground personnel understand a flashing aircraft beacon means extreme caution - engines are running, or engine start is imminent.

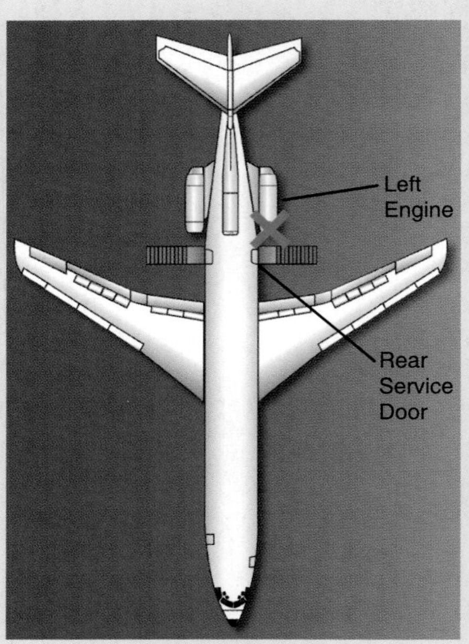

Students should be advised to taxi slowly on snow or slush, so water and ice does not spray onto the control surfaces and landing gear. Remind students who fly retractable gear airplanes to avoid getting slush into the wheel wells, where it can freeze and obstruct the gear.

Point out that taxiing too fast on a wet taxiway can lead to hydroplaning. Hydroplaning occurs when a thin layer of standing water separates an airplane's tires from the surface. This reduces friction and makes steering and braking difficult.

You can compare taxiing on ice to driving on icy roads. Remind your students that the airplane tires have little or no traction on areas of ice. Discuss the sources of weather and airport information, such as flight service or ATIS, which report whether braking action is good, fair, poor, or nil, if icy, snowy or wet taxiways or runways exist.

Figure 4-14. Do not forget to address the hazards of varied surface conditions with your students. Depending on the season and airport location, your students may not encounter wet or icy conditions during training.

and use the tow bar. However, at a large airport, when following a wide, uncongested taxiway to a runway two miles away, taxi speed may be increased somewhat. In addition, strong surface winds or slippery pavement are good reasons to advise your students to decrease taxi speed [Figure 4-14]

Since students easily can forget to apply wind corrections during taxi, it is important that you monitor their control positions and remind them of the importance of this procedure. On days when there is no wind, you can ask students to assume there is a wind from a certain direction and demonstrate the proper control positions. *Climb into the wind, dive away from it,* is an easy rule to teach your students taxiing tailwheel airplanes. The rule for tricycle gear airplanes is similar except that in a headwind, students should use neutral, not up, elevator deflection to keep weight on the nosewheel. [Figure 4-15]

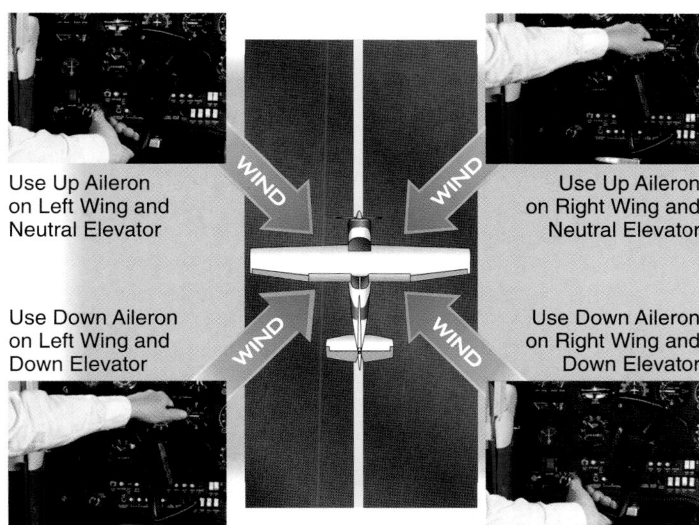

QUARTERING HEADWIND

Upward deflection of the upwind aileron prevents the wind from lifting this wing.

A quartering headwind striking the rudder can cause the airplane to weathervane into the wind. Neutral elevator helps keep sufficient weight on the nosewheel to maintain directional control.

QUARTERING TAILWIND

Downward deflection of the upwind aileron helps prevent the wind from getting under the wing and causing the airplane to tip over onto the nosewheel and one of the main wheels.

Downward deflection of the elevator causes the wind to strike the top of the elevator and exert a tail-down force to keep the tail from being lifted.

Figure 4-15. If you explain how the control surfaces are deflected to compensate for the effects of the wind, it may be easier for your students to remember the correct procedures.

RUNWAY INCURSION AVOIDANCE

A **runway incursion** is any occurence at an airport involving an aircraft, vehicle, person, or object on the ground that creates a collision hazard or results in loss of separation with an aircraft taking off, intending to take off, landing, or intending to land. Runway incursions are primarily caused by errors with clearances, communication, airport surface movement, and positional awareness. Two-thirds of runway incursion incidents involve general aviation pilots and normally occur at large, complex airports with multiple runways and complicated taxi routes. [Figure 4-16]

Figure 4-16. To prevent runway incursions, the FAA urges you to discuss and encourage good surface movement procedures with your students.

Make sure your students consistently do the following:

1. Read back all runway crossing and/or hold short instructions.
2. Review airport layouts as part of preflight planning, while descending to land, and while taxiing.
3. Know airport signage.
4. Review NOTAMs for information on runway/ taxiway closures and construction areas.
5. Request progressive taxi instructions when unsure of a taxi route.
6. Complete as many checklist items as possible before taxi or while holding short.
7. While taxiing, concentrate on primary responsibilities. Do not become absorbed in other tasks, or conversation, while the aircraft is moving.
8. Check for traffic before entering any runway or taxiway. Whether operating at controlled or uncontrolled airports, monitor the radios to maintain situational awareness of other traffic.
9. Turn on aircraft lights, including rotating beacons and strobe lights, while taxiing. Also, use the landing light when on final so aircraft on the ground can see your aircraft more easily.
10. Promptly clear the active runway upon landing. Taxi the entire aircraft over the holding position lines, then stop and wait for taxi instructions before further movement. Stay on the tower frequency until instructed to change frequencies.
11. Study and use proper radio phraseology, as described in the AIM.
12. Report deteriorating or confusing airport markings, signs, and lighting to the airport operator or FAA officials. Also report confusing or erroneous airport diagrams and instructions.
13. Understand the procedures for land and hold short operations (LAHSO). While LAHSO is not authorized for student solo operations, your students need to understand these procedures once they are certificated pilots.

LAND AND HOLD SHORT OPERATIONS

Land and hold short operations (LAHSO) refer to landing and then holding short of an intersecting runway, taxiway, predetermined point, or an approach/departure flight path. While LAHSO clearances can increase airport capacity and maintain system efficiency, specific knowledge-based training is required before these operations can be conducted safely. To ensure your students will be qualified to accept LAHSO clearances after they become certificated pilots, you should provide appropriate ground training, including a review of airport signs, lighting, and markings.

After they are trained in LAHSO and become certificated pilots, your students can accept a LAHSO clearance, which indicates they fully understand the clearance, including all related procedures. This means they know the **available landing distance (ALD)** and do not have the slightest doubt they can safely land and stop within that distance. [Figure 4-17]

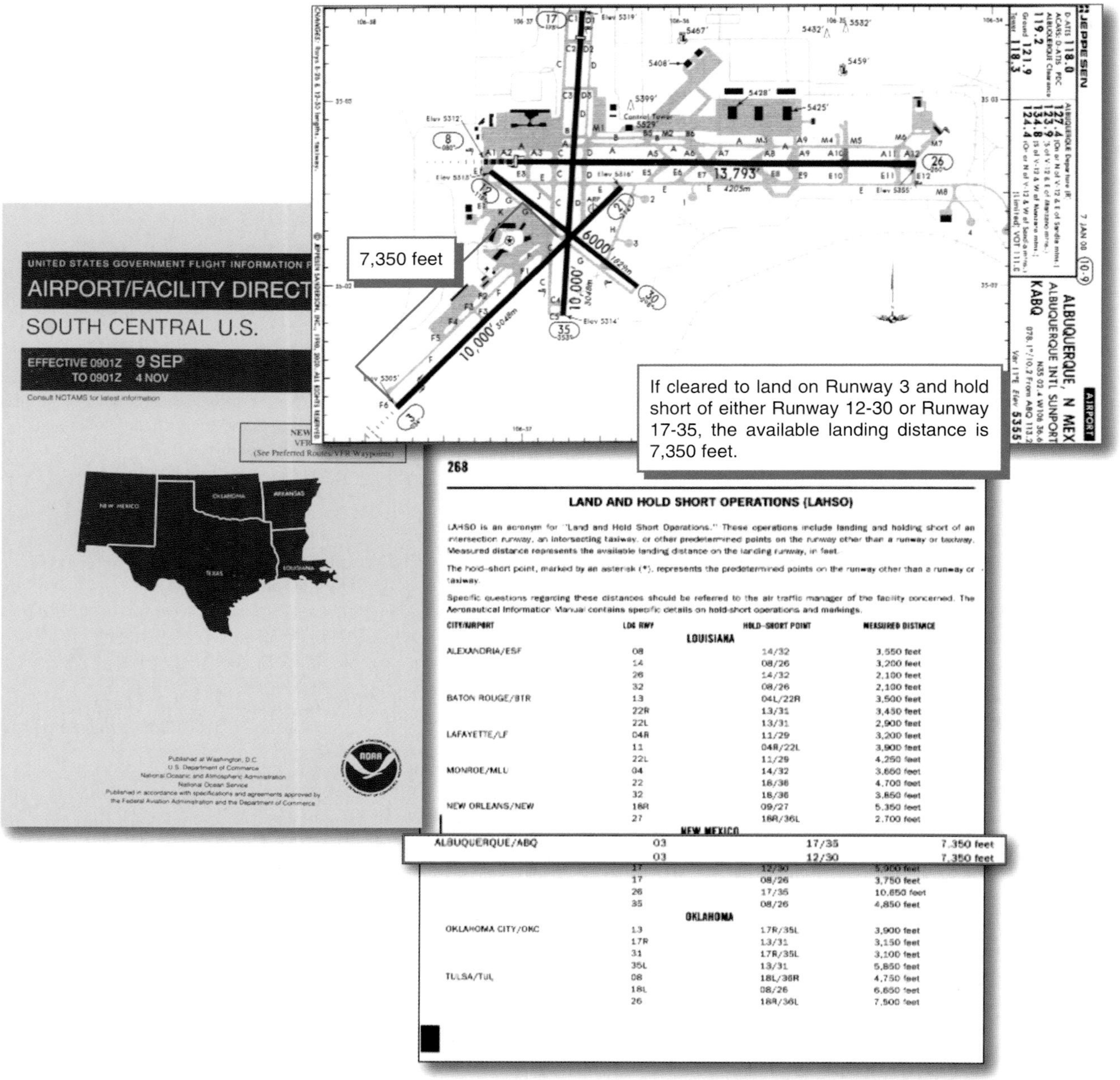

7,350 feet

If cleared to land on Runway 3 and hold short of either Runway 12-30 or Runway 17-35, the available landing distance is 7,350 feet.

UNITED STATES GOVERNMENT FLIGHT INFORMATION
AIRPORT/FACILITY DIRECT
SOUTH CENTRAL U.S.
EFFECTIVE 0901Z 9 SEP
TO 0901Z 4 NOV

268

LAND AND HOLD SHORT OPERATIONS (LAHSO)

LAHSO is an acronym for "Land and Hold Short Operations." These operations include landing and holding short of an intersection runway, an intersecting taxiway, or other predetermined points on the runway other than a runway or taxiway. Measured distance represents the available landing distance on the landing runway, in feet.

The hold-short point, marked by an asterisk (*), represents the predetermined points on the runway other than a runway or taxiway.

Specific questions regarding these distances should be referred to the air traffic manager of the facility concerned. The Aeronautical Information Manual contains specific details on hold-short operations and markings.

CITY/AIRPORT	LDG RWY	HOLD-SHORT POINT	MEASURED DISTANCE
		LOUISIANA	
ALEXANDRIA/ESF	08	14/32	3,550 feet
	14	08/26	3,200 feet
	26	14/32	2,100 feet
	32	08/26	2,100 feet
BATON ROUGE/BTR	13	04L/22R	3,500 feet
	22R	13/31	3,450 feet
	22L	13/31	2,900 feet
LAFAYETTE/LF	04R	11/29	3,200 feet
	11	04R/22L	3,900 feet
	22L	11/29	4,250 feet
MONROE/MLU	04	14/32	3,650 feet
	22	18/36	4,700 feet
	32	18/36	3,850 feet
NEW ORLEANS/NEW	18R	09/27	5,350 feet
	27	18R/36L	2,700 feet
		NEW MEXICO	
ALBUQUERQUE/ABQ	03	17/35	7,350 feet
	03	12/30	7,350 feet
	17	12/30	5,900 feet
	17	08/26	3,750 feet
	26	17/35	10,850 feet
	35	08/26	4,850 feet
		OKLAHOMA	
OKLAHOMA CITY/OKC	13	17R/35L	3,900 feet
	17R	13/31	3,150 feet
	31	17R/35L	3,100 feet
	35L	13/31	5,850 feet
TULSA/TUL	08	18L/36R	4,750 feet
	18L	08/26	6,650 feet
	26	18R/36L	7,500 feet

Figure 4-17. The FAA expects pilots to know whether LAHSO is being conducted at the destination airport, and to determine the ALD as part of preflight preparation. Your students can find ALD information in aeronautical publications such as the *Airport/Facility Directory*.

Upon accepting a LAHSO clearance, a pilot is obligated to comply with it, although this does not preclude a rejected landing. Unless directed otherwise, your students should land and exit the runway at the first convenient taxiway before reaching the hold short

point. Explain to your students that if it is not possible to exit the runway before reaching the hold short line, they must stop at this point. [Figure 4-18] If a rejected landing becomes necessary after accepting a LAHSO clearance, it is essential to maneuver to maintain safe separation from other aircraft or vehicles, and promptly notify the controller. Students should be aware that a go-around may be dangerous if ATC is expecting an airplane to hold short of a crossing runway or taxiway. For this and other safety reasons, many pilots and commercial aircraft operators do not accept LAHSO clearances. [Figure 4-19]

This aircraft is cleared to land using the full length of the runway.

27-9

27-9

You are cleard to land on Runway 27 and hold short of Runway 23.

5-23

5-23

Runway Holding Positon Sign

Figure 4-18. To help your students understand LAHSO procedures, you may want to provide them with a diagram that illustrates a typical land and hold short situation.

ATC: *"Sundowner 1523 Sierra, cleared to land Runway 6 Right, hold short of Taxiway Bravo for crossing traffic, a Baron."*

Pilot: *"Sundowner 1523 Sierra, wilco, cleared to land Runway 6 Right to hold short of Taxiway Bravo."*

Emphasize to your students that since the pilot in command is the final authority as to the safe operation of the aircraft, they should not feel pressured to accept any clearance they feel is unsafe. Additionally, student pilots and pilots not trained in LAHSO must refuse these clearances:

ATC: *"Sundowner 1523 Sierra, cleared to land Runway 6 Right, hold short of Taxiway Bravo for crossing traffic, a Baron."*

Pilot: *"Sundowner 1523 Sierra, unable to hold short."*

Advise your students that while they should have the published ALD and runway for all LAHSO runway combinations at each airport of intended landing, controllers can confirm ALD data upon request.

ATC: *"Sundowner 1523 Sierra, cleared to land Runway 6 Right, hold short of Taxiway Bravo for crossing traffic, a Baron."*

Pilot: *"Sundowner 1523 Sierra, please say available landing distance."*

ATC: *"Sundowner 1523 Sierra, ALD 4,000 feet.*

Pilot: *"Sundowner 1523 Sierra, wilco, cleared to land Runway 6 Right to hold short of Taxiway Bravo."*

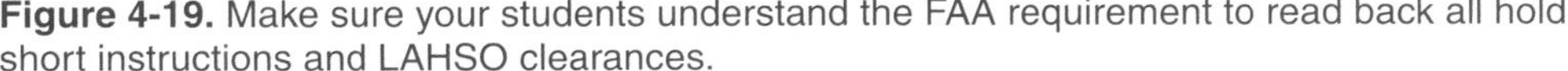

Figure 4-19. Make sure your students understand the FAA requirement to read back all hold short instructions and LAHSO clearances.

If you are flying with a student, or as part of a multi-person crew, you should know that effective intra-cockpit communication is also critical. Research has shown that in several instances, the pilot responsible for operating the radios accepted a LAHSO clearance and forgot to tell the pilot flying the aircraft. As you can imagine, failure to conduct LAHSO properly can result in a collision with fatalities. You may need to review the AIM's latest LAHSO policies and procedures with all of your students, regardless of their level of training.

SITUATIONAL AWARENESS PAYS OFF

In Providence, Rhode Island, a regional airline crew refused a takeoff clearance from the tower, knowing that another airliner had just landed and was lost somewhere in the dark, foggy field. The regional pilots had been monitoring the communication between the landing aircraft and ATC, and were unconvinced that anyone really knew exactly where the airplane was. The local controller insisted it was safe to take off, and cleared a cargo jet for takeoff on the same runway on which the regional crew had refused the clearance. The cargo jet flew directly over the lost airplane, which had wandered back onto the active runway.

In Los Angeles, California, a Boeing 757 rotated abruptly during its takeoff roll to avoid an MD-80 that had inadvertently taxied onto the active runway. The 757 passed only 60 feet above the encroaching aircraft.

Whether on the ground or in flight, maintaining situational awareness is imperative for both you and your students. One technique you can use while instructing is to compete with your students and see who can spot the most aircraft during training flights. You can also ask about the positions of other aircraft that are transmitting on the same frequency to determine if your students are aware of operations around them.

AIRPORT SIGNS, LIGHTING, AND MARKINGS

To avoid runway incursion incidents and problems with LAHSO operations, your students need a thorough understanding of airport signs, lighting, and markings. You can quiz your students about the significance of airport signs during taxi, and point out various runway and taxiway markings as you overfly airports. Take the controls so your students can focus on the markings without having to concentrate on flying the airplane. You also should explain the various types of airport lighting. Daytime lessons are a good time to begin showing your students the lights, even though they are not operating. [Figure 4-20]

Figure 4-20. During the day, students can see the light fixtures, including the color of the lenses, and their location relative to runways and taxiways. Make sure you emphasize the various lights that lead to the landing threshold, possibly pointing out these lights during a low approach.

WAKE TURBULENCE

It is essential you teach students about the hazards of **wake turbulence**, as well as keep up-to-date on the latest research regarding wake turbulence generation. To effectively avoid the dangers of wake turbulence, students must have a thorough understanding of how it is formed. As you know, any airplane generating lift produces **wingtip vortices**. These whirlpools of air are most intense from aircraft that are heavy, clean, and slow. The greatest wake turbulence danger is encountered when following large commercial jets taking off or landing. The peak vortex tangential speeds of such aircraft can exceed 300 feet per second. This can cause a smaller aircraft with a relatively short wingspan to roll inverted, especially when its heading is aligned with the generating aircraft's flight

path. Under these conditions, the encountering aircraft may lack sufficient aileron control authority to counteract the rolling moment from the vortices.

How large does an airplane need to be to present a hazard? Students should understand that any aircraft generates a wake, and the bigger the difference in size between the leading and trailing airplanes, the more caution is required. Wakes from large transport and military aircraft, as well as helicopters, should always be avoided, but other aircraft also can create hazardous vortices. [Figure 4-21]

In Van Nuys, California, the wake from a King Air upset a Piper Arrow that was close behind and below its approach path, resulting in a crash landing of the Arrow.

While executing a visual approach to Runway 32 at Salt Lake City International Airport, a Cessna 182 encountered wake turbulence while crossing the flight path of a B-757 on final for Runway 35. The 182 crashed short of the runway. The flight path of the 182 was slightly above that of the 757 at the point of crossing.

The pilots of a B-767 temporarily lost control when the airplane encountered wake turbulence while in trail of a B-777 at FL370. The 767 was 10 miles behind the 777 when it experienced an uncommanded roll which the crew was unable to counter with full right aileron. The bank angle reached 45° before the turbulence subsided.

Figure 4-21. Wake turbulence avoidance must be exercised with all jet aircraft and all large aircraft (greater than 12,500 pounds). Some turbulence can exist even behind light airplanes. Providing specific examples to your students allows you to emphasize the importance of exercising caution when following a variety of aircraft.

Your students must learn to avoid areas where they are likely to encounter wake turbulence. Vortex cores descend at several hundred feet per minute behind a landing aircraft, until about 900 feet below the aircraft, where they begin to break up and dissipate. Vortices that are generated in calm wind conditions near the ground settle to within about 200 feet of the ground and then move laterally outward. A crosswind decreases the lateral movement of the upwind vortex and increases the movement of the downwind vortex. [Figure 4-22].

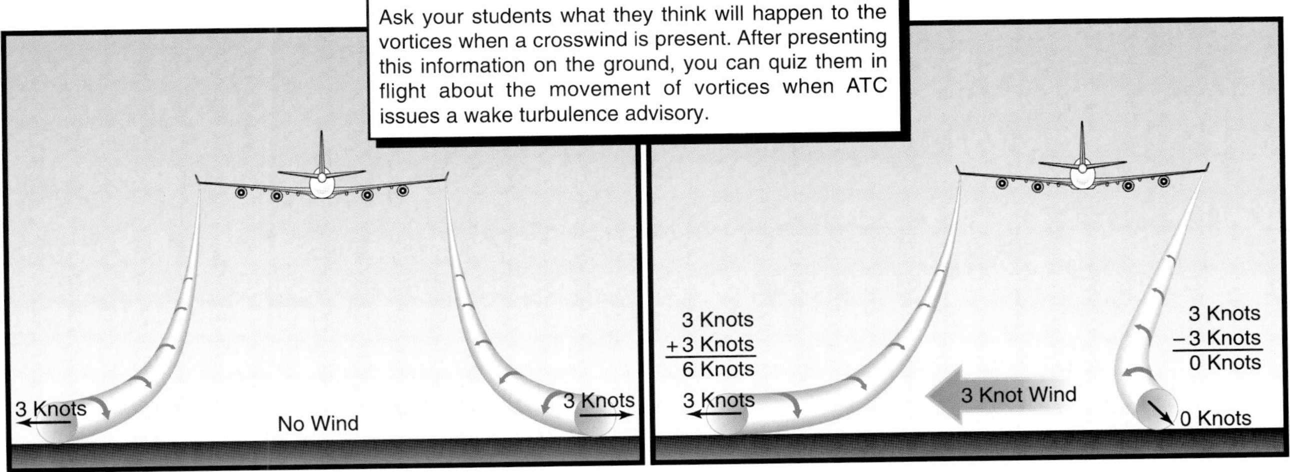

Figure 4-22. A diagram can help your students visualize the movement of vortices. A light wind of three to seven knots can hold the upwind vortex in the touchdown zone while hastening the drift of the downwind vortex toward another runway.

While an illustration may be helpful to introduce wake turbulence avoidance procedures, an effective method to reinforce these operations is to ask your students to apply their knowledge during a flight. Depending on the type of operations common to the airport at which you conduct training, you may encounter situations while taking off or landing

behind large aircraft to test your students' knowledge, or you may need to present your students with scenarios during a flight lesson. [Figure 4-23]

Figure 4-23. Prior to takeoff or landing, you can ask your students what action they would take if a large aircraft was taking off or landing ahead of them.

WAKE TURBULENCE RESEARCH

Why do dangerous vortex encounters continue, even while pilots follow established wake turbulence avoidance procedures? One reason is that the classic advice to rotate prior to the point where the large airplane becomes airborne and then climb above its flight path is often impractical. While it may have been possible to outclimb some of the early jet transports, modern turbofan-powered aircraft can climb at steeper angles than most small airplanes, even with an inoperative engine. You should advise your students that since it is unlikely their training aircraft can outclimb a jet, it is necessary to turn upwind of the large airplane's flight path.

Another concern regarding wake turbulence involves the study of certain accidents and NASA research which have challenged the notion that vortices always sink. It is believed that some vortices, depending on their intensity, can actually bounce back into the air after ground contact. It should also be remembered that the diameter of a vortex's flow field usually is equal to the wingspan of the generating airplane. This means trailing aircraft may be in danger of a vortex encounter even if slightly above the flight path of the generating aircraft. [Figure 4-24]

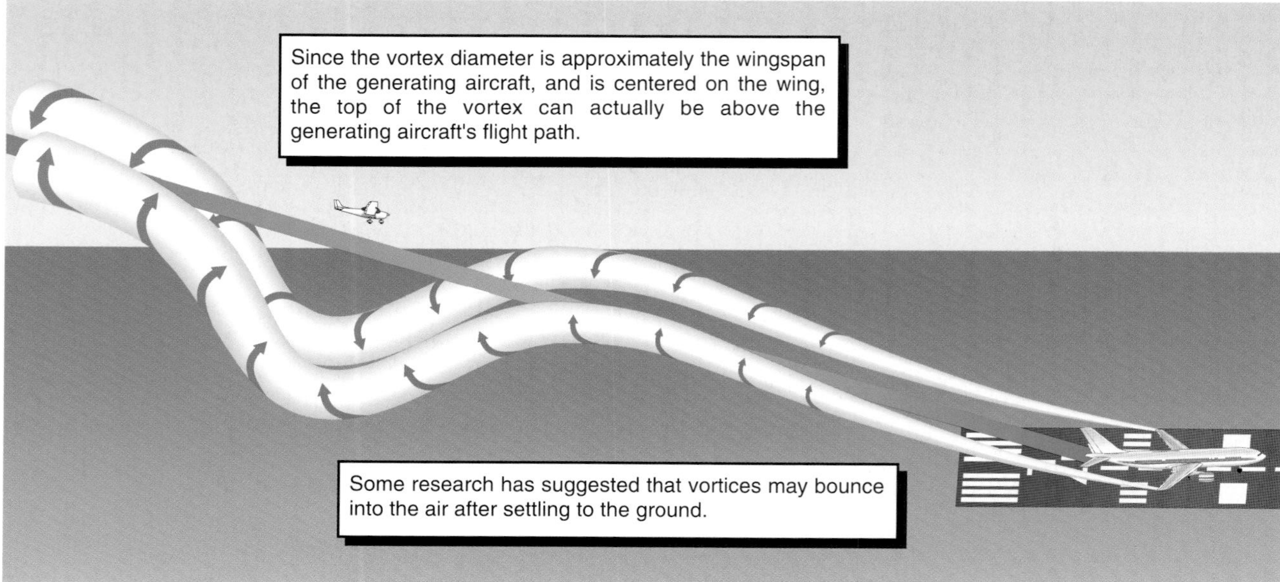

Figure 4-24. Some aspects of vortex behavior still are unknown. Instruct your students to remain well above the generating aircraft's flight path.

Additional research has shown that vortices retain nearly all of their hazardous strength until the time they dissipate, and this is sometimes longer than the delay times allotted by ATC for wake avoidance. This research carries some serious implications: established procedures for avoiding wake turbulence upsets may be insufficient.

With proper precautions, the probability of flying directly into a vortex core is relatively small. While most pilots will never suffer a vortex encounter, it is extremely hazardous to those who do. Your students may be under the impression that as they transition to larger aircraft they will not be affected by vortices. NTSB reports indicate that all but the biggest transport jets can be victims of wake turbulence. However, upsets of large airplanes are relatively rare. For example, only one DC-9 following an L-1011 was included in a report of 51 wake turbulence accidents and incidents investigated by the NTSB over a 10-year period.

HELICOPTER VORTICES

Your wake turbulence discussion is not complete without addressing the vortices caused by helicopters. In a slow hover-taxi or stationary hover near the surface, helicopter main rotor(s) generate high-velocity downwash. When this downwash hits the surface, the resulting **outwash vortices** extend to a distance approximately three times the diameter of the rotor. They behave similar to wingtip vortices from fixed-wing aircraft, except they act in all directions. In forward flight, departing or landing helicopters produce a pair of strong, high-speed trailing vortices which are similar to the wingtip vortices of large fixed-wing aircraft. Make sure your students understand they should stay at least three rotor diameters away from hovering or slow-moving helicopters, and that they should avoid the wake behind landing and departing helicopters. Typically, specific procedures for helicopter departures and arrivals are established for a particular airport. You can alert your students to these operations and point out the routes that helicopters normally follow. [Figure 4-25]

Figure 4-25. Helicopter routing normally does not conflict with fixed-wing traffic. However, students should still exercise caution, especially at uncontrolled airports where military helicopters conduct training.

Just as on a fixed-wing aircraft, helicopter vortices formed at low airspeeds are initially stronger than those generated at higher airspeeds, heavier helicopters produce stronger wake vortices than those that are lighter, and larger helicopters create an increased vortex size. However, there are important differences between rotary wake and the wake

Figure 4-26. Research using smoke to make vortices visible has shown that the left and right vortices are distinctly different in helicopters.

Since the retreating blade operates at a much lower relative airspeed, it must maintain a higher angle of attack to produce as much lift as the advancing blade.

The retreating blade creates a vortex with a larger diameter, less dense smoke marking, and a greater cross section.

The vortex behind the advancing rotor blade is normally smaller, tighter, and more coherent, especially when the helicopter's forward speed is above 80 knots.

formed by fixed-wing aircraft. Research indicates that the wake reacts differently depending on whether the helicopter is climbing or descending. The vortex cores move farther apart during descents and closer together during climbs. [Figure 4-26]

JET ENGINE BLAST

Jet engine blast is a related hazard that you must address with your students. It can damage or even overturn a small airplane if it is encountered at close range. To avoid excessive jet blast, make sure your students stay several hundred feet behind a jet with its engines operating, even when they are at idle thrust. [Figure 4-27] If you pursue an airline career, and find yourself in the cockpit of a jet transport airplane, be aware of the aircraft behind you. Do not apply large amounts of thrust until moving clear of other aircraft.

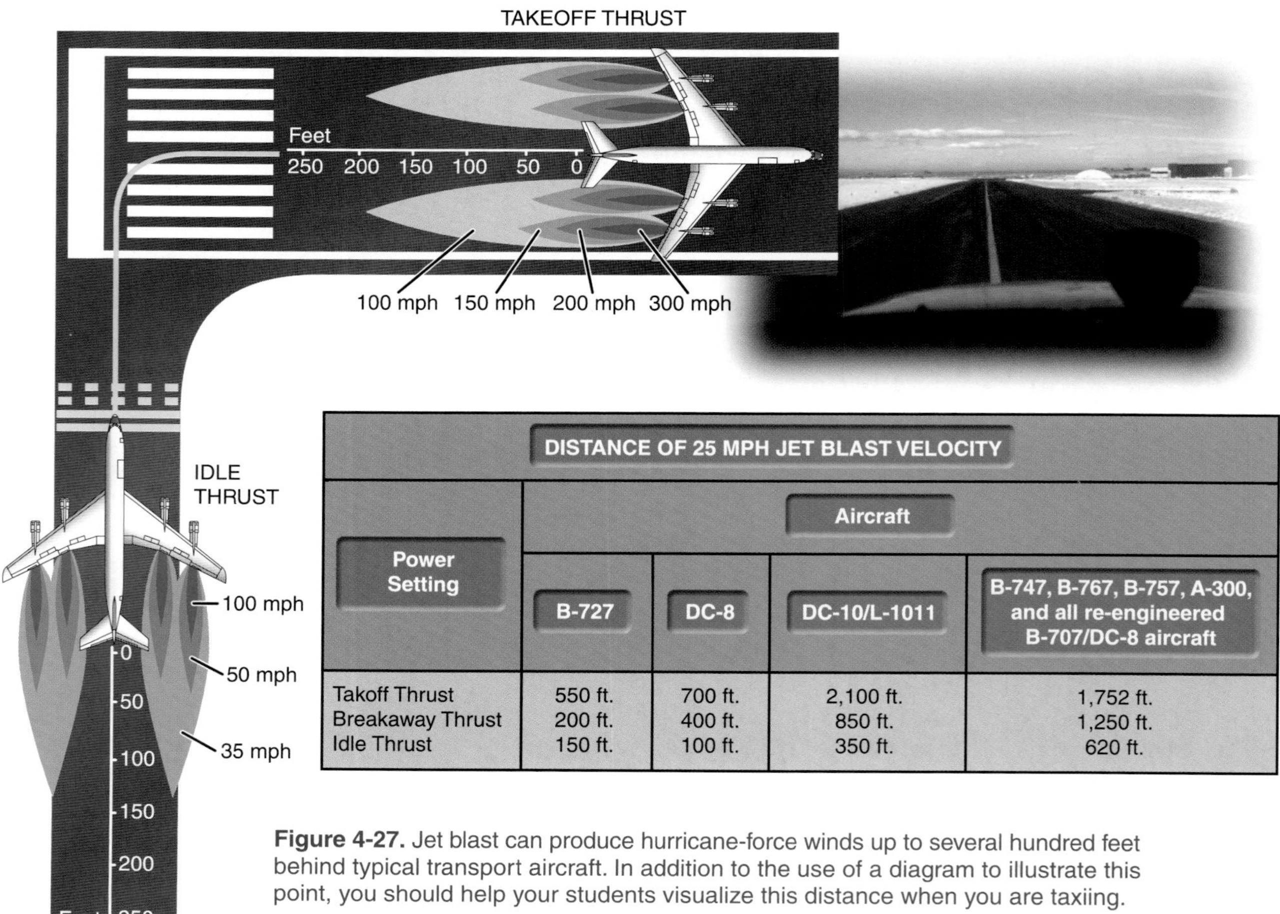

Power Setting	Aircraft: B-727	Aircraft: DC-8	Aircraft: DC-10/L-1011	Aircraft: B-747, B-767, B-757, A-300, and all re-engineered B-707/DC-8 aircraft
DISTANCE OF 25 MPH JET BLAST VELOCITY				
Takoff Thrust	550 ft.	700 ft.	2,100 ft.	1,752 ft.
Breakaway Thrust	200 ft.	400 ft.	850 ft.	1,250 ft.
Idle Thrust	150 ft.	100 ft.	350 ft.	620 ft.

Figure 4-27. Jet blast can produce hurricane-force winds up to several hundred feet behind typical transport aircraft. In addition to the use of a diagram to illustrate this point, you should help your students visualize this distance when you are taxiing.

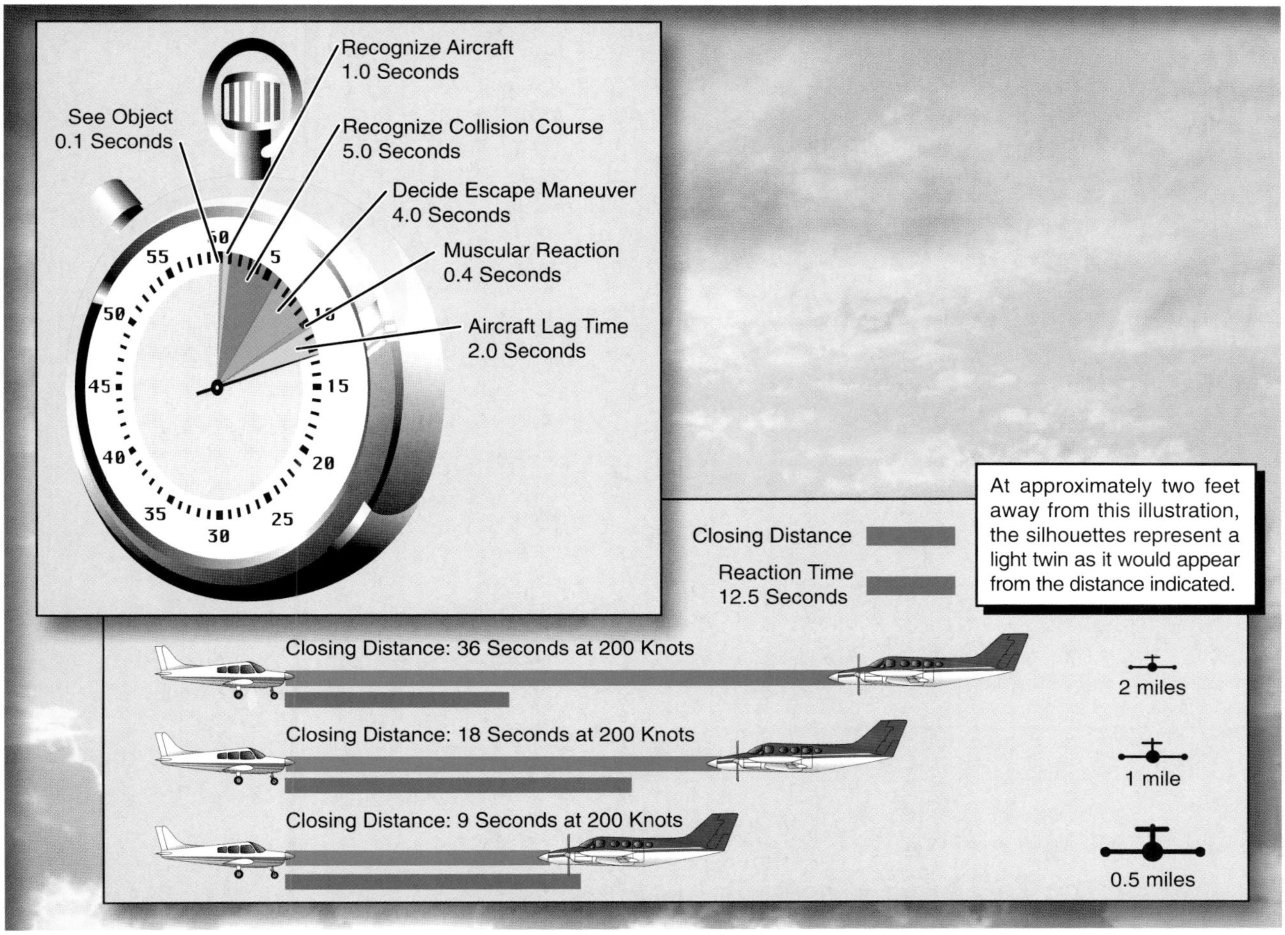

Figure 4-28. Surprisingly, 82% of midair collisions are at overtaking or converging angles and do not involve the high rate of closure shown here. This suggests that a consistent habit of looking outside the cockpit could avert most collisions.

COLLISION AVOIDANCE

It is important to teach collision avoidance procedures beginning with a student's first flight. While every aircraft has some risk of an in-flight collision, your students can act to avoid this type of accident. Most midair collisions occur near airports, during daylight hours, and in VFR conditions. Explain to your students that early detection is crucial to avoiding certain collisions, since it takes about 12.5 seconds to realize that you are on a collision course with another airplane and to do something about it. [Figure 4-28]

During flight training, your students are busy learning, and you are busy teaching and evaluating. You need to divide your attention so this does not detract from collision avoidance. Since you are ultimately responsible for the safety of flight, you must bear 100% of the burden to avoid other traffic during early training fights. It is important that your students see you taking this duty seriously. Move your head conspicuously as you look around aircraft blind spots for traffic and explain that your students need to do this as well. Point out other aircraft and ask students to do the same for you. Challenge students to spot other aircraft before you do. Watch their head and eye movements to ensure they are exercising proper scanning techniques, especially if it appears they are having difficulty seeing other aircraft. As instruction progresses, students become skilled in visual scanning and gradually begin to perform their share of this vital task. Obviously, they must be exercising solid collision avoidance procedures prior to solo. The AIM suggests pilots spend no more than 1/4 to 1/3 of their scan time on visual tasks inside the cockpit when flying in VFR conditions. As an instructor, you can encourage this habit by the way you teach basic maneuvers.

VISUAL SCANNING

Without proper training, students may have a natural tendency to simply sweep their eyes across the sky. Since this is not an effective way to see and avoid other aircraft, your students must learn **visual scanning** techniques. The more time they spend developing their scan during early flight training, the more natural it will become later. The FAA recommends eye movements of 10°, focusing one to two seconds on each segment of the sky. Be sure that your students' scan pattern covers all of the sky that can be seen from the cockpit, with particular emphasis on the area 60° to the left and right of the center visual area and 10° up and down from your flight path. [Figure 4-29]

To scan using the side-to-side method, start at the far left of the windshield and make a methodical sweep to the right, pausing in each block of viewing area to focus your eyes.

An alternative scanning method is to start in the center block of the windshield, move to the left, focusing in each block, then swing quickly to the center block after reaching the last block on the left and repeat this action to the right.

Figure 4-29. You can begin teaching your students visual scanning on the ground, where they can focus on learning the techniques without any distractions.

Another important aspect of teaching visual scanning is ensuring students understand the eye's limitations. For example, although the eye can see in an arc of approximately 200°, it can clearly focus on only the center 10°. Beyond that visual acuity drops rapidly to the point where your students may not notice objects in their peripheral vision unless there is some relative motion. This can be a problem, since an aircraft on a collision course appears almost stationary; the most serious threat is the one that is most difficult to see. [Figure 4-30]

In addition to the limitations of the visual field, students should be aware of factors that can affect their ability to see traffic. **Accommodation** is the time required to focus on a distant object after looking at the instrument panel. Your students can combat accommodation by focusing on exterior parts of the aircraft as a transition from inside to outside the cockpit. It also is important that your students understand **empty field myopia**. When conditions are hazy, the eyes can relax and focus 10 to 30 feet ahead of the aircraft. Under these conditions, an aircraft must be two or three times closer before a pilot will see it. To help avoid empty field myopia, teach your students to consciously increase their scan rate and focus alternately from far to near. Also, make sure the windscreen is clean, since smudges and bugs could hide traffic.

Stand this textbook on the edge of a table and have your student sit in a chair about five feet away. The width of the book represents an area approximately 10° wide — the relatively small area in which the eyes can focus sharply. Now direct your student to focus on the Guided Flight Discovery logo. Ask your student if he can see the words Flight Instructor Manual in the upper right corner. Your student will not be able to see the printed title clearly while focused on the logo.

To demonstrate the limitations of peripheral vision, ask your student to close his eyes. You can then position your hand about two feet away, level with his ear. Ask him to open his eyes and remain focused straight ahead. How well can he see your hand when it is stationary compared to when it is moving? This exercise illustrates the difficulty in perceiving objects peripherally when there is no relative motion.

Figure 4-30. You can demonstrate the limitations of the visual field to your students by performing these experiments.

When encountering traffic, the most effective evasive maneuver usually is a change in altitude, often combined with a turn. Until your students gain experience, you probably will have to direct their actions to avoid other aircraft. Point out that the other pilot might not react as expected. When taking evasive action, students should watch the other aircraft for unusual maneuvers, and consider that there may be more than one potential collision hazard in an area at the same time.

BLIND SPOTS AND AIRCRAFT DESIGN

Since most students have experience with driving, the concept of **blind spots** is familiar. [Figure 4-31] Teach your students to move their heads frequently to look around door posts and other cockpit obstructions. Set a good example for your students from the first lesson by lifting the wing of a high-wing airplane in the direction of the turn and clear the area for other aircraft. If your students begin a turn without looking for traffic first, ask them to stop the turn and clear the area before continuing. When beginning a turn in a low-wing airplane, your students also should look carefully in the direction of the turn for conflicting traffic.

Figure 4-31. During flight, point out how both the fuselage and wings block portions of your view. Since you may instruct in both high- and low-wing airplanes, you must be aware of the blind spots associated with each design.

The differences in blind spots caused by aircraft design can develop into a serious problem, particularly during the approach and landing phases of flight. When a high-wing airplane is below a low-wing airplane on approach to landing or during a departure, both airplanes can easily remain out of sight of each other. Teach your students to make shallow S-turns and avoid climbing or descending at steep angles. These are good methods of reducing the possibility of a collision during extended climbs or descents. [Figure 4-32]

The pilots of two training airplanes in Florida were fortunate enough to walk away from a normally fatal midair collision that occured while both planes were on final for touch-and-go landings on the same runway, The low-wing Piper PA-28 Cadet descended onto a Cessna 152. The Piper's nosegear shattered the Cessna's windshield, and the two planes became stuck together. Neither pilot saw the other aircraft prior to the collision.

The collision occured at an altitude of about 200 feet AGL. The instructor in the Cessna took control from his student pilot and safely landed the interlocked aircraft in the grass near the runway.

Amazingly, both aircraft sustained only minor damage. One reason the Cessna was able to carry the weight of the larger Piper is that the student in the Piper aircraft applied go-around power after contacting the Cessna. This accident, like most midair collisions, occured in good visibility

Figure 4-32. To reinforce the importance of understanding blind spots to your students, present a scenario or cite a specific example of a hazardous situation caused by the failure of pilots to recognize this collision factor.

You may even wish to consider visibility as a factor in choosing a training airplane. Some airplanes have large windows or canopies that improve visibility. Others have rear windows, giving you a 360° view. Slower training airplanes have an increased risk of collisions from the rear. If your airplane does not allow a rear view, make sure your students conduct S-turns if there is any possibility of conflicting traffic behind you.

MANEUVERS IN THE PRACTICE AREA

It is important your students not only maintain their scan, but also that they clear an area for traffic prior to and while practicing maneuvers. It is essential that you teach your students to make **clearing turns** before performing maneuvers in the practice area. Keep emphasizing this until they conduct these turns without your prompting. As minutes pass while performing maneuvers, students must continue clearing the area around the aircraft. It is easy for them to become complacent when they think you are watching for traffic, so you must continually stress student responsibility for collision avoidance.

REDUCING COLLISION RISK

Besides maintaining an effective scan, there are other techniques you can teach your students to avoid collisions. In addition to sky condition, the contrast an aircraft has with its background affects its likelihood of being clearly seen. High-intensity strobe lights can increase your aircraft's contrast by as much as ten times, day or night. [Figure 4-33]

Figure 4-33. While it is relatively easy to see aircraft below you over sparse terrain, it can be very difficult to see them against other backgrounds. Point out the problem areas at the airports where your students will regularly operate.

COLLISION AVOIDANCE IN THE TRAFFIC PATTERN

Since most collisions occur near airports, it is important that your students learn to enter and fly traffic patterns properly. Approximately 80% of traffic pattern collisions occur on final approach, and two-thirds of collisions near airports occur at uncontrolled airports, so particular vigilance is required here. Provide your students with opportunities to practice traffic pattern procedures at uncontrolled fields if you conduct training at a tower-controlled airport. Maintaining situational awareness in the traffic pattern is especially important. If your students pay attention to radio communication and can discern that other pilots are having trouble seeing them, they can maneuver their aircraft to make it appear larger, or to flash the sun's reflection. Banking the aircraft for a minor heading change not only makes the wings more visible, but also changes the aircraft's relative motion, which could help other pilots see it more easily. [Figure 4-34]

Collision Avoidance Checklist

- ✓ Before taxiing onto a runway, check for traffic on final or on the runway.
- ✓ During climbout, accelerate to cruise-climb speed upon reaching a safe altitude to improve forward visibility and perform shallow S-turns if the pitch attitude is too high to see directly ahead.
- ✓ Familiarize yourself with special procedures at airports where you intend to operate.
- ✓ Check NOTAMs for such items as parachute and glider operations.
- ✓ Never overfly an airport where skydivers may be landing, but stay clear and perform a normal 45° downwind entry.
- ✓ Use your landing light when near an airport to make your aircraft more visible.
- ✓ At uncontrolled airports, report your position on the CTAF or Local Airport Advisory (LAA) frequency. Be alert for aircraft not using a radio.
- ✓ Descend to pattern altitude several miles before reaching the airport. Do not descend into the traffic pattern.
- ✓ Avoid continuous turns of more than 90° while in the traffic pattern.

Figure 4-34. When you conduct lessons on traffic pattern procedures, provide your students with a collision avoidance checklist.

COLLISION AVOIDANCE TOOLS

Where ATC radar services are available, flight following can help your students concentrate their scan in a specific sector when conflicting traffic is reported. Make sure your students look for ATC-reported traffic based on the aircraft's ground track, if it differs from the aircraft's heading due to wind correction. Other tools, such as the **traffic and collision alert device (TCAD)** and even variations of the **traffic alert and collision avoidance system (TCAS)** are becoming increasingly affordable, and may appear in more general aviation cockpits. As this equipment becomes more commonplace, it is important that you understand its operation so you can provide your students, especially those who are pursuing aviation careers, with up-to-date, accurate information.

The FAA developed TCAS in the early 1970s to help prevent midair collisions. TCAS I is required on most corporate and smaller commuter aircraft, while the more expensive TCAS II is required on airplanes with more than 30 passenger seats. TCAS interrogates nearby transponder-equipped aircraft to determine bearing, distance, and altitude, and provides the crew with advance warning of potential conflicts. TCAS II also issues resolution advisories (RAs), which command the crew to climb or descend to avoid conflicting traffic. TCAS II can even coordinate evasive maneuvers with another TCAS II aircraft, via the Mode S transponder's datalink. For example, it can command one aircraft to climb and the other to descend.

The general aviation version of TCAS, called TCAD (traffic collision avoidance device) is less complicated, since it does not interrogate other aircraft and is therefore significantly less expensive. As a passive system, it receives all transponder replies in the local area and then presents altitude and distance of targets within the designated traffic shield on the display. TCAD is different from TCAS in that it does not provide the pilot with the relative bearing or clock position of the threat aircraft. Distance information can be inaccurate for aircraft with strong or weak transponder signals, and since TCAD does not itself interrogate other transponders, it does not function in non-radar environments. Since adjusting altitude is usually the most effective method of avoiding a collision, the TCAD traffic altitude information can be very valuable. There is now a TCAD system available with a directional antenna that provides an approximate bearing to conflicting aircraft. [Figure 4-35]

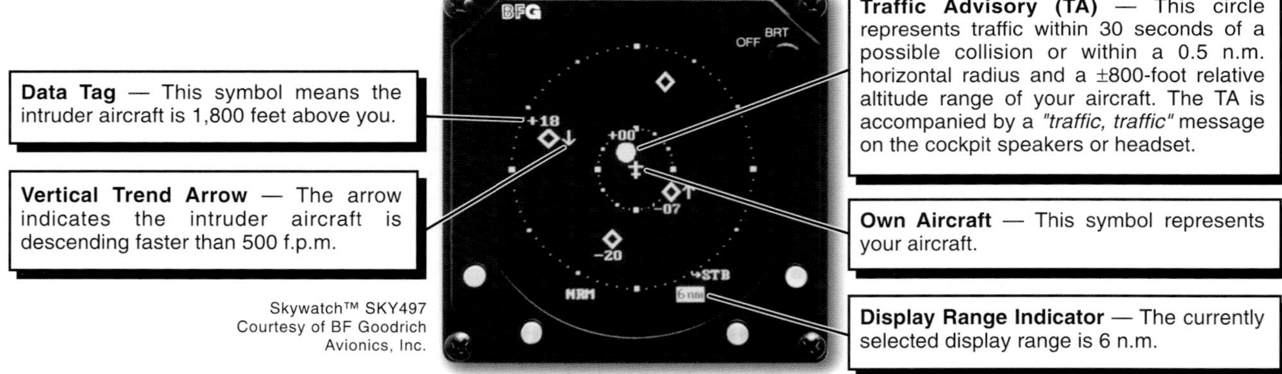

Figure 4-35. Emphasize to your students that TCAD should be used only as a supplemental tool to increase scanning effectiveness. While you should encourage your students to utilize all available resources, you also should caution them to avoid the complacency that can accompany radar or TCAD traffic advisories, especially in busy Class B and Class C airspace.

WIND SHEAR

Many beginning students may have heard the term wind shear associated with aircraft accidents. It is important that you define wind shear for your students and provide them with tools for predicting the presence of this hazard. **Wind shear** is a sudden, drastic shift in wind speed and/or direction that occurs over a short distance. It can be found at any altitude and either in a vertical or horizontal plane. Students should be aware that wind shear can subject their aircraft to sudden updrafts, downdrafts, or extreme horizontal wind components, causing loss of lift or violent changes in vertical speed or altitude.

The phenomenon can be associated with convective precipitation, a jet stream, or a frontal zone. Wind shear can also be encountered when climbing or descending between calm air at the surface and a strong flow aloft.

Typically, the worst wind shear is associated with thunderstorms, which can induce powerful downdrafts that strike the ground and spread horizontally. A **microburst** is a downdraft less than 1 mile in diameter as it descends from the cloud base to about 1,000 to 3,000 feet above the ground. In the transition zone near the ground, the downdraft changes to a horizontal outflow that can extend to approximately 2.5 miles in diameter. Downdrafts can be as strong as 6,000 feet per minute, with horizontal winds near the surface approaching 45 knots. This would result in a 90-knot shear as the wind changes from a headwind to a tailwind passing through the microburst. [Figure 4-36]

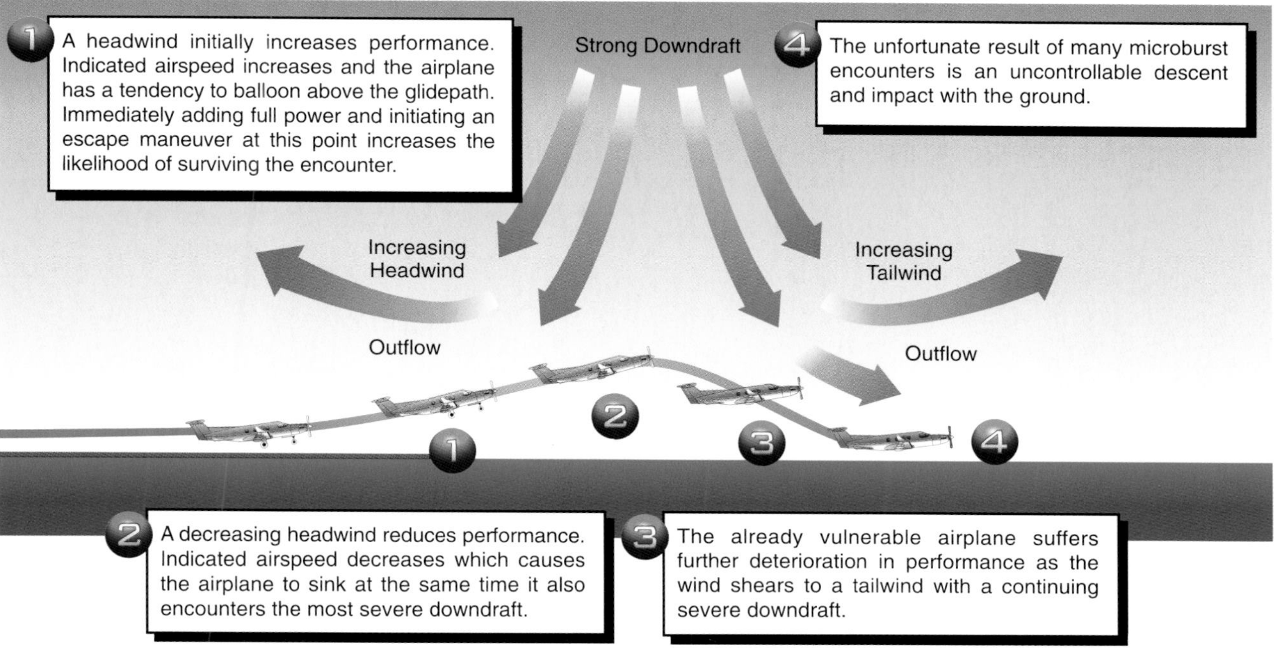

Figure 4-36. An effective way to explain the wind shear associated with a microburst is to use a diagram and discuss step-by-step how an aircraft is affected when flying through the shear.

An important consideration for your students is that microbursts seldom last longer than 15 minutes from the time they strike the ground until dissipation. Because of their short life, it is normally possible to land safely by simply waiting for the downdrafts to dissipate before operating near the airport. However, microbursts can occasionally be concentrated into a line structure and the activity can continue for as long as an hour. Once microburst activity starts, multiple microbursts in the same general area are possible.

Predicting Wind Shear

Once you teach your students the effect that an encounter with wind shear can have on an aircraft, they will understand the importance of predicting the occurrence of this phenomena so it can be avoided. Non-frontal wind shear may exist any time strong winds aloft overrun calm or different-direction surface winds. With frontal wind shear, the most critical period is one to three hours following a cold frontal passage and up to six hours preceding warm frontal passage. Wind shear with a warm front causes the most problems, since it lasts longer and frequently occurs with low ceilings and poor visibility.

Microbursts can occur quickly and without fully developed cumulonimbus clouds. Seemingly innocuous rain showers can induce severe downdrafts with wind shear. One aircraft may successfully complete an approach and landing, while an aircraft less than two minutes behind meets disaster.

As a result of a number of major airline accidents, the FAA has installed low level wind shear alert systems (LLWAS) and terminal doppler weather radar (TDWR) at busier airports where microbursts and wind shear are likely to occur. In areas without LLWAS or TDWR, it is essential to look for visual indications. Point out to your students that rainshafts and virga extending from the bases of clouds and dust rings on the ground can indicate microbursts. [Figure 4-37] Since downdrafts spread horizontally across the ground, low-level wind shear may be found beyond the boundaries of the visible rainshaft.

Figure 4-37. While a rainshaft or virga indicates the possibility of a microburst, visual indications may not always be available. Make sure your students avoid any area suspected to contain hazardous wind shear, even if there is no visible evidence.

It is essential that your students learn to exercise their pilot-in-command authority to avoid encounters with hazardous wind shear. In July 1988, five air carrier flights were approaching to land in Denver and all flight crews received a microburst warning from the tower with their landing clearance. Three of the five continued the approach, despite their airline's prohibition against approaches through microburst activity. Fortunately, these three flight crews successfully conducted escape maneuvers at the first sign of wind shear. All five aircraft held, waited for the microburst to dissipate, and landed safely. Your students can learn from this event; they should be prepared to refuse an approach or landing clearance and delay their landing if hazardous wind shear is expected.

ENCOUNTERING WIND SHEAR

While all aircraft must remain clear of thunderstorms and other severe wind shear activity, minor wind shear is manageable for skilled pilots in light aircraft. Your students may encounter wind shear when descending below the tree line or into an inversion layer from strong winds aloft. Teach them to visualize the wind at the surface and the winds aloft. If taking off with calm wind at the surface, it is best to fly into the wind aloft. A shear to a headwind is normally benign; it increases aircraft performance during penetration. However, a shear to a tailwind could cause an aircraft to lose altitude and even stall. Advise your students that if they are taking off or landing in adverse wind shear or gusty conditions, they should maintain an extra margin of airspeed of approximately half the gust factor, and minimize the use of flaps. [Figure 4-38]

Your instrument students should monitor the power and vertical velocity required to maintain the glide path on an approach. If encountering an unexpected wind shear, it may be difficult to stay on the glide path at normal power and descent rates. If there is any doubt of regaining a reasonable rate of descent and landing without abnormal maneuvering, they should immediately apply full power and abandon the approach. Once the aircraft is stabilized, encourage your students to report the encounter to ATC. This information could prevent an aircraft following you from experiencing an accident. [Figure 4-39]

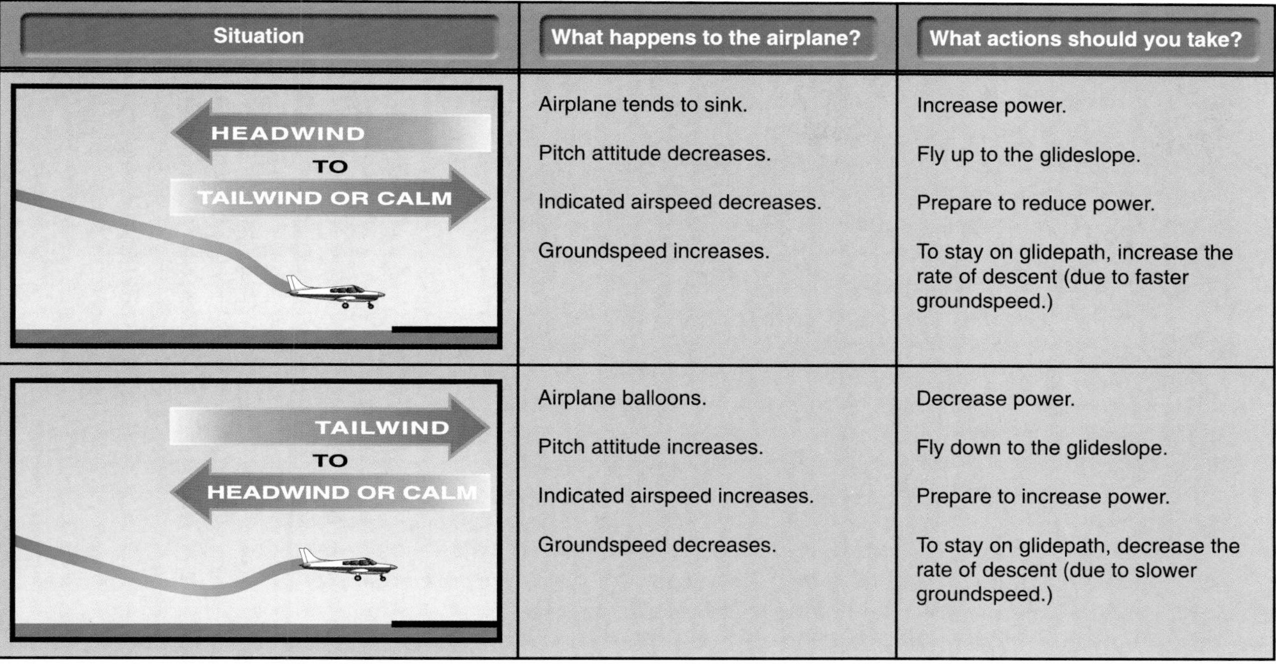

Situation	What happens to the airplane?	What actions should you take?
HEADWIND TO TAILWIND OR CALM	Airplane tends to sink. Pitch attitude decreases. Indicated airspeed decreases. Groundspeed increases.	Increase power. Fly up to the glideslope. Prepare to reduce power. To stay on glidepath, increase the rate of descent (due to faster groundspeed.)
TAILWIND TO HEADWIND OR CALM	Airplane balloons. Pitch attitude increases. Indicated airspeed increases. Groundspeed decreases.	Decrease power. Fly down to the glideslope. Prepare to increase power. To stay on glidepath, decrease the rate of descent (due to slower groundspeed.)

Figure 4-38. While you should teach your students never to attempt an approach into hazardous wind shear conditions, if they inadvertently encounter wind shear during approach the FAA recommends specific procedures to follow.

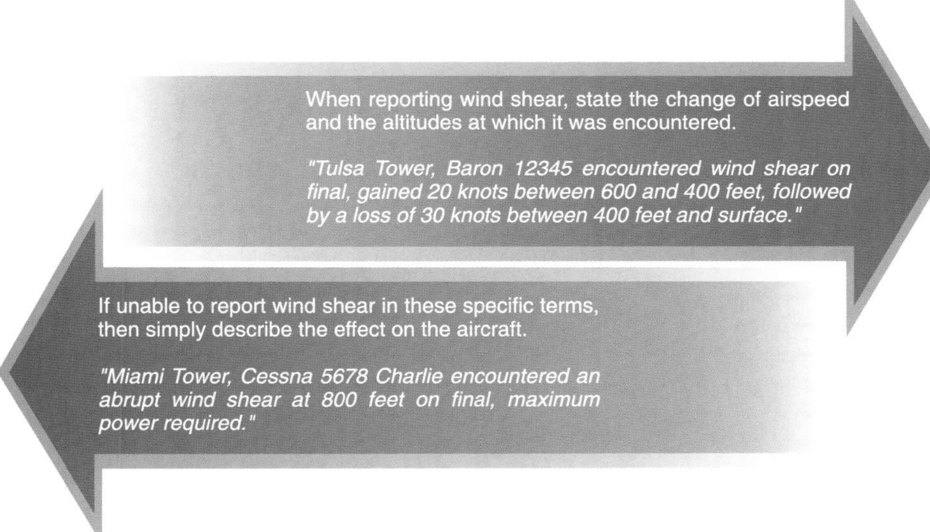

Figure 4-39. When analyzing wind shear reports from other pilots, have your students consider the type of aircraft when evaluating the severity of the encounter. If a high-performance jet requires full thrust to escape the shear, it is quite likely it will be hazardous to pilots in aircraft with less performance capability.

Stall/Spin Awareness

Stall/spin awareness is an important safety issue for pilots at all levels of training. The FAA reference for this subject is AC 61-67, *Stall and Spin Awareness Training*. This publication explains the training required by the FARs and offers you guidance to provide this instruction. You should emphasize that the techniques and procedures for each aircraft may differ, and your students should be aware of the flight characteristics of each aircraft flown. Single-engine stalls should not be demonstrated or practiced in multi-engine

1. Definitions
   a. Angle of attack
   b. Airspeed
   c. Configuration
   d. V-speeds
   e. Load factor
   f. Center of gravity (CG)
   g. Weight
   h. Altitude and temperature
   i. Snow, ice or frost on the wings
   j. Turbulence
2. Distractions
3. Stall Recognition
4. Types of Stalls
   a. Power-off (approach to landing)
   b. Power-on (departure stalls)
   c. Accelerated
5. Stall Recovery
6. Secondary Stalls
7. Spins
   a. Weight and balance
   b. Primary cause
8. Types of spins
   a. Incipient spin
   b. Fully developed spin
   c. Flat spin
9. Spin Recovery

Figure 4-40. The FAA recommends these ground-training subjects for stall/spin awareness.

airplanes. Engine-out minimum control speed demonstrations in multi-engine airplanes should not be attempted when the density altitude and temperature are such that the engine-out minimum control speed is close to the stall speed, since loss of directional or lateral control could result. The flight training required by FAR Parts 61 and 141 does not entail the actual practicing of spins for other than flight instructor — airplane and flight instructor — glider applicants, but emphasizes stall and spin avoidance. Your regulatory responsibility is to conduct the required ground training so your students understand spins and spin recovery, and to provide the required stall avoidance training. The intention of the regulations is for you to emphasize recognition of situations that could lead to inadvertent stalls and spins. [Figure 4-40]

STALL AVOIDANCE AT SLOW AIRSPEEDS

Flight at critically slow airspeeds is a very effective stall avoidance practice. It gives your students a feel for how the aircraft performs when a stall is imminent. Make sure all stalls, as well as slow flight maneuvers that can lead to inadvertent stalls, are conducted at sufficient altitude to enable recovery above 1,500 feet AGL in single-engine airplanes and above 3,000 feet in multi-engine airplanes. [Figure 4-41]

REALISTIC DISTRACTIONS

The FAA recommends you teach your students to avoid inadvertent stalls by creating distractions while your students are practicing slow flight and maneuvering in the traffic pattern on an approach. There are a number of distracting tasks you can assign. [Figure 4-42]

FUEL EXHAUSTION

Fuel exhaustion is an extremely rare accident cause for U.S. airlines, with zero occurrences in most years, but according to the AOPA Air Safety Foundation, this type of accident claimed 110 general aviation aircraft in 1997. Fuel exhaustion occurs because of improper preflight planning, or failure to adjust to unexpected conditions during flight. If there is a silver lining, it is that most forced landings that result from fuel exhaustion are not fatal; 6 persons died in 5 of these 110 accidents.

Many NTSB reports of fuel exhaustion blame inadequate preflight planning for these accidents, but this assessment of cause may not tell the whole story. Many of these pilots did what most pilots consider reasonable flight planning. They calculated the distance for their flight, obtained a weather briefing, and made sure at least the required fuel reserve was on board, based on the reported and forecast conditions. In many of these

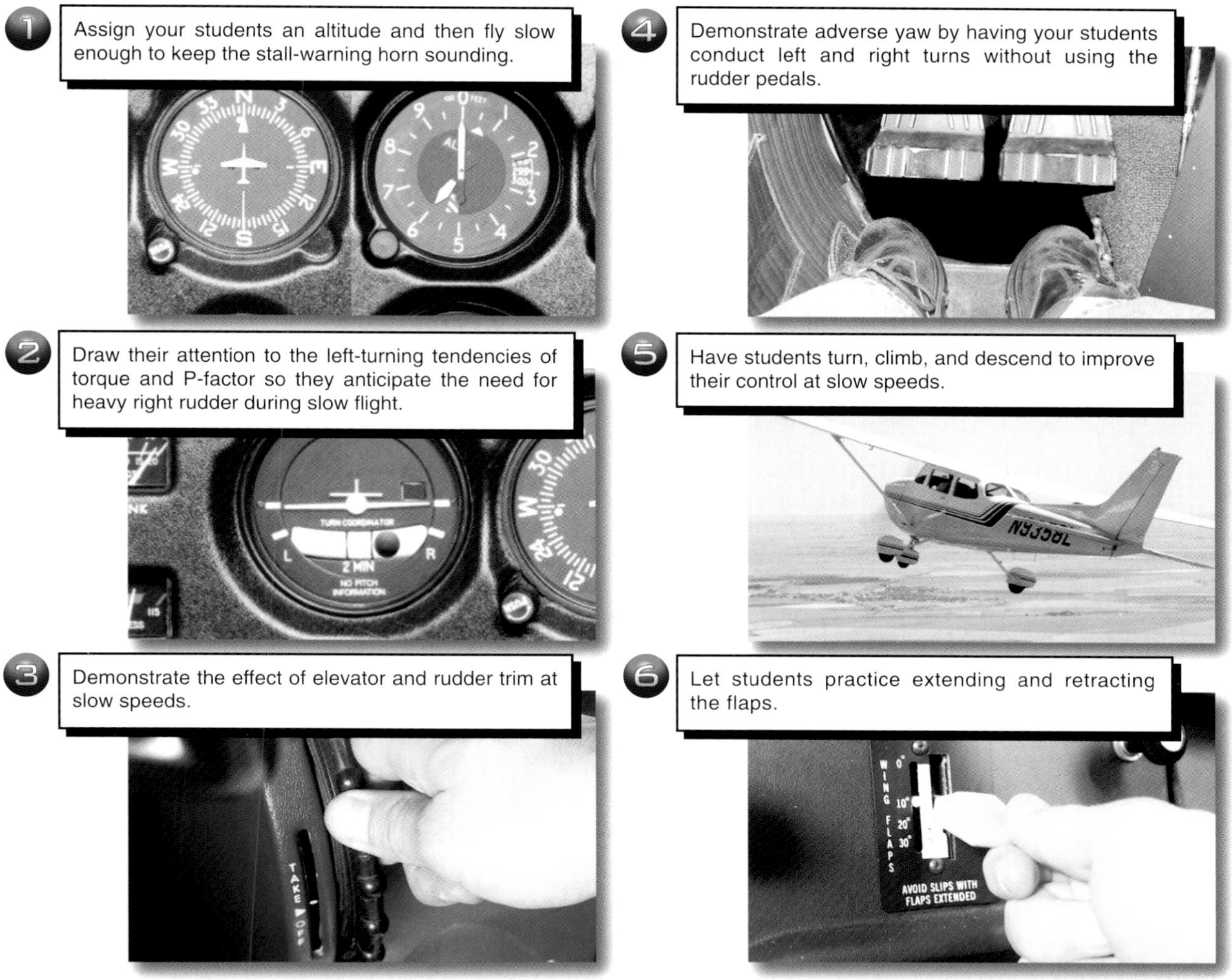
1
Assign your students an altitude and then fly slow enough to keep the stall-warning horn sounding.
2
Draw their attention to the left-turning tendencies of torque and P-factor so they anticipate the need for heavy right rudder during slow flight.
TURN COORDINATOR
2 MIN
3
Demonstrate the effect of elevator and rudder trim at slow speeds.
TAKE OFF
4
Demonstrate adverse yaw by having your students conduct left and right turns without using the rudder pedals.
5
Have students turn, climb, and descend to improve their control at slow speeds.
6
Let students practice extending and retracting the flaps.
WING FLAPS
AVOID SLIPS WITH FLAPS EXTENDED

Figure 4-41. Flying near stall speed can help your students recognize and avoid stalls later.

N98969
N98969
N98969

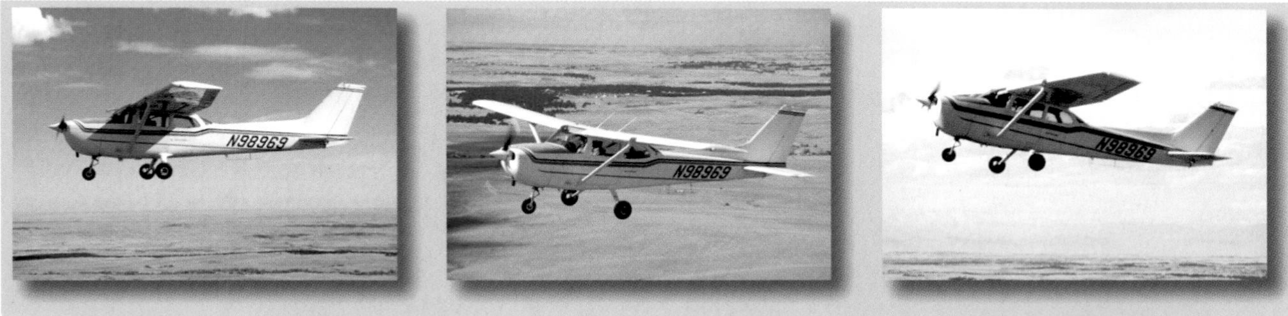

1. Begin at or above 2,000 feet AGL to ensure recovery from any unintentional stall above 1,500 feet AGL.
2. Establish an airspeed 10 to 15% below a normal approach airspeed.
3. Begin a turn with a bank of 20°, as though turning from base to final.
4. Explain that an aircraft just reported turning final and have your student look for the traffic.
5. Return to straight-and-level flight at the initial airspeed.
6. Ask your student to change the radio frequency, as though the tower requested an alternate frequency.
7. Return to straight-and-level flight at the initial airspeed, if necessary.
8. Instruct your student to check and reset the heading indicator to correspond with the magnetic compass.
9. Return to straight-and-level flight at the initial airspeed, if necessary.
10. Tell your student to obtain a chart or A/FD from the back seat to verify pattern altitude.
11. Recover to normal cruise airspeed, and straight-and-level flight.

Figure 4-42. You can create an exercise simulating several different distractions that could occur during a routine flight.

OUT OF OPTIONS

From the files of the NTSB . . .

Aircraft: *Piper PA-32-260*

Narrative: *The aircraft collided with a railroad bridge overpass during a forced landing after fuel exhaustion. The flight departed NC for NJ with an enroute stop to drop off a passenger. The pilot was unable to refuel at this stop as planned and departed and overflew other sighted airports because he could not make contact on UNICOM. Approach control gave the pilot the vector of 288 degrees for the airport. During this time, the right fuel tank ran dry and pilot switched tanks to continue flight. When [approach] could not be raised on UNICOM the pilot continued on the 288 degree heading until fuel exhaustion. He declared an emergency and was vectored to 110 degrees for the nearest airport. The pilot could not reach this airport and crashed on a railroad bridge attempting to land on a four-lane highway. An on-scene investigation confirmed the state of fuel exhaustion. The aircraft departed with 50 gallons and flew 4.1 hours. Fuel burn is 12 GPH.*

While sharing reports such as this one with your students may be a little unsettling, it will certainly emphasize the point of the importance of effectively applying ADM principles. The pilot in this case had many opportunities to rectify the situation, but made the wrong decision in each case, ultimately leading to an accident. First, the pilot opted to depart an airport without refueling. Then he overflew a number of airports where he could have safely landed. Finally, with few options left, he chose an emergency landing site that did not prove successful. By showing your students examples of what not to do, you can call attention to what the proper actions are to avoid getting into a hazardous situation.

cases, the pilots were accurate in their fuel consumption calculations; the aircraft ran out of gas at the expected time. Instead, unforeseen circumstances and failure to exercise other options led these pilots to accidents.

To address fuel exhaustion with your students, you may begin by posing the following scenario. You are enroute on a cross-country and land at a proposed fuel stop, only to discover that the FBO is closed and you are unable to obtain fuel. You cannot continue your flight to your destination without refueling. What action would you take? Obviously it is better to stay on the ground, regardless of the inconvenience. However, you can find accidents, some fatal, where a pilot did take off under these circumstances and was forced down due to fuel exhaustion. While you hope to teach your students not to make poor decisions such as this, you know there are situations where the temptation can be overwhelming. For that reason, preflight planning needs to extend beyond the weather briefing and flight log. Your students need to know all the options for obtaining fuel before leaving the ground, even if they do not expect to need them. [Figure 4-43]

Figure 4-43. Consulting flight information publications for the names of FBOs is a good start for exploring fueling options, but the planning should not stop there. A phone call verifying that an FBO has the required fuel grade available at the ETA is a good idea. It is also wise to know pricing and payment information before taxiing up to an unfamiliar pump.

You also need to teach your students to be flexible. There are plenty of reasons a properly planned flight may not have enough fuel to reach the intended destination. Do not let your students be counted among those that overflew perfectly good airports in a failed attempt to reach their destination after unexpected headwinds or other delays put it out of range.

Fuel starvation occurs when the engine stops due to an interruption of the fuel supply to the engine, even though fuel remains available in one or more of the aircraft's fuel tanks. In 1997, fuel starvation resulted in 59 general aviation accidents, with 9 fatalities. One possible reason fuel starvation accidents have a higher rate of fatalities than fuel exhaustion accidents is that fuel starvation often occurs unexpectedly. With impending fuel exhaustion, pilots know they are in trouble and are already preparing for a forced landing. Fuel starvation may occur shortly after takeoff due to mechanical problems, improper fuel management, lack of pilot understanding of the fuel system, or a combination of these problems. [Figure 4-44]

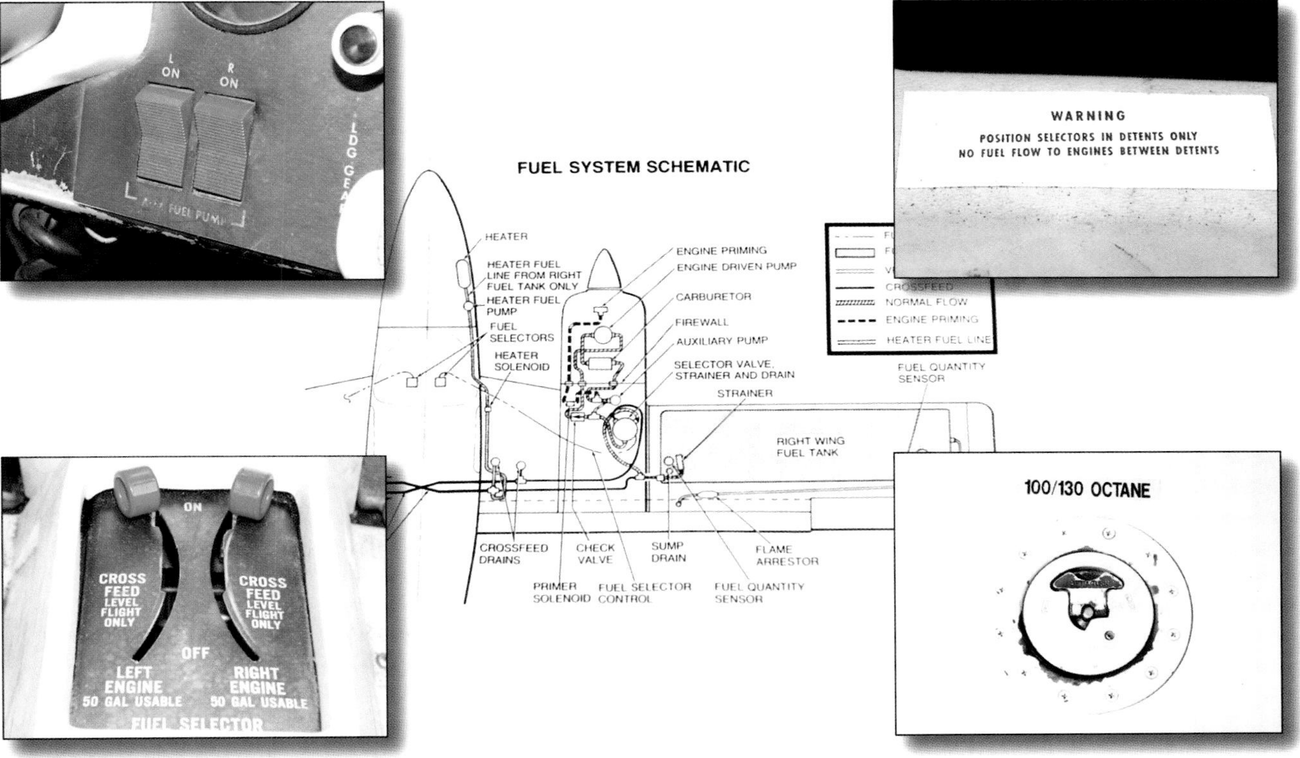

Figure 4-44. Thorough training in the design and operation of the aircraft's fuel system is the best way to make sure your students do not experience fuel starvation.

You may train your students in an aircraft with a simple, gravity-feed fuel system that can draw fuel from both tanks at once. Your students may later transition to an aircraft that requires more complex fuel management techniques. Some single-engine airplanes can be switched to only one tank at a time, and the manufacturer typically recommends taking off and landing on the fuller tank. However, if there is adequate fuel in the currently selected tank immediately before takeoff or landing, many pilots prefer to leave the fuel selector valve alone. Fuel starvation could occur at a critical phase of flight if the valve is inadvertently turned off, or changed to a tank with a fuel problem. The engine may run just long enough to allow takeoff and then quit a couple of hundred feet above the ground.

Another aspect of fuel management is switching tanks on a routine basis if the aircraft does not permit simultaneous selection of both tanks. Your students should do this at a precise, regular interval, such as every half hour or hour during the flight. This keeps the aircraft laterally balanced and also provides assurance that a certain amount of fuel remains in the other tank in the event the currently selected tank runs dry earlier than expected.

DEVELOPING JUDGMENT SKILLS

While it is relatively easy to teach and evaluate your students' ability to perform flight safety procedures, such as checklist use or collision avoidance techniques, it is more difficult to ensure that they have developed effective judgment and decision-making skills, especially in emergency situations. As you learned in Chapter 3, there are a variety of techniques you can use to teach ADM concepts to enhance your students' flight safety. Many of these methods involve discussions and review of flight scenarios on the ground.

Prudent flight instructors avoid practicing certain emergency procedures in the air, since this can be sufficiently risky and outweigh the benefits of the training. For example, while it may be more realistic to simulate fuel starvation by pulling the mixture or turning off the fuel valve, these actions cause an actual engine failure with the accompanying risk that the engine may not be restarted in time to avoid a forced landing. [Figure 4-45]

Figure 4-45. You may have access to personal computer-based aviation training devices (PCATDs), flight training devices (FTDs), or simulators that allow you to expose your students to emergency situations that cannot be safely attempted in the airplane itself.

TOO REALISTIC

From the files of the NTSB . . .

Aircraft: *Cessna 152*

Narrative: *While practicing simulated engine failures from 4,800 feet above mean sea level, the instructor pilot pulled the mixture lever to the cutoff position, causing the engine to shut down. The instructor and student pilot continued with "simulated" engine-out procedures until 2,500 feet when an attempt was made to restart the engine. After several unsuccessful attempted restarts, the instructor maneuvered the airplane toward the original simulated forced landing area. However, he overshot the field, and the airplane impacted trees. The post-accident examination of the engine revealed it was capable of normal operation.*

Although the NTSB cited poor planning as a probable cause, poor judgment definitely played a role. It is possible that better planning during this exercise would have resulted in a forced landing with no aircraft damage. However, using better judgment in the first place would have eliminated the need to exercise the superior pilot skills required for an accident-free outcome.

Because of training regimens that include instruction in human factors concepts, crew resource management, and simulations of multiple system failures and emergencies, airlines and corporate flight operations continue to improve their safety records. General aviation can benefit from this type of training. While it is not possible to teach every eventuality in the cockpit, or even in a simulator, experience coping with unlikely scenarios will help your students develop the judgment to be safer pilots.

SUMMARY CHECKLIST

✓ Flight safety is directly linked to the pilot's ability to exercise good judgment and make effective decisions.

✓ Briefings that contain potentially adverse weather are great opportunities to teach your students sound go/no-go decision skills.

✓ To help students become more aware of fuel quantity issues, ask them to compute a required landing time for each flight.

✓ It is essential to teach effective checklist use beginning with the first flight. Consider having your students write their own checklists based on the POH.

✓ Teach your students methods to avoid propeller hazards, such as stopping the engine prior to allowing passengers to board or disembark and verifying the ignition is off before examining the propeller.

✓ Students should look around the airplane and yell *"Clear"* before engaging the starter, as well as turn on the beacon light, and, if the flight is at night, the position lights.

✓ A runway incursion is any occurrence at an airport involving an aircraft, vehicle, person, or object on the ground that creates a collision hazard or results in loss of separation with an aircraft taking off, intending to take off, landing, or intending to land. To prevent runway incursions, discuss and encourage good surface movement procedures with your students.

✓ Land and hold short operations (LAHSO) refer to landing and then holding short of an intersecting runway, taxiway, predetermined point, or an approach/departure flight path.

✓ The FAA expects pilots to know whether LAHSO is being conducted at the destination airport, and to determine the available landing distance (ALD) as part of preflight preparation.

✓ You may need to review the AIM's latest LAHSO policies and procedures with all of your students, regardless of their level of training.

✓ To avoid runway incursion incidents and problems with LAHSO operations, your students need a thorough understanding of airport signs, lighting, and markings.

✓ It is essential you teach students about the hazards of wake turbulence, as well as keep up-to-date on the latest research regarding wake turbulence generation.

✓ While an illustration may be helpful to introduce wake turbulence avoidance procedures, an effective method to reinforce these operations is to ask your students to apply their knowledge during a flight.

✓ Some aspects of vortex behavior still are unknown. The study of certain accidents and NASA research indicate that some vortices, depending on their intensity, can actually bounce back into the air after ground contact.

✓ There are important differences between rotary wake and that formed by fixed-wing aircraft.

✓ Jet blast can produce hurricane force winds up to several hundred feet behind typical transport aircraft. In addition to the use of a diagram to illustrate this point, you should help your students visualize this distance when you are taxiing.

✓ The AIM suggests pilots spend no more than 1/4 to 1/3 of their scan time on visual tasks inside the cockpit when flying in VFR conditions.

✓ Your students must learn visual scanning techniques to effectively see and avoid other aircraft.

✓ Since you may instruct in both high- and low-wing airplanes, you must be aware of the blind spots associated with each design.

✓ It is essential that you teach your students to make clearing turns before performing maneuvers in the practice area.

✓ Another important aspect of teaching visual scanning is ensuring students understand the eye's limitations. For example, although the eye can see in an arc of approximately 200°, it can clearly focus on only the center 10°.

✓ Since most collisions occur near airports, it is important that your students learn to enter and fly traffic patterns properly. Eighty percent of traffic pattern collisions occur on final approach, so particular vigilance is required here. Two-thirds of collisions near airports occur at uncontrolled airports.

✓ It is important that you understand the operation of traffic and collision alert device (TCAD) and traffic collision avoidance system (TCAS) equipment so you can provide your students, especially those who are pursuing aviation careers, with up-to-date, accurate information.

✓ Students should be aware that wind shear can subject their aircraft to sudden updrafts, downdrafts, or extreme horizontal wind components, causing loss of lift or violent changes in vertical speed or altitude.

✓ An effective way to explain the wind shear associated with a microburst is to use a diagram and discuss step-by-step how an aircraft is affected when flying through the shear.

✓ While you should teach your students never to attempt an approach into hazardous wind shear conditions, if they inadvertently encounter wind shear during approach the FAA recommends specific procedures to follow.

✓ AC 61-67 *Stall and Spin Awareness Training* explains the stall/spin training required by the FARs and offers you guidance to provide this instruction.

✓ The FAA-recommended method of teaching stall/spin avoidance includes making sure your students can safely conduct slow flight with realistic distractions.

✓ Fuel exhaustion occurs because of improper preflight planning, or failure to adjust to unexpected conditions during flight.

- ✓ Fuel starvation occurs when the engine stops due to an interruption of the fuel supply to the engine, even though fuel remains available in one or more of the aircraft's fuel tanks.
- ✓ Thorough training in the design and operation of the aircraft's fuel system is the best way to make sure your students do not experience fuel starvation.
- ✓ While it is relatively easy to teach and evaluate your students' ability to perform flight safety procedures, such as checklist use or collision avoidance techniques, it is more difficult to ensure that they have developed effective judgment and decision making skills, especially in emergency situations.
- ✓ You may have access to personal computer-based aviation training devices (PCATDs), flight training devices (FTDs), or simulators that allow you to expose your students to emergency situations that cannot be safely attempted in the airplane itself.

KEY TERMS

Flight Safety

Checklist Use

Runway Incursion

Land and Hold Short Operations (LAHSO)

Available Landing Distance (ALD)

Wake Turbulence

Wingtip Vortices

Outwash Vortices

Jet Engine Blast

Collision Avoidance Procedures

Visual Scanning

Accommodation

Empty Field Myopia

Blind Spots

Clearing Turns

Traffic and Collision Alert Device (TCAD)

Traffic Alert and Collision Avoidance System (TCAS)

Wind Shear

Microburst

Stall/Spin Awareness

Fuel Exhaustion

Fuel Starvation

QUESTIONS

1. Select the true statement regarding preflight weather briefings.

   A. Instruct students to cancel flight lessons if marginal conditions are forecast nearby.
   B. If the weather appears good, students should not be required to obtain a weather briefing.
   C. Weather briefings that contain potentially adverse conditions can have great instructional value.

2. What is one method you can use to help students become more aware of fuel quantity issues before flight lessons?

3. List at least three precautions your students can take to avoid propeller hazards on the ground.

4. How would you define the term runway incursion to a student?

5. True/False. The FAA now requires your students to obtain solo experience in land and hold short operations (LAHSO) in order to obtain a private pilot certificate.

6. Select the true statement regarding wake turbulence.

   A. Airplanes that weigh more than 12,500 pounds cannot be upset by the wake of other aircraft.
   B. Research has shown that vortices may not always sink and can bounce back into the air after ground contact.
   C. Remaining even a few feet above the flight path of another aircraft guarantees you will not encounter that aircraft's wake.

7. True/False. Helicopter vortices exhibit the exact same behavior as fixed-wing vortices.

8. Name at least five actions you can teach your students to take to avoid a collision with another aircraft.

9. True/False. TCAD equipment interrogates nearby transponder-equipped aircraft to determine bearing, distance, and altitude.

10. Select the true statement regarding teaching your students about wind shear.

    A. Explain to your students that if no visual indications exist, they are unlikely to encounter hazardous wind shear.
    B. You can teach your students specific procedures to follow should they inadvertently encounter wind shear during approach.
    C. Since all wind shear is hazardous, it is not necessary for your students to determine what type of aircraft was involved when analyzing a pilot report of a wind shear encounter.

11. True/False. Your private and commercial students may be required to perform spins on their practical tests if they cannot adequately describe stall/spin entry and recovery.

12. List at least 5 realistic distractions you can provide to your students as they are performing slow flight.

13. Explain the difference between fuel exhaustion and fuel starvation.

SECTION C

DEVELOPING A PROFESSIONAL IMAGE

It may be difficult to adjust to the fact that once you have passed your flight instructor practical test, you are considered a professional pilot. In addition to the knowledge and flight skills that you possess, you will have the responsibility of developing and maintaining an image which will enable you to earn the respect of your students, as well as other professionals in the aviation industry. Since your students tend to consider you a role model, it is imperative that you set an example worthy of emulation. The word **professional** conjures up all sorts of images. [Figure 4-46]

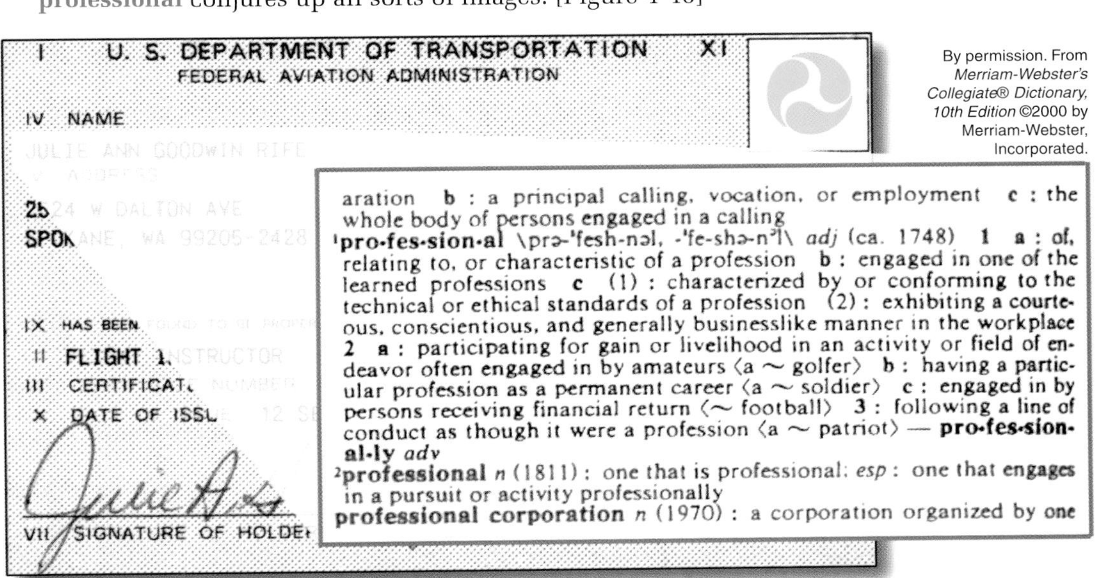

I U. S. DEPARTMENT OF TRANSPORTATION XI
FEDERAL AVIATION ADMINISTRATION
IV NAME
IX HAS BEEN
II FLIGHT I
III CERTIFICAT
X DATE OF ISSU
VII SIGNATURE OF HOLDE

aration **b** : a principal calling, vocation, or employment **c** : the whole body of persons engaged in a calling
[1]**pro·fes·sion·al** \prə-ˈfesh-nəl, -ˈfe-shə-nᵊl\ *adj* (ca. 1748) **1 a** : of, relating to, or characteristic of a profession **b** : engaged in one of the learned professions **c** (1) : characterized by or conforming to the technical or ethical standards of a profession (2) : exhibiting a courteous, conscientious, and generally businesslike manner in the workplace **2 a** : participating for gain or livelihood in an activity or field of endeavor often engaged in by amateurs ⟨a ~ golfer⟩ **b** : having a particular profession as a permanent career ⟨a ~ soldier⟩ **c** : engaged in by persons receiving financial return ⟨~ football⟩ **3** : following a line of conduct as though it were a profession ⟨a ~ patriot⟩ — **pro·fes·sion·al·ly** *adv*
[2]**professional** *n* (1811) : one that is professional; *esp* : one that engages in a pursuit or activity professionally
professional corporation *n* (1970) : a corporation organized by one

Figure 4-46. The word professional has many meanings, several of which should apply to you as a flight instructor. Your concept of what it means to be a professional may be different from someone else's.

Learning How to Fly Wright

The first well-known flight instructors were the Wright brothers, Orville and Wilbur. In 1911, they established a flight training program for both civil and military customers. One of the military students, Lieutenant Henry H. "Hap" Arnold of the U.S. Army, described his experience at the Wright flying school.

The training actually began at the Wright factory in Dayton, Ohio. "*. . . in addition to learning to fly we found we would have to master the construction and maintenance features on the Wright machine.*"

Flight training began with an old airplane mounted on a sawhorse. *"The lateral controls were connected with small clutches at the wingtips, and grabbed a moving belt running over a pulley. A forward motion, and the clutch would snatch the belt, and down would go the left wing. A backward pull, and the reverse would happen. The jolts and teetering were so violent that the student was kept busy just moving the lever back and forth to keep on an even keel. That was primary training."*

After the simulation instruction in the factory, Arnold completed his flight training course in 10 days. During those 10 days, he logged 28 training flights for a total of 3 hours and 48 minutes of dual time. The last three flights he *"landed without assistance."*

The Wright brothers were probably more qualified than anyone to give flight instruction in the early 1900s. They had the experience, know-how, dedication, and other qualifications commonly attributed to professionals.

Quoted excerpts from Arnold in his autobiography Global Mission (New York Harper & Brothers, 1949).

Courtesy of U.S. Air Force Academy Special Collections

PROFESSIONAL QUALIFICATIONS

You should carefully consider what traits you must possess as a professional flight instructor. If you attempt to instruct without considering these qualifications, your performance will be degraded, and you may deprive your students of essential training. Professional flight instructors constantly work on preparation, and strive for improved performance. [Figure 4-47]

- Professionalism exists only when a service is performed for someone, or for the common good.
- Professionalism is achieved only after extended training and preparation.
- True performance as a professional is based on study and research.
- Professionalism presupposes an intellectual requirement. Professionals must be able to reason logically and accurately.
- Professionalism requires the ability to use good judgment when making decisions. Professionals cannot limit their actions and decisions to standard patterns and practices.
- Professionalism demands a code of ethics. Professionals must be true to themselves and to those they serve. Anything less than a sincere performance is quickly detected, and immediately destroys its effectiveness.

Figure 4-47. There are many concepts, personal qualifications, and activities that define professionalism.

There is no such thing as the ideal flight instructor for every situation. For example, you may excel at relating to people and be comfortable teaching a wide variety of students, while your technical knowledge in certain subject areas may be limited. Another instructor may have an excellent

grasp of many technical concepts, but has difficulty explaining information to students who do not already have an understanding of these subjects. As a professional, you learn to recognize your limitations and work to eliminate them. You also realize what you can do best, and often concentrate your training activities accordingly.

You may feel overwhelmed by the responsibilities and expectations incumbent on a flight instructor. At the same time, remember you have been through a rigorous certification process. Once you are certificated, you have a solid foundation of knowledge and skill. Your experience may be limited and initially you may lack confidence, but as a rule, beginning flight instructors do a good job. They normally exhibit a high level of enthusiasm and compensate for either real or perceived deficiencies by taking extra care to be well prepared for each lesson.

SINCERITY

Sincerity is a quality or state of being sincere, honest, and genuine. Attempting to hide some inadequacy behind a smokescreen of unrelated details will diminish your ability to command the respect and full attention of your students. The student-instructor relationship is based upon acceptance that you are a competent, qualified teacher and an expert pilot. [Figure 4-48]

Anything less than a sincere performance degrades your effectiveness as a professional flight instructor.

Figure 4-48. Any appearance of pretentiousness, whether it is real or mistakenly assumed by your students, will immediately cause them to lose confidence in you, and their learning will be adversely affected. You should strive to be honest in every way.

INTEGRITY

Integrity is the quality or state of being complete. When applied to a person, it usually implies commendable behavioral characteristics, including sound moral principles, forthrightness, honesty, and sincerity. It also extends to other traits, such as having the courage to back up your convictions, taking responsibility for your actions, and being held accountable. People who possess integrity do not cover up embarrassing incidents, or promulgate misleading information.

CREDIBILITY

When applied to a professional, credibility refers to qualities such as reliability, reputation, trustworthiness, and even appearance. Often your credibility is based on your education, experience, achievement, or status.

From the Moon to the Classroom

It's a strange, eerie sensation to fly a lunar landing trajectory — not difficult, but somewhat complex and unforgiving. — Neil Armstrong

It can be a strange sensation to transition from the role of student to your new role as an instructor. Teaching individuals to fly can be complex and unforgiving at times. Neil Armstrong may have felt this same way, and not only about his moon landing. In addition to his historic first steps on the moon, Armstrong took steps to be a worthy role model as a teacher. The following story, as related by a former student, Tom Black, clearly illustrates that Professor Armstrong possessed the traits of a truly professional instructor.

I was a sophomore in high school (or would be in another 2 months) in July 1969 when Neil Armstrong took his famous "small step." In the fall of 1972, I entered the University of Cincinnati as an aerospace engineering major, from where I graduated in 1977 with a BS in Aerospace Engineering (U.C. has a 5-year engineering program). During my time there I was privileged (and I do mean that) to study under Professor Neil Armstrong.

Neil truly has a gift for teaching, and I never heard him try to "snow" a student when answering a question. If he didn't know, he said so -—but you could be sure he would have looked up the answer before the next class and would stop you on the way in the door to tell you where to find the answer (what book, what chapter, and that he had put that book on reserve for you in the college's library!). He had a policy that if more than half the class missed a question on one of his exams he would throw that question out, telling us, "I obviously didn't cover that well enough. Let's go over it again." You could bet that question — or a version of it — would be on the next exam, though. He even spent extra time — a precious commodity in his busy schedule — with several of us in his Flight Test Engineering class who were pilots, briefing us on how to fly routine flight test maneuvers in the light aircraft we flew and reviewing the results with us afterwards to show us how to fly the maneuvers more accurately in order to collect the best engineering data.

Tom Black is an aerospace engineer and former student of Neil Armstrong's at the University of Cincinnati. In 1983, Armstrong sponsored Black for membership in the Society of Experimental Test Pilots.

PERSONAL APPEARANCE AND HABITS

Your **personal appearance** has a significant effect on your image. Many of your students will be successful professionals, and they will expect you to look and act professionally — to be neat, clean, and well dressed. Dressing professionally does not necessarily mean you must wear a business suit. You may instruct at a flight school or club where there is no specific dress code, or a particular uniform or tie may be required. You should adopt attire appropriate to your professional status as a flight instructor and realize that your appearance, even when you are not working, affects your credibility with your students. [Figure 4-49]

How confident would you be of this instructor's abilities?

Would you be more comfortable learning to fly from this CFI now that his appearance is more professional?

Figure 4-49. Imagine you are a new student concerned about the safety of learning to fly and you must select an instructor.

Personal habits also have an effect on your professional image. The exercise of common courtesy is perhaps as important as any habit. Be on time for lessons and make sure you answer the phone properly. If you are rude, thoughtless, and inattentive you cannot hold the respect of students, regardless of your ability as a pilot or instructor. Personal cleanliness is important to aviation instruction. Frequently, you and your students work in close proximity, and even little annoyances such as body odor, excessive perfume or cologne, and bad breath can cause serious distractions. In addition, the use of alcohol in public, especially around an airport, has a seriously negative impact on your image.

DEMEANOR

Demeanor refers to your outward behavior or conduct. Your professional image requires development of a calm, thoughtful, and disciplined demeanor that puts your students at ease. You must constantly portray competence in the subject matter and genuine interest in the students' well-being. Avoid erratic behavior and mood swings, distracting speech habits, behaving in an overbearing manner, or acting flippantly. [Figure 4-50]

Figure 4-50. Avoid any tendency toward frequently countermanding directions, reacting inconsistently to similar errors at different times, demanding unreasonable performance or progress, or criticizing your students unfairly.

RESPONSIBILITY TO YOUR STUDENTS

Your main task during flight or ground instruction is to teach. Your instruction must be appropriate to the needs of your students. This means your instruction should be tailored to each individual student, and to the circumstances under which it is given.

ACCEPTANCE OF THE STUDENT

You must accept students as they are, which includes all their faults and problems. Your students are people who want to learn and you are the person who is available to help in the learning process. Beginning with this understanding, the professional relationship between you and your students should be based on a mutual acknowledgement that you are both important to each other, and you are both working toward the same objective. Under no circumstance should you do anything that implies disregard for your students.

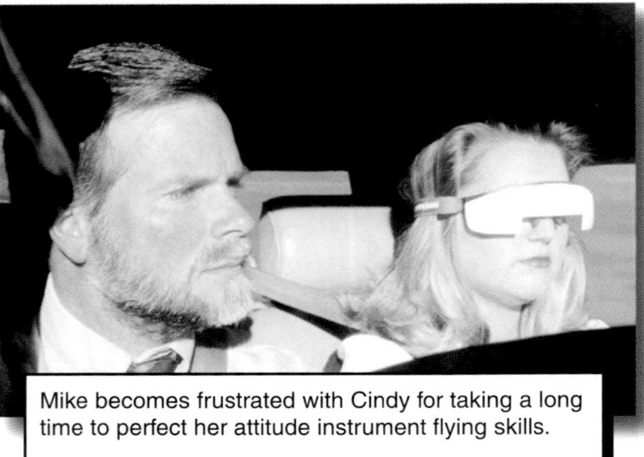
Mike becomes frustrated with Cindy for taking a long time to perfect her attitude instrument flying skills.

Since Tim is having a difficult time with VOR tracking in the airplane, Peggy suggests that he spend some time practicing in the simulator.

Figure 4-51. You must treat your students with respect, regardless of whether they are quick to learn or slow and apprehensive.It is important to realize that not all of your students learn at the same rate. Some of your students need more practice than others.

Acceptance, rather than ridicule, and support, rather than reproof, will encourage learning. [Figure 4-51]

PROPER LANGUAGE

In flight instruction, as in other professional activities, the use of profanity should be avoided. The use of such language generally shows a lack of self-control. To many people, such language is actually objectionable to the point of being painful. You must talk normally, without inhibitions, and develop the ability to speak positively and descriptively without excesses of language.

BECOME A POSITIVE ROLE MODEL

Whether you like it or not, you are a **role model**. Your every action is observed, and when your students see that you take pride in your profession and show enthusiasm for aviation, they are favorably impressed. Throughout their flying careers, your students will remember your attitude, and be influenced by what you have taught them.. You can be remembered as a positive influence who encouraged your students and instilled in them a sense of the beauty and excitement of aviation. Or, you can have a negative impact, causing your students to feel unsuccessful in their efforts and to view flight training as stressful and difficult. The aviation industry needs good, solid role models to help develop competent and safe pilots for the future. [Figure 4-52]

Jennifer enthusiastically relates stories to her students about her experiences as a pilot and the positive impact aviation has on her life. She discusses how much she enjoys flight instructing and its many rewards.

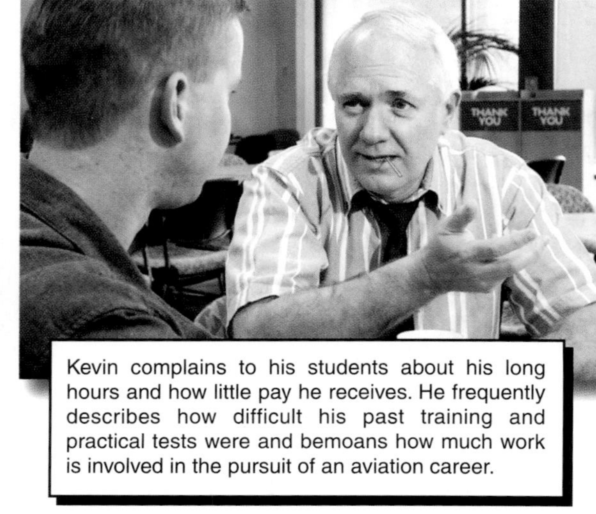

Kevin complains to his students about his long hours and how little pay he receives. He frequently describes how difficult his past training and practical tests were and bemoans how much work is involved in the pursuit of an aviation career.

Figure 4-52. What do you remember about your flight instructors? What do you want your students to remember about you?

ENHANCING YOUR QUALIFICATIONS

Once you become a CFI, you must resist the temptation to become complacent or satisfied with your current status and capabilities. A good pilot never stops learning, and this is especially true for successful flight instructors. Look for ways to upgrade your professional qualifications. Normally you need to build aeronautical experience, expand your technical knowledge, improve your teaching skills, and polish your professional image.

BUILDING AERONAUTICAL EXPERIENCE

Upgrading your pilot certificate or adding a rating to your existing certificate is an excellent way to enhance your piloting skills. Advanced training also demonstrates your commitment to aviation, and improves your professional status. [Figure 4-53]

An additional flight instructor rating can lead to new instructing opportunities. You must log at least 15 hours as pilot in command (PIC) in the category and class of aircraft appropriate to the instructor rating sought.

Courtesy of Schweizer Aircraft Corporation

To provide instruction to a student toward the issuance of a certificate or rating in a multi-engine airplane, helicopter, or powered-lift aircraft, you must have at least 5 hours of pilot-in-command time in the specific make and model of aircraft.

You can obtain an additional category or class rating or work toward achieving an airline transport pilot (ATP) certificate.

Receiving a tailwheel or high-altitude endorsement, as well as seeking instruction in aerobatics or mountain flying can allow you to gain experience in unique airplanes and expand your teaching repertoire.

Figure 4-53. Never become complacent regarding your own qualifications or abilities. You have the opportunity and responsibility to introduce new procedures and techniques to your students as you gain experience.

Another way to add to your aeronautical experience is through the **Pilot Proficiency Award Program**, or Wings Program, which is described in AC 61-91. You can complete a phase of the Wings Program by obtaining three hours of specific flight training, including one hour of air work, one hour of takeoffs and landings, and one hour of instrument training. You must also attend an approved Aviation Safety Seminar, a mountain flying course with both flight and ground training, or an FAA-approved physiological training course conducted by the FAA or at a military facility. As a CFI, you can substitute completion of a flight instructor refresher clinic or renewal program for the safety seminar. In addition, you can satisfy the flying portions of the first three phases by providing the instruction for three Wings candidates — a minimum of nine hours of instruction. Phases IV through XX can be accomplished by taking an evaluation or proficiency flight with a designated flight instructor examiner or an FAA operations inspector.

EXPANDING YOUR TECHNICAL KNOWLEDGE

You can stay informed about various FAA programs and policies by reviewing advisory circulars available through your local Flight Standards District Office, by subscription, or on the FAA web site. You also can obtain current FARs, airworthiness directives, and *The General Aviation Inspector's Handbook* from the Internet. By logging on to the NTSB web site, you can review accident statistics and summaries and you can explore subjects ranging from aircraft design to human factors research by looking up NASA on the Internet. [Figure 4-54]

Photos Courtesy of NASA and NASA Dryden Research Center

Figure 4-54. Topics such as aircraft design, aerodynamics, aviation history, human factors research and, of course, space flight can be found on NASA's website.

When you participate in the FAA program called **Operation Raincheck**, you can expand your knowledge of ATC services by visiting facilities such as control towers, approach control, or air route traffic control centers. By taking part in a similar program called **Operation Takeoff**, you can interact with weather briefers at a local flight service station and learn tips and techniques to get the most out of the services they provide. The insight you gain by touring an ATC or FSS facility can be beneficial to pass on to your students. [Figure 4-55]

Figure 4-55. You may elect to arrange a group tour of a control tower or a flight service station for your students.

IMPROVING YOUR TEACHING SKILLS

Taking advantage of continuing education courses offered through colleges and universities is a good way to sharpen your instructing skills. Classes which focus on topics such as communication, learning styles, testing, and student motivation can be valuable in improving your teaching techniques. Computer courses can help increase your productivity by enabling you to unlock resources on the Internet, or take advantage of software to develop effective instructional presentations.

POLISHING YOUR IMAGE

Becoming an **aviation safety counselor** is an excellent way to polish your professional image. Aviation safety counselors are volunteers from the aviation community who help promote safety in a variety of ways. As a safety counselor, your responsibilities may include helping to conduct aviation safety seminars, providing remedial training for pilots who have violated regulations, and offering advice and guidance regarding aviation safety. You can also strive to obtain a **gold seal instructor certificate**, which identifies you as an experienced instructor with a high student pass rate. [Figure 4-56]

I U. S. DEPARTMENT OF TRANSPORTATION XI
FEDERAL AVIATION ADMINISTRATION
IV NAME
CARL EDWARD ARMSTRONG
V ADDRESS
12345 MAIN ST.
PALM SPRINGS, FL 33461
VI NATIONALITY USA
D.O.B. 11 DEC 1938
SEX M HEIGHT 69 WEIGHT 200 HAIR BROWN EYES HAZEL
IX HAS BEEN FOUND TO BE PROPERLY QUALIFIED TO EXERCISE THE PRIVILEGES OF
II GROUND INSTRUCTOR
III CERTIFICATE NUMBER 357568714CFI
X DATE OF ISSUE 22 JAN 1995
VII SIGNATURE OF HOLDER
XIV
VIII ADMINISTRATOR

You have to hold a ground instructor certificate with an advanced or instrument rating.

According to the general guidelines in AC 61-65, *Certification: Pilots and Flight and Ground Instructors*, to obtain a gold seal designation you must have trained and recommended at least 10 students for practical tests within the previous 24 months and at least 8 of these students must have passed on the first attempt.

Figure 4-56. Once you earn a gold seal designation, it is reissued each time you renew your flight instructor certificate.

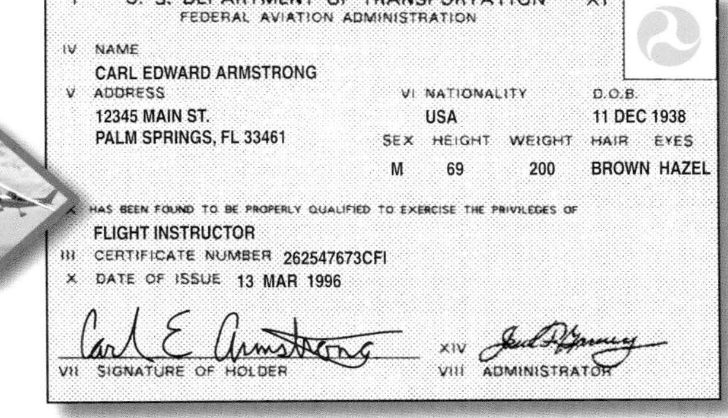
I U. S. DEPARTMENT OF TRANSPORTATION XI
FEDERAL AVIATION ADMINISTRATION
IV NAME
CARL EDWARD ARMSTRONG
V ADDRESS
12345 MAIN ST.
PALM SPRINGS, FL 33461
VI NATIONALITY USA
D.O.B. 11 DEC 1938
SEX M HEIGHT 69 WEIGHT 200 HAIR BROWN EYES HAZEL
HAS BEEN FOUND TO BE PROPERLY QUALIFIED TO EXERCISE THE PRIVILEGES OF
FLIGHT INSTRUCTOR
III CERTIFICATE NUMBER 262547673CFI
X DATE OF ISSUE 13 MAR 1996
VII SIGNATURE OF HOLDER
XIV
VIII ADMINISTRATOR

These are only some suggestions for enhancing your qualifications. Your main objective should be to expand your knowledge and credibility as a professional instructor. At some point, you may find a niche for your experience and skills and decide to specialize in a particular type of training. This might be instrument training, multi-engine instruction, or some facet of simulation or computer-based education. In any event, the opportunities for professional instructors are wide open and ready for you to explore.

SUMMARY CHECKLIST

✓ The word professional has many meanings, several of which should apply to you as a flight instructor.

✓ Anything less than a sincere performance degrades your effectiveness as a professional flight instructor.

✓ If you have integrity, you possess sound moral principles, forthrightness, honesty, and sincerity. You also have the courage to back up your convictions, take responsibility for your actions, and be held accountable.

✓ Credibility refers to qualities such as reliability, reputation, trustworthiness, and even appearance.

✓ Your personal appearance and habits have a significant effect on your image.

✓ Demeanor refers to your outward behavior or conduct. Your professional image requires development of a calm, thoughtful, and disciplined demeanor that puts your students at ease.

✓ Acceptance and support of students, rather than ridicule and reproof, will encourage learning.

✓ In flight instruction, as in other professional activities, proper language should be used and profanity should be avoided.

✓ As a role model, your every action is observed, and when your students see that you take pride in your profession and show enthusiasm for aviation, they are favorably impressed.

✓ Upgrading your pilot certificate or adding a rating to your existing certificate is an excellent way to enhance your piloting skills.

✓ Another way to add to your aeronautical experience is through the Pilot Proficiency Award Program, or Wings Program, which is described in AC 61-91.

✓ You can stay informed about various FAA programs and policies by reviewing advisory circulars available through your local Flight Standards District Office, by subscription, or on the FAA web site. You also can obtain current FARs, airworthiness directives, and *The General Aviation Inspector's Handbook* from the Internet.

✓ By logging on to the NTSB web site you can review accident statistics and summaries, and by looking up NASA on the Internet you can explore subjects ranging from aircraft design to human factors research.

- ✓ The insight you gain by touring an ATC or FSS facility through Operation Raincheck or Operation Takeoff can be beneficial to pass on to your students.

- ✓ Taking advantage of continuing education courses offered through colleges and universities is a good way to sharpen your instructing skills.

- ✓ As an aviation safety counselor, your responsibilities may include helping conduct aviation safety seminars, providing remedial training for pilots who have violated regulations, and offering advice and guidance regarding aviation safety.

- ✓ To obtain a gold seal certificate, you must have trained and recommended at least 10 students for practical tests within the previous 24 months, and at least 8 of these students must have passed on their first attempt. You also must hold a ground instructor certificate with an advanced or instrument rating.

KEY TERMS

Professional

Sincerity

Integrity

Credibility

Personal Appearance

Personal Habits

Demeanor

Role Model

Pilot Proficiency Award Program

Operation Raincheck

Operation Takeoff

Aviation Safety Counselor

Gold Seal Instructor Certificate

QUESTIONS

1. Describe at least three of the qualities that a professional flight instructor should possess.

2. True/False. As long as you are knowledgeable, your personal appearance and habits will not affect how your students perceive you.

3. Your responsibilities to your students normally include which of the following?

   A. Accepting students for who they are
   B. Guaranteeing your students will complete their training within a specific number of hours
   C. Both answers A and B

4. List at least five ways you can enhance your professional qualifications.

5. Explain some of the ways you can stay informed about FAA policies, aviation safety, and other aviation-related subjects.

6. Briefly describe the FAA Operation Raincheck and Operation Takeoff programs.

7. True/False. To obtain a gold seal flight instructor certificate, you must hold a ground instructor certificate with an advanced or instrument rating.

8. Select the true statement about obtaining a gold seal flight instructor certificate.

   A. You must have trained and recommended at least 10 students for practical tests within the previous 12 months and at least 8 must have passed on their first attempt.
   B. You must have trained and recommended at least 20 students for practical tests within the previous 24 calendar months and at least 10 must have passed on their first attempt.
   C. You must have trained and recommended at least 10 students for practical tests within the previous 24 calendar months and at least 8 must have passed on their first attempt.

SECTION D

EXERCISING INSTRUCTOR PRIVILEGES

A person who holds a flight instructor certificate is authorized within the limitations of that flight instructor certificate and ratings, to give training and endorsements...

— FAR Part 61.193 FLIGHT INSTRUCTOR PRIVILEGES

The attitude you adopt about your responsibilities deeply influences the quality and scope of the flight training you provide. You are actively shaping the future of your students and influencing their attitudes about the flight careers they may pursue. You are responsible for ensuring your students have a positive and productive training experience. [Figure 4-57]

Figure 4-57. You are held accountable for providing supervision, evaluation, and test recommendations for your students.

PREPARING TO INSTRUCT

You should refer to FAR Part 61, Subpart H or FAR Part 141, Appendices F and G for specific information on eligibility, aeronautical knowledge, and flight proficiency requirements. Obtaining a flight instructor – airplane certificate under Part 61 and 141 requires that you possess either a commercial certificate and an instrument rating or an airline transport pilot certificate (ATP). You also must receive and log training on the fundamentals of instruction and possess the aeronautical knowledge applicable to recreational, private, and commercial pilot certificates.

CERTIFICATES AND RATINGS

Part 61 lists the pilot certificates and ratings that may be issued to applicants who satisfactorily accomplish the training and certification requirements specified in the FARs. As a flight instructor, you need to study the regulations in order to become familiar with pilot and flight instructor certificates and the associated category and class ratings that may be placed on them. [Figure 4-58]

Your certifications must be in the same aircraft category and class rating as the flight instructor certificate sought. For example, if you apply for a multi-engine instructor – airplane

Pilot Certificates

Student pilot
Recreational pilot
Private pilot
Commercial pilot
Airline transport pilot

Flight instructor certificates
Ground instructor certificates

Aircraft Type Ratings

Aircraft type ratings are listed in AC 61-1 and are classified as follows:

Large aircraft (other than lighter-than-air)
Turbojet-powered airplanes

Other aircraft type ratings may be specified by the Administrator through the aircraft type certification procedures.

Category and Class Ratings

The following ratings can be placed on pilot certificates initially or may be acquired later as an additional rating to add an aircraft category, class, or type:

Aircraft Category Ratings:
- Airplane
- Rotorcraft
- Glider
- Lighter-than-air
- Powered lift

Airplane Class Ratings:
- Single-engine land
- Multi-engine land
- Single-engine sea
- Multi-engine sea

Rotorcraft Class Ratings:
- Helicopter
- Gyroplane

Lighter-Than-Air Class Ratings:
- Airship
- Balloon

Intrument Ratings (On Private and Commercial Certificates Only):
- Instrument–Airplane
- Instrument–Helicopter
- Instrument–Powered-lift

Flight Instructor Ratings:

Aircraft Category Ratings:
- Airplane
- Rotorcraft
- Glider
- Powered-lift

Airplane Class Ratings:
- Single-engine
- Multi-engine

Rotorcraft Class Ratings:
- Helicopter
- Gyroplane

Instrument Ratings:
- Instrument–Airplane
- Instrument–Helicopter
- Instrument–Powered-lift

Ground Instructor Ratings:
- Basic
- Advanced
- Instrument

Figure 4-58. Part 61.5 shows the relationships between pilot and flight instructor certificates and the aircraft category and class ratings that may be placed on those certificates.

rating you must have an airplane – multi-engine rating on your commercial certificate. In addition, you must have logged 15 hours of PIC time in the category and class of aircraft appropriate to the flight instructor rating sought.

If you apply for an additional rating on your flight instructor certificate, you must have a minimum of 15 hours as pilot in command in the category and class of aircraft appropriate to the rating sought.

YOUR MEDICAL CERTIFICATE

FAR 61.23 lists operations that require a medical certificate and states which class of certificate applies to each operation. Part 67 describes the standards governing issuance of medical certificates. This regulation is used by **aviation medical examiners (AMEs)** in determining fitness standards for pilot certificate qualifications.

The FAA requires only that you possess a valid third-class medical when acting as pilot in command (PIC) in the course of providing instruction. It is not necessary for you to possess a current medical to instruct if you do not act as pilot in command or act as a required crewmember. If you elect to instruct without a medical certificate, your student must be a certificated pilot who is rated in the aircraft and able to act as PIC. This is not to say that a flight instructor without a medical cannot log pilot-in-command time. It is legal for you to log PIC time as an instructor and not act as PIC of the aircraft. The only situations in which you are required to act as PIC are during training of a student pilot and when giving instrument instruction to a non-instrument-rated student while operating under an IFR flight plan, regardless of whether IFR conditions exist.

Regulations are silent on the issue of compensation for instructors since the FAA does not set rates or prevent free instruction. However, the FAA has determined that providing flight instruction does not constitute pilot services. Therefore, you may be compensated for your instructional services without regard to your medical status, as long as you are not acting as PIC or functioning as a required crewmember. [Figure 4-59]

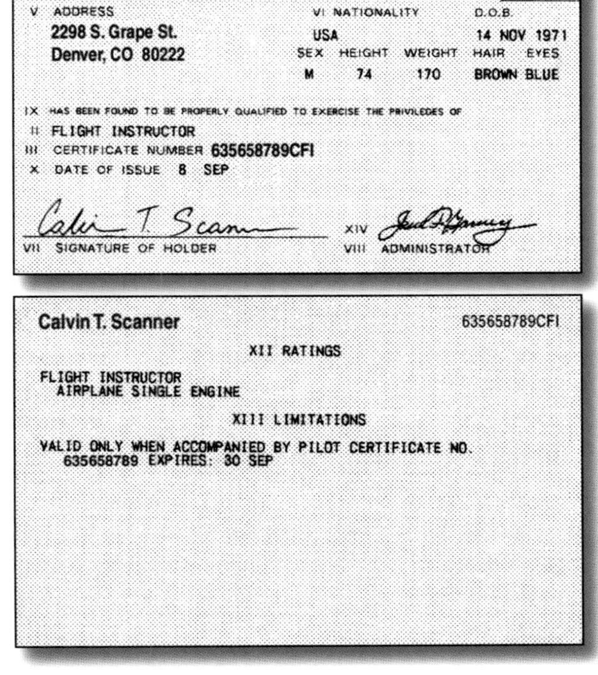

I U. S. DEPARTMENT OF TRANSPORTATION XI
FEDERAL AVIATION ADMINISTRATION
IV NAME
Calvin T. Scanner
V ADDRESS VI NATIONALITY D.O.B.
2298 S. Grape St. USA 14 NOV 1971
Denver, CO 80222 SEX HEIGHT WEIGHT HAIR EYES
M 74 170 BROWN BLUE
IX HAS BEEN FOUND TO BE PROPERLY QUALIFIED TO EXERCISE THE PRIVILEGES OF
II FLIGHT INSTRUCTOR
III CERTIFICATE NUMBER 635658789CFI
X DATE OF ISSUE 8 SEP
VII SIGNATURE OF HOLDER XIV VIII ADMINISTRATOR

Calvin T. Scanner 635658789CFI
XII RATINGS
FLIGHT INSTRUCTOR
AIRPLANE SINGLE ENGINE
XIII LIMITATIONS
VALID ONLY WHEN ACCOMPANIED BY PILOT CERTIFICATE NO. 635658789 EXPIRES: 30 SEP

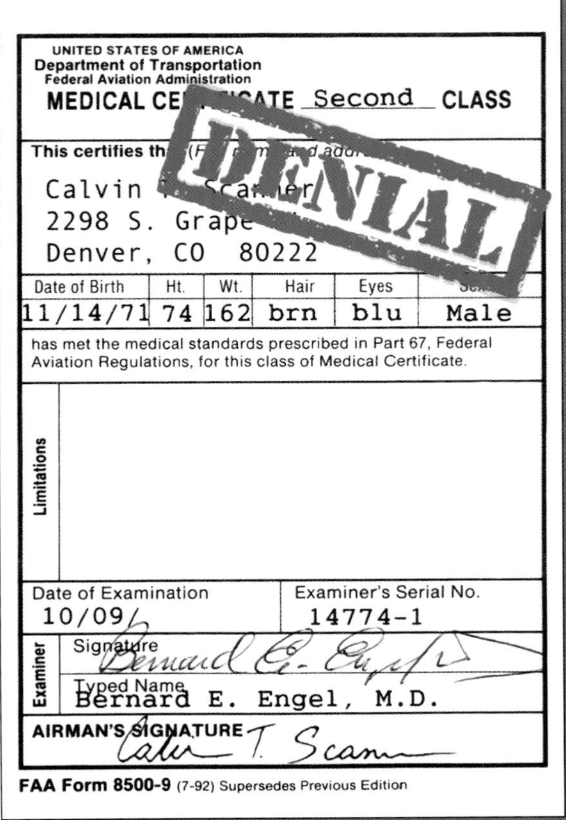

UNITED STATES OF AMERICA
Department of Transportation
Federal Aviation Administration
MEDICAL CE[...]ATE Second CLASS
DENIAL
This certifies th[...]
Calvin [...] Sca[...]er
2298 S. Grape
Denver, CO 80222

Date of Birth	Ht.	Wt.	Hair	Eyes	Sex
11/14/71	74	162	brn	blu	Male

has met the medical standards prescribed in Part 67, Federal Aviation Regulations, for this class of Medical Certificate.

Limitations

Date of Examination 10/09/ Examiner's Serial No. 14774-1
Examiner Signature
Typed Name Bernard E. Engel, M.D.
AIRMAN'S SIGNATURE
FAA Form 8500-9 (7-92) Supersedes Previous Edition

Figure 4-59. The compensation you receive for flight instruction is not in exchange for piloting the aircraft. As a result, denial of a medical certificate does not prevent you from instructing under certain circumstances.

Once you begin flight instruction, FAR 61.195 allows a maximum of 8 hours of flight training in any 24-hour period. Remember to schedule your instruction time to remain within this limit. Conducting flight training beyond the 8-hour requirement, particularly on successive days, may affect your mental and physical status to the point where you are no longer medically fit for flight.

As an instructor, you are only permitted to flight instruct 8 hours in a 24-hour period.

PROVIDING INSTRUCTION UNDER PART 61 AND PART 141

The requirements for the issuance of pilot and flight instructor certificates and ratings are prescribed by Part 61. In addition, Part 61 states the conditions under which those certificates and ratings are necessary, as well as the associated privileges and limitations. Part 141 governs the certification of **approved pilot schools** and sets forth the rules under which they operate. Since approved pilot schools must conduct flight and ground training under specific guidelines and meet rigid operational requirements, graduates of these schools are permitted certification with less total flight experience than that specified in Part 61. See FAR 61.71 for special rules that apply to graduates of approved schools.

AERONAUTICAL KNOWLEDGE REQUIREMENTS

The aeronautical knowledge requirements are essentially the same in terms of content for each certificate or rating whether your student trains under Part 61 or Part 141. However, the regulations differ with regard to ground training time. Part 61 does not specify a given number of hours of ground instruction as a requirement for a pilot or flight instructor rating. It does, however, specify the general subjects in which an applicant must have either received ground instruction or completed a home study course. [Figure 4-60]

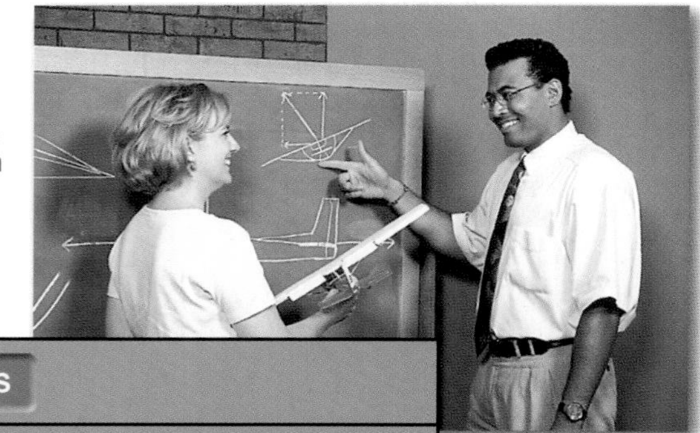

Figure 4-60. Part 141 lists the general subjects which must be included in most approved courses of training. It also specifies the number of hours of ground instruction an approved school applicant must receive for a pilot or flight instructor certificate or rating.

GROUND TRAINING REQUIREMENTS

Certificate or Rating	FAR Part 61 Reference	FAR Part 141 Time Requirements
Student Pilot Certification	61.87(b)	N/A
Recreational Pilot Certification	61.97(b)	20 hours
Private Pilot Certification	61.105(b)	35 hours
Commercial Pilot Certification	61.125(b)	35 hours
Flight Instructor Certification	61.185(a)	40 hours
Airline Transport Pilot Certification	61.155(c)	40 hours
Instrument Rating	61.65(b)	30 hours
Additional Instructor Ratings	61.191(b)	20 hours

HOME STUDY COURSES

Under FAR 61.35, a **home study course** may be used to meet the prerequisites for a knowledge test. In fact, home study curriculums may be developed individually by students from material described in the applicable FAA knowledge test guide. Usually, home study courses are designed by pilot schools, colleges and universities, aviation

organizations, publishers, or individual ground or flight instructors. The home study course may feature printed material, video, or computer-based training provided on CDs or accessed over the Internet. Regardless of the medium, students must show the course has been satisfactorily completed and obtain an endorsement from an authorized instructor. Refer to *Certification: Pilots and Flight Instructors* (AC 61-65) which describes several methods students can use to show evidence of having satisfactorily completed home study courses.

AERONAUTICAL EXPERIENCE REQUIREMENTS

The eligibility and experience required for each certificate and rating are defined explicitly in Part 61 and Part 141. Aeronautical experience requirements vary depending on the regulations under which you are training. [Figure 4-61]

Commercial Requirements	
Total (FAR Part 61)	**250 hours**
Simulator/FTD maximum	50 hours
Powered aircraft	100 hours
In airplanes	50 hours
Dual	20 hours
Complex airplane	10 hours
Instrument training	10 hours
In airplanes	5 hours
Day VFR cross country	*2 hours
Night VFR cross country	*2 hours
Practical test preparation	3 hours
Pilot in command	100 hours
In airplanes	50 hours
Cross country	50 hours
In airplane	10 hours
Solo	**10 hours
Night, VFR	***5 hours

*Must be more than 100 n.m. straight-line distance from original point of departure.

**Includes one cross-country flight of not less than 300 n.m., with landings at a minimum of three points, one of which is a straight-line distance of at least 250 n.m. from the original departure point.

***Includes 10 takeoffs and landings (with each landing involving a flight in the traffic pattern) at an airport with an operating control tower.

Commercial Requirements	
Total (FAR Part 141)	**120 hours**
Simulator maximum	36 hours
FTD maximum	24 hours
Dual	55 hours
Complex airplane	10 hours
Instrument training	5 hours
Day VFR cross country	*2 hours
Night VFR cross country	*2 hours
Practical test preparation	3 hours
Solo	**10 hours
Night, VFR	***5 hours

*Must be more than 100 n.m. straight-line distance from original point of departure.

**Includes one cross-country flight with landings at three points, and one segment must consist of a straight-line distance of at least 250 n.m.

***Includes 10 takeoffs and landings (with each landing involving a flight in the traffic pattern) at an airport with an operating control tower.

John has held a private pilot certificate for several years and has been flying regularly for business and pleasure. He has already logged enough flight time to meet the total aeronautical experience requirements for a commercial certificate.

Under Part 141, John can receive credit for no more than 25% of the flight time requirements for the approved course. This would mean John would have to obtain as much as 142 hours of additional flight time. In this case, training under Part 61 would be the most economical.

Randy recently obtained a private pilot certificate under Part 141 and is planning to use veteran's educational benefits to pursue a commercial certificate.

The Veterans Administration (VA) normally awards benefits only for training conducted under Part 141. Since 250 hours of flight time is required for a commercial certificate under Part 61, he is definitely a good candidate for the Part 141 course.

Figure 4-61. You should evaluate your students' prior experience and the requirements of Part 61 and Part 141 to determine the most efficient course of training.

When your students transfer from one approved school to another, the receiving school may credit as much as 50% of their previous training under ideal circumstances. First, the previous school must certify that the kind and amount of training was in accordance with the approved course. Also, the result of each stage check and end-of-course check must be provided. Finally, the amount of training credit that is granted to your transferring student must also be based on an evaluation, which includes a proficiency test, knowledge test, or both. Maximum credit for prior training may not be justified in certain cases.

Prior Part 61 training experience may be credited for no more than 25% of Part 141 approved course requirements. Regulations also require you to evaluate your student with the same knowledge and/or proficiency tests mentioned previously. The 25% credit toward training is not automatic; it must be justified. The 25% maximum credit rule can be a big drawback to your Part 61 student who has completed substantial training. The thing to remember is that even though you work for a Part 141 school, you can still provide Part 61 instruction to your transfer students if that best serves their interests.

Regulations require Part 141 schools to publish and distribute detailed safety procedures to all new students. This handout must include weather minimums for dual and solo flights, safety procedures for starting and taxiing on the ramp, fire precautions, and instructions for unscheduled landings on and off airports. It must also include procedures for noting aircraft discrepancies, guidelines for securing aircraft when not in use, minimum fuel reserves for local and cross-country flights, collision-avoidance techniques, altitude limitations, and emergency landing instructions, as well as a description of designated practice areas. Regardless of whether you are instructing under Part 141 or Part 61, this type of orientation is beneficial.

AUTHORIZED INSTRUCTOR

The term **authorized instructor** is frequently referred to in regulations regarding who is qualified to provide ground or flight training under Part 61 and 141. FAR 61.1 provides an official definition of the term and also defines a number of other important terms relevant to training activities. Keep in mind that the terms certificated ground instructor or certificated flight instructor are also valid, but authorized instructor is used in a broad sense to indicate a person qualified to provide training under specific regulatory authority.

RECORDS

Documentation of training is a common area between Part 61 and Part 141. Part 61 governs your personal record-keeping requirements regarding the ground and flight instruction you provide your students. FAR 61.189 requires you to endorse the logbook of each student to whom you have provided ground or flight instruction. How detailed your logbook entries should be depends upon the type of training environment in which you are teaching. If you are teaching in a Part 61 school and do not follow a training syllabus that details each lesson, then you must explain each maneuver accomplished during every flight. You are not obligated to write a full page for each lesson, only a short list or summary of the training accomplished. [Figure 4-62]

E OF FLIGHT		NR INST. APP.	REMARKS AND ENDORSEMENTS	NR T/O	NR LDG	AIRCRAFT SINGLE-ENGINE LAND	
M	TO						
	LCL		slow flight, stalls, forced landing CFI489244386 Exp 2-01		1	1	2
	LCL		VOR nav, hood, pilotage CFI489244386 Exp 2-01		1		8
	PUB		x-country, procedures, VOR nav, pilotage CFI489244386 Exp 2-01		1	1	0
	APA		x-country, lost procedures, forced landing CFI489244386 Exp 2-01		1	1	1
	LCL		takeoffs and landings CFI489244386 Exp 2-01		6		7

Figure 4-62. The FAA requires you to log each lesson given. The log should include a description of the training given and the length of the training lesson, as well as your signature, certificate number, and certificate expiration date.

Keeping a written record documents lesson conduct, content, and completion standards. When instructing at an approved school, you are required to keep a separate and accurate up-to-date training record for all of your students. Your student's logbook is not an acceptable record in this case. [Figure 4-63]

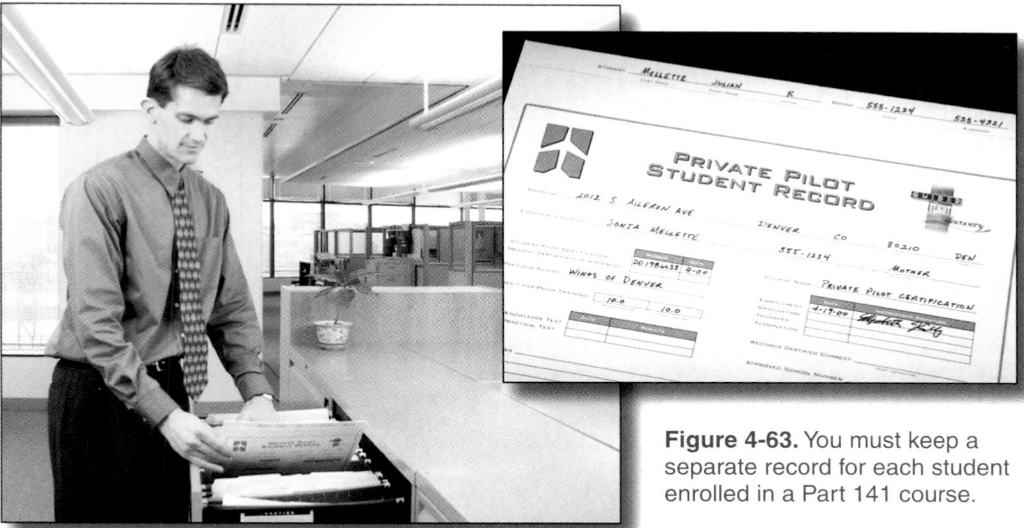

Figure 4-63. You must keep a separate record for each student enrolled in a Part 141 course.

Part 61 requires that you keep a record of all endorsements you have made in logbooks and on student pilot certificates to authorize solo flight privileges, as well as those authorizing students to take knowledge or practical exams. This detailed record can be kept in a separate notebook or in your logbook and must be retained for at least three years. Your record entries should include the name of the person receiving the endorsement, the date, and type of endorsement. [Figure 4-64]

You must keep a record of all endorsements you have made in logbooks and on student pilot certificates to authorize solo flight privileges, as well as those authorizing students to take knowledge or practical exams. This record must be retained for at least three years.

Figure 4-64. For knowledge and practical exam endorsements, your record must include the kind of test, date, and the results.

CFI RENEWAL

One of your most important responsibilities is **CFI renewal**. Your flight instructor certificate is only valid for 24 calendar months. CFI renewal is not automatic by any means, since it requires a specific certificate action by the FAA. Renewal of your certificate should be in accordance with FAR 61.197 by any of the following methods. You can present to the FAA your record of training, and show that you endorsed at least 5 students for a practical test for a certificate or rating and at least 80% of the students passed on their first attempt. You can also show the FAA a satisfactory record as a Part 121 or 135 check pilot, chief flight instructor, check airman or flight instructor, or that you are in a position involving the regular evaluation of pilots. Graduation from an approved **flight instructor refresher course (FIRC)** consisting of at least 16 hours of ground and/or flight training also may be the basis of renewing your certificate at the discretion of the FAA.

At some point in your career you may no longer see the need to maintain your flight instructor certificate. Remember, if you should rethink your decision after your certificate has lapsed, you will have to take the CFI checkride all over again. Keeping your certificate current may be a much wiser decision. Maintaining your instructor certificate compels you to continually educate yourself on current regulations and safety procedures, which enhances your piloting and instructing skills throughout your flight career. [Figure 4-65]

You may renew your flight instructor certificate by any of the following methods:

(1) Presenting a record of training to the FAA showing that you endorsed at least 5 students for a practical test for a certificate or rating and at least 80% of the students passed on their first attempt.

(2) Showing a satisfactory record to the FAA as a Part 121, or 135 check pilot, chief flight instructor, check airman, or flight instructor.

(3) Graduating from an approved flight instructor refresher course consisting of at least 16 hours of ground and/or flight training.

Your flight instructor certificate is valid for 24 calendar months from the month in which it was issued or renewed. If your flight instructor certificate expires, you may exchange that certificate for a new one only by passing the appropriate practical test.

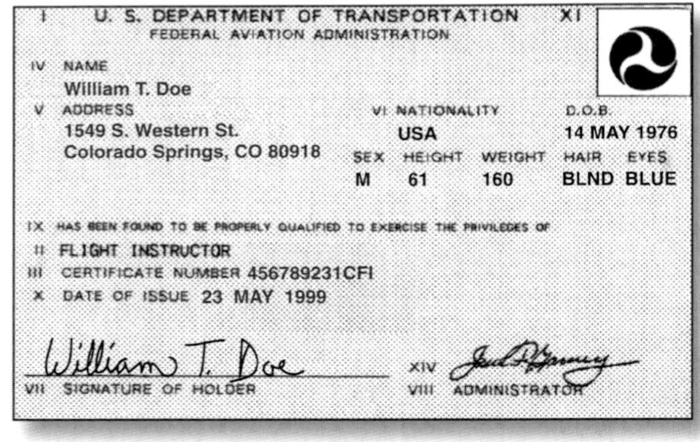

I U. S. DEPARTMENT OF TRANSPORTATION XI
FEDERAL AVIATION ADMINISTRATION
IV NAME
William T. Doe
V ADDRESS
1549 S. Western St.
Colorado Springs, CO 80918
VI NATIONALITY USA
D.O.B. 14 MAY 1976
SEX M HEIGHT 61 WEIGHT 160 HAIR BLND EYES BLUE
IX HAS BEEN FOUND TO BE PROPERLY QUALIFIED TO EXERCISE THE PRIVILEGES OF
II FLIGHT INSTRUCTOR
III CERTIFICATE NUMBER 456789231CFI
X DATE OF ISSUE 23 MAY 1999
William T. Doe
VII SIGNATURE OF HOLDER
XIV
VIII ADMINISTRATOR

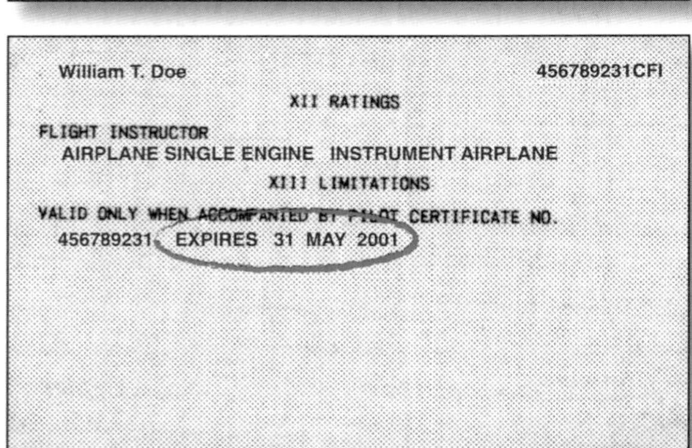

William T. Doe 456789231CFI
XII RATINGS
FLIGHT INSTRUCTOR
AIRPLANE SINGLE ENGINE INSTRUMENT AIRPLANE
XIII LIMITATIONS
VALID ONLY WHEN ACCOMPANIED BY PILOT CERTIFICATE NO.
456789231, EXPIRES 31 MAY 2001

Figure 4-65. In the event you allow the renewal deadline to pass and your flight instructor certificate expires, a practical test is required to reinstate your certificate. At the FAA inspector's or designated examiner's discretion, one or all of the ratings held may be reinstated.

MAY

S	M	T	W	T	F	S
	1	2	3	4	5	6
7	8	9	10	11	12	13
14	15	16	17	18	19	20
21	22	23	24	25	26	27
28	29	30	31			

GROUND INSTRUCTORS

You need to qualify for at least a second-class medical to obtain a commercial pilot certificate, which is a prerequisite for obtaining an initial flight instructor certificate. Of

course, if you obtain a flight instructor certificate, you are qualified to provide ground instruction within the limitations of your certificate. If you are unable to obtain a medical certificate, and still wish to pursue a career in aviation, you may consider becoming a ground instructor.

The areas of requisite knowledge are the same as for flight instructors, and a knowledge test, as well as a practical test, is required. As a **basic ground instructor** you are authorized to provide ground training on knowledge areas for procurement of a recreational or private pilot certificate and you may also endorse students for the recreational and private knowledge tests. As an **instrument ground instructor** you may provide ground training for the issuance of an instrument rating and ground training for an instrument competency check, as well as recommend students for instrument knowledge tests. Lastly, an **advanced ground instructor** is authorized to provide ground training for any certificate or rating under Part 61 and ground training for any flight review, as well as recommendations for any knowledge test issued under Part 61.

The aeronautical knowledge and training required for ground instructors under Part 141 includes 20 hours of training if the course is for an initial issuance of a ground instructor certificate, or 10 hours of training if the course is for an additional ground instructor rating. To maintain currency as a ground instructor, you must serve as a ground instructor for 3 months within the preceding 12 months, or receive an endorsement from an authorized ground or flight instructor certifying that you have demonstrated satisfactory proficiency in the subject areas prescribed in 61.213 (a)(3) and (a)(4).

When you hold a ground instructor certificate with a basic rating you are authorized to provide the ground training required for all aeronautical knowledge areas for a recreational or private pilot certificate.

When you hold a ground instructor certificate with an advanced rating you are authorized to provide ground training in aeronautical knowledge areas for any pilot certificate or rating.

When you hold a ground instructor certificate with an advanced rating, you are authorized to provide the ground training required for any flight review.

You may not exercise the privileges of a ground instructor certificate unless you have served at least 3 months as a ground instructor within the preceding 12 months or have received an endorsement from an authorized ground or flight instructor certifying that you have demonstrated satisfactory proficiency in the subject areas prescribed in 61.213 (a)(3) and (a)(4).

TRAINING STUDENT PILOTS

New students have little knowledge about what to expect during pilot training, what equipment is required, or what steps to take to ensure the training program maintains the continuity needed for them to progress steadily toward the goal of becoming a pilot. In order to commence pilot training, they will need guidance from you to obtain student pilot and medical certificates.

STUDENT PILOT AND MEDICAL CERTIFICATES

Your students normally should undergo a medical examination within the first few weeks of flight training. This may save them from unnecessary expense if they find they possess a pre-existing physical condition that would prevent them from qualifying for a medical certificate. A student pilot certificate is usually issued by an AME as part of a medical certificate. However, an aviation safety inspector (ASI) or a designated examiner also may issue student pilot certificates if your students already possess a third-class medical.

LIMITATIONS AND WAIVERS

Medical certificates can be issued to students who do not fully meet FAA medical standards. Your students can have a medical certificate issued requiring they adhere to certain limitations. For instance, students who are unable to distinguish certain colors may have a limitation preventing them from flying an aircraft at night.

The official term for a waiver is **statement of demonstrated ability (SODA)**. This actually is a form which may be issued in conjunction with your students' medical. SODAs can only be issued by the FAA's federal air surgeon, not an AME, and are granted for a condition normally requiring a denial that is not necessarily a safety factor. In this situation, your students must continually prove to the FAA that their medical status is under control and does not create a safety problem each time they obtain a new medical. [Figure 4-66]

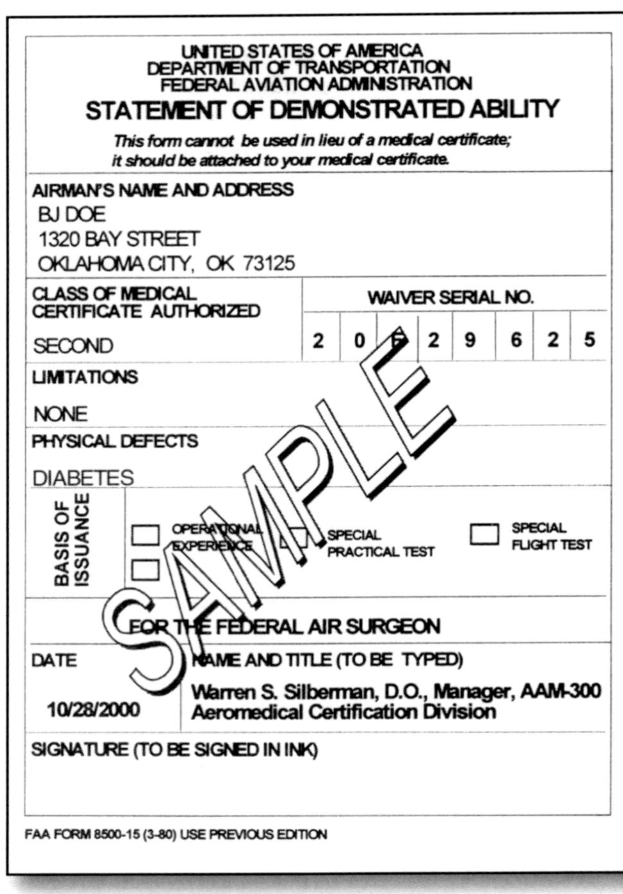
UNITED STATES OF AMERICA
DEPARTMENT OF TRANSPORTATION
FEDERAL AVIATION ADMINISTRATION
STATEMENT OF DEMONSTRATED ABILITY
This form cannot be used in lieu of a medical certificate; it should be attached to your medical certificate.

AIRMAN'S NAME AND ADDRESS
BJ DOE
1320 BAY STREET
OKLAHOMA CITY, OK 73125

CLASS OF MEDICAL CERTIFICATE AUTHORIZED: SECOND
WAIVER SERIAL NO.: 2 0 6 2 9 6 2 5

LIMITATIONS: NONE

PHYSICAL DEFECTS: DIABETES

BASIS OF ISSUANCE: ☐ OPERATIONAL EXPERIENCE ☐ SPECIAL PRACTICAL TEST ☐ SPECIAL FLIGHT TEST ☐

FOR THE FEDERAL AIR SURGEON

DATE: 10/28/2000
NAME AND TITLE (TO BE TYPED): Warren S. Silberman, D.O., Manager, AAM-300 Aeromedical Certification Division

SIGNATURE (TO BE SIGNED IN INK)

FAA FORM 8500-15 (3-80) USE PREVIOUS EDITION

SAMPLE

Figure 4-66. Students with diabetes may receive a SODA if they can prove that their condition is stable and does not pose a threat to safety.

Always advise your students to ask an AME about the specific details concerning the need for a particular waiver. It is quite possible, through a SODA, for a disabled person to receive a medical certificate. Naturally, it depends on the type and the extent of the disability. If a medical can be issued, it probably will include some limitation.

ADVISING YOUR STUDENTS

Inform your students that if there is any change in their medical condition, they need to determine whether they are medically fit for flight. A medical condition, such as a broken arm or serious infection, may temporarily void their medical certificate until they are well. [Figure 4-67]

If you suspect a more serious health problem, encourage your students to visit an AME. During your flight career, you or your students may develop medically disqualifying conditions, which would prevent legal flight. A more serious medical problem can be

dealt with and flight status may be maintained with an AME's help, which is preferable to hoping a condition will go away on its own. An AME should be able to assess the problem and tell whether it is safe to fly and may be able to give a prognosis for when flight status may be resumed.

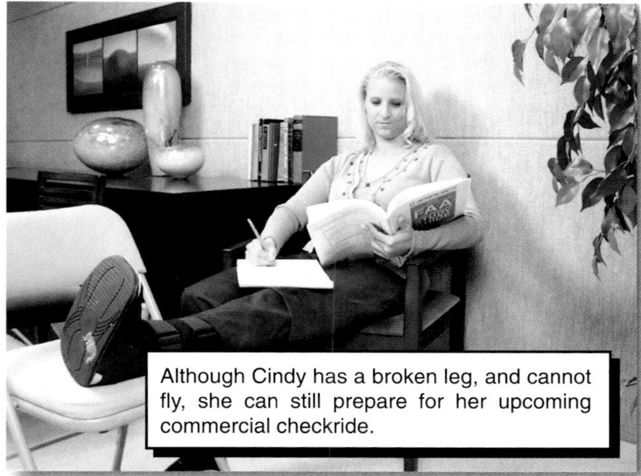

Figure 4-67. You may want to mention to your students that if they are currently medically unfit for flight, they should ground themselves until the condition subsides.

FLYING UNDER THE INFLUENCE

From the files of the NTSB . . .

Narrative: *A student pilot flying a Cessna 150 was returning from the northwest, entering the downwind for Runway 01, when he saw an airplane coming towards him. The student executed evasive maneuvers, but collided with the tail section of a Cessna 172 that had just departed Runway 01 and was turning from the left crosswind to the downwind leg for Runway 01.*

The Cessna 172 descended to the ground, killing all three occupants on board. The student pilot in the 150 made a forced landing at the airport and was uninjured. Toxicology tests performed on the pilot of the C-172 revealed a high level of an over-the-counter antihistamine with sedative side effects.

The NTSB listed the following contributing factors of the accident:

1. The failure of both pilots to see and avoid each other,
2. the C-172 pilot's impairment due to medication.

NTSB reports such as this one can impress upon your students that holding a current medical certificate does not ensure they are fit for flight. Even a simple cold and over-the-counter medication can adversely affect flight safety. If your students are unsure of whether the medication they are taking is safe for flight, it is best to err on the cautious side and postpone the flight.

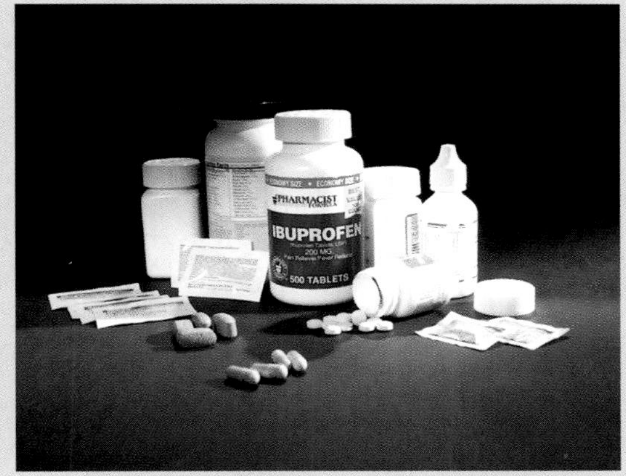

MEDICAL APPLICATION FORM

Before you send your students to obtain a medical exam, spend a few minutes going over FAA Form 8500-8 with them, since the application can be very confusing. It is important your students have a good understanding of exactly what the form entails before they fill it out. There are several suggestions you can give your students to make the process easier. [Figure 4-68]

 The information on the certificate is typed in by the AME. Your student will sign the certificate after satisfactory completion of the exam.

 Your students may want to apply for a first class medical to confirm they meet the requirements, especially if they intend to pursue a career in aviation.

 If your students wear corrective lenses, be sure they bring them for the exam.

 Anytime your students check Yes to any of the conditions in this box, the AME will typically have them supply a more detailed explanation.

 The FAA normally wants to know about doctor's visits for serious medical problems.

 This box requires your students to list any and all alcohol related motor vehicle actions (MVAs), or administrative actions. Omitting motor vehicle actions or administrative actions is more damaging than an honest declaration of the event.

 This box is the declaration, which gives express consent to the FAA to obtain information from the National Drivers Register (NDR) to verify your students' motor vehicle history.

Applicant Must Complete ALL 20 Items (Except For Shaded Areas) **PLEASE PRINT** Approved OMB No. 2120-0034

Copy of FAA Form 8500-9 (Medical Certificate) or FAA Form 8420-2 Medical Student Pilot Certificate) issued. **FF-**

MEDICAL CERTIFICATE_____CLASS AND STUDENT PILOT CERTIFICATE

This certifies that ***(Full name and address):***

Date of Birth	Height	Weight	Hair	Eyes	Sex

has met the medical standards prescribed in part 67, Federal Aviation Regulations, for this class of Medical Certificate.

Limitations

Examiner: Date of Examination | Examiner's Designation No | Signature | Typed Name

Airman's Signature

1. Application For: ☐ Airman Medical Certificate ☐ Airman Medical and Student Pilot Certificate

2. Class of Medical Certificate Applied For: ☐ 1st ☐ 2nd ☐ 3rd

3. Last Name First Name Middle Name

4. Social Security Number - -

5. Address Telephone Number ( ) -

Number/Street

City State/Country Zip Code

6. Date of Birth__________ MM/DD/YYYY Citizenship___________

7. Color of Hair

8. Color of Eyes

9. Sex

10. Type of Airman Certificate(s) You Hold

☐ None ☐ Airline Transport ☐ Commercial ☐ ATC Specialist ☐ Fight Engineer ☐ Flight Navigator ☐ Flight Instructor ☐ Private ☐ Student ☐ Recreational ☐ Other ____________

11. Occupation

12. Employer

13, Has Your FAA Airman Certificate Ever Been Denies, Suspended, or Revoked? ☐ Yes ☐ No If yes, give date__________ MM/DD/YYYY

Total Pilot Time(Civilian Only) 14. To Date 15. Past 6 Months

16.Date of Last FAA Medical Application __________ MM/DD/YYYY ☐ No Prior Application

17.a. Do You Currently Use Any Medication (Prescription or Nonprescription)?

Yes No (If yes, below list medication(s) used and check appropriate box) 17.b. Do You Previously Reported Yes ☐ ☐ ☐ ☐ No ☐ ☐ ☐ ☐

(If more space is required, use 17.a. on the instruction sheet).

17.b. Do You Ever Use Near Vision Contact Lens(es) While Flying? ☐ Yes ☐ No

18. Medical History - HAVE YOU EVER IN YOUR LIFE BEEN DIAGNOSSED WITH, HAD, OR DO YOU PRESENTLY HAVE ANY OF THE FOLLOWING? Answer "yes" or "no" for every condition listed below. In the EXPLANATIONS box below, you may note "PREVIOUSLY REPORTED, NO CHANGE" only if the explanation of the condition was reported on a previous application for an airman medical certificate and there has been no change in your condition. **See Instructions Page**

Yes	No	Condition	Yes	No	Condition	Yes	No	Condition	Yes	No	Condition
a. ☐	☐	Frequent or severe headaches	g. ☐	☐	Heart or vascular trouble	m. ☐	☐	Mental disorders of any sort; depression, anxiety, etc.	r. ☐	☐	Military medical discharge
b. ☐	☐	Dizziness or fainting spells	h. ☐	☐	High or low blood pressure	n. ☐	☐	Substance dependence or failed a drug test ever, or substance abuse or use of illegal substance in the last 2 years	s. ☐	☐	Medical rejection by military service
c. ☐	☐	Unconsciousness for any reason	i. ☐	☐	Stomach, liver, or intestinal trouble				t. ☐	☐	Rejection for life or health insurance
d. ☐	☐	Eye or vision trouble except glasses	j. ☐	☐	Kidney stone or blood in urine	o. ☐	☐	Alcohol dependence or abuse	u. ☐	☐	Admission to hospital
e. ☐	☐	Hay fever or allergy	k. ☐	☐	Diabetes	p. ☐	☐	Suicide attempt	x. ☐	☐	Other illness, disability, or surgery
f. ☐	☐	Asthma or lung disease	l. ☐	☐	Neurological disorders; epilepsy, seizures, stroke, paralysis, etc.	q. ☐	☐	Motion sickness requiring medication			

Conviction and/or Administrative Action History - See Instructions Page

Yes	No		Yes	No	
v. ☐	☐	History of (1) any conviction(s) involving driving while intoxicated by, while impaired by, or while under the influence of alcohol or a drug; or (2) history of any conviction(s) or administrative action(s) involving an offense(s) which resulted in the denial, suspension, cancellation, or revocation of driving privileges or which resulted in attendance at an educational or a rehabilitation program.	w. ☐	☐	History of nontraffic conviction(s) (misdemeanors or felonies).

Explanations: See Instructions Page FOR FAA USE Review Action Codes

19. Visits to Health Professional Within Last 3 Years ☐ Yes (Explain Below) ☐ No See Instructions Page

Date Name, Address, and Type of Health Professional Consulted Reason

- NOTICE -
Whoever in any matter within the jurisdiction of any department or agency of the United States knowingly and willfully falsifies, conceals or covers up by any trick, scheme, or device a material fact, or who makes any false, fictitious or fraudulent statements or representations, or entry, may be fined up to $250,000 or imprisoned not more than 5 years, or both (18 U.S. Code Sec. 1001; 3571

20. Applicant's National Driver Register and Certifying Declarations
I hereby authorize the National Driver Register (NDR), through a designated State Department of Motor Vehicles, to furnish to the FAA information pertaining to my driving record. This consent constitutes authorization for a single access to the information contained in the NDR to verify information provided in this application. Upon my request, the FAA shall make the information received from the NDR, if any, available for my review and written comment. Authority: 23 U.S. Code 401, Note

NOTE: ALL persons using this form must sign it. NDR consent, however, does not apply unless this form is used as an application for Medical Certificate or Medical Certificate and Student Pilot Certificate.

I hereby certify that all statements and answers provided by me on this application are complete and true to the best of my knowledge, and I agree that they are to be considered part of the basis for issuance of any FAA certificate to me. I have also read and understand the Privacy Act statement that accompanies this form.

Signature of Applicant Date______________ MM / DD / YYYY

FAA Form 8500-8 (3-99) Supersedes Previous Edition NSN: 0052-00-670-6002

 The back of the form is typed by your AME, signed, and sent to the FAA for processing.

 If the AME is unable to issue a medical certificate for any reason, it is either deferred to the FAA for further evaluation or denied.

NOTE: FAA/Original Copy of the Report of Medical Examination Must be TYPED.

REPORT OF MEDICAL EXAMINATION

21. Height (inches)	22. Weight (pounds)	23. Statement of Demonstrated Ability (SODA) ☐ Yes ☐ No Defect Noted:	24. SODA Serial No.

CHECK EACH ITEM IN APPROPRIATE COLUMN	Normal	Abnormal	CHECK ITEM IN APPROPRIATE COLUMN	Normal	Abnormal
25. Head, face, neck, and scalp			37. Vascular system (Pulse, amplitude and character, arms, legs, others)		
26. Noses			38. Abdomen and viscera (including hernia)		
27. Sinuses			39. Anus (Not including digital examination)		
28. Mouth and throat			40. Skin		
29. Ears, general (Internal and external canals; Hearing under item 49)			41. G-U System (Not including pelvic examination)		
30. Ear Drums (Perforation)			42. Upper and lower extremities (Strength and range of motion)		
31. Eyes, general (Vision under items 50 to 54)			43. Spine, other musculoskeletal		
32. Ophthalmoscopic			44. Identifying body marks, scars, tattoos (Size & location)		
33. Pupils (Equality and reaction)			45. Lymphatics		
34. Ocular motility (Associated parallel movement, nystagmus)			46. Neurologic (Tendon reflexes, equilibrium, senses, cranial nerves, coordination, etc.)		
35. Lungs and chest (Not including breast examination			47. Psychiatric (Appearance, behavior, mood, communication, and memory)		
36. Heart (Precordial activity, rhythm, sounds, and murmurs)			48. General systemic		

NOTES: Describe every abnormality in detail. Enter applicable item number before each comment. Use additional sheets if necessary and attach to this form.

49. Hearing	Record Audiometric Speech Discrimination Score Below		Right Ear					Left Ear				
Conversational Voice Test at 6 Feet ☐ Pass ☐ Fail		Audiometer Threshold in decibels	500	1000	2000	3000	4000	500	1000	2000	3000	4000

50. Distant Vision	51.a. Near Vision	51.b. Intermediate Vision	52. Color Vision
Right 20/ Corrected to 20/ Left 20/ Corrected to 20/ Both 20/ Corrected to 20/	Right 20/ Corrected to 20/ Left 20/ Corrected to 20/ Both 20/ Corrected to 20/	Right 20/ Corrected to 20/ Left 20/ Corrected to 20/ Both 20/ Corrected to 20/	☐ Pass ☐ Fail

53. Field of Vision ☐ Normal ☐ Abnormal	54. Heterophoria 20' (in prism diopters)	Esophoria	Exophoria	Right Hyperphoria	Left Hyperphoria

55. Blood Pressure (Sitting, mm of Mercury) Systolic / Diastolic	56. Pulse (Resting)	57. Urinalysis (if abnormal, give results) ☐ Normal ☐ Abnormal	Albumin	Sugar	58. ECG (Date) MM DD YYYY

59. Other Tests Given

60. Comments on History and Findings: AME shall comment on all "YES" answers in the Medical History section and for abnormal findings of the examination. (Attach all consultation reports, ECGs, X-rays, etc., to this report before mailing.)

FOR FAA USE
Pathology Codes:
Coded By:
Clerical Reject

Significant Medical History ☐ Yes ☐ No Abnormal Physical Findings ☐ Yes ☐ No

61. Applicant's Name

62. Has Been Issued - ☐ Medical Certificate ☐ Medical & Student Pilot Certificate
☐ No Certificate Issued - Deferred for Further Evaluation
☐ Has Been Denied - Letter of Denial Issued (Copy Attached)

63. Disqualifying Defects (List by item number)

64. Medical Examiner's Declaration - I hereby certify that I have personally reviewed the medical history and personally examined the applicant named on this medical examination report. This report with any attachment embodies my findings completely and correctly.

Date of Examination MM DD YYYY	Aviation Medical Examiner's Name			Aviation Medical Examiner's Signature
	Street Address			AME Serial Number
	City	State	Zip Code	AME Telephone ( )

FAA Form 8500-8 (3-99) Supersedes Previous Edition NSN: 0052-00-670-6002

Figure 4-68. The medical application form comes with an instruction sheet, but few new pilots understand the phraseology.

It is important to advise students that in addition to providing information regarding their medical history, they must also declare any alcohol-related motor vehicle actions on the medical application form. To enhance air safety and monitor pilots with multiple violations, the Department of Transportation in 1986 began auditing pilots with alcohol-related motor vehicle offenses. The FAA established a drug and alcohol-abatement program in 1988 to address the findings of the audit. In order to monitor pilots who had an alcohol-related action, Congress revised the National Drivers Register (NDR) and allowed the FAA to match the names of pilots who had completed recent medical applications against a database of the NDR. This is known as the DUI/DWI compliance program that was established in November of 1990.

DOCUMENTATION OF TRAINING

It is particularly important that you document all the flight maneuvers and associated ground school discussions when you conduct ground and flight training with student pilots. Keeping your documentation up to date provides you and your students with a checklist of elements accomplished and items required for course completion. If you provide flight training in an aircraft, flight simulator or flight training device, or provide ground training, you must certify that the instruction was given.

If you provide flight training in an aircraft, flight simulator or flight training device, or provide ground training, you must certify that the instruction was given.

For the Record in the Early Days

Providing and documenting pilot training have been ongoing since the beginning of aviation. Even before there were regulations, flight instructors annotated the flight instruction given and signed the logbooks of their students. Logbooks probably began as a way for pilots to prove they had accumulated a certain amount of training and solo experience in order to fly someone else's aircraft. Some interesting logbook documentation from the early days of aviation, circa 1929, shows the signature of E.B. Jeppesen — flight instructor and company founder — in the logbook of one of his students, Tony L. McKay.

Also note who signed Jeppesen's original pilot certificate #7034 — Orville Wright. The certificate is dated January 29, 1929 and was issued by the authority of the Federation Aeronautic Association of the U.S.A. Written eight years after his first flight in 1921, Jeppesen received his certificate, purchased a "Jenny" for $500 and began barnstorming.

ENDORSEMENTS

As a flight instructor you are allowed to provide **endorsements** for certain flying activities, as well as recommend your students for practical tests. Accompanying this privilege of furnishing endorsements is an obligation to the students receiving the endorsements. Regardless of the endorsement or recommendation, it should ensure that your students have received all of the training specified in the FARs and are fully proficient for the operation being authorized.

Your endorsements are required on student pilot certificates and logbooks for various operations. For example, you may authorize students for solo operations or solo cross-country flight, and you are responsible for making sure these endorsements are made accurately. Rules governing endorsements are contained in Part 61, and Part 141. A list of required endorsements from *Certification: Pilots and Flight Instructors* (AC 61-65) is reproduced for your use in Appendix C. Endorsements do not need to be worded exactly as those in the AC. For example, changes in regulatory requirements may affect the wording, or you may customize the endorsement for any special circumstances of the student.

PRE-SOLO KNOWLEDGE TEST

The FARs require your student pilots to complete a knowledge test prior to flying solo. The test must evaluate your students' comprehension of Parts 61 and 91, airspace rules and procedures for the airport where the solo flight will be conducted, and the flight characteristics and operational limitations for the make and model of aircraft to be flown. The purpose of the pre-solo written test is to determine fitness for solo flight and not to assign a grade. It is important that the test properly evaluates a full range of possible flight situations that may be encountered. An adequate sample of questions regarding the general operating rules, safety issues pertaining to the local airspace environment, and aircraft emergencies should be included in the pre-solo written test. When you create the test, consider the complexity of the airplane, and the type of airport from which you operate. [Figure 4-69]

You are responsible for administering a pre-solo knowledge test and reviewing the incorrect answers with your student before endorsing your student's logbook and student pilot certificate for solo flight.

The pre-solo knowledge test must cover applicable regulations, and local airport and airspace rules and procedures, as well as the flight characteristics and operational limitations of the make and model of aircraft to be flown.

PRESOLO WRITTEN EXAM

AIRPORT AND LOCAL AIRSPACE QUESTIONS

Instructions: Flight instructors may assign only those questions that pertain to the student's airport environment and surrounding local area. However, if necessary, instructors may assign additional questions for a particular flying area.

1. What are the traffic patterns for each runway at your airport? What is the MSL altitude for the traffic pattern?

2. How do you enter and exit the traffic pattern at your airport? What, if any, radio communications are required?

3. What radio calls are recommended in the traffic pattern at an uncontrolled airport? What

Susan needs a significant amount of knowledge to solo a complex airplane at a busy, controlled airport.

Since Mike operates a basic trainer from a quiet, uncontrolled field, his test will be tailored to his flying environment.

Figure 4-69. You are allowed a fair amount of flexibility with regard to the pre-solo knowledge test. The number, type, and difficulty of the questions are left to your judgment.

SOLO PRIVILEGES

Two of the first and most important endorsements you may provide as an instructor are those authorizing a student pilot to fly solo. Prior to performing solo operations, your student's logbook and student pilot certificate must be endorsed to confirm that the necessary training requirements outlined in FAR 61.87 have been met. In order to make these endorsements, you must have given your student flight training in the type of aircraft involved. Also, keep in mind that completing the paperwork is secondary to ensuring the student is fully proficient for the solo privileges being endorsed.

To endorse your students' logbook for solo flight, you are required to have given them flight training in the type of aircraft involved.

Prior to your student's first solo, you must endorse the student pilot certificate and logbook for the specific make and model of aircraft to be flown. Thereafter, your student's logbook must be endorsed every 90 days to retain solo flight privileges. The solo endorsement on the student pilot certificate is a one-time endorsement. [Figure 4-70]

Prior to first solo, you are required to endorse your student's logbook and student pilot certificate for the specific make and model of aircraft to be flown. Thereafter, your student's logbook must be endorsed every 90 days to retain solo flight privileges.

If you find it necessary or advantageous to have your student practice takeoffs and landings at

Prior to solo flight, your student must have received flight instruction in ground reference maneuvers.

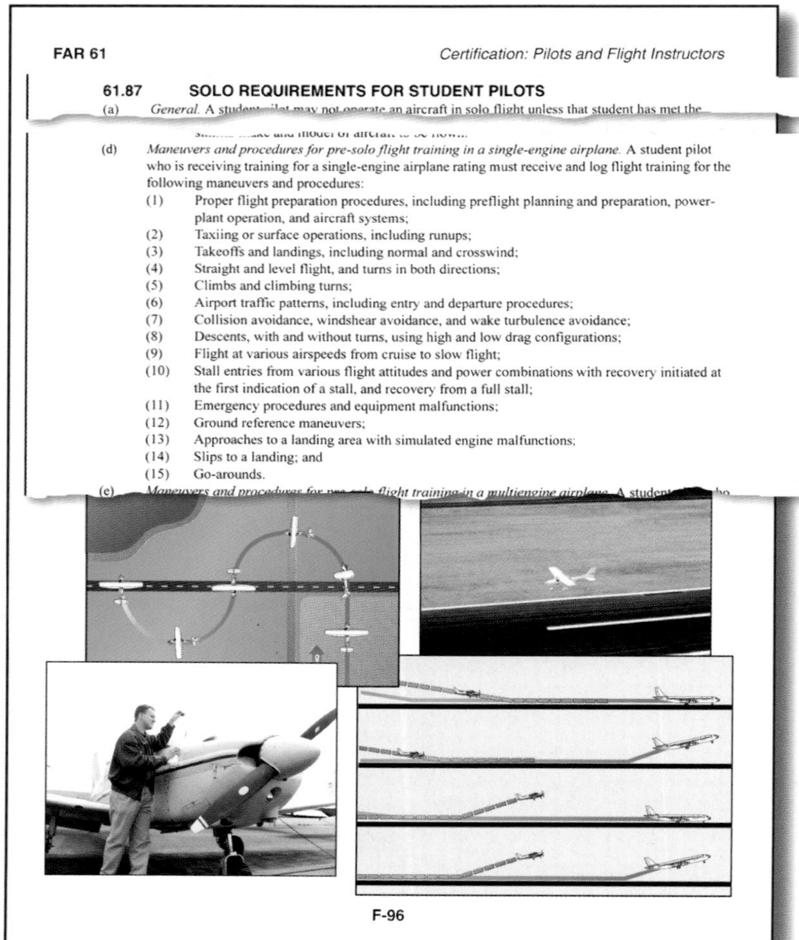

FAR 61 *Certification: Pilots and Flight Instructors*

61.87 SOLO REQUIREMENTS FOR STUDENT PILOTS

(a) *General.* A student pilot may not operate an aircraft in solo flight unless that student has met the

(d) *Maneuvers and procedures for pre-solo flight training in a single-engine airplane.* A student pilot who is receiving training for a single-engine airplane rating must receive and log flight training for the following maneuvers and procedures:

(1) Proper flight preparation procedures, including preflight planning and preparation, powerplant operation, and aircraft systems;
(2) Taxiing or surface operations, including runups;
(3) Takeoffs and landings, including normal and crosswind;
(4) Straight and level flight, and turns in both directions;
(5) Climbs and climbing turns;
(6) Airport traffic patterns, including entry and departure procedures;
(7) Collision avoidance, windshear avoidance, and wake turbulence avoidance;
(8) Descents, with and without turns, using high and low drag configurations;
(9) Flight at various airspeeds from cruise to slow flight;
(10) Stall entries from various flight attitudes and power combinations with recovery initiated at the first indication of a stall, and recovery from a full stall;
(11) Emergency procedures and equipment malfunctions;
(12) Ground reference maneuvers;
(13) Approaches to a landing area with simulated engine malfunctions;
(14) Slips to a landing; and
(15) Go-arounds.

(e) *Maneuvers and procedures for pre-solo flight training in a multiengine airplane.* A student

F-96

Figure 4-70. Prior to solo flight, student pilots should be able to demonstrate consistent ability in all maneuvers and procedures listed in FAR 61.87(d) including preflight preparation, slow flight, stalls, and ground reference maneuvers. In addition, they must be proficient in coping with flight situations ranging from collision avoidance, wind shear, and wake turbulence avoidance to equipment malfunctions and emergencies.

an airport other than your home base airport, you must provide your student with an endorsement. Your endorsement essentially states that you have trained your student specifically for this operation and your student can navigate from the home base to the other airport and back again. The satellite airport must be within 25 nautical miles and this operation is not considered a cross-country. [Figure 4-71]

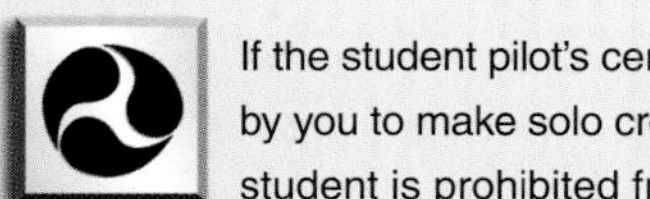

If the student pilot's certificate is not endorsed by you to make solo cross-country flights, your student is prohibited from flying solo beyond 25 nautical miles from the original point of departure.

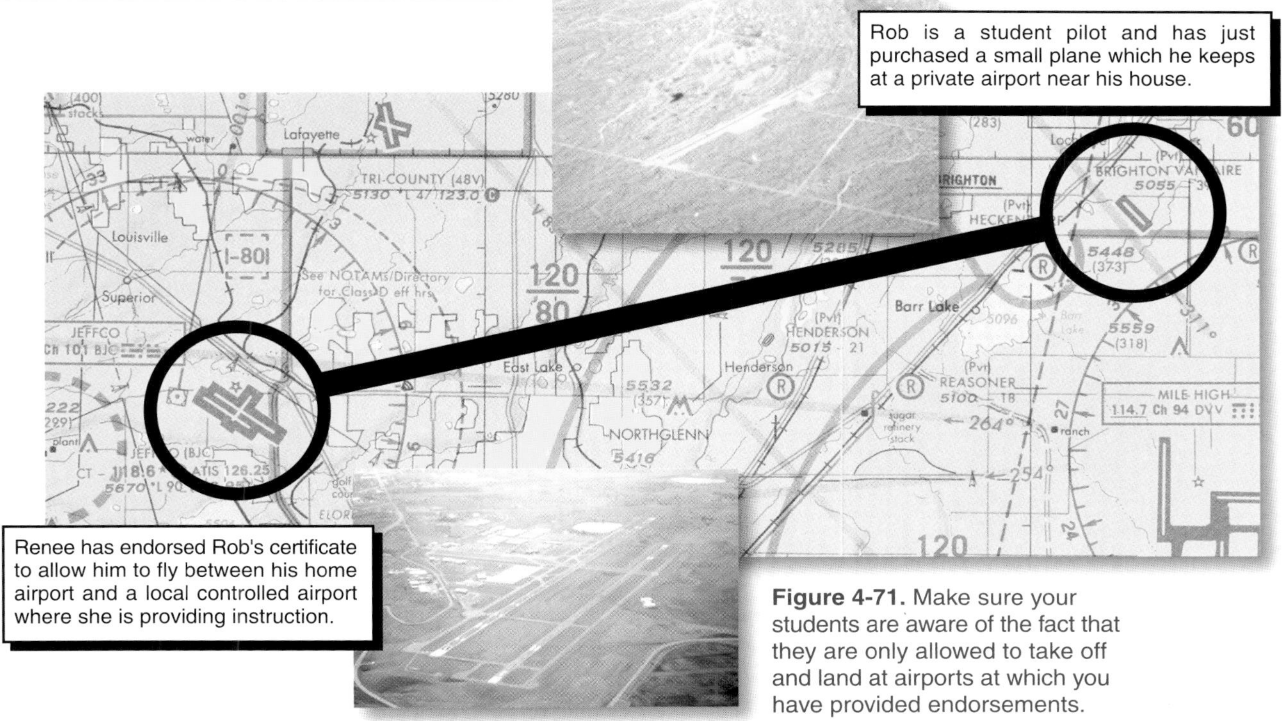

Figure 4-71. Make sure your students are aware of the fact that they are only allowed to take off and land at airports at which you have provided endorsements.

SOLO CROSS-COUNTRY

To meet the aeronautical experience requirements for a private pilot certificate, cross-country time consists of any flight that includes a point of landing that is at least a straight-line distance of more than 50 nautical miles from the original point of departure and involves the use of dead reckoning, pilotage, electronic navigation aids, radio aids, or other navigation systems. In order for your students to be ready for solo cross-country flight, they must undergo training on specific maneuvers and procedures outlined in the regulations.

When your students have satisfactorily accomplished all required training for solo cross-country operations, you may endorse their logbook and student pilot certificate for cross-country flight. The endorsement on the certificate is an endorsement for solo cross-country privileges in the specific category of aircraft to be flown, and the make and model of aircraft need not be included. The endorsement in the logbook should be for the specific make and model of aircraft to be flown.

To endorse your student for solo cross-country privileges, you are required to determine that your student's preparation, planning, and procedures are adequate for the proposed flight under the existing conditions.

In addition to the general endorsements which authorize your students to conduct solo cross-country flight, you are required to review their cross-country planning for each flight they make. You must endorse their logbook to state that their preflight planning and preparation are correct that they are prepared to make the flight safely under the known conditions. You must have reviewed the current and forecast conditions and have determined the flight can be completed under VFR conditions. If the weather deteriorates enroute it may put your students in a hazardous situation, and prevent them from completion of the flight. [Figure 4-72] In addition, this endorsement states that any limitations you have stipulated for your students have been met and you have confirmed that your students' cross-country and solo endorsements are current and apply to the appropriate make and model of aircraft.

Figure 4-72. If your student must spend the night away from the home base due to weather or maintenance problems, keep in mind that the cross-country planning endorsement is no longer current for the next day. You may need to fly to the airport with another instructor so you can accompany your student on the return trip and recover both airplanes.

If for some reason you are unavailable to review your student's cross-country planning, you may ask a fellow instructor to endorse your student's logbook for you. Providing an endorsement which confirms proper flight planning does not require the signing instructor to fly with your student. However, the signing instructor must verify that all the conditions have been met to permit your student to complete the flight safely. [Figure 4-73]

Figure 4-73. If you endorse a student's flight planning with whom you have not flown, you are assuming full responsibility for the training provided by the student's instructor.

Your responsibility toward your students regarding solo operations does not end with endorsements. In order to provide supervision, you should require your students to notify you when they embark on a solo flight. It is a good idea to include a preflight briefing and post-flight critique for each student training flight.

REPEATED SOLO CROSS-COUNTRY FLIGHTS

At some point you may find yourself training students who live a considerable distance away from your home base. After solo, you can authorize repeated solo cross-country flights to enable your students to fly to the airport at which you will conduct training. These flights can be made without receiving an endorsement from you for each flight, provided the destination airport is no more than 50 nautical miles from the point of departure.

Repeated solo cross-country flights over the same route may be made by your students without receiving an endorsement from you for each flight, if the destination airport is no more than 50 nautical miles from the point of departure and instruction was given in both directions over the route.

You must provide instruction along the route both to and from each airport, as well as discuss with your students the acceptable weather conditions, and other associated safety concerns. When all of the training requirements are met, you may then endorse them for repeated solo cross-country flights. This endorsement permits your students to fly this route without you reviewing their planning, or the weather, prior to each flight. The repeated solo cross-country endorsement allows a greater amount of freedom for both you and your students, but it also incurs a higher risk for your students' safety.

CLASS B AIRSPACE

To operate an aircraft on a solo flight within Class B airspace, student pilots must have a logbook endorsement showing that they have received ground instruction on, and flight instruction in, that specific airspace for which solo flight is authorized. For example, you cannot train your students on Class B operations in Seattle, Washington, endorse them, and then allow them to fly into Denver, Colorado Class B airspace. One endorsement does not fit all situations. In addition to this endorsement, your students must obtain an appropriate ATC clearance, and their aircraft must be equipped with an operating transponder with automatic altitude-reporting equipment and an operating two-way radio.

To operate on a solo flight within Class B airspace, your students must have a logbook endorsement from you. The endorsement must show that they have received ground instruction on, and flight instruction in, that specific airspace for which solo flight is authorized.

A separate endorsement is required to allow your students to operate solo from or to an airport located within Class B airspace. You must provide ground training on the operations specific to that airport and flight training at the airport. Both the endorsement allowing your students to operate within Class B airspace, and the one enabling them to operate at the airport, must be made within 90 days preceding the date of their intended flight.

KNOWLEDGE TESTS

Preparing your students to take the airmen knowledge test is a part of the ground instruction process. You can set up question-and-answer sessions covering all items required for the exam. There are many study materials and computer software programs on the market to aid in preparation for the exam. Since all knowledge exams are now administered on a computer, a tutorial might be in order to help students who are not experienced with computers.

To help your students determine where they can take a knowledge exam, most flight schools have a listing of the local test centers, or you can call your local **Flight Standards**

District Office (FSDO). Ensure that your students bring to the testing center a written endorsement certifying that they have accomplished the appropriate ground training or home study course. In addition, they must provide identification that includes a photo, signature, residential address, and date of birth. The date of birth ID must show that they meet the age requirement for the certificate sought before the expiration date of the knowledge test report. [Figure 4-74]

Figure 4-74. In addition to identification and an endorsement, ensure that your students bring the pilot supplies necessary to take the exam, such as a simple calculator, plotter, and mechanical or electronic flight computer.

To take a knowledge test, your students must bring to the testing center a written endorsement certifying that they have accomplished the appropriate ground training or home study course.

You may remind students that after they become rated pilots, short added-rating tests may be administered in some situations to avoid repetitive testing. A short test is designed to avoid duplication of subject areas on which your student has already been tested during previous FAA knowledge tests. Short tests are available for the instrument rating as well as the airline-transport pilot and flight-instructor certificates. However, the designated examiner for the practical test will also accept a full test for these certificates or ratings. [Figure 4-75]

Carol is applying for a flight instructor – instrument rating. In addition to an endorsement from her instructor, the testing center will require her pilot and flight instructor certificates to qualify her for the short instrument knowledge test.

Figure 4-75. Advise your students to contact the testing center for specific information on the necessary qualifications for short tests. Ensure that your students fully communicate to the testing centers that they are adding a rating to an existing certificate, and are not seeking initial certification.

The computer test results always identify subject areas in which your student answered the questions incorrectly. This is done through the use of subject matter knowledge codes. The subject matter knowledge codes represent a broad area of airman knowledge, not specific test questions, and they do not identify the correct answers. Giving a subject matter area of deficient answers, rather than a specific test question, forces you and your student to perform a more detailed analysis of the topic. This will enhance the review required for the practical test and/or a retake. In the event your student fails the knowledge test, you must conduct a review of deficient areas. The computer test report provides an endorsement form on the bottom section, allowing you to endorse your student to retake the exam. [Figure 4-76]

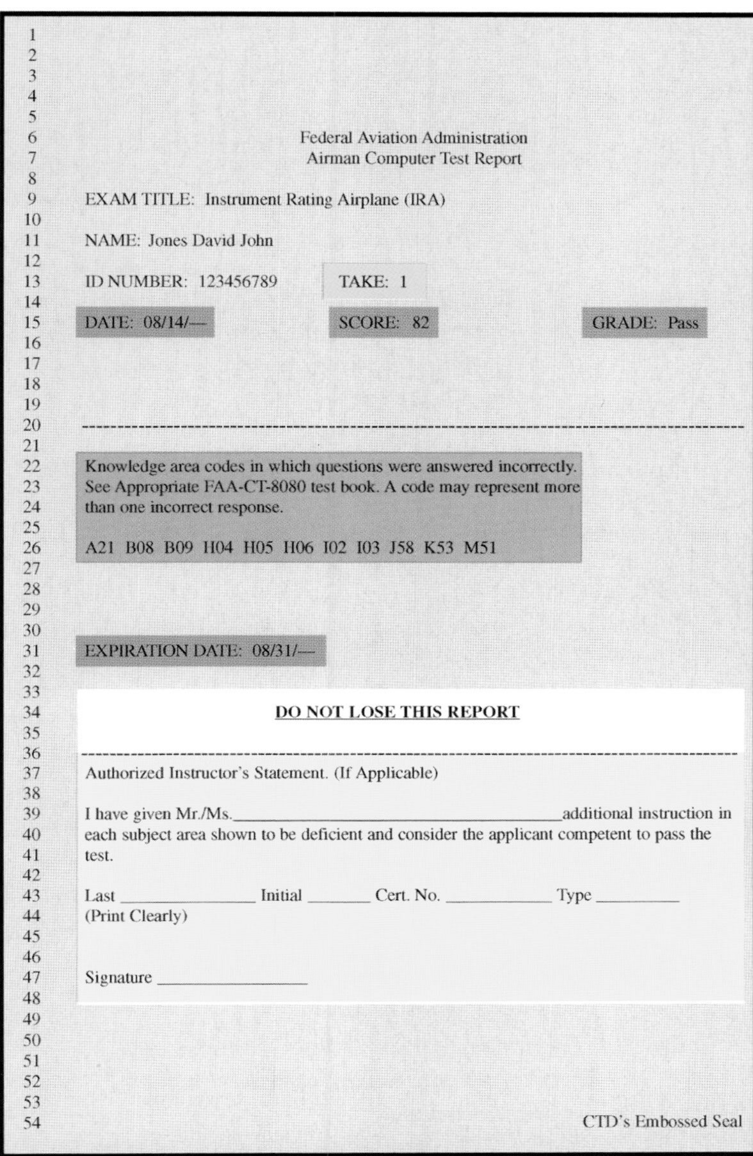

Federal Aviation Administration
Airman Computer Test Report

EXAM TITLE: Instrument Rating Airplane (IRA)

NAME: Jones David John

ID NUMBER: 123456789 TAKE: 1

DATE: 08/14/— SCORE: 82 GRADE: Pass

Knowledge area codes in which questions were answered incorrectly. See Appropriate FAA-CT-8080 test book. A code may represent more than one incorrect response.

A21 B08 B09 H04 H05 H06 I02 I03 J58 K53 M51

EXPIRATION DATE: 08/31/—

DO NOT LOSE THIS REPORT

Authorized Instructor's Statement. (If Applicable)

I have given Mr./Ms.____________________additional instruction in each subject area shown to be deficient and consider the applicant competent to pass the test.

Last ________ Initial ____ Cert. No. _______ Type ______
(Print Clearly)

Signature __________

CTD's Embossed Seal

Figure 4-76. Upon completion of the knowledge test, the results are available almost immediately.

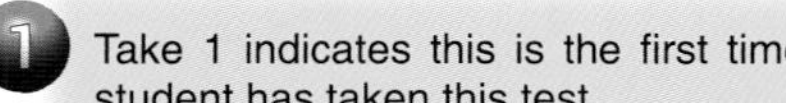

1 Take 1 indicates this is the first time your student has taken this test.

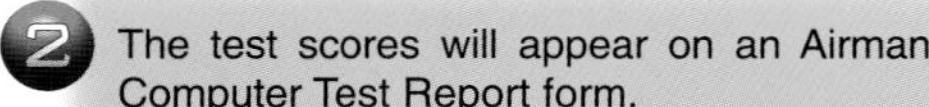

2 The test scores will appear on an Airman Computer Test Report form.

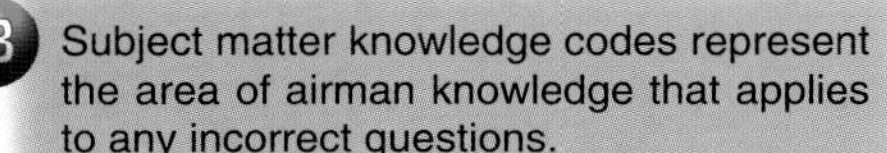

3 Subject matter knowledge codes represent the area of airman knowledge that applies to any incorrect questions.

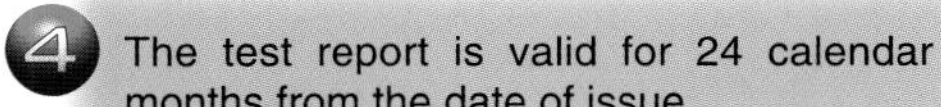

4 The test report is valid for 24 calendar months from the date of issue.

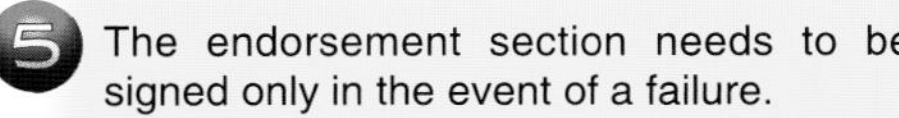

5 The endorsement section needs to be signed only in the event of a failure.

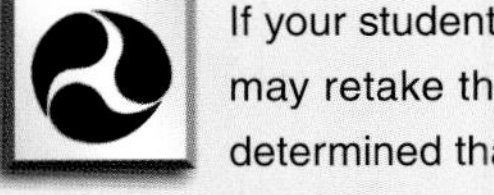

If your students fail a knowledge test, they may retake the exam. After you have determined that they have reviewed the deficient areas and they possess sufficient knowledge to pass the test, you may endorse them for a retake.

To be eligible for a practical test under Part 61, your student must have passed the appropriate knowledge test (when required) within the preceding 24 calendar months.

Often your students are ready for the knowledge test well in advance of the practical test for the rating sought. It is a good idea to recommend that your students take the knowledge test as soon as they are able, allowing a seamless transition from the completion of flight training to the practical test. After passing the knowledge test, your students have 24 calendar months to take the corresponding practical exam.

PRACTICAL TESTS

Once your students accomplish the requirements of Part 61 pertaining to private pilot certification, they are ready for their practical test. A written statement from you certifying that your students have received the required training in preparation for a practical test must be dated within 60 days preceding the date of the application. Typically, you make this statement by endorsing your students' logbook. In addition, you must sign your students' application form.

When making final arrangements for a practical test, carefully analyze your student's records to verify that all flight time, ground time, and endorsements are completed properly and meet the requirements of Part 61. For example, your student, who is preparing for a private pilot practical test in a single-engine airplane, has received 3.5 hours of cross-country solo flight training, including flights of 1.9 hours, 1.0 hours, and 0.6 hours. You student is not eligible to take the practical test because at least 5 hours of solo cross-country time is required.

When making final arrangements for a practical test, carefully analyze your student's records. Verify that all flight time, ground time, and endorsements are completed properly and meet the requirements of Part 61 of the regulations. Verify eligibility requirements of FAR 61.103, confirm flight proficiency as per FAR 61.107, and double check flight time and aeronautical experience. For example, your student must have received 3 hours of night flight training and 10 takeoffs and landings at night to be eligible to take the private pilot practical test. It would be unfortunate if your student was turned away from the test due to a clerical error, lack of flight time or landings, or another item that could have been quickly remedied.

Your students are not eligible to take the private pilot practical test, until they have received 3 hours of night flight training and 10 takeoffs and landings at night.

A written statement from you certifying that your student has received the required training in preparation for a practical test must be dated within 60 days preceding the date of the application.

THE 8710-1 FORM

It is important to assist your student when filling out an Airman Certificate and/or Rating Application, **FAA Form 8710-1**. The front page requires information pertaining to your student and the back page requests information from you. Your student may need help filling out the front side of this form properly. Refer to the example shown for filling the form out correctly. [Figures 4-77]

PREPARATION

Never rush a student into a practical test. Keep in mind that well-prepared students are a reflection of your instructional abilities. Unprepared students could give the impression to the examiner that you are a poor instructor. When your students pass their checkrides, it is attributed to their knowledge and skill as pilots. When your students fail, it is generally attributed to poor instruction and lack of preparation on your part. When too many of your students fail their checkrides, you look unprofessional. Ensure your success and that of your students by thorough preparation in all areas relating to the practical test.

Examiners usually welcome questions from instructors and students regarding practical tests. You may interview a few examiners to discover some of the weak areas they have observed with recent applicants, and discuss these areas with your students to help them avoid similar difficulties. If you train and prepare your students on the subjects outlined in the appropriate practical test standards, they should not have any problems passing their test.

PRACTICAL TEST STANDARDS

The purpose of the **practical test standards (PTS)** is to standardize the conduct and performance of the FAA inspectors and **designated examiners** conducting the tests for certificates and ratings. The standards are set at a level that is already very high. They are not minimum standards and they do not represent a floor of acceptability. A practical test recommendation based on anything less than practical test standards compromises the students' chances of passing the test.

1. Type or print in ink when filling out the 8710-1.
2. You students' middle name must be spelled out. If they have no middle name, the letters "NMN" must be indicated. DO NOT USE MIDDLE INITIAL.
3. The city and state within the U.S. must be included. Include city and country outside the U.S.
4. Do not use a P.O. box or rural route UNLESS a statement of physical location is provided.
5. Spell out hair and eye color.
6. Enter class shown on your students' medical certificate (i.e. 1st, 2nd, 3rd), if required.
7. Items U. and V. DO NOT apply to alcohol related offenses (DWI or DUI).
8. Check that your students' flight time is sufficient for the certificate or rating.
9. Make sure your students sign the form.
10. The date signed by your students should be within 60 days prior to the date of the practical test.

TYPE OR PRINT ALL ENTRIES IN INK — Form Approved OMB No: 2120-0021

US Department of Transportation
Federal Aviation Administration

Airman Certificate and/or Rating Application

I. Application Information ☐ Student ☐ Recreational ☒ Private ☐ Commercial ☐ Airline Transport ☐ Instrument
☐ Additional Aircraft Rating ☒ Airplane Single-Engine ☐ Airplane Multiengine ☐ Rotorcraft ☐ Glider ☐ Lighter-Than-Air
☐ Flight Instructor ____ Initial ____ Renewal ____ Reinstatement ☐ Additional Instructor Rating ☐ Ground Instructor
☐ Medical Flight Test ☐ Reexamination ☐ Reissuance of ________ Certificate ☐ Other ________

A. Name (Last, First, Middle): Doe, John David
B. SSN (US Only): 223-45-6678
C. Date of Birth (Mo. Day Year): 11/25/
D. Place of Birth: Bakersfield, CA
E. Address (Please See Instructions Before Completing): 1234 North Street
City, State, Zip Code: Alltown, PA 62534
F. Nationality (Citizenship): ☒ USA ☐ Other ____ Specify
G. Do you read, speak and understand English? ☒ Yes ☐ No
H. Height: 68 In.
I. Weight: 165 Lbs.
J. Hair: Blonde
K. Eyes: Blue
L. Sex: ☒ Male ☐ Female
M. Do you now hold, or have you ever held an FAA Pilot Certificate? ☒ Yes ☐ No
N. Grade Pilot Certificate: Student
O. Certificate Number: BB07138
P. Date Issued: 06-15-
Q. Do you hold a Medical Certificate? ☒ Yes ☐ No
R. Class of Certificate: Third
S. Date Issued: 6-15-
T. Name of Examiner: Thomas C. Smith, MD
U. Have you been convicted for violation of Federal or State statutes relating to narcotic drugs, marijuana, or depressant or stimulant drugs or substances ☐ Yes ☒ No
V. Date of Final Conviction
W. Glider or Free Balloon Pilots only: *Medical Statement: I have no known physical defect which makes me unable to pilot a glider or free balloon.* Signature X. Date

II. Certificate or Rating Applied For on Basis of:

☒ A. Completion of Required Test — 1. Aircraft to be used (if flight test required): Cessna 152; 2a. Total time in this aircraft: 55 hours; 2b. Pilot in command: 24 hours
☐ B. Military Competence Obtained in — 1. Service; 2. Date Rated; 3. Rank or Grade and Service Number; 4. Has flown at least 10 hours as pilot in command during the past 12 months in the following military aircraft.
☐ C. Graduate of Approved Course — 1. Name and Location of Training Agency or Training Center; 1a Certification Number; 2. Curriculum From Which Graduated; 3. Date
☐ D. Holder of Foreign License Issued By — 1. Country; 2. Grade of License; 3. Number; 4. Ratings
☐ E. Completion of Air Carrier's Approved Training Program — 1. Name of Air Carrier; 2. Date; 3. Which Curriculum ☐ Initial ☐ Upgrade ☐ Transition

III. Record of Pilot time *(Do not write in the shaded areas.)*

	Total	Instruction Received	Solo	Pilot in Command	Second in Command	Cross Country Instruction Received	Cross Country Solo	Cross Country Pilot in Command	Instrument	Night Instruction Received	Night Take-off/ Landing	Night Pilot in Command	Night Take-off/ Landing Pilot in Command	Number of Flights	Number of Aero-Tows	Number of Ground Launches	Number of Powered Launches	Number of Free Flights
Airplanes	55	31	24	24		5	12	12	3	4	12							
Rotor-craft																		
Gliders																		
Lighter than Air																		
Training Device Simulator																		

IV. Have you failed a test for this certificate or rating? ☐ Yes ☒ No **Within the Past 30 days?** ☐ Yes ☒ No

V. Applicant's Certification — I certify that all statements and answers provided by me on this application form are complete and true to the best of my knowledge, and I agree that they are to be considered as part of the basis for issuance of any FAA certificate to me. I have also read and understand the Privacy Act statement that accompanies this form.

Signature of Applicant: John David Doe John David Doe — Date: 04-12-

FAA Use Only

EMP	REG	D.O.	SEAL	CON	ISS	ACT	LEV	TR	S.H	SRCH	#RTE	RATING (1)

FAA Form 8710-1 (7-95) Supersedes Previous Edition — NSN: 0052-00-682-5006

Figure 4-77. A correctly completed 8710-1 and an organized logbook with the proper endorsements will give the examiner a good first impression. Emphasize to your students the importance of maintaining accurate logbooks and other documentation throughout their flying careers.

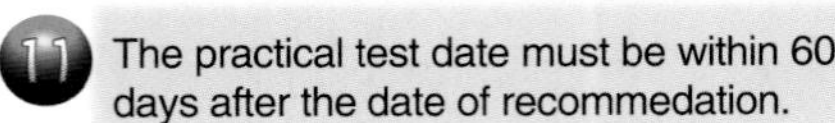
The practical test date must be within 60 days after the date of recommedation.

Your full printed name should be included with your signature.

Your instructor's certificate must be current on the date of recommendation.

Instructor's Recommendation

I have personally instructed the applicant and consider this person ready to take the test.

Date	Instructor's Signature	Certificate No:	Certificate Expires
4-11-_____	*James E. Jones* James E. Jones	1234567 CFI	05-31-_____

Air Agency's Recommendation

The applicant has successfully completed our __________ course, and is recommended for certification or rating without further __________ test.

Date	Agency Name and Number	Official's Signature
		Title

Designated Examiner's Report

☐ Student Pilot Certificate Issued *(Copy attached)*

☒ I have personally reviewed this applicant's pilot logbook, and certify that the individual meets the pertinent requirements of FAR 61 for the pilot certificate or rating sought.

☐ I have personally reviewed this applicant's graduation certificate, and found it to be appropriate and in order, and have returned the certificate.

☒ I have personally tested and/or verified this applicant in accordance with pertinent procedures and standards with the result indicated below.

☒ Approved—Temporary Certificate Issued *(Copy Attached)*

☐ Disapproved—Disapproval Notice Issued *(Copy Attached)*

Location of Test *(Facility, City, State)*	Duration of Test: Ground	Simulator	Flight
Alltown, PA	2.6	0	2.1

Certificate or Rating for Which Tested	Type(s) of Aircraft Used	Registration No.(s)
Private Pilot	Cessna 152	N12345

Date	Examiner's Signature	Certificate No.	Designation No.	Designation Expires
04-12-_____	Henry L. Smith *Henry L. Smith*	332345678	AE-01-1123	01-31-_____

Evaluator's Record For Airline Transport Certificate/Rating Only

	Inspector	Examiner	*Signature*	Date
Oral	☐	☐		
Approved Simulator/Training Device Check	☐	☐		
Aircraft Flight Check	☐	☐		
Advanced Qualification Program	☐	☐		

Inspector's Report

I have personally tested this applicant in accordance with or have otherwise verified that this applicant complies with pertinent procedures, standards, policies, and or necessary requirements with the result indicated below.

☐ **Approved**—Temporary Certificate Issued ☐ **Disapproved**—Disapproval Notice Issued

Location of Test *(Facility, City, State)*	Duration of Test: Ground	Simulator	Flight

Certificate or Rating for Which Tested	Type(s) of Aircraft Used	Registration No.(s)

☐ Student Pilot Certificate issued
☐ Examiner's Recommendation
☐ ACCEPTED ☐ REJECTED
☐ Reissue or Exchange of Pilot Certificate
☐ Special medical test conducted—report forwarded to Aeromedical Certification Branch, AAM-130

☐ Certificate or Rating Based on
☐ Military Competence
☐ Foreign License
☐ Approved Course Graduate
☐ Other Approved FAA Qualification Criteria
☐ Certificate Issued
☐ Certificate Denied

☐ Instructor ☐ Flight ☐ Ground
☐ Renewal ☐ Approved
☐ Reinstatement ☐ Disapproved
Instructor Renewal Based on
☐ Activity ☐ Training Course
☐ Acquaintance ☐ Test

Training Course (FIRC) Name	Graduation Certificate No.	Date

Date	Inspector's Signature	FAA District Office

Attachments:

☐ Student Pilot Certificate (copy)
☒ Report of Written Examination
☒ Temporary Pilot Certificate (copy)

☒ Airmans Identification (ID)
Pennsylvania Drivers License
Form of ID
223456678
Number
11-25-_____
Expiration Date

☐ Notice of Disapproval
☐ Superseded Pilot Certificate
☐ Answer Sheet Graded
☐ Answer Sheet Graded (Foreign Instrument)

FAA Form 8710-1 (7-95) Supersedes Previous Edition NSN: 0052-00-682-5006

☆ U.S. GOVERNMENT PRINTING OFFICE: 1997-668-108

Figure 4-77. Continued.

You are expected to use PTS publications when preparing your students for practical tests. Make sure that both you and your students possess a current copy of the PTS for the certificate or rating sought. Current PTS documents can be accessed on the Internet using FAA web sites. Introducing the PTS to your students early in training can prove to be very helpful in accomplishing the desired results. Ensuring that your students use the PTS makes the learning process easier because the goals are well defined. This simplifies your job as an instructor because your students are better informed and are active

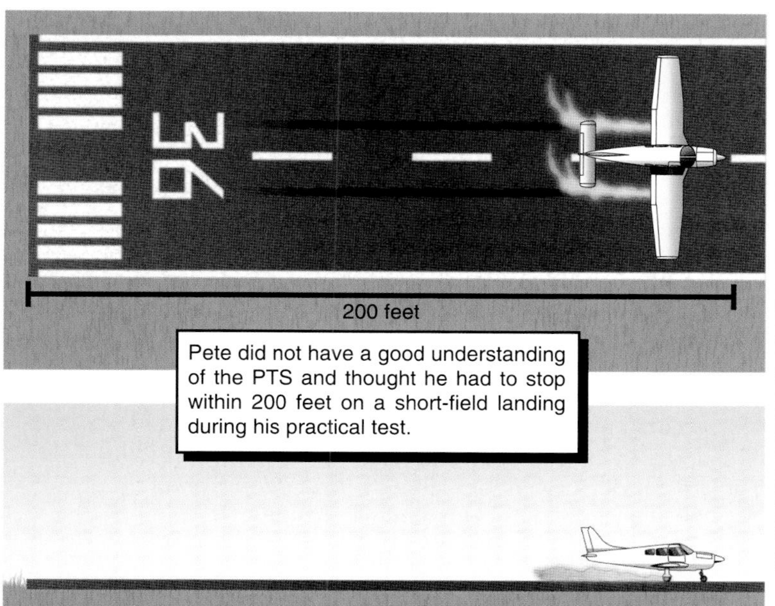

F. TASK: SHORT-FIELD APPROACH AND LANDING

REFERENCES: AC 61-21; Pilot's Operating Handbook, FAA-Approved Airplane Flight Manual.

Objective. To determine that the applicant:

1. Exhibits knowledge of the elements related to a short-field approach and landing.
2. Considers the wind conditions, landing surface and obstructions, and selects the most suitable touchdown point.
3. Establishes the recommended approach and landing configuration and airspeed, and adjusts pitch attitude and power as required.
4. Maintains a stabilized approach and the recommended approach airspeed, or in its absence not more than 1.3 V_{SO}, +10/-5 knots, with gust factor applied.
5. Makes smooth, timely, and correct control application during the roundout and touchdown.
6. Touches down smoothly at the approximate stalling speed, at or within 200 feet (60 meters) beyond a specified point, with no side drift, and with the airplane's longitudinal axis aligned with and over the runway centerline.
7. Applies brakes, as necessary, to stop in the shortest distance consistent with safety.
8. Maintains crosswind correction and directional control throughout the approach and landing.
9. Completes the appropriate checklist.

Figure 4-78. Your students should not encounter anything unexpected during the practical test.

participants in the learning process. If your students have a good understanding of what is expected from the start, their chances of success are greatly improved. [Figure 4-78]

The PTS for aeronautical certificates and ratings include **areas of operation** and **tasks** that reflect the requirements of Part 61. Areas of operation define phases of the practical test arranged in a logical sequence within each standard. Tasks are knowledge areas, flight procedures, and/or maneuvers appropriate to an area of operation. Also included within each task are references to the applicable regulations or publications. Areas of operation run the gamut from preflight preparation to postflight procedures. The examiner, however, may conduct the practical test in any sequence that results in a complete and efficient test. [Figure 4-79]

IV. AREA OF OPERATION: TAKEOFFS, LANDINGS, AND GO-AROUNDS

A. TASK: NORMAL AND CROSSWIND TAKEOFF AND CLIMB

NOTE: If a crosswind condition does not exist, the applicant's knowledge of crosswind elements shall be evaluated through oral testing.

...perating Handbook, FAA-

...nt:

...nts related to a normal and

...e existing wind conditions;

...eoff position and aligns the

...takeoff power.

... airspeed, lifts off, and accelerat... to V_Y.

6. Establishes the pitch attitude for V_Y and maintains V_Y, +10/-5 knots, during the climb.
7. Retracts the landing gear, if retractable, and flaps after a positive rate of climb is established.
8. Maintains takeoff power to a safe maneuvering altitude.
9. Maintains directional control and proper wind-drift correction throughout the takeoff and climb.
10. Complies with noise abatement procedures.
11. Completes the appropriate checklist.

61.107 FLIGHT PROFICIENCY

(a) *General.* A person who applies for a private pilot certificate must receive and log ground and flight training from an authorized instructor on the areas of operation of this section that apply to the aircraft category and class rating sought.

(b) *Areas of operation*

(1) *For an airplane category rating with a single-engine class rating:*

(i) Preflight preparation;
(ii) Preflight procedures;
(iii) Airport and seaplane base operations;
(iv) Takeoffs, landings, and go-arounds;

Figure 4-79. The roman numerals preceding each area of operation relate that subject to the corresponding regulatory requirement.

In addition to covering the areas of operation and tasks with your students, you should familiarize them with the first section of the PTS publication. This section includes such items as an explanation of the PTS concept, a definition of CRM, and a description of the examiner's responsibility during the practical test. The **applicant's practical test checklist** also is available in the PTS publication for your students to confirm they have everything ready for their checkride. [Figure 4-80]

APPLICANT'S PRACTICAL TEST CHECKLIST

APPOINTMENT WITH EXAMINER:

EXAMINER'S NAME____________________

LOCATION ____________________

DATE/TIME ____________________

ACCEPTABLE AIRCRAFT

- ☐ Aircraft Documents:
  Airworthiness Certificate
  Registration Certificate
  Operating Limitations
- ☐ Aircraft Maintenance Records:
  Logbook Record of Airworthiness Inspections and AD Compliance
- ☐ Pilot's Operating Handbook, FAA-Approved Airplane Flight Manual
- ☐ FCC Station License

PERSONAL EQUIPMENT

- ☐ View-Limiting Device
- ☐ Current Aeronautical Charts
- ☐ Computer and Plotter
- ☐ Flight Plan Form
- ☐ Flight Logs
- ☐ Current AIM, Airport Facility Directory, and Appropriate Publications

PERSONAL RECORDS

- ☐ Identification - Photo/Signature ID
- ☐ Pilot Certificate
- ☐ Current and Appropriate Medical Certificate
- ☐ Completed FAA Form 8710-1, Airman Certificate and/or Rating Application with Instructor's Signature (if applicable)
- ☐ AC Form 8080-2, Airman Written Test Report, or Computer Test Report
- ☐ Pilot Logbook with Appropriate Instructor Endorsements
- ☐ FAA Form 8060-5, Notice of Disapproval (if applicable)
- ☐ Approved School Graduation Certificate (if applicable)
- ☐ Examiner's Fee (if applicable)

1-vii *FAA-S-8081-14*

Figure 4-80. Both you and your students should use the applicant's practical test checklist during checkride preparation.

SATISFACTORY PERFORMANCE

Your students must demonstrate mastery of the aircraft, with the successful outcome of each performed task never seriously in doubt. They must show satisfactory proficiency and competency, exhibit sound judgment; and prove single-pilot competence. Satisfactory performance is based on your students' ability to safely perform the areas of operation within the approved standards.

UNSATISFACTORY PERFORMANCE

If in the judgment of the examiner, your student does not meet the standards of performance for any task performed, the associated area of operation is failed and, therefore, the practical test is failed. The examiner or your student may discontinue the test any time after the failure of an area of operation makes your student ineligible for the certificate or rating sought. The test is continued beyond this point with your student's consent. Whether the test is continued or discontinued, your student is entitled to credit for only those tasks satisfactorily performed. However, during the retest and at the discretion of the examiner, any task may be re-evaluated, including those previously passed.

Unsatisfactory performance and grounds for disqualification are any action or lack of action by your student that requires corrective intervention by the examiner. Some typical areas where a student fails a checkride are: improper and ineffective visual scanning techniques to clear the area before and while performing maneuvers, consistently exceeding tolerances stated in the objectives, and failure to take prompt corrective action when tolerances are exceeded.

There also is a broad range of material that is covered in ground school of which your students should have a working knowledge prior to the checkride. As the recommending flight instructor, you should verify that your students know and understand all the materials requested of them in the ground portion of the practical test. Many students fail their checkride before the flight begins. For example, their inability to read and analyze weather and make a go/no-go decision is disqualifying. When a disapproval notice is issued, the examiner records your student's unsatisfactory performance in

Mark was deficient in some areas of operation during his private pilot practical test.

With some additional instruction and an endorsement from his instructor, Mark passed his practical test 10 days later.

Figure 4-81. In the event your student fails a practical test, review the deficient area/areas in a timely manner, sign a new application form, and endorse your student's logbook again.

terms of the area of operation appropriate to the practical test conducted. Meeting with the examiner and your students to discuss the area/areas failed is important for test review. [Figure 4-81]

A student who fails a practical test may reapply for testing after receiving the necessary instruction and an endorsement from you.

ADDITIONAL TRAINING AND ENDORSEMENTS

As a new instructor, your primary focus will be on student and private pilots. Obviously there are other areas of flight and ground training. As you gain experience as an instructor, you will receive requests for a wide variety of training. You may provide tailwheel checkouts, complex and high-performance aircraft instruction, high-altitude training, flight reviews, instrument proficiency checks, and even instruction for students seeking airline transport pilot certificates. When you provide training in these areas, you are offering specialized instructional services, which are covered in Chapter 5, Section E. In addition, you may train students pursuing recreational pilot certificates, initial instructor certificates, or additional CFI ratings.

RECREATIONAL PILOTS

Occasionally you may encounter a student who wishes to pursue a recreational pilot certificate instead of a private pilot certificate. Since the recreational pilot certificate has not proved to be as popular as the private, you may have a few questions on proper endorsements and training. Part 61, Subpart D includes the regulations governing flight and ground training for recreational pilots. The requirements for aeronautical knowledge and experience are different than those for your private pilot students. You still endorse your recreational students for solo privileges. You also may endorse them for solo cross-country operations once they obtain their recreational pilot certificate, provided you give them the required training for cross-country flight. [Figure 4-82]

Kevin received his recreational pilot certificate 6 months ago and is required to receive an endorsement from his instructor every 180 days until he accumulates 400 hours. If he chooses to pursue a private certificate in the future, he will need further training as well as additional endorsements.

Figure 4-82. Once your students obtain a recreational pilot certificate, you may encounter some unusual requirements.

FLIGHT INSTRUCTOR TRAINING

FAR 61.195 requires a certain level of experience before you can instruct applicants for an initial CFI certificate. To provide ground training, you must have held a current ground or flight instructor certificate with the appropriate rating for at least 24 months and have given at least 40 hours of ground training. An alternate way of meeting this requirement is to hold a current ground or flight instructor certificate with the appropriate rating and have given at least 100 hours of ground training in an FAA-approved course.

To provide initial CFI flight training, you must have held the appropriate flight instructor certificate and rating for at least 24 months and given at least 200 hours of flight training as a CFI. This requirement applies to airplane, rotorcraft, or powered-lift category ratings. If you serve as a CFI in an approved school, there is an alternate requirement. You must have given at least 400 hours of flight training as a CFI, have trained and endorsed at least 5 applicants for a practical test for a pilot certificate, flight instructor certificate, ground instructor certificate, or additional rating, and had at least 80% of the applicants pass the test on the first attempt. More information on training flight instructors, including spin training, is presented in Chapter 5, Section F.

To prepare a student for an initial flight instructor certificate, you must have held a flight instructor certificate for at least 24 months and have given a minimum of 200 hours of flight training.

SUMMARY CHECKLIST

✓ You should refer to FAR Part 61, Subpart H or FAR Part 141, Appendices F and G for specific information on eligibility, aeronautical knowledge, and flight proficiency requirements.

✓ FAR 61.23 lists operations that require a medical certificate and which class of certificate applies to each operation.

✓ You may be compensated for your instructional services without regard to your medical status, as long as you are not acting as PIC or functioning as a required crewmember.

✓ Part 141 governs the certification of approved pilot schools and sets forth the rules under which they operate.

✓ The aeronautical knowledge requirements are essentially the same in terms of content for each certificate or rating area whether your student trains under Part 61 or Part 141.

✓ The term authorized instructor is frequently referred to in regulations regarding who is qualified to provide ground or flight training.

✓ FAR 61.189 requires you to endorse the logbook of each student to whom you have provided flight or ground instruction.

✓ When instructing at an approved school, you are required to keep a separate and accurate up-to-date training record for all your students.

✓ Your flight instructor certificate is only valid for 24 calendar months. Renewal of your certificate should be in accordance with FAR 61.197 and can be accomplished by several methods, including graduation from a flight instructor refresher course (FIRC).

✓ If you are unable to obtain a medical certificate and still wish to pursue a career in aviation, you may consider becoming a ground instructor.

- ✓ As a basic ground instructor you are authorized to provide ground training on knowledge areas for procurement of a recreational or private pilot certificate and may also endorse students for the recreational and private knowledge tests.
- ✓ As an instrument ground instructor you may provide ground training for the issuance of an instrument rating, ground training for an instrument competency check, and recommend students for instrument knowledge tests.
- ✓ An advanced ground instructor is authorized to provide ground training for any certificate or rating under Part 61, as well as ground training for any flight review, and recommendations for any knowledge test issued under Part 61.
- ✓ A student pilot certificate is usually issued by an AME as part of a medical certificate. However, an aviation safety inspector (ASI) or a designated examiner also may issue student pilot certificates, if your students already possess a third class medical.
- ✓ A statement of demonstrated ability (SODA) is issued by the FAA's federal air surgeon and is granted for a condition normally requiring a denial of a medical certificate that is not necessarily a safety factor.
- ✓ Inform your students that if there is any change in their medical condition, they need to determine whether they are medically fit for flight.
- ✓ It is important that you review FAA Form 8500-8 with your students before they obtain a medical certificate.
- ✓ As a flight instructor, you are allowed to provide endorsements for certain flying activities as well as recommend your students for practical tests.
- ✓ Prior to solo, student pilots must complete a knowledge test which evaluates their comprehension of Parts 61 and 91, airspace rules and procedures for the airport where the solo flight will be conducted, and the flight characteristics and operational limitations for the make and model of aircraft to be flown.
- ✓ Prior to performing solo operations, your student's logbook and student pilot certificate must be endorsed to confirm that the necessary training requirements outlined in FAR 61.87 have been met.
- ✓ When your students have satisfactorily accomplished all required training for solo cross-country operations you may endorse their logbook and student pilot certificate for cross-country flight.
- ✓ Your students may make repeated cross-country flights without receiving an endorsement from you for each flight if they meet specific training requirements and the destination airport is no more than 50 nautical miles from the point of departure.
- ✓ To operate an aircraft on a solo flight within Class B airspace, student pilots must have a logbook endorsement showing that they have received ground instruction on, and flight instruction in, that specific airspace for which solo flight is authorized.
- ✓ Preparing your students to take the airmen knowledge test is a part of the ground instruction process.
- ✓ The subject matter knowledge codes represent a broad area of airman knowledge, not specific test questions, and they do not identify the correct answers.

- ✓ A written statement from you certifying that your student has received the required training in preparation for a practical test must be dated within 60 days preceding the date of the application.
- ✓ It is important to assist your students when filling out an Airman Certificate and/or Rating Application, FAA Form 8710-1.
- ✓ The purpose of the practical test standards (PTS) is to standardize the conduct and performance of the FAA inspectors and designated examiners conducting the tests for certificates and ratings.
- ✓ The PTS for aeronautical certificates and ratings include areas of operation and tasks that reflect the requirements of Part 61.
- ✓ In the event your student fails a practical test, review the deficient area/areas in a timely manner, sign a new application form, and endorse your student's logbook again.
- ✓ To provide initial CFI flight training, you must have held the appropriate flight instructor certificate and rating for at least 24 months and given at least 200 hours of flight training as a CFI.

KEY TERMS

Aviation Medical Examiner (AME)

Approved Pilot School

Home Study Course

Authorized Instructor

CFI Renewal

Flight Instructor Refresher Course (FIRC)

Basic Ground Instructor

Instrument Ground Instructor

Advanced Ground Instructor

Statement of Demonstrated Ability (SODA)

FAA Form 8500-8

Endorsements

Flight Standards District Office (FSDO)

Subject Matter Knowledge Codes

FAA Form 8710-1

Practical Test Standards (PTS)

Designated Examiner

Areas of Operation

Tasks

Applicant's Practical Test Checklist

QUESTIONS

1. When acting as PIC in the course of providing instruction, what class of medical certificate are you required to possess?

2. According to FAR 61.195, you are allowed to instruct a maximum of how many hours in a 24-hour period?

   A. 6 hours
   B. 8 hours
   C. 12 hours

3. What does FAR Part 141 govern?

4. True/False. A student who has previously trained under Part 61 cannot receive credit for that instruction when transferring to a Part 141 approved school.

5. For how long are you required to maintain records of endorsements you have provided?

6. How long is your flight instructor certificate valid and what methods can you use to renew it?

7. True/False. A limitation on your students' medical certificate renders them unfit for flight.

8. Select the true statement regarding the endorsements that authorize your students for solo flight.

   A. The logbook endorsement specifies the make and model of aircraft and is valid for 90 days.
   B. The endorsement on the student pilot certificate specifies the make and model of aircraft and is valid for 90 days.
   C. The endorsement on the student pilot certificate specifies aircraft category only and is a one-time endorsement.

9. True/False. The only endorsement you are required to provide for your students' solo cross-country flights is an endorsement that says you have verified your students' fight planning.

10. What is required of your students to conduct solo operations within Class B airspace? To take off and land at an airport within Class B airspace?

11. True/False. If your students fail an airman knowledge test, they may retake the exam upon receiving an endorsement from you stating you have reviewed the deficient areas and find them competent to pass the test.

12. How long is an endorsement for a private pilot practical test valid?

    A. 60 days
    B. 30 days
    C. It does not expire.

13. What is the difference between an area of operation and a task as described in the PTS?

14. True/False. During a practical test, a designated examiner must direct applicants to perform tasks in the order shown in the PTS.

15. If your student fails a practical test, how long must they wait to retake the checkride?

    A. 30 days
    B. 60 days
    C. Your student can retake the test after receiving the necessary instruction and endorsement from you.

16. What qualifications must you possess to provide initial CFI training?

CHAPTER 5

THE BASIC INSTRUCTOR

Flight Instructor
Volume 3 — Instructing the Private Student

Flight Instructor
Volume 4 — Instructing the Commercial Student

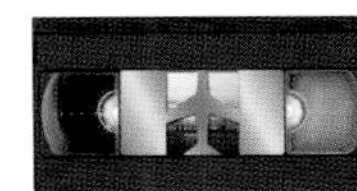

SECTION A
PRESENTING PRIVATE KNOWLEDGE

Teaching private students can be one of the most rewarding and challenging endeavors you will undertake as a CFI. It can be very satisfying to watch beginning students gain knowledge and understanding based on your instruction and guidance. This section does not attempt to address all aspects of private pilot knowledge. Rather, it contains practical and creative methods to teach difficult and complex subjects in a way private students can easily understand. You should refer to the Guided Flight Discovery *Private Pilot Manual* for specific information pertaining to private pilot knowledge.

TEACHING THE PRIVATE STUDENT

Typically, students seeking their private pilot certificate come to you with no aviation background or knowledge. Often, they have a very limited understanding of general aviation. What comes naturally to you can be foreign and confusing to a new student. For example, something that seems simple to you, like airspace, can be a challenge for the beginning student to grasp. [Figure 5-1]

Figure 5-1. If you ever lose sight of how your students may feel, remember your first few lessons and think of a concept you found particularly complicated.

EXPLAINING AIRPLANE SYSTEMS

Private students typically have questions and concerns about how an airplane operates before the first lesson. Many new students are somewhat fearful of small airplanes

because they lack this knowledge. For example, many people believe a single-engine airplane would plummet to the earth in the event of an engine failure. By providing your students with knowledge of **airplane systems** from the beginning of their training, you may be able to alleviate some of their fears. When teaching your students about systems there are several techniques that can be helpful. [Figure 5-2]

One of the most effective ways to teach systems is by incorporating a visit to the maintenance hangar into your lesson. An airplane with the cowling removed can be an excellent teaching tool, because it gives your students a chance to see various machanical parts.

Sitting in the airplane, using the panel and POH as guides, is an excellent way to organize a systems discussion.

When you describe systems, use some type of visual aid, such as a good full-color textbook.

Figure 5-2. Keep in mind that it is usually best to discuss systems with your student while on the ground. Trying to teach systems in the air is generally counterproductive.

Keep in mind that some students may have an extensive mechanical or engineering background, while some may be confused by mechanical systems. During systems lessons, it might be beneficial for you to pair a knowledgeable student with a student that has trouble understanding systems. You also can relate certain airplane components to systems and equipment with which your students may already be familiar. [Figure 5-3]

The fuel systems of cars and airplanes share many common characteristics. Fuel is stored in a tank and then fed to the engine via fuel lines. Typically, airplanes use fuel pumps to transport fuel from the tanks to the engine, just like an automobile. Remember that some high-wing airplanes rely on gravity to feed fuel to the engine.

A carburetor on an automobile operates almost exactly like the carburetor on an airplane.

The alternator and charging system on a training airplane are similar in operation to those on many automobiles.

The brakes on some automobiles are hydraulically actuated disc brakes, just like those used on training airplanes.

You should point out to your students that magnetos are a self-sustaining ignition source. Even in the event of total electrical failure, the airplane's magnetos still function normally. An automobile typically requires a source of electricity to operate its ignition system.

Figure 5-3. You can relate many parts used in automobiles to those found in a single-engine airplane. These types of analogies can help students associate concepts they may know about their cars to the airplane.

POWERPLANTS

Understanding the operation of the powerplant can be challenging for many students. You may have to spend more time explaining basic engine concepts to certain students. Be sure you know the background of your audience, so that you can teach powerplant-related material at the proper pace. For example, a private student that is an automotive technician would probably become bored with a discussion about basic engine operation. [Figure 5-4]

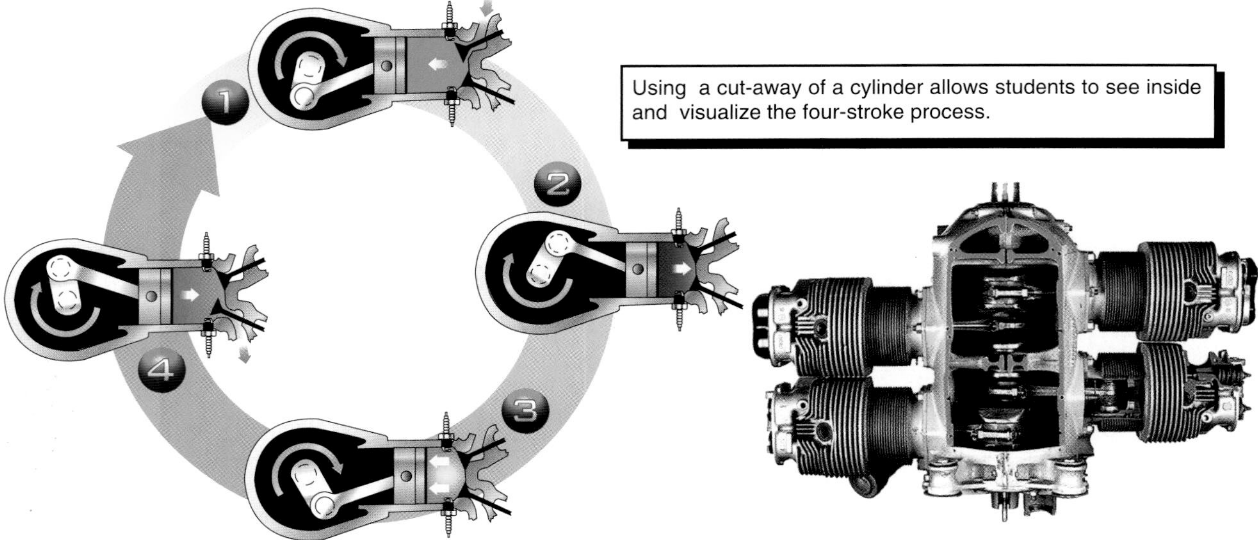

Figure 5-4. Using a cut-away drawing or picture can help students with a limited understanding of powerplants comprehend what is actually happening inside the engine. If you have access to an actual cut-away model of a typical aircraft engine, it can serve as a useful teaching tool.

Engine Evolution

In the years after World War II, reciprocating engine development reached its peak. The Pratt & Whitney R-4360 is widely regarded as the most technologically advanced reciprocating aircraft engine ever produced in large numbers. This engine was used to power numerous military and commercial airplanes, including the C-119, B-36 and the Boeing 337 Stratocruiser. [Figure A]

The R-4360 Wasp Major had a staggering 28 cylinders. Some models of the R-4360 were rated as high as 3,800 horsepower, and this engine typically weighed in around 3,600 pounds. So, why were large radial engines phased out in favor of turboprop engines? One reason is power-to-weight ratio. For instance, the engines on the Saab-340 produce approximately 2.3 horsepower for each pound they weigh. [Figure B] Another reason turboprops are favored is reliability and simplicity of operation.

TROUBLESHOOTING PROBLEMS

Some of your private students may wonder why they need such a thorough understanding of the airplane's systems. They may be thinking, *"I drive my car, and I don't really know how it works, so why do I need to know how the airplane works?"* What students often fail to realize is that in-depth knowledge of systems is a valuable asset when troubleshooting problems that may arise during the flight. [Figure 5-5]

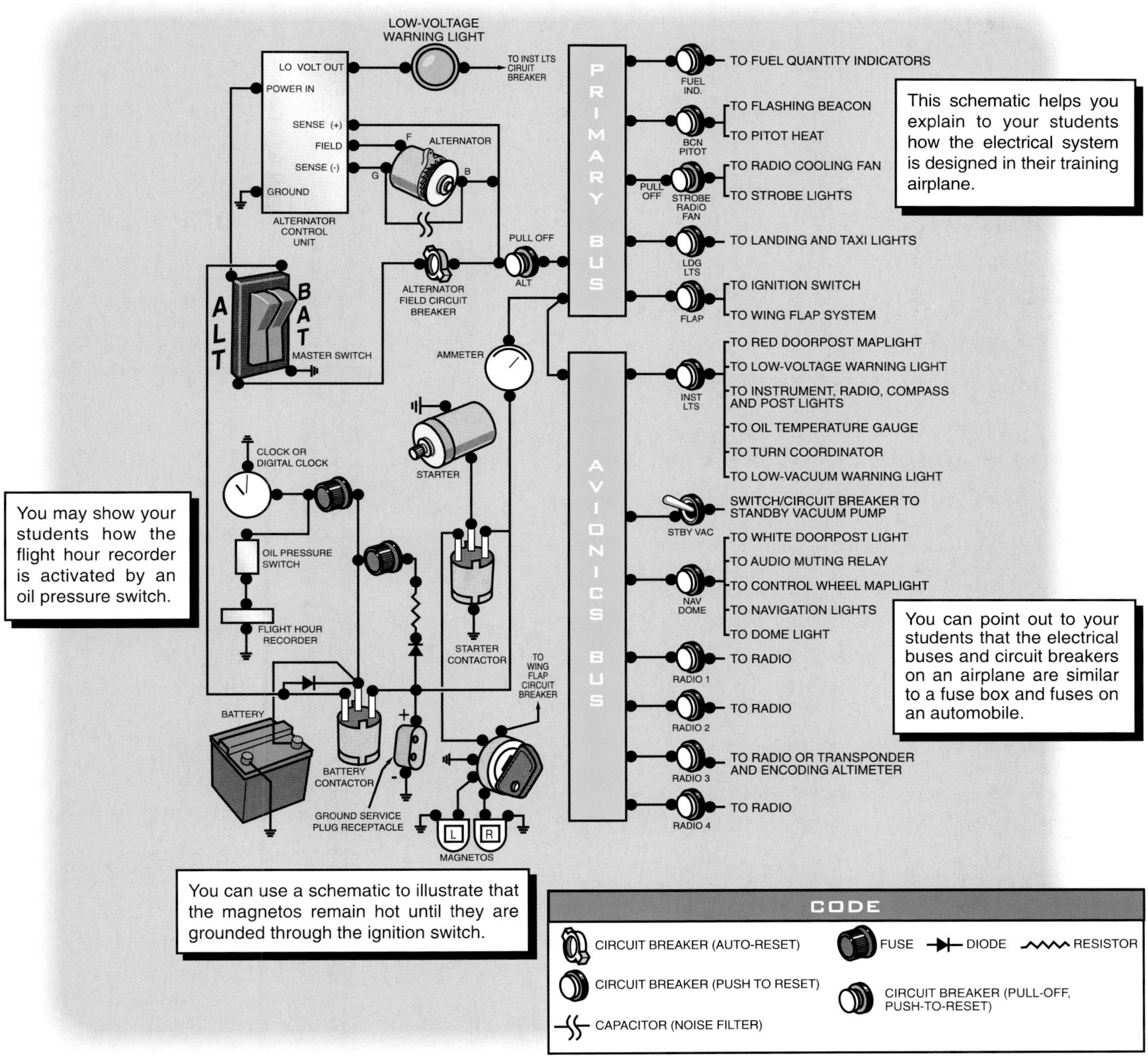

This schematic helps you explain to your students how the electrical system is designed in their training airplane.

You may show your students how the flight hour recorder is activated by an oil pressure switch.

You can point out to your students that the electrical buses and circuit breakers on an airplane are similar to a fuse box and fuses on an automobile.

You can use a schematic to illustrate that the magnetos remain hot until they are grounded through the ignition switch.

CODE

CIRCUIT BREAKER (AUTO-RESET) · FUSE · DIODE · RESISTOR

CIRCUIT BREAKER (PUSH TO RESET) · CIRCUIT BREAKER (PULL-OFF, PUSH-TO-RESET)

CAPACITOR (NOISE FILTER)

Figure 5-5. Make sure your students are familiar with the system schematics for the airplane they fly. By having a mental picture of how the system works, your students will likely develop effective troubleshooting skills.

Knowing how to troubleshoot problems can be considered the correlation phase of learning aircraft systems. Your students must be able to associate the meaning of a particular warning light or indication with the correct action to take. For example, an ammeter displaying an excessive rate of charge typically calls for the alternator to be turned off. If the gauge reflects a discharge, the master switch is usually cycled in an attempt to reactivate the charging system.

INTRODUCING AERODYNAMICS

Aerodynamics can be an intimidating subject for some private students because it largely involves theories and concepts. Typically, you cannot take your students out to the ramp and physically show them an example of aerodynamics. Rather, your students must be able to envision aerodynamic principles. Often a simple model airplane can be an effective way for you to help your students visualize concepts such as angle of attack and the four forces of flight.

How does an airplane generate lift? Your private students are sure to pose this question to you during the course of their training. Your response may include an explanation of Bernoulli's principle and the air accelerating over the wing's curvature causing a decrease in pressure. However, there is more to creating lift than Bernoulli's principle. Newton's third law, which states for every action there is an equal and opposite reaction, also has a place in describing the generation of lift. In fact, if Bernoulli's principle was the only reason airplanes flew, the wing on a typical small training airplane would have to have a much greater curvature along its upper surface to provide enough lift. [Figure 5-6]

LIFT

Upwash

Remember to illustrate to your students how lift is generated perpendicular to the relative wind, not the chord line of the wing.

FLIGHT PATH

RELATIVE WIND

Angle of Attack

Downwash

Figure 5-6. In addition to the lowered pressure, a downward-backward flow of air also is generated from the top surface of the wing. The reaction to this downwash results in an upward force on the wing which demonstrates Newton's third law of motion.

Generally, students confuse flight attitude with flight path, which causes difficulty in understanding angle of attack. You must ensure that your students can picture the relative wind acting parallel and in the opposite direction of the flight path. [Figure 5-7]

This Duchess has a relatively level flight attitude, but a descending flight path, and this F-16C is displaying a vertical climb.

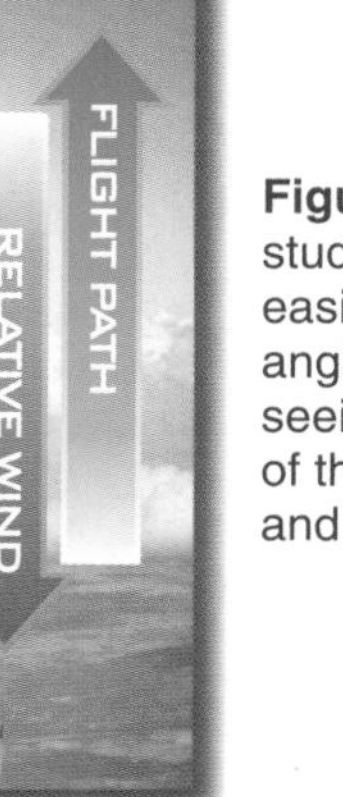

Your student may think the Duchess has a small angle of attack, while this F-16C is operating at an extreme angle of attack, but an analysis of the flight path and relative wind reveals just the opposite.

Figure 5-7. Some students may find it easier to visualize angle of attack by seeing a diagram of the relative wind and the flight path.

Your students need to have a good understanding of why an airplane flies, so they can operate the airplane safely and extract from it the desired performance. It is usually best to introduce aerodynamics using basic principles and concepts, only adding advanced topics when students show understanding and interest. For instance, a discussion of boundary layer control devices would probably not be appropriate for most beginning students.

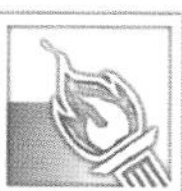

DESIGN YOUR OWN AIRPLANE

Creating an exercise that enables students to design their own airplane can be an effective way to foster their interest in aerodynamics. Students are able to learn about a variety of aerodynamic topics, such as why some airplanes have a canard design, or why some airplanes use a swept wing instead of a straight wing. [Figure 5-8]

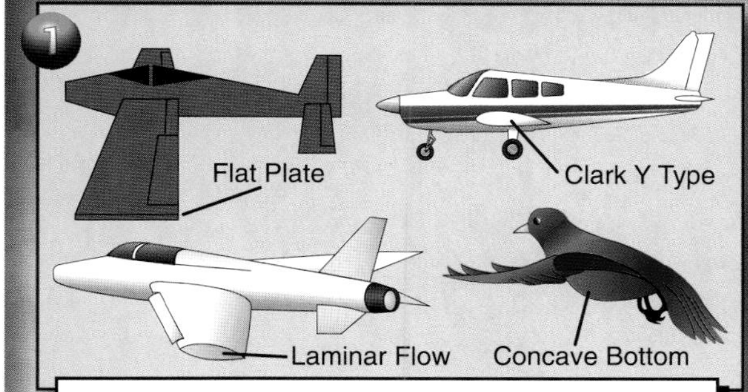

1
Flat Plate
Clark Y Type
Laminar Flow
Concave Bottom

You can begin designing the airplane by discussing with your student the advantages and disadvantages of various wing shapes. For example, the concave bottom produces the most amount of lift, but is generally not suited for high-speed flight.

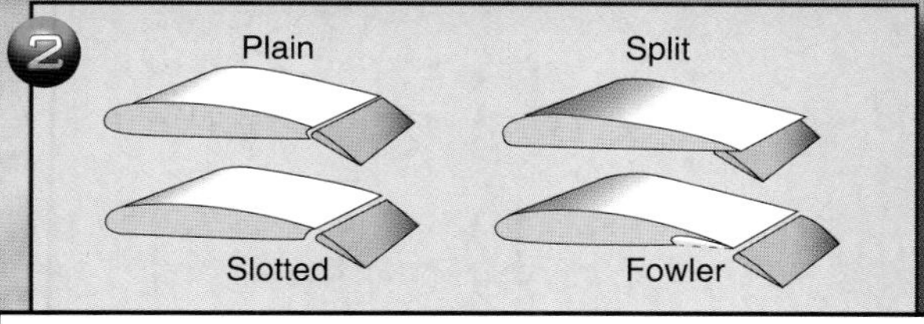

2
Plain
Split
Slotted
Fowler

Next, you can move into flap types. Discuss the advantages and disadvantages that flaps provide. It might be advantageous to not incorporate flaps into your design. For example, some areobatic and military airplanes do not have flaps because of the weight-saving advantage. Heavy jet transports typically have very complicated flap systems to give them desirable flight characteristics at low airspeeds.

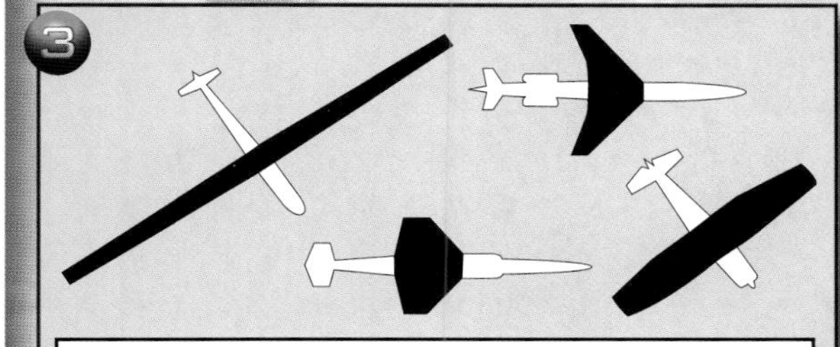

3

Then, you can discuss wing planforms. The discussion may include items like stall patterns associated with various planforms, and aspect ratio. For example, discuss why a glider has a long, thin wing and a fighter has a relatively short, stubby wing.

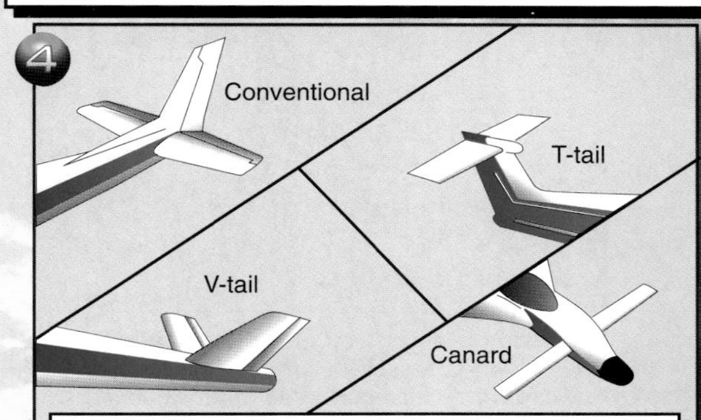

4
Conventional
T-tail
V-tail
Canard

Lastly, you can cover different tail configurations. For instance, point out why a canard has certain benefits over an airplane with a conventional tail.

Figure 5-8. Before you begin this exercise with your student, make sure you emphasize that airplanes are designed to perform distinct functions efficiently within specific flight regimes. For example, a delta wing would probably make a poor planform design for a basic training airplane, due to its poor stall and slow flight characteristics.

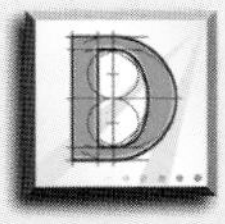

Flyboy

Scientists have begun to discover that flies and other airborne insects have a very interesting method of producing lift. Through the use of wind tunnels and robots that simulate the motion of insect wings, researchers have determined that bugs produce lift very differently than airplanes.

A moth in flight tilts its wings steeply forward . . .

before a downstroke,

then it tilts its wings backward . . .

before an upstroke.

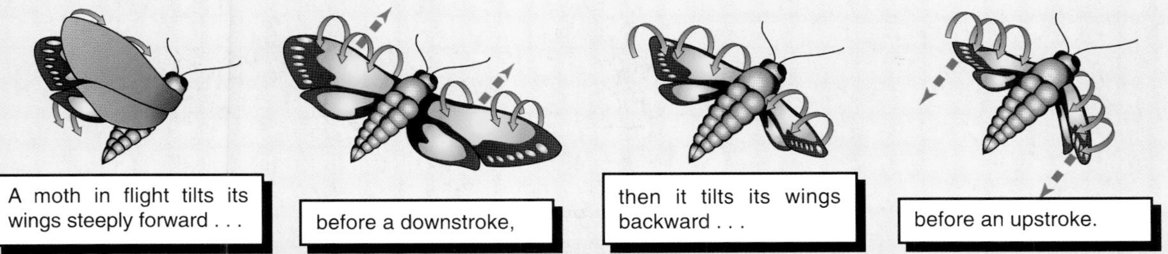

The motion of flapping insect wings produces a vortex along the wings' leading edge, which creates the majority of lift. The vortex then spirals outward, toward the tip of the wings. This spiraling motion keeps the vortex from detaching from the wing.

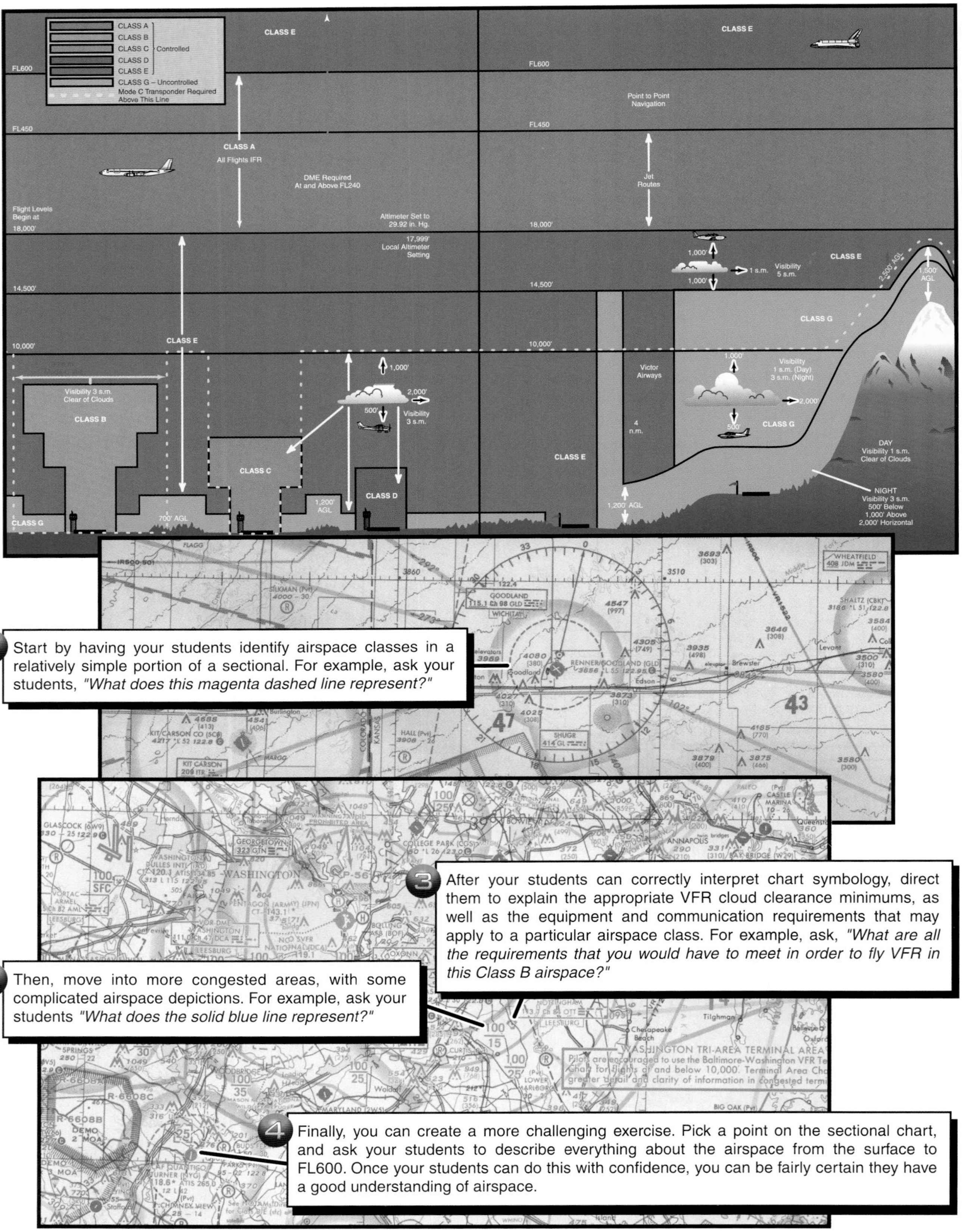

1. Start by having your students identify airspace classes in a relatively simple portion of a sectional. For example, ask your students, *"What does this magenta dashed line represent?"*

2. Then, move into more congested areas, with some complicated airspace depictions. For example, ask your students *"What does the solid blue line represent?"*

3. After your students can correctly interpret chart symbology, direct them to explain the appropriate VFR cloud clearance minimums, as well as the equipment and communication requirements that may apply to a particular airspace class. For example, ask, *"What are all the requirements that you would have to meet in order to fly VFR in this Class B airspace?"*

4. Finally, you can create a more challenging exercise. Pick a point on the sectional chart, and ask your students to describe everything about the airspace from the surface to FL600. Once your students can do this with confidence, you can be fairly certain they have a good understanding of airspace.

Figure 5-9. When describing airspace to students, using a sectional chart in conjunction with an airspace diagram can be an effective teaching tool.

DESCRIBING AIRSPACE

Due to the complexity of modern airspace, new students can sometimes be overwhelmed. It takes most private students a fair amount of instruction and study to feel fully comfortable with this subject. Students often have no relevant experiences to help them understand airspace classification, and the concept is difficult for some students to grasp since airspace dimensions are invisible. For example, your students cannot look up in the sky and determine what kind of airspace they are standing in. Your students must be able to decipher charted symbols and correlate their actual position with their location on the chart.

Before you begin a lesson on airspace, have a plan of how to present the subject. You might find it useful to begin with the least restrictive airspace and work up to the most restrictive. For example, beginning with Class G, cover all the VFR cloud clearance minimums. As you continue to describe each airspace class, add other requirements, such as those for communication and specific equipment, until you finish your discussion with Class A. [Figure 5-9]

Once your students have an understanding of airspace dimensions, you can quiz them while flying. For example, on the way to the practice area, you may ask, *"What airspace class are we in right now?"* or *"What are your VFR cloud clearance minimums?"* Oral quizzing in flight forces your students to maintain situational awareness, in addition to testing their knowledge of airspace.

PRACTICING RADIO PROCEDURES

Teaching radio procedures to private students has many different facets. You may be instructing at a busy controlled airport with jet traffic, or you may be teaching at an uncontrolled airport with a grass runway. Either way, your students need to gain experience and confidence in their radio skills and procedures.

Some of your private students will probably have difficulty learning the radio procedures used in the traffic pattern. There is a lot for your students to concentrate on while they are flying the traffic pattern, and often they simply get overloaded with tasks. An effective and entertaining way for your students to overcome this problem is to create a practice traffic pattern. [Figure 5-10]

Figure 5-10. By laying out a rectangle on the floor with tape, you can have your students walk along the pattern and recite various radio calls for uncontrolled airports, as well as respond to your sample control tower instructions for controlled airports. This technique is probably best suited to a classroom setting.

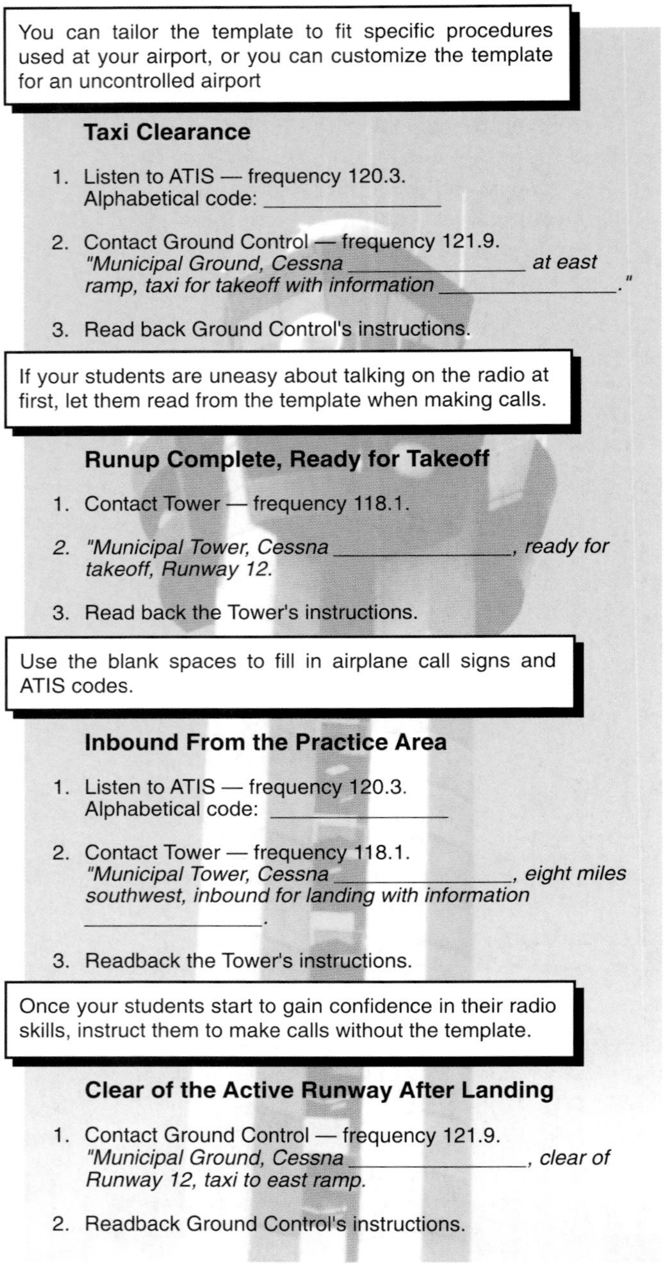

You can tailor the template to fit specific procedures used at your airport, or you can customize the template for an uncontrolled airport

Taxi Clearance

1. Listen to ATIS — frequency 120.3.
   Alphabetical code: ________________
2. Contact Ground Control — frequency 121.9.
   "Municipal Ground, Cessna ________________ at east ramp, taxi for takeoff with information ________________."
3. Read back Ground Control's instructions.

If your students are uneasy about talking on the radio at first, let them read from the template when making calls.

Runup Complete, Ready for Takeoff

1. Contact Tower — frequency 118.1.
2. *"Municipal Tower, Cessna ________________, ready for takeoff, Runway 12.*
3. Read back the Tower's instructions.

Use the blank spaces to fill in airplane call signs and ATIS codes.

Inbound From the Practice Area

1. Listen to ATIS — frequency 120.3.
   Alphabetical code: ________________
2. Contact Tower — frequency 118.1.
   "Municipal Tower, Cessna ________________, eight miles southwest, inbound for landing with information ________________.
3. Readback the Tower's instructions.

Once your students start to gain confidence in their radio skills, instruct them to make calls without the template.

Clear of the Active Runway After Landing

1. Contact Ground Control — frequency 121.9.
   "Municipal Ground, Cessna ________________, clear of Runway 12, taxi to east ramp.
2. Readback Ground Control's instructions.

Training at a controlled airport presents some additional challenges for your students. For many private students, learning how to communicate with ATC is a daunting task. Some students are so focused on using the correct phraseology they lose sight of the message they are trying to communicate. Others may be afraid of saying something wrong and aggravating the controller. Whether or not you are operating from an airport with a control tower, there are some teaching techniques you can use to help your students gain confidence in their radio communication skills.

Suggest your students listen to the tower or CTAF frequency on the ground as a good way to learn radio procedures. Not only is a handheld radio a great tool for this, it is certainly beneficial to have in the event of a radio malfunction in flight. [Figure 5-11]

Figure 5-11. You can create a radio phraseology template that your students can use to study at home.

When teaching radio procedures, you should avoid the temptation to help your students too much. For instance, when students miss a radio transmission from ATC, you should have them call back for clarification, rather than relying on you to answer. Even though this may seem unproductive, remember you are not always going to be in the airplane to help your students. Teach your students to anticipate what calls ATC is going to make. For example, when you call inbound to the airport, standard procedure may be to *"report three miles out, expect left downwind."* Another effective teaching method involves you playing the role of ATC and asking your students to provide responses. Give them some unusual calls and scenarios to see if they answer properly. Finally, stress to your students that they never should accept a clearance that makes them uncomfortable. For instance, ATC may ask your students to land on a runway that has a slight tailwind, in order to expedite departures. The tailwind landing makes your students uncomfortable, yet they may feel compelled to help ATC, and accept the clearance. In this scenario, your students should not accept the clearance and request another runway for landing.

WERE WE CLEARED?

This excerpt from an ASRS report reinforces how important it is for you and your students to maintain situational awareness when operating in a busy traffic pattern.

". . . After approximately 4 touch and goes on Runway 11, my student told me on the upwind that he thought we had not been cleared to land. He was right, we had not been cleared to land, or for the option, for that touch and go. I had completely forgotten and tower said nothing, so I told my student to say nothing over the radio and continue as before. Tower cleared us for the option approaching base on the next landing and the flight continued without further incident. While not too dangerous by itself, our uncleared landing was dangerous considering how busy the airport was. Tower departed 1 aircraft off of Runway 11 while we were on final, another was landing behind us, there was the usual steady stream of airline departures and arrivals on Runway 12R, and several aircraft were stacked up on Runway 12L for departure. Tower simply forgot about that Cessna in the pattern, and we forgot to get cleared to land as we were busy with the difficult patterns and watching for traffic. Not exactly my finest moment as the all powerful, student-mistake-catching CFI.

Fortunately, this report had a happy ending, but as the CFI implied, it could have turned out much worse. With the large amount of diverse traffic operating at airports like this, it is very important that ATC is cognizant of where you are, and what you intend to do.

PREDICTING WEATHER

Students often lack the skills for making **weather predictions** based on weather data and direct observations of weather. Your students should be able to create a basic weather forecast based on atmospheric trends such as pressure, position of highs and lows, and frontal activity. Also, avoid limiting your instruction to certain weather phenomena which dominates your local area. For example, if you fly in San Francisco you would likely teach your students about fog, but you may fail to mention mountain wave activity. A good technique to help your students learn how to predict the effects of major weather systems is to have them monitor national weather patterns. [Figure 5-12]

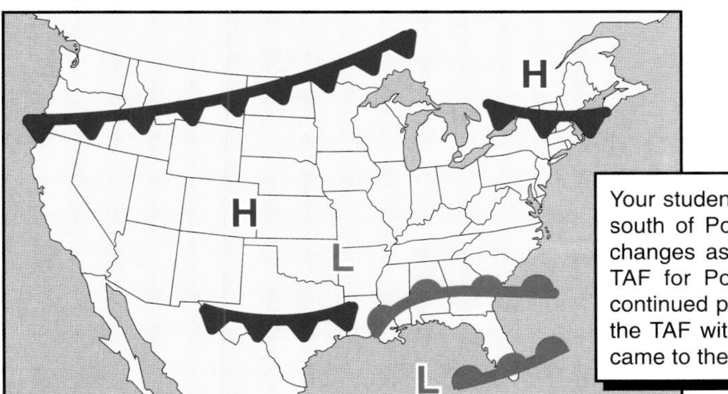

Your students should be able to identify a cold front passing just south of Portland, and be capable of predicting some weather changes associated with a cold front passage. Notice how the TAF for Portland, Oregon (KPDX) is predicting a wind shift, continued precipitation, and strong, gusty winds. You can review the TAF with your students and see how close their predictions came to the TAF.

```
METAR KPDX 011755Z 15022G29KT 1 3/4SM +RA BR BKN016 OVC027
      20/19 A2944 RMK A02 PK WND 16040/1818 TWR VIS 2 1/2 PRESFR
      SLP972 P0030 T02000189

TAF KPDX 011730Z 011818 15030G35KT 4SM OVC040 TEMPO 1819 1SM
      OVC020
      FM1900 27025G30KT P6SM -RA OVC040 TEMP 1820 3SM OVC030
      FM2000 33015KT 3SM RA BR OVC005
      FM0600 34010KT P6SM BKN100 TEMPO 0608 BKN010 3SM -RA
```

Figure 5-12. When a major system moves through an area, your students can predict various flight and ground conditions. As the system progresses, you and your students can compare the actual weather reports with their predictions.

On days when the weather is too poor to fly, you can find some interesting weather reports and forecasts to discuss with your students. Often, these reports contain symbols and abbreviations that are not normally seen on fair weather days. You can create a valuable learning experience for your students by researching unusual weather reports.

TEACHING FARs

Typically, the **Federal Aviation Regulations (FARs)** are not the most exciting and glamorous topic you will teach your private students, but nevertheless, they must have a thorough and complete understanding of the regulations that affect them while flying. Most students are unfamiliar with the nomenclature used in the FARs; therefore, you should begin by explaining the differences between Parts 1, 61, 91, and NTSB 830. You may point out that the FARs are identified by a specific title number (Aeronautics and Space Title 14) within the larger group of rules contained in the Code of Federal Regulations (CFR). Your students may encounter references to regulations which use the abbreviation CFR, such as 14 CFR part 61 or 14 CFR section 91.125. To help your students learn, you can provide them with examples of the FARs at work in day-to-day flight operations. [Figure 5-13]

FAR 91.155 (c) states: Except as provided in 91.157, no person may operate an aircraft beneath the ceiling under VFR within the lateral boundaries of controlled airspace designated to the surface for an airport when the ceiling is less than 1,000 feet.

FAR 91.155 (d) states: Except as provided in 91.157 of this part, no person may take off or land an aircraft, or enter the traffic pattern of an airport, under VFR, within the lateral boundaries of the surface areas of Class B, Class C, Class D, or Class E airspace designated for an airport —

(1) Unless ground visibility at that airport is at least 3 statute miles; or

(2) If ground visibility is not reported at that airport, unless flight visibility during landing or takeoff, or while operating in the traffic pattern is at least 3 statute miles.

Figure 5-13. If you teach at a controlled airport, your students may notice the airport beacon on during the day, which usually signifies that the ceiling is less than 1,000 feet and/or the visibility is less than 3 statute miles. So, where can your students find information explaining the ceiling and visibility requirements of 1,000 and 3?

CALCULATING PERFORMANCE DATA

Some CFIs incorporate the use of performance charts into one or two lessons, and then the subject is abandoned until preparations begin for the practical test. This tends to give the impression that performance calculations are not important to the safety of each flight. A better technique is to require your students to arrive at every lesson with at least takeoff and landing distance calculations for the flight. This not only illustrates the importance of calculating performance data, but it also gives your students realistic practice using the charts. When teaching the use of performance charts, provide examples based on the actual flying your student plans to do. For example, if your student intends to fly to high-elevation airports, create scenarios that illustrate the effects of high-density altitude on aircraft performance.

Failure to calculate **performance data** properly can have dire consequences, especially when operating in high-density altitude conditions, or when the airplane is operated

near maximum weight. This point can be illustrated by having your student analyze an accident or incident scenario where neglecting to obtain performance data was determined to be a contributing factor. While the NTSB reports are excellent tools, you may also elect to create your own scenarios. [Figure 5-14]

Figure 5-14. You can use the following example as a guideline for presenting a realistic situation that emphasizes the importance of using aircraft performance data. Ask your students to determine the cause of the accident by calculating takeoff distance under the flight conditions given.

During initial climb, a Cessna 172 crashed into trees 60 feet in height after departing a grass strip of 2,100 feet in length. An investigation of the events leading to this accident revealed that the pilot took off with a 5-knot tailwind, the temperature was 95°F (35°C), and the pressure altitude was 4,900 feet. In addition, the airplane was loaded 35 pounds over the maximum certificated takeoff weight.

PLANNING CROSS-COUNTRY FLIGHTS

Cross-country flight planning requires your students to utilize much of the aeronautical knowledge they have acquired throughout their training. In order for your students to successfully plan a cross-country, they must be competent in many areas, including reading weather reports, calculating aircraft performance, knowledge of FARs, and chart interpretation.

Some students may have trouble visualizing the cross-country planning process. As a result, they tend to get confused about the planning sequence to which they need to adhere. For example, your students must obtain winds aloft values before they can compute groundspeeds and headings. [Figure 5-15]

CROSS-COUNTRY FLIGHT PLANNING

a. DETERMINE COURSE LINE
   1. Draw course line.
   2. Determine true course.
   3. Measure total distance.

b. DETERMINE ALTITUDE
   1. True course + or - variation gives magnetic course (east is least, west is best).
   2. Select altitude based on VFR cruising altitude rules and terrain.

c. PERFORMANCE
   1. Determine TAS and fuel burn from cruise performance chart.
   2. Determine level-off point, fuel used in climb, time to level-off point.
   3. Determine takeoff and landing distances.
   4. Perform weight and balance for departure and arrival.

d. CURRENT SECTIONAL CHART
   1. Mark level-off point.
   2. Mark remaining checkpoints.
   3. Measure distance between checkpoints.

e. CALL FSS FOR A STANDARD WEATHER BREIFING
   1. Determine wind correction angle.
   2. Determine ground speed.
   3. Determine ETE between checkpoints.
   4. Determine fuel burn between checkpoints.

f. AIRPORT INFORMATION
   1. Find runway lengths (A/FD).
   2. Determine traffic pattern directions.
   3. Find applicable frequencies.
   4. Read all airport remarks.

Figure 5-15. You can develop a checklist for your students to follow when they plan cross-country flights. Using this method ensures your students complete the planning in the proper order and accomplish all the necessary steps.

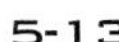

PRIVATE PILOT AERONAUTICAL DECISION MAKING

From the first lesson, you should strive to make your private students aware of **aeronautical-decision-making (ADM)** principles, and you should have them routinely practice their judgment skills just as they would maneuvers and procedures. For example, you can require your students to obtain a weather briefing before each lesson and determine whether the flight can be completed safely. In addition, during ground lessons, you can describe to your students situations they may encounter as pilots and ask them to make choices regarding these scenarios.

Consider creating a file which contains a wide variety of ADM scenarios you have written, as well as appropriate NTSB and ASRS reports. Determine to which phase of pilot training each account applies and label the example appropriately. This way you have a valuable resource available at each lesson. You may even provide your students with copies of the scenarios and ask them to evaluate the situations as study assignments. [Figure 5-16]

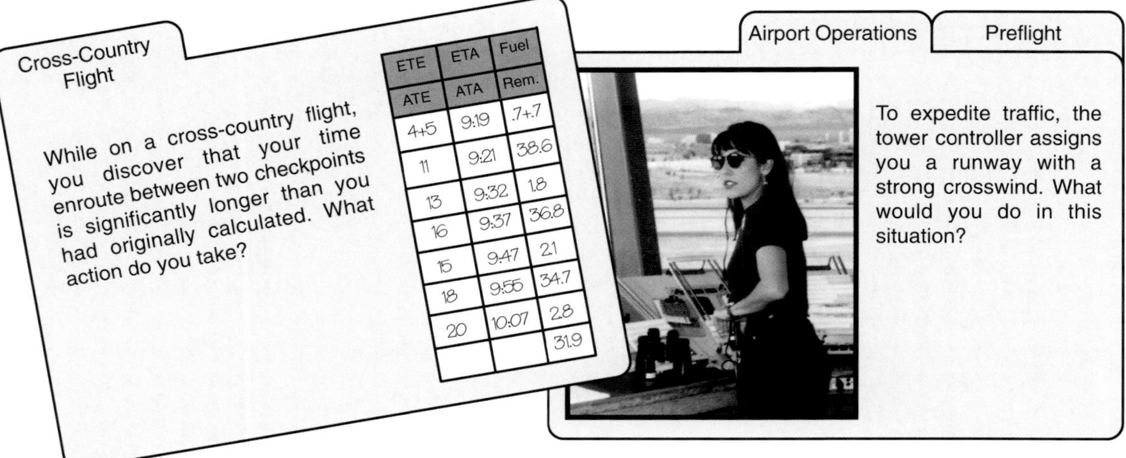

Figure 5-16. To enable your students to practice aeronautical decision making throughout their course of training, present specific scenarios which apply to each subject area you introduce.

SUMMARY CHECKLIST

- ✓ By providing your students with knowledge of airplane systems from the beginning of their training, you may be able to alleviate some of their fears about the safety of aircraft.
- ✓ You can relate certain airplane components to systems and equipment with which your students may already be familiar.
- ✓ Knowing how to troubleshoot problems can be considered the correlation phase of learning aircraft systems.
- ✓ Using a cut-away drawing or model can help students with a limited understanding of powerplants comprehend what is actually happening inside the engine.
- ✓ Make sure your students are familiar with the system schematics for the airplane they fly.

- ✓ Try to incorporate a model airplane and illustrations into your aerodynamics lessons.
- ✓ Explain to your students that there is more to creating lift than Bernoulli's principle. Newton's third law, which states for every action there is an equal and opposite reaction, also has a place in describing the generation of lift.
- ✓ Creating an exercise that enables students to design their own airplane can be an effective way to foster their interest in aerodynamics.
- ✓ Before you begin a lesson on airspace, have a plan of how to present the subject. You might find it useful to begin a lesson that covers airspace by describing the least restrictive airspace first and then work up to the most restrictive.
- ✓ When describing airspace to students, using a sectional chart in conjunction with an airspace diagram can be an effective teaching tool.
- ✓ Oral quizzing in flight forces your students to maintain situational awareness, in addition to testing their knowledge of airspace.
- ✓ Creating a practice traffic pattern is an effective and entertaining way for your students to overcome the difficulty of learning radio procedures in the airport environment.
- ✓ Suggest your students listen to the tower or CTAF frequency on the ground as a good way to learn radio procedures.
- ✓ You can create a radio phraseology template that your students can use to study radio procedures at home.
- ✓ An effective method for teaching radio procedures involves you playing the role of ATC and asking your students to provide responses.
- ✓ Try not to help your student too much when they are learning radio procedures. Your students may begin to rely on you if they miss radio transmissions.
- ✓ Your students should be able to create a basic weather forecast based on direct observations of weather and atmospheric trends such as pressure, position of highs and lows, and frontal activity.
- ✓ A good technique to help your students learn how to predict the effects of major weather systems is to have them monitor national weather patterns.
- ✓ Students must have a thorough and complete understanding of the Federal Aviation Regulations (FARs) that affect them while flying. Begin by explaining the differences between Parts 1, 61, 91, and NTSB 830.
- ✓ You may point out that the FARs are identified by a specific title number (Aeronautics and Space Title 14) within the larger group of rules contained in the Code of Federal Regulations (CFR).
- ✓ Requiring your students to arrive at every lesson with at least takeoff and landing distance calculations for the flight not only illustrates the importance of calculating performance data, but also gives your students realistic practice using the charts.
- ✓ When teaching the use of performance charts, provide examples based on the actual flying your student plans to do.

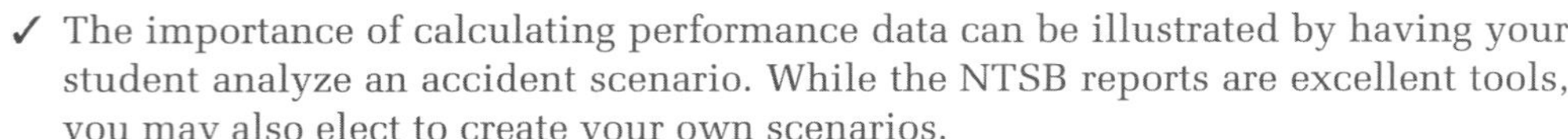

- ✓ The importance of calculating performance data can be illustrated by having your student analyze an accident scenario. While the NTSB reports are excellent tools, you may also elect to create your own scenarios.
- ✓ You can develop a checklist to ensure your students complete cross-country planning in the proper order and accomplish all the necessary steps.
- ✓ To enable your students to practice aeronautical decision making throughout their course of training, present specific scenarios which apply to each subject area you introduce.
- ✓ Consider creating a file which contains a wide variety of ADM scenarios you have written, as well as appropriate NTSB and ASRS reports.

KEY TERMS

Airplane Systems

Aerodynamics

Airspace

Radio Procedures

Weather Predictions

Federal Aviation Regulations (FARs)

Performance Data

Cross-Country Flight Planning

Aeronautical Decision Making (ADM)

QUESTIONS

1. Describe at least two techniques you can use to teach your students about aircraft systems.
2. Why is it important that students gain an in-depth knowledge of their airplane's systems.
3. List at least two aircraft design features that your students can learn about if they participate in an exercise to design their own airplane.
4. Select the true statement regarding teaching airspace to private students.
   - A. Using a sectional chart in conjunction with an airspace diagram can be an effective teaching tool.
   - B. Most private students have relevant experiences that help them to understand airspace classification.
   - C. Oral quizzing during flight is not an effective way to help your students understand airspace.
5. Describe two methods that you can use to help your students learn radio procedures.
6. True/False. So as not to confuse your students, you should limit your discussions regarding weather to conditions prevalent in your local area.
7. Explain how an accident or incident scenario can help you emphasize the importance of aircraft performance calculations to your students.
8. What is one way you can teach your students on the ground about ADM principles which apply to flight operations?

SECTION B
BUILDING FLIGHT SKILLS

INSTRUCTING THE STUDENT PILOT

This section is designed to provide you with techniques to help you instruct students who are pursuing private pilot certificates. Teaching student pilots how to control an airplane with precision and skill is challenging as well as extremely rewarding. You may remember your initial flight training, and the tremendous feelings of satisfaction and accomplishment you gained each time you mastered a new maneuver. You may also recall some anxiety and frustration as you were introduced to certain procedures. Keep these recollections in mind as you prepare to teach student pilots. Your students likely will experience a similar sense of achievement as well as some of the same concerns that you had as a student pilot.

This section is not intended to explain private pilot ground and flight operations in the detail required for a student to master each maneuver and procedure. Rather, it is designed as a guideline for instructing student pilots which provides you with examples of specific teaching techniques, common student errors, and tips to help you make your students' flight training a positive experience. For specific information on private pilot knowledge and step-by-step descriptions of private pilot maneuvers,consult the Guided Flight Discovery *Private Pilot Manual* and the *Private Pilot Maneuvers Manual* respectively.

INTRODUCING GROUND OPERATIONS

Your students are exposed to **ground operations** early in the training process. Some of the first operations they learn are performing a preflight inspection, starting the engine, taxiing, accomplishing the before takeoff check, and completing postflight procedures. When first learning to refer to checklists during ground operations, students may have difficulty locating various items in the cockpit, such as the primer or the suction gauge. A good technique to alleviate this problem is to recommend your students sit in the airplane on their own time to simulate following the checklists. You may also suggest they include notes or additional items on the standard checklist to help them recall the correct procedures. [Figure 5-17]

Figure 5-17. When operating from a high-elevation airport, the mixture is typically leaned for taxi operations to prevent spark plug fouling. Students may forget this procedure unless it is added to their checklist.

During engine start, make sure your students are very careful about clearing the area around the airplane, and instruct them to turn on the airplane's anti-collision lights to signify the engine is running. Make certain you discuss the dangers of hand propping with your students. Point out to your students that this procedure is rarely necessary since safer alternatives normally exist, such as using an external power source, enlisting the assistance of a maintenance technician, requesting another rental airplane, or simply canceling the flight. Emphasize that they must never attempt to turn the propeller by hand to start the engine, unless they have received instruction on the correct procedure and a qualified pilot is at the controls.

As your students begin to taxi the airplane, make sure they perform a brake check immediately after the airplane begins to move. During taxi some students tend to ride the brakes, which can lead to excessive wear and overheating. It is better to control the speed during taxi with the power. Since your students need to have their hands on the yoke to practice proper crosswind taxi techniques, they are often tempted to try to steer the airplane with the yoke. This is a common student error and should be corrected early in the flight training process.

You must teach students about some of the basic taxiway and runway markings as early as the first lesson. Experience with markings found on roads may both hinder and help your students learn about airport markings. For example, your students may initially attempt to taxi the airplane to the right side of the taxiway, so you must ensure they are vigilant about keeping the nosewheel on the centerline. In other circumstances, you can use your students' familiarity with road markings to your advantage. [Figure 5-18]

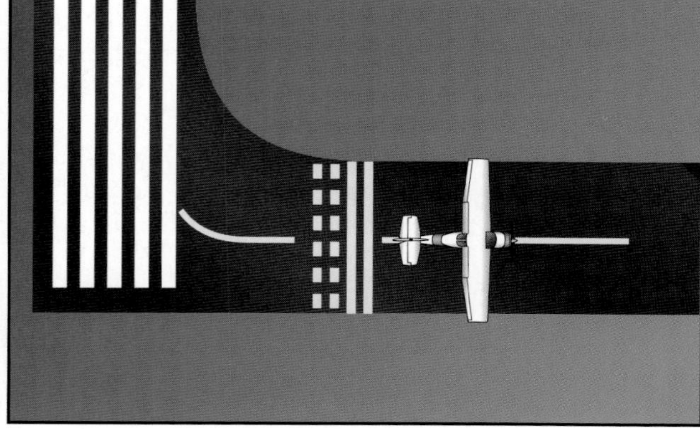

Figure 5-18. The use of hold lines can be a confusing subject for new students to grasp. A good analogy to use when explaining this important airport marking is the centerline painted on most roads. They may cross a dashed line, but not a solid line.

TEACHING PRIVATE PILOT MANEUVERS

Student pilots gain proficiency and confidence in their piloting skills by practicing **private pilot maneuvers**. Your students first learn the most basic tasks such as straight-and-level flight, climbs, descents, and turns. Then they build upon those skills by performing maneuvers, such as slow flight, stalls, and steep turns, until they are able to operate the airplane competently by themselves.

LOCATING THE PRACTICE AREA

Typically, flight schools have an area designated for refining maneuvers, usually referred to as the **practice area**. Early in their flight training, you should introduce your students to the location of the practice area, as well as explain safety considerations associated with this area. Be sure to show your students any significant landmarks and reporting points associated with the practice area. They should know exactly where the practice area is in relation to the airport, and where the boundaries of this area are located. To further enhance your students' familiarity with the practice area, you can use a street map to find roads that may not be depicted on an aviation chart. Also, take into account any IFR approach and holding procedures, as well as enroute operations on Victor airways that may take place in the area.

Stress to your students the importance of collision avoidance in the practice area, since numerous training flights may be operating simultaneously. Also, you and your students should be vigilant while flying between the airport and the practice area, as this route can sometimes be congested with training flights.

Although most practice areas are situated over sparsely populated locations, you still need to be cognizant of the minimum safe altitude rules stipulated in the FARs, especially when practicing ground reference maneuvers. Altitudes for performing maneuvers are specified in the Private Pilot PTS. For example, slow flight, stalls, and steep turns must be completed by 1,500 feet AGL and ground reference maneuvers should be entered at 600 to 1,000 feet AGL. In addition, most general aviation airports that are in or near populated areas have noise abatement procedures that should be adhered to while traveling between the airport and the practice area. [Figure 5-19]

Figure 5-19. Keep in mind noise abatement while operating in the practice area. For example, try not to use a farmhouse as a reference point for turns around a point. The intersection of two isolated roads is a better choice.

PERFORMING BASIC MANEUVERS

Your students will begin to grasp fundamental airplane control concepts by performing the **basic maneuvers**: straight-and-level flight, climbs, descents, and turns. These four maneuvers form the foundation of the development of all piloting skills. Each flight maneuver, regardless of its complexity, is composed of combinations of the basic maneuvers. Your students must master these maneuvers before proceeding to more challenging procedures.

Since establishing the proper airplane attitude is routine to you, it may be easy to forget that you need to point out to beginning students the visual and instrument references they should use to perform basic maneuvers. Most students do not automatically refer to the horizon as an indicator of aircraft attitude and they may not associate changes in the nose's position relative to the horizon as significant. In addition, interpreting the instrument indications will be completely unfamiliar to most beginning students. [Figure 5-20]

Figure 5-20. You can use several techniques to effectively teach the basic maneuvers.

Practicing airspeed changes by increasing or decreasing the power provides an excellent means of developing proficiency in straight-and-level flight at various speeds. Students must learn that significant changes in airspeed will require changes in pitch attitude and trim to maintain altitude.

To demonstrate the effects of torque and P-factor, ask your students to raise the nose of the airplane to a climb attitude with their feet off the rudder pedals.

Introduce partial power descents first and then teach your students to perform power-off glides.

When teaching turns, observe your students' posture. Initially your students may lean away from the turn in an attempt to remain upright in relation to the ground, rather than ride with the airplane. Ensure your students are using a reference point directly in front of them instead of using the center of the nose, and point out how the nose attitude appears different in left and right turns. Your students may attempt to compensate for parallax error, which causes the nose to appear to rise when making left turns and appear to descend when making right turns. For example, students may dive during left turns and use excessive back pressure on the yoke while performing right turns. [Figure 5-21]

During level turns in side-by-side airplanes, students often dive during left turns since the nose appears to be rising during entry.

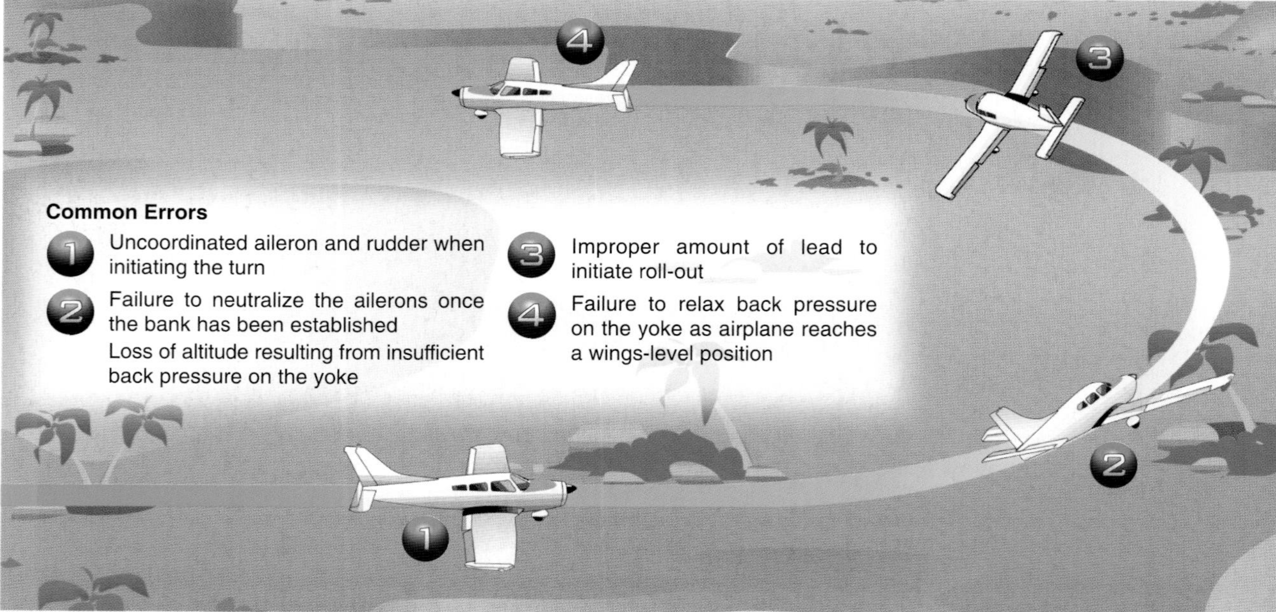

Figure 5-21. If turning errors are not corrected during the early stages of flight training, students will continue to have problems as they are introduced to more complex maneuvers.

One of the most common errors that new students exhibit during the first phases of flight training is fixating on the flight instruments. Your students must learn to use the natural horizon as the primary attitude reference, while cross-checking the instruments and scanning for traffic. In addition, new students often have difficulty using the trim properly. Some students use the trim wheel to fly the airplane, while others must be constantly reminded to relieve control pressures. [Figure 5-22]

Figure 5-22. An effective way for students to remember the proper sequence for using trim is the abbreviation for apartment — APT. For example, for your students to transition to a climb from straight-and-level flight, they establish the proper pitch attitude, simultaneously set climb power, and finally adjust the trim to relieve control pressures.

PERFORMING FLIGHT MANEUVERS

When your students begin to gain confidence and proficiency in the basic maneuvers, you should introduce the **flight maneuvers**: slow flight, power-off stalls, power-on stalls, demonstration stalls, and steep turns. These flight maneuvers continue to challenge and enhance your students' piloting ability.

MANEUVERING DURING SLOW FLIGHT

Slow flight can be broadly defined as flight at an airspeed below the normal cruise speed. However, the speed used for the private pilot practical test, $1.2V_{S1}$, is sufficiently slow so that any significant reduction in speed or power, or increase in load factor, results in stall indications. You should have your students practice maneuvering at this speed, as well as at airspeeds and in configurations which are encountered during takeoffs, climbs, descents, go-arounds, and approaches to landing.

The primary purpose of practicing operations at reduced airspeed is to enable your students to become familiar with appropriate control techniques, and the rapidity with which control effectiveness can be lost.

For slow flight training to be most effective, it is important your students understand why they are practicing this maneuver. The primary purpose of teaching slow flight is to familiarize your students with the appropriate control techniques for flight at slow airspeeds, and learn how rapidly control effectiveness can be lost. Performing slow flight prepares your students for flying at reduced speeds, including the airspeeds appropriate for landing approaches. In addition, by being able to recognize the sounds and visual cues associated with the airplane at slow airspeeds, the chance of inadvertently entering a stall is decreased. [Figure 5-23]

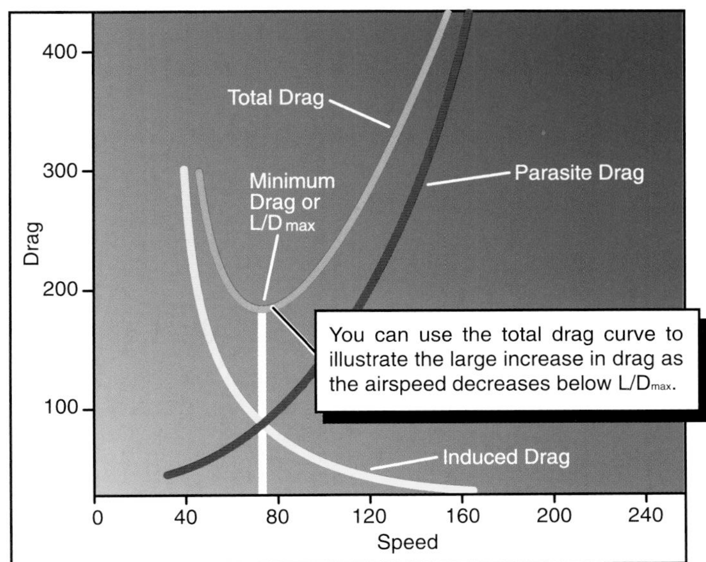

Figure 5-23. It can be helpful to discuss the drag curve when introducing slow flight. You can also use this diagram to illustrate why it is dangerous to get low and slow on final approach.

During a demonstration of slow flight, you should point out the loss of control effectiveness due to the reduced velocity of the airflow over the control surfaces. Students may have difficulty maintaining coordinated flight due to the large rudder displacement needed to overcome left-turning tendencies. When stabilized in straight-and-level flight at the specified slow flight airspeed, ask your students to perform shallow turns, climbs (if possible), and descents. Some common errors associated with slow flight include not enough rudder correction, too much bank angle in turns, and maintaining an airspeed faster than recommended.

Performing slow flight prepares your students for flying at reduced speeds, including the airspeeds appropriate for landing approaches.

PRACTICING STALLS

Students may be apprehensive about practicing stalls and without a proper explanation from you, they may feel the goal of stall training is to become proficient at performing stalls. Make sure you explain that the objective of this instruction is to enable your students to recognize the cues of an impending stall and initiate proper recovery procedures, if an inadvertent stall occurs. In addition, students may be more enthusiastic about performing stalls if they understand this training helps prepare them for flying the traffic pattern and landing the airplane.

Emphasize to your students that although an airplane can be stalled in any attitude, at any airspeed, and with any power setting, inadvertent stalls are most likely to occur with a nose-high attitude. This unusually high pitch attitude is the most obvious visual cue to an approaching stall. In addition, students should be alerted to other impending stall indications, such as the decrease in tone and sound volume of the airflow and the rapid decay of control effectiveness.

Have your students practice both power-off and power-on stalls straight ahead and in turns. These training sessions will be more effective if your students understand the practical application of the stall practice. You should discuss situations during which inadvertent stalls are most likely to occur. For example, power-off stalls normally are associated with approach to landing situations, such as faulty turns from base to final, while power-on stalls could occur due to a poorly executed go-around, or during takeoff and climbout. [Figure 5-24]

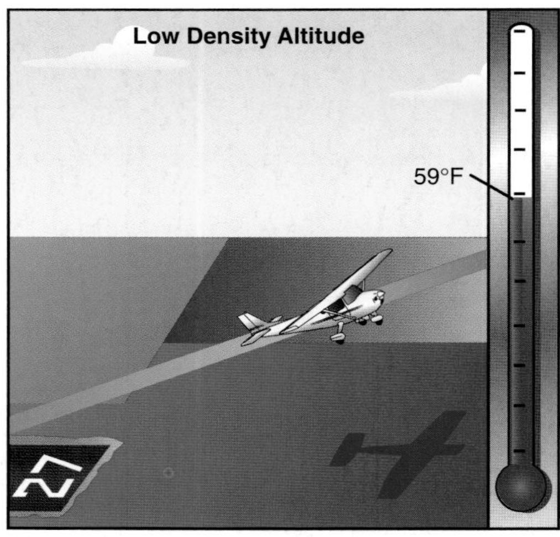

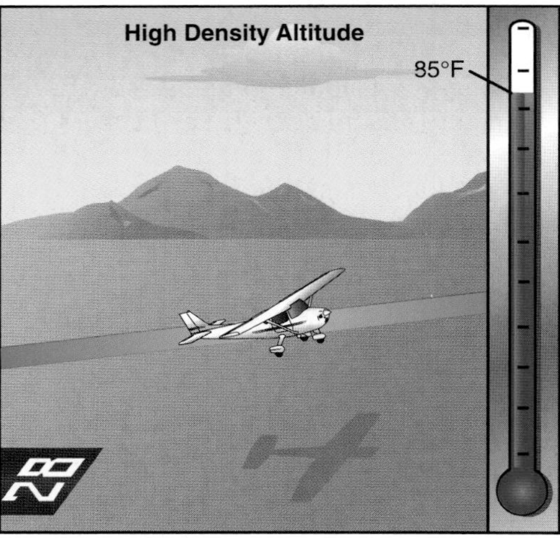

Figure 5-24. At a high density altitude, a flatter pitch may be required during climbout. If your students fail to monitor the airspeed indicator, and maintain the steeper climb pitch they are accustomed to when the air is denser, a power-on stall could occur.

Typically, you may begin stall practice by performing only approaches to stalls, with recovery initiated as soon as the first buffeting or partial loss of control is recognized. In this way, your students can become familiar with the indications of an impending stall without actually stalling the airplane. You may consider initially practicing recovery

without the addition of power. This method places emphasis on the concept that decreasing the angle of attack is the action that enables the airplane to recover from the stall and that power is necessary to maintain altitude or initiate a climb.

After students are comfortable with the feel of the stall and understand the basic recovery procedure, you can ask them to perform stalls in configurations which apply to realistic flight situations. For example, they should initiate power-off stalls from a glide to simulate a landing approach and configure the airplane for landing with full flaps and landing gear extended (if applicable). [Figure 5-25]

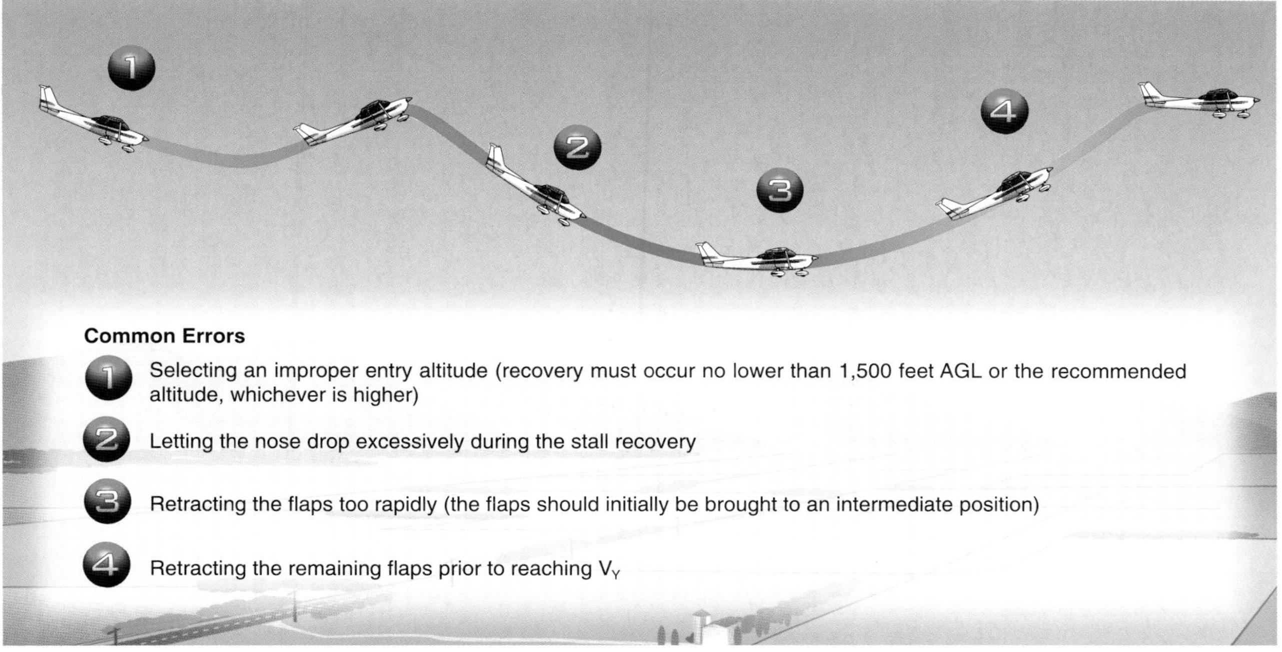

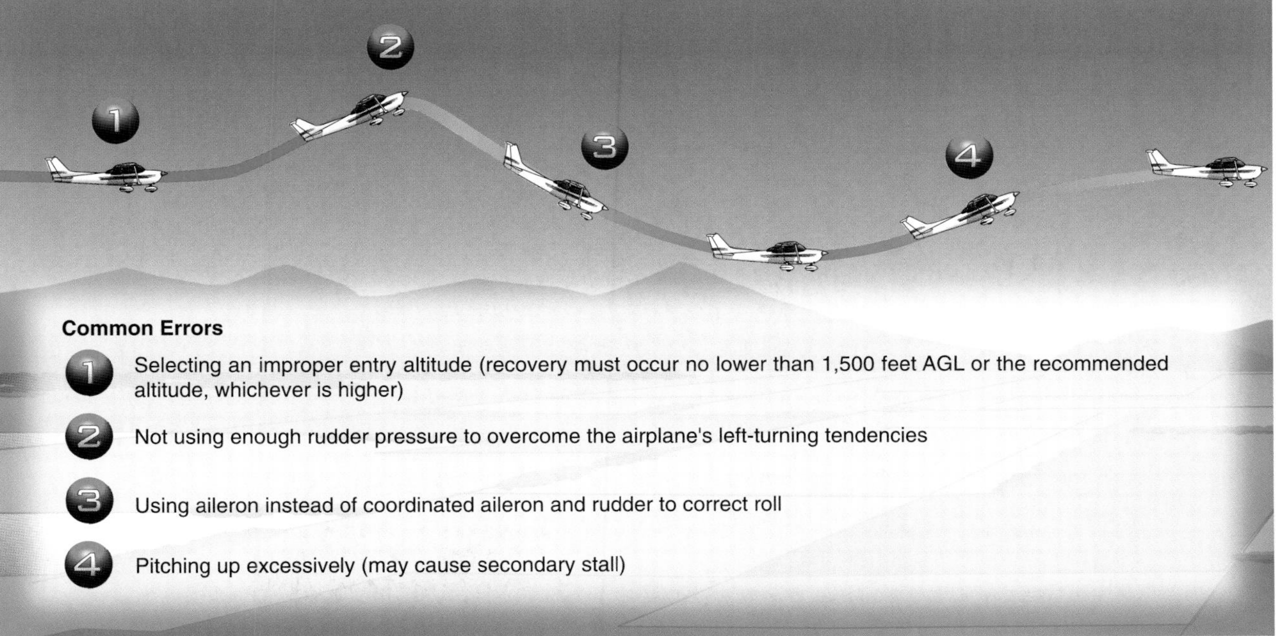

Figure 5-25. Errors in stall recovery can lead to secondary stalls. For example, attempting to recover from a stall and initiate a climb without retracting the flaps or retracting the flaps too quickly are both actions which could lead to a secondary stall.

Demonstration stalls include secondary stalls, accelerated maneuver stalls, crossed-control stalls, and elevator trim stalls. You may demonstrate these stalls to enhance your students' stall/spin awareness, however under no circumstances should students be allowed to practice these maneuvers in solo flight. A more detailed discussion of demonstration stalls can be found in Section F of this chapter, *Preparing Future Flight Instructors*. [Figure 5-26]

The objective of a crossed-control stall demonstration is to show the effect of improper control technique and emphasize the importance of executing coordinated turns.

If your student stalls the airplane in a slipping right turn with insufficient right rudder, the ball is displaced to the right, and the left wing drops, even though the airplane is initially banked to the right.

Figure 5-26. A spin that occurs from a crossed-control situation results in rotation in the same direction as any excessive rudder force, i.e. opposite the displacement of the ball in the inclinometer. Performing a crossed-control stall is a useful way to demonstrate the effect of improper control technique and emphasize the importance of making coordinated turns.

If your student stalls the airplane during a skidding right turn to final, the excessive right rudder displaces the ball to the left, and the right wing drops.

Your students need to have aeronautical knowledge training in stall awareness, spin entry, spins, and spin recovery techniques. It is your decision whether to incorporate spins into your students' flight training. If you do demonstrate spins to your students, be absolutely certain that you are familiar with the spin characteristics of the airplane, and that you are comfortable performing the maneuver.

EXECUTING STEEP TURNS

The objective of performing steep turns is to help your students develop smooth, coordinated control techniques, as well as learn how to maintain orientation, and properly divide their attention. During their practical test, private pilot applicants are required to perform turns in either direction with an angle of bank of 45° ±5°. Steep turns are also required for commercial pilot applicants, however a bank angle of 50° ±5° is used. Since the procedures (other than the bank angle used) and common errors associated with steep turns are the same for both private and commercial students, the primary discussion of steep turns can be found in Section D of this chapter, *Enhancing Flight Skills.*

FLYING GROUND REFERENCE MANEUVERS

Ground reference maneuvers include rectangular courses, S-turns, and turns around a point. Ground reference maneuvers are designed to develop your students' ability to maintain a desired track along the ground by compensating for the effects of the wind. In addition, each of the ground reference maneuvers requires your students to maintain situational awareness by dividing their attention between controlling the airplane and observing ground objects or features. Your students' ability to successfully fly the traffic

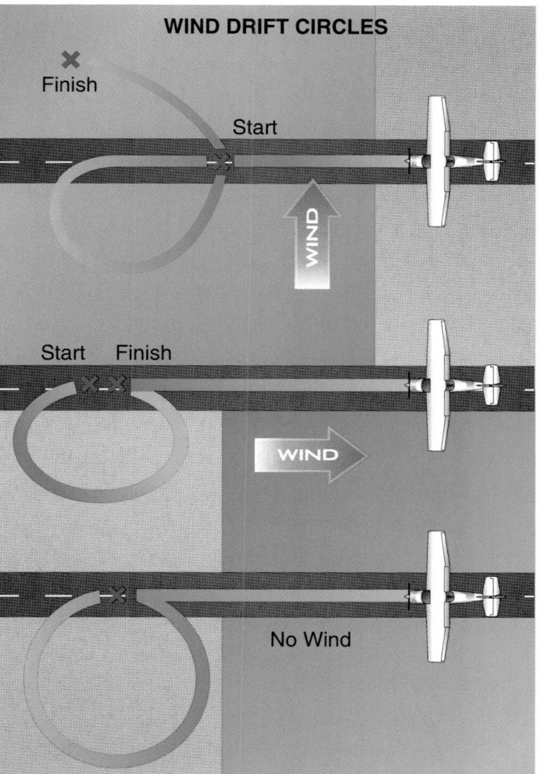

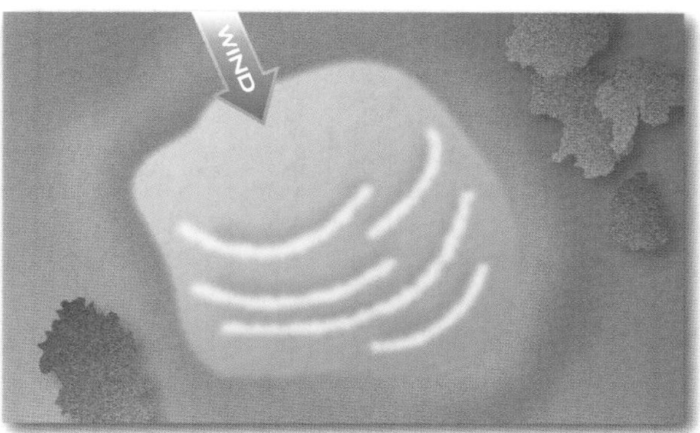

Figure 5-27. Being able to determine the wind direction and velocity is a key element of flying ground reference maneuvers.

pattern and perform accurate landings relies on mastering the skills gained from flying ground reference maneuvers. [Figure 5-27]

Referring to the practical test standards which apply to rectangular courses, S-turns, and turns around a point may help you determine how to teach certain aspects of these maneuvers. For example, the PTS states that all ground reference maneuvers should be performed at an altitude of 600 to 1,000 feet AGL and an emergency landing site must be located within gliding distance. To ensure your students use no more than a 45° bank angle at the steepest point, you should instruct them to begin a turn around a point downwind. In addition, the first turn of each maneuver should be made to the left. [Figure 5-28]

To ensure your students use no more than a 45° bank angle at the steepest point, you should instruct them to begin a turn around a point downwind.

ACCOMPLISHING EMERGENCY PROCEDURES

Whether they apply to a Boeing 737 or a Cessna 152, **emergency procedures** have one common element — control of the airplane must be maintained. When you teach emergency procedures to your students, you should stress that flying the airplane is the first priority.

In an emergency situation, your students need to understand the importance of using a checklist, and they also should know why certain checklist items are accomplished. For example, explain why some POHs call for the doors to be unlatched prior to touchdown during an emergency landing. Also, discuss emergencies and abnormal situations that may not be specifically covered in the POH. For instance, you may ask your students, *"What would you do if the airspeed indicator suddenly went to zero?"* or *"What action would you take if ATC informed you that they were not receiving your transponder signal?"* You should have your students consult the emergency procedures checklists

RECTANGULAR COURSE

Shallowest Bank
No Crab
Crab Left
Crab Right
Steepest Bank
No Crab
WIND
Common Errors
1 Entering the maneuver improperly (enter 45° to the downwind leg, left turns, 600 to 1,000 feet AGL)
2 Improperly judging wind direction and speed
3 Uncoordinated turns
4 Failure to maintain selected altitude and airspeed
5 Improper wind drift correction

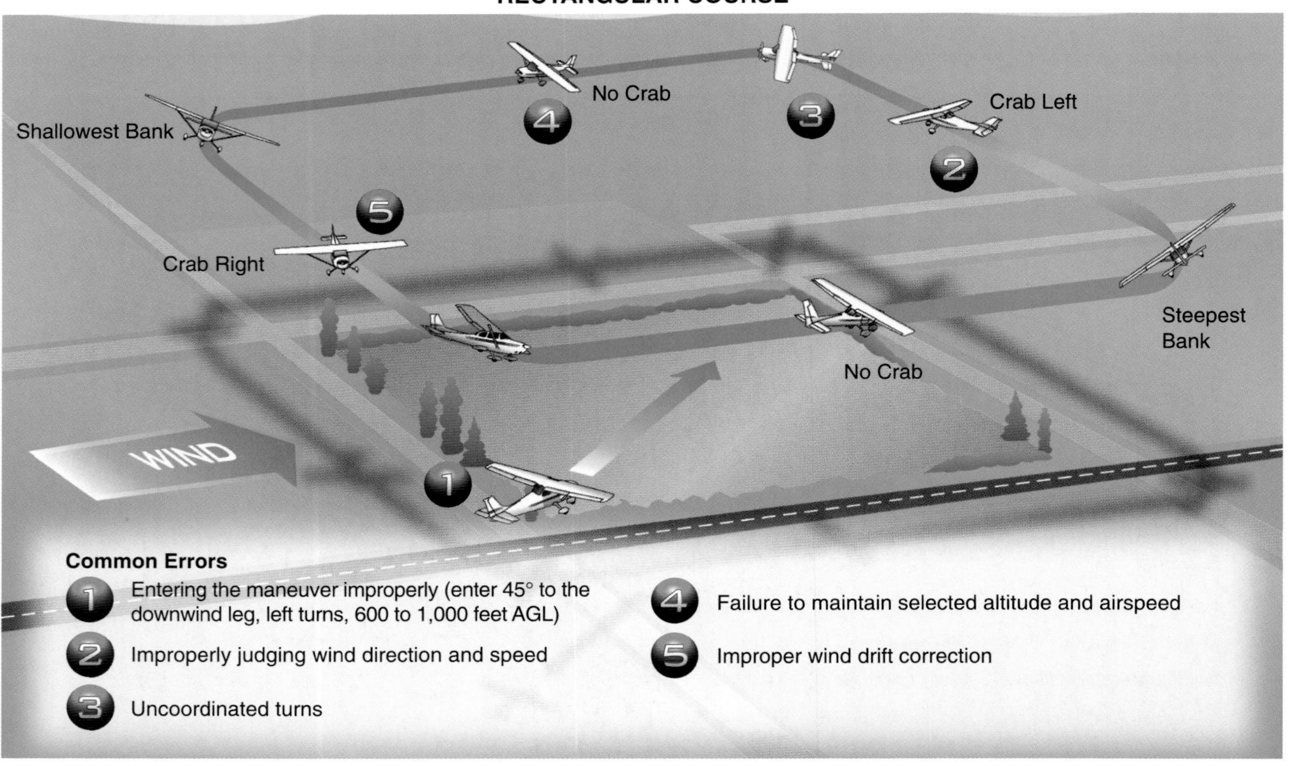

S-TURNS

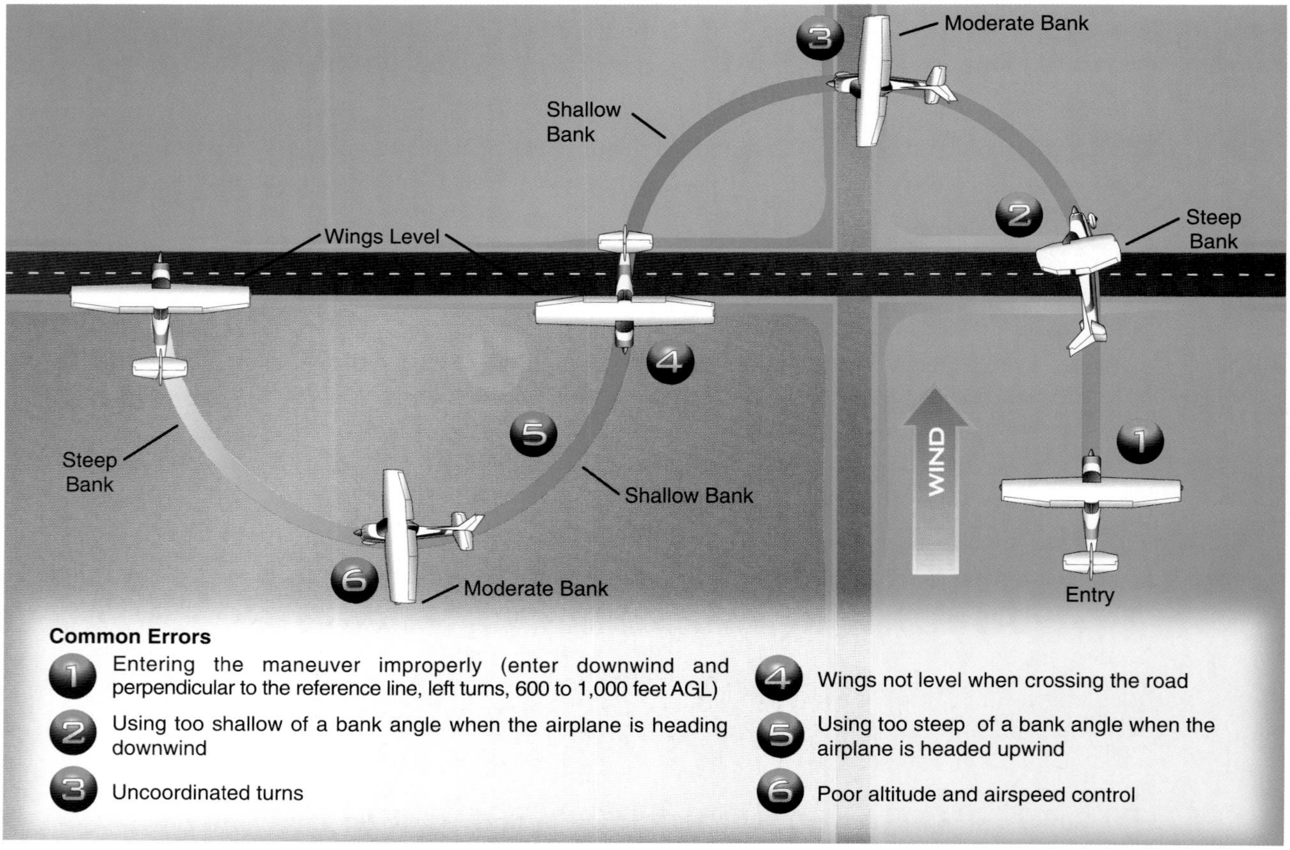

Moderate Bank
Shallow Bank
Steep Bank
Wings Level
WIND
Steep Bank
Shallow Bank
Moderate Bank
Entry
Common Errors
1 Entering the maneuver improperly (enter downwind and perpendicular to the reference line, left turns, 600 to 1,000 feet AGL)
2 Using too shallow of a bank angle when the airplane is heading downwind
3 Uncoordinated turns
4 Wings not level when crossing the road
5 Using too steep of a bank angle when the airplane is headed upwind
6 Poor altitude and airspeed control

Figure 5-28. In addition to the errors shown here, students may have difficulty performing ground reference maneuvers when only a light wind exists. For example, students may automatically change the airplane's bank angle as they have been taught to do when encountering a strong wind.

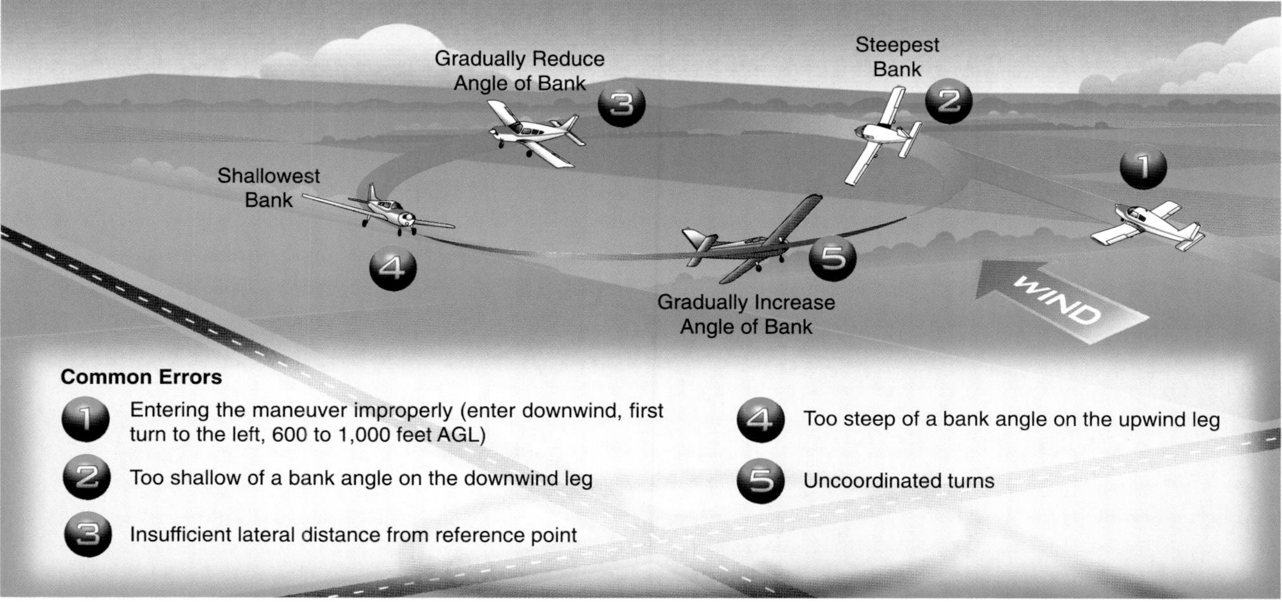

Figure 5-28. Continued.

whenever practical, but during some emergencies your students must react quickly. For instance, your students should memorize the emergency procedures for an engine failure, but not necessarily the procedure for a low voltage light illumination.

Ensure your students are familiar with the lost communication procedures at your airport. For example, many controlled airports have specific actions recommended by ATC, in addition to the standard procedures listed in the FARs. Posing various scenarios to your students can be an effective way to teach them emergency procedures. Oral quizzing keeps your students alert and helps to alleviate complacency. [Figure 5-29]

Figure 5-29. You can test your students' knowledge by posing various emergency situations. Remember that emergencies can also occur on the ground.

CONDUCTING AIRPORT OPERATIONS

Gaining proficiency in **airport operations** can be one of the most challenging and exciting aspects of flight training for student pilots. Most of your students will require a fair amount of time dedicated to mastering traffic patterns, normal takeoffs and landings, and crosswind takeoffs and landings.

OPERATING IN THE TRAFFIC PATTERN

While students are probably familiar with the legs of the traffic pattern by this stage of training, you now need to introduce some of the specific procedures and special considerations which apply to traffic pattern operations, such as emergency procedures.

For example, explain to your students that if a loss of power or engine failure occurs at pattern altitude, they most likely can maneuver the airplane to the runway. However, an engine failure immediately after takeoff is normally survivable only if they land straight ahead with minor deviations around obstacles. They need to understand that, prior to the crosswind leg, it is unlikely they could make it back to the runway, and attempting to do so would dramatically increase the risk of a stall/spin accident that would almost certainly be fatal. To make this point, demonstrate an attempted turn back after simulating an engine failure at a safe altitude in the practice area. Students will quickly see how much altitude is lost during such an attempt. They also should see how rapidly airspeed decays when an engine fails during climb and why they must immediately pitch down to the attitude for best glide speed. [Figure 5-30]

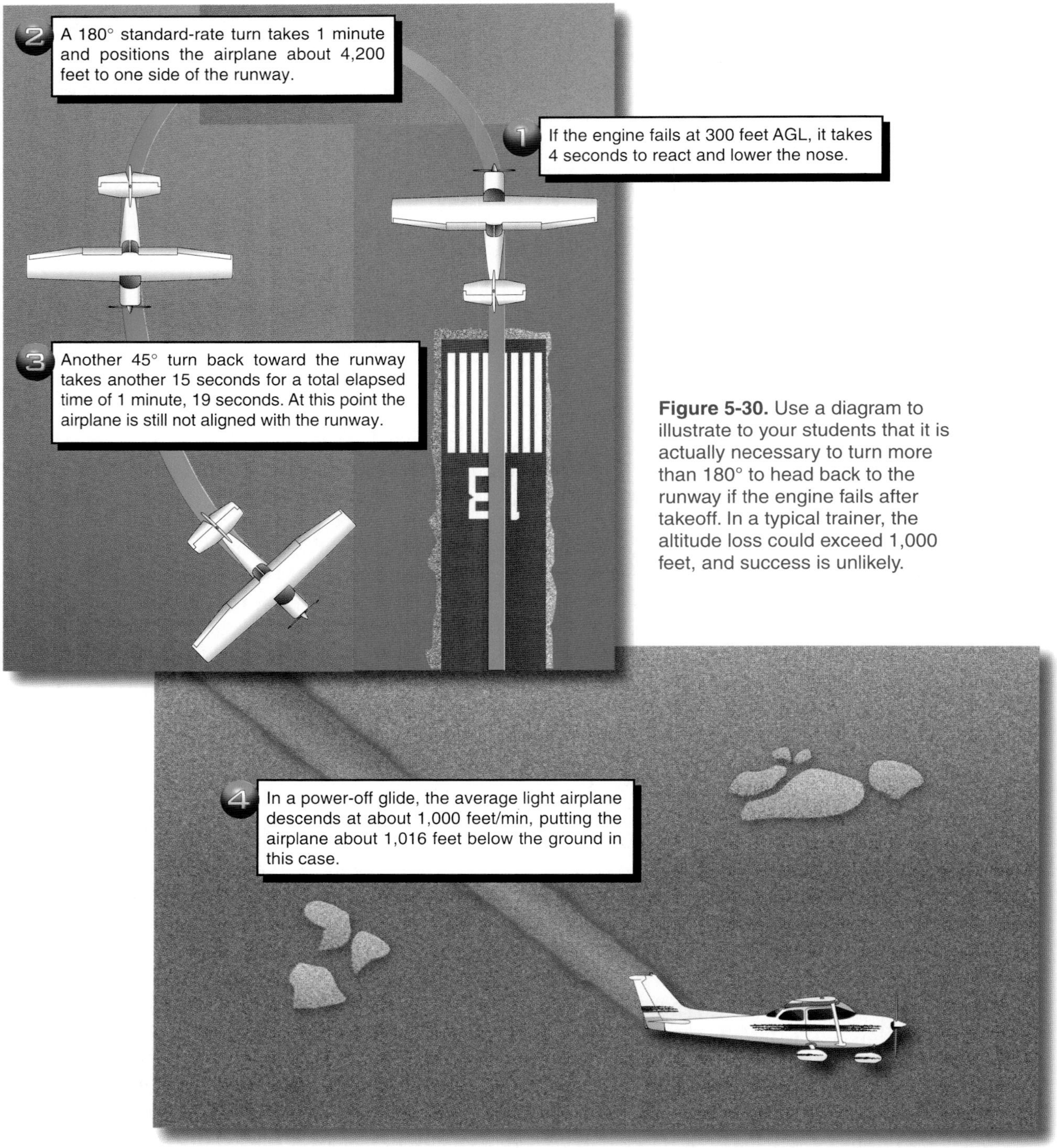

Figure 5-30. Use a diagram to illustrate to your students that it is actually necessary to turn more than 180° to head back to the runway if the engine fails after takeoff. In a typical trainer, the altitude loss could exceed 1,000 feet, and success is unlikely.

When your students begin to feel comfortable with flying traffic patterns, you can expose them to other airports in the local area. To help your students with situational awareness, have them review the layout of unfamiliar airports before the flight. Since your students become accustomed to visual references and procedures at their home base, exposing your students to a variety of different airports during training, helps lessen anxiety during cross-country flights to unfamiliar airports. [Figure 5-31]

Figure 5-31. When you teach students about uncontrolled airport operations, stress the importance of making proper radio calls and traffic pattern entry procedures.

A PATTERN OF DECISIONS

Operating in the traffic pattern provides numerous opportunities for your students to employ ADM principles. A simple task, such as following traffic, requires the decision-making process. For example, your students must decide if they have proper spacing on downwind, or what actions to take if they land behind a corporate jet.

Your students' situational awareness skills are developed while operating in a busy traffic pattern. For instance, they must keep track of their sequence in the pattern and know what traffic to follow, in addition to listening for radio calls, monitoring airplane systems, and observing the weather.

TAKING OFF

Most student pilots have more difficulty mastering landings than they do takeoffs. Nonetheless, there are some important concepts regarding takeoffs you need to teach your students. Loss of directional control is more often associated with landings, but it can also occur during takeoff. Sometimes students possess the mindset that once they begin the takeoff roll, they are committed to continue. If they begin to lose directional control, they often try to pull the airplane into the air prematurely, instead of simply aborting the takeoff and stopping on the runway. Stress to your students that they almost always have the option of aborting the takeoff, and allow them to practice this procedure so they will be prepared to discontinue the takeoff, if necessary. [Figure 5-32]

TAKEOFF

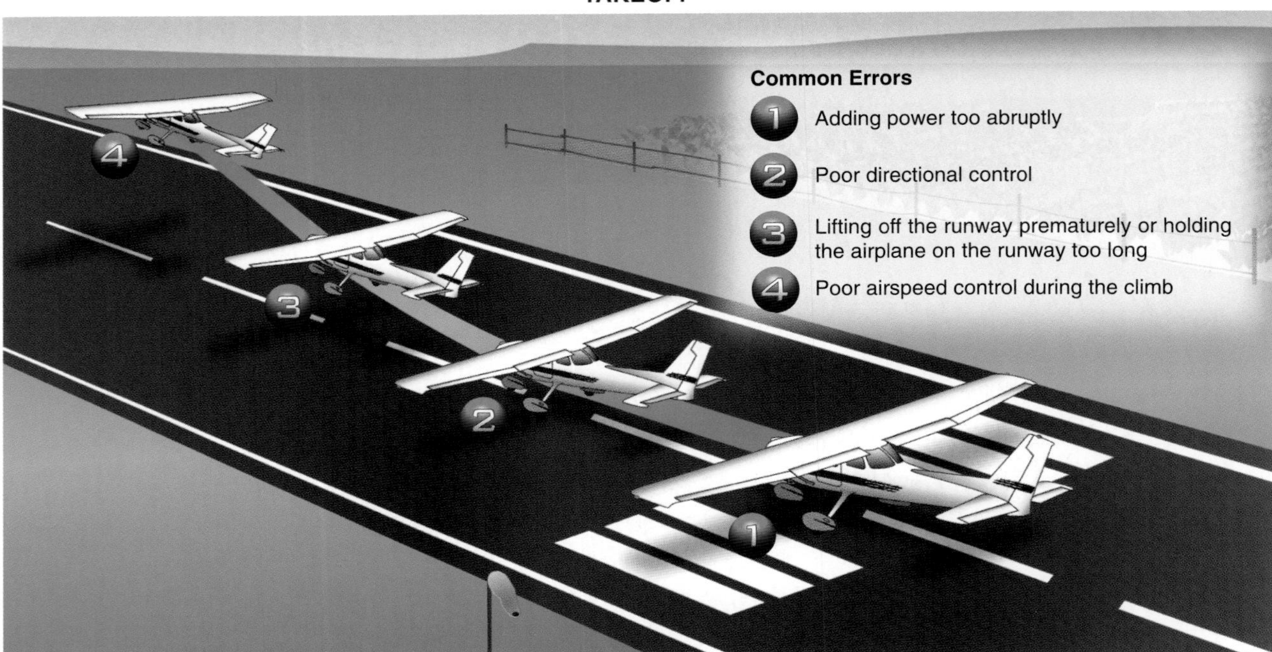

Figure 5-32. While the takeoff may be one of the easiest maneuvers to teach, you must still be alert for student errors.

To help your students maintain situational awareness during takeoff, ensure they develop the habit of performing a check of engine power instruments after takeoff power is applied. You may request that your students verbally confirm the power check has been completed and the airspeed indicator is functioning. In addition, once your students have gained proficiency performing takeoffs, you can simulate engine failure on takeoff by suddenly retarding the throttle. This helps students mentally prepare for the possibility of an engine failure and exposes them to the sudden transition from acceleration to deceleration.

The key element of crosswind takeoffs is maintaining directional control with the proper wind-drift correction throughout the takeoff and climb. If a crosswind exists, you should teach your students to hold the airplane on the runway until they attain a slightly higher-than-normal liftoff speed. This allows your students to have increased control authority and also reduces the chance of the airplane skipping sideways during rotation. Then, have your students establish a wind correction angle that maintains the desired track over the extended runway centerline.

LANDING

Typically, learning how to land the airplane is the biggest challenge student pilots face. This phase of training requires patience and understanding on your part, and most importantly, it demands keen observation and analysis. You must be able to effectively spot your students' errors and recommend corrective actions.

You should stress to your students that a good landing starts with executing a stabilized approach, which is defined as an approach using a constant power setting, constant rate of descent, and constant airspeed for each leg of the approach. [Figure 5-33] You should recommend power and flap settings for your students to use during the approach. Also, it is a good idea to establish minimum altitude checkpoints at various points in the pattern. This way, your students know if they are getting too low during any portion of the approach. Simply judging altitude by maintaining a constant rate of descent does not always work. For example, your students may be instructed to extend downwind. If they begin descending at the same point on downwind they are accustomed to, at the same constant rate, then obviously they will be low on the base leg.

Figure 5-33. You know your students are making a stabilized approach when the aiming point appears to be stationary.

Consider using full-stop-taxi-backs when you practice landings with your students. Full-stop-taxi-backs let you observe how well your students maintain directional control of the airplane during the landing roll. In addition, as you taxi back to the runway for takeoff, your students have time to relax and collect themselves, and you have an opportunity to effectively critique the landing.

Make sure to emphasize the importance of a go-around. Sometimes students are so committed to the approach and landing they forget that a go-around is nearly always an option. Too often, trying to salvage a poor approach leads to executing a poor landing, which could have been easily prevented by simply going around. Probably the most common error associated with landings is students not focusing the proper distance down the runway. Often students focus on references that are too close or they look directly down, which may result in beginning the flare too high. Other times, they may focus too far ahead during the landing approach, which makes it difficult to judge the closeness of the ground resulting in a nose-first touchdown. [Figure 5-34 on Page 5-32]

If your students focus too close or look directly down during landing, they may tend to begin the flare too high.

Your students may have difficulty judging the closeness of the ground if they focus too far ahead during a landing approach. This often results in a nose-first touchdown.

FLYING SOLO

Your students' **first solo** is likely one of the most memorable and exciting events of their flight training. It is a major milestone on their way to becoming a private pilot, and for most students, their solo comes after many long hours of practicing and perfecting flight maneuvers and much studying. It is hard to top the feeling of satisfaction you receive when your students emerge from the airplane, grinning uncontrollably, after successfully completing their first solo flight.

Before your students solo, they must consistently demonstrate proficiency in all the required maneuvers and procedures. However, even if your students meet the requirements

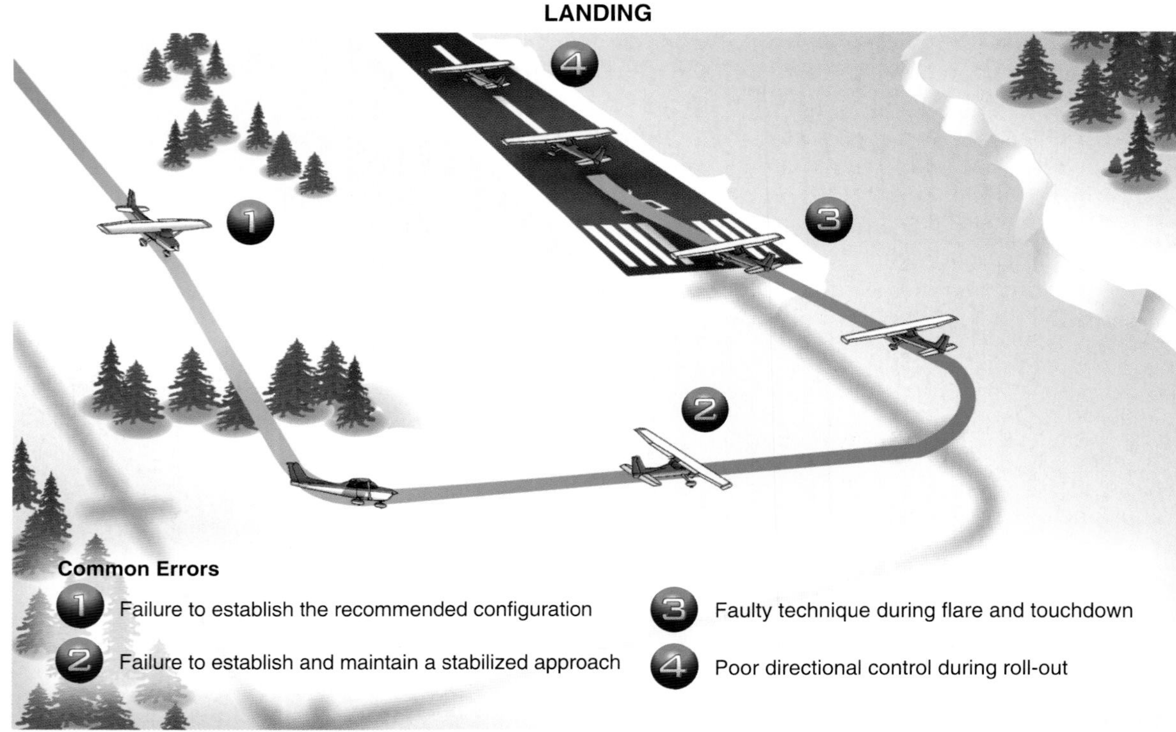

Figure 5-34. You must become skilled at recognizing student errors and explaining corrective actions. Students quickly gain proficiency once they are able to evaluate their own performance and correct their mistakes.

Pilots and Penguins

The early days of aviation, before and during World War I, saw the rapid development of flight training techniques as well as airplanes.

Flight schools were meadows and open fields. Airplanes had no brakes, but were slowed by the drag of their non-steerable tail skids. Even some of the best airplanes had no throttles or ailerons. In most flight training establishments, airplanes with dual controls were still far in the future. However, the aircraft were equipped with various safety devices — skids under the nose prevented prop damage and kept the airplanes from nosing over, and skids under the wingtips minimized damage during inevitable ground loops.

The following quotes from *Jane's All the World's Aircraft* of 1913 give some insight into the state of the new art:

"One month is probably the utmost effective life of an aeroplane on hard active service and it may well be a good deal less."

About the French military aviation school: *"The principal school is at St. Cyr, which was specially selected because the ground is rough and mostly covered with small shrubs; it being held important to train officers from the first to rise and land on ground similar to that most likely to be found in war time."*

One of the methods used to train new aviators was practicing in the Penguin (Pingouin in French), a low-powered, single seat airplane with small wings incapable of generating enough lift for flight. The student learned to taxi the Penguin, and when the instructors judged him proficient, the craft could be fitted with larger wings permitting flight in ground effect. Shown here is an American version of the Penguin concept. The Breese Penguin was created in 1918 for the U.S. Army.

Figure 5-35. Can your students cope with congestion in the traffic pattern, a wind shift, or unusual radio instructions? It is a good idea to have another CFI objectively evaluate your students before they solo.

of the FARs, they may not be ready to fly the airplane by themselves. There are some factors in addition to those stated in the FARs that you should consider. [Figure 5-35]

In addition to preparing your students for their first solo, you also need to prepare yourself. For example, you should determine how you will supervise your students, and what action you will take to stop the lesson if you deem it necessary. For example, you may observe your students from the control tower, or monitor the CTAF frequency on a handheld radio while watching the airplane from an appropriate location on the ground.

When the time comes for you to exit the airplane and send your students on their first solo, shut down the engine, explain to your students where you will be, where to meet after the lesson, and exactly what you want them to do. For example, direct them to accomplish three full-stop-taxi-back landings, and then taxi to the ramp. Also, to help your students' confidence, have them follow the same routine to which they are accustomed. For instance, instruct them to complete the before starting engine checklist and runup procedures just as they have done for every dual lesson.

What a Thrill!

During the 1930s, William J. Powell, a prominent black entrepreneur and pilot, worked relentlessly to encourage black awareness of aviation and founded the Bessie Coleman Aero Club to promote flying within the black community. The following excerpt from his 1934 book, *Black Wings*, describes his experience during his memorable first solo flight.

. . .What a thrill! Up in the air all alone! A thousand thoughts passed through his mind . . . Around the field at 1,000 feet and then land, Bill thought. The first time around he made himself quite at home looking over the side of the ship at those on the ground watching him. He even waved. Yes, he's getting too smart right at the start. He's coming in now for a landing. Everybody is out of the hangars and shops watching Bill solo — he's way too high — he'll land way out in the weeds on the rough ground — probably he'll nose over, break a propeller, probably the ship will catch fire. He is side-slipping, but he's too high, even at that. The instructor is watching him very calmly. But Bill, too, has noticed that he cannot make the field from that height, and so he gives her the gun and goes around again, and Monteith [his instructor] heaves a sigh of relief.

William J. Powell, as quoted in *Black Wings*, Ivan Deach, Jr., Los Angeles, 1934.

EXECUTING PERFORMANCE TAKEOFFS AND LANDINGS

Performance takeoffs and landings, which consist of short-field and soft-field takeoffs and landings, require your students to master new techniques. Try to make this training as realistic as possible. For example, if possible, take your students to a grass strip, or perhaps to an airport with a relatively short runway. Of course both of these techniques can be simulated, but operating from an actual short or soft field is a more effective learning experience.

When you teach short and soft-field techniques, refer to the airplane's POH and instruct your students to fly the airplane in accordance with approved procedures. Also, explain why different procedures and techniques are used for performance takeoffs and landings. For example, tell your student that lowering the nose immediately after liftoff during a soft-field takeoff keeps the airplane in ground effect, thus allowing the airplane to fly at a slightly lower airspeed. [Figure 5-36]

SHORT-FIELD TAKEOFF

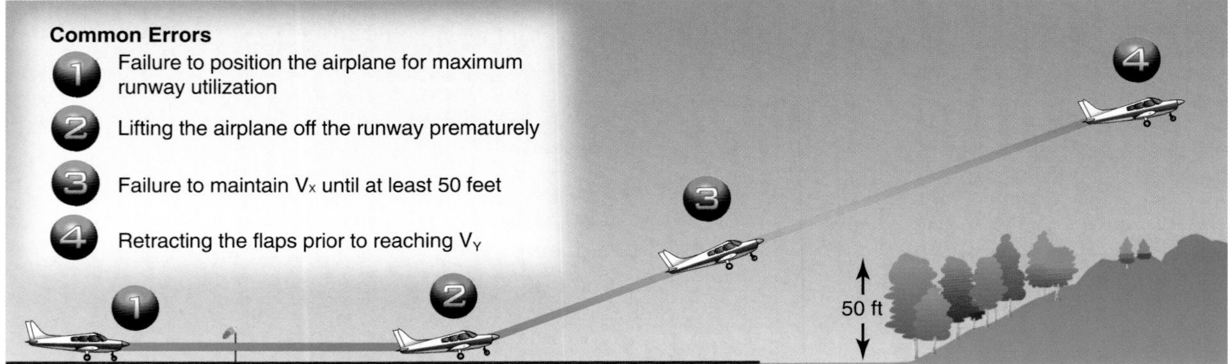

SHORT-FIELD LANDING

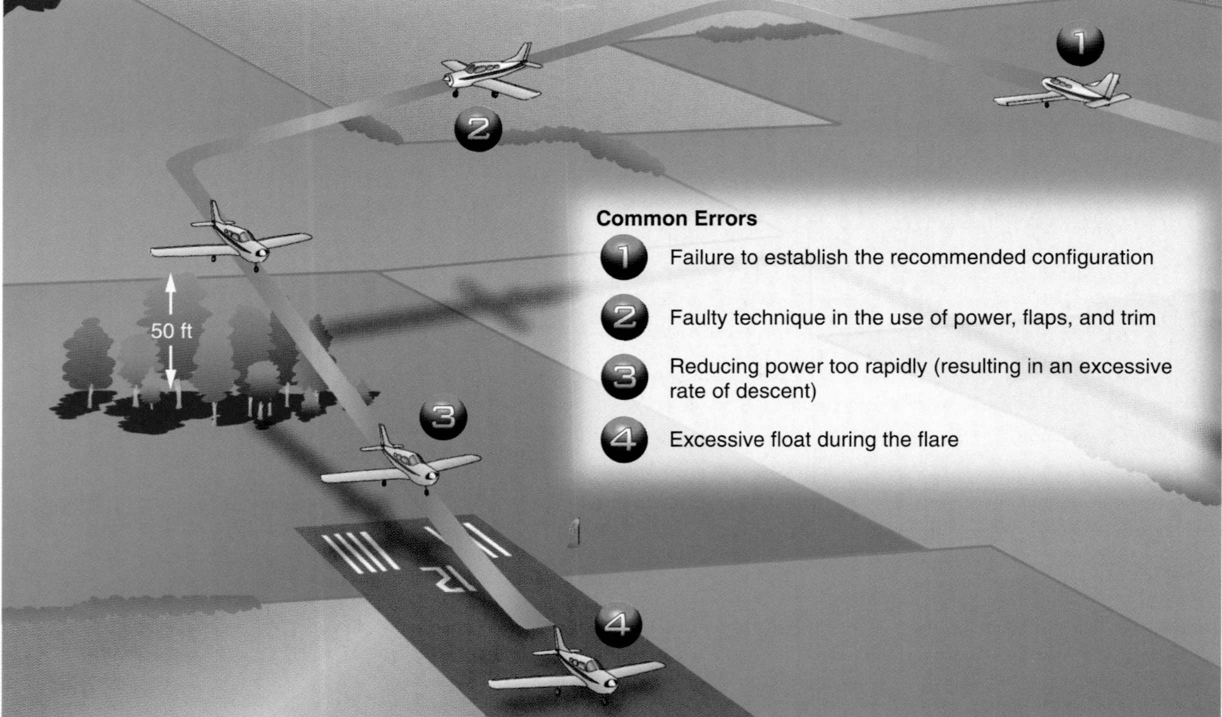

Figure 5-36. Keep in mind that some students may become frustrated while trying to learn the new techniques necessary for performance takeoffs and landings after they have finally mastered normal takeoff and landing procedures.

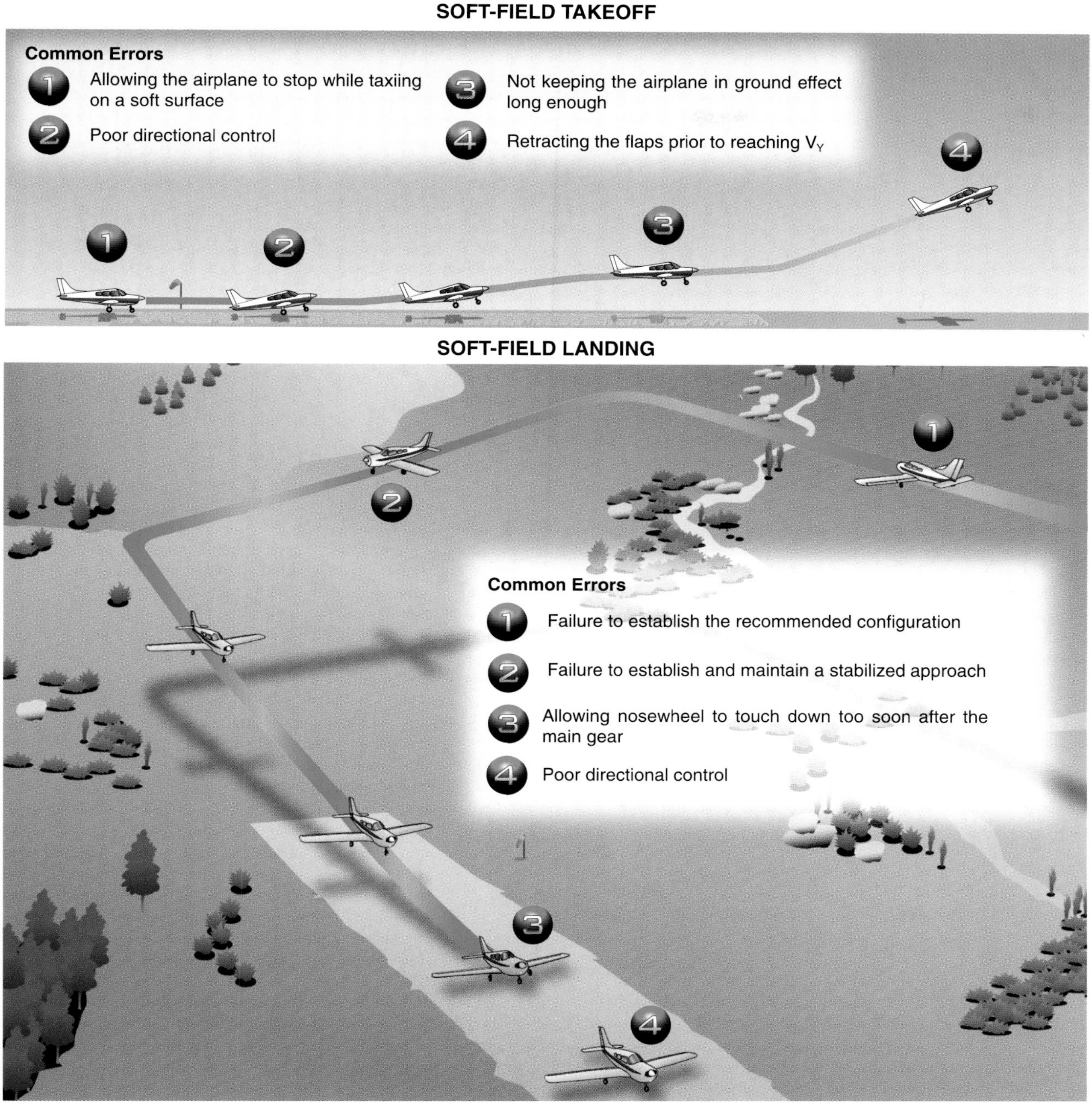

SOFT-FIELD TAKEOFF

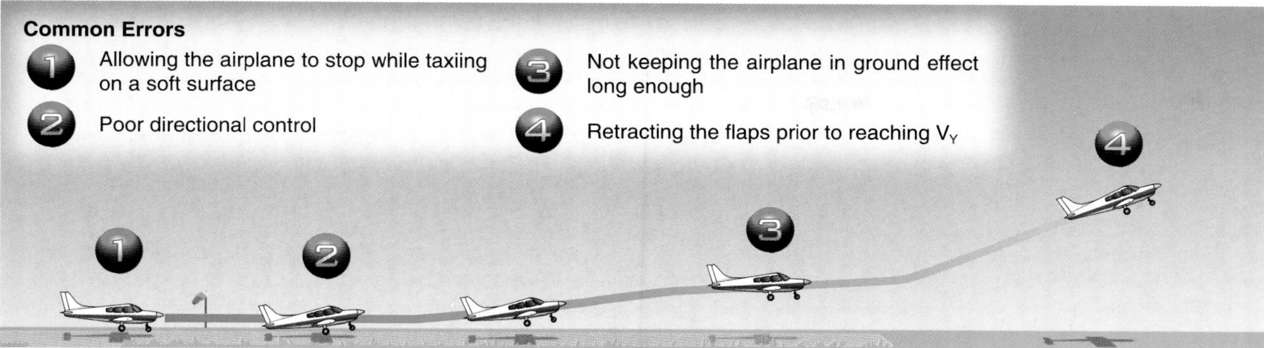

SOFT-FIELD LANDING

Common Errors

1 Failure to establish the recommended configuration

2 Failure to establish and maintain a stabilized approach

3 Allowing nosewheel to touch down too soon after the main gear

4 Poor directional control

Figure 5-36. Continued.

INTRODUCING SPECIAL FLIGHT OPERATIONS

Your private students are required to receive training in both attitude instrument flying and night flying. Keep in mind that the minimum night flying instruction required by the FARs is not adequate for most students to become proficient at all night operations. You should encourage your students to seek additional night flying instruction after they receive their private pilot certificate.

FLYING AT NIGHT

Flying at night is often a peaceful, enjoyable experience that also presents some unique challenges. Many students do not realize how different **night flying** is from flight during the day. The loss of visual cues at night can surprise many student pilots. You should

Controlled Crash

Landing a high-performance jet fighter aboard an aircraft carrier could certainly be described as the ultimate short-field landing. Imagine approaching 800 feet of pitching and rolling runway at 150 knots, and descending around 1,000 feet per minute. Now imagine doing all this at night or in poor weather conditions. Navy and Marine aviators make this daunting task look easy.

Most pilots strive to make smooth touchdowns. *"Nice landing"* is music to any pilot's ears. However, for pilots that land on aircraft carriers, finesse is the furthest thing from their mind. They want to do one thing: put the airplane on the deck, while catching one of the arresting wires. Hence the term controlled crash.

make sure your students are well aware of other night flying considerations, such as physiological effects, the additional equipment required for night flying, and dealing with emergencies at night. [Figure 5-37]

Figure 5-37. Probably the most common error associated with learning to land at night is misjudging when to begin the flare.

When you practice landings at night with your students, make sure they can land without the aid of the landing light. In most training airplanes the landing light has a fairly short life span. You should also simulate a complete loss of electrical power by turning off all the cockpit lights during a night flight. Furthermore, stress how important preflight planning is to night operations. For example, a simple item like fresh batteries in a flashlight can be easily overlooked.

USING INSTRUMENT REFERENCES

VFR pilots that continue flight into IFR conditions are likely to become disoriented within a matter of minutes. Unfortunately, this occurrence often results in dire consequences. During training, you have the opportunity to educate your students about the hazards of attempting instrument flight without being properly qualified. Your private students are required to have three hours of **instrument training** that must include: straight-and-level flight, constant airspeed climbs and descents, turns to headings, recovery from unusual attitudes, radio communication, and the use of navigation systems/facilities and radar services appropriate to instrument flight.

Be sure to stress how quickly unqualified pilots can become disorientated without visual references. A good exercise to illustrate this concept is to ask your students find a frequency on a chart or to retrieve an item from the floor, while flying with a view limiting device. Some common errors you may encounter when teaching attitude instrument flying to student pilots include over-controlling the airplane, fixating on one instrument, and looking outside the airplane.

CONTINUED VFR INTO IMC...A DEADLY MIX

From the files of the NTSB...

Aircraft: Beechcraft F33A

Narrative: *After takeoff, the pilot requested radar flight following service for his flight from Torrence through the Banning Pass to Palm Springs. Clouds were present in the Banning Pass area. At 1435:21, while proceeding at 7,600 feet in an easterly direction, the pilot asked the controller "We on course through the Banning Pass?" The controller responded at 1435:26 and informed the pilot "... you're not through the Banning Pass but the Banning Pass is at eleven o'clock and eight miles." There were no further communications from the pilot. The airplane continued cruising about 7,600 feet (mode C transponder altitude) on an east-north-easterly course until impacting terrain about 3.5 miles from the western side of Mt. San Jacinto (peak elevation: 10,804 feet).*

The probable cause, according to the NTSB, was continued VFR flight by the pilot into instrument meteorological conditions (IMC), and his failure to maintain proper altitude or clearance from the mountainous terrain. The instrument training required for a private certificate is not intended to make your students skilled instrument pilots. Rather, it is meant to provide them with the ability to survive an inadvertent encounter with clouds or reduced visibility by making a 180° turn back to VFR conditions.

TEACHING CROSS-COUNTRY FLYING

The **cross-country** phase usually occurs near the end of your students' training. After countless stalls, S-turns, takeoffs, and landings, your students finally are able to experience what an airplane is especially good at: traveling from point A to point B in a minimal amount of time. When determining a cross-country flight for your students to plan, you can ask other instructors what routes they have used in the past. Consider having your students plan a cross-country flight during which they must negotiate various types of airspace. If your students are training at an uncontrolled field, have them plan a trip to an airport with a control tower. Also, keep in mind the FAR requirements for distance, number of legs, and the amount of cross-country time your students must log for private pilot certification. [Figure 5-38]

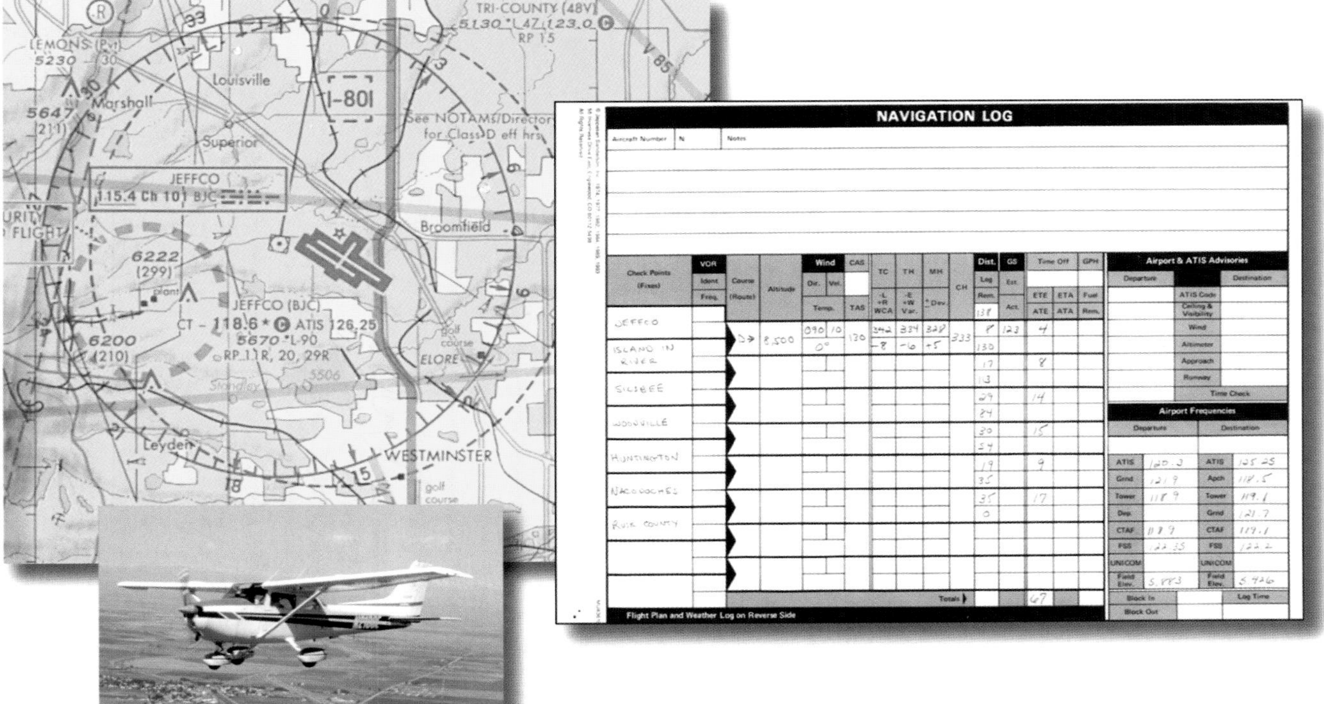

Figure 5-38. Ask your students if there is anywhere they would like to go on a cross-country. Of course the trip must be reasonable, and satisfy the FAR requirements.

The cross-country phase of private pilot flight training is typically the first occasion for students to use their new flying skills in a practical way. The dual cross-country should include navigation by pilotage, dead reckoning, and radio aids. You may wish to break the trip into three legs, and use a different navigation method for each leg. [Figure 5-39] Your students' first solo cross-country flight should have at least one leg in common with the dual cross-country. Keep in mind that your students are required to have one dual night cross-country of at least 100 nautical miles in total distance.

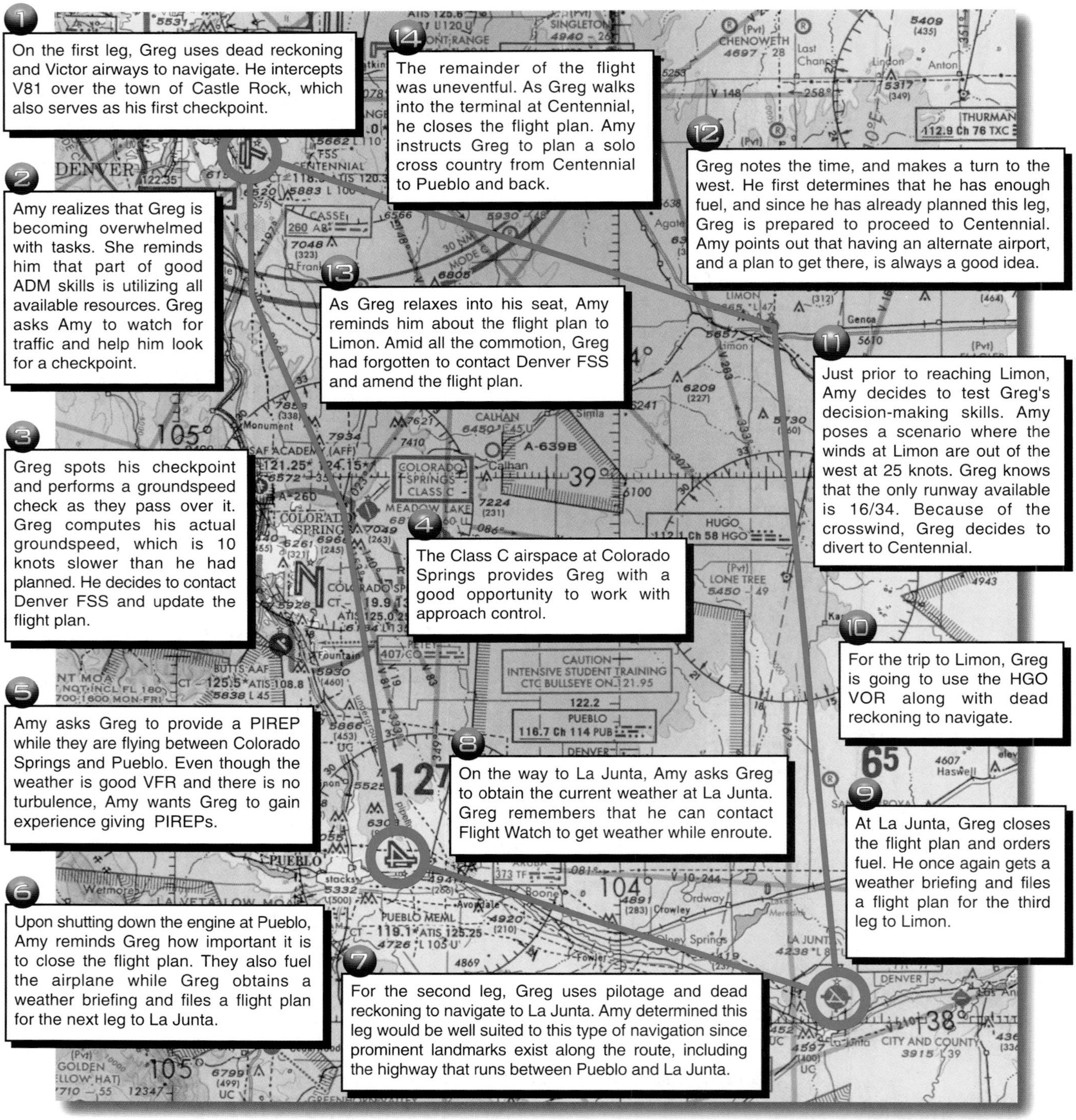

1 On the first leg, Greg uses dead reckoning and Victor airways to navigate. He intercepts V81 over the town of Castle Rock, which also serves as his first checkpoint.

2 Amy realizes that Greg is becoming overwhelmed with tasks. She reminds him that part of good ADM skills is utilizing all available resources. Greg asks Amy to watch for traffic and help him look for a checkpoint.

3 Greg spots his checkpoint and performs a groundspeed check as they pass over it. Greg computes his actual groundspeed, which is 10 knots slower than he had planned. He decides to contact Denver FSS and update the flight plan.

4 The Class C airspace at Colorado Springs provides Greg with a good opportunity to work with approach control.

5 Amy asks Greg to provide a PIREP while they are flying between Colorado Springs and Pueblo. Even though the weather is good VFR and there is no turbulence, Amy wants Greg to gain experience giving PIREPs.

6 Upon shutting down the engine at Pueblo, Amy reminds Greg how important it is to close the flight plan. They also fuel the airplane while Greg obtains a weather briefing and files a flight plan for the next leg to La Junta.

7 For the second leg, Greg uses pilotage and dead reckoning to navigate to La Junta. Amy determined this leg would be well suited to this type of navigation since prominent landmarks exist along the route, including the highway that runs between Pueblo and La Junta.

8 On the way to La Junta, Amy asks Greg to obtain the current weather at La Junta. Greg remembers that he can contact Flight Watch to get weather while enroute.

9 At La Junta, Greg closes the flight plan and orders fuel. He once again gets a weather briefing and files a flight plan for the third leg to Limon.

10 For the trip to Limon, Greg is going to use the HGO VOR along with dead reckoning to navigate.

11 Just prior to reaching Limon, Amy decides to test Greg's decision-making skills. Amy poses a scenario where the winds at Limon are out of the west at 25 knots. Greg knows that the only runway available is 16/34. Because of the crosswind, Greg decides to divert to Centennial.

12 Greg notes the time, and makes a turn to the west. He first determines that he has enough fuel, and since he has already planned this leg, Greg is prepared to proceed to Centennial. Amy points out that having an alternate airport, and a plan to get there, is always a good idea.

13 As Greg relaxes into his seat, Amy reminds him about the flight plan to Limon. Amid all the commotion, Greg had forgotten to contact Denver FSS and amend the flight plan.

14 The remainder of the flight was uneventful. As Greg walks into the terminal at Centennial, he closes the flight plan. Amy instructs Greg to plan a solo cross country from Centennial to Pueblo and back.

Figure 5-39. Amy, a CFI, has her student, Greg, plan a dual cross-country from Centennial (APA) with stops at Pueblo (PUB), La Junta (LHX), and Limon (LIC). Amy wanted to expose Greg to several different facets of cross-country flying, including VOR navigation, pilotage, dead reckoning, and diversion procedures. Amy also instructed Greg to plan fuel stops at each airport.

PREPARING FOR THE PRACTICAL TEST

The best way to tell if your students' knowledge and flying skills meet private pilot standards is to reference the Private Pilot PTS. You should also have another CFI, typically the chief instructor, give your students a mock practical test to evaluate their performance objectively. Before you send your students for their practical test, be sure to review their FAA 8710-1 form for accuracy and review their logbook to verify they meet the requirements listed in the FARs.

SUMMARY CHECKLIST

✓ To help them become familiar with the locations of various items in the cockpit, recommend your students sit in the airplane on their own time to simulate following the checklists.

✓ During engine start, make sure your students are very careful about clearing the area around the airplane, and instruct them to turn on the airplane's anti-collision lights to signify the engine is running.

✓ Make certain you discuss the dangers of hand propping with your students. Point out to your students that hand propping is rarely necessary since safer alternatives normally exist, such as using an external power source, enlisting the assistance of a maintenance technician, requesting another rental airplane, or simply canceling the flight.

✓ Emphasize to your students that they must never attempt to turn the propeller by hand to start the engine unless they have received instruction on the correct procedure and a qualified pilot must always be at the controls during the procedure.

✓ Students are often tempted to try to steer the airplane with the yoke. This is a common student error and should be corrected early in the flight training process.

✓ A good analogy to use when explaining the purpose of hold lines is the centerline painted on most roads. You may cross a dashed line, but you may not cross solid lines.

✓ You should introduce your private students to the location of the practice area, as well as some safety considerations associated with this area, early in their flight training.

✓ Minimum altitudes are stipulated in the FARs as well as in the PTS: recovery by 1,500 AGL for flight maneuvers, and 600 to 1,000 feet AGL for ground reference maneuvers.

✓ The basic maneuvers of straight and level flight, climbs, descents, and turns, form the foundation of the development of all piloting skills.

✓ You need to point out to beginning students the visual and instrument references they should use to perform basic maneuvers.

✓ While performing turns, ensure your students are using a reference point directly in front of them instead of using the center of the nose. Point out how the nose attitude appears different in left and right turns.

✓ Due to parallax error, your students may dive during left turns and use excessive back pressure on the yoke while performing right turns.

- ✓ One of the most common errors that new students exhibit during the first phases of flight training is fixating on the flight instruments.
- ✓ An effective way for students to remember the proper sequence for using trim is the abbreviation for apartment — APT (attitude, power, trim).
- ✓ The speed used for slow flight during the private pilot practical test, $1.2V_{S1}$, is sufficiently slow so that any significant reduction in speed or power, or increase in load factor, results in stall indications.
- ✓ The primary purpose of teaching slow flight is so your students become familiar with the appropriate control techniques for flight at slow airspeeds, and learn how rapidly control effectiveness can be lost.
- ✓ Some common errors associated with slow flight include not enough rudder correction, too much bank angle in turns, and maintaining an airspeed faster than recommended.
- ✓ Make sure you explain that the objective of this instruction is to enable your students to recognize the cues of an impending stall and recover from a stall, should one inadvertently occur.
- ✓ You should discuss situations during which inadvertent stalls are most likely to occur.
- ✓ Demonstration stalls include secondary stalls, accelerated maneuver stalls, crossed-control stalls, and elevator trim stalls. Under no circumstances should students be allowed to practice these maneuvers in solo flight.
- ✓ Your private students need to have aeronautical knowledge training in stall awareness, spin entry, spins, and spin recovery techniques.
- ✓ Private pilot applicants are required to perform turns in either direction with an angle of bank of 45° ±5° during their practical test.
- ✓ Ground reference maneuvers are designed to develop your students' ability to maintain a desired track along the ground by compensating for the effects of the wind.
- ✓ Each of the ground reference maneuvers requires your students to maintain situational awareness by dividing their attention between controlling the airplane and observing ground objects or features.
- ✓ Being able to determine the wind direction and velocity is a key element in flying ground reference maneuvers.
- ✓ To ensure your students use no more than 45° bank at the steepest point, you should instruct them to begin each maneuver downwind, and the first turn of each maneuver should be made to the left.
- ✓ When you teach emergency procedures to your students, you should stress that flying the airplane is the first priority.
- ✓ You should have your students consult the emergency procedures checklist whenever practical, but during some emergencies your students must react quickly.
- ✓ To emphasize why students should land straight ahead if an engine failure occurs on takeoff, demonstrate an attempted turn back to the runway after simulating an engine failure at a safe altitude in the practice area.

- ✓ Since your students become accustomed to visual references and procedures at their home airport, operating at different airports is a good idea.
- ✓ Stress to your students that they almost always have the option of aborting during the takeoff roll and practice this procedure so students will be prepared to discontinue the takeoff, if necessary.
- ✓ If a crosswind exists, you should teach your students to hold the airplane on the runway until they attain a slightly higher-than-normal liftoff speed to allow increased control authority and reduce the chance of the airplane skipping sideways during rotation.
- ✓ To help your students maintain situational awareness during takeoff, ensure they develop the habit of performing a check of engine power instruments after full throttle is applied on takeoff.
- ✓ You should stress to your students that a good landing starts with executing stabilized approach, which is defined as an approach using a constant power setting, constant rate of descent, and constant airspeed for each leg of the approach.
- ✓ Full-stop-taxi-backs let you observe how well your students maintain directional control of the airplane during the landing roll. In addition, as you taxi back to the runway for takeoff, your students have time to relax and collect their themselves, and you have an opportunity to effectively critique the landing.
- ✓ Probably the most common error associated with landings is students not focusing at the proper distance down the runway.
- ✓ Prior to their first solo, you should determine how you will supervise your students, and what action you will take to stop the lesson if you deem it necessary.
- ✓ When you teach short and soft-field techniques, refer to the airplane's POH and teach your students to fly the airplane in accordance with approved procedures.
- ✓ Probably the most common error associated with learning to land at night is misjudging when to begin the flare.
- ✓ Your private students are required to have three hours of instrument training that must include straight-and-level flight, constant airspeed climbs and descents, turns to headings, recovery from unusual attitudes, radio communication, and the use of navigation systems/facilities and radar services appropriate to instrument flight.

KEY TERMS

Ground Operations	Airport Operations
Private Pilot Maneuvers	First Solo
Practice Area	Performance Takeoffs and Landings
Basic Maneuvers	Night Flying
Flight Maneuvers	Instrument Training
Ground Reference Maneuvers	Cross-Country
Emergency Procedures	

QUESTIONS

1. True/False. You should emphasize to your students that items should never be added to the aircraft manufacturer's checklist.

2. According to the Private Pilot PTS, your students must be able to complete a stall by what minimum altitude?

   A. 1,000 feet AGL
   B. 1,500 feet AGL
   C. 2,500 feet AGL

3. Select the true statement about teaching students how to perform turns.

   A. You should ensure your students are using the center of the nose for a reference.
   B. Students may initially dive during left turns since the nose appears to rise during entry.
   C. Students may initially dive during right turns since the nose appears to rise during entry.

4. List at least three difficulties that beginning students may have in performing a basic maneuver, such as straight-and-level flight.

5. What speed is used to perform slow flight for the private pilot practical test?

6. Explain, as you would to your students, the purpose of practicing stalls.

7. List at least three common errors students may exhibit when performing power-off stalls.

8. True/False. Your students need to demonstrate spins during their private pilot practical test.

9. Select the true statement regarding ground reference maneuvers.

   A. The PTS states that these maneuvers should be performed at an altitude of 1,500 feet AGL.
   B. A common student error when performing S-turns is using too shallow of a bank angle when the airplane is headed downwind.
   C. To ensure your students use no more than a 45° bank at the steepest point, you should direct them to begin turns around a point upwind.

10. For each of the three ground reference maneuvers, list at least two applicable common errors.

11. What should you emphasize to your students as the first step in the event of an inflight emergency?

12. Describe a method you can use to explain the hazards of attempting a turn back to the runway should the engine fail after takeoff.

13. True/False. Aborting the takeoff is an option that students should consider if they lose directional control on the runway.

14. Describe the benefits of practicing full-stop-taxi-backs with your students.

15. True/False. A common error associated with short-field takeoffs is lifting the airplane off the runway prematurely.

16. What operations must be covered during the three hours of instrument training required for the private pilot certificate?

SECTION C

IMPARTING COMMERCIAL KNOWLEDGE

Teaching commercial students presents challenges different from those you face when conducting private pilot training. While many private students begin instruction with little or no aviation background, your commercial students may have a wide range of experience levels. Some students may still be accumulating the flight time required for the commercial certificate, while others may have extensive experience in a wide variety of aircraft. Consequently, the amount and type of aeronautical knowledge that your commercial students possess may also vary significantly. When teaching some students, you may need to review basic private pilot knowledge of such subjects as systems, aerodynamics, and airspace before proceeding to more advanced discussions appropriate for commercial pilots. With other students, you may need to only address topics which apply to commercial pilot training. [Figure 5-41]

Figure 5-41. Before you can instruct commercial students, you must evaluate their experience and knowledge levels. You can then outline a plan of action which enables your students to meet the requirements found in the FARs and provides them with the knowledge necessary to effectively operate as commercial pilots.

This section does not attempt to address all aspects of commercial pilot knowledge. Rather, it focuses on several topics of particular concern to commercial students and includes practical and creative methods to teach these subjects. You should refer to the Guided Flight Discovery *Instrument/Commercial Manual* for specific information pertaining to commercial pilot knowledge.

TEACHING THE COMMERCIAL STUDENT

One of the first topics you may need to discuss with potential commercial students is **commercial pilot privileges**. Many students may not understand the types of operations in which they are permitted to engage after receiving a commercial pilot certificate. You need to explain that while a commercial pilot certificate is the foundation of an aviation career, additional training usually is necessary to qualify for one of the many jobs available to pilots. While some commercial operations are governed by FAR Part 91, many others must meet additional requirements described in FAR Parts 119, 121, 125, 129, 135, and 137. [Figure 5-42]

FAR Part 119 — Certification: Air Carriers and Commercial Operators
FAR Part 121 — Operating Requirements: Domestic, Flag, and Supplemental
FAR Part 125 — Certification and Operation: Airplanes Having a Seating Capacity of 20 or More Passengers or a Maximum Payload Capacity of 6,000 Pounds or Greater
FAR Part 129 — Operations: Foreign Air Carriers and Foreign Operators of U.S.-Registered Aircraft Engaged in Common Carriage
FAR Part 135 — Operating Requirements: Commuter and On-Demand Operations
FAR Part 137 — Agricultural Aircraft Operations

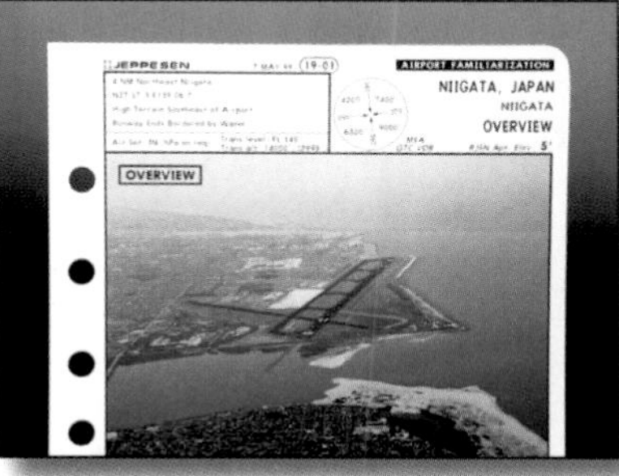

Figure 5-42. While your students normally do not need to study these regulations for commercial pilot certification, you should ensure they understand what types of operations these FARs cover.

INTRODUCING ADVANCED AIRPLANE SYSTEMS

Your students are required to receive at least 10 hours of flight training in an airplane with retractable gear, flaps, and a controllable pitch propeller. If they pursue careers as pilots, they most likely will be piloting increasingly complex aircraft capable at operating at high speeds and high altitudes. For these reasons, it is essential you ensure your students have a thorough understanding of **advanced airplane systems**. You need to

From Wilderness Trail to Busy Highway

As the expense of lifting payloads into orbit comes down, demand for easier access to space is increasing. With the development of reusable launch vehicles and larger expendable rockets, launch facilities are gearing up to handle the additional load.

In the near future, commercial and scientific space launches may outpace those supporting military and intelligence goals at Cape Canaveral, Florida, America's busiest space launch facility. Launches in each of those categories are expected to average 30 per year at the Cape over the next few years. While more than half of the workload at Cape Canaveral and the Eastern Test Range still centers around intelligence gathering, human space launch, and ballistic missile testing, the demand for commercial and scientific space launches is expected to continue to increase.

Aging equipment and an overburdened work force have been factors that limit the number of launches that can be accomplished. Ironically, some of the same range equipment used to launch John Glenn in 1962 was also used to launch him in 1998—over 36 years later. It requires enormous effort on the part of launch facility personnel to keep the old equipment functioning. However, as demand for launches increases, construction of new facilities can be justified.

The trail into space has been blazed, and in coming decades the trail must turn into a highway. NASA predicts that by 2040 there will be no clear line of distinction between a commercial launch vehicle and a commercial airliner. Safety, reliability, turn-around times, flight availability, and the need for ground support should be comparable to the airlines of the future. Perhaps some of the students you train will crew those vehicles.

Courtesy of NASA

familiarize your commercial students with high performance engines, constant-speed propellers, retractable gear, and flaps, as well as environmental and ice control systems.

You should begin by addressing, in detail, the systems found on the airplane in which your students are training. One way to organize this discussion is to use the POH as an outline. Simply proceed in order through the systems descriptions with your students. [Figure 5-43]

Reviewing the POH, studying a schematic, and discussing general operating principles provides your students with a solid foundation in systems knowledge. However, preparing your students to operate aircraft equipment safely and efficiently, as well as furnishing them with the necessary knowledge to effectively troubleshoot and correct problems, may require you to utilize some unique teaching methods. [Figure 5-44]

HIGH PERFORMANCE POWERPLANTS

Many of your commercial students may have logged the majority of their flight time in relatively low performance aircraft. As your students pursue commercial certification and continue their aviation careers, they are likely to progress to flying complex and

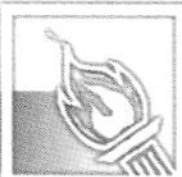

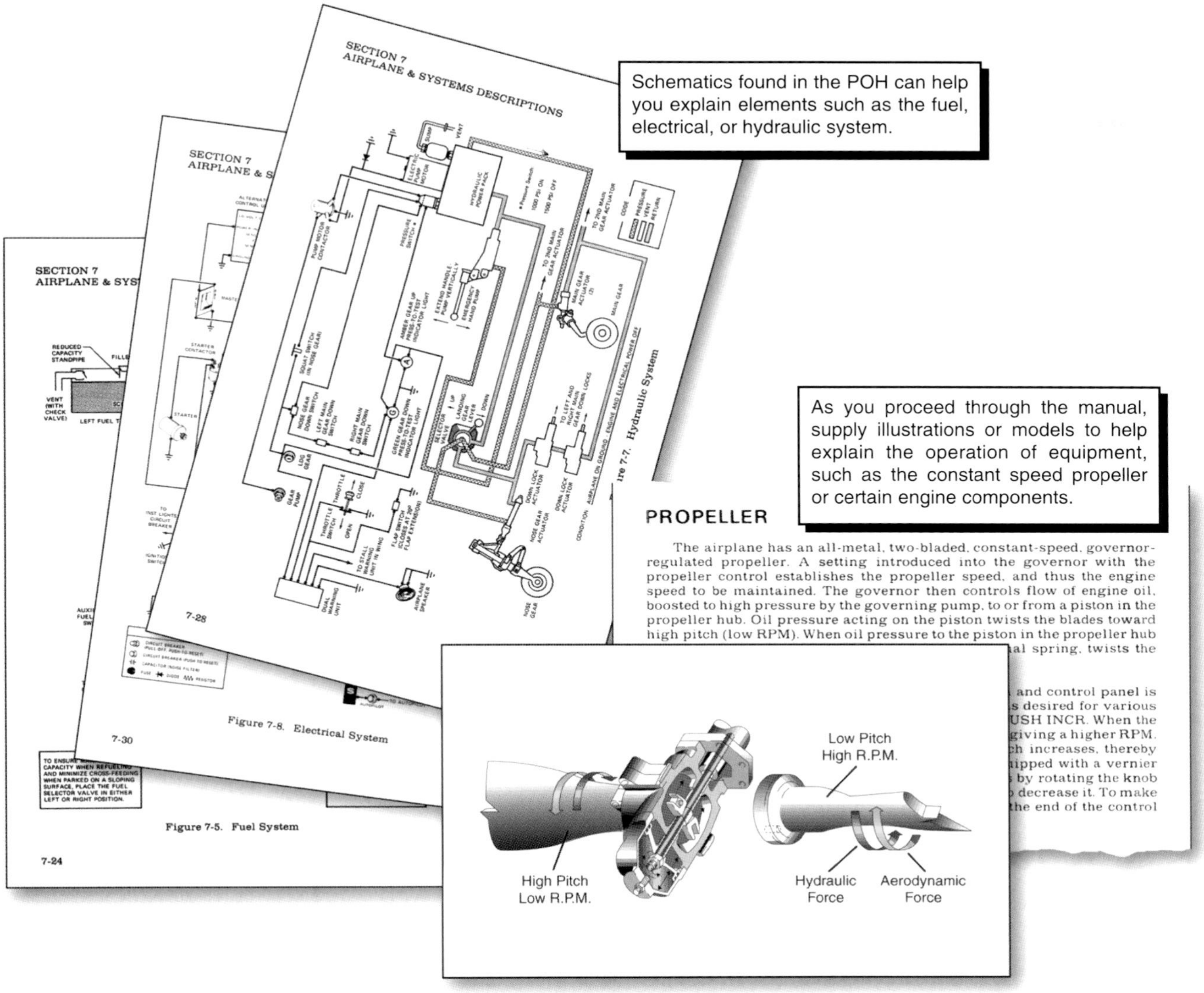

Schematics found in the POH can help you explain elements such as the fuel, electrical, or hydraulic system.
SECTION 7
AIRPLANE & SYSTEMS DESCRIPTIONS
Figure 7-8. Electrical System
Figure 7-5. Fuel System
7-24
7-30
7-28
As you proceed through the manual, supply illustrations or models to help explain the operation of equipment, such as the constant speed propeller or certain engine components.
PROPELLER
The airplane has an all-metal, two-bladed, constant-speed, governor-regulated propeller. A setting introduced into the governor with the propeller control establishes the propeller speed, and thus the engine speed to be maintained. The governor then controls flow of engine oil, boosted to high pressure by the governing pump, to or from a piston in the propeller hub. Oil pressure acting on the piston twists the blades toward high pitch (low RPM). When oil pressure to the piston in the propeller hub
Low Pitch
High R.P.M.
High Pitch
Low R.P.M.
Hydraulic Force
Aerodynamic Force

Figure 5-43. Be prepared to use supplementary teaching aids to enhance discussions on some of the more complex systems.

Ask your students to create a list of questions regarding the operation of specific aircraft systems and equipment.

What are some of the advantages of a turbocharged engine?

What is shock cooling and how can you prevent it from occurring?

Add to this list by posing realistic scenarios which reflect systems and equipment malfunctions and unique operating procedures.

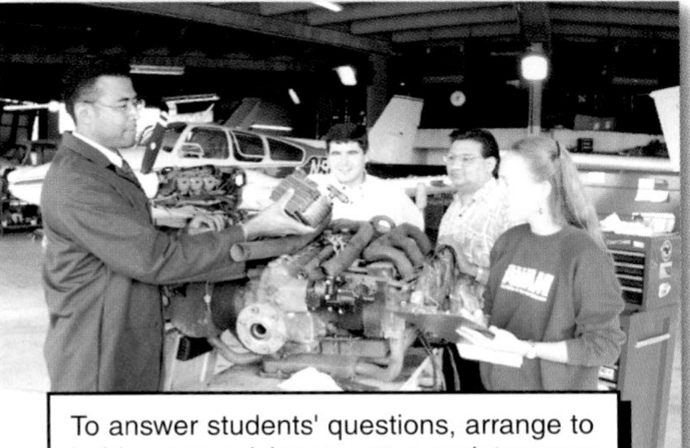

To answer students' questions, arrange to hold a ground lesson at a maintenance hangar or ask an AMT to attend a ground school class you are conducting.

Figure 5-44. To create an effective and interesting learning experience, enlist the assistance of an aviation maintenance technician (AMT) in this learning exercise.

In addition to familiarizing your students with the basic components . . .

A switch that allows for selection of various output rates often controls the fuel injection system's auxiliary fuel pump.

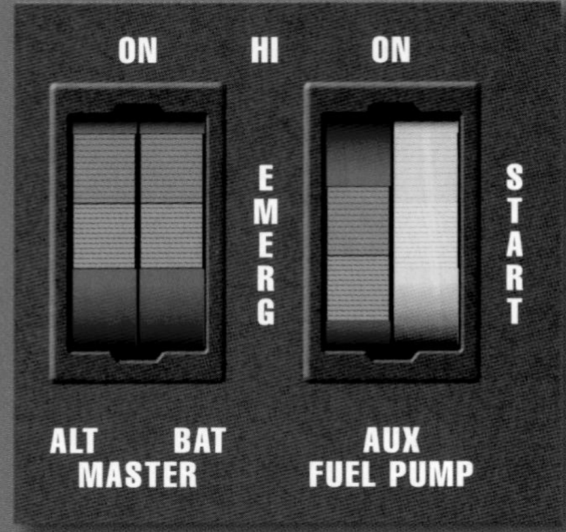

. . . you must address how the system's design affects operating procedures.

With some injection systems, if high output is selected on the auxiliary fuel pump while the engine-driven pump is also operating, the fuel pressure developed by both pumps may cause an excessively rich mixture. This may cause the engine to lose performance or to quit operating.

high performance airplanes. Such aircraft are most likely equipped with fuel injected and possibly turbocharged engines. Operating these **high performance powerplants** requires procedures different from those to which your students have been exposed in the past. [Figure 5-45]

Figure 5-45. If your students understand the reasons for certain procedures, it is more likely they will remember and correctly execute these actions when necessary.

Your students must understand terms such as manifold absolute pressure (MAP), overboost, and critical altitude before they can properly operate a turbocharged engine. Impress upon them that damage can occur to a turbocharged engine if the proper procedures are not followed, particularly during power advancement. [Figure 5-46]

Figure 5-46. Your students may have questions about the operation of a turbocharged engine that are not answered by referring to the POH or a systems diagram.

ASK AN AMT
Turbocharging Systems

1. What are some of the advantages of a turbocharged engine?

The main advantage is that sea level engine performance can be maintained as the airplane climbs. Also, a turbocharged airplane allows you to fly at higher altitudes that offer advantages such as, higher true airspeeds, favorable winds aloft, and the ability to navigate around adverse weather. Some disadvantages include the added complexity of the turbocharging equipment, and increased operational requirements on the pilot.

2. Can a turbocharged engine generate excessive manifold pressure? If so, what effect does that have on the engine?

If a manual wastegate is left closed after descending from a high altitude, it is possible to produce a manifold pressure that exceeds the engine's limitations. An automatic waste gate system is less likely to experience an overboost condition. However, if you try to apply takeoff power while the engine oil temperature is below the normal operating range, the cold oil may not flow out of the waste gate actuator quickly enough to prevent an overboost. You should advance the throttle cautiously to prevent exceeding the maximum manifold pressure limits. An overboost can produce severe detonation as a result of the leaning effect due to the increased air density.

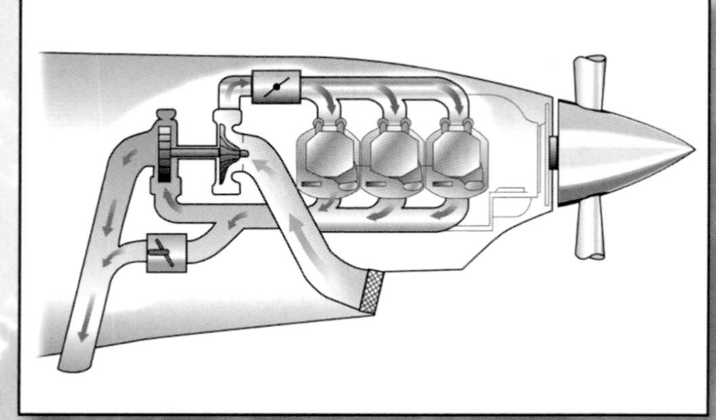

3. What is shock cooling and how can you prevent it from occurring?

Shock cooling occurs when the source of heat to a piece of equipment is suddenly removed. This sudden cooling causes abnormal wear since various metals cool at different rates. Suddenly reducing the power to idle can cause damage to any reciprocating engine, especially turbocharged engines that generally operate at relatively high temperatures. It is preventable by planning descents in advance so that it is not necessary to reduce the power abruptly.

The operation of turbine-powered engines is a totally new experience for pilots who have flown only reciprocating engines in the past. Though most students are unlikely to accomplish their commercial training in turbine-powered aircraft, they may wish to expand their knowledge of these systems to prepare for future endeavors as commercial pilots. Understanding the basic operating principles of these powerplants will enable you to help your students in this pursuit. In addition, you should be prepared to offer your students assistance in locating reference material which can help answer any questions they may have.

CONSTANT-SPEED PROPELLERS

When introducing **constant-speed propellers**, explain to your students the advantages of this design. Fixed-pitch propellers are usually optimized for either high power situations such as takeoff, or for economy circumstances such as cruise. In some cases, a compromise is attempted, but usually this results in a combination that does not perform well in either regime. Constant-speed propellers allow your students to set the propeller blade pitch to the best angle for any phase of flight. You can help your students to best utilize the advantages of the constant-speed propeller by making certain they understand how the system works. [Figure 5-47]

ASK AN AMT
Constant-Speed Propellers

1. Why is the propeller and throttle control sequence so important when conducting power changes?

If the throttle is advanced without decreasing the pitch of the propeller blades to increase r.p.m., the manifold pressure increases as the propeller mechanism attempts to keep r.p.m. constant by increasing the blade angle. The combination of high manifold pressure and low r.p.m. can cause engine damage due to high internal cylinder pressures.

2. What is meant by the term overspeeding, and how can this phenomenon be prevented?

Overspeeding is exceeding the maximum r.p.m. limits of the engine. Typically an overspeed is a result of a malfunctioning propeller governor or a loss of engine oil pressure. In the event of a propeller overspeed, most POHs call for the throttle to be reduced until the r.p.m. reaches a safe value.

3. What occurs to the propeller blade angle if hydraulic pressure is lost inside the hub?

On most single-engine aircraft, aerodynamic forces tend to move the propeller blades to the low pitch, high r.p.m. position, while hydraulic pressure provides an opposing force that moves the blades to high pitch, low r.p.m. position. Therefore, the loss of hydraulic pressure results in a low pitch, high r.p.m., setting.

Figure 5-47. Since improper usage of the constant-speed propeller can cause serious engine damage or dangerous degradation of flight characteristics, proficiency in the operation of such propellers is required of your commercial students.

RETRACTABLE LANDING GEAR

Begin a discussion of **retractable landing gear** by explaining the types of systems commonly used to operate the gear. For example, the gear may be operated either through a hydraulic system or an electric motor, or a hybrid of the two methods. Visiting a maintenance hangar, or simply strolling on the ramp, may allow you to point out aircraft that employ various types of gear systems. Next, review the POH for your students'

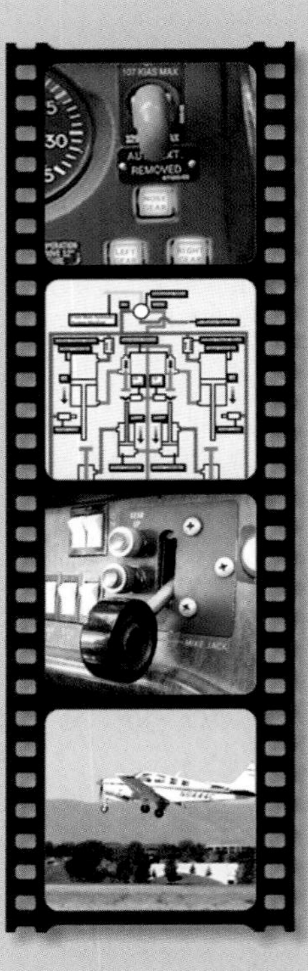

Figure 5-48. Students must have a comprehensive knowledge of the landing gear system to be able to correctly answer questions regarding malfunctions.

Is there more than one reason that a gear indicator light may fail to illuminate?

What does a flickering gear indicator light mean?

What signs might indicate a slow leak of hydraulic fluid?

What will happen to the landing gear if all the hydraulic fluid in the system is lost?

While on the ground, if you inadvertently move the cockpit gear switch to the retract position, what will happen to the gear?

If you leave the gear switch in the retract position during takeoff, what can happen?

What could cause a failure of the gear to

training airplane and explore the landing gear system in detail. Pose landing gear malfunction scenarios to your students to help prepare them to troubleshoot problems. [Figure 5-48]

ENVIRONMENTAL SYSTEMS

As students pursue commercial pilot certification and continue to fly increasingly complex aircraft, they most likely will encounter aircraft capable of flying at higher altitudes than those they have previously flown. Understanding how oxygen and pressurization systems operate is essential to the safety of flight in these aircraft.

OXYGEN SYSTEMS

Your students need to be aware that **oxygen systems** for aircraft are available in three basic configurations: continuous-flow, diluter-demand, and pressure-demand. Your students may be most familiar with the continuous-flow system, since it is primarily installed on reciprocating-engine airplanes due to its low cost and simplicity. Continuous-flow systems provide adequate respiration up to 25,000 feet and are available in three styles: constant flow, adjustable flow, and altitude-compensated. The components of the diluter-demand and pressure-demand oxygen systems are essentially the same as those used with continuous-flow systems. Exceptions include a different style of oxygen mask, and the replacement of the distribution outlet with a special regulator unit. [Figure 5-49]

CABIN PRESSURIZATION

Commercial students are probably more familiar with the use of onboard oxygen than they are with **cabin pressurization**. For most commercial operations at high altitude, passenger comfort demands the use of pressurized aircraft; so, your students need to have a basic understanding of how pressurization systems work. If you are instructing your students in a pressurized aircraft, emphasize knowledge of the specific procedures required in the event of a loss of pressurization. While in the cockpit on the ground, you

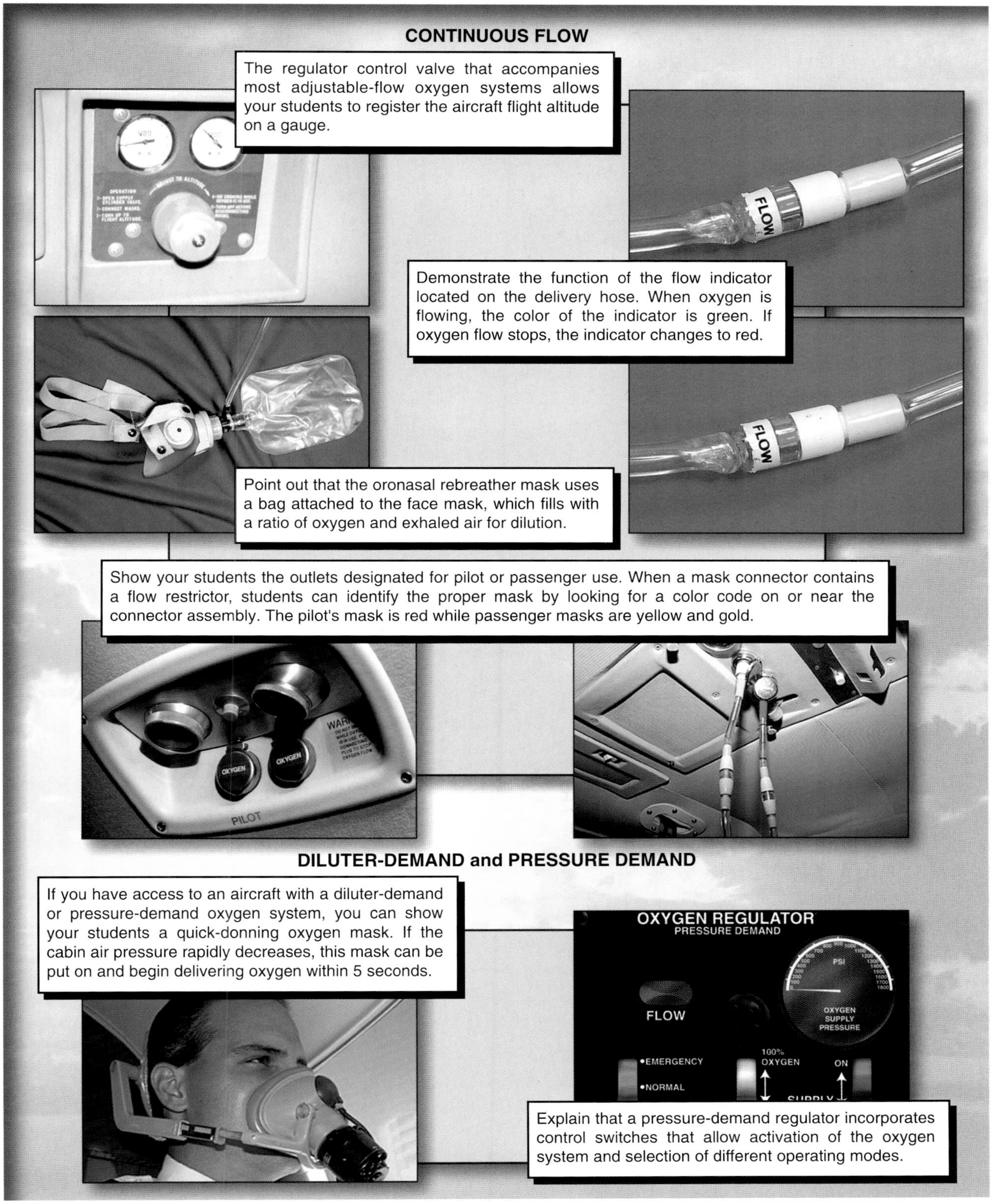
CONTINUOUS FLOW
The regulator control valve that accompanies most adjustable-flow oxygen systems allows your students to register the aircraft flight altitude on a gauge.
FLOW
Demonstrate the function of the flow indicator located on the delivery hose. When oxygen is flowing, the color of the indicator is green. If oxygen flow stops, the indicator changes to red.
FLOW
Point out that the oronasal rebreather mask uses a bag attached to the face mask, which fills with a ratio of oxygen and exhaled air for dilution.
Show your students the outlets designated for pilot or passenger use. When a mask connector contains a flow restrictor, students can identify the proper mask by looking for a color code on or near the connector assembly. The pilot's mask is red while passenger masks are yellow and gold.
OXYGEN
OXYGEN
PILOT
DILUTER-DEMAND and PRESSURE DEMAND
If you have access to an aircraft with a diluter-demand or pressure-demand oxygen system, you can show your students a quick-donning oxygen mask. If the cabin air pressure rapidly decreases, this mask can be put on and begin delivering oxygen within 5 seconds.
OXYGEN REGULATOR
PRESSURE DEMAND
PSI
FLOW
OXYGEN SUPPLY PRESSURE
•EMERGENCY
•NORMAL
100% OXYGEN
ON
Explain that a pressure-demand regulator incorporates control switches that allow activation of the oxygen system and selection of different operating modes.

Figure 5-49. If you have the opportunity, introduce your students to the various oxygen systems by showing them the equipment from several different airplanes.

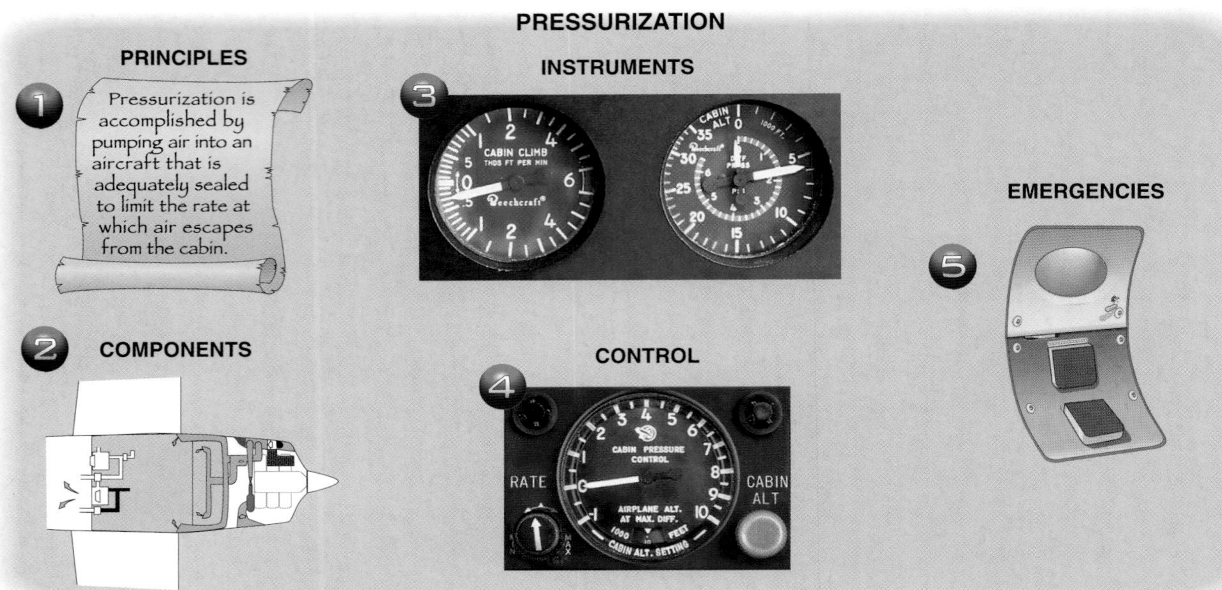

Figure 5-50. Consider organizing your discussion on cabin pressurization in the manner shown here. Use illustrations and time spent in the airplane on the ground to teach this topic.

should rehearse the necessary steps to be taken if a slow, rapid, or explosive cabin decompression occurs. Commercial students must be particularly aware of the actions they should take to assist passengers in an emergency situation. [Figure 5-50]

ICE CONTROL SYSTEMS

Commercial operations can take place in a wide variety of weather conditions, and your students will be flying aircraft that may be equipped with several types of **anti-icing equipment** and **de-icing equipment**. Prior to addressing ice control systems, ensure your students have a solid foundation of knowledge regarding the generation of aircraft icing. Some students may have covered this topic in detail during training for their instrument rating, while others may have limited knowledge in this area. After a review of icing, introduce the types of ice control systems by exploring them on the flight line, if possible. A trip to a maintenance facility may afford your students an opportunity to see systems, such as de-icing boots, in operation. [Figure 5-51]

EXPLORING ADVANCED AERODYNAMICS

As your students transition to larger, more complex aircraft capable of performing at increasingly higher airspeeds, they must enhance their knowledge of the aerodynamic principles which apply to operation of these aircraft. Understanding the performance and limitations of the wide variety of airplanes they may operate as commercial pilots is essential to flight safety.

In order to effectively explore **advanced aerodynamics** with your commercial students, you must first ensure they possess a solid foundation of knowledge regarding the four forces of flight. One way to approach this discussion with your commercial students is to initially ask them to explain the four forces to you. In this way, you may determine how well they understand basic aerodynamic principles and identify areas that need review. While pilots must apply their knowledge of such aeronautical subjects as systems or airspace on a routine basis during flight, they normally are not required to directly apply their knowledge of aerodynamic principles on a regular basis. A review of the basic principles typically covered during private pilot training may be in order prior to proceeding to explanations of more advanced concepts. [Figure 5-52]

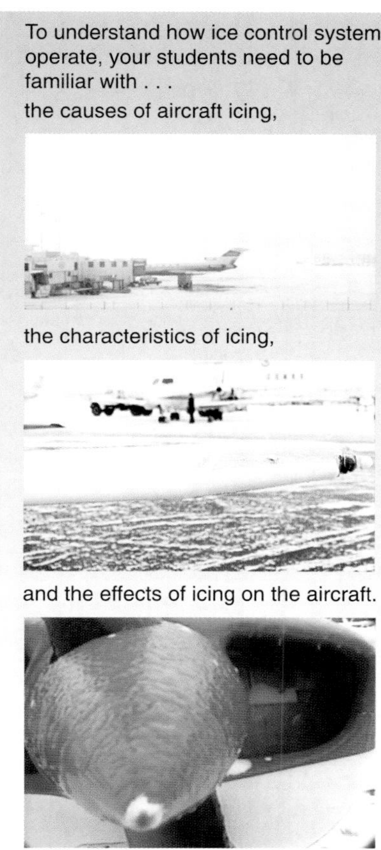

To understand how ice control systems operate, your students need to be familiar with . . .

the causes of aircraft icing,

the characteristics of icing,

and the effects of icing on the aircraft.

Ensure you explain the difference between . . .

de-icing equipment and

anti-icing equipment.

It is important to emphasize that . . .

although an aircraft may be equipped with ice control systems, it may not be certified to fly in icing conditions. To determine if your airplane is certified to operate in icing conditions, you should consult the FAA-approved POH.

Even if certified, icing conditions pose significant hazards. When encountered, always seek out regions where meteorological conditions are less conducive to ice formation.

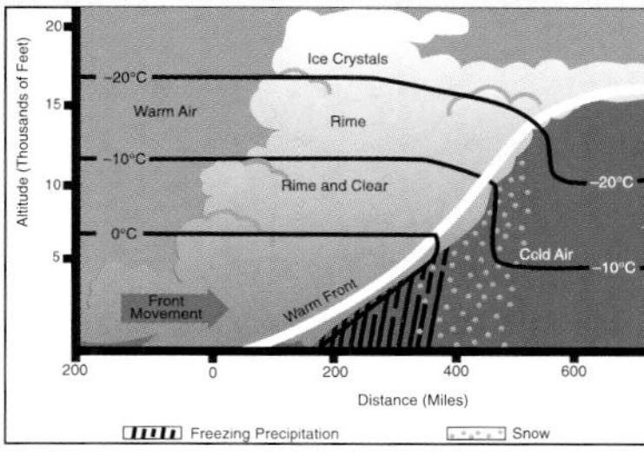

Figure 5-51. There are several important issues to address with students when you explain ice control systems.

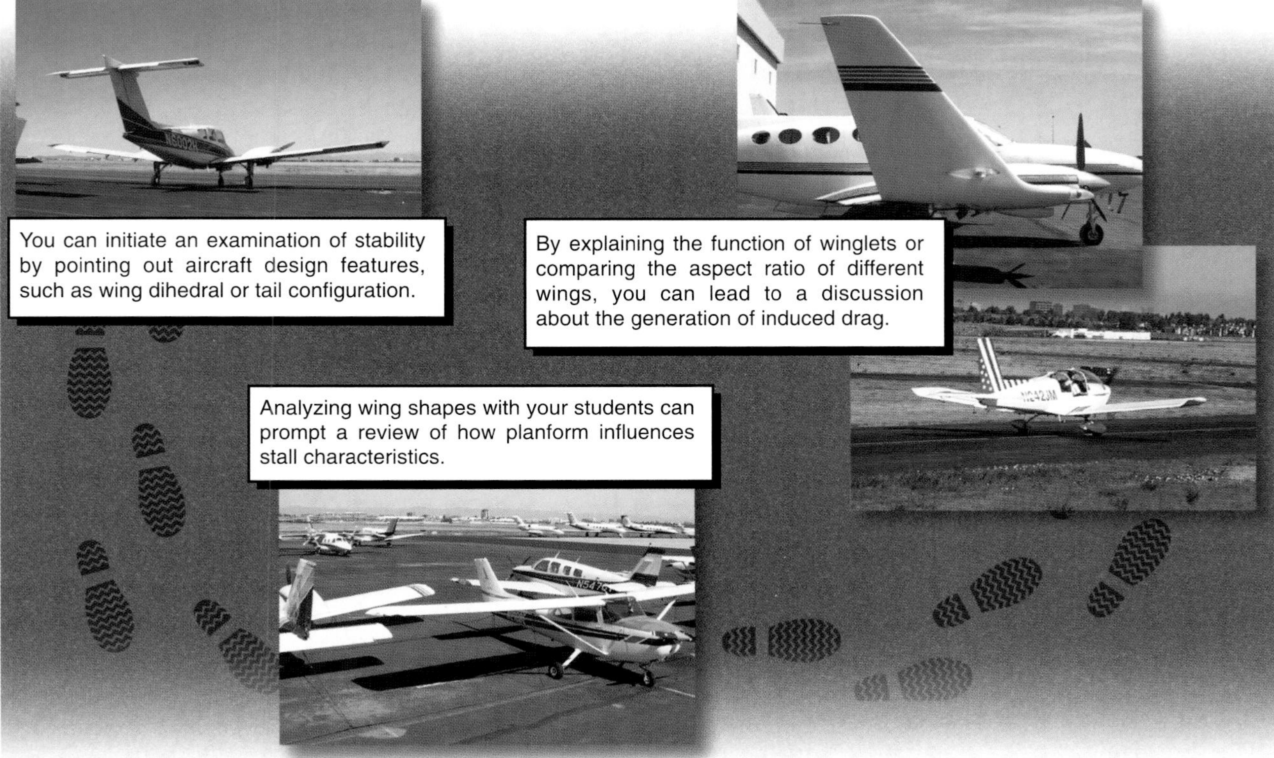

You can initiate an examination of stability by pointing out aircraft design features, such as wing dihedral or tail configuration.

By explaining the function of winglets or comparing the aspect ratio of different wings, you can lead to a discussion about the generation of induced drag.

Analyzing wing shapes with your students can prompt a review of how planform influences stall characteristics.

Figure 5-52. If you have the opportunity to observe a wide variety of aircraft at your local airport, a stroll on the flight line is one good way to launch a review of aerodynamic concepts.

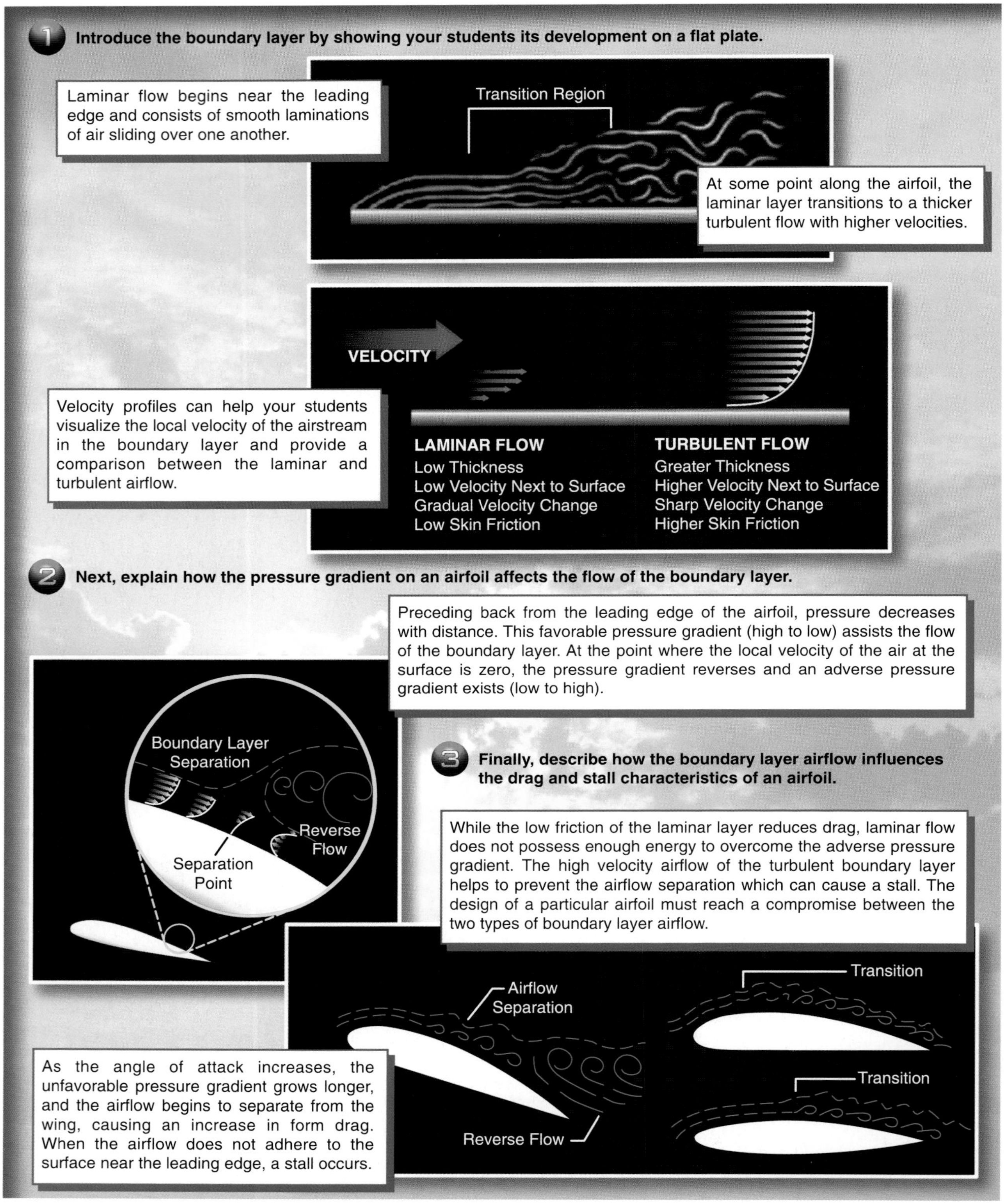

Figure 5-53. Using a diagram to explain the characteristics of the boundary layer in steps can greatly enhance student understanding of this complex subject.

LIFT

Exploring the generation of lift in detail with your commercial students is essential to their future understanding of the high lift and high drag devices found on many advanced aircraft. One aspect of lift which may not have been addressed during private

pilot training is the boundary layer. The **boundary layer** is air next to the surface of an airfoil, which shows reduction of speed due to the air's viscosity, or thickness. As the air flows from front to back on the upper surface of a wing, the boundary layer goes through a transition from smooth airflow to turbulent airflow. [Figure 5-53]

HIGH LIFT DEVICES

In most airplanes, the only way to change the lift characteristics of the wing is by employing **high lift devices**, such as trailing edge flaps or leading edge devices. Your students probably are quite familiar with the use of the trailing edge flaps found on aircraft they have flown. However, as they transition to a wide range of airplanes during their flying careers, students will most likely encounter a variety of flap configurations, and they should be familiar with the aerodynamic characteristics associated with each. [Figure 5-54]

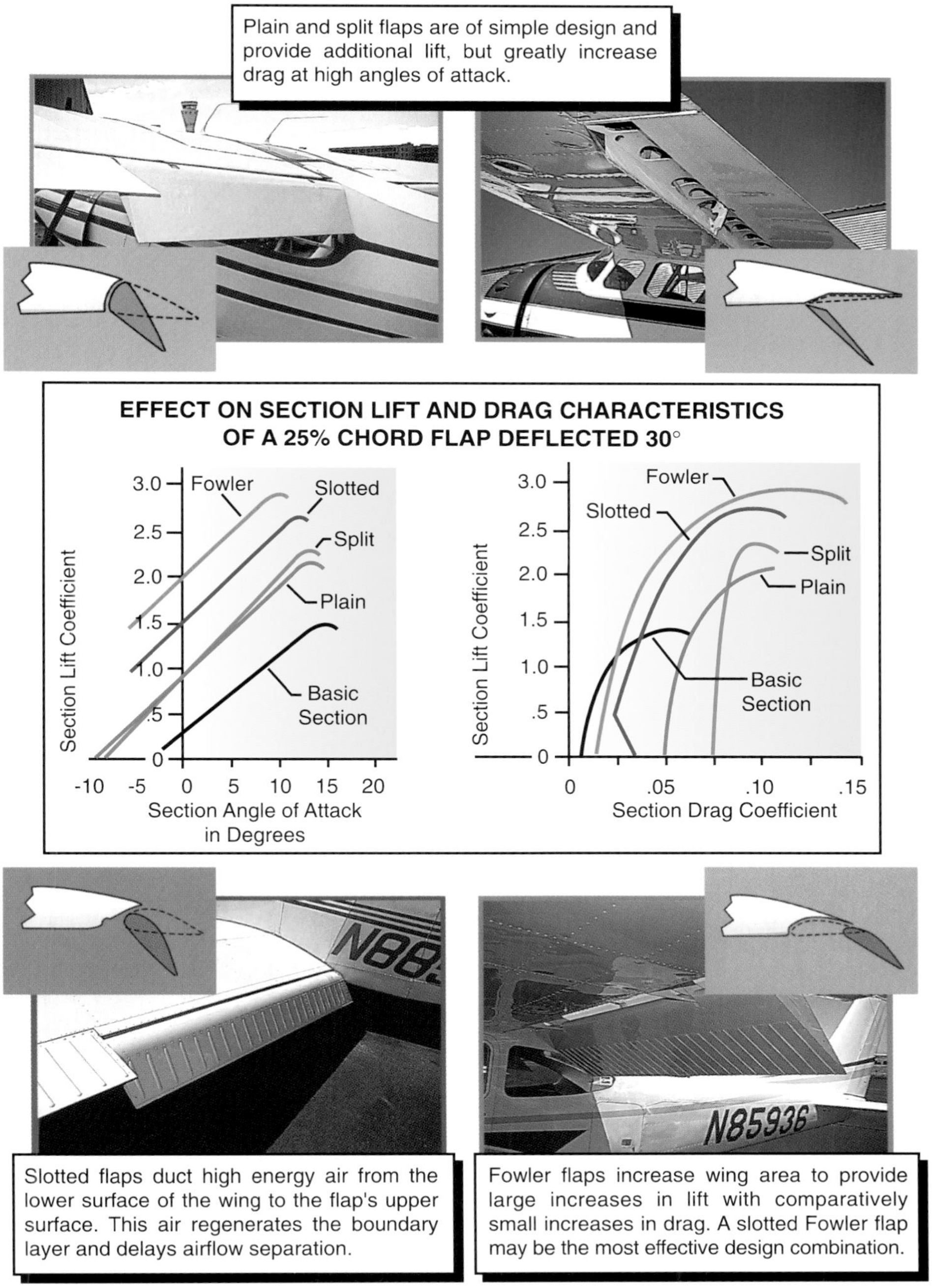
Plain and split flaps are of simple design and provide additional lift, but greatly increase drag at high angles of attack.
EFFECT ON SECTION LIFT AND DRAG CHARACTERISTICS OF A 25% CHORD FLAP DEFLECTED 30°
Fowler
Slotted
Split
Plain
Basic Section
Section Lift Coefficient
Section Angle of Attack in Degrees
Section Drag Coefficient
3.0
2.5
2.0
1.5
1.0
.5
0
-10
-5
0
5
10
15
20
.05
.10
.15
N85936
Slotted flaps duct high energy air from the lower surface of the wing to the flap's upper surface. This air regenerates the boundary layer and delays airflow separation.
Fowler flaps increase wing area to provide large increases in lift with comparatively small increases in drag. A slotted Fowler flap may be the most effective design combination.

Figure 5-54. You can use this diagram to show your students the efficiency of each flap design.

Since low performance aircraft seldom employ leading edge devices, these components may be unfamiliar to many of your students. Leading edge flaps, fixed slots, and movable slats are three of the more common leading edge devices. Explain to your students that these devices usually operate in concert with trailing edge flaps to change the coefficient of lift of the wing. [Figure 5-55]

The fixed slot conducts the flow of high-energy air into the boundary layer and delays airflow separation to a higher angle of attack.

Leading edge flaps are used to increase camber to increase lift. This type of leading edge device is used frequently in conjunction with trailing edge flaps and can reduce the nose-down pitching moment.

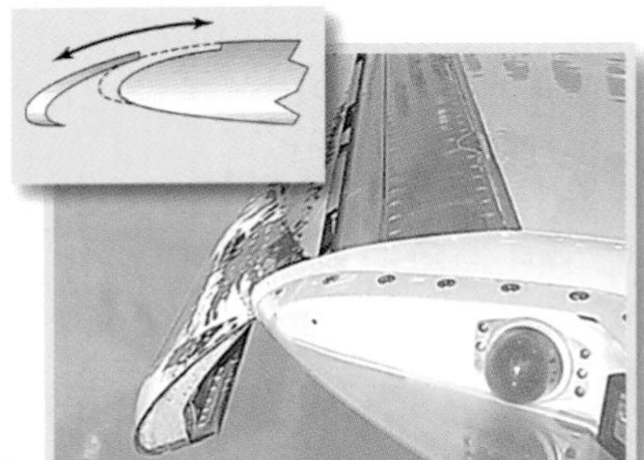

A movable slat consists of a leading edge segment which is free to move on tracks. At high angles of attack, either a low pressure area at the wing's leading edge or pilot-operated controls force the slat to move forward. This opens a slot and allows air below the wing to flow over the wing's upper surface, delaying airflow separation.

Figure 5-55. Your students' learning experience will be enhanced if you have the opportunity to show them examples of leading edge devices on aircraft. If this is not possible at your local airport, the use of photos or models in addition to illustrations can greatly increase understanding.

Your students may ask about the vortex generators they see on a wide variety of aircraft. Those placed on the upper wing surface of turbojet airplanes delay the airflow separation which occurs with shock-induced separation when operating at high speeds. The vortex generators found on many propeller-driven airplanes improve low-speed handling characteristics, especially during single-engine flight in multi-engine airplanes and slow flight operations in single-engine airplanes. [Figure 5-56]

Blood vessels stabilize the membranes in the wings of a worker bee and increase the energy of the turbulent boundary layer.

A golf ball's roughness from dimpling forces a premature transition from laminar to turbulent flow and delays airflow separation, reducing form drag.

Vortices are formed at the tips of vortex generators which add energy to the boundary layer to prevent or delay airflow separation.

Figure 5-56. Your students may find it interesting to learn that boundary layer control is not unique to the aviation environment.

HIGH DRAG DEVICES

While they may not encounter or **high drag devices** until much later in their flying careers, your students may have questions about this equipment that you should be prepared to address. Begin a discussion of high drag devices by posing the following

questions: Since aircraft designers normally strive to eliminate as much drag as possible, why is it necessary to create mechanisms solely to produce additional drag? In what situations would the deployment of high drag devices be beneficial to flight operations? Most likely your students will determine that high drag devices are useful anytime it is necessary for aircraft to descend without gaining speed, such as during a landing approach. [Figure 5-57]

Figure 5-57. Explain to your students that speed brakes and spoilers are some of the most common high drag devices.

HIGH SPEED/HIGH ALTITUDE FLIGHT

The transition to high performance airplanes may be accompanied by a transition to flight at higher speeds and higher altitudes than those to which your students are accustomed. If your students plan to act as PIC of a pressurized airplane that has a service ceiling or maximum operating altitude, whichever is lower, above 25,000 MSL, you must provide specific ground training as specified in FAR 61.31 (f). Even if it is not necessary to provide a high altitude checkout to your commercial students, you may consider discussing some of the factors involved with **high speed/high altitude flight**. [Figure 5-58]

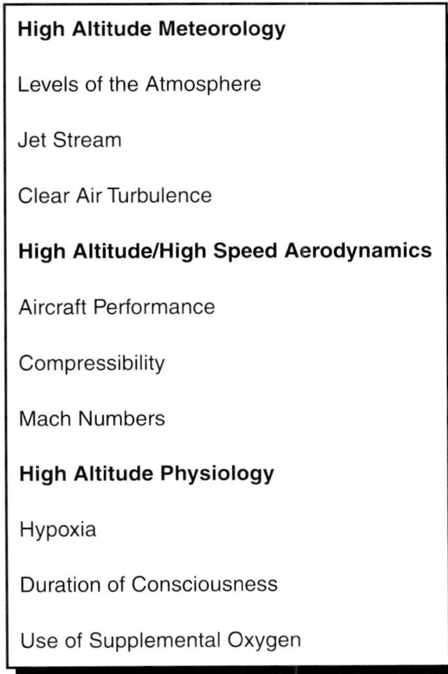

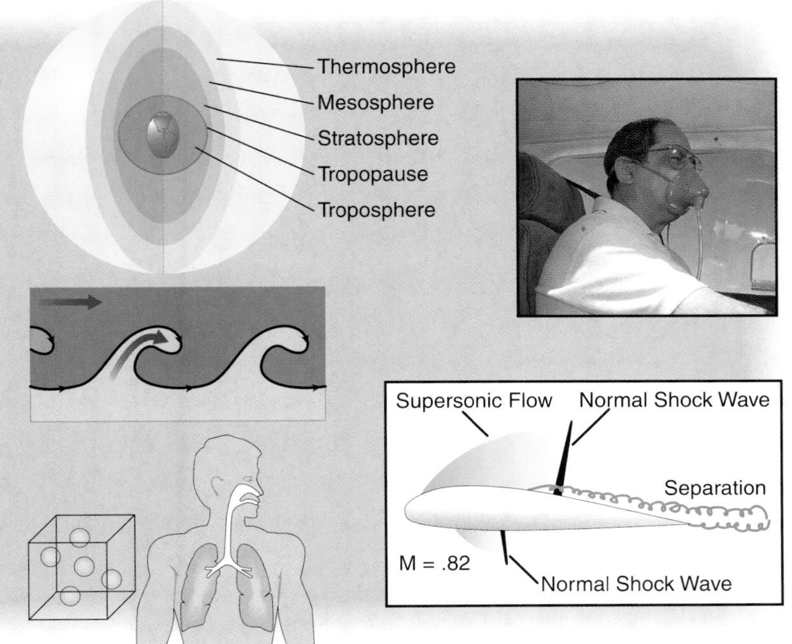

Figure 5-58. To expand your students' knowledge of flight at increased speeds and high altitudes, you may consider addressing several different subject areas.

PLANNING FLIGHTS

The ability to effectively prepare for and accurately plan flights is essential to commercial pilots. Many of your commercial students may have only limited flight planning experience. You may encounter students who have met their cross-country flight time requirements by repeatedly traveling to a familiar airport in the same airplane. Your students may begin their professional pilot careers performing charter operations, air ambulance missions, or corporate flights. They may be required to plan flights involving a wide variety of aircraft, airports, and flight conditions. While you cannot prepare your students for every contingency, you can provide them with the tools necessary to safely and efficiently plan and execute cross-country flights.

Your students need practical flight planning experience with conditions they may realistically encounter as commercial pilots. For example, filling the aircraft fuel tanks may not be an option due to the weight of passengers or cargo. One of the best ways to prepare your students for commercial flight planning is to develop scenarios and ask your students to perform all aspects of the preparation for each flight. [Figure 5-59]

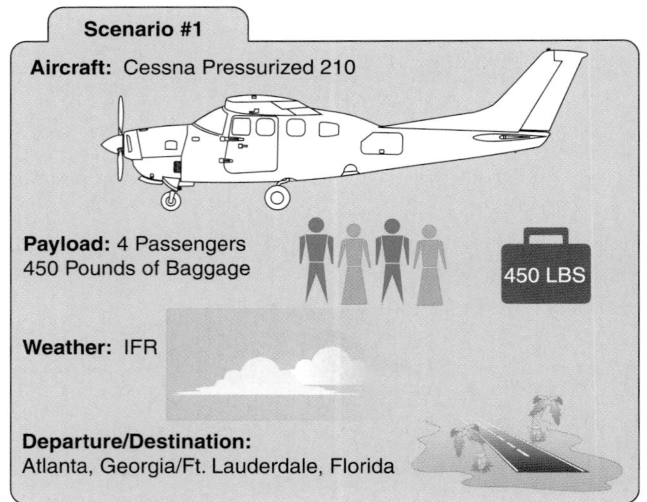

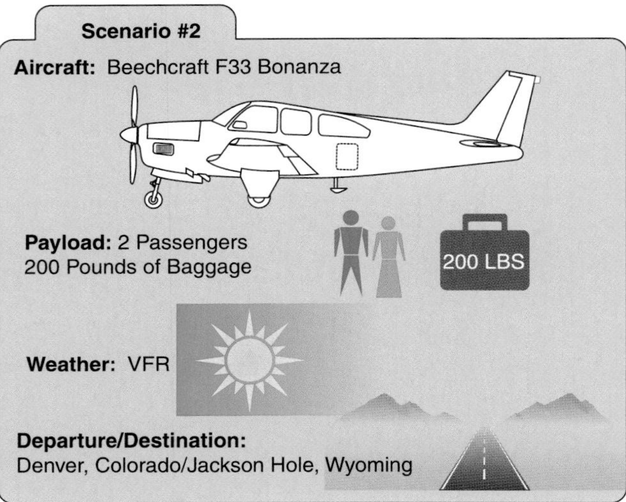

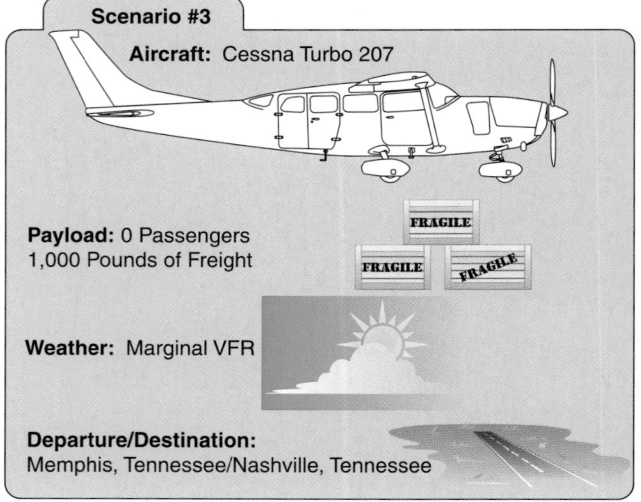

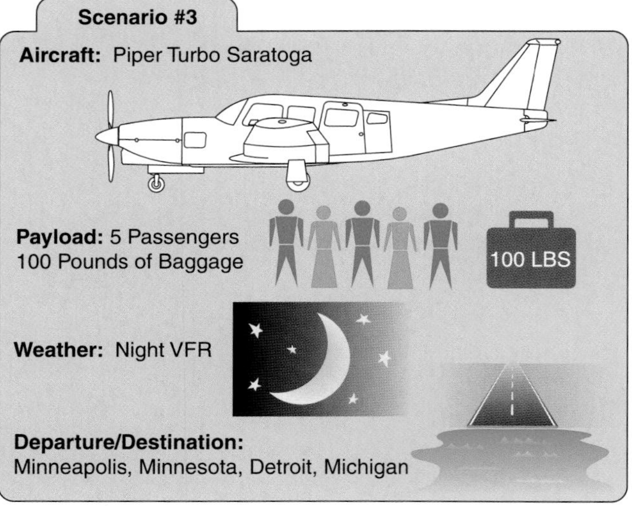

Figure 5-59. Flight planning scenarios should require students to compute takeoff and landing distances, determine climb and cruise performance, and perform weight and balance calculations.

COMMERCIAL PILOT ADM

Your commercial students may have varying backgrounds in regard to aeronautical decision making. Many may have had comprehensive human factors and ADM training while pursuing private pilot certificates or instrument ratings and extensive experience making

inflight decisions. Others may not have received any organized ADM instruction and may have only limited experience implementing decisions as PIC. You may need to review basic ADM concepts such as the decision-making process and the poor judgment chain with some students. In other cases, you may begin immediately exploring ADM concepts which relate specifically to commercial operations.

Explain to your students that when they become professional pilots, decision making becomes increasingly complex. They must balance public perceptions of aviation, their company's demands, passenger comfort, and their own desire to conduct safe flight operations. In addition, relying upon flying for their income may affect their ability to make sound decisions. They may need to make the sometimes difficult and unpopular choice to cancel a flight or divert to an alternate. You may consider enlisting a friend or acquaintance who is a professional pilot to describe to your students some of the types of decisions required during commercial operations. [Figure 5-60]

Although he has no mountain-flying experience, Jeff believes he is competent to fly to an airport located in the mountains after completing his checkout in a high performance airplane.

Figure 5-60. Even if your students do not intend to pursue aviation careers, they may be tempted to take additional risks as they develop commercial piloting skills and begin to operate airplanes with advanced equipment and systems.

THE HUMAN ELEMENT IN SPACE

From the very beginning, American astronauts have argued for control of their spacecraft. On the first American orbital flight, John Glenn had to deal with serious emergencies and use his own skill to manually position his Mercury spacecraft for re-entry into the atmosphere. Even today, the last minute of every Space Shuttle flight is flown manually by a human pilot. While visionary airplane pilots might hope for long careers as commercial space pilots, the prospects seem dim for the near future. Even career astronauts are limited to a few flights due to the radiation exposure they receive on each mission.

Historically, the overwhelming majority of space launches have had no human pilots. At first, the rockets were too small to carry anything but small payloads. When larger rockets came along, the enormous cost of putting each pound into orbit made it too expensive to add crew, especially considering the additional life support and recovery systems needed to return them safely to Earth!

Even in spacecraft that have crews, the pilot's principal task during launch has been to monitor the automated systems and handle any emergencies, and there have been mercifully few of those. Most of the designs for commercial launch vehicles of the future have no flight crews. Even vehicles that will carry human crews to and from the International Space Station have no provision for human pilots.

It can be difficult to make a case for human pilots in an environment where an error or hesitation of a fraction of a second can mean the difference between success and disaster. Computers are fast, logical, and have exquisitely sensitive nervous systems running throughout the vehicle. In the time it takes a human pilot to see and respond to an alarm, the computers can run through millions of calculations and evaluate hundreds of options.

On the other hand, software errors and minor equipment failures have resulted in the loss of several multi-million dollar spacecraft and important interplanetary probes. Perhaps a resourceful human pilot on board could have saved them. As reusable launch vehicles are developed and the cost per pound of getting into orbit comes down, there may be increased latitude for human pilots on commercial launches.

Courtesy of NASA

Possibly the greatest potential career for ambitious astronaut/pilots will be in space tourism. Already several designs are taking shape for suborbital passenger spacecraft that will take well-heeled adventurers for short ballistic flights into space. Most designs include a pilot, who not only manages the spacecraft, but also sees to the needs of the passengers and acts as tour guide and coach during the flight.

If your students pursue aviation careers, they most likely will transition from acting as sole authority in the cockpit to operating as part of a crew. You can prepare them for the crew environment by practicing crew coordination with your students. While crew coordination is crucial during emergency situations, it can be just as important during completion of routine tasks since the failure to ensure that essential duties have been accomplished can lead to serious in-flight problems. In light of this concern, commercial air carriers include **line-oriented flight training (LOFT)** within their ongoing training curricula. LOFT was first developed in the late 1970s after a serious airline accident focused attention on CRM issues. The program is organized to evaluate how crews work together during legs of a typical trip. For example, a first officer transitioning from domestic to international routes may join a captain and (if applicable) a second officer to review the dispatch for an actual flight segment, such as a trip from San Francisco to Tokyo. After a detailed briefing, they conduct the flight in a simulator, while being evaluated by an instructor. Once the flight is completed, the crew is debriefed on their performance. [Figure 5-61]

1 Assign your students the task of planning a specific trip. Each student must work the performance calculations necessary for the flight.

2 Prior to the simulation, observe your students as they participate in a preflight briefing. Ensure they discuss the division of responsibilities for the flight.

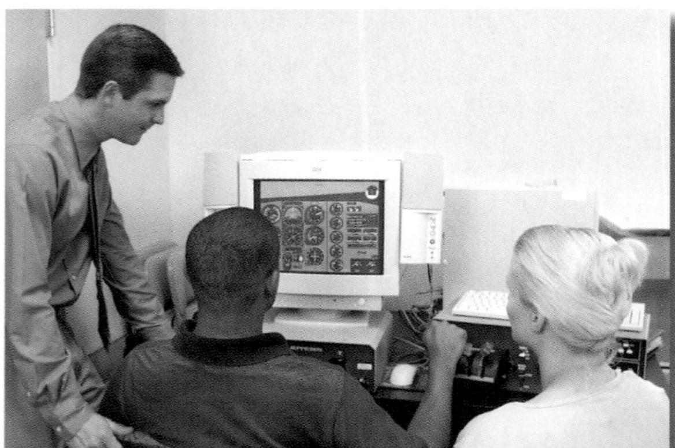

3 Play the role of ATC as your students rehearse the flight in the PCATD. They should conduct all departure, enroute, and arrival procedures as you observe their performance and issue ATC instructions. Evaluate how well your students use crew coordination techniques, such as the challenge-response method of performing checklists.

4 After the session, debrief your students on their performance. Be open to their input regarding the flight and offer suggestions as to how they may improve coordination and communication.

Figure 5-61. You can hold your own LOFT sessions with your commercial students. Ask one student to play the role of the captain and the other to act as the first officer during a session using a flight training device (FTD), PCATD, or simulator. If you cannot enlist two students, you can assume one of the roles.

SUMMARY CHECKLIST

✓ Before you can instruct commercial students, you must evaluate their experience and knowledge levels.

✓ While your students normally do not need to study FAR Parts 119, 121, 125, 129, 135, and 137 for commercial pilot certification, you should ensure they understand what types of operations these regulations cover.

✓ To create an effective and interesting learning experience, enlist the assistance of an aviation maintenance technician (AMT) to teach advanced aircraft systems.

✓ If your students understand the reasons for certain system operating procedures, it is more likely they will remember and correctly execute these actions when necessary.

✓ Understanding the basic operating principles of turbine-powered engines will enable you to help answer students' questions.

✓ Your commercial students must be proficient in the operation of constant-speed propellers since improper usage can cause serious engine damage or dangerous degradation of flight characteristics.

✓ To help prepare your students to troubleshoot problems, you may consider posing landing gear malfunction scenarios.

✓ If you have the opportunity, introduce your students to the various oxygen systems by showing them the equipment from several different airplanes.

✓ For most commercial operations at high altitude, passenger comfort demands the use of pressurized aircraft, so your students need to have a basic understanding of how pressurization systems work.

✓ Exploring the generation of lift in detail with your commercial students is essential to their future understanding of the high lift and high drag devices found on many advanced aircraft.

✓ The boundary layer is air next to the surface of an airfoil which shows reduction of speed due to the air's viscosity, or thickness.

✓ The high velocity airflow of the turbulent boundary layer helps to prevent the airflow separation which can cause a stall. The design of a particular airfoil must reach a compromise between the two types of boundary layer airflow.

✓ Leading edge flaps, fixed slots, and movable slats are three of the more common leading edge devices which usually operate in concert with trailing edge flaps to change the coefficient of lift of the wing.

✓ Vortices are formed at the tips of vortex generators which add energy to the boundary layer to prevent or delay airflow separation.

✓ High drag devices are useful anytime it is necessary for aircraft to descend without gaining speed, such as during a landing approach.

- ✓ To expand your students' knowledge on flight at increased speeds and high altitudes, you may consider addressing several different subject areas, such as high altitude meteorology, high altitude/high speed aerodynamics, and high altitude physiology.
- ✓ One of the best ways to prepare your students for commercial flight planning is to develop scenarios and ask your students to perform all aspects of the preparation for each flight, such as computing takeoff and landing distances, determining climb and cruise performance, and performing weight and balance calculations.
- ✓ Aeronautical decision making (ADM) can be complex for commercial pilots, since they must balance public perceptions of aviation, their company's demands, passenger comfort, and their own desire to conduct safe flight operations.
- ✓ You can hold your own line-oriented flight training (LOFT) sessions with your commercial students by asking one student to play the role of the captain and the other to act as the first officer during a session using a flight training device (FTD), PCATD, or simulator.

KEY TERMS

Commercial Pilot Privileges

Advanced Airplane Systems

High Performance Powerplants

Constant-Speed Propellers

Retractable Landing Gear

Oxygen Systems

Cabin Pressurization

Anti-Icing Equipment

De-Icing Equipment

Advanced Aerodynamics

Boundary Layer

High Lift Devices

High Drag Devices

High Speed/High Altitude Flight

Line-Oriented Flight Training (LOFT)

QUESTIONS

1. True/False. Commercial pilot applicants are required to know the regulations governing commercial operations described in FAR Parts 119, 121, 125, 129, 135, and 137.
2. Explain some of the methods you can use to teach your students about advanced aircraft systems.
3. State at least two questions you could ask a student to prompt them to think about retractable landing gear malfunctions.
4. What are the primary types of oxygen systems with which your students should be familiar?
5. State at least two issues that are important to address with students when you explain ice control systems.

6. Select the true statement regarding characteristics of the boundary layer.

    A. Turbulent flow begins near the leading edge of the airfoil, and at some point along the wing transitions to laminar flow.
    B. The high velocity airflow of the turbulent boundary layer helps to prevent the airflow separation which can cause a stall.
    C. Proceeding back from the leading edge of the airfoil, pressure increases with distance, creating a favorable pressure gradient.

7. How do vortex generators benefit the generation of lift by an airfoil?

    A. They delay the transition from the laminar to the turbulent boundary layer.
    B. They reverse the pressure gradient on the wing resulting in an adverse pressure gradient (low to high).
    C. They add energy to the boundary layer to prevent or delay airflow separation which can result in increased form drag and eventually a stall.

8. True/False. Leading edge flaps, fixed slots, and movable slats are three of the more common high drag devices.

9. Create a scenario you could use to teach your students about the aspects of flight planning.

10. What is one method you can use to help your students develop crew coordination skills?

SECTION D

ENHANCING FLIGHT SKILLS

INSTRUCTING THE COMMERCIAL STUDENT

This section is designed to provide you with methods to help you instruct students who are pursuing commercial pilot certificates. When flying with commercial students, you may assume they are current and competent pilots capable of performing to the level and standards of at least that of a private pilot. However, this may not always be the case. It is a good idea to spend some time interviewing students to assess their knowledge and currency level, and to find out what goals they hope to accomplish after they earn their commercial certificate. [Figure 5-62]

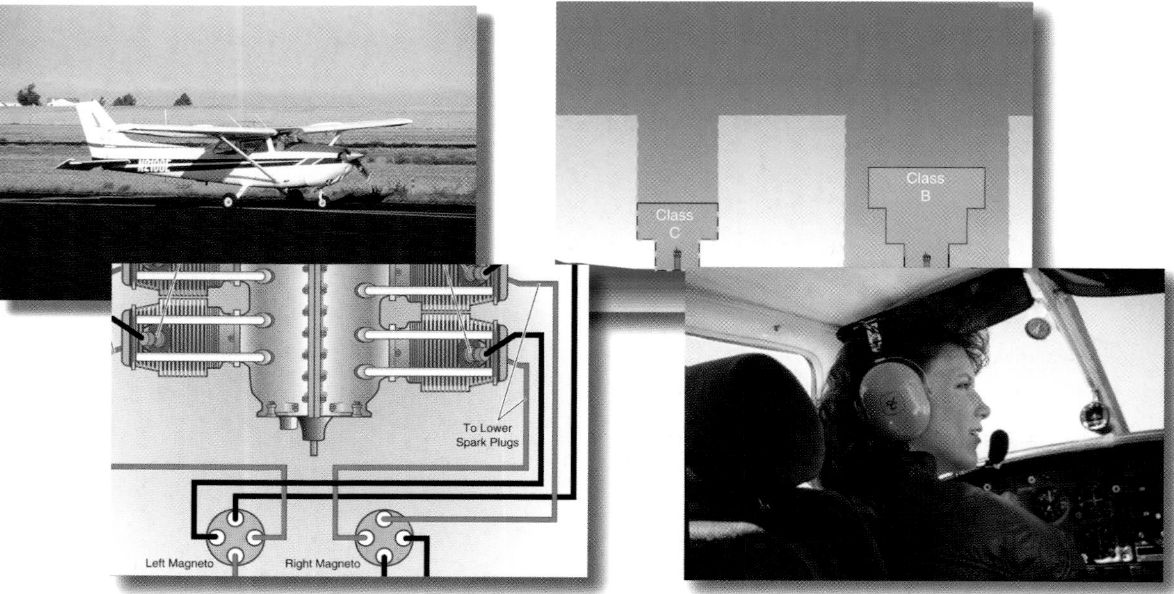

Figure 5-62. Keep in mind that your commercial students may need remedial instruction in many areas, including taxiing, radio work, operating airplane systems, flying in various types of airspace, or even a general review of maneuvers.

This section is not intended to explain commercial pilot ground and flight operations in the detail required for a student to master each maneuver and procedure. Rather, it is designed as a guideline for instructing students that provides you with examples of specific teaching techniques, common student errors, and tips to help you make your

students' commercial flight training a positive experience. Your students must perform several maneuvers which are required for both private pilot and commercial pilot certification. This section covers only those maneuvers which apply specifically to commercial pilot training. Detailed discussions on maneuvers such as slow flight and stalls, as well as takeoffs and landings, can be found in Section B of this chapter. For specific information on commercial pilot knowledge and step-by-step descriptions of commercial pilot maneuvers, consult the Guided Flight Discovery *Instrument/Commercial Manual.*

INTO THE WILD BLACK YONDER

Learning to fly the Space Shuttle is very similar to checking out in any large, complex airplane — and also very different. As in an airplane, much of the rookie astronaut's training consists of learning systems and memorizing procedures. Up to three quarters of formal training time can be classroom work, supplemented by long nights of homework and study. In addition to learning the details of every system in the orbiter, the new astronaut will also learn orbital mechanics, rocket propulsion, flight dynamics, spaceflight physiology, life support essentials, and how to observe features on the Earth from space.

As with commercial airplanes, simulators play a large part in the training. NASA's Johnson Space Center has only two full-motion shuttle simulators, so most practice sessions use single-task trainers that simulate a particular system or aspect of the flight. Many of the simulators are unique to the equipment and experiments that will be flown on a specific mission. [Figure A]

A

Since the Shuttle takes off vertically and lands horizontally, the cockpit and mid-deck simulators can be locked with their noses pointed up at the ceiling to practice getting into the seats for launch, or getting out fast in case of an emergency during launch. CRM and teamwork are essential to each flight, so crews train together once they are assigned to a mission.

B

Pilot astronauts are expected to fly a minimum of 15 hours per month to keep their skills sharp. A specially modified Grumman Gulfstream jet simulates the landing characteristics of the Shuttle Orbiter, and the pilots usually practice at least 300 landings before their first flight in the Shuttle. [Figure B]

Getting acquainted with microgravity is done in two different ways. Flights in a modified Boeing KC-135, affectionately known as the "Vomit Comet," give brief tastes of zero-G as the airplane describes parabolic arcs in the sky. About a third of the participants get sick on their first few flights. Wearing spacesuits underwater in huge neutral bouyancy tanks simulates working in space. [Figure C]

C

The curriculum is rounded out with wilderness survival training, eating space food, and parachute practice.

As the launch date gets closer, the crew spends more and more time in the full mission simulator, wearing full spacesuits and rehearsing every aspect of the mission and every conceivable emergency and combination of emergencies. After their flights, astronauts have commented that the training is quite realistic. They say the major differences are that there is more noise and vibration during launch, and continuous microgravity while in orbit. And of course, you can not beat the view!

Thorough, careful training and detailed planning are often cited as major factors in a successful Shuttle mission. The same can be said for successful airplane flights within the atmosphere. As an instructor, you will share responsibility for that training, and when former students apply the skills and habits you helped them learn, you will share in their success.

Before you begin flight training with your students, you may need to do some recurrent training of your own. If you have not flown a **complex airplane**, or **high performance airplane** for a while, it is a good idea to spend some time reviewing pertinent operational items. A flight lesson with an experienced instructor is a good way to polish your skills as well as identify some of your weak areas. More advanced airplanes tend to be heavier and faster, so it may be a good idea to spend some time practicing takeoffs, landings, emergency procedures, and reviewing systems before teaching your commercial students.

TEACHING IN COMPLEX AIRPLANES

Often, the first time your students operate a complex airplane is in conjunction with commercial flight training. Since your commercial students need to receive at least 10 hours of training in an airplane with retractable landing gear, flaps, and a controllable pitch propeller, you have a unique opportunity to introduce them to a complex, and possibly a high performance, airplane. [Figure 5-63]

Figure 5-63. A high performance airplane, as defined by the FARs, has an engine with more than 200 horsepower. A complex airplane has retractable landing gear, flaps, and a controllable pitch propeller.

In order for your students to act as PIC of either a complex or a high performance air-plane, they must receive instruction and a logbook endorsement stating that they are com- petent to pilot such an airplane. Your students' flight training should focus primarily on operation of systems which are new to them, such as retractable landing gear, and a constant-speed propeller.

At first, your commercial students may be overwhelmed with tasks when flying advanced airplanes. This is simply due to the increased speed at which the airplane flies, and the greater complexity of the systems. As your students learn to operate these more advanced systems, it is essential that you stress the importance of checklists. As an example, since retractable gear will most likely be a new system to your students, the proper use of a checklist will keep them from overlooking this important item. As your students gain experience operating advanced airplanes, they will generally begin to operate the airplane with greater efficiency and skill. If your students continue to fall behind the airplane after several lessons, you may want to suggest they spend some time in the cockpit reviewing procedures while the airplane is on the ground.

RETRACTABLE LANDING GEAR

Chapter 2 of your airplane's POH is a good place to introduce your students to the recommended operating procedures for **retractable landing gear**. This section lists the airspeed limitations for gear retraction, extension, and normal operation. One thing you should discuss with your students is the length of time it takes for retraction and extension

LANDING GEAR

MAXIMUM GEAR EXTENDED SPEED		155 MPH
MAXIMUM GEAR OPERATING SPEED	EXTENSION	155 MPH
	RETRACTION	130 MPH

Figure 5-64. Airplane manufacturers include landing gear operating speed limitations in the POH as well as on a placard in the cockpit.

of various gear systems. It should include a discussion that some gear systems actually create more drag during extension or retraction due to the action of the gear doors. Also, many aircraft have marked pitch changes as the gear is retracted or extended. [Figure 5-64]

When first instructing your students on operating the landing gear, it is a good idea to define clearly when to retract and when to extend the landing gear. On takeoff, instruct your students not to retract the landing gear until they are out of available runway. That way, if the engine fails immediately after takeoff, an emergency landing may be made on the remaining runway.

WEIGHTY DECISIONS

Encourage your students to think about the trade-off between the performance gained by cleaning up the airplane immediately after takeoff, versus the safety of leaving the gear down until there is no longer any usable runway. Additionally, when some airplane gear doors open, drag is temporarily increased, thus reducing airplane performance. The following ASRS report illustrates this point.

Accelerated to full power, 10 degrees of flaps, and rotated at 70 knots. Pulled gear up at approximately 10-15 feet in the air. Sank into the ground at full power, in effect a gear-up landing. After the incident, the airplane contents were weighed, and the actual weight was such that the airplane was 150 lbs. over gross.

The fact that the airplane was over gross certainly contributed to this incident. However, if the gear had been left in the down position, the airplane would have likely settled onto its wheels instead of the belly of the airplane.

While operating in the traffic pattern, you should generally instruct your students to ensure the landing gear is extended upon reaching mid-field downwind. Additionally, your students must take into account important airspeed limitations, such as V_{LO} and V_{LE}. If your students are making a straight-in approach, they must be able to determine an appropriate point to lower the landing gear. Usually it is better to have them lower the gear early in the approach, rather than at the last minute. The landing gear can also be used to control airspeed and descent rates. For example, if speed reduction is desired, extending the landing gear is an excellent means to achieve a slower airspeed without reducing power. [Figure 5-65]

Figure 5-65. Stress the importance of the proper timing of checklist items and enlist the manufacturer's recommendations as an aid in determining proper speed and required time for gear extension.

Emphasize the importance to your students of some type of gear and flap identification, either verbal, visual or both, when extending or retracting the landing gear and flaps. Devise a routine of stating, "*Identifying landing gear, gear up*" or "*Identifying flap handle, flaps retract*" to prevent inadvertently extending or retracting the wrong equipment. Another helpful tip to teach your students is to never rush through cleaning up an airplane after landing. Wait for the airplane to come to a complete stop, clear of the runway, before retracting the flaps, unless the airplane's POH recommends otherwise. Also, when your students extend the landing gear, have them leave their hand on the gear handle until the landing gear is visually confirmed down and locked, and then have them state, "*Gear down and locked.*" Do not allow them to run though the checklist without verifying their actions. [Figure 5-66]

Figure 5-66. When on short final it is a good idea to have your students say and verify: "*Landing gear down and locked, propeller full forward, mixture rich, cleared to land.*" A check like this ensures a safe landing or go-around.

There are times while performing maneuvers in the practice area that the gear warning horn will sound because of throttle and/or flap position. Anytime a warning horn sounds, or an annunciator light illuminates, your students should verify what is causing the warning, and what action is required to correct the situation. If the landing gear warning horn is silenced or ignored, it could easily create a scenario for a gear-up landing. Have your students practice **emergency landing gear extension** on a regular basis. Be sure they use the checklist, and most importantly, continue to fly the airplane during the emergency extension. If your students are comfortable using the emergency extension system, their stress level during an actual emergency will most likely be significantly reduced.

Constant-Speed Propeller Operation

Typically, your commercial students are accustomed to flying airplanes with fixed-pitch propellers. It may take several training flights for your students to be comfortable operating a **constant-speed propeller**. Often students have trouble with the sequence of adjusting power and r.p.m. For example, when increasing power, students may try to increase manifold pressure without first increasing the r.p.m. [Figure 5-67]

Encourage your students to take some time during the before takeoff check to verify the propeller and governor operations. Most POHs include a pre-takeoff propeller cycling check and instructions in the airplane checklist that verify adequate governor and propeller operation. During takeoff have your students position the throttle and propeller control full forward so the engine can turn at its maximum r.p.m., while also developing the maximum amount of horsepower. Then, to help establish the airplane in a climb after takeoff, explain to your students that they should retard the throttle and propeller controls, as per manufacturer's recommendations, in order to achieve more economical fuel consumption. [Figure 5-68]

Tell your students that to help prevent excessive internal cylinder pressures, they should first verify that the manifold pressure is within allowable limits before they decrease the

PROPELLER

The airplane has an all-metal, two-bladed, constant-speed, governor-regulated propeller. A setting introduced into the governor with the propeller control establishes the propeller speed, and thus the engine speed to be maintained. The governor then controls flow of engine oil, boosted to high pressure by the governing pump, to or from a piston in the propeller hub. Oil pressure acting on the piston twists the blades toward high pitch (low RPM). When oil pressure to the piston in the propeller hub is relieved, centrifugal force, assisted by an internal spring, twists the blades toward low pitch (high RPM).

A control knob on the center area of the switch and control panel is used to set the propeller and control engine RPM as desired for various flight conditions. The knob is labeled PROP RPM, PUSH INCR. When the control knob is pushed in, blade pitch will decrease, giving a higher RPM. When the control knob is pulled out, the blade pitch increases, thereby decreasing RPM. The propeller control knob is equipped with a vernier feature which allows slow or fine RPM adjustments by rotating the knob clockwise to increase RPM, and counterclockwise to decrease it. To make rapid or large adjustments, depress the button on the end of the control knob and reposition the control as desired.

Figure 5-67. Remind your students to always refer to the POH for specific constant-speed propeller operating instructions.

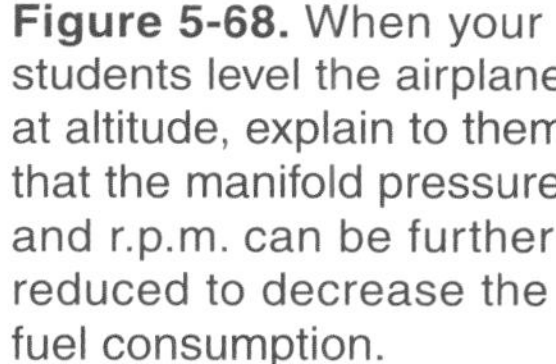

Figure 5-68. When your students level the airplane at altitude, explain to them that the manifold pressure and r.p.m. can be further reduced to decrease the fuel consumption.

engine's r.p.m. with the propeller control. For example, to establish a climb after takeoff, the throttle should be retarded first to establish the climb manifold pressure. Once adjusted, your students can adjust the propeller control to obtain a lower r.p.m. Conversely, when your students are increasing the throttle to a high power setting, they should first verify that the engine's r.p.m. is high enough to permit the increased manifold pressure. This means that before they fully advance the throttle, the propeller control should be positioned full forward, to the low pitch, high r.p.m. position. [Figure 5-69]

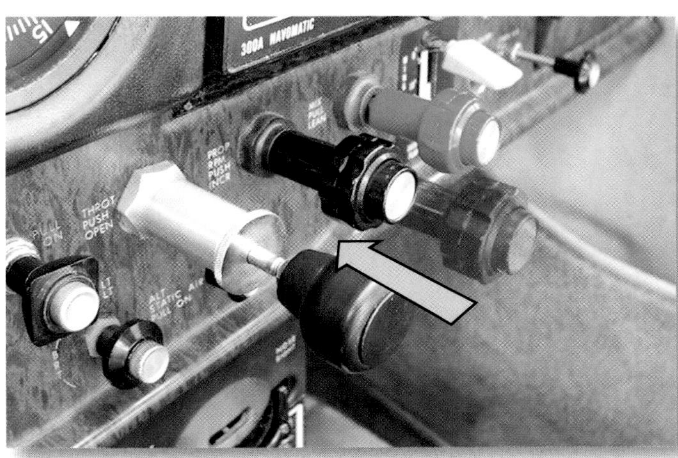

Figure 5-69. The propeller control should be full forward before landing so your students can apply full throttle without causing engine damage in case a go-around is initiated.

Additionally, have your students consider the reasons behind avoiding rapid throttle movements when making power adjustments. Harmonic balance weights are often installed in the engine's crankshaft. These weights are designed to position themselves by the inertia generated during crankshaft rotation, in order to effectively absorb and dampen crankshaft vibration. If your students abruptly move the throttle, the balance weights may shift away from the optimum position, causing the crankshaft to receive a large amount of vibration-induced stress.

TEACHING COMMERCIAL PILOT MANEUVERS

Commercial pilot maneuvers require smoother control inputs and have more stringent completion standards than private maneuvers. For example, your commercial students are required to reduce their landing distance on a short-field landing, and there are smaller altitude deviations allowed for slow flight and stalls. Remember that before every maneuver your students should visually clear the area.

PERFECTING STEEP TURNS

Steep turns are designed to develop your students' ability to accurately control the airplane while operating near its performance limits. You need to stress to your students the importance of performing steep turns at or below V_A. When flying above V_A, it is possible to exceed the airplane's load limit.

A common error associated with steep turns is trying to regain lost altitude without decreasing the bank angle. When teaching students how to recover from a nose-low attitude during a steep turn, have them first reduce the angle of bank and then apply back pressure to attain the desired pitch attitude. You should also teach your students that during a steep turn to the right, the rudder is normally used to prevent yawing. [Figure 5-70]

When teaching students how to recover from a nose-low attitude during a steep turn, have them first reduce the angle of bank and then apply back pressure to attain the desired pitch attitude.

You should teach your students that throughout a level, 720° steep turn to the right, the rudder is normally used to prevent yawing.

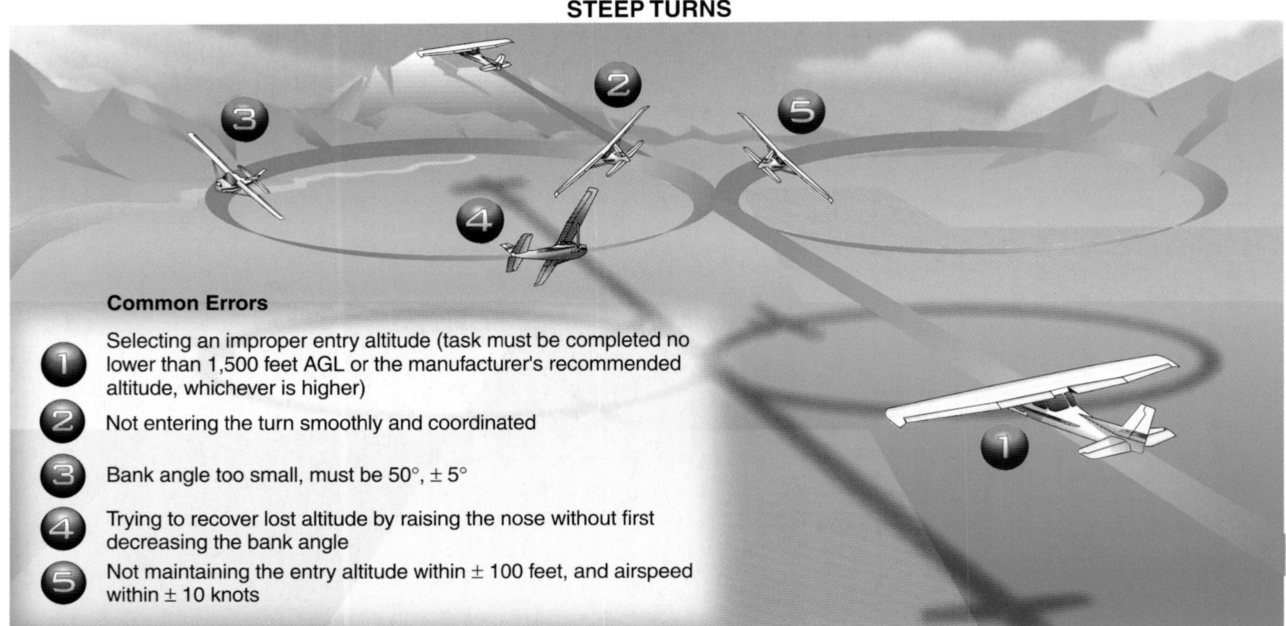

Figure 5-70. After your students complete one 360° turn, they should immediately roll into a steep turn in the opposite direction.

Looping the Loop

In the very early days of flying, about the only way a pilot could make money was by charging for public exhibitions. At first the astonishing spectacle of a machine lifting itself off the ground was enough, but soon pilots began trying to outdo each other with feats of airmanship.

The first loop was flown on September 21, 1913, when Adolphe Pegoud of France performed the maneuver in his Bleriot XI-2. [Figure A] (A month before, he had become the first person to parachute from an airplane.) His aerobatics and flying exhibitions made him a celebrity in both France and England. In America, Marjory and Katherine Stinson were popular female stunt pilots. (After World War I, they would become the operators of the successful Stinson Airplane Company.)

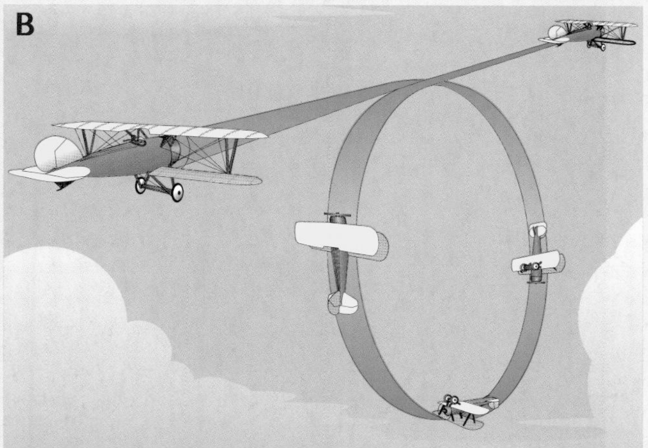

World War I saw the mastery of ever more complex maneuvers. A half loop combined with a half roll became known as an Immelman, after the German fighter ace Max Immelman. The French *vrille* was used by pilots of both sides to escape when the combat became too hot. In English, we call the maneuver a spin.

The postwar years gave rise to barnstorming aerial circuses, and rapidly advancing technology led to stronger, more capable airplanes. The legendary Jimmy Doolittle is generally credited with flying the first outside loop in a Curtiss P-1 Hawk, in May 1927, a few days after Lindbergh's transatlantic flight. [Figure B]

The first major international aerobatic competition was held in 1934 in Vincennes, France. By then, left and right spins, outside loops, and inverted 360-degree turns were compulsory maneuvers. Gerhard Fieseler of Germany became the first World Aerobatic Champion at that contest. (Fieseler went on to become a noted airplane designer, and although he retired from competition after that 1934 victory, he remains a steadfast supporter of sport aerobatics.)

After the Second World War, competitive aerobatics emerged as a sport distinct from airshow stunt-flying. Uniform scoring systems and standardized judging criteria placed more emphasis on precision and control than risk and danger. The Aresti Aerocryptographic System made it possible to draw and describe any aerobatic routine easily and neatly, both for consistent judging and for reference in the cockpit during the flight. Capable new airplanes such as the Pitts Special and Zlin Akrobat came to dominate international competitions in the 1960s and 1970s, gradually edging out mature veterans like the Bucker Jungmeister and Yak 18. [Figure C] Mira Slovak got the attention of the aviation world in the late 1960s with his Lomcevak, hailed as the first truly new aerobatic maneuver in decades.

In the last 20 years, sturdy monoplanes with amazingly stiff composite structures have replaced wood, fabric and steel biplanes, but precision, physical stamina, an intimate understanding of their airplane, and a deft touch on the controls still are defining characteristics of successful aerobatic pilots. [Figure D]

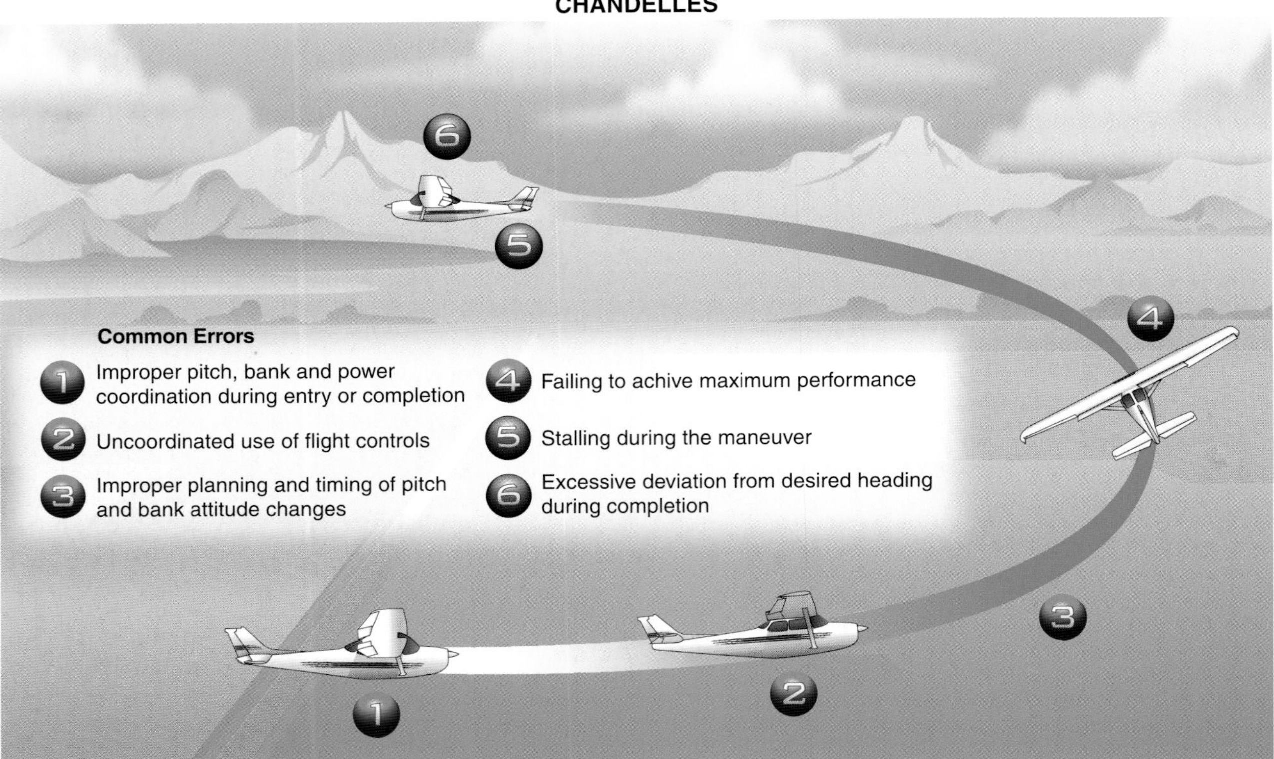

Figure 5-71. Your students should be consistent with the entry airspeed and power setting they select when performing chandelles.

PERFORMING CHANDELLES

The objective of a **chandelle** is to help your students develop good coordination skills and refine the use of the airplane's flight controls. Explain to your students that during a chandelle, the airspeed gradually decreases from the entry speed to a few knots above stall speed at the completion of the 180° turn. While performing chandelles, your students use full power in an airplane with a fixed-pitch propeller, or climb power in an airplane equipped with a constant-speed propeller. To control the airspeed they must adjust the pitch attitude of the airplane. Therefore, maintaining the proper pitch attitude is a key element of this maneuver. Due to variables, such as atmospheric density and airplane performance, altitude gain is not a criterion for successful completion of a chandelle.

Have your students choose an altitude which allows them to complete the maneuver no lower than 1,500 feet AGL. Demonstrate that wind has little or no effect on chandelles, but your students should be made aware that it is in their best interest to begin the maneuver by turning into the wind, which helps them remain inside the intended practice area. [Figure 5-71]

FLYING LAZY EIGHTS

The **lazy eight** is a maneuver that requires your students to possess a high degree of piloting skill and a sound understanding of the associated performance factors. The objective of this maneuver is to develop and improve your students' coordination, orientation, planning, division of attention, and ability to maintain precise airplane control. Point out to your students that the maneuver is called a lazy eight due to the longitudinal axis of the airplane appearing to fly a pattern about the horizon that resembles a figure eight lying on its side. Some students perform lazy eights with too much emphasis on mechanics, rather than feel. They may develop a better sense for a proper lazy eight if you have them visualize the smooth, sloping curves that the airplane traces in the sky.

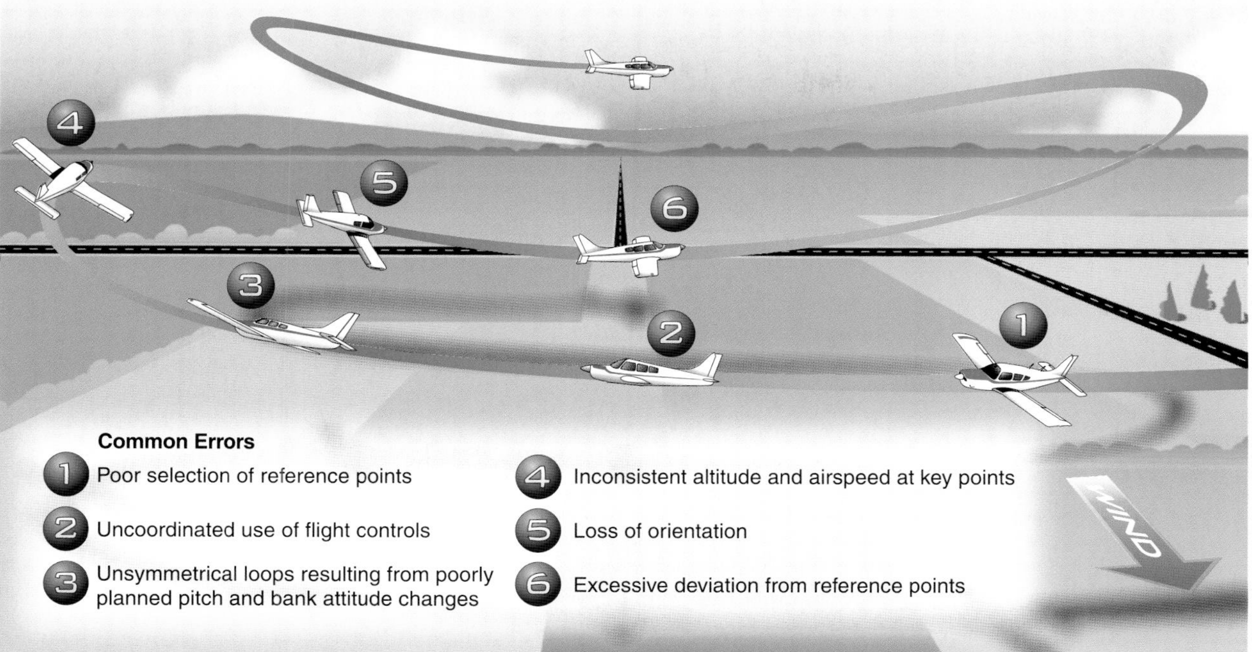

Figure 5-72. Throughout a lazy eight, airspeed, altitude, bank angle and pitch attitude, as well as control pressures, constantly change.

Ensure that your students select an altitude that allows them to perform the maneuver at no lower than 1,500 feet AGL or an altitude recommended by the airplane manufacturer, whichever is higher. Emphasize continual scanning for traffic, and be sure to have your students select reference points to help them identify the 45°, 90°, and 135° points on the horizon. Your students should make turns into the wind, so the airplane remains inside the intended practice area. [Figure 5-72]

EXECUTING EIGHTS-ON-PYLONS

When your students learn **eights-on-pylons** they begin refining their ability to control the airplane at traffic pattern altitude over a varied ground track, while dividing their attention between instrument indications and visual cues outside the airplane. Recommend to your students to choose a reference point on or near the wingtip, so their line of sight through the reference point is parallel to the lateral axis of the airplane. Point out to your students that the reference varies considerably on different airplanes. Also, be sure your students know how to approximate pivotal altitude: TAS (in m.p.h.)^2 ÷ 15 = pivotal altitude. [Figure 5-73]

Figure 5-73. The reference point may be above the wingtip on a low-wing airplane, below the wingtip on a high-wing airplane, and ahead of the wingtip on a tapered-wing airplane.

EIGHTS-ON-PYLONS

Common Errors

1. Faulty entry technique
2. Poor planning, orientation, and division of attention
3. Uncoordinated flight control application
4. Use of improper line-of-sight reference
5. Application of rudder alone to maintain line-of-sight on the pylon
6. Improper timing of turn entries and rollouts
7. Improper correction for wind drift between pylons
8. Selection of pylons where there is no suitable emergency landing area within gliding distance

WIND

Figure 5-74. Your students should choose pylons that are perpendicular to the wind, and the pylons should be spaced to provide a few seconds of straight-and-level flight between the turns.

Help your students choose pylons in an open area, clear of any hills or obstructions. Point out the benefits of choosing pylons at approximately the same elevation, to avoid the added burden of adjusting altitude for variations in terrain. [Figure 5-74]

REFINING EMERGENCY PROCEDURES

Your commercial students are required to demonstrate knowledge of the emergency procedures listed in the Commercial Pilot PTS. You should make sure your students are competent in all areas of emergency operations required for commercial certification,

WHERE'S THE GPS?

In this day and age, transatlantic crossings are commonplace. Huge jet airliners carry passengers in pampered luxury, while the flight crew is assisted by an autopilot and sophisticated navigation equipment. All the while there is the reassurance that someone on the ground is tracking the progress of the flight.

In 1927, Charles Lindbergh was afforded no such luxuries when he piloted the *Spirit of St. Louis* from New York City to Paris. The resources available to Lindbergh were very primitive compared to today's standards, and he primarily relied on his own knowledge and skills to complete the flight.

Lindbergh's flight was the first successful nonstop crossing of the Atlantic Ocean by airplane. The flight took 33 hours and 29 minutes and covered 3,600 miles. Lindbergh's accomplishment was truly amazing considering he relied on nothing more than pilotage and dead reckoning as navigation tools, and approximated winds aloft by watching the white caps and foam on the ocean surface.

such as emergency descents, emergency approaches and landings, systems and equipment malfunctions, and the use of emergency equipment and survival gear. While there are some general guidelines to follow when performing these operations, you should ensure your students are familiar with the specific procedures outlined by their airplane's POH. A thorough discussion of commercial pilot emergency procedures can be found in the Guided Flight Discovery *Instrument/Commercial Manual.*

CONDUCTING THE LONG CROSS-COUNTRY FLIGHT

Prior to endorsing your commercial students for their commercial pilot practical test you are required to verify they have met the various flight time requirements, cross-country and distance requirements, and any other eligibility requirements found in FAR Part 61 or 141. FAR 61.129(4) requires your commercial students to conduct a solo cross-country flight of at least 300 nautical miles total distance, with one leg equal to or greater than 250 nautical miles from the original point of departure. Some training airplanes are capable of making this flight without planning a fuel stop and remaining well within the required fuel reserve minimums for flight. However, as a commercial pilot your students will likely be making flights where they must determine a fuel stop. One of the challenges you face with your commercial students is getting them to think like commercial pilots and plan accordingly. [Figure 5-75]

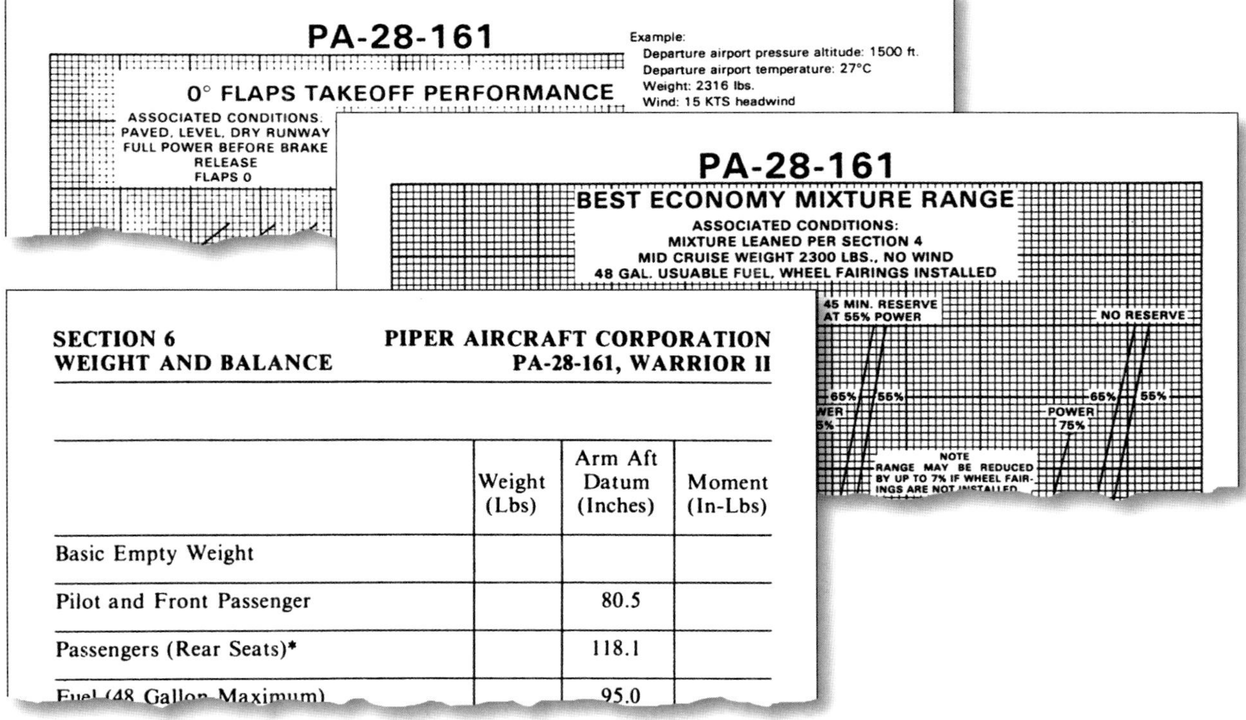

Figure 5-75. While the cross-country flights your students will fly in preparation for commercial certification are similar to those they have flown in the past, there will be some additional considerations. Items such as takeoff performance, range, and weight and balance should all be examined in greater detail.

At this level of their flight training, your commercial students should already be well versed in cross-country flying procedures. However, they may not have any experience with cross-country legs that are 250 nautical miles long. When your students fly a route of this distance, it becomes more crucial to monitor items like actual groundspeed, fuel burn, and weather along the route and at the destination. Remind your students that commercial pilots should always maintain good situational awareness, and have an alternate plan of action readily available, should an unplanned event occur during the flight.

SUMMARY CHECKLIST

✓ If you have not flown a complex airplane, or high performance airplane in a while, it is a good idea to spend some time reviewing pertinent operational items.

✓ Since your commercial students need to receive at least 10 hours of training in an airplane with retractable landing gear, flaps, and a controllable pitch propeller, you have a unique opportunity to introduce them to a complex, and possibly a high performance, airplane.

✓ In order for your students to act as PIC of either a complex or a high performance airplane, they must receive instruction and a logbook endorsement stating that they are competent to pilot such an airplane.

✓ A high performance airplane, as defined by the FARs, has an engine with more than 200 horsepower. A complex airplane has retractable landing gear, flaps, and a controllable pitch propeller.

✓ When first instructing your students on operating the landing gear, it is a good idea to define clearly when to retract and when to extend the landing gear.

✓ Devise a routine of stating: "*Identifying landing gear, gear up*" or "*Identifying flap handle, flaps retract*" to prevent inadvertently extending or retracting the wrong equipment.

✓ If your students are comfortable using the emergency extension system, their stress level during an actual emergency will most likely be significantly reduced.

✓ Always refer to the POH for specific constant-speed propeller operating instructions.

✓ The propeller control should be full forward before landing so your students can apply full throttle without causing engine damage in case a go-around is initiated.

✓ Commercial maneuvers require smoother control inputs and have more stringent completion standards than private maneuvers.

✓ Steep turns are designed to develop your student's ability to accurately control the airplane while operating near its performance limits.

✓ The objective of a chandelle is to help your students develop good coordination skills and refine the use of the airplane's flight controls.

✓ The objective of lazy eights is to develop and improve your students' coordination, orientation, planning, division of attention, and ability to maintain precise airplane control.

✓ When your students learn eights-on-pylons, they begin refining their ability to control the airplane at traffic pattern altitude over a varied ground track while dividing their attention between instrument indications and visual cues outside the airplane.

✓ FAR Part 61.129(4) requires your commercial students to conduct a solo cross-country flight at least 300 nautical miles total distance, with one leg equal to or greater than 250 nautical miles from the original point of departure.

KEY TERMS

Complex Airplane

High Performance Airplane

Retractable Landing Gear

Emergency Landing Gear Extension

Constant-Speed Propeller

Commercial Pilot Maneuvers

Steep Turn

Chandelle

Lazy Eight

Eights-on-Pylons

QUESTIONS

1. As defined by the FARs, what is a high performance airplane?

2. A complex airplane must have which of the following components?

   A. Constant-speed propeller, flaps
   B. Retractable landing gear, flaps, fixed-pitch propeller
   C. Controllable pitch propeller, flaps, retractable landing gear

3. True/False. For your students to act as PIC of a complex airplane, they must receive instruction and a logbook endorsement stating that they are competent to pilot a complex airplane.

4. True/False. Manufacturers are not required to include a placard with the landing gear operating speed limitations in the cockpit.

5. True/False. During the pre-takeoff check, it is not recommended to verify adequate governor and propeller operation, since it may damage the propeller.

6. When making power reduction adjustments during climbout, what should be retarded first, the propeller control or the throttle control?

7. What is a common error associated with chandelles?

   A. Improper planning and timing of pitch and bank attitude changes
   B. Excessive deviation from desired heading during completion
   C. Both A and B

8. True/False. The objective of lazy eights is to help your students develop and improve on their coordination, orientation, planning, division of attention, and ability to maintain precise airplane control.

9. What is the formula for estimating pivotal altitude?

10. Select the true statement about the cross-country required by FAR 61.129(4).

    A. The total distance of the flight needs to be no more than 250 nautical miles.
    B. One leg of the cross-country must be equal to or greater than 250 nautical miles from the original point of departure.
    C. The flight must have a total distance of at least 300 nautical miles with each leg equal to or greater than 100 nautical miles from the original departure point.

SECTION E
PROVIDING SPECIALIZED INSTRUCTION

As a future flight instructor, you may associate training activity with students who are seeking initial certification. With experience, you will begin to realize there is a broad range of **specialized instructional services** that you can also provide. Some examples include flight reviews, instrument proficiency checks, and transition training. Others involve aircraft checkouts for tailwheel, complex, high performance, and high altitude airplanes. In addition, you may help experienced military pilots transition to general aviation aircraft or you may have an opportunity to provide instruction in homebuilt airplanes. Regional or local checkouts are additional areas where specialized instruction can benefit pilots and increase safety. You may find providing these services to your students diversifies your schedule and expands your experience as an instructor.

CONDUCTING FLIGHT REVIEWS

FAR 61.56 requires that each certificated pilot successfully complete a **flight review**, consisting of a minimum of one hour of ground training, and one hour of flight training every 24 calendar months. A flight review is not a checkride — a flight review is a knowledge and skill refresher, and it should provide a learning experience for the pilot. [Figure 5-76]

You are allowed a fair amount of freedom with regard to the content of a flight review. With this in mind, you should tailor a flight review to fit the pilot's background and experience level. While preparing to give a flight review, it may be helpful to interview the pilot to find out if there is an academic area or a particular maneuver that the pilot wants to review. During the interview, you should ask the pilot about the type of equipment flown, and the nature of the flight operations. For example, the areas of operation emphasized for a pilot who normally flies local VFR flights from an uncontrolled field should be different from the areas of operation emphasized for a pilot who flies cross country under IFR to airports located in busy terminal areas.

You should also ask about the amount and recency of the pilot's flight experience. For instance, a private pilot who does not periodically practice stalls or short-field landings may need more time during the flight review dedicated to these procedures. Lastly, you and the pilot should agree on the content and scope of the flight review. In addition to interviewing the pilot, you should also refer to *Currency and Additional Qualification Requirements for Certificated Pilots* (AC 61-98), which provides additional information and a sample plan for conducting a flight review.

The flight review must be accomplished in an aircraft in which both you and the pilot are rated. For example, if you want to give a flight review in a multi-engine airplane, then you must hold the appropriate category and class ratings on your pilot and CFI certificate. Before you give a flight review in an aircraft in which you are not current, or with which

Since Phil is a private pilot that rarely flies more than 50 miles from his home airport, Mary feels a review of sectional charts and cross-country planning procedures is appropriate for the ground portion of the flight review.

Phiil has not reviewed emergency landing procedures since his last flight review, so he is a little rusty. Mary reminds Phil to locate a suitable landing spot before attempting to call ATC.

Even though Phil required a little help with certain procedures, Mary feels that overall he is a competent and safe pilot. She endorses his logbook to indicate satisfactory completion of a flight review.

Figure 5-76. At a minimum, a flight review must include coverage of the current general operating and flight rules of FAR Part 91, and performance of the flight maneuvers and procedures that, at your discretion, are necessary to demonstrate safe operation of the aircraft.

you are not familiar, you should obtain sufficient knowledge of its limitations, flying characteristics, and performance.

If the pilot completes the flight review satisfactorily, you should endorse the pilot's logbook. The endorsement should be in accordance with the current edition of AC 61-65. You should not make any logbook entries that show unsatisfactory performance. Instead, record the flight as instruction given and inform the pilot that additional training is required in those areas you find deficient.

While you need to know when a flight review is required, you should also be aware of the instances when one is not required. There are situations where a pilot may have been flying for several years without ever having accomplished a flight review. [Figure 5-77]

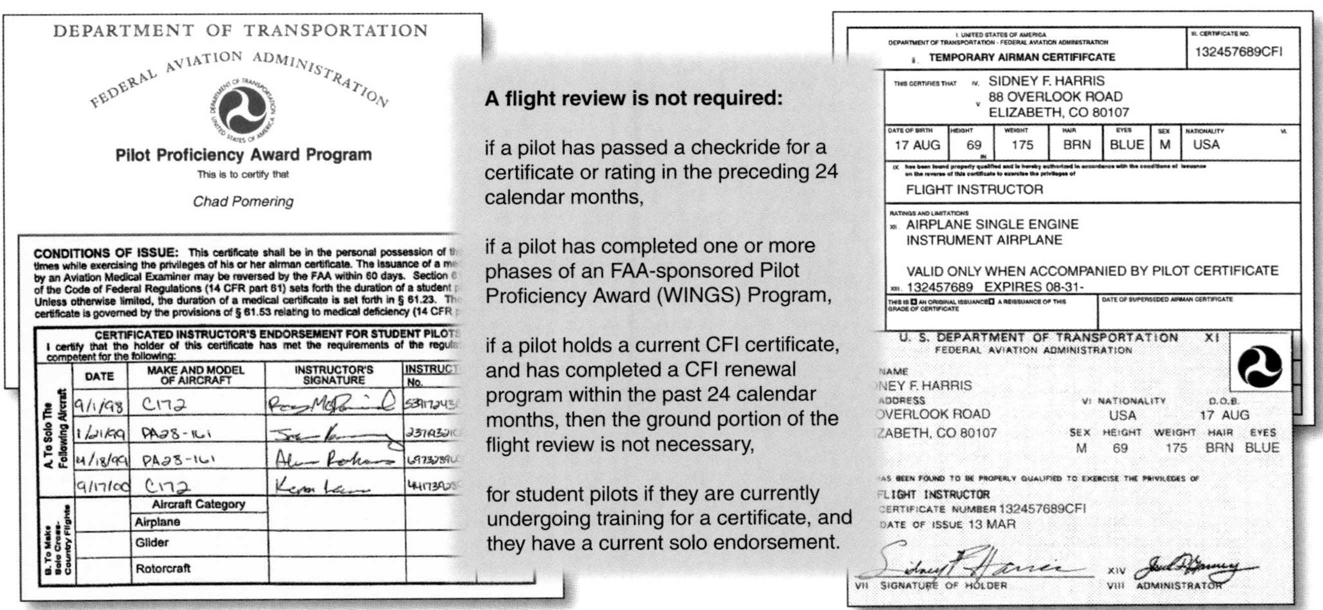

Figure 5-77. The regulations require pilots to obtain a flight review every 24 months, with certain exceptions.

PERFORMING INSTRUMENT PROFICIENCY CHECKS

To maintain instrument currency, instrument-rated pilots must have performed and logged the following under actual or simulated instrument conditions within the past 6 calendar months: 6 instrument approaches, holding procedures, and intercepting and tracking courses using navigation systems. As an alternative, a pilot may elect to take an **instrument proficiency check (IPC)** to maintain currency. However, if a pilot has not been instrument current for more than 6 calendar months, then an IPC becomes mandatory to regain currency. [Figure 5-78]

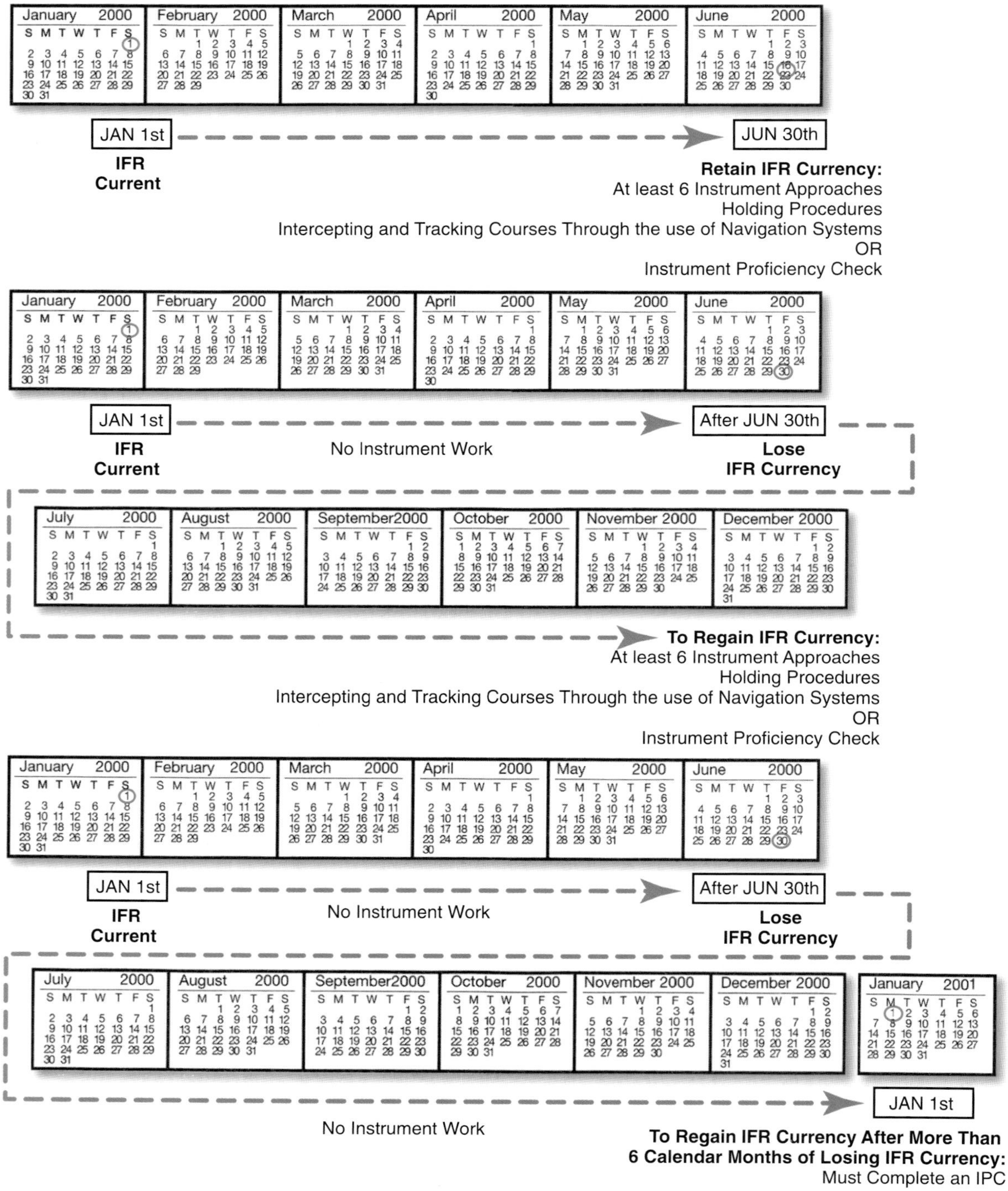

January 2000 | February 2000 | March 2000 | April 2000 | May 2000 | June 2000

JAN 1st → JUN 30th

IFR Current

Retain IFR Currency:
At least 6 Instrument Approaches
Holding Procedures
Intercepting and Tracking Courses Through the use of Navigation Systems
OR
Instrument Proficiency Check

January 2000 | February 2000 | March 2000 | April 2000 | May 2000 | June 2000

JAN 1st → After JUN 30th

IFR Current — No Instrument Work — Lose IFR Currency

July 2000 | August 2000 | September2000 | October 2000 | November 2000 | December 2000

To Regain IFR Currency:
At least 6 Instrument Approaches
Holding Procedures
Intercepting and Tracking Courses Through the use of Navigation Systems
OR
Instrument Proficiency Check

January 2000 | February 2000 | March 2000 | April 2000 | May 2000 | June 2000

JAN 1st → After JUN 30th

IFR Current — No Instrument Work — Lose IFR Currency

July 2000 | August 2000 | September2000 | October 2000 | November 2000 | December 2000 | January 2001

→ JAN 1st

No Instrument Work

To Regain IFR Currency After More Than 6 Calendar Months of Losing IFR Currency:
Must Complete an IPC

Figure 5-78. Diagramming the IFR currency requirements can be an effective way to present the subject to your students.

To give an IPC, you must be an authorized instructor, meaning you must possess an appropriate instrument rating on your pilot and CFI certificates. The airplane used for the IPC should meet all of the Part 91 equipment requirements for IFR operations. As an alternative, all or part of the IPC may be accomplished in a simulator or flight training device (FTD) that is representative of the aircraft category and approved by the FAA for such use.

When you are planning an IPC, there are some items you should consider. If the IPC is conducted under actual IFR weather conditions, and the pilot receiving the IPC is out of instrument currency, you will be the PIC, and, therefore, you must be instrument current. Because there are no established performance criteria for IPCs, you and the pilot should discuss and establish completion standards based on the Instrument Rating PTS. The final step is to prepare a plan for conducting the IPC, which typically consists of a knowledge or ground portion, and a skill or flight portion. You should also refer to AC 61-98 for additional guidance and a sample plan for conducting IPCs. [Figure 5-79]

John is an experienced instrument pilot who primarily operates at rural, uncontrolled airports, and rarely utilizes DPs or STARs. Because of this, Mike decides to quiz John on various aspects of DPs and STARs.

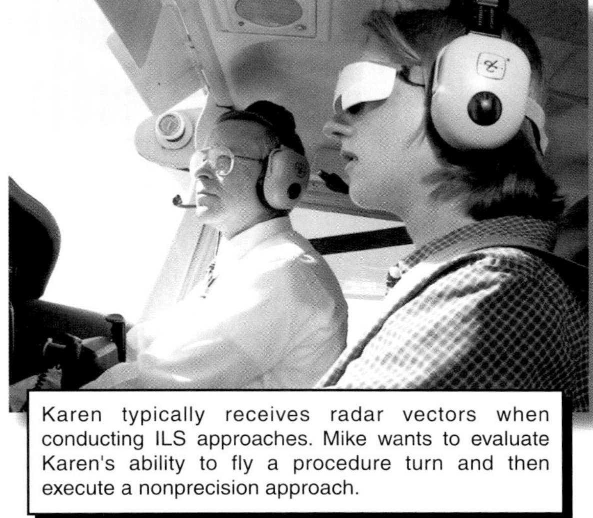

Karen typically receives radar vectors when conducting ILS approaches. Mike wants to evaluate Karen's ability to fly a procedure turn and then execute a nonprecision approach.

Figure 5-79. An instrument proficiency check should be tailored to the needs of the pilot, much like a flight review. Because of this, the content of an IPC may vary considerably from one individual to another. When developing a plan for an IPC, you should reach a mutual agreement with the pilot on the scope of the check and the standards used to measure performance.

An IPC should provide a learning experience, as well as an evaluation session for the pilot. If the pilot gives an unsatisfactory performance, you should endorse the pilot's logbook to record the instruction given, but not to reflect an unsatisfactory IPC. Satisfactory completion of an IPC should be indicated by a logbook endorsement that is in accordance with the current edition of AC 61-65.

TEACHING AIRCRAFT TRANSITIONS

As pilots gain flight experience and confidence in their flying skills, it is natural for them to seek **transition training** so they can fly different makes and models of airplanes. AC 61-98 provides information and a sample training plan for providing transition training to pilots who want to fly complex and high performance airplanes. You may also want to consult the *Transition Training Master Syllabus*, produced by the General Aviation Manufacturers Association (GAMA). Information on obtaining this document may be found in the current edition of AC 61-103 or on the GAMA website. The *Transition Training Master Syllabus* is intended to assist you in developing training guidelines for individual makes and models of high performance airplanes. It also provides structured differences training for pilots who wish to transition between similar makes and models of a given manufacturer. For example, transitioning from a C-210 to a P-210 would require differences training for pressurization and turbocharging. Pilots who want to transition into complex or high performance airplanes, pressurized airplanes that are capable of flight at high altitude, or tailwheel airplanes are required to obtain ground instruction, flight instruction, and a logbook endorsement from an authorized instructor. [Figure 5-80]

Figure 5-80. To be authorized to give flight instruction in airplanes like these, you must have the appropriate endorsements in your own logbook, unless you meet the grandfather requirements. In addition, you must have the appropriate ratings on your pilot and flight instructor certificates.

PERFORMING AIRCRAFT CHECKOUTS

There are no regulatory requirements for aircraft checkouts, but there are some guidelines to keep in mind. If you are not completely comfortable with the flying characteristics of the airplane or its systems, then you should seek a comprehensive checkout from an experienced CFI. For example, different airplanes offer different visual perspectives during the landing flare. You can only get the proper feel for an airplane by obtaining a thorough checkout. You may also have to do research on unfamiliar avionics, such as sophisticated GPS units or moving map systems.

Sometimes checkouts go beyond learning about a particular airplane, and move into learning how to fly in a specific region. Before you fly or give flight instruction in any environment that is unfamiliar, you should obtain a regional checkout from a qualified CFI. For example, mountain flying offers some breathtaking scenery and wonderful experiences, but it also has some unique challenges and can be extremely dangerous to inexperienced pilots. When flying in the mountains, you must take these additional hazards into account: rapidly changing weather, mountain wave activity, high elevation airport operations, and reduced aircraft performance. If you provide training only in areas of the country that are comparatively flat, you should warn your students about the dangers of mountain flying and advise them that a thorough mountain checkout is an absolute necessity prior to conducting flight operations in mountainous regions.

SUMMER DEPARTURE FROM LAKE COUNTY AIRPORT

From the files of the NTSB . . .

Aircraft: *C-172RG*

Location: *Leadville, CO*

Narrative: *Before takeoff from a high altitude (9,927 feet MSL, 12,400 feet density altitude) airport on a mountain flying training flight, the CFI noted that the airport elevation was higher than the takeoff data charts provided for. During takeoff, the aircraft was rotated and settled back to the ground three times during takeoff roll. On the fourth rotation, which was at the departure end of the runway, the aircraft became airborne and descended down the side of an incline where it struck a power line and came to rest in a flat rocky area.*

The NTSB declared that inadequate training of the CFI and high density altitude were among the causative factors in this accident. Unfortunately, there are no standards or requirements that CFIs need to meet in order to teach mountain flying.

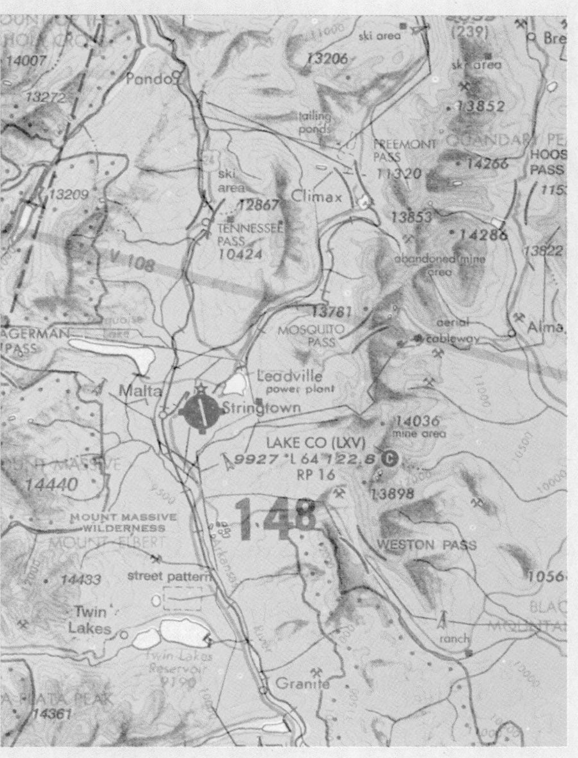

COMPLEX AND HIGH PERFORMANCE CHECKOUTS

In 1997, the FAA, citing vastly different operating characteristics between **complex and high performance airplanes**, revised FAR 61.31 to require separate endorsements for each airplane configuration. Further justification arose from the fact that there are turbine-powered aircraft that are high performance but are not considered complex because they utilize fixed gear. In any event, the two checkouts each require a separate endorsement regardless of whether they can be accomplished in the same aircraft. For example, a complex aircraft with more than 200 horsepower could be used to satisfy both training requirements, but two endorsements would still be required. Also, keep in mind that when you provide these types of checkouts, you must provide ground training as well as flight training, and the training must be logged. FAR 61.31(e) and (f) are very specific regarding the type of training and documentation required for complex and high performance airplanes. Also note that pilots with experience prior to August 4, 1997 in these airplanes are exempt from the requirement.

TAILWHEEL CHECKOUTS

To act as PIC of a tailwheel airplane, you are required by FAR 61.31(g) to demonstrate competency in normal and crosswind takeoffs and landings, wheel landings (unless the manufacturer has recommended against such landings), and go-around procedures. You should seek a comprehensive **tailwheel checkout** from a qualified instructor for each make and model of tailwheel airplane in which you intend to give instruction. Remember, if you have logged PIC time in a tailwheel airplane prior to April 15, 1991, then you are not required to have a tailwheel endorsement in your logbook.

There are some unique features of tailwheel airplanes that need to be considered during the checkout, such as the pronounced left-turning tendency that may occur on takeoff.

Other features include a greater surface area behind the main gear, which may cause weathervaning in gusty or crosswind conditions, and the location of the center of gravity, which can affect directional control, especially in the after-landing roll. [Figure 5-81]

Figure 5-81. A checkout for each make and model of tailwheel aircraft is recommended due to differences in operating characteristics.

High Altitude Checkouts

FAR 61.31(f) requires specific ground and flight training for a pilot to act as PIC of a pressurized airplane that has a service ceiling or maximum operating altitude, whichever is lower, above 25,000 MSL. **High altitude checkouts** require both ground and flight training. Included in the ground training is a thorough review of the physiological aspects of high-altitude flight. An overview of these effects is contained in Chapter 8 of the *Aeronautical Information Manual* (AIM) and AC 61-107, *Operations of Aircraft at Altitudes Above 25,000 Feet MSL and/or MACH Numbers (Mmo) Greater Than .75.* AC 61-107 contains a recommended outline for a high-altitude training program. To give flight instruction in a pressurized airplane that has a service ceiling or maximum operating altitude above 25,000 feet MSL, you need an endorsement for high-altitude operations in your logbook.

Military to Civilian Transitions

Military or former military pilots may apply for civilian certificates and ratings based on their military flight training and experience. The application process typically includes taking a knowledge test, and providing evidence that shows acceptable completion of a U.S. military pilot check and instrument proficiency check within the preceding 12 calendar months. Since there are many stipulations to the application process, you should refer to FAR 61.73 for specific requirements so you can provide the appropriate guidance.

With regard to obtaining a CFI certificate, military instructor pilots (IPs) must meet the same requirements as civilian pilots. There are no provisions for military or former military IPs to apply for a civilian CFI certificate based on their military instructing experience. This is because military IPs typically teach in a much different environment than their civilian counterparts. Most military flight training is done in high-performance jet aircraft, performing various maneuvers at high altitude. Conversely, civilian CFIs

Formation Flying

Formation flying is a specialized skill that should not be entered into lightly. Before you consider formation flying, you should seek instruction from a qualified CFI. Military demonstration teams, like the Thunderbirds and Blue Angels, may make formation flying look easy, but, in reality, they are performing complex maneuvers with intense precision and coordination. In fact, formation flying is extremely dangerous when the pilots have not received concentrated formation training from experienced instructors who have themselves accumulated a considerable amount of formation flying time. Many hours of training and preparation go into making precision formation flying look effortless.

According to the FARs, you may not operate an airplane in formation flight unless prior arrangements have been made with the PIC of each airplane in the formation. Also, no person may operate an airplane in formation flight while carrying passengers for hire. These seemingly matter-of-fact provisions may lead pilots to believe formation flying is easy. Nothing could be further from the truth, and each year several midair collisions occur as a direct result of formation flying by inexperienced pilots, as well as professionals.

typically spend their time in general aviation training airplanes at low altitude, teaching basic maneuvers such as slow flight, stalls, steep turns, and ground reference maneuvers.

INSTRUCTING IN HOMEBUILT AIRCRAFT

There are more than 22,000 **homebuilt airplanes**, which are certified by the FAA in the experimental category. As the price of production airplanes continues to rise, many pilots are turning to homebuilding as a cost-effective solution to ownership. Since the number of homebuilt airplanes continues to grow, your chances of obtaining a student that desires instruction in such an airplane also continues to increase. Most homebuilt aircraft operate on experimental airworthiness certificates, which means they must follow a stricter set of regulations than aircraft operating under normal airworthiness certificates, such as most production aircraft. Therefore, before you teach in a homebuilt, it is important that you fully understand your privileges and limitations with respect to instructing in an airplane with an experimental airworthiness certificate. [Figure 5-82]

Figure 5-82. Designers of homebuilt airplanes typically sell their product in one of two ways. The first method is providing only the plans for the airplane, with the builder fabricating all the parts. The second method is selling the airplane as a kit, and providing pre-fabricated parts in addition to plans. However, for an airplane to be considered a homebuilt, the builder must construct at least 51% of the airplane, and the manufacturer of the kit may not construct more than 49% of the total airplane.

Can you instruct in a homebuilt airplane? This is a question that forces you to interpret the FARs, which typically do not tell you what to do, but rather, what you cannot do. In many cases, you may infer that an action is allowed simply because it is not specifically prohibited by regulation.

The operating limitations for homebuilts are typically issued in two phases. The first phase is considered the flight-testing phase, which prohibits the carriage of any person not required for flight. Therefore, you could not instruct in a homebuilt during the flight-testing phase. However, after the flight testing is completed successfully, the airplane may be operated with passengers.

Experimental certificates must display the intended purpose of flying the aircraft, such as air racing, exhibition, or operating amateur-built aircraft. FAR 91.319(a)(1) prohibits operating an experimental airplane in a manner that contradicts the purpose for which its experimental certificate was issued. The FAA definition of operating amateur-built aircraft is operating an aircraft, the major portion of which has been fabricated and assembled by persons who undertook the construction project solely for their own education or recreation. From this definition you may infer that someone who builds an airplane for personal education and recreation would operate the airplane for the same reasons. Therefore, if a pilot wants to obtain flight instruction in a homebuilt airplane, it would be consistent with education, and in accordance with the purpose for which the experimental certificate was issued.

The Experimental Aircraft Association

In 1953, a group of 36 pilots got together in Milwaukee, Wisconsin to form a club. Their purpose was to support each other in building and flying their own airplanes.

Through the 1950s and '60s the EAA focused on homebuilt airplanes, but as the organization grew, it gradually became the primary organization for sport aviation in general. The EAA is about grassroots flying. This is the organization for those who enjoy aerobatics, antique and classic airplanes, ultralights, warbirds, and other recreational flying. Guided since the beginning by its founder, Paul Poberezny, the organization has also established itself as the voice for recreational aviation.

The EAA has grown from that original group of 36 pilots in Milwaukee into a huge international organization with more than 170,000 members. Located at the Oshkosh, Wisconsin, Airport, the EAA operates one of the finest aviation museums in the country. The group held its first fly-in a few months after that initial meeting in 1953, and in less than 50 years, that annual event has grown to attract more than 12,000 aircraft each year. Today the annual EAA AirVenture convention and fly-in at Oshkosh is the largest aviation event in the world.

Courtesy of the EAA and Mike Husar

The issue of providing flight instruction in homebuilt airplanes is further clarified in FAA Order 8700.1, *The General Aviation Operations Inspector's Handbook.* It states that a pilot or owner may use the services of a CFI to receive instruction in an experimental airplane; however, a flight school or FBO may not provide an experimental airplane for the purpose of flight instruction for hire. Essentially this also means that experimental aircraft cannot be rented from an FBO, flight school, or private party. This document specifically states that an aircraft with an experimental airworthiness certificate may be used for crew training or flight instruction when no charges or remuneration for use of the aircraft are involved. Further, a pilot or owner may use the services of an instructor to receive instruction in an experimental aircraft; however, a commercial operator may not provide such an aircraft for the purpose of flight instruction for hire.

FAR 91.319(a)(2) prohibits carrying persons or property for compensation or hire in experimental aircraft. This rule may restrict you from receiving payment under certain conditions. However, FAR 91.319 does not prohibit you from giving free instruction.

To summarize, all sources indicate that flight instruction may be given for all certificates and ratings in an amateur-built airplane provided that the flight testing period is complete, and you do not charge for your services. In spite of this, there are certain cases where an instructor may legally receive compensation. [Figure 5-83]

1. IS THIS OPERATION FOR HIRE?

2. WHO IS THE OPERATOR?

3. WHAT IS THE PURPOSE OF THE FLIGHT?

Figure 5-83. FAR 1.1 provides a test for determining if an operation is for compensation or hire. You must determine if the carriage by air is merely incidental to the pilot's other business or is, in itself, a major enterprise for profit. Now, apply this test to the owner of a homebuilt airplane seeking flight instruction. The pilot of the homebuilt presumably initiates the training flight for the primary purpose of increasing proficiency, not as a major enterprise for profit. The fact that you are paid is merely incidental to the primary purpose of the flight.

You could not receive compensation for giving flight instruction in a homebuilt airplane that you own. This action would be perceived as an operation conducted primarily for your profit, and, therefore, violates FAR 91.319(a)(2).

INSTRUCTING AIRLINE TRANSPORT PILOTS

While you may aspire to obtain an **airline transport pilot (ATP)** certificate in the future, you are allowed to instruct ATP applicants as one of your flight instructor privileges. One unique aspect of preparing your students for an ATP certificate is that once they have completed the required training, they do not need a recommendation from you to take either the knowledge or the practical test, unless they are applying for a retest.

A flight instructor recommendation is not required for your ATP student except when applying for a retest.

An important thing to remember when instructing your students for an ATP certificate is they are not students in the traditional sense, but experienced pilots. While they need instruction to meet the regulatory requirements, you are likely to have little or no new material to present, unless the ATP applicant is also transitioning into a new airplane for the checkride. You are mainly looking for procedural problems or techniques that may need some fine-tuning prior to their practical test. If your students do not have an instructor certificate and are applying

An airline transport pilot certificate is required to act as a pilot in command in passenger-carrying operations of a turbojet airplane, or an airplane having a passenger seating configuration, excluding any pilot seat, of 10 seats or more, or a multi-engine aircraft operated by a commuter air carrier.

for an ATP certificate, they will now be authorized to give limited types of instruction. Their authorization to instruct is limited to instructing other pilots in air transportation service, in aircraft of the category, class, and type for which they are rated. ATP pilots without flight instructor ratings are prohibited from instructing under Part 61 or 141. [Figure 5-84]

Figure 5-84. An airline transport pilot certificate allows your students a larger range of privileges than their commercial certificate. As an ATP, your students can act as pilot in command and/or serve as director of operations or chief pilot of an aircraft operating under Part 121 or Part 135.

SUMMARY CHECKLIST

✓ In addition to giving instruction to students seeking a certificate or rating, there is a wide variety of specialized instructional services that you can provide.

✓ Each certificated pilot must complete a flight review every 24 calendar months. You and the pilot must hold ratings appropriate for the airplane used for the flight review.

✓ To give an instrument proficiency check, you must possess an appropriate instrument rating on your flight instructor certificate and pilot certificate. If a pilot has not been IFR current for more than six calendar months, then an instrument proficiency check becomes mandatory to regain currency.

✓ As pilots gain flight experience and confidence in their flying skills, it is natural for them to seek transition training so they can fly different makes and models of airplanes.

✓ To give instruction in certain airplanes, you must have the appropriate endorsements in your logbook. For example, to give instruction in a tailwheel airplane, you must have a tailwheel endorsement in your logbook, unless you have logged PIC time in such an airplane prior to April 15, 1991.

✓ To act as PIC of complex and high performance airplanes, a separate endorsement for each configuration is required, unless you have logged PIC time in these types of airplanes prior to August 4, 1997. A complex airplane with more than 200 horsepower could be used to satisfy both training requirements; however, two endorsements would still be needed.

✓ Before you fly or give flight instruction in an environment that is unfamiliar, you should obtain a regional checkout from a qualified CFI, especially in mountainous areas.

✓ Generally, you may be compensated and provide flight instruction in an experimental airplane as long as your student owns the airplane.

✓ An ATP applicant does not require a recommendation from you to take the written and practical examinations.

KEY TERMS

Specialized Instructional Services

Flight Review

Instrument Proficiency Check (IPC)

Transition Training

Differences Training

Aircraft Checkout

Regional Checkout

Complex and High Performance Airplanes

Tailwheel Checkout

High Altitude Checkout

Homebuilt Airplanes

Airline Transport Pilot (ATP)

QUESTIONS

1. To act as PIC, how often is each certificated pilot required to complete a flight review?

   A. Once every year
   B. Once every 24 calendar months
   C. Whenever a pilot applies for a new certificate or rating

2. True/False. Flight instructors who have completed a CFI renewal program within the preceding 24 calendar months are exempt from the flight review requirement.

3. If an instrument-rated pilot has not been IFR current for seven months, what action(s) are required to regain IFR currency?

4. True/False. You should record an unsatisfactory instrument proficiency check by making an endorsement in the pilot's logbook in accordance with the current edition of AC 61-65.

5. What publication would likely be helpful when designing a training plan for pilots transitioning to high performance airplanes?

   A. AIM
   B. AC 61-98
   C. Instrument Rating PTS

6. Under which situation may you give instruction in a homebuilt airplane?

   A. If the student owns the airplane
   B. If you own the airplane and give instruction for hire
   C. If the FBO or flight school owns the airplane and provides it for hire

SECTION F

PREPARING FUTURE FLIGHT INSTRUCTORS

When you train individual students to become pilots, your actions as a flight instructor have a profound effect on the way they fly for the rest of their careers. When you advance to teaching flight instructors, you not only shape the way your own students fly, but the way future generations fly, since the knowledge you impart is passed along by each of your CFI students. The flight instructor experience can be far more challenging and inspirational if you approach it as more than an initial stepping-stone in your career as a professional pilot. In fact, many professional pilots remain active as instructors long after they obtain corporate or airline employment. Others like to stay active in general aviation, training pilots at all levels, and most importantly, training the flight instructors of the future. If you remain an active CFI throughout your career, your instructional expertise continues to grow and your influence reaches literally hundreds of pilots. When you train CFI applicants, you are truly passing the torch to the next generation of aviators.

WHO SHOULD BECOME A FLIGHT INSTRUCTOR?

You may believe that flight instructing is not for everyone. Good instructors possess patience and the ability to learn from mistakes, along with a deep desire to impart what they know to others. Some students who approach you to become flight instructors may not display these qualities at first glance. You, as a mentoring flight instructor, can help your students develop those characteristics through careful nurturing. As you begin training new instructors, remember to use the same tools that you found helpful during your own training, such as this textbook. Throughout this section, you may wish to refer back to relevant chapters or sections to focus your instruction and start your CFI students in the right direction. [Figure 5-85]

It is interesting to note that you are not permitted to provide training to flight instructor applicants until you have acquired a certain amount of instructing experience. Refer to Chapter 4, Section D, for the experience prerequisites under FAR Part 61 and 141 for teaching CFI applicants.

GROUND INSTRUCTION

Like other certificates and ratings, the training for a flight instructor certificate begins on the ground. The bulk of what new instructors need to know is academic, since they have presumably covered all of the private and commercial maneuvers while acquiring their own flight experience. Rather than having to train your student to fly, you need to show them how to teach and then help them make the necessary refinements to their flying skills before the practical test. [Figure 5-86]

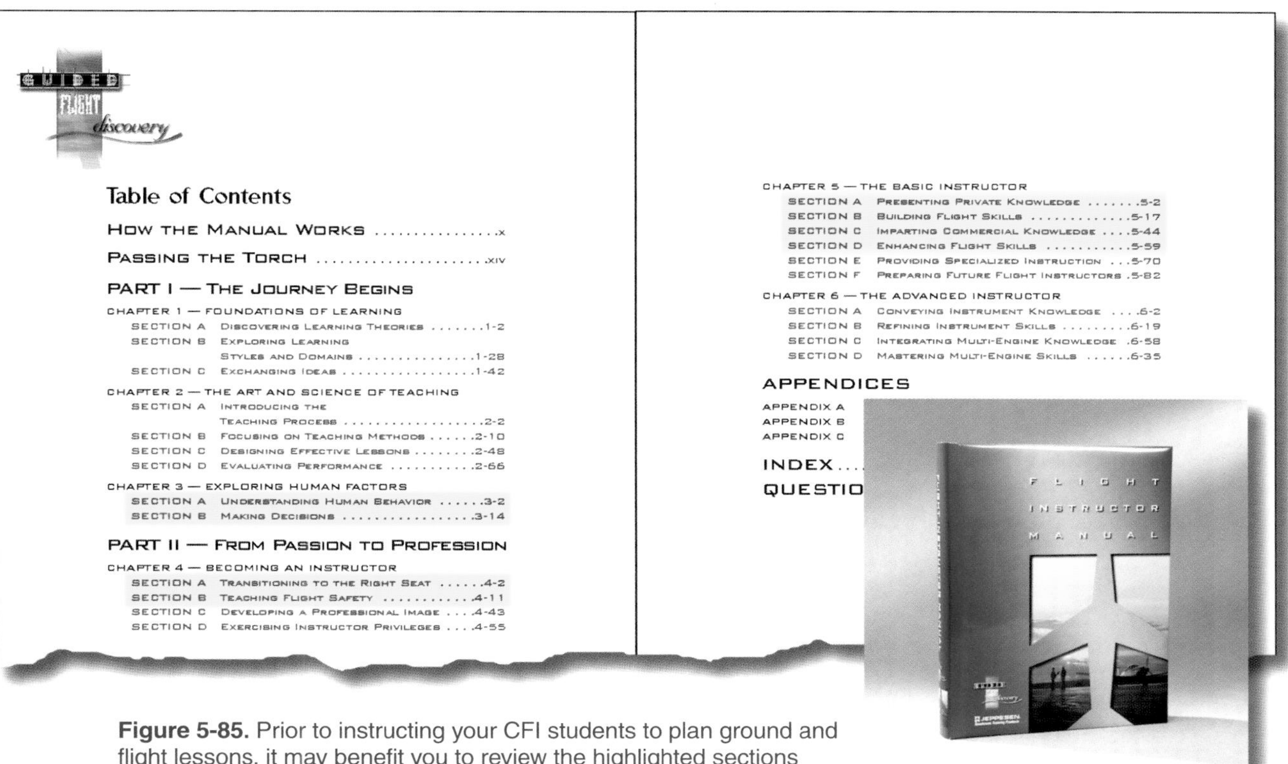

Table of Contents

Figure 5-85. Prior to instructing your CFI students to plan ground and flight lessons, it may benefit you to review the highlighted sections shown in this table of contents.

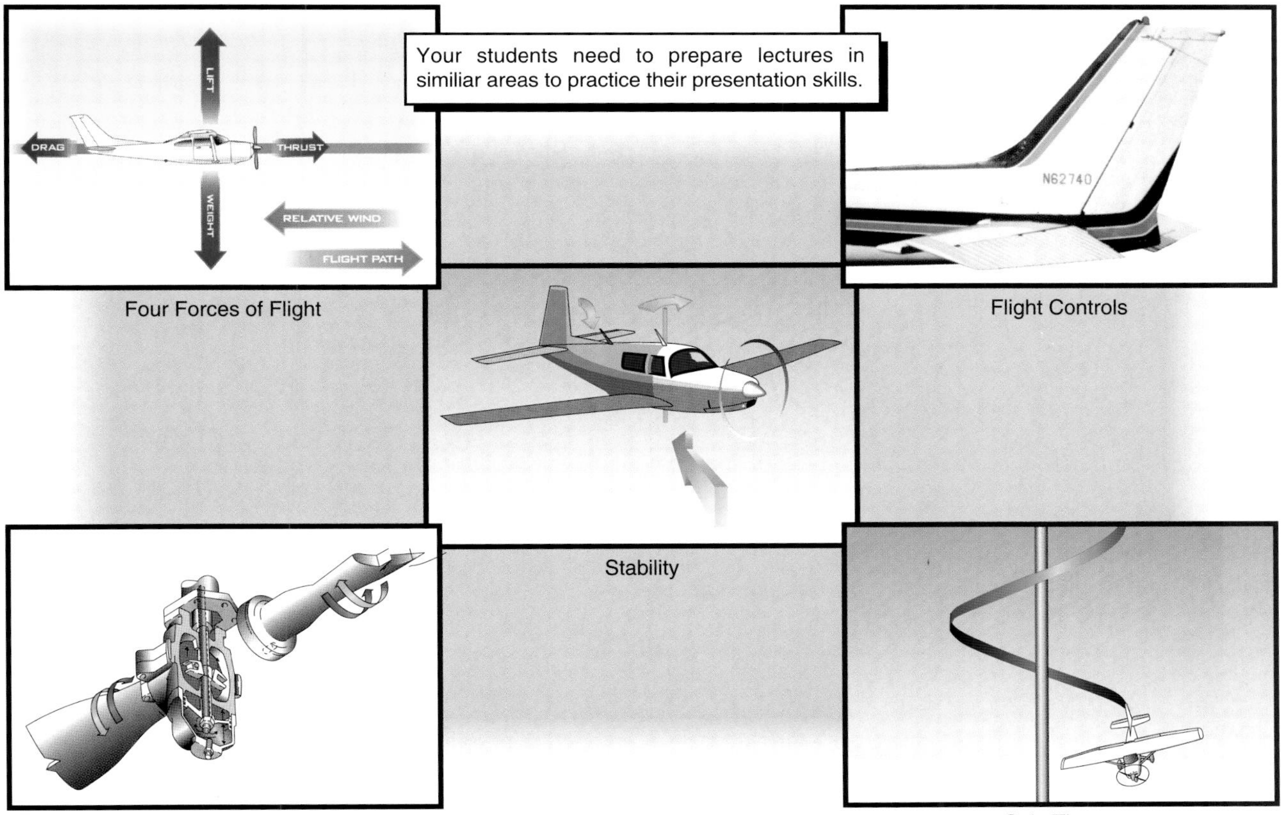

Your students need to prepare lectures in similiar areas to practice their presentation skills.

LIFT

DRAG

THRUST

WEIGHT

RELATIVE WIND

FLIGHT PATH

Four Forces of Flight

N62740

Flight Controls

Stability

Airplane Systems

Spin Theory

Figure 5-86. For the first segment of instruction, you focus on several areas of emphasis to help your students become proficient in giving ground instruction.

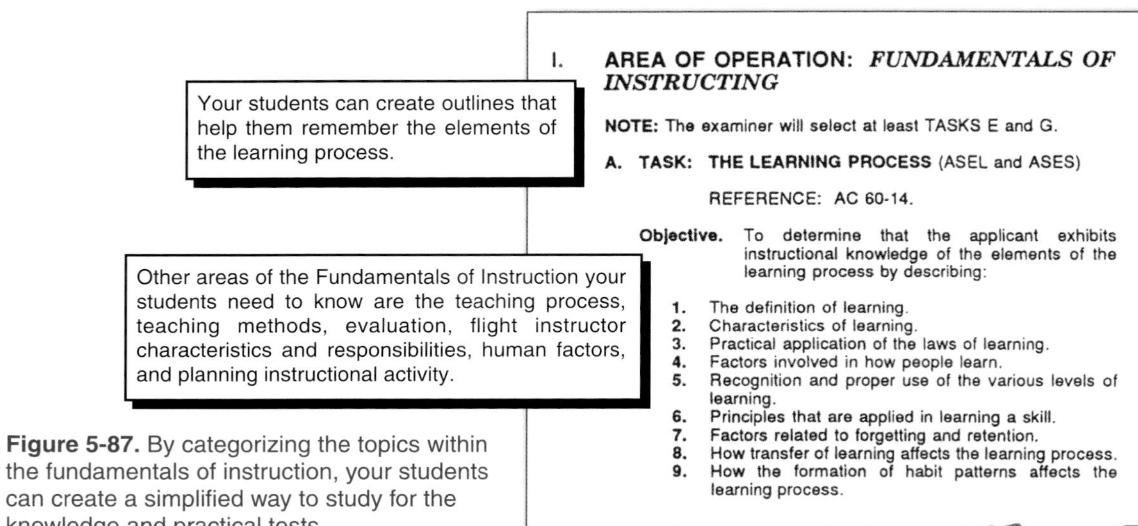

I. **AREA OF OPERATION: *FUNDAMENTALS OF INSTRUCTING***

NOTE: The examiner will select at least TASKS E and G.

A. TASK: THE LEARNING PROCESS (ASEL and ASES)

REFERENCE: AC 60-14.

Objective. To determine that the applicant exhibits instructional knowledge of the elements of the learning process by describing:

1. The definition of learning.
2. Characteristics of learning.
3. Practical application of the laws of learning.
4. Factors involved in how people learn.
5. Recognition and proper use of the various levels of learning.
6. Principles that are applied in learning a skill.
7. Factors related to forgetting and retention.
8. How transfer of learning affects the learning process.
9. How the formation of habit patterns affects the learning process.

Figure 5-87. By categorizing the topics within the fundamentals of instruction, your students can create a simplified way to study for the knowledge and practical tests.

FUNDAMENTALS OF INSTRUCTION

Just as you learned the **fundamentals of instruction** in depth for your initial flight instructor checkride, your students need to acquaint themselves fully with the contents of Part I of this textbook. You may start by reviewing this area of operation in the PTS to determine where to focus your instruction. The PTS also helps you sort the various technical subjects within the fundamentals of instruction into manageable chunks to use as the basis for ground lessons. Your students may find it helpful to outline the applicable sections, so as to increase their understanding and to give them a quick study reference as they prepare for the oral portion of the practical test. [Figure 5-87]

PRACTICE LESSONS

One of the most challenging transitions for someone to make while becoming an instructor is to explain the elements of flight rather than simply understand them. Relating complex topics such as aerodynamics and weather requires a correlation level of comprehension. Your student may only possess knowledge to the understanding level when training. The best way to determine a CFI student's expertise within a topic is to assign **practice lessons**.

You should begin by explaining the structure of a typical ground lesson, and you may incorporate a discussion of the various teaching methods you expect your students to use. Once they have a good grasp of the key elements of a lesson, give them a topic to present to you at an upcoming session. You may choose aerodynamics or another common topic, but be sure your practice lessons cover the most difficult subjects to teach. When your students present lessons, take note of areas in their presentation that are weak or incomplete, and ask questions which test their understanding and simulate common questions from students. After a presentation is complete, go over your notes with them, fill in the gaps in their presentation, and give them some of your personal techniques for teaching certain concepts.

Practice lessons also serve another purpose: to encourage your students to develop lesson plans. Your students need to compile a comprehensive collection of lesson plans covering the subjects likely to be discussed during the oral portion of the CFI checkride. Presentation of these lesson plans during the checkride lends an air of professionalism to your applicant, and compiling the plans adequately prepares most students for giving a ground lesson to the examiner. You should also ask your students questions that test material from several lesson plans at once. Examiners are fond of asking complex and potentially esoteric questions, intended to test the depth of an applicant's knowledge and ability to correlate and apply information to unique situations. [Figure 5-88]

Figure 5-88. You should require your students to maintain a binder for their lesson plans and other reference materials. Not only is this binder useful during the checkride, but new flight instructors can refer to it often and use it to stay organized once they begin teaching.

FARs AND ENDORSEMENTS

As you have learned in your own training, knowledge of FARs and required endorsements is an important part of a CFI's expertise. As pilots, your students may only have a casual acquaintance with the endorsements in their logbooks, and similarly, they may only be knowledgeable about FARs under which they operate on a regular basis. However, your students and other pilots often call upon you, as a CFI, to interpret the regulations. Therefore, you need to lead your CFI students through a detailed study of the regulations and endorsements that apply to the certificates and ratings they will be teaching. Keep in mind that your CFI students do not need an endorsement to take the CFI knowledge test, or the fundamentals of instruction knowledge test, but they do need an endorsement from you verifying they have received the appropriate instruction prior to taking the practical test. [Figure 5-89]

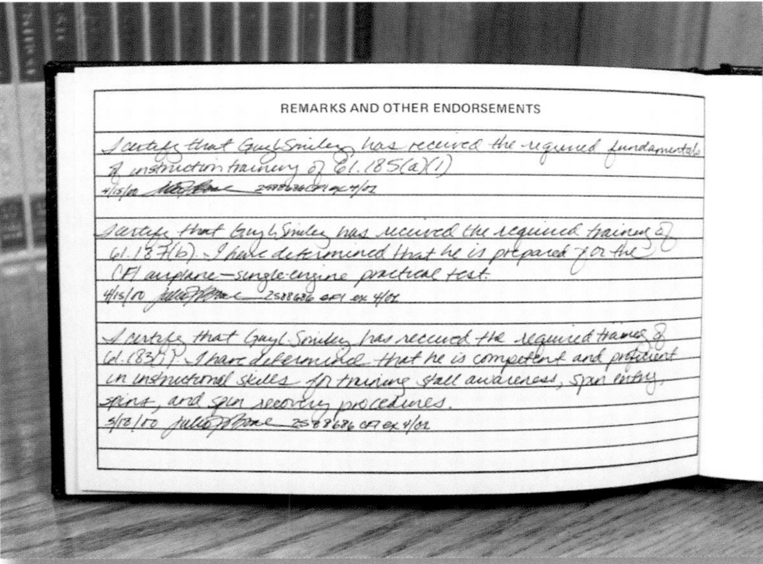

Figure 5-89. An applicant pursuing a flight instructor certificate must have extensive knowledge of endorsements, including student, recreational, private, commercial, and flight instructor entries. Covering these endorsements serves as a good lead-in for discussions with your students, and enables you to make sure their logbooks are in order before the practical test.

One technique you can use to help your students sort through the regulations is to encourage them to outline the sections they will be using most often, such as Parts 1, 61, 91, 141, and NTSB 830. You should also encourage them to read through the FARs thoroughly, highlighting pertinent phrases and noting commonly used paragraphs. By doing so, they can refer to the FARs quickly during the checkride and during future discussions with students. A complete list of FAR-recommended endorsements, including FAR Part 61 references, is reproduced from AC 61.65 in Appendix C at the back of this textbook.

FLIGHT INSTRUCTION

Teaching your students to fly as instructors is much more than a matter of familiarizing them with controlling the airplane from the right seat. Your students come to you with a wide range of experience; many of them may not have flown with other pilots recently and are now unaccustomed to sharing the cockpit. Since discussing and analyzing maneuvers are primary to giving instruction, you need to help your students develop these skills. They master these techniques by talking you through maneuvers as if you were a student, and, in some cases, by observing flight instruction given by others. [Figure 5-90]

Figure 5-90. Your students may come to you right after obtaining their commercial certificates, or they may have had extensive experience flying in commercial operations before seeking an initial flight instructor certificate. Every CFI student is unique, and you need to vary your approach to address these differences.

PRACTICE INSTRUCTION

How you train your CFI student to teach maneuvers could have a broad impact on flight safety. For example, there are a number of ways to simulate an engine failure. On one hand, your student can demonstrate an emergency approach by retarding the throttle to idle at a safe altitude over the practice area, where there are numerous fields suitable for an actual off-airport landing if the maneuver goes awry. Conversely, your CFI student could initiate an actual engine failure by turning off the fuel. In most cases, the engine will start again once the procedure is complete, but the risk associated with using idle power is far less, and demonstrates a conservative approach to flight instruction.

AERONAUTICAL DECISION MAKING

Throughout the course of training, you not only need to emphasize emergency procedures but also promote the ability to think critically about in-flight situations. Stress to your CFI applicants that one of the most important skills they can foster in their future students is good judgment. You can accomplish this by modeling your own behavior. Ask your CFI students "what if" questions that apply to them as flight instructors, such as, *"What if your student pilot calls you from an unfamiliar airport, having been forced to land there during a cross-country flight due to weather?"* How your CFI students answer this question opens the door for a discussion about teaching pilots to make wise decisions. Also, ensure they know the importance of helping their students identify options and know how to keep several options open during every flight.

HOW SAFE IS FLIGHT TRAINING?

According to the 1999 Nall Report published by the AOPA Air Safety Foundation, flight training accounted for 13.4% of the accidents in 1998 as compared to 14.1% in 1997. The proportion of fatal accidents suffered during instructional flights remained virtually unchanged with 5.7% in 1997 to 5.6% in 1998. These figures are well below the 22% of the flying that is done for instructional purposes.

Following is a list of some noteworthy figures.

Instructional flights accounted for 39 (14.9 %) of the 262 total takeoff/climb accidents in all types of operations. In 24 of these cases, the accidents occurred during a dual flight.

Stalls/spins accounted for 9 instructional accidents, but fortunately they resulted in only 1 serious and 5 minor injuries.

Engine failure for mechanical/maintenance reasons accounted for 11 accidents. Another 10 accidents resulted from engine failures due to unknown reasons.

Fuel mismanagement was a causal factor in 9 accidents, resulting in 3 minor injuries. Three of these accidents, including 2 with minor injuries, were during dual flights.

Instructional activity suffered 8 go-around accidents, 6 during dual flights and 2 during solo flights.

Flight instruction may appear benign to a beginning instructor, but it actually carries a significant risk according to accident statistics. This is why you should set safety as a priority for you and your students on every flight.

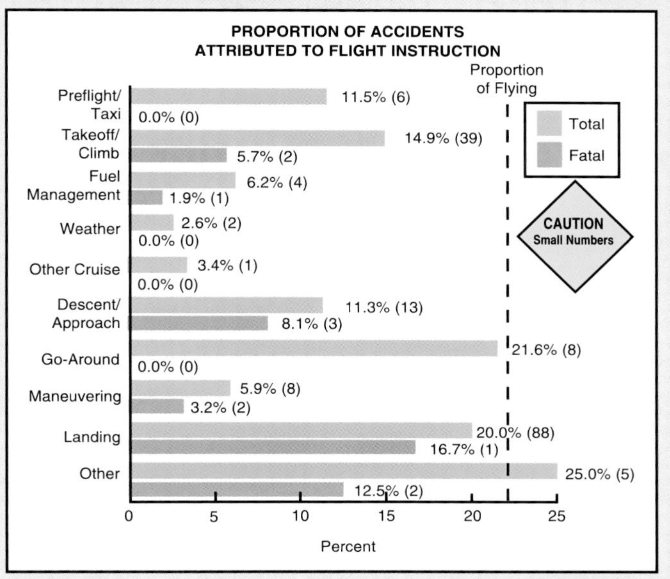

Courtesy of AOPA Air Safety Foundation

LANDINGS

As you may expect, one of the most challenging maneuvers to cover thoroughly with a new flight instructor is normal and crosswind landings. The complexity of a landing requires that instructors learn how to first cover all the basics, then work to combine these pieces to create a safe approach and touchdown. Your challenge is to help your students learn how to diagnose what is going wrong with a landing. They must learn to balance their ability to make verbal corrections that their student can follow with the capability to make those correct inputs in a timely fashion when their student fails to follow through. You also need to give your CFI students techniques for explaining to student pilots how to accomplish a good landing while they are acquiring the visual cues necessary to make these landings consistently. [Figure 5-91]

Students should focus their eyes farther down the runway, which allows them to take in more visual cues.

Some students may focus too close to the nose of the airplane.

Figure 5-91. When your students begin instructing, they will notice that their primary students learning how to land for the first time focus on the ground immediately to the left and in front of the nose. These students need to relax their eyes, allowing them to focus farther down the runway. This technique helps them to sense the visual cues provided by their peripheral vision.

HUMAN FACTORS FOR CFI APPLICANTS

When you begin training flight instructors, you need to assess each CFI student's personal knowledge of human factors. Depending on your students' previous training experience, they may possess a good foundation for expanding their knowledge to the flight instructor level. For example, if their prior training involved Guided Flight Discovery materials and was led by an instructor who had developed strong skills for teaching human factors, your job is much easier. On the other hand, some students may not have received appropriate instruction on **human factors concepts** during previous training programs. When this is the case, you need to make an extra effort to increase their knowledge of human factors to an acceptable level. Chapter 3 — Exploring Human Factors is a detailed and comprehensive review of these concepts. There are several other text references on the subject that you can assign to your CFI students for outside reading.

APPLYING HUMAN FACTORS KNOWLEDGE

Of course, a sound foundation in the knowledge of human factors concepts is of little value unless your students can apply this information, and teaching your students this application may be challenging. During your beginning sessions with aspiring instructors, establish human factors training as a priority. Be specific about assigning at least one human factors element in each practice ground or flight lesson. You should spend considerable time rehearsing decision-making scenarios appropriate for student pilots and commercial students. In your role as instructor, as well as your student role playing, be sure you cover ways to evaluate student judgment.

STALL/SPIN AWARENESS TRAINING

When you begin teaching your CFI students how to present **stall/spin awareness** training, you have an opportunity to make a lasting impact on aviation safety. If all of your students receive a comprehensive education on the subject, and they, in turn, orient their own students properly, the benefits are enormous in terms of saving lives. For this reason, stall/spin awareness is a very important part of pilot training. Many stall/spin accidents occur as a result of pilot distraction while maneuvering at slow speeds close to the ground. Your CFI students should realize that while their students need to be able to describe a spin, it is far more critical for them to understand the causes of a spin, warnings of an approaching stall, and how to recover if they inadvertently enter a spin. The objective of stall/spin awareness training should be to instill in the students' minds a trigger, or early warning, that causes them to react to potential stall/spin situations in an immediate, positive way. By having their students initially practice imminent stalls, your CFI applicants can reinforce this concept.

GROUND TRAINING

Your CFI applicants should help their students build a foundation of knowledge during ground training that they may apply throughout their flying careers. Perhaps the best way to organize stall/spin ground lessons is to develop an outline and enhance it as you gain experience. *Stall/Spin Awareness Training* (AC 61-67), which was referenced earlier in Chapter 4, Section B, provides some content guidelines for beginning instructors.

DEMONSTRATION STALLS

Your students are now required to demonstrate specific stall maneuvers, which fall into two categories. Proficiency stalls are intended for student practice and skill development. **Demonstration stalls** are also meant for student practice, but the instructor demonstrates these stalls mainly as an in-flight portion of stall/spin awareness training. The flight instructor PTS lists these stalls, categorizes them, and explains the knowledge and skill associated with successful performance. Student pilots should be advised that demonstration

Spinning From the Beginning

Stall/spin awareness training is as old as flight itself. Stall/spin accidents claimed many of the early aviation pioneers, and even today, spins continue to exact an unacceptable toll of pilots and flight instructors alike. Most flight instructors have very definite ideas regarding the best way to teach stall/spin awareness. Some feel that all pilots should be required to demonstrate proficiency in spins, including entry and recovery, at some point in their training. Others cite statistical evidence, which seems to point to stall/spin avoidance training as being the most effective overall.

Originally, spin demonstrations were required for private and commercial pilot certification. But in 1949 the Civil Aeronautics Board (CAB), predecessor of the FAA, eliminated the spin test requirements for private and commercial pilots. The basis for the decision was that greater improvements in safety would be achieved by stressing recognition and recovery than by continuing to require pilots to perform spins during their flight tests. It was also envisioned that the change would stimulate manufacturers to build spin-resistant aircraft. The spin demonstration requirement for flight instructors remained in effect.

In 1976, the FAA conducted a General Aviation Pilot Stall Awareness Training Study (Report No. FAA-RD-77-26). This study was really in response to an NTSB Special Study of Stall/Spin Accidents and a subsequent recommendation which urged the FAA to evaluate the feasibility of requiring at least minimal spin training for all pilot applicants. At that time, the FAA found that mandatory spin demonstrations for all pilot applicants were not feasible or justified by the accident statistics.

Since the 1940s there has, in fact, been a significant reduction in the percentage of fatal stall/spin accidents compared to all fatal accidents. It fell from 48 percent for the 1945 –1948 period to 22 percent for the 1967 – 1969 period. This trend continued through the '70s, '80s, and '90s, showing that 12 – 13% of all fatal accidents resulted from stall/spin scenarios.

In 1991, the FAA amended the regulations to further improve the effectiveness of stall/spin awareness training for recreational, private, and commercial students who were seeking airplane or glider category ratings. These provisions required additional ground training in stall awareness, spin entry, spins, and spin recovery techniques. Students were required to receive additional instruction in slow flight with realistic distractions providing exposure to situations where inadvertent stalls are likely. The FAA also revised *Stall/Spin Awareness Training* (AC-61-67) to provide guidance for implementing the regulatory changes.

stalls are not to be practiced in solo flight. Like other flight maneuvers, demonstration stalls should be performed at an altitude that allows for recovery above 1,500 ft. AGL.

SECONDARY STALL DEMONSTRATION

The **secondary stall** occurs as a result of increasing the angle of attack beyond the critical angle during recovery from a preceeding stall. Tell your CFI applicants that these maneuvers should only be demonstrated when their students have a strong understanding of secondary stalls. They should coach their students to perform every stall as if actually maneuvering in the traffic pattern. Once their students are proficient at the stall and recovery, some realistic distractions can be added to the maneuver. Teach your applicants to provide proper critique of their students' performance, and to analyze these stalls as though they were occurring at pattern altitude. As their students become proficient in performing stalls as maneuvers, they may become very comfortable with them and react more casually. They may not fully understand the danger presented by stalling at low altitude. Your CFI applicants should emphasize early warning and detection in their analysis of their students' performance.

ELEVATOR TRIM STALL DEMONSTRATION

The **elevator trim stall** simulates the danger zone defined by a go-around. It is demonstrated safely at altitude with the airplane configured and trimmed for a typical final approach

to landing. Have your CFI applicant emphasize to their students that forward elevator pressure must be used to establish the correct pitch attitude. This produces the manufacturer's recommended rejected landing climb speed, which is often lower than V_Y. The more practice students receive in go-arounds, the less likely they are to become distracted and make a critical error, such as an elevator trim stall, during solo operations. [Figure 5-92]

Figure 5-92. Point out to your CFI students that since full power is already applied, recovery from an elevator trim stall is accomplished simply by lowering the nose and flying out of the stall with coordinated controls.

CROSSED-CONTROL STALL DEMONSTRATION

During a power-off stall, a gliding turn is used to simulate the approach-to-landing danger zone in which a **crossed-control stall** may occur. Show your CFI student that, as in slow flight, an imminent stall can be avoided with release of back pressure and/or application of power. Stress that at low altitudes and for practice, students should always use full power, and recover with smooth control inputs. By permitting the stall to occur with properly coordinated controls, your CFI students can demonstrate that the wing on the outside of the turn stalls first, because it has a higher angle of attack due to the turn. The result is that the airplane rolls out of the turn during the stall, and recovery can be initiated by releasing back pressure and using coordinated aileron and rudder. [Figure 5-93]

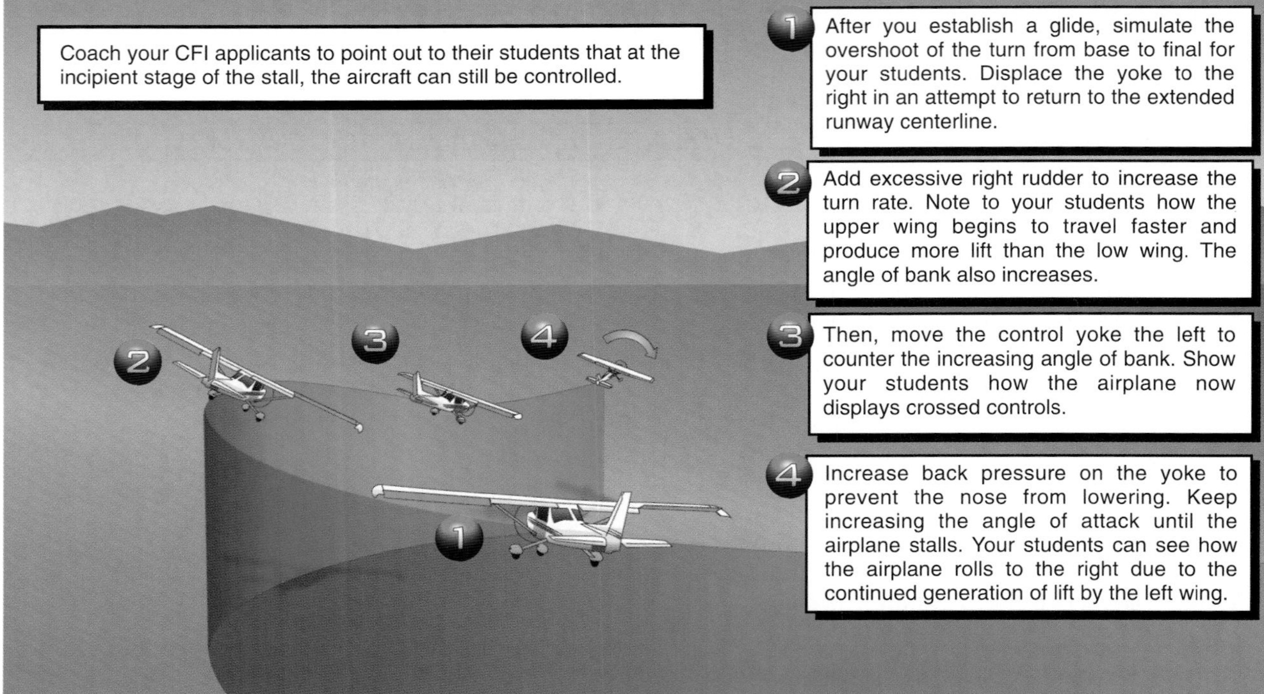

Figure 5-93. A second demonstration with the controls crossed shows the additional risk of spinning.

On the CFI practical test, your students must exhibit instructional knowledge of these types of stalls by demonstrating and simultaneously explaining them. An important part of these demonstrations is the selection of the appropriate landing gear and flap configurations. The idea behind these demonstrations is to expose students to situations where unintentional stalls and spins could develop. Refer to the Flight Instructor PTS for specific performance criteria.

SPIN TRAINING

When applying for an initial flight instructor certificate, your CFI students need to accomplish specific **spin training** in accordance with FAR 61.183. If you are not checked out in an airplane certified for spins, or do not have access to one, you may have another flight instructor accomplish this training. As long as your CFI students receive the

PUTTING A NEW SPIN ON TRAINING

Many flight instructors introduce spins to their recreational, private, or commercial students as a safety precaution and as a confidence builder. They may feel that the benefits outweigh the risks. The decision to spin or not to spin is largely up to you and your student, although flight schools and/or aircraft owners may have policies prohibiting actual spin training.

If you and your student decide that performing spins is desirable, there are some important considerations. Use the following to assess your personal risk in providing spin training to a student.

Pilot — Are you properly trained in the procedure? If not, find another instructor who is qualified to train you, or give the training to your student directly.

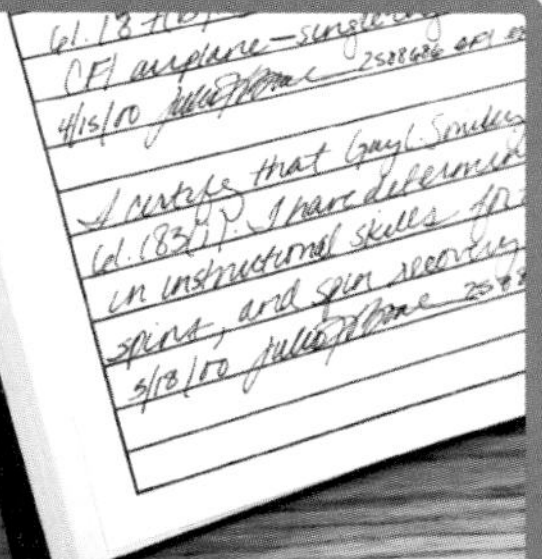

Aircraft — Is the airplane certificated in the utility category and approved for spins? Be sure to follow the manufacturer's procedural recommendations.

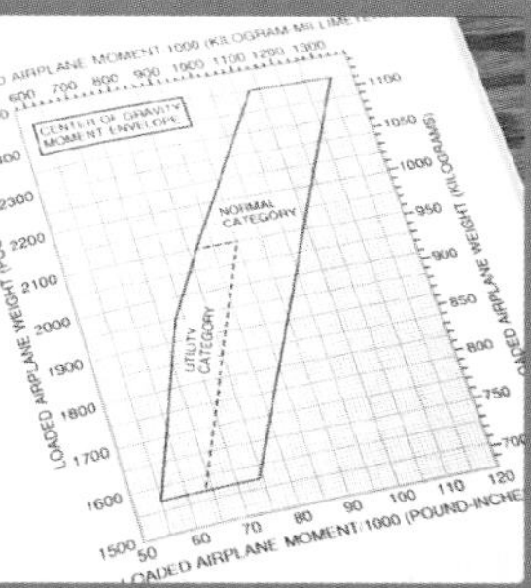

Environment — Does the flight school, FBO, or aircraft owner prohibit spins in the airplane? You may need to check the insurance requirements to determine if there are any notations concerning spin training.

Operation — Are you familiar enough with the specific airplane to be used to ensure safety? After you are sure of the instructor, consider the student. Does the student have the maturity for this type of training?

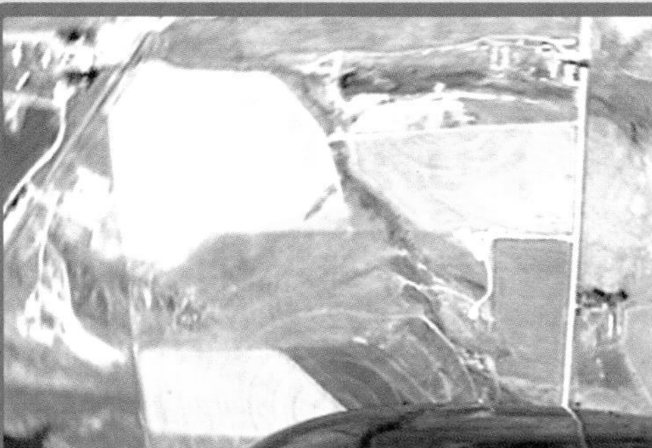

Situation — Once you have determined that the risks associated with spin training are acceptable, you can assess where and when to accomplish this training. Practice spins on a day with good VFR conditions, perform them in an open area, and begin at a safe altitude.

specific endorsement from that instructor, you may still endorse them for the practical test. [Figure 5-94] Of course, this is another enhancement you may consider for upgrading your knowledge and abilities if you plan on working with many flight instructor applicants. Your students may not need to demonstrate spins on the flight instructor – airplane practical test, but if they fail to show instructional proficiency in stall awareness, spin entry, spins, or spin recovery during the initial test, FAR 61.49 requires them to demonstrate spins in an airplane during the retest.

A power-on or power-off stall must be performed during a flight instructor – airplane practical test.

A flight instructor applicant must demonstrate spins in an airplane when being retested for deficiencies in instructional proficiency on stall awareness during an initial test.

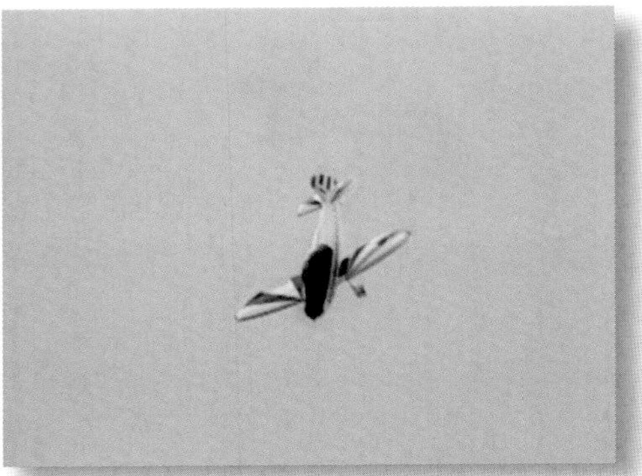

Figure 5-94. If you can, try to have your CFI applicants practice some spin recoveries in airplanes like the ones they will be flying.

SPIN AERODYNAMICS

Your CFI students already possess some knowledge about spins and, depending on their previous instruction, may have performed spins. However, you still need to review spin aerodynamics with all of your students. You can begin by explaining that during an uncoordinated stall, the resulting roll and slip of the airplane creates yaw by weathervane effect. The weathervaning produces rotation about the vertical axis of the airplane, and the uncoordinated condition causes the stall of one wing before the other, resulting in roll. The combination of rolling, slipping, and yawing produces the autorotation characteristic of the spin. In the incipient stage of the spin, the motions about the vertical and longitudinal axis are developing and changing. During the fully developed spin, the airspeed and motions are stabilized, producing a consistent cycle of rotation, and the flight path is nearly vertical. [Figure 5-95]

Figure 5-95. This illustration shows spin forces at work during the incipient stage of the spin which results from a crossed-control stall. The roll, yaw, and slip are the beginning of the autorotation of the spin. Because of the slip, the relative wind causes the airplane to weathervane, adding to the rotation.

Explain to your CFI students that during the incipient spin, the airplane flight path is changing from horizontal to vertical, and the spin rotation is increasing from zero to the fully developed spin rate. The incipient spin usually occurs rapidly in light airplanes (about 4 to 6 seconds) and consists of approximately the first two turns. At about the half-turn point, the airplane is pointed almost straight down but the angle of attack is usually above that of the stall because of the inclined flight path. As the one-turn point is approached, the nose may come back up and the angle of attack continues to increase. As the airplane begins the second turn, the flight path becomes more nearly vertical, and the pitching, rolling, and yawing motions become more repetitive and approach those of the fully developed spin. [Figure 5-96]

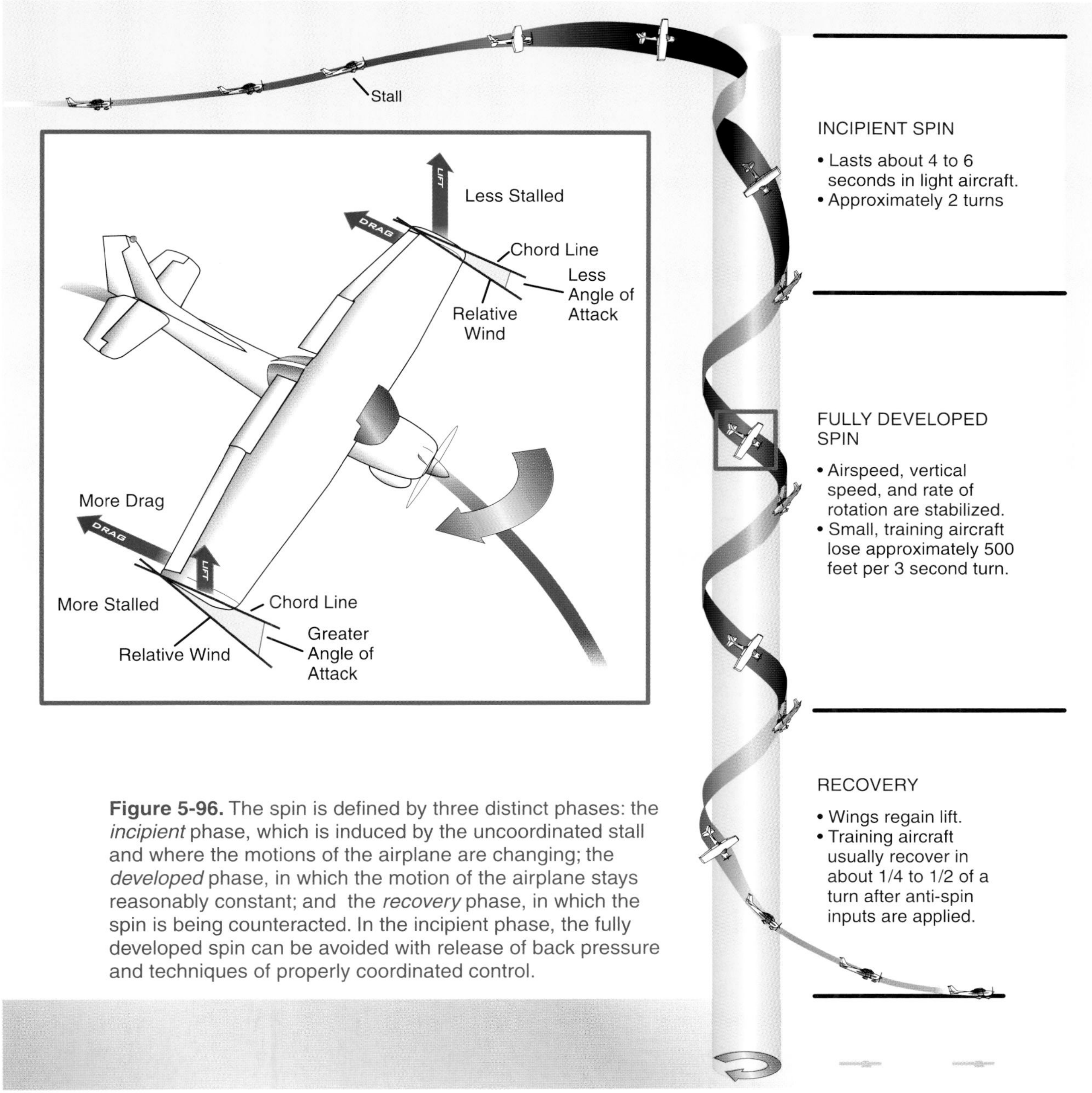

Stall

Less Stalled

LIFT

DRAG

Chord Line

Less Angle of Attack

Relative Wind

More Drag

DRAG

LIFT

More Stalled

Chord Line

Greater Angle of Attack

Relative Wind

INCIPIENT SPIN

- Lasts about 4 to 6 seconds in light aircraft.
- Approximately 2 turns

FULLY DEVELOPED SPIN

- Airspeed, vertical speed, and rate of rotation are stabilized.
- Small, training aircraft lose approximately 500 feet per 3 second turn.

RECOVERY

- Wings regain lift.
- Training aircraft usually recover in about 1/4 to 1/2 of a turn after anti-spin inputs are applied.

Figure 5-96. The spin is defined by three distinct phases: the *incipient* phase, which is induced by the uncoordinated stall and where the motions of the airplane are changing; the *developed* phase, in which the motion of the airplane stays reasonably constant; and the *recovery* phase, in which the spin is being counteracted. In the incipient phase, the fully developed spin can be avoided with release of back pressure and techniques of properly coordinated control.

After the spin has developed, specific control movement is required to counteract and recover from the spin. Spin recovery techniques, which are specific to the airplane make and model, are found in the airplane's POH. The FAA describes standard spin recovery techniques in AC 61-67. You should review all the applicable techniques of spin recovery with your CFI students.

Emphasize to your CFI students that a spin is a complex aerodynamic phenomenon. Not only do rolling and yawing moments act on the airplane, but centrifugal and gyroscopic forces also come into play. It has been estimated that several hundred factors actually contribute to spinning, and for this reason, the spin is not very amenable to accurate theoretical analysis. However, modern aerodynamic theory does provide insights that your CFI applicants may share with their students to help them understand spins.

SPIN TRAINING SEQUENCE

When you introduce spins to your flight instructor applicants, keep in mind that your objective is broader than simply teaching your students to spin safely. You should have your CFI students teach stall/spin awareness first and then demonstrate spin entries, spins, and spin recoveries. [Figure 5-97]

CFI Student Spin Training Guidelines

1. Spin training must be accomplished in an airplane which is approved for spins.
2. Begin the training by practicing both power-on and power-off stalls to familiarize your student with the airplane's stall characteristics.
3. Incipient spins should be practiced to train your CFI applicants to recover from a student's poorly performed stall or unusual attitude that could lead to a spin.
4. You should demonstrate spin entry, spins, and spin recovery, and your students should repeat these maneuvers in both directions.

Figure 5-97. These guidelines provide a good framework for training your CFI students. After you cover these items, switch roles with your students and give them the opportunity to practice their own demonstrations of stall/spin awareness and spins.

SPIN LIMITATIONS

There are numerous things that flight instructors need to be cautious about in regards to spin training, and you need to strongly convey these hazards to your CFI students. The accident record for flight instructors providing spin training shows that, over the years, many CFIs have made serious errors in judgment which have proved fatal to themselves and their students.

CERTIFICATION CATEGORY

One of the first errors stems from a CFI misunderstanding the normal and utility category **spin certification** requirements for light airplanes. Many pilots mistakenly believe that some normal and all utility category airplanes are acceptable for spin training. This concept is false. No normal category airplane is approved for spins, and an airplane certificated in the utility category is not necessarily approved for spins.

NORMAL CATEGORY

In general, single-engine **normal category** airplanes are placarded against intentional spins. The placard is required to be in clear view of the pilot, stating, *"No acrobatic maneuvers, including spins, approved."* However, to provide a margin of safety when recovery from a stall is delayed, most airplanes are tested during certification and must be able to recover from a 1 turn or a 3-second spin, whichever takes longer, in not more than one additional turn with the controls used in the manner normally used for recovery. Since airplanes certificated under these rules have not been tested for more than a 1 turn or 3-second spin, their performance characteristics beyond these limits are unknown. This is the primary reason they are placarded against intentional spins. If an airplane is not tested for spins during flight testing, it is normally because the manufacturer has demonstrated an Equivalent Level of Safety, by an alternate means than normal spin recovery procedures, if the airplane departs controlled flight. This situation is noted in the airplane's Approved Flight Manual (AFM) or POH when it exists.

UTILITY CATEGORY

Utility category airplanes are typically approved for certain acrobatic maneuvers. For example, maneuvers which may involve more than 60° of bank, including steep turns, chandelles, lazy eights, and spins, may be approved, provided the airplane is operated according to the applicable utility category limitations.

One source of confusion involving certification in the utility category stems from the fact that Part 23 permits airplanes to be type-certificated in more than one category if the requirements of each are met. In addition, a utility category airplane may meet the spin requirements for either the normal or acrobatic category, which means it may not be approved for spins. In fact, if the utility category airplane went through the certification process after March 1978 and does not meet acrobatic category spin requirements, a placard, displayed in clear view of the pilot, states that spins are prohibited. A utility category certification prior to that date does not require the placard, even though the airplane is not approved for spins. This is another good reason to always review the AFM or POH prior to conducting spin training in a particular airplane. [Figure 5-98]

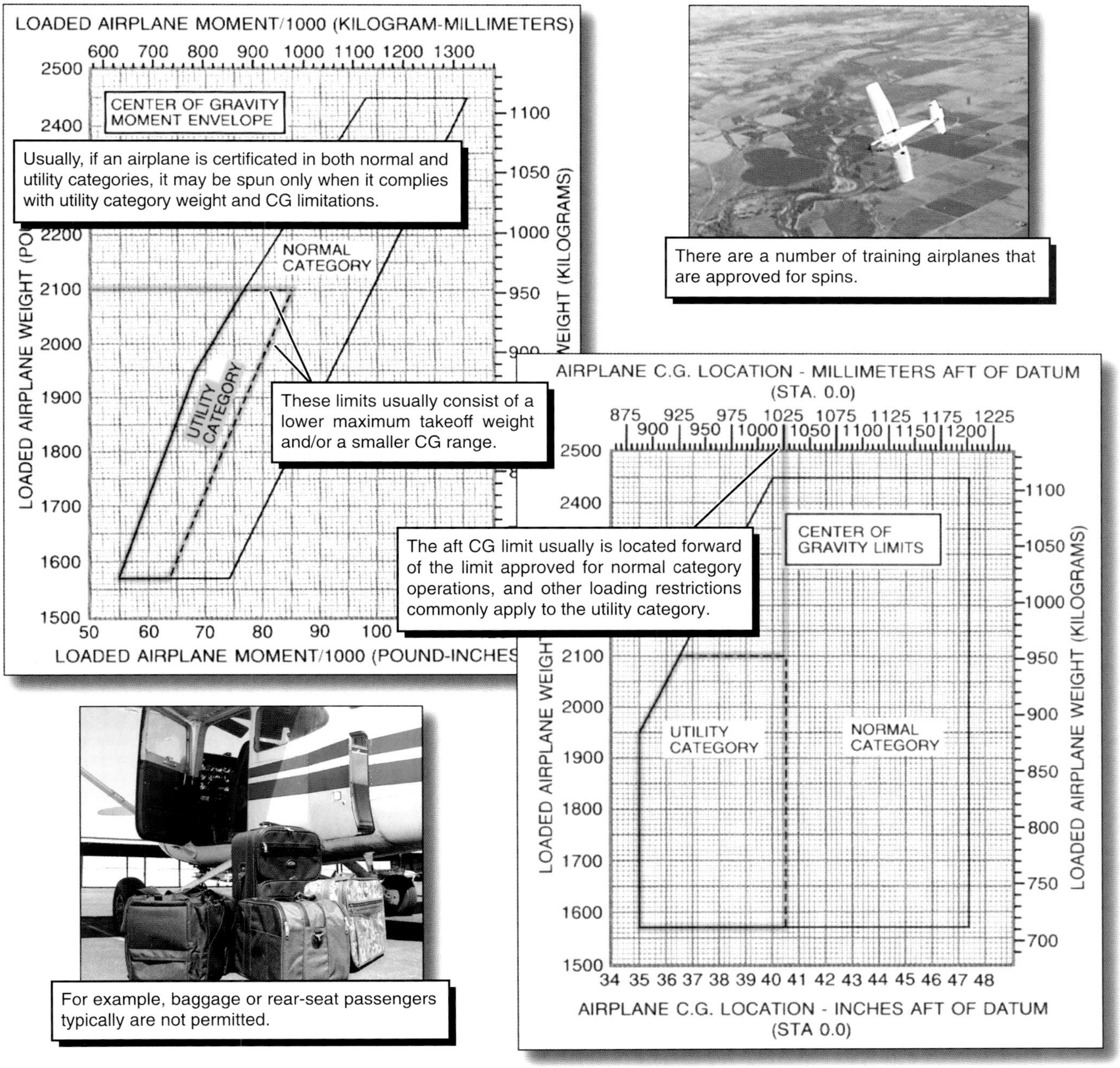

Usually, if an airplane is certificated in both normal and utility categories, it may be spun only when it complies with utility category weight and CG limitations.

These limits usually consist of a lower maximum takeoff weight and/or a smaller CG range.

The aft CG limit usually is located forward of the limit approved for normal category operations, and other loading restrictions commonly apply to the utility category.

For example, baggage or rear-seat passengers typically are not permitted.

There are a number of training airplanes that are approved for spins.

Figure 5-98. When a normal/utility airplane is operated according to the limitations of the normal category, certain maneuvers often are prohibited. For instance, acrobatics, spins, or spins with flaps extended may not be authorized. All of these limitations are listed in the POH, AFM, and/or indicated by specific markings and placards. Since procedures vary with different airplanes, it is important to follow the manufacturer's recommendations.

Your CFI students need to know the specific limitations of the training airplane they use for both normal and utility category operations, and when these limitations apply. In an airplane that is certificated for spins, a CG only slightly aft of the approved range could make recovery from a fully developed spin improbable. If an airplane is not certificated for spins, you have no assurance that recovery from a spin is possible.

ACROBATIC CATEGORY

For certification in the **acrobatic category**, the airplane must recover from any point in a spin in not more than 1-1/2 additional turns after normal recovery application of the

Hitting the Silk

The parachute dates back to the 15th century when Leonardo da Vinci sketched a description of a man-carrying parachute. The dimensions were quite close to that of the parachute used today. Although some early jumps from balloons took place, it was not until the invention of the airplane that interest in parachutes heightened. During the early years of powered airplanes, many lives were lost when aircraft separated in flight. As a result, the parachute had its first application for airplane pilots as a rescue device.

Leo Stevens came up with an idea that a parachute could be packed in a container that fit under the wing of an airplane. A harness worn by the pilot was attached to the parachute. It was designed so the weight of the pilot would extract the parachute from its container if the pilot needed to escape from the aircraft. The device was successfully demonstrated in 1912 at an army post, influencing the use of the container parachute in World War I. This design was also used in jumps from observation balloons during the war. Eventually, it became apparent that it took the pilot/jumper too long to get rigged into a safe position during an actual emergency. Soon after, others were inspired to improve upon the concept, and a man named Charles Broadwick was credited with the backpack/container parachute in April 1914, just a few months before World War I began. The device was successfully demonstrated before the U.S. Army. However, at that particular point in history, the army failed to adopt the concept and U.S. pilots flew into combat a few years later without parachutes. During this war, only Germany provided parachutes for its aircrews.

Before the war concluded in 1918, Colonel William (Billy) Mitchell, in charge of Allied Air Units, attempted to break the longstanding tradition and tried to obtain parachutes for his aviators. He believed the parachute was not only beneficial in a lifesaving event, but could also be used as a strategic device in offensive operations. On October 17, 1918, Col. Mitchell met with General John Pershing for approval, but the meeting was unsuccessful. Although, the war ended 25 days later, the United States Army did not completely abandon the idea, and in 1919 began researching the most suitable parachute for U.S. aviators.

The first free-fall parachute was demonstrated by a circus performer, known as "Sky High" Irvin, who had been jumping since the age of 16. Irvin made a delayed-opening jump from 1,500 feet, in a parachute which had a 32-foot diameter with 24 suspension lines. The free-fall concept required that the jumper manually activate the release of the canopy with a ripcord versus a static line. This particular model and design used a harness as opposed to a coat. The board signed a contract with Irvin for 300 parachutes. By 1922, a parachute was a required part of the uniform for military and airmail pilots.

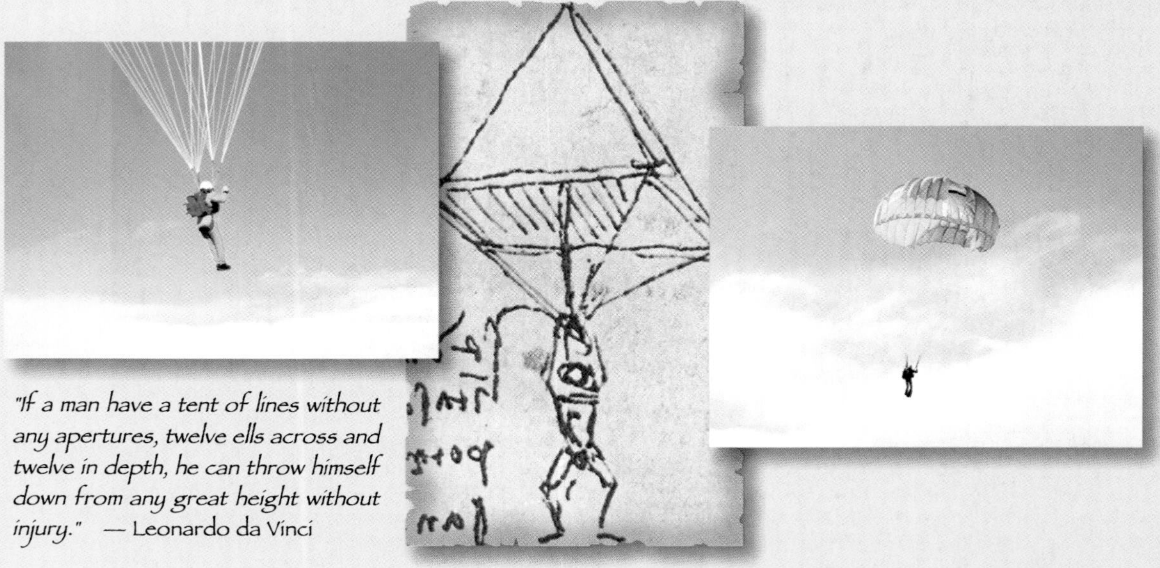

"If a man have a tent of lines without any apertures, twelve ells across and twelve in depth, he can throw himself down from any great height without injury." — Leonardo da Vinci

controls. Prior to initiating the recovery, the test pilot must allow the spin to develop for 6 turns or 3 seconds, whichever takes longer, with flaps retracted, and 1 turn or 3 seconds, with flaps extended. However, beyond 3 seconds, the spin may be discontinued when spiral characteristics appear with flaps retracted. Since airplanes certificated under these rules have not been tested for more than 6 turns or 3 seconds, their performance characteristics beyond these limits are unknown. This is something to keep in mind if you give spin training to your CFI students in acrobatic airplanes.

SAFE ALTITUDE

FAR 91.303 prohibits acrobatic flight below an altitude of 1,500 feet AGL. Spin recovery should commence well before reaching that altitude. A safe spin entry altitude depends on the airplane's spin characteristics, the number of turns used, the current density altitude, and the entry/recovery techniques applied. During spin training, always give yourself and your CFI students an extra margin of safety beyond the manufacturer's recommendations. Even the slightest complication or delay in recovery greatly increases the altitude used during the spin. Also, remember that your students could react improperly to the spin and further upset the recovery process.

PARACHUTES AND SPIN TRAINING

FAR Part 91.307 prohibits pilots of civil aircraft from executing spin maneuvers unless each occupant is wearing an **approved parachute**. However, this regulation states that the parachute requirement does not apply when CFIs give spin instruction or instruction involving other flight maneuvers required by the regulations for any certificate or rating. Consequently, a CFI may provide spin instruction to a person who holds either a student, recreational, private, or commercial pilot certificate without either the instructor or the student wearing a parachute. [Figure 5-99]

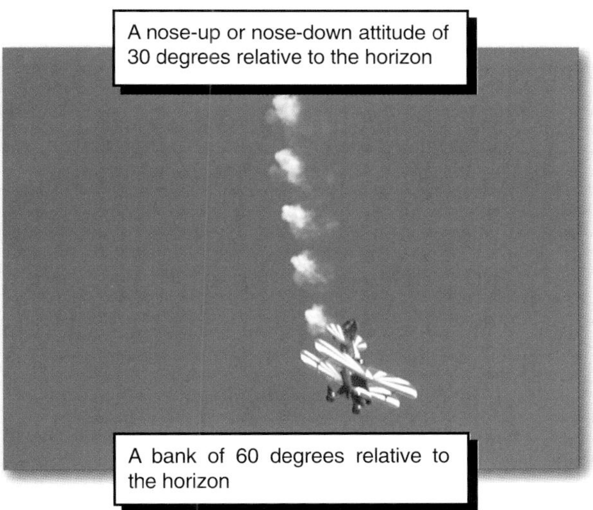

Figure 5-99. As an instructor, make sure all your students understand that, without an instructor onboard, parachutes are required when carrying any person, other than a crewmember, for any intentional maneuver that exceeds these parameters.

SUMMARY CHECKLIST

✓ As you begin training new instructors, remember to use the same tools that you found helpful during your own training.

✓ The bulk of what new instructors need to know is academic, since they have presumably covered all of the private and commercial maneuvers while acquiring their own flight experience.

✓ The PTS helps you sort the various subjects within the fundamentals of instruction into manageable chunks that you can use as the basis for ground lessons.

✓ When your students present lessons, take note of areas in their presentation that are weak or incomplete, and ask questions which test their understanding and simulate common questions from students.

✓ You should require your students to maintain a binder for their lesson plans and other reference materials. Not only is this binder useful during the checkride, but new flight instructors can refer to it often and use it to stay organized once they begin teaching.

✓ One technique you can use to help your students sort through the regulations is to encourage them to outline the Parts they will be using most often, such as Parts 1, 61, 91, 141, and NTSB 830.

✓ Since discussing and analyzing maneuvers is primary to giving instruction, you need to help your students develop these skills.

✓ During your beginning sessions with aspiring instructors, establish human factors training as a priority. Be specific about assigning at least one human factors element in each practice ground or flight lesson.

✓ Many stall/spin accidents occur as a result of pilot distraction while maneuvering at slow speeds close to the ground.

✓ The objective of stall/spin awareness training should be to instill a trigger in students' minds that causes them to react to potential stall/spin situations in an immediate, positive way.

✓ Demonstration stalls are also meant for student practice, but the instructor demonstrates these stalls mainly as an in-flight portion of stall/spin awareness training.

✓ The secondary stall occurs as a result of increasing the angle of attack beyond the critical angle during recovery from a preceeding stall.

✓ The more practice students receive in performing go-arounds, the less likely they are to become distracted and make a critical error, such as an elevator trim stall, during solo operations.

✓ By permitting a crossed-control stall to occur, your CFI student can demonstrate that the wing on the outside of the turn stalls first because it has a higher angle of attack due to the turn.

✓ Your students may not need to demonstrate spins on the flight instructor – airplane practical test, but if they fail to show instructional proficiency in stall awareness, spin entry, spins, or spin recovery during the initial test, FAR 61.49 requires them to demonstrate spins in an airplane during the retest.

✓ The FAA describes standard spin recovery techniques in AC 61-67. You should review all the applicable techniques of spin recovery with your CFI students.

✓ No normal category airplane is approved for spins, and an airplane certificated in the utility category is not necessarily approved for spins.

✓ Since airplanes certificated in Part 23 in the acrobatic category have not been tested for more than 6 turns or 3 seconds, their performance characteristics beyond these limits are unknown.

✓ A safe spin entry altitude depends on the airplane's spin characteristics, the number of turns used, the current density altitude, and the entry/recovery techniques applied.

✓ The requirement to wear parachutes does not apply when CFIs give spin instruction or instruction involving other flight maneuvers required by the regulations for any certificate or rating.

KEY TERMS

Fundamentals of Instruction

Practice Lessons

Human Factors Concepts

Stall/Spin Awareness

Demonstration Stalls

Secondary Stall

Elevator Trim Stall

Crossed-Control Stall

Spin Training

Spin Certification

Normal Category

Utility Category

Acrobatic Category

Approved Parachute

QUESTIONS

1. True/False. You are able to provide training for flight instructor applicants as soon as you become a CFI.
2. What is the best way to determine a CFI student's expertise in a subject area?

   A. Observe their checkride
   B. Assign them practice lessons
   C. Check their logbook for lesson completion

3. What are some of the characteristics of a good instructor?
4. Select the area where primary students tend to focus their eyes when learning to land for the first time.

   A. Inside the cockpit
   B. Far down the runway toward the horizon
   C. On the ground immediately to the left and in front of the nose

5. How should your CFI applicants help their students recognize an approaching stall in flight?

   A. By practicing imminent stalls
   B. By discussing stall/spin accidents in ground training
   C. By discouraging students from practicing slow flight and stalls

6. True/False. Trimming the airplane during the initial phase of the go-around may distract students from the more immediate requirements of maintaining positive control over airspeed, power, and flap retraction procedures.
7. Above what altitude should all stall demonstrations and practice be conducted to enable sufficient altitude for recovery?

8. True/False. Student pilots must understand that they should not practice demonstration stalls during solo operation.

9. Select the stall that occurs as a result of increasing the angle of attack beyond the critical angle during recovery from a preceeding stall.

   A. A power-on stall
   B. A secondary stall
   C. A crossed-control stall

10. True/False. In the incipient phase, the fully developed spin can be avoided with release of back pressure and properly coordinated control techniques.

11. Describe the initial development of a spin.

12. An airplane is undergoing certification in the utility category. Which spin testing requirements must the airplane manufacturers meet under Part 23?

    A. Utility category requirements
    B. Normal category requirements
    C. Normal or acrobatic requirements

13. Parachutes are required when carrying any person, other than a crewmember, for any intentional maneuver that exceeds which two parameters?

CHAPTER 6

THE ADVANCED INSTRUCTOR

Flight Instructor
Volume 5 — Instrument/Multi-Engine Instructor

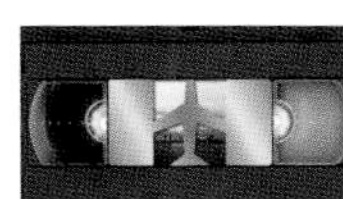

SECTION A

CONVEYING INSTRUMENT KNOWLEDGE

Meeting the knowledge and skill requirements for an instrument rating is challenging for both you and your beginning instrument students. Flying under IFR in today's airspace system requires a high level of instrument proficiency. Your instrument students also must acquire detailed knowledge of the ATC system and the use of instrument charts and procedures before conducting instrument flight operations. How effectively you convey these concepts to your students has a great impact on their instrument training experience. This section is not intended to be a review of instrument knowledge areas contained in the Guided Flight Discovery *Instrument/Commercial Manual.* It is meant to provide instructional examples in areas that are beneficial to your students during instrument ground and flight training.

UNDERSTANDING INSTRUMENTS

Teaching the fundamentals is the first step toward creating a successful instrument pilot. Fully understanding flight and navigation instruments is a basic requirement for your students. While they learned about airplane systems and flight instruments during their previous pilot training, they need to have more in-depth knowledge to become successful instrument pilots. It is essential that students know how the instruments work, which ones are likely to fail at the same time due to a system malfunction, and how they behave upon failing.

You should discuss with your students the instruments required for IFR flight, and review the difference between gyroscopic and pitot-static instruments. Make sure students understand how the various instruments back each other up in the event one instrument or system fails. [Figure 6-1]

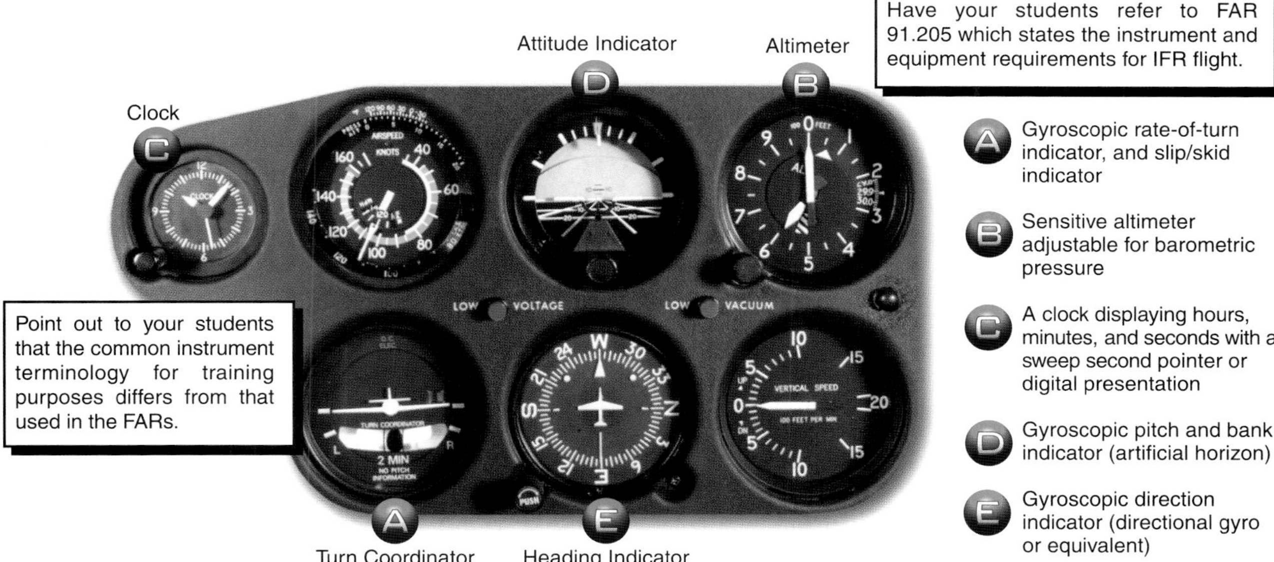

Figure 6-1. In addition to the instruments required for VFR flight, your students will need to be aware of the instruments required for flight under IFR.

Your students need to have a good understanding of the two fundamental concepts of gyroscopes-rigidity in space and precession. Then, discuss how gyroscopes are mounted inside the instruments to provide the appropriate indications. You may find it useful to visit an instrument repair station and examine instruments that have been disassembled or set up demonstrations of gyroscopic principles at work. [Figure 6-2]

Figure 6-2. You can demonstrate gyroscopic rigidity in space and precession using a spinning bicycle wheel. Show your students how an attempt to tilt the spinning wheel creates a resultant force 90° in the direction of rotation.

ATTITUDE INDICATOR

Explain how the gyroscope is mounted on dual gimbals inside this instrument so that it is free to spin in a plane parallel to the horizon, regardless of airplane movement about the lateral and longitudinal axes. Also, show them how the pendulous vanes erect the gyro so it spins in the horizontal plane. [Figure 6-3]

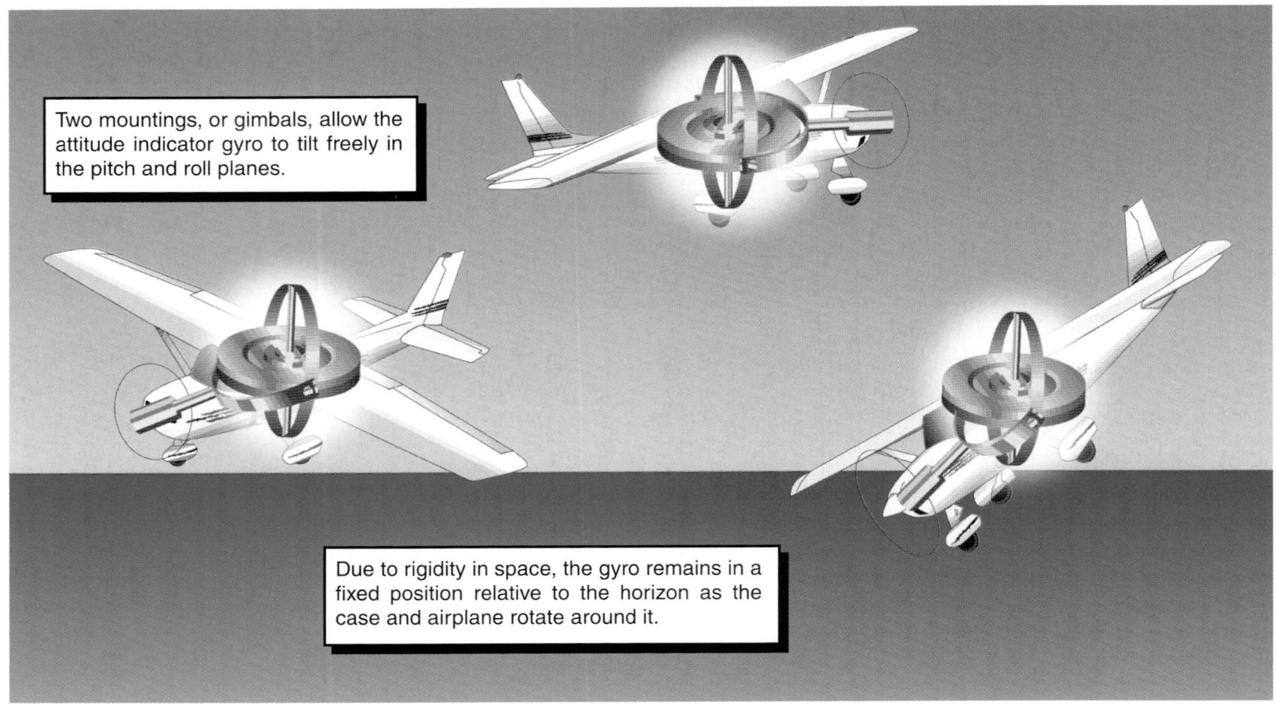

Figure 6-3. A gyroscope remains fixed in the plane in which it is spinning.

Generally, attitude indicator errors are very small, but your students should be aware of them. The small error that occurs when completing a 180° turn is easily compensated for by cross-checking the heading and turn indicators. During acceleration, the attitude indicator may indicate a slight climb attitude. Unfortunately, this reinforces the somatogravic illusion a pilot can experience during acceleration, which could lead to establishing an insufficient nose-up attitude during a missed approach. Your students need a good instrument cross-check in order to detect when the attitude indicator is not giving entirely accurate information.

HEADING INDICATOR

The heading indicator is usually vacuum powered and senses rotation about the airplane's vertical axis. Rigidity in space keeps the gyro pointing in the same direction as the airplane turns. Your students need to develop the habit of regularly comparing the heading indicator with the magnetic compass, since precision can cause the compass card to drift. [Figure 6-4]

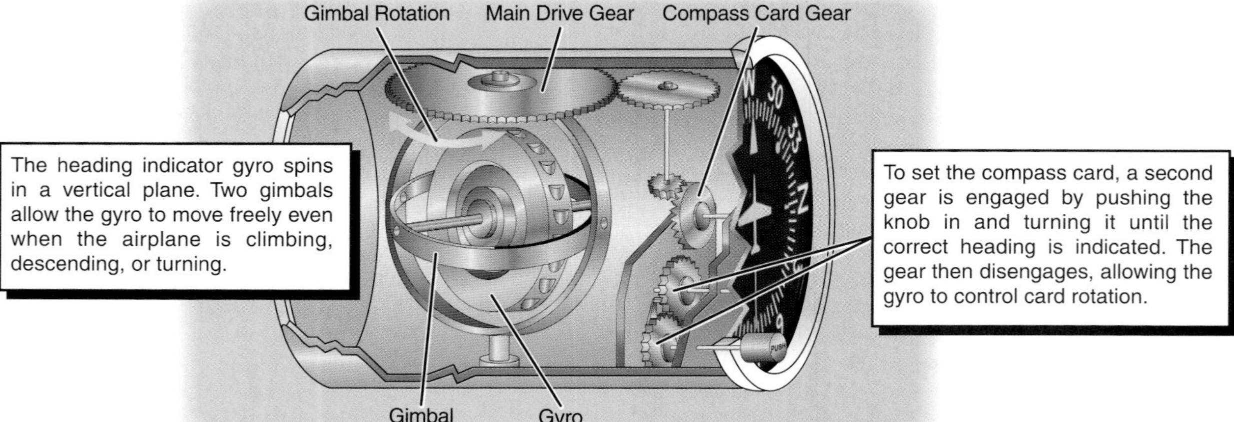

Figure 6-4. Explain to your students that the heading indicator case revolves around the gyro. This motion is translated into a heading indication by an internal gear train.

TURN INDICATORS

When examining a disassembled turn indicator, your students can easily see how precession forces acting on the gyro allow it to sense rate of turn. Some students will need help with standard-rate turn arithmetic. Give them practice problems; ask the time for a 20°, 45°, or 60° turn at 3 degrees per second. If the degrees to turn are not evenly divisible by 3, have students choose the nearest full number. For example, the time for a 20° standard-rate turn is approximately 7 seconds (21 ÷ 3). [Figure 6-5]

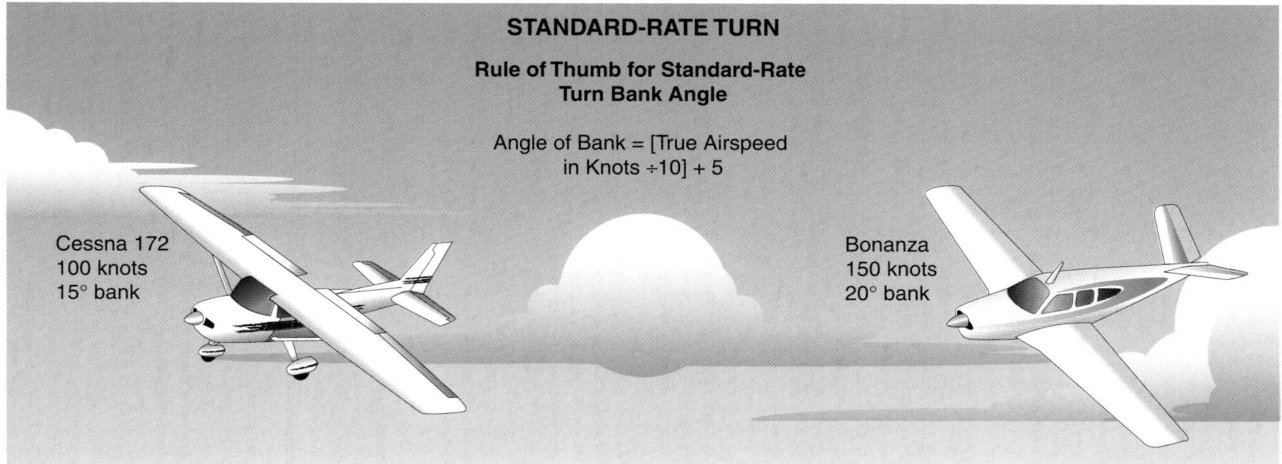

Figure 6-5. The bank required to maintain a standard-rate turn increases with true airspeed (TAS).

VERTICAL SPEED INDICATOR

Some pilots discount the value of the VSI because of its inherent lag, but the concept of lag is often misunderstood. The VSI responds immediately to changes in pitch and indicates the direction of a pitch deviation. This is called trend information, and is extremely useful during instrument flight. However, it takes several seconds before the pointer moves to the actual value for the rate of climb or descent. This is called lag. If you train your students in the proper use of this instrument, lag will not be a problem. Your students should understand that this instrument responds immediately to pitch changes and shows small deviations before they are apparent on other instruments.

AIRSPEED INDICATOR

You should have your students check the POH to verify that, at typical approach speeds, there is normally very little difference between calibrated airspeed (CAS) and indicated airspeed (IAS). Under these circumstances, your students normally can use indicated airspeed for calculating true airspeed.

The difference between indicated and true airspeed (TAS) may be significant if conducting an approach to a high-altitude airport. True airspeed increases over CAS/IAS nearly 2% for each 1,000-foot increase in altitude. You could give your students an example of flying an approach into Denver's Centennial Airport (5,883 feet MSL) at 90 knots IAS. True airspeed at the outer marker would be about 100 knots and, assuming no wind, they would need to use the 100-knot speed from the approach chart for timing from the FAF to the MAP.

ATTITUDE INSTRUMENT FLYING

One of your initial challenges is to train students in the cognitive processes of instrument flying. Such training will enable your students to efficiently gather necessary information from the instruments and to provide appropriate, precise inputs to achieve airplane control. You should prepare your students by giving them progressively more complex tasks.

Your students must master three fundamental skills — instrument cross-check, instrument interpretation, and airplane control. They should be able to recite these to you, in the order they use them. Thinking about the process of attitude instrument flying actually helps your students become better instrument pilots. More information on teaching these skills is presented in Section B of this chapter.

INSTRUMENT CROSS-CHECK

Instrument scan, or **cross-check** is the first fundamental skill of attitude instrument flying. A good scan requires logical and systematic observation of the instrument panel. It saves time and reduces the workload of instrument flying, because your students look for necessary information on the most appropriate instruments rather than looking at instruments in a random sequence. There are two generally accepted methods in use for teaching instrument cross-check during attitude instrument training. Both methods use the same flight instruments, and both require the same responses for attitude control. However, they differ in the degree of reliance on the attitude indicator.

The first method of attitude instrument flying regards the attitude of the airplane as a function of pitch, bank, and power control. For a given maneuver, there are specific pitch, bank, and power instruments that you must teach your students to use in order to control the airplane and obtain the desired performance. Those instruments, which provide the most pertinent and essential information during a given condition of flight, are termed primary instruments. Those which back up and supplement the primary instruments are termed supporting instruments. As a result, this method is termed the **primary/support concept** of attitude instrument flying, and is recommended by the FAA for instrument training conducted in light aircraft with low operating speeds. This method of attitude instrument flying does not lessen the value of any individual instrument. The attitude indicator, for example, is still the instrument that provides basic attitude reference. [Figure 6-6]

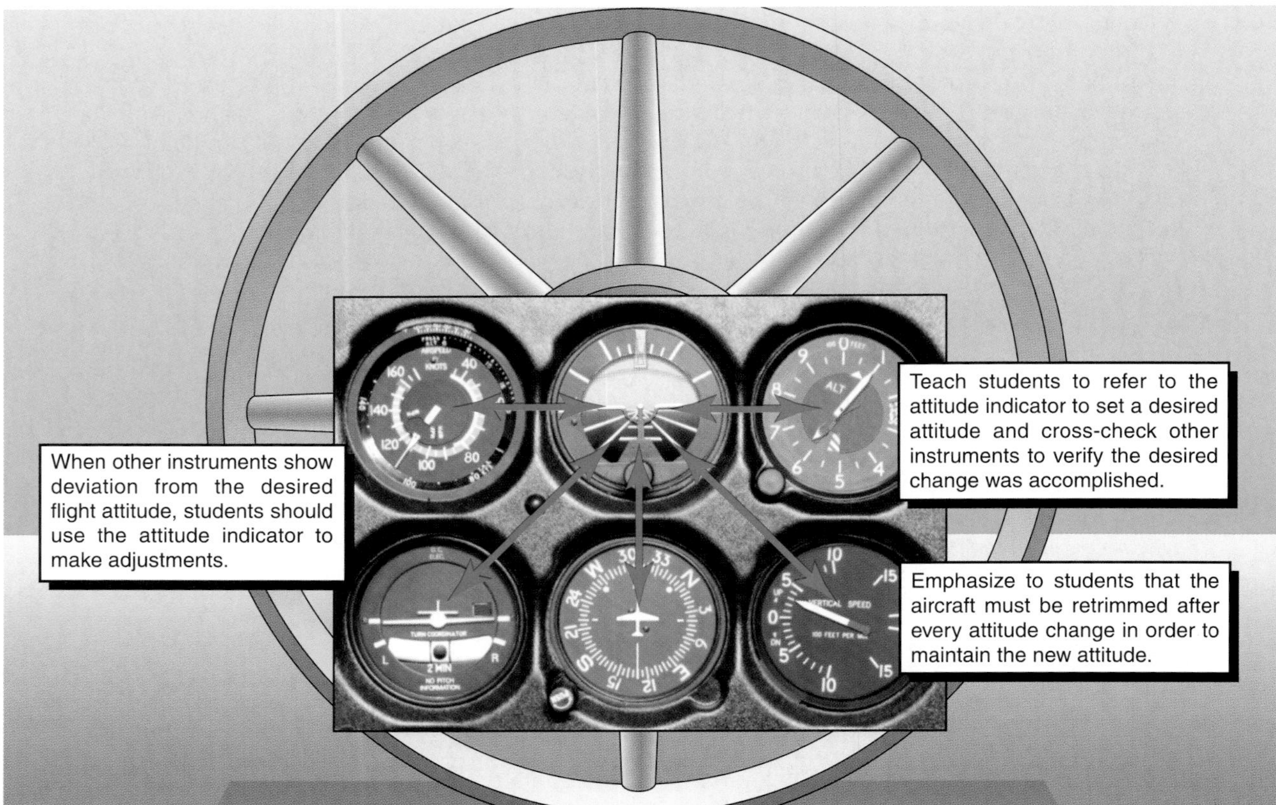

Figure 6-6. You can point out to your students that the attitude indicator is analogous to the hub of a wheel and the other instruments are the spokes. Since it is the only instrument that provides instant and direct aircraft attitude information, the attitude indicator should be considered primary during any change in pitch or bank attitude. After the new attitude is established, other instruments become primary, and the attitude indicator usually becomes a supporting instrument.

The second method is based on the concept that airplane performance depends on how you control the attitude and power relationships of the airplane. Widely used by military pilots, the **control and performance concept** of attitude instrument flying focuses on controlling attitude and power as necessary to produce the desired performance. This concept is well suited to high performance airplanes, since these aircraft tend to have a more precisely calibrated attitude indicator as well as a backup attitude indicator; so heavy reliance on that instrument is more prudent. The control and performance concept divides the instruments into three categories: control, performance, and navigation. Control instruments directly indicate pitch and power. Performance instruments indicate how the aircraft responds to changes in pitch and power. Navigation instruments indicate the position of the aircraft relative to a navigational facility or fix.

Regardless of the method you use with your students, you can help them make the transition to instrument flying by relating their VFR experience to IFR flight. When learning VFR flying, your students used the horizon as a reference for every flight maneuver. Without any special effort, VFR pilots are aware of the natural horizon, even when they are not consciously looking at it. It requires little or no interpretation by a pilot who has mastered basic flight maneuvers. In IFR conditions, your students need to get the same information from the attitude indicator. However, since the attitude indicator is a somewhat abstract representation of the natural horizon, and because it is much smaller, it requires more effort by your students to use it precisely. You should discuss this with your students in order to help them develop the mental discipline to devote appropriate attention to this instrument.

INSTRUMENT INTERPRETATION

Instrument interpretation is easier for your students if you demonstrate how each instrument operates. Help your students learn the instrument indications that represent the desired pitch and bank attitudes for the airplane. Discuss the limitations of each instrument, and identify other instruments to cross-check for additional information. Understanding the relationships between pitch and bank instruments helps your students identify instrument indications that are inconsistent. This helps them recognize instrument failure when it occurs. For example, to confirm bank attitude, teach them to refer to the heading indicator and turn coordinator in addition to the attitude indicator. The altimeter, vertical speed indicator, and airspeed indicator should be consulted to confirm level flight. If a level flight indication on the attitude indicator is maintained over a period of time, the other instruments will validate that condition unless an instrument has failed.[Figure 6-7]

Figure 6-7. If the attitude indicator fails when the airplane is flying in a wings-level climb attitude, these indications will be observed on the other instruments in the order shown.

AIRCRAFT CONTROL

Aircraft control is the third fundamental skill of attitude instrument flying. Before flying with new instrument students, determine what they know about the pitch and power settings for different flight configurations on the airplane. These settings serve as a basis for controlling the performance of the airplane. Section B of this chapter discusses how these values can be determined through experimentation, and covers other techniques for refining the way your students handle the airplane. The importance of trim should

Figure 6-8. If the airplane is not trimmed, the attitude of the airplane will likely change as soon as your student looks away from the attitude indicator.

also be discussed with your students. Even the most proficient instrument pilots will have trouble maintaining control of the airplane if trim is not used to maintain the flight attitude. [Figure 6-8]

PITOT-STATIC SYSTEM FAILURE

Knowledge of the pitot-static instruments is essential if your students are to understand the effects of certain instrument malfunctions. Since it may not be possible to adequately simulate instrument failures, it is important that you discuss the operation of the pitot-static system with your students and verify that they understand how the instruments are affected if a blockage in a system line occurs. [Figure 6-9]

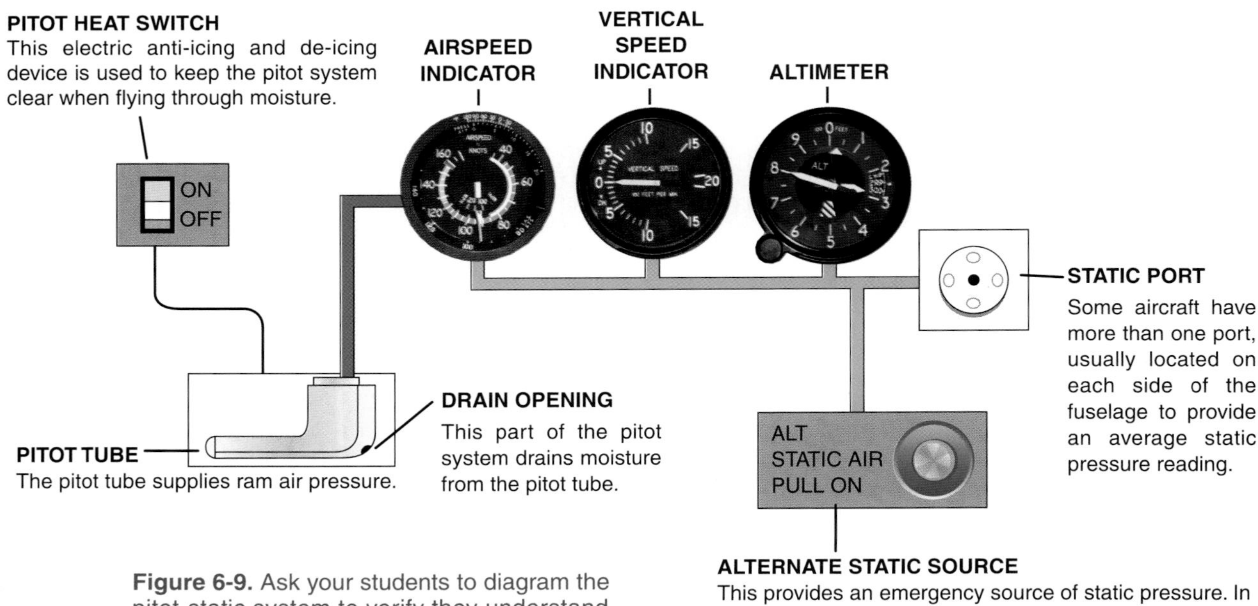

Figure 6-9. Ask your students to diagram the pitot-static system to verify they understand its operation.

Your students need to understand that loss of the airspeed indicator is manageable, provided other instruments are functional. If they have learned the approximate airspeed performance to expect in various phases of flight (climb, cruise, descent, and approach in a landing configuration), they should be able to set the controls and have a fairly accurate estimate of their airspeed. [Figure 6-10]

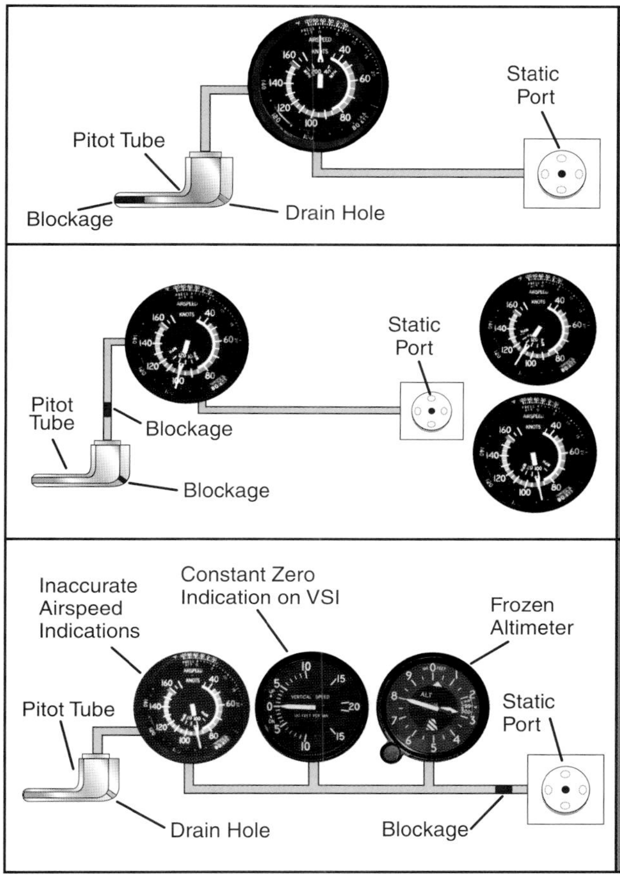

	PROBLEM	RESULTS	CORRECTIVE ACTIONS
Static Port Pitot Tube Blockage Drain Hole	Pitot tube blocked, drain open	Only airspeed is affected. Airspeed drops to zero.	Turn on pitot heat. If blockage is due to ice, indications should return to normal.
Static Port Pitot Tube Blockage Blockage	Both pitot tube and drain blocked	Only airspeed is affected. If climbing, airspeed indication increases. In level flight, airspeed indication freezes at time of blockage and no longer indicates airspeed changes. If descending, airspeed indication decreases.	If blockage is due to freezing moisture, pitot heat should return indications to normal.
Inaccurate Airspeed Indications Constant Zero Indication on VSI Frozen Altimeter Pitot Tube Static Port Drain Hole Blockage	Static system blocked	Airspeed indicator functions, but not correctly. If the aircraft climbs or descends from the altitude where blockage occurs, airspeed indications are lower than actual above the altitude and too high below the altitude. Altimeter freezes at altitude indicated when blockage occurred and is unusable. The VSI freezes at zero, and is unusable.	Switch to alternate static source if airplane is so equipped. If not equipped with alternate static air source, breaking the glass on VSI will return airspeed and altimeter to normal operation if aircraft is non-pressurized

Figure 6-10. Different types of pitot-static system blockages have different results. Unless your students can anticipate pitot-static equipment failures and are trained to compensate with other instruments, they could lose control of the airplane.

GYROSCOPIC INSTRUMENT FAILURE

Although training provides some preparation for flying with a gyroscopic instrument failure, it is difficult to accurately simulate instrument failure the same way it might occur during actual instrument conditions. While your students know an instrument failure is being simulated when you cover the attitude and heading indicators, actual failures usually are not as obvious.

An attitude indicator failure can be as subtle as continuing to indicate wings level while the airplane gradually drifts off into a diving spiral. It is important that your students are taught to continually monitor all the instruments to make sure the attitude indications correspond to other instrument indications. When there is a conflict, your students must apply their knowledge of instrument operational characteristics to determine which instruments have failed.

When your students are troubleshooting a suspected problem, a small control input should be made and the other instruments checked to verify the input. In the case of an attitude indicator failure, knowing how instrument systems work would also lead your students to suspect other vacuum-driven instruments, such as the heading indicator.

Students should cross-check the heading indicator against the indications of the magnetic compass. If the attitude indicator responds as expected, it may be working, but there could still be inaccurate indications due to precession. Ultimately, students must analyze the indications from different instruments and systems and accept those that correlate with each other.

ATTITUDE INDICATOR FAILURE

If an attitude indicator fails, your students must not let the erroneous indications distract them from airplane control. This is a particularly critical issue when flying in IFR conditions. If the airplane is equipped with an electrically-powered attitude indicator, resetting the circuit breaker may be all that is needed to restore operation of the indicator. Some light airplanes have a backup vacuum system that may be utilized in the event the main vacuum pump fails. Since students may still include the malfunctioning attitude indicator in their scan a recommended practice is to cover the failed instrument to prevent the conflicting indications from being a distraction. Point out that the suction-cup instrument covers that you may have used when simulating instrument failure are ideal for this purpose.

HEADING INDICATOR FAILURE

Heading indicators also tend to fail in subtle ways. Since the heading indicator in most small general aviation airplanes is a directional gyro with no magnetic slaving, your students should periodically check the heading against the magnetic compass. One technique is to compare the heading indicator with the magnetic compass after any change in heading along the route being flown. For the most part, this will preclude being surprised by a heading indicator failure.

When you cover the attitude indicator and/or heading indicator, your students are forced to fly the airplane with reference to the remaining instruments. This practice is necessary for your students to become proficient at partial panel flying, but this does little to prepare them for the unexpected failure of these instruments. However, training devices or simulators are well suited for giving this type of instruction. These devices may be a flight training device (FTD), or a personal computer-based aviation training device (PCATD), that is approved by the FAA for limited credit toward instrument flight training time. [Figure 6-11]

Figure 6-11. Use of a PCATD, FTD, or other flight simulator allows you to provide your students with unannounced, insidious failures of primary flight instruments.

INSTRUMENT NAVIGATION

Another skill that was introduced during your students' private pilot training is instrument navigation. As an instructor, it is your responsibility to make certain your students

understand navigation instruments, and are able to use them accurately to fly the airplane along a precise track with no outside visual reference. Instrument navigation procedures are designed to ensure terrain and obstacle clearance. It is helpful to your students if you point out the necessity for precise navigation and close adherence to altitudes and climb gradients. Some avionics, like ADF and GPS, require additional training to be used effectively under IFR. As an instructor, you need to possess thorough, up-to-date knowledge to pass on to your students.

EXPLORING THE FLIGHT ENVIRONMENT

Your instrument students will need a review of the flight environment from an IFR perspective. Instrument flight operations require your students to become familiar with new facets of airports, airspace, and flight information. In addition, they must acquire new knowledge of the air traffic control system and ATC clearances.

AIR TRAFFIC CONTROL SYSTEM

One of the best ways to teach your students to gain an understanding of the ATC system is to take them to visit FAA facilities. The FAA has two formal programs: Operation Takeoff for educating pilots on how to utilize Automated Flight Service Stations, and Operation Raincheck to familiarize pilots with the ATC system. Beyond these formal programs, tower and air traffic control facilities are usually more than willing to accommodate visits from instructors and their students.

Radio procedures can prove extremely challenging for many instrument students. The rapid exchange of pilot/controller communication in the ATC system requires your students to develop improved listening skills. To help students, you can act as the controller and practice communication by issuing clearances, taxi instructions, and amendments to clearances.

In addition to practice, there are several things you can do to help your students make radio communication easier. Teach your students to anticipate ATC's radio calls. The message sent may not always be exactly what is expected, but if students have an idea of what the next transmission will be, understanding it is easier. A factor that may be overlooked is the difference between listening to transmissions over the airplane's speaker and the relative ease of listening to transmissions through headsets. If your students do not have a headset, strongly encourage them to obtain this equipment.

ATC CLEARANCES

The ability to file a flight plan and obtain an IFR clearance are fundamental skills for instrument pilots. Copying and understanding a clearance will be much easier for your students if you teach them the format of the clearance and show them shorthand for writing it down. You can quiz your students by dictating clearances for them to copy, or by tuning a radio or scanner to the clearance delivery frequency of a nearby airport to allow them to practice copying clearances. Many training publishers also offer ATC clearances on audio tapes or computer-based training programs, which allows students to learn clearance shorthand and practice writing sample clearances. [Figure 6-12]

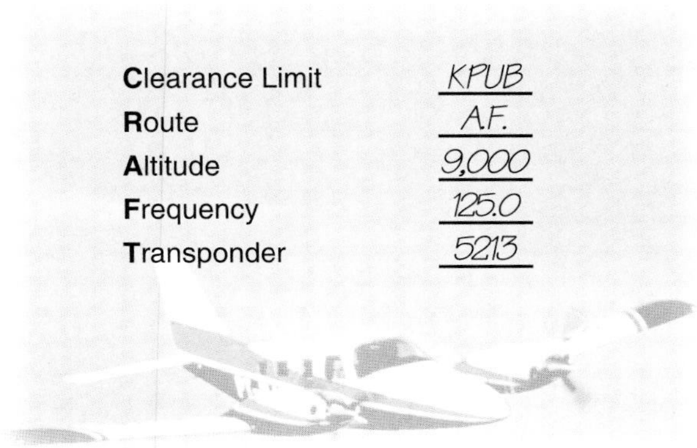

Figure 6-12. Acronyms, like CRAFT, can help your students keep track of the items in an IFR clearance.

INTERPRETING INSTRUMENT CHARTS AND PROCEDURES

Whether your students use NOS or Jeppesen charts, you must help them become intimately familiar with charted information. They will be unable to precisely navigate the airplane if they are struggling with chart interpretation. Your students need to know how to safely conduct the various instrument operations, from departure procedures (DPs) to approaches.

DEPARTURE PROCEDURES

Unless you teach your students the reasons for specific altitudes and climb gradients, they may not fully appreciate the importance of a properly executed **departure procedure (DP)**. They must understand how to climb to a safe altitude in poor visibility while

Departures According to TERPS

Obstacle clearance for all instrument departures is based on an aircraft passing the departure end of the runway (DER) at least 35 feet AGL, climbing to 400 feet above the airport elevation before turning, and climbing at least 200 feet per nautical mile (f.p.n.m.), unless a higher climb gradient (greater than 200 f.p.n.m.) is specified, or unless required to level off by a crossing restriction.

A 40:1 slope begins at 35 feet above the DER and slopes upward at 152 f.p.n.m. until reaching the minimum IFR altitude or entering the enroute structure. This 40:1 slope is an imaginary plane, which not only slopes upward, but also fans out from the runway centerline. In the *U.S. Standard for Terminal Instrument Procedures* (TERPS), the slope is called an obstacle identification surface (OIS). [Figure A] As specified in TERPS, objects which penetrate the OIS shall be considered in the departure procedure. In these cases, a climb gradient of greater than 200 f.p.n.m. is necessary to provide the required obstacle clearance, (ROC). The ROC at one nautical mile from the end of the runway is 48 feet (200 -152 = 48). At two miles from the end of the runway, the ROC is 96 feet. Thus, the ROC, or clearance from the OIS is 48 feet for each nautical mile of distance from the end of the runway. [Figure B]

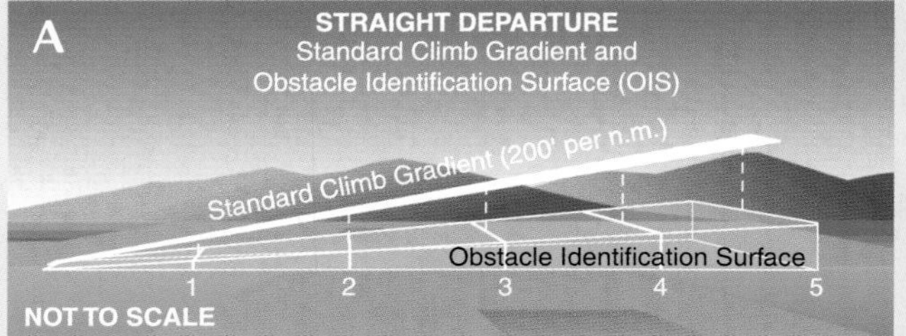

B

Distance From Runway	1 n.m.	2 n.m.	3 n.m.	4 n.m.	5 n.m.
Standard Climb Gradient	200'	400'	600'	800'	1,000'
40:1 OIS	152'	304'	456'	608'	760'
Required Obstacle Clearance	48'	96'	144'	192'	240'

There are numerous variations of departure procedures. Some involve course guidance from a navaid located on or near the airport, others in fact most, include a turn. When a turn is necessary, specific TERPS criteria are applied to both the straight and the turning segments.

Figure C shows the required obstacle clearance area for a typical departure. This is an example of a combined straight and turning procedure, which includes a navigational fix at the end of the straight segment. When a navigational fix is not available, the start of the turning may depend on reaching a specified attitude.

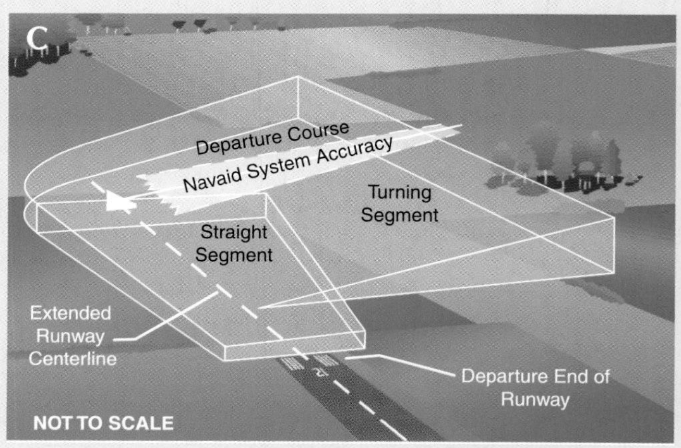

avoiding obstacles. You should make certain that your students know how to comply with required **climb gradients** that are published for many of these procedures.

One of the most important habits you can instill in your students is to visualize and critically analyze each clearance received from ATC. Just as it is prudent to look again before driving your car into an intersection when you have a green light, it is always best to double-check any ATC clearance issued. One critical clearance to question is a departure clearance. Many accidents have occurred when a pilot was confused about a departure clearance and failed to obtain clarification prior to departure. Warn your students that these situations can easily result in a controlled flight into terrain (CFIT) accident.

ENROUTE CHARTS AND PROCEDURES

The increase in the number of navaids and the complexity of the airway and airspace system have made specialized enroute charts a necessity for flight under IFR. In addition to making it possible to keep track of position, enroute charts provide the information to operate at a safe altitude and to maintain navigational aid signal reception. In the process of reviewing enroute charts, ask your students questions concerning the data found on the end panels, such as special use airspace, part-time terminal airspace hours, and communication frequencies.

HOLDING PATTERNS

Do you remember how difficult holding patterns were when you were first learning instrument flight? This is an area where you can count on your students needing extra help. Holding patterns are difficult because they require your students to visualize their position in relation to the fix and plan the correct entry procedure, all while flying the airplane. The best time to introduce holding patterns is during ground training, where you can have your students determine the type of entry procedure appropriate to the direction of flight. FTDs and PCATDs are also effective for this type of training. [Figure 6-13] In the classroom, you may develop other creative techniques for explaining holding pattern procedures. [Figure 6-14 on Page 6-14]

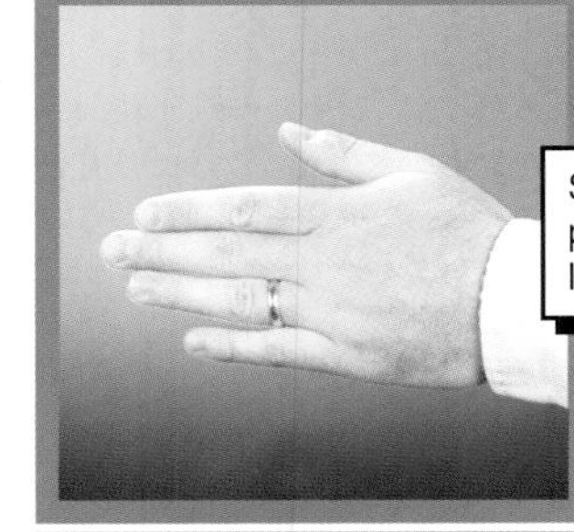

Signal the direction of the holding pattern turns. For example, signal left turns with left hand.

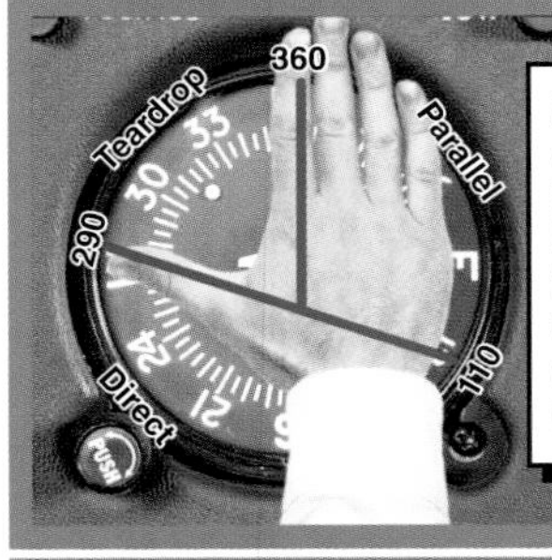

Have your students place their *other* hand (in this case their right hand) on the heading indicator like so. The natural angle between the outstretched thumb and forefinger form the teardrop entry range. From this, the other entries may by visualized.

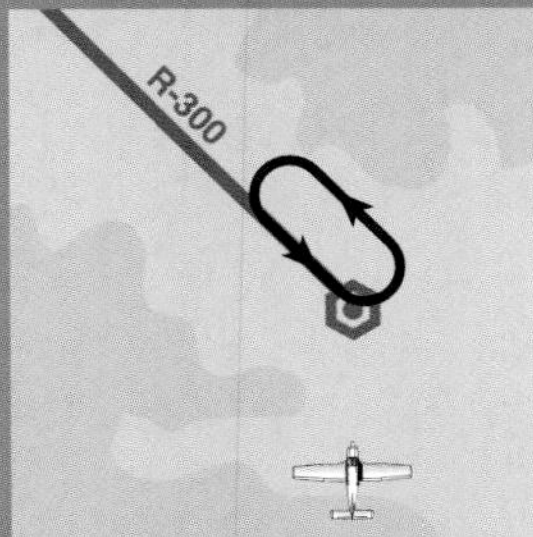

In this example, the airplane is approaching a VOR from the south. If the hold is on the 300¡ radial with the left turns, your student can easily determine that a teardrop entry is appropriate.

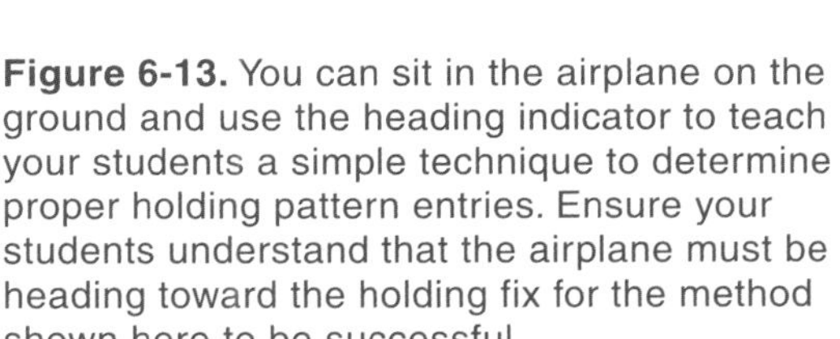

Figure 6-13. You can sit in the airplane on the ground and use the heading indicator to teach your students a simple technique to determine proper holding pattern entries. Ensure your students understand that the airplane must be heading toward the holding fix for the method shown here to be successful.

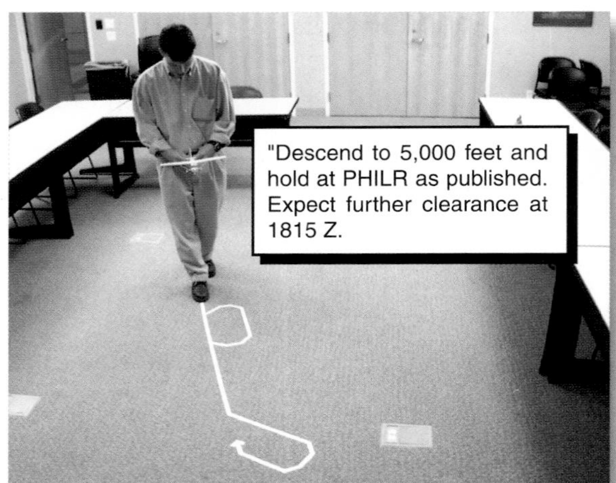

Figure 6-14. One way to teach your students about holding procedures is to use a diagram on the floor of the classroom.

ARRIVAL CHARTS AND PROCEDURES

Arrival charts provide a smooth transition between the enroute structure and busy terminal areas, simplifying complex clearances and supplying an expected plan of action to both pilots and controllers. Knowing how to integrate these charts into a flight plan enables your students to fly IFR into congested airspace with confidence.

Depending on where you conduct training, your students may not have the opportunity to fly **standard terminal arrival routes (STARs)**. Many of these procedures are intended for high altitude airplanes and would not be routinely assigned to a light aircraft. For this reason, your ground school discussions of how to fly an arrival procedure may be especially important.

Even if you do not have an opportunity in your local area to fly STARs with your students, it is essential that they be taught to plan their arrivals well ahead of time. If you can instill the habit of gathering information about what approaches are in use, and of reviewing the chart for the expected arrival before it is time to fly it, your students' workload is dramatically reduced. [Figure 6-15]

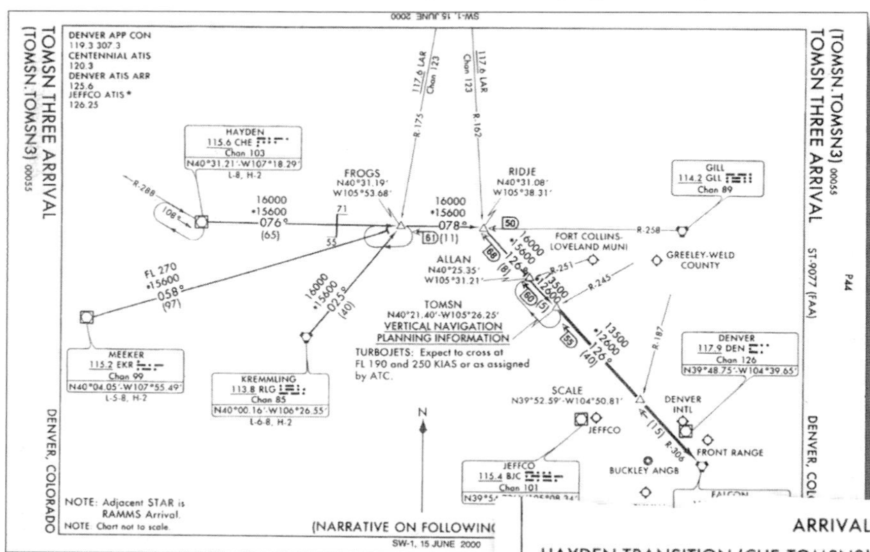

ARRIVAL DESCRIPTION

HAYDEN TRANSITION (CHE.TOMSN3): From over CHE VOR/DME via CHE R-076 and GLL R-258 to RIDJE INT; then via FQF R-306 to TOMSN INT. Thence . . . .
KREMMLING TRANSITION (RLG.TOMSN3): From over RLG VORTAC via RLG R-025 and GLL R-258 to RIDJE INT; then via FQF R-306 to TOMSN INT. Thence . . . .
MEEKER TRANSITION (EKR.TOMSN3): From over EKR VOR/DME via EKR R-058 and GLL R-258 to RIDJE INT; then via FQF R-306 to TOMSN INT. Thence . . . .
. . . . From over TOMSN INT via FQF R-306 to FQF VORTAC. Expect radar vectors to the final approach course at or before FQF VORTAC.

Figure 6-15. STAR charts provide established transitions from the enroute structure to a segment of an instrument approach.

APPROACH CHARTS AND PROCEDURES

How well your students learn to fly instrument approaches is often proportionate to how well they understand the approach charts and how well they understand the design of instrument approach procedures. Presenting your students with information about the *U.S. Standards for Terminal Instrument Approaches (TERPS)* design criteria, including the purpose for each approach segment, will improve their situational awareness. Also, make sure your students understand all of the data presented on instrument approach charts. This helps them handle the wide variety of approaches they may encounter later when they begin exercising their instrument privileges. Some of the areas that you must be certain your students have operational knowledge of include: approach segments, chart layout, airport information, approach clearances, radar vectors, course reversals, landing minimums, inoperative components, circling and sidestep maneuvers, and visual/contact approaches.

APPROACH SEGMENTS

Approach segments may be viewed as the building blocks of the approach structure. It is important for your students to understand the different approach segments that make it possible to transition from the enroute portion of a flight to the landing portion. Detailed descriptions and design criteria for approaches can be found in the TERPS.

Although **feeder routes** technically are not considered approach segments, they are an integral part of many approaches and need to be discussed with your students. Many approaches include them as a means of transitioning from the enroute segment to the initial approach fix (IAF) when this fix is not part of the enroute structure. You can provide sample approach clearances, and then ask your students to explain how they would transition from the enroute portion to the IAF. During the approach, they should only be making brief references to the approach chart while concentrating on precise navigation and aircraft control. [Figure 6-16]

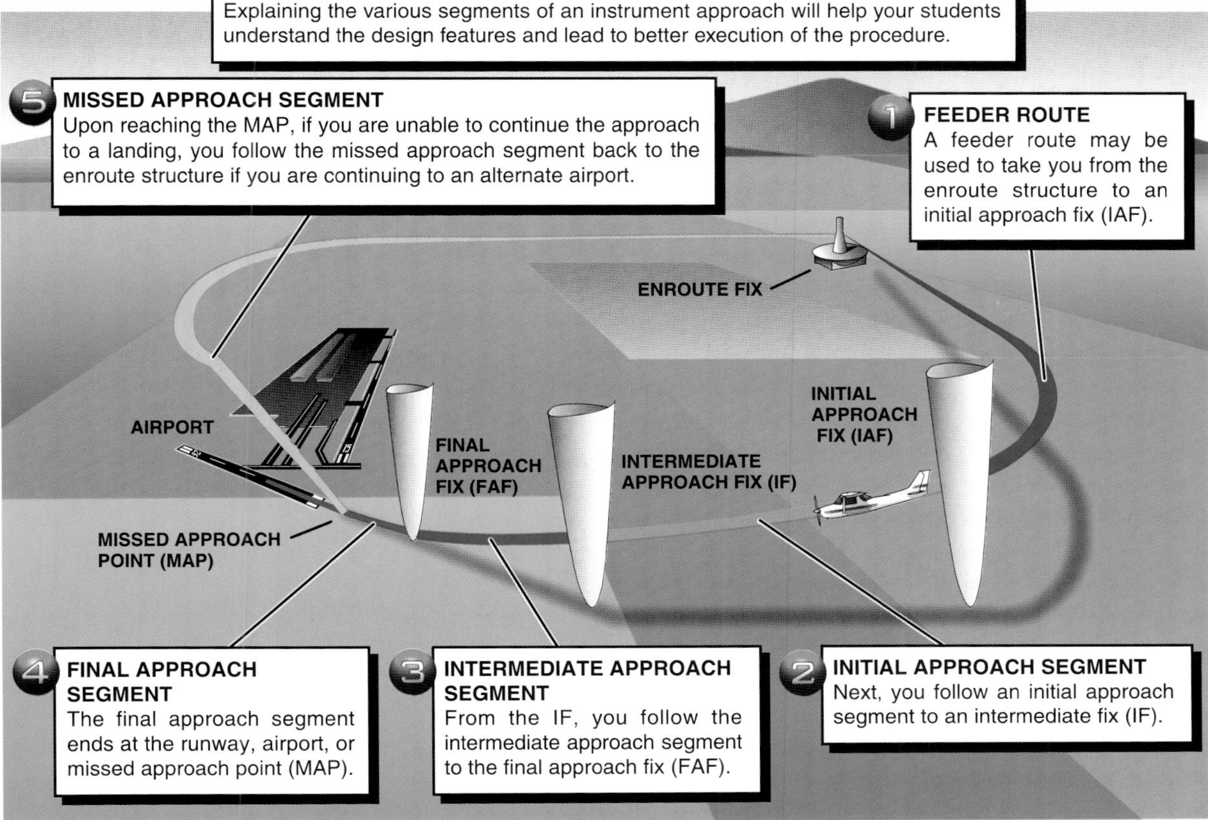

Figure 6-16. The approach procedure is divided into segments, each of which is designed so the airplane can navigate from the initial approach fix to either a landing or missed approach.

Chart Layout

Your students will need to be able to read and understand approach charts whether they are in the Jeppesen or NOS format. Your students will be much more comfortable with the use of these charts if they have a thorough knowledge of where information is located and what it means. Once you have provided your students with a solid foundation in chart symbology, a good technique is to select charts at random and have your students explain the approach procedures. [Figure 6-17]

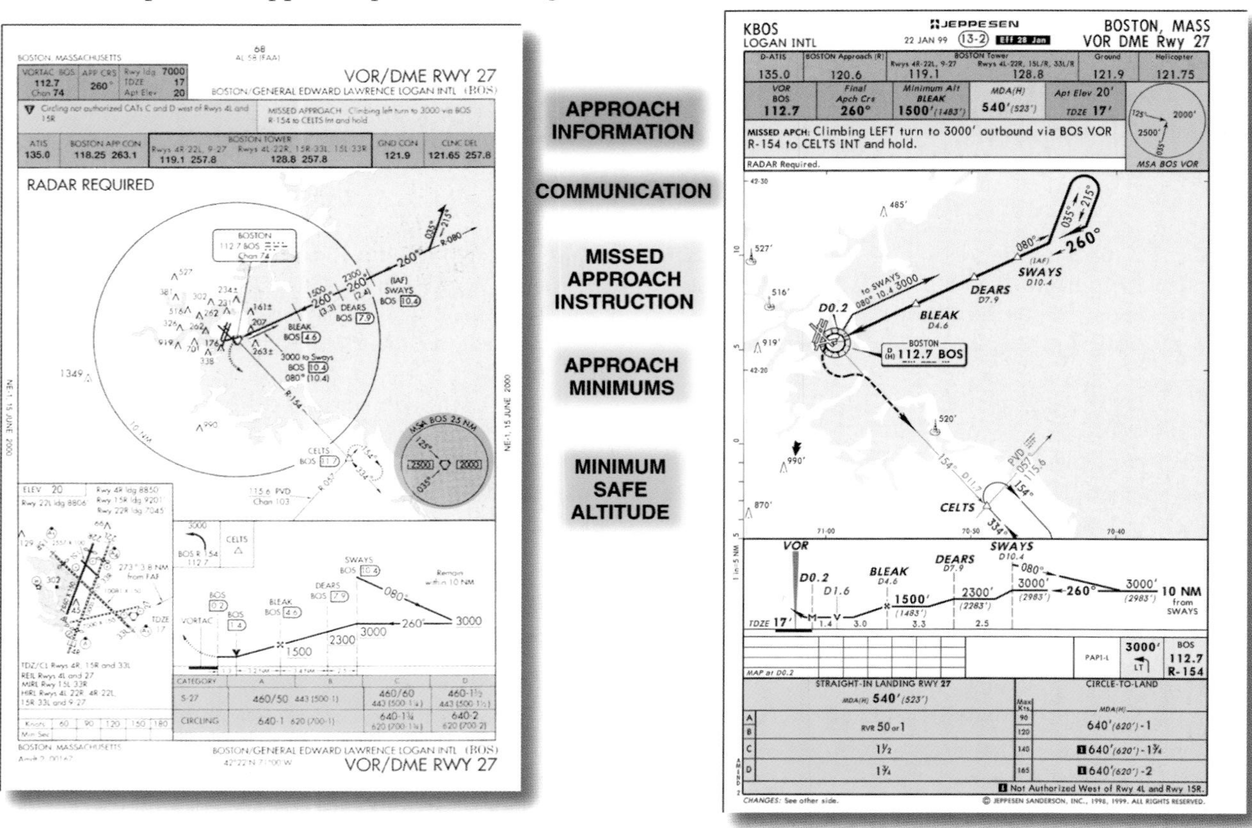

Figure 6-17. Although NOS and Jeppesen charts are slightly different in format, they both contain essential information. Regardless of format, your students must be able to interpret the procedure and understand the information depicted.

Airport Information

Both NOS and Jeppesen have detailed diagrams of the airport associated with each approach. By making certain that your students form the habit of acquiring a good working knowledge of the destination airport, they are less likely to be involved in a runway incursion incident. They also can anticipate the appearance of the runway environment better as they descend toward minimums. Discuss with your students the definition of runway environment as it relates to meeting the requirements that allow them to transition to a visual landing.

Approach Clearance

Whether your students receive a clearance for a specific approach into an airport or are cleared for any approach, it is important that they know what the clearance means from an operational standpoint. You need to make certain they understand that unless they are being radar vectored, they are expected to fly the entire charted procedure.

Radar Vectors to Approach

All instrument approaches are required to have positive course guidance to the IAF. Sometimes radar vectors may provide this guidance. Discuss with your students the importance of maintaining situational awareness when using radar vectors. There is a tendency, even for inexperienced pilots, to become complacent when being continuously

radar vectored. This complacency could result in them not knowing where they are or what actions to take, if radar contact or communication is lost. Some preparation for maintaining situational awareness can be accomplished by reviewing a number of approach charts with your students and raising "*what if*" questions. Emphasis should be on maintaining positional awareness, especially during vectors to the final approach course. [Figure 6-18]

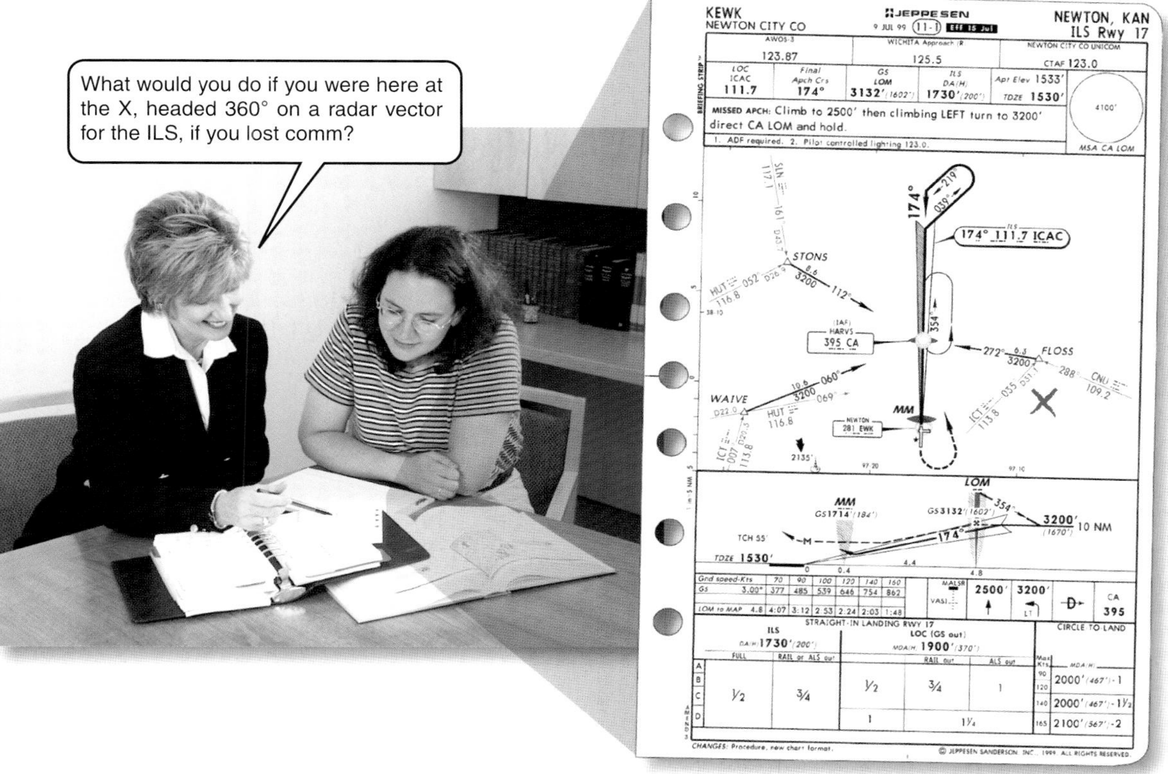

Figure 6-18. Quizzing your students on what they would do if they lost radio contact while being radar vectored to the final approach course helps them prepare for handling the same situations in flight.

COURSE REVERSALS

If the procedure being flown by your students is not a straight-in approach to the final approach course and radar vectors are not available, a **course reversal** is usually depicted on the approach chart. If the reversal is in the form of a procedure turn, the point where your students begin the turn and type and rate of turn are optional as long as the airplane remains in protected airspace. However, your students need to be aware that if the reversal is depicted as a holding pattern or teardrop, they need to fly it exactly as shown. You also need to discuss the descent procedures with your students. If they are above the course reversal altitude, they may begin the descent procedure after passing the IAF.

UNDERSTANDING LANDING MINIMUMS

The purpsose of the final approach segment is to position the airplane for landing. Too often, students get into a mindset that an approach procedure ends with a missed approach at the DH or MDA. You must afford them the opportunity to learn to transition between flying with reference to instruments and making a normal landing. The best way of doing this is to have your students fly approaches in actual instrument meteorological conditions (IMC). Failing to have the opportunity for this, you can be as realistic as possible by having your students remove their view limiting devices at the DH or MDA and complete a landing. You can also use FTDs or PCATDs, if available. Many of these devices are very realistic in their visual presentations of this transition and can simulate the changeover to visual cues for approach to landing, if not to the landing itself.

INOPERATIVE COMPONENTS

Another area with which your students should be familiar in regard to landing minimums is **inoperative components**. Your students will have little trouble realizing that landing minimums usually increase when a required component or visual aid becomes inoperative. ILS glide slope inoperative minimums are published on instrument charts as localizer minimums. However, you need to teach them that the loss of other items, such as approach lights, also affects landing minimums. You need to discuss with your students the differences in how these higher minimums are presented on NOS and Jeppesen approach charts. [Figure 6-19]

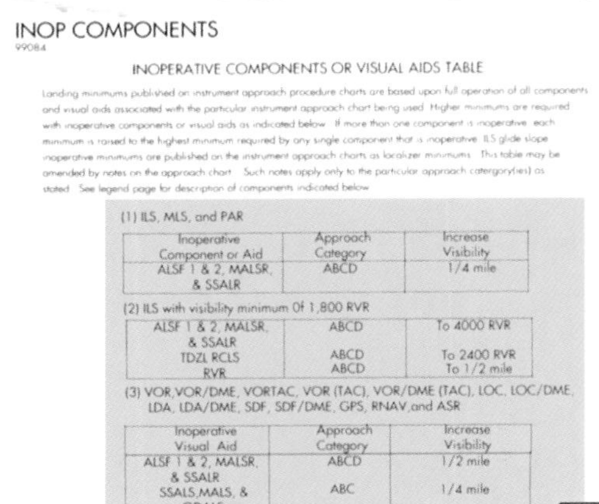

INOP COMPONENTS

99084

INOPERATIVE COMPONENTS OR VISUAL AIDS TABLE

Landing minimums published on instrument approach procedure charts are based upon full operation of all components and visual aids associated with the particular instrument approach chart being used. Higher minimums are required with inoperative components or visual aids as indicated below. If more than one component is inoperative, each minimum is raised to the highest minimum required by any single component that is inoperative. ILS glide slope inoperative minimums are published on the instrument approach charts as localizer minimums. This table may be amended by notes on the approach chart. Such notes apply only to the particular approach catergory(ies) as stated. See legend page for description of components indicated below.

(1) ILS, MLS, and PAR

Inoperative Component or Aid	Approach Category	Increase Visibility
ALSF 1 & 2, MALSR, & SSALR	ABCD	1/4 mile

(2) ILS with visibility minimum Of 1,800 RVR

ALSF 1 & 2, MALSR, & SSALR	ABCD	To 4000 RVR
TDZL RCLS	ABCD	To 2400 RVR
RVR	ABCD	To 1/2 mile

(3) VOR, VOR/DME, VORTAC, VOR (TAC), VOR/DME (TAC), LOC, LOC/DME, LDA, LDA/DME, SDF, SDF/DME, GPS, RNAV, and ASR

Inoperative Visual Aid	Approach Category	Increase Visibility
ALSF 1 & 2, MALSR, & SSALR	ABCD	1/2 mile
SSALS, MALS, & ODALS	ABC	1/4 mile

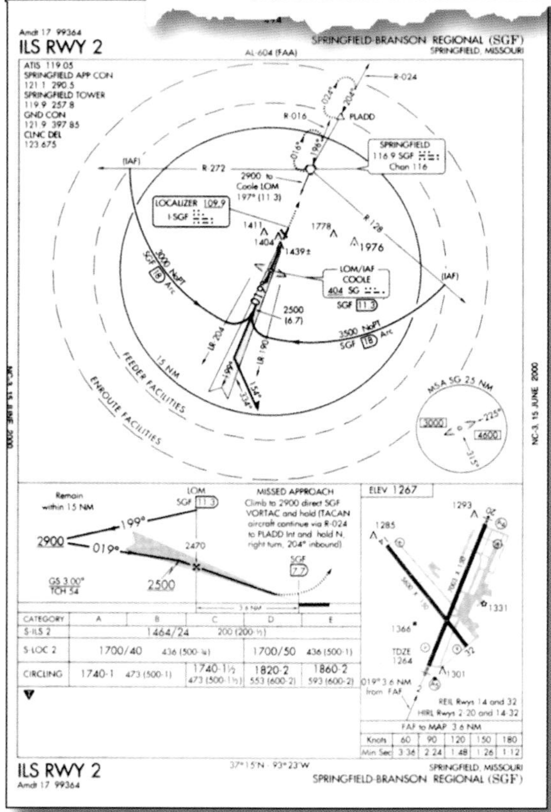

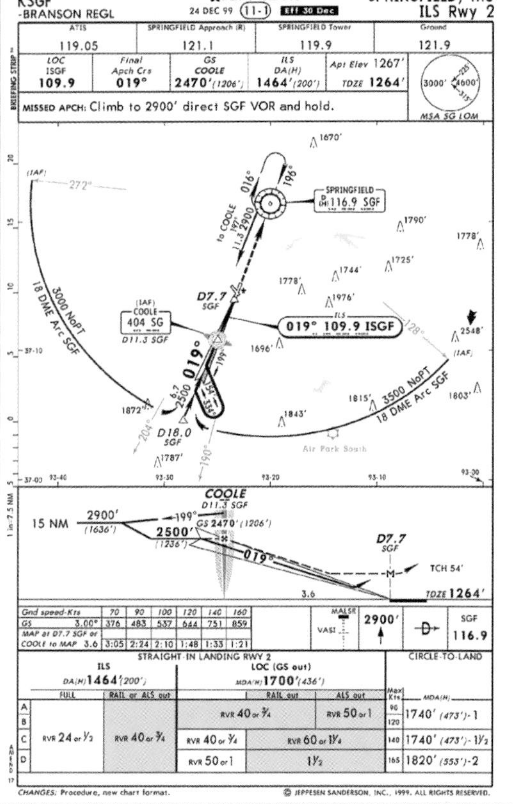

Figure 6-19. While Jeppesen depicts inoperative component minimums on the approach chart, NOS provides a separate inoperative components table in each chart volume.

CIRCLING AND SIDESTEP MANEUVERS

The transition from flying with reference to instruments to landing the airplane visually is challenging in low visibility, and more difficult when the landing runway is not aligned with the final approach course. Actually performing circling and sidestep maneuvers is the best way for your students to master them. However, explaining these

procedures during ground training is good preparation. In the case of a circling approach, it is beneficial to discuss terrain clearance concerns and how the radius of turns relates to the circling approach protected airspace.

VISUAL AND CONTACT APPROACHES

A visual or contact approach is not technically part of an instrument approach procedure, but you should make certain your students know the differences between these two approaches. Your students need to understand that while they may request a **contact approach**, the controller can clear them for a **visual approach** whether or not it has been requested. Be certain your students are aware that they can refuse the visual approach. Discuss examples of situations when they may consider refusing a visual approach, such as marginal and intermittent visibility, lack of familiarity with the airport, or uncertainty in identifying the preceding aircraft.

VOR AND NDB APPROACHES

Much of the time with your students is spent flying nonprecision approaches. It is important that you teach your students not only how to interpret the approach charts, but also to understand why the approach is designed the way it is. It is a good technique to select approach charts that can be analyzed for format. [Figure 6-20]

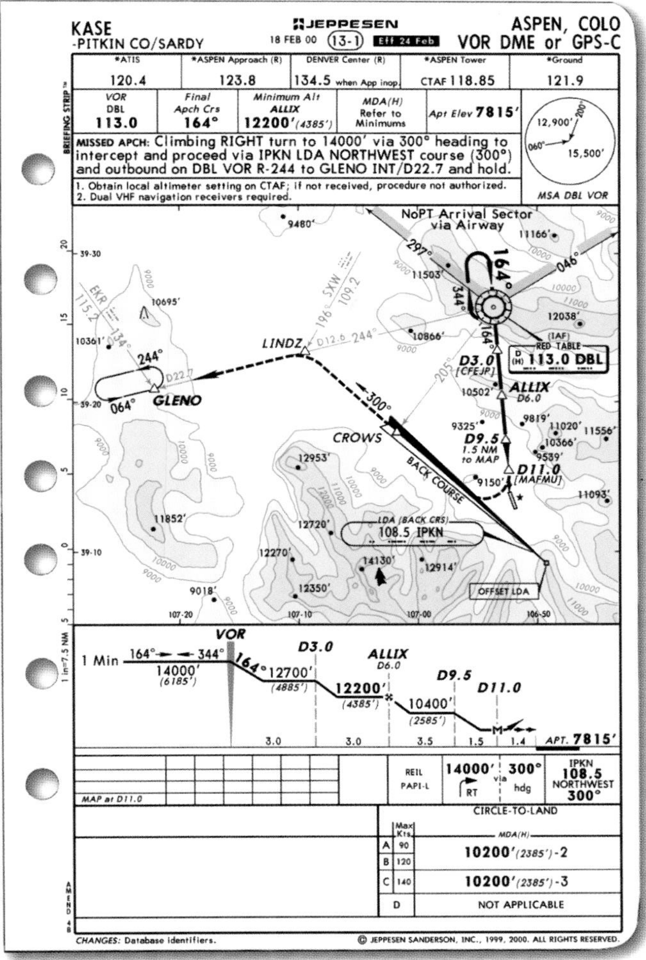

Figure 6-20. The approach and missed approach procedures on this chart are designed to keep the airplane safely in the valley between the higher ground to the east and the southwest.

Your students need to be aware of the two schools of thought on descent to the MDA. Explain the relative merits of descending promptly to the MDA, leveling off, and proceeding to the MAP vs. setting up a descent rate that has the airplane arriving at the MDA simultaneously with reaching a point where a visual landing can be made.

ILS APPROACHES

There are some unique operational requirements for ILS approaches that are not encountered on nonprecision approaches. For example, you can emphasize to your students the increased sensitivity of course guidance as the airplane gets closer to the runway. Also, alert your students to the fact that the glide slope indications become progressively more sensitive as the airplane approaches the runway.

Once your students start looking at back course procedures, you need to point out that the back course localizer is much more sensitive for a given distance from the runway. This is because the transmitter is at the approach end of the runway, as opposed to being at the departure end for a front course ILS approach. Another area to emphasize and explain to your students is the reverse sensing of a conventional VOR/ILS indicator when flying inbound on the back course or outbound on the front course.

GPS and RNAV Approaches

GPS and RNAV approaches are becoming available for more and more airports, including small airports. The FAA is including **GPS approaches** with **RNAV approaches** since both are systems essentially independent of navigation aids located at the landing airport. One of the worst problems your students can have while flying such approaches is loss of situational awareness. The more complex the navigation equipment is and the more workload it alleviates, the more important it is for your students to maintain an awareness of location and what is happening during the approach. You can teach your students the perils of not maintaining situational awareness by failing the RNAV or GPS while practicing in a simulation device, or telling your students during an approach briefing that they have lost the equipment and require them to explain what actions they would take. Another point to impress upon your students is that the equipment is no better than the information programmed into it. The GPS equipment can tell your exact location but cannot tell you where to go unless it has been properly programmed. In addition, you should stress the fact that the GPS/RNAV equipment is not standardized. Therefore, it is important to know how to use the specific equipment in your airplane.

Radar Approaches

Radar approaches, during which ATC provides horizontal, and, in some cases, vertical course guidance can be obtained at a limited number of airports. Your students need to know how to perform these approaches since in the event of a partial panel emergency, these are often the best option. The radar approach, which may include no-gyro-procedures, has the advantage of another person (the controller) assisting your students during a critical phase of flight.

Evaluating Weather Considerations

By now, your students have gained some experience in judging weather. Most have made go/no-go decisions, and many are seeking instrument training so they can operate in less than VFR conditions. One myth you need to promptly dispel is that an instrument rating makes it possible for a pilot to safely fly in any type of weather. The fact is, an instrument rating will allow your students to fly in a wider variety of weather conditions, some of which present dangers not faced by fair-weather pilots. In addition, explain that restricted visibility can create a hazard, even to instrument-rated pilots. That is why your students need to understand the conditions under which an alternate airport is required, and the qualifications for listing an airport as an alternate.

Understanding Weather Phenomena

Judging weather is more complicated for instrument pilots. Because your students could be entering the clouds, they need to pay more attention to weather phenomena that do not present a hazard to VFR pilots. For example, airplanes remaining outside the clouds normally can avoid icing and embedded thunderstorms. Instrument pilots must use additional care to avoid these hazards. Although some students may not see the importance of expanding their weather knowledge and improving their interpretive skills, these are the keys to utilizing their newfound instrument capabilities to the

maximum. Their ability to fly in instrument conditions has expanded, but the limitations on the types of conditions the airplane can fly in have not changed. By understanding weather systems and how to interpret weather reports and charts, your students will be able to exercise their instrument privileges safely.

Destination Airport: Cape Canaveral, Florida
Alternate Airport: Zaragoza, Spain

Every Space Shuttle Mission includes planning for unscheduled landings due to such things as adverse weather conditions at the primary and secondary landing sites or mechanical problems during the launch or recovery.

One mode of unscheduled landing is called the Transoceanic Abort Landing (TAL). This landing would be made if one of the Shuttle's engines failed or if some other major piece of equipment failed which would preclude satisfactory continuation of the mission. The TAL would be for missions aborted between two and a half minutes and eight minutes after liftoff.

A TAL would be made at one of four sites: Ben Guerir Air Base, Morocco; Yundum International Airport, Banjul, The Gambia; Moron Air Base, Spain; or Zaragoza Air Base, Spain. Each of these sites has been prepositioned with Shuttle specific equipment including special navigation and landing aids, automated weather equipment, a shuttle orbiter arresting system (a net barrier installed prior to launch and dismantled after a successful launch); dedicated ground support equipment; and fire, crash, and rescue resources. In addition, Department of Defense C-130s are used to transport TAL ground personnel between sites and for any necessary medical evacuation. TAL sites are activated about one week prior to a launch, but actual declaration of a TAL would be only about 20 to 25 minutes before landing.

Once a TAL has been declared, a pre-loaded reentry program goes into effect. About 200 miles out from landing, the Shuttle will update its inertial guidance system from the landing site's TACAN.

The Shuttle will enter the terminal area about 6 minutes before landing at an altitude of 82,000 feet and Mach 2.5. About 5 minutes before landing, the Shuttle will pass over the center of the runway and slow to Mach 1. At 4 minutes prior to touchdown the crew will take over manual control of the Shuttle. Final approach begins 2 minutes before touchdown at 13,000 feet and a glide angle of 17 degrees. At an altitude of 1,800 feet and 7,500 feet horizontally out from touchdown, glide angle is reduced to 1 1/2° and touchdown is at 195 knots.

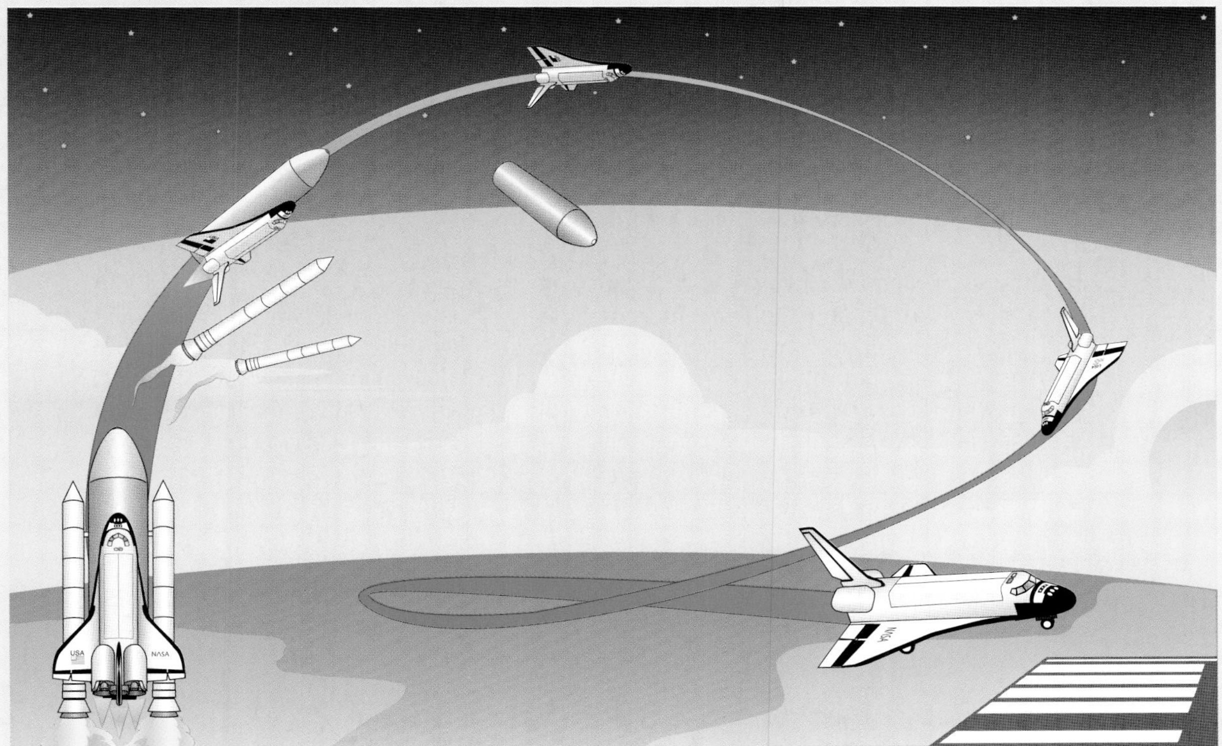

EXAMINING IFR FLIGHT CONSIDERATIONS

It is important that you teach your students to distinguish between instrument flight rules (IFR), and instrument meteorological conditions (IMC). Remind your students that the terms VFR and IFR are often used to define weather conditions as well as the FARs under which pilots operate. In order to fly legally in controlled airspace when IMC exists or under IFR, a pilot must be instrument rated, fly an airplane with approved equipment, and be cleared by ATC to operate in the IFR system. Another advantage of being instrument rated is the ability to fly in the IFR system whether it is IMC or VMC. The advantages of flying under IFR, such as advisories and separation from all IFR traffic, facilitates easier routing through controlled areas along the route of flight, sequencing into high traffic airports, and assistance in case of emergency. [Figure 6-21]

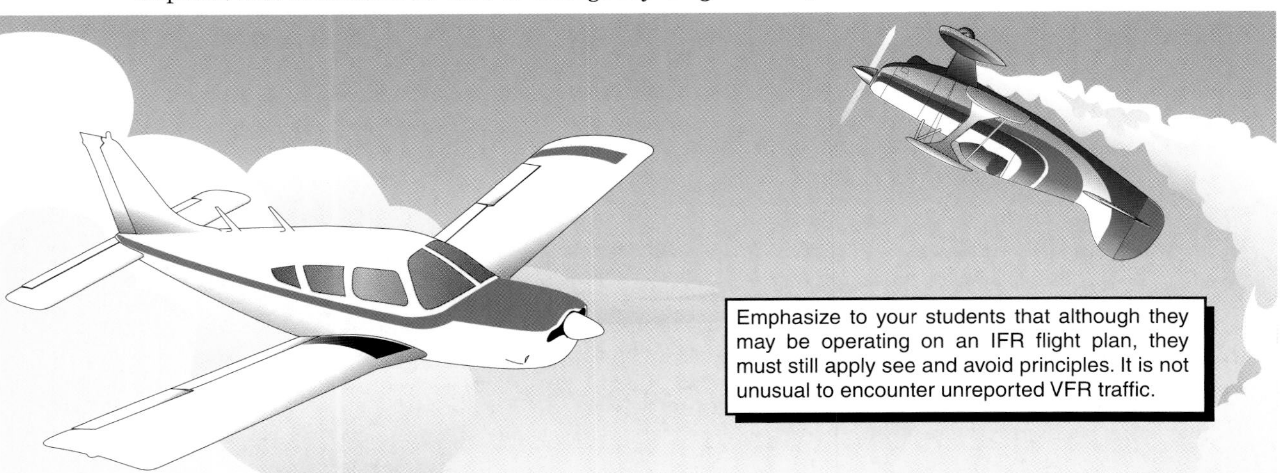

Figure 6-21. When flying under IFR, your students still have a responsibility for traffic separation when in visual conditions.

Statistics show that most IFR accidents occur when instrument-rated pilots fail to file an IFR flight plan when conditions warrant, or when they cancel their IFR clearance prematurely and continue flight into poor weather. You should train your students that the best way of maintaining their instrument proficiency, as well as their currency, is to fly under IFR as often as possible. By filing an IFR flight plan every time they fly cross-country, they will ensure maximum safety as well as currency. They also should seek instrument refresher training periodically.

IFR EMERGENCIES

No one likes to think they might be required to deal with an emergency during instrument flight. However, proper planning and sound knowledge of emergency procedures can help your students complete a flight safely should an emergency occur. Your students must be aware of the requirements in FAR 91.187 for notifying ATC of any malfunction of navigational, approach, or communication equipment occurring during flight in controlled airspace under IFR. The main benefit of this rule is that ATC may be able to assist in resolving any problems encountered. [Figure 6-22]

IFR DECISION MAKING

Aviation differs from most pursuits because it demands higher quality decisions, especially within the IFR system. The complexity of these decisions is one of the reasons your students must exhibit a high level of competence and obtain appropriate experience before they can become instrument-rated pilots. Flying in poor weather, without visual references, exposes them to situations they would never encounter flying in VFR conditions. They also will operate in a more structured environment, and collaborate with ATC throughout the course of a flight. [Figure 6-23]

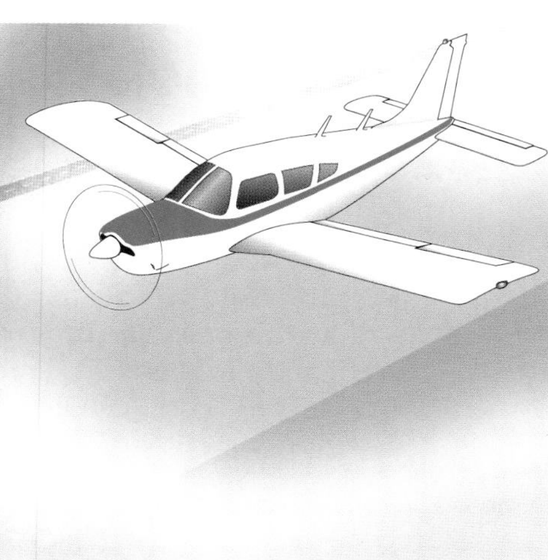

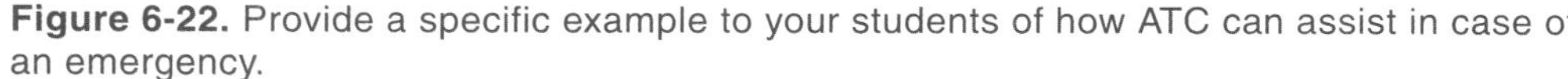

Figure 6-22. Provide a specific example to your students of how ATC can assist in case of an emergency.

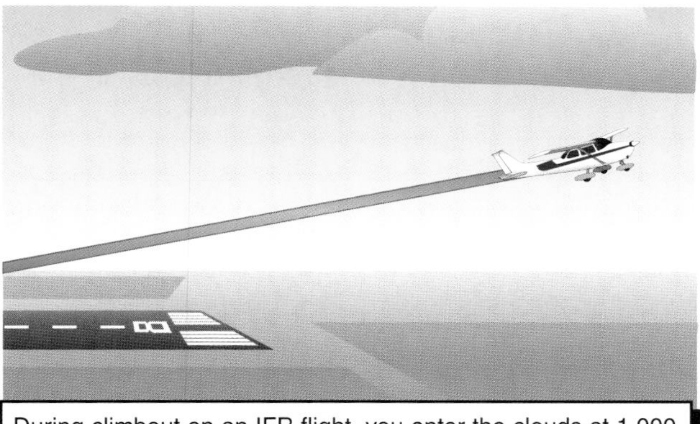

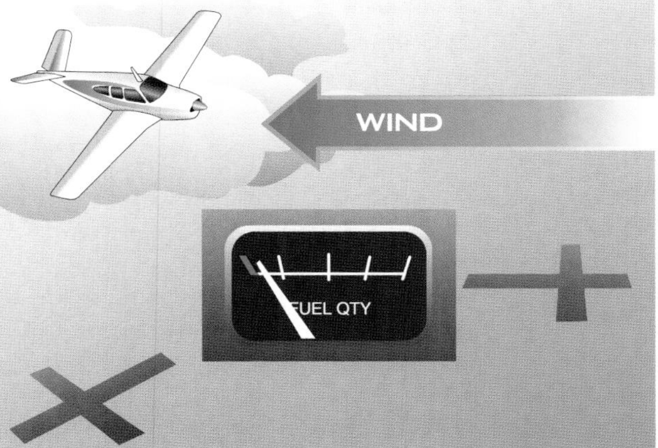

Figure 6-23. As an exercise to develop decision-making skills, discuss different scenarios with your students.

IFR FLIGHT PLANNING

In some ways, IFR planning is easier than VFR planning. Your students can read the distances and courses directly off an enroute chart, rather than measuring them with a plotter. However, they are likely to plan flights over longer distances, closer to the range of the airplane, and must consider potential ATC delays, alternate airports, and other factors when calculating the required fuel for a trip. IFR flight planning emphasizes route selection, the collection of communication and navigation information, knowledge of charts and flight publications, and, above all, the gathering of timely and accurate weather information. Your students are required by regulations to perform numerous preflight actions and be familiar with a variety of information. Airplane performance, knowledge of current and forecast weather conditions, and planned alternates are items to which they should pay special attention during the IFR flight planning process.

SUMMARY CHECKLIST

✓ A spinning bicycle wheel can be used to demonstrate gyroscopic rigidity in space and precession.

✓ The bank required to maintain a standard-rate turn increases with true airspeed (TAS).

✓ True airspeed increases over CAS/IAS nearly 2% for each 1,000-foot increase in altitude.

✓ An instrument scan, or cross-check, is the first fundamental skill of attitude instrument flying. A good scan requires logical and systematic observation of the instrument panel.

✓ The primary/support concept of attitude instrument flying is recommended by the FAA for instrument training in light aircraft with low operating speeds.

✓ The control and performance concept divides the instruments into three categories: control, performance, and navigation.

✓ An attitude indicator failure can be as subtle as continuing to indicate wings level while the airplane gradually drifts off into a diving spiral.

✓ Because of turning error and the associated problems with use of the magnetic compass, a timed turn is the most accurate way to turn to a specific heading without the use of the heading indicator.

✓ Use of a PCATD, FTD, or flight simulator allows you to provide your students with unannounced, insidious failures of primary flight instruments.

✓ The best way to introduce holding patterns is during ground training where you can have students determine the type of entry procedure appropriate to the direction of flight.

✓ The approach procedure is divided into segments, each of which is designed so the airplane can navigate from the initial approach fix to either a landing or missed approach.

✓ Your students must be able to interpret the procedure and understand the information depicted, on both NOS and Jeppesen charts.

- ✓ The transition from flying with reference to instruments to landing the airplane visually is challenging in low visibility and even more difficult when the landing runway is not aligned with the final approach course.
- ✓ The back course localizer is much more sensitive for a given distance from the runway. This is because the transmitter is at the approach end of the runway as opposed to being at the departure end for a front course ILS approach.
- ✓ The more complex the navigational equipment is and the more workload it alleviates, the more important it is for your students to maintain an awareness of location and what is happening during an approach.
- ✓ The radar approach, which may include no-gyro-procedures, has the advantage of another person (the controller) helping out during a critical phase of flight.
- ✓ One myth about an instrument rating is that it is possible for a pilot to safely fly in any type of weather. The fact is, an instrument rating will allow your students to fly in a wider variety of weather conditions, some of which present dangers not faced by fair-weather pilots.
- ✓ Statistics show that most IFR accidents occur when instrument-rated pilots fail to file an IFR flight plan when conditions warrant, or when they cancel their IFR clearance prematurely and continue flight into poor weather.
- ✓ IFR flight planning emphasizes route selection, the collection of communication and navigation information, knowledge of charts and flight publications, and, above all, the gathering of timely and accurate weather information.

KEY TERMS

Standard-Rate Turn

Calibrated Airspeed (CAS)

Indicated Airspeed (IAS)

True Airspeed (TAS)

Cross-Check

Primary/Support Concept

Control and Performance Concept

Instrument Interpretation

Aircraft Control

Departure Procedure (DP)

Climb Gradients

Standard Terminal Arrival Route (STAR)

U.S. Standards for Terminal Procedures (TERPS)

Feeder Routes

Course Reversal

Inoperative Components

Contact Approach

Visual Approach

GPS Approach

RNAV Approach

QUESTIONS

1. Name at least one method you can use to teach your students about gyroscopic principles?

2. What three fundamental skills must your students master when learning attitude instrument flying?

3. What are the two generally accepted methods in use for teaching instrument cross-check during attitude instrument training?

4. What advantage do PCATDs, FTDs, and flight simulators have over demonstrating instrument failures in flight?

5. One of the best ways to teach pilots to gain an understanding of the ATC system is to visit FAA facilities. What are the names of the two formal programs used by the FAA?

6. State at least one method you can use to teach students holding pattern entry procedures.

7. Select the true statement regarding instructing your students on approach procedures.

   A. Students only need to be familiar with one type of approach chart format.
   B. An understanding of approach segments is not necessary for your students to effectively learn approach procedures.
   C. Students should be aware that complacency can lead to a loss of situational awareness when they are receiving radar vectors to the IAF.

8. Provide an example of a scenario which you can pose to your students to help their decision-making skills in the IFR environment.

SECTION B
REFINING INSTRUMENT SKILLS

Once your students have learned about instrument operations on the ground, it is time to apply this knowledge in the airplane. This is not to imply that all of the knowledge related to instrument flying should be covered prior to the first instrument training flight. On the contrary, you should continue to conduct ground training along with flight lessons. As you probably recall from your previous flight training, pursuing an instrument rating can be quite challenging. Your instrument students must understand a wide variety of new procedures, master advanced skills of flying with reference to instruments, and learn how to utilize aircraft equipment in ways they have not done before.

As an instructor, you also face new challenges and new rewards as your students gain proficiency, increase their confidence level, and enhance their flight safety on their way to becoming instrument-rated pilots. This section is not intended to explain instrument flight operations in the detail required for a student to master each maneuver and procedure. Rather, it is designed as a guideline for instructing instrument students. In this section, you will find examples of specific teaching techniques, common student errors, and tips to help you make your students' instrument flight training successful. For specific information on instrument operations consult the Guided Flight Discovery *Instrument/Commercial Manual.*

PREPARING FOR INSTRUMENT INSTRUCTION

Success during instrument instruction largely depends on the amount of time spent in preparation for flight lessons. While a student pilot may be able to perform turns, slow flight, and even stalls without explanations of these maneuvers on the ground prior to flight, it is unlikely that an instrument student will successfully execute holding or approach procedures without extensive ground preparation. In addition to traditional ground lessons, you can employ several other methods to help effectively prepare your students for instrument instruction in flight.

USING PCATDS AND FTDS

You may be utilizing a syllabus that includes use of a **personal computer-based aviation training device (PCATD)** and/or a **flight training device (FTD)**. These devices, when properly used, are excellent for introduction of new maneuvers and procedures. The advantages to using a PCATD or FTD include the ability to reposition the airplane, freeze the simulation, conduct safe emergency instruction, control the training environment, and provide more lesson versatility. These benefits allow you to avoid the distractions that can occur in the airplane and concentrate on areas of training that need to be emphasized.

A PCATD that meets the established criteria of AC-61-126, *Qualification and Approval of PCATDs*, may be used for 10 hours of the instrument training time that ordinarily would be acquired in an airplane. If your organization has an FTD that meets the requirements of FAR 141.41(b), you may reduce the flight training hour requirements for a Part 141 instrument-rating course by up to 40%. For Part 61 training, up to 20 hours of instrument training accomplished in an FTD can be used to meet instrument flight time requirements.

FLIGHT PLANNING

Another way to help your students prepare for instrument flight instruction is to incorporate elements of basic **flight planning** into each lesson. Depending on the lesson, you may incorporate such planning activities as checking weather reports and forecasts, computing takeoff and landing distances, calculating fuel requirements, and determining available

Simulator Training Comes Down to Earth

In 1997, the FAA recognized the potential for computer-based aviation training devices (PCATDs) by issuing AC-61-126, *Qualification and Approval of Personal Computer-Based Aviation Training Devices.* This AC provides that some training time on PCATDs meeting acceptable FAA standards may be used to reduce the total flight hours that otherwise would have to be accomplished in an aircraft or a flight training device in order to meet the requirement for an instrument rating under FAR 61 or 141. PCATDs determined to meet the criteria established by this AC may be used in lieu of, and for not more than, 10 hours of time that ordinarily may be acquired in a flight simulator or flight training device authorized for use under FAR 61 or 141.

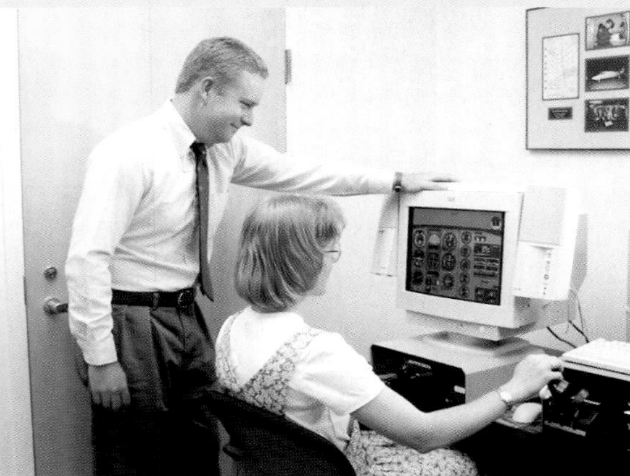

Using a PCATD before an instrument training flight allows your students to absorb new information and become familiar with the objectives of the lesson in a low-stress environment. The PCATD also can be used to review a lesson after the flight, which helps the student to lock in their new knowledge. It also allows you to go over specific details, pausing or repeating as necessary. With an approved PCATD, your students may develop valuable instrument skills and log time that counts toward their rating.

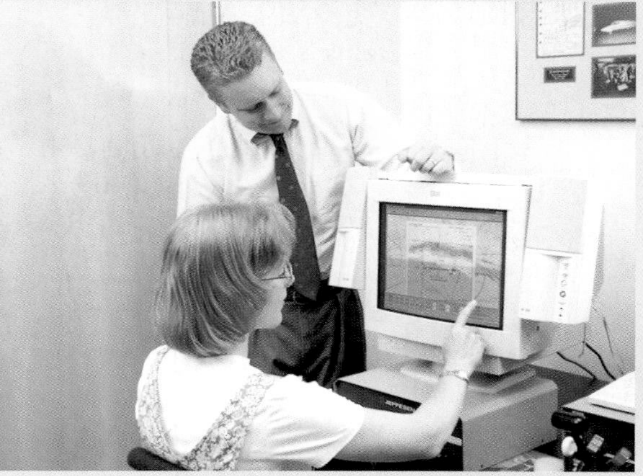

One of the unique features provided by some PCATD manufacturers includes IFR simulation software which contains printable instrument charts for simulator use. You can superimpose your student's flight path on-screen over the selected chart and review both the ground track and profile. With a comprehensive information database, the software lets you use approach charts, airport diagrams, SIDs/DPs, and STARS for almost any airport in the world.

FAA-sanctioned studies have shown that PCATDs can reduce the total hourly training time required in an airplane to achieve an instrument rating. When properly utilized, PCATDs provide a more efficient learning environment, and can be very beneficial for solving individual problems encountered by instrument students.

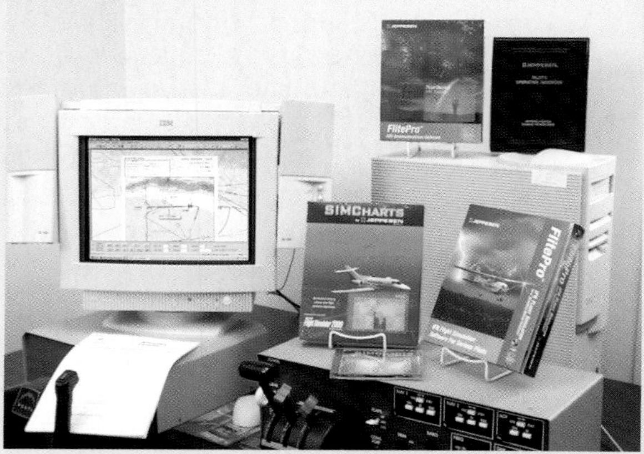

alternatives if the flight cannot be completed as planned. As students gain experience in instrument operations, you can add elements of instrument flight planning, such as checking pertinent NOTAMs, reviewing departure, arrival, and approach charts, and planning flights using navaids. By including elements of flight planning into each lesson, you help to instill habit patterns in your students that ensure they are well prepared for each instrument flight. [Figure 6-24]

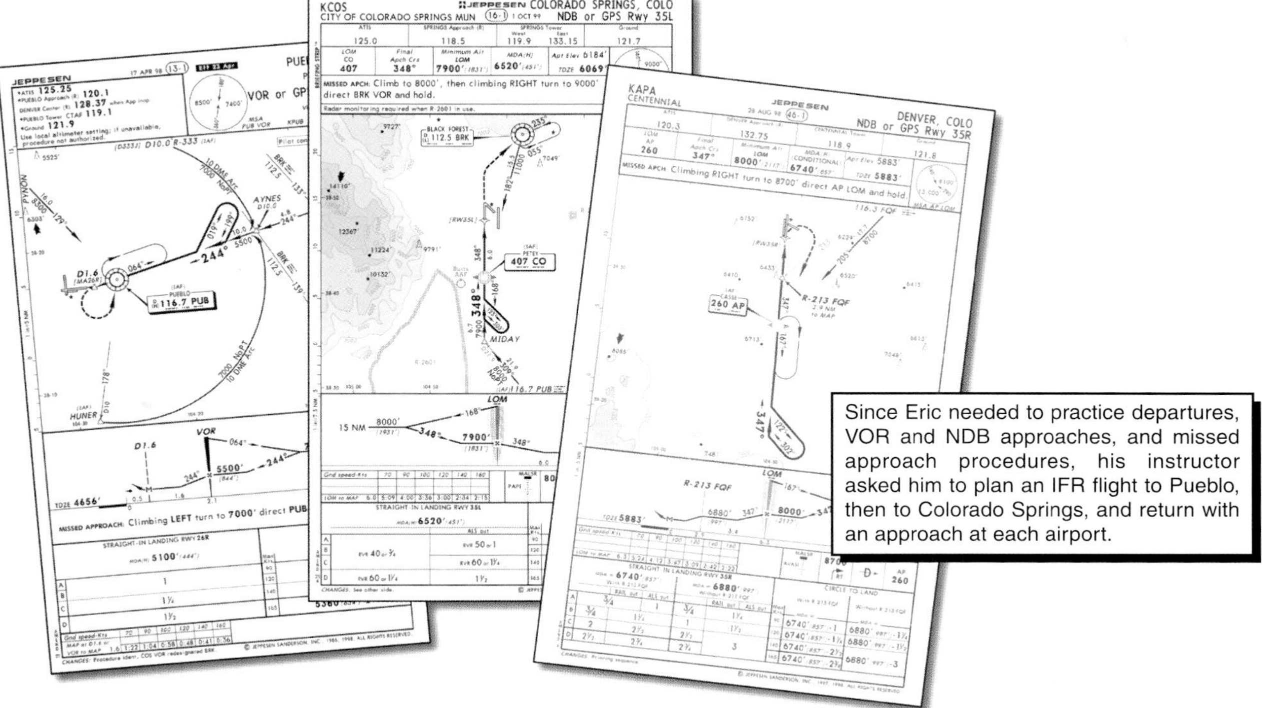

Figure 6-24. Once you have completed the initial instrument training flights, have your students plan and file flights under IFR to accomplish specific lesson objectives.

INSPECTING THE AIRPLANE

Beginning with the first instrument training flight, instruct your students to preflight the airplane and perform instrument and equipment checks as if they are about to embark on a flight under IFR. Since students with no IFR flight experience may not understand the importance of these inspections, it is essential that you explain the hazards that may result if equipment is not operating properly. Specific examples of the consequences of instrument and equipment malfunctions in IFR conditions derived from your own experience or obtained from ASRS or NTSB reports may help emphasize how crucial these checks are. [Figure 6-25 on Page 6-30]

DEVELOPING INSTRUMENT FLIGHT SKILLS

Your students learn instrument flying skills best when you utilize a building block concept of instruction. These blocks begin with the development of basic attitude instrument flying skills, followed by instrument navigation proficiency. Ultimately, these abilities provide the foundation for training in departure, arrival, and approach procedures.

ATTITUDE INSTRUMENT FLIGHT

Basic attitude instrument flight maneuvers are similar to basic visual maneuvers — straight-and-level flight, climbs, descents, leveloffs, and turns, as well as climbing and descending turns. Keep in mind that private pilot certification requires only three hours of flight training on the control and maneuvering of an airplane solely by reference to

INSTRUMENT AND EQUIPMENT CHECKS

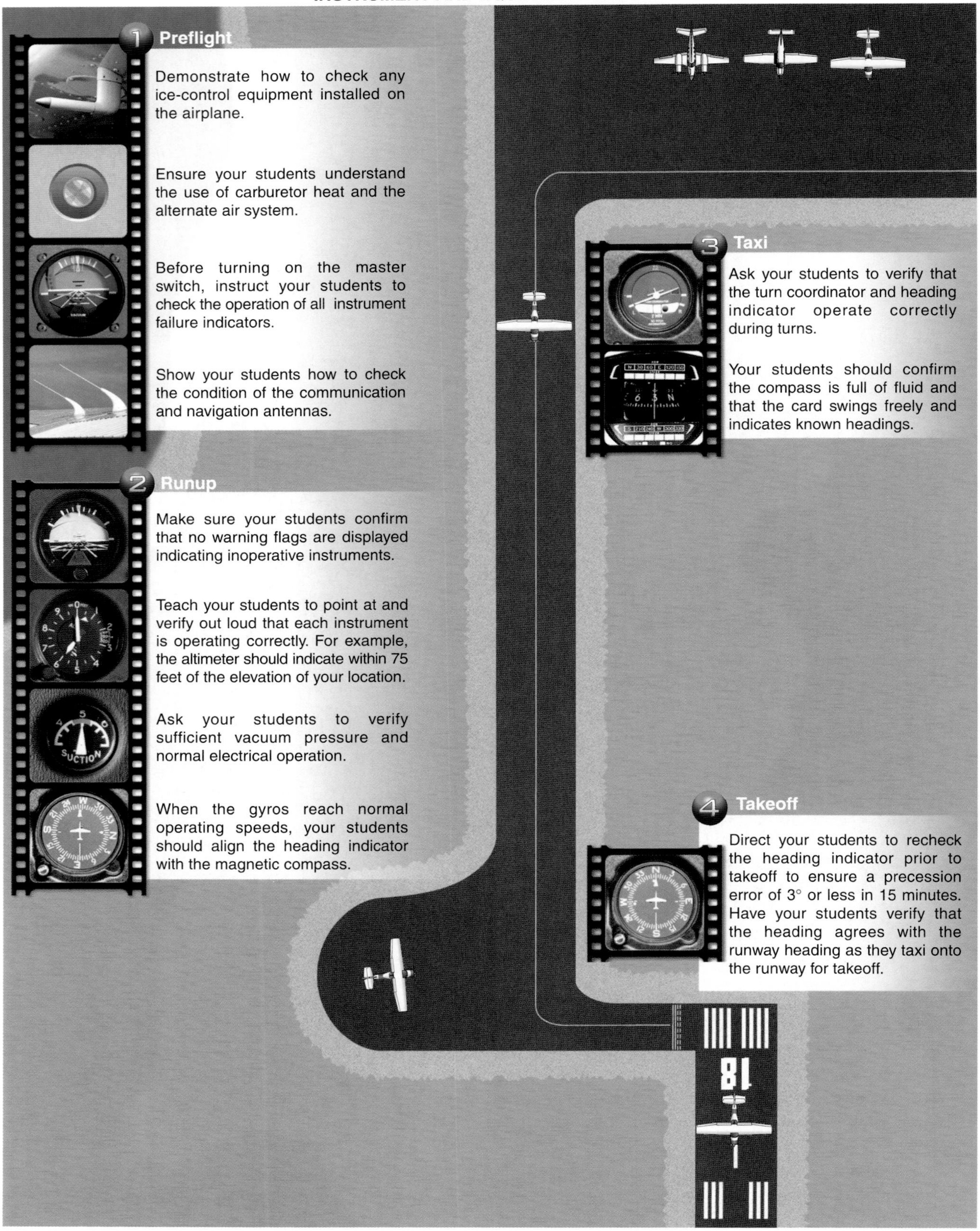

1 Preflight

Demonstrate how to check any ice-control equipment installed on the airplane.

Ensure your students understand the use of carburetor heat and the alternate air system.

Before turning on the master switch, instruct your students to check the operation of all instrument failure indicators.

Show your students how to check the condition of the communication and navigation antennas.

2 Runup

Make sure your students confirm that no warning flags are displayed indicating inoperative instruments.

Teach your students to point at and verify out loud that each instrument is operating correctly. For example, the altimeter should indicate within 75 feet of the elevation of your location.

Ask your students to verify sufficient vacuum pressure and normal electrical operation.

When the gyros reach normal operating speeds, your students should align the heading indicator with the magnetic compass.

3 Taxi

Ask your students to verify that the turn coordinator and heading indicator operate correctly during turns.

Your students should confirm the compass is full of fluid and that the card swings freely and indicates known headings.

4 Takeoff

Direct your students to recheck the heading indicator prior to takeoff to ensure a precession error of 3° or less in 15 minutes. Have your students verify that the heading agrees with the runway heading as they taxi onto the runway for takeoff.

Figure 6-25. A recommended practice is to help your students develop their own expanded checklist for preflight of instruments and equipment prior to all flights under IFR.

instruments. Although some private pilots may have considerably more training, their overall competence is generally well below that needed to safely fly in IFR conditions. For example, your students may not have received any partial panel training. In addition, they may have developed some bad habits and will need to review effective scanning techniques.

With these considerations in mind, one of your primary tasks during the early part of instrument flight raining is to evaluate your students' overall proficiency in basic attitude instrument flying. It is usually easy to enumerate deficiencies, but the more important part of your job is to determine why your students are making mistakes. You need to analyze errors and make constructive recommendations on how to correct them. Determining the probable cause of mistakes is often the most difficult step. However, if you remember that for each maneuver there is a generally acceptable cross-check, any deviation from the normal cross-check should show where the problem lies. The sooner you can identify problems and suggest corrections, the more successful your students will be.

COMMON SCANNING ERRORS

The common instrument scanning errors are fixation, omission, and emphasis. Most beginning instrument students tend to emphasize the attitude indicator as the central focus of their scan. However, it is important to avoid fixation on this instrument. You can tell if your students are fixating on the attitude indicator if large deviations in airspeed, altitude, or heading occur before corrections are initiated. While it is true that carefully controlling power and attitude leads to the desired conditions, small deviations are inevitable with time. That is why it is necessary to cross-check the airspeed indicator, the heading indicator, and altimeter every few seconds and correct any deviations using specific adjustments, including changes in power if necessary. You can identify fixation on other instruments by observing that your students overcorrect as they attempt to make adjustments. [Figure 6-26]

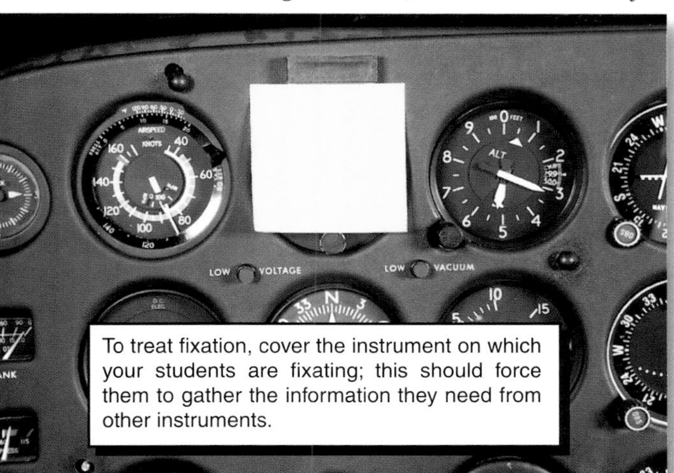

Figure 6-26. If your students are fixating on the airspeed indicator during a climb, they find it difficult to maintain the correct airspeed. This is because they are not using the attitude indicator to make small pitch adjustments.

While fixation neglects all but the instrument on which a student is focusing, omission drops only one instrument from the scan. For example, if the heading indicator is omitted, deviations in heading may occur, even though your student continues to control altitude. While performing VOR navigation, your student may chase the indicator needle, rather than using a specific heading to track or intercept the course. [Figure 6-27]

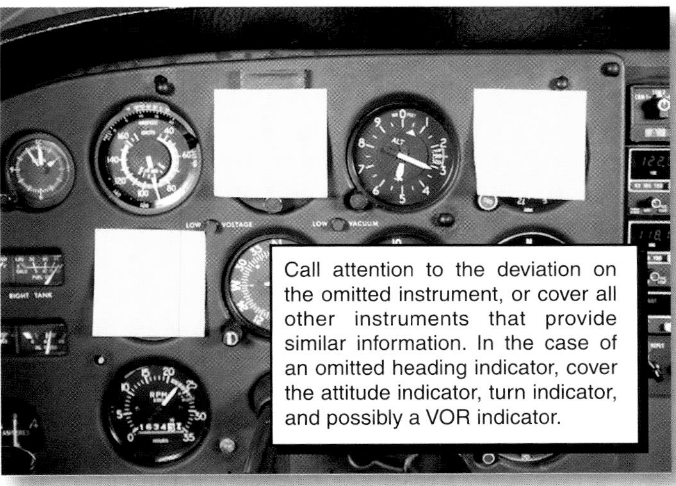

Figure 6-27. To treat omission, refocus your student's attention on the omitted instrument.

Emphasis is somewhat like fixation. Instead of looking at a combination of instruments, students tend to rely on the instrument they prefer. This is particularly true during initial stages of training. For example, students may place too much emphasis on the attitude indicator for altitude control, when they should be relying primarily on the altimeter.

USING TRIM

Since proper use of trim is especially important in instrument flying, you need to teach your students good trimming habits. If the aircraft is not trimmed, it starts to vary from the attitude selected and frequent corrections have to be made. As an experienced pilot, you can normally tell when the airplane is trimmed, even if you are not touching the controls. If you suspect the aircraft is out of trim, ask your students to let go of the controls. This reminds them of the importance of maintaining proper trim. Being able to establish and maintain an attitude is essential in order to become successful at attitude instrument flying. It is natural for your students to grip the yoke tightly when they are tense. This works against them by inducing fatigue, as well as unintended control inputs, which further destabilize the aircraft. If you observe that your students are overcontrolling the airplane or making unintended attitude changes, check their grip on the yoke. [Figure 6-28]

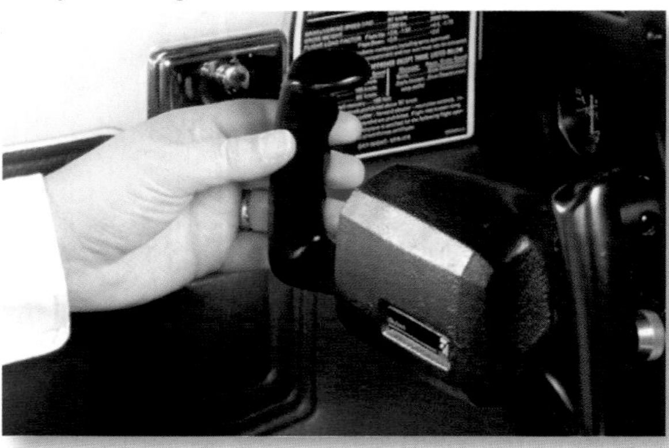

Figure 6-28. When you notice your students gripping the yoke too tightly, ask them to hold the control with only their fingertips.

GETTING TO KNOW THE AIRCRAFT

Before your students can control an airplane with the precision required for instrument flight, they must be familiar with the pitch and power settings required for certain operations. You may need to re-introduce your students to an airplane they have already flown. For example, when asked to perform a descent at a specific airspeed, your students need to be able to promptly adjust the throttle to obtain a specific r.p.m. or manifold pressure, rather than aimlessly increasing and reducing power until the airplane eventually obtains the correct speed. In addition, your students should have a specific pitch attitude in mind for the airspeed they are trying to maintain.

Prior to flying with a view-limiting device, have your students operate the airplane with the variety of airspeeds and configurations used for instrument procedures. Take a notepad and write down the specific pitch and power settings required for each maneuver. For example, if an ILS approach is typically flown at 90 knots with a 500 f.p.m. descent, take note of the power setting used to obtain this airplane performance. Remind your students that these settings are only approximations. After initially placing the throttle, they may need to make minor adjustments to achieve the desired performance. When your students have memorized some basic settings and can easily configure the airplane to perform various flight maneuvers in VFR conditions, introduce these maneuvers by instrument reference.

UNDERSTANDING THE PTS

Introduce your students to the practical test standards for attitude instrument flight early in their training. Without specific goals in mind, your students may become frustrated performing basic maneuvers repeatedly, and wonder why they cannot proceed to more complicated procedures. In addition to the tolerances for such elements as altitudes, headings, and airspeeds, you should make sure your students are familiar with the other

objectives for each maneuver. Instrument rating applicants must exhibit adequate knowledge of the elements relating to attitude instrument flying, use proper instrument cross-check and interpretation, and apply the appropriate pitch, bank, power, and trim corrections. [Figure 6-29]

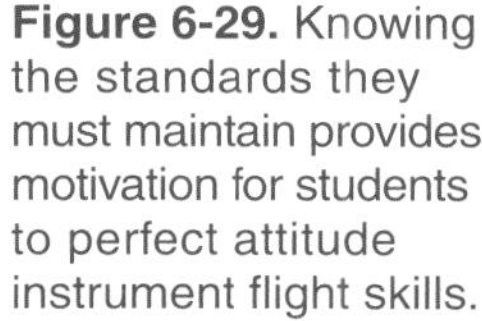

Airspeed ± 10 knots

Altitude ± 100 feet (when appropriate)

Bank Angle ± 5° (when a bank is specified)

Heading ± 10° (where a constant heading is required)

Rate of Climb/Descent ± 100 f.p.m. (for rate climbs/descents)

Figure 6-29. Knowing the standards they must maintain provides motivation for students to perfect attitude instrument flight skills.

It's All In Your Attitude

Most attitude indicators have a horizon bar (wings and center fuselage dot) with a thickness of 2°. A logical question is, what vertical velocity does a 2° pitch change provide? The answer depends on true airspeed or Mach number.

Actually, a 1° pitch change results in a change in vertical velocity equal to the Mach number times 1,000. For example, a 1° pitch change at Mach .3 equals a 300 f.p.m. change in vertical velocity. This is useful information if you are flying an airplane with a Mach indicator, but what if you do not have one?

Check out the following table based on standard day temperatures. It shows some representative slower true airspeeds, the equivalent Mach number, and the corresponding vertical velocity for 1°, 2°, and 4° pitch changes.

Now you have some numbers that might be useful for precise pitch changes using the attitude indicator. For example, if you want to use a rate of climb of 400 f.p.m. while cruising at 130 KTAS, a 2° (one horizon bar) correction on the attitude indicator would be appropriate. If you need to begin a 500 f.p.m. rate of descent at 65 KTAS, the adjustments in your attitude indicator would be 5°, or a pitch down equal to the thickness of 2 -1/2 horizon bars.

Knots TAS	Mach Number	1° Pitch Change (f.p.m.)	2° Pitch Change (f.p.m.)	4° Pitch Change (f.p.m.)
65	.1	100	200	400
130	.2	200	400	800
200	.3	300	600	1,200
300	.45	450	900	1,800

STRAIGHT-AND-LEVEL FLIGHT

Do not underestimate the value of straight-and-level flight as a learning tool. This maneuver is especially effective in teaching your students how to properly use the attitude indicator. Determine if your students understand the meaning of the indications on the attitude indicator and how to use this instrument effectively. For example, ask them what the thickness (in degrees) is of the wings and center fuselage dot of the horizon bar. And, how can they use this information to make an appropriate correction for a 100-foot deviation from their desired altitude?

Explain to your students that a 100-foot correction to get back to their desired attitude while in straight-and-level flight requires only a small change on the attitude indicator. For example, at a cruise airspeed of 130 knots, a pitch change of 1° (1/2 horizon bar) is recommended. This provides a 200 f.p.m. vertical velocity. For a deviation of more than 100 feet, a 2° (full horizon bar) correction generally is recommended under the same or similar flight conditions.

Once your students are competent flying straight and level at a constant airspeed, teach them how to perform airspeed transitions and configuration changes. Another good exercise is to practice maneuvering during slow flight. Before proceeding to any other maneuvers, ensure that your students can perform at a level that meets PTS criteria. [Figure 6-30]

Instruction
"Increase airspeed by 10 knots while maintaining straight-and-level flight."

Student Action
Your student adds power and the airplane begins to climb.

Error Analysis
Your student did not adjust the pitch nor trim the airplane while adding power.

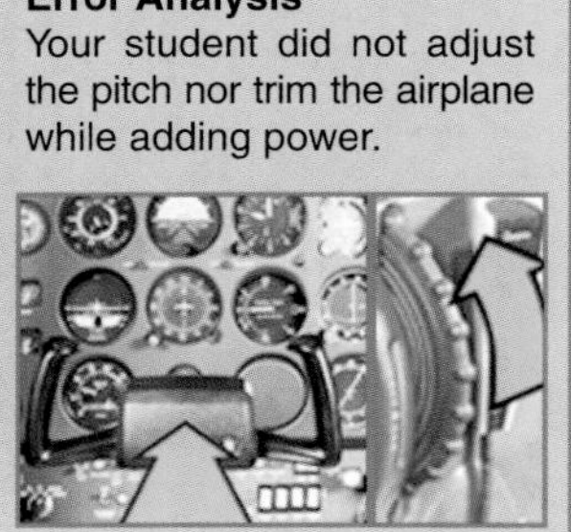

Figure 6-30. To become proficient at basic attitude instrument flight, your students must be able to determine the causes of their errors.

CLIMBS AND DESCENTS

Your students must be proficient at performing both constant airspeed and constant rate climbs and descents. Although you may wish to vary the procedure, constant airspeed climbs/descents are usually practiced with a constant power setting. So, your students must vary the pitch attitude to maintain the airspeed. In contrast, constant rate maneuvers are generally flown with variable power and pitch as necessary to maintain a specific airspeed and vertical speed. You should have your students practice these maneuvers using airspeeds, configurations and altitudes that are common in actual instrument flight.

Leveloff procedures are similar whether climbing or descending. To help your students avoid overshooting their desired altitude, it is important to teach them to anticipate the leveloff point and begin leveling off prior to reaching the new altitude. The amount of lead they use depends on the airplane, pilot technique, and the desired leveloff speed. As a guide, teach them to use 10% of the vertical velocity when they intend to maintain the airspeed during leveloff. For example, if their vertical velocity is 500 f.p.m., they should begin to level off 50 feet before reaching the desired altitude. The attitude indicator is their primary pitch instrument during the transition to level flight, and the tachometer or manifold pressure gauge is primary for power as they move the throttle to the setting they estimate will provide the desired airspeed in level flight. [Figure 6-31]

TURNS TO HEADINGS

Prior to practicing turns under a view-limiting device, ensure your students have a good understanding of the dynamics of turning flight. Review the concept of a standard-rate turn and how the turn coordinator indicates rate of turn, while angle of bank is displayed on the attitude indicator. A rule of thumb for determining the angle of bank for a standard-rate turn is to divide the true airspeed by 10 and add 5 to the result. At 110 knots, performing a standard-rate turn requires a bank angle of 16° (110 ÷10 = 11 + 5 =116). Explain to your students that while this rule works well for low-speed training airplanes, for high-speed airplanes, they must add 7 instead of 5.

Instruction
"Descend at 90 knots to 7,500 feet."

Student Action
Although your student levels off at the appropriate altitude, the airspeed decreases by 20 knots.

Error Analysis
Your student did not add enough power during the leveloff nor adjust the pitch attitude.

Figure 6-31. Failure to adjust the power while leveling off during climbs and descents can result in a failure to maintain the desired airspeed in level flight.

Normally, you should have your students use a lead of 1/2 the angle of bank to roll out of a turn. With practice, your students should develop a consistent rate to roll in and roll out of turns. Once your students have mastered turns, climbs, and descents, they should combine these maneuvers to perform climbing and descending turns. [Figure 6-32]

Instruction
"Turn right heading 270, climb and maintain 7,600."

Student Action
Your student levels off at the requested altitude and rolls out of the turn at the same time, prior to reaching the desired heading.

Error Analysis
While fixating on the altimeter during the leveloff, your student failed to notice that the airplane was rolling out of the bank.

Figure 6-32. Pay close attention as your students reach their target altitudes and headings during climbing and descending turns. Students often have difficulty leveling off while continuing the turn or rolling out of a bank while maintaining a climb or descent.

PRACTICE PATTERNS

You can develop lessons which provide your students with motivation to perfect attitude instrument flight. For example, furnish students with copies of flight patterns which model procedures such as holding and instrument approaches. Create exercises based on published approach procedures. Your students fly the basic ground track and profile of the approach, changing headings, altitudes, and airspeeds based on your directions. This can be accomplished at safe altitudes in the local practice area, with or without the use of navigation aids. As your students practice the pattern, assume the role of ATC and ask them to repeat altitude and heading changes. As proficiency is gained, you can provide distractions by requesting your students change a radio frequency or reset the clock. Finally, this pattern can be flown as your students practice partial panel skills. [Figure 6-33 on Page 6-36]

PERFORMING ADVANCED INSTRUMENT MANEUVERS

Once your students gain proficiency in basic attitude instrument flight, they are ready to practice more challenging maneuvers. Performing steep turns and vertical S maneuvers helps students to refine their aircraft control skills and perfect their instrument scan. Practicing stalls and recoveries from unusual attitudes prepares students to recognize potentially hazardous situations in IFR conditions and take the appropriate corrective actions.

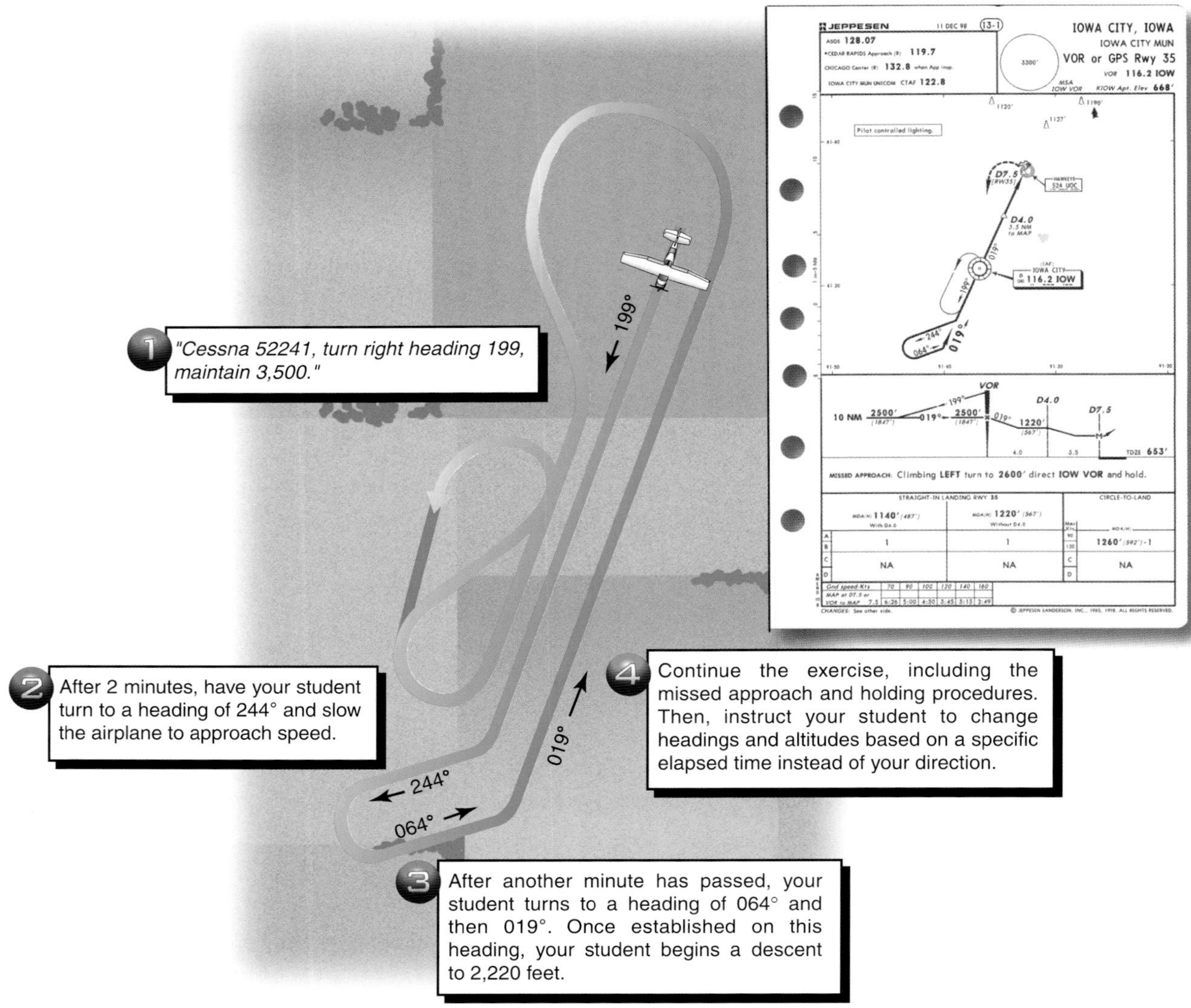

Figure 6-33. This exercise is based on the VOR approach to Runway 35 at Iowa City Municipal Airport. For the practice session, 1,000 feet have been added to the altitudes indicated on the approach chart.

STEEP TURNS

During instrument training, students practice steep turns using a 45° angle of bank. **Steep turns** magnify errors in pitch control, and require students to speed up their cross-check, interpret the instruments accurately, and apply prompt, smooth control pressures. You should stress control pressure technique and use of trim. The vertical speed indicator normally provides the first indication of a pitch deviation. Use of the VSI is particularly important during steep turns, since the attitude indicator does not provide precise pitch information. If the VSI is omitted from your students' scan, you may find that they have to make large corrections in pitch. Drawing their attention to this instrument should help them improve performance and fly more smoothly.

VERTICAL S MANEUVERS

Vertical S maneuvers are good exercises to teach your students to transition from one set of flight conditions to another. These maneuvers are designed to improve your students' instrument cross-check and aircraft control. The basic vertical S begins with a climb at a constant airspeed and rate of climb. Once a particular cardinal altitude is reached, the climb is reversed and a constant rate, constant airspeed descent is begun. The amount of altitude between reversals can be varied. [Figure 6-34]

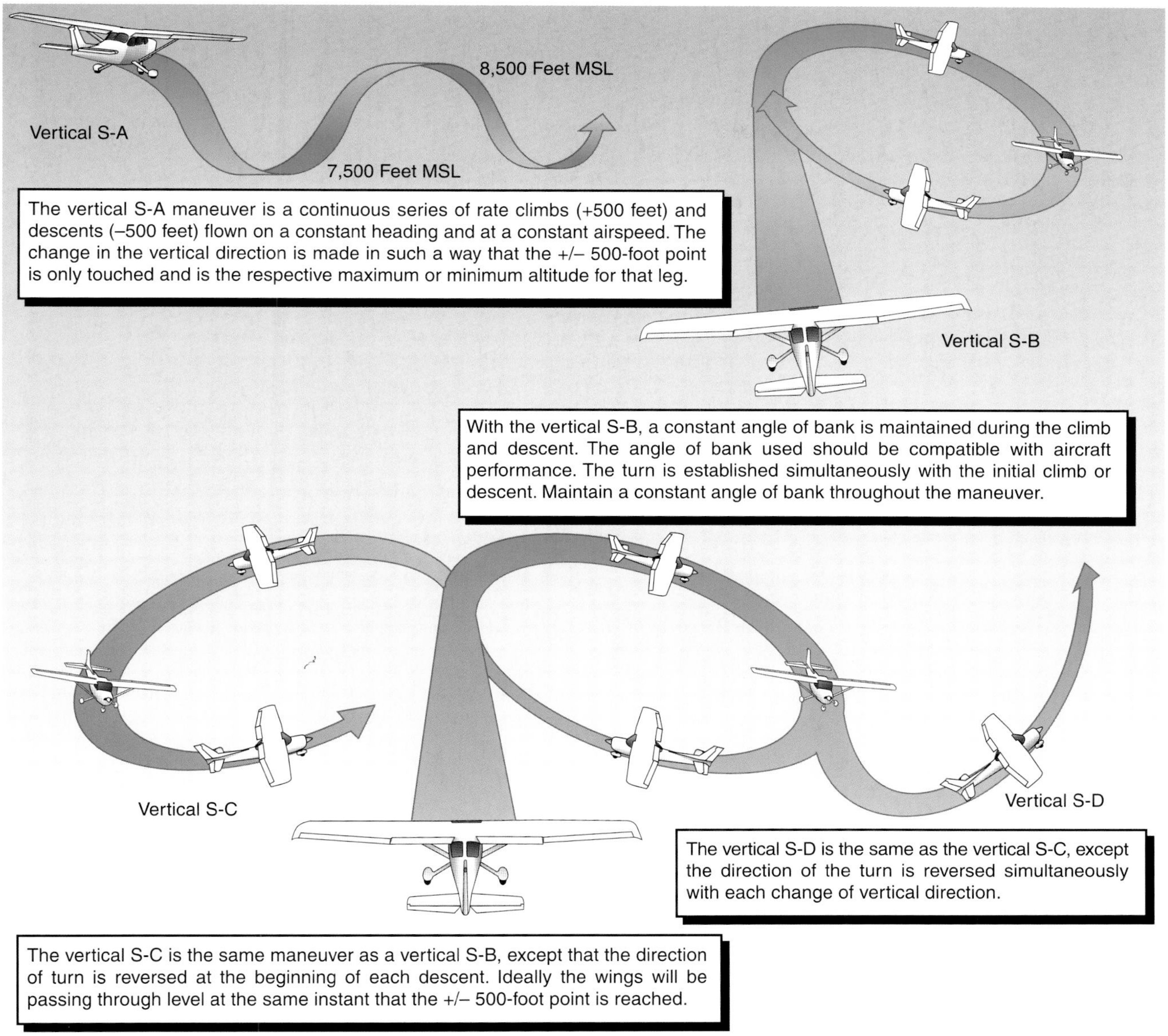

8,500 Feet MSL

Vertical S-A

7,500 Feet MSL

The vertical S-A maneuver is a continuous series of rate climbs (+500 feet) and descents (–500 feet) flown on a constant heading and at a constant airspeed. The change in the vertical direction is made in such a way that the +/– 500-foot point is only touched and is the respective maximum or minimum altitude for that leg.

Vertical S-B

With the vertical S-B, a constant angle of bank is maintained during the climb and descent. The angle of bank used should be compatible with aircraft performance. The turn is established simultaneously with the initial climb or descent. Maintain a constant angle of bank throughout the maneuver.

Vertical S-C

Vertical S-D

The vertical S-D is the same as the vertical S-C, except the direction of the turn is reversed simultaneously with each change of vertical direction.

The vertical S-C is the same maneuver as a vertical S-B, except that the direction of turn is reversed at the beginning of each descent. Ideally the wings will be passing through level at the same instant that the +/– 500-foot point is reached.

Figure 6-34. Vertical S maneuvers are excellent for assessing your students' ability to cross-check the instruments and maintain an effective scan.

STALLS

You should have your students practice **stalls** during instrument training to help them recognize the instrument indications associated with an approaching stall and to illustrate that recovery procedures are the same as during VFR conditions. To perform stalls, instruct your students to configure the airplane to reflect realistic in-flight situations. For example, to practice power-off stalls, your students should configure the airplane as they would for an instrument approach, including use of the proper power setting and airspeed, as well as extending the approach flaps and landing gear, if appropriate.

RECOVERY FROM UNUSUAL FLIGHT ATTITUDES

An **unusual flight attitude** can occur even with a properly trained instrument pilot at the aircraft controls. Common causes include failure of the attitude indicator, disorientation, wake turbulence, lapse of attention, or abnormal trim. To become instrument-rated, your students must demonstrate recovery from unusual attitudes with or without the attitude indicator.

To effectively teach recovery from unusual flight attitudes, you should instruct your students to close their eyes, and remove their hands and feet from the controls, while you maneuver the aircraft in such a way as to induce disorientation. Then, have your students open their eyes, take control of the airplane, and make a proper recovery. Another method that works quite well is to have your students close their eyes and turn their head to rest on their shoulder while continuing to fly the airplane. Direct them to make some gentle turns, climbs, and descents. Once an unusual attitude has been reached (and it usually will happen fairly quickly), instruct your students to open their eyes and initiate recovery.

The indications of a nose-high unusual attitude are decreasing airspeed, rapid gain of altitude, a high rate of climb, and a nose-high pitch attitude on the attitude indicator. The indications of a nose-low attitude are increasing airspeed, rapid loss of altitude, a high rate of descent, and a nose-low pitch attitude. During recovery from an unusual attitude, ensure your students evaluate *all* of the instrument indications to determine the type of unusual attitude. Since one of the primary causes of an unusual attitude is the failure of one or more of the instruments, it is very important all instruments be compared. You may find it helpful to have your students call out the indications and state the attitude they believe the airplane has assumed. You should emphasize to your students that, although prompt recovery is essential, they should not overcontrol the airplane, especially during recovery from a nose-low attitude. [Figure 6-35]

NOSE-HIGH ATTITUDE

Add power.

Since they are focused on leveling the wings, students may forget to adjust power and airspeed will continue to decrease.

Lower the nose.

The addition of power may cause the pitch attitude to increase if students do not lower the nose quickly. If students lower the nose without adding power, they will begin a descent.

Correct the bank attitude with coordinated aileron and rudder pressure.

Often, students focus on leveling the wings to the exclusion of actions to control the pitch attitude. Students may try to correct with aileron only, resulting in uncoordinated flight.

NOSE-LOW ATTITUDE

Reduce power.

Students may not adjust power, resulting in an increased rate of descent and excessive airspeed.

Correct the bank attitude with coordinated aileron and rudder pressure.

Often, students focus on leveling the wings to the exclusion of actions to control the pitch attitude. Students may try to correct with aileron only, resulting in uncoordinated flight.

Raise the nose to a level flight attitude.

Raising the nose too abruptly without reducing power or leveling the wings first can overstress the airplane.

Return to the original altitude and heading.

Students may forget this step. They are relieved to have recovered from the unusual attitude and continue to fly at the heading and altitude that was established immediately after recovery.

Figure 6-35. Explain that at a high airspeed during a nose-low recovery, it is possible to overstress the aircraft quite easily. Emphasize the danger of a diving spiral and the reasons for rolling the wings level prior to pulling the nose back up to the horizon.

PARTIAL PANEL FLYING

You have a responsibility as an instructor to provide your students with effective training in flying **partial panel**, from a safety standpoint as well as in preparation for the practical

test. When you begin partial panel training with your students, it becomes obvious whether or not they have acquired an effective instrument scan. If your students tend to fixate on one instrument such as the attitude indicator, they have difficulty when it is taken away. This is a good time to reemphasize to your students the importance of a good, consistent cross-check. Not only will they be able to detect when one or more of the instruments have become inoperative, they will be better at interpreting the indications of the remaining instruments. The best thing you can do for your students is to teach them the relationships between the different instruments. For example, your students should immediately take note when the VSI, altimeter, heading indicator, or turn coordinator disagrees with the attitude indicator.

Flight training aircraft generally are equipped with only a single-source vacuum system for the attitude indicator and the heading indicator. Failure of these gyroscopic instruments may not be readily apparent, and can be critical when flying in IFR conditions. This is why partial-panel instrument skills are required for an instrument rating. Make sure your students understand the severity of gyroscopic system failure and how it can lead to spatial disorientation. Loss of the heading indicator is a problem, but the magnetic compass, when properly used, is a reliable backup. Loss of the attitude indicator is more serious.

Without the attitude indicator, your students will have difficulty at first maintaining pitch attitude, since the remaining instruments do not provide immediate indications of pitch changes. Often, the first problem is timely recognition and acceptance of the failure. Stress to your students that they will have to modify their scan patterns and omit, or cover up, the attitude indicator. Without the attitude indicator, the altimeter, VSI, and airspeed indicator become the best instruments for pitch information. Since these instruments are fairly slow to provide pitch information, it is important to emphasize to your students the need for small changes in pitch. They also must keep the airplane trimmed, and have patience to wait and see the results before changing pitch again.

COMPASS TURNS

Executing turns without benefit of the attitude indicator and heading indicator may be easier for your students than maintaining the proper pitch attitude. Your students should be accustomed to the indications of the turn coordinator as it relates to the attitude indicator. The magnetic compass gives good heading information but only when in steady, straight-and-level flight. When turning, the compass is less reliable. [Figure 6-36]

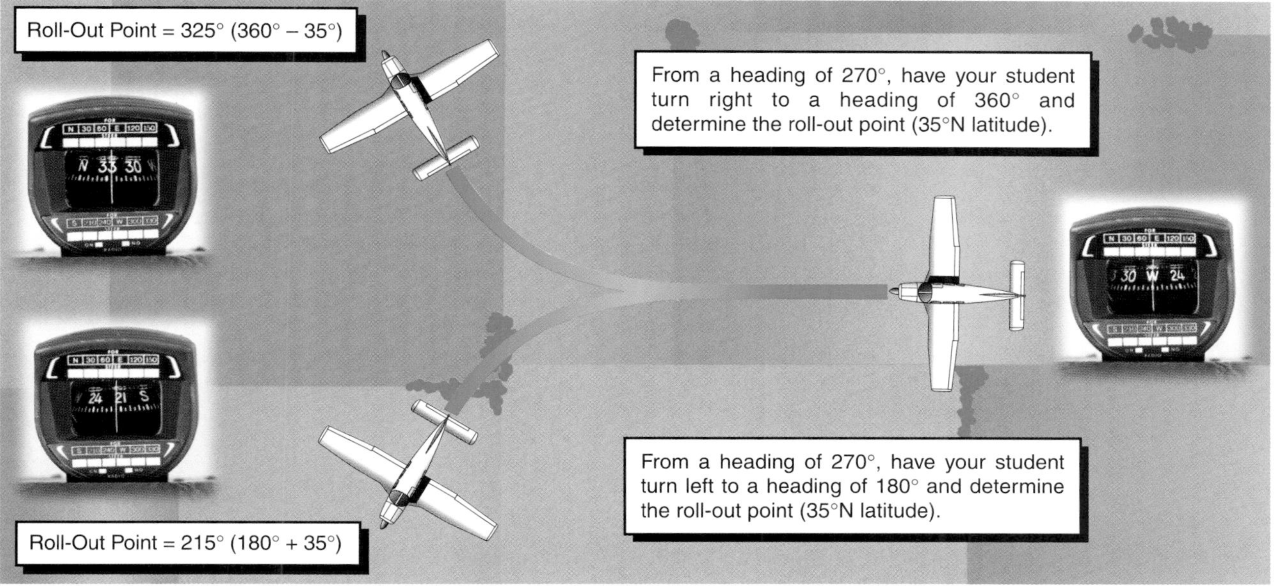

Figure 6-36. To help with compass turns, teach your students the acronym, OSUN (Overshoot South, Undershoot North).

TIMED TURNS

Another technique that students should practice is the timed turn. Have them practice standard and one-half standard rate turns by using the turn and slip indicator, or the turn coordinator. Then have them use timing to make turns a specific number of degrees. For example, a standard-rate turn (3° per second) of 30° requires 10 seconds, and half standard-rate turn (1-1/2° per second) of 30° would require 20 seconds.

PARTIAL PANEL UNUSUAL ATTITUDE RECOVERY

Anyone who has ever had a flight instrument fail can relate how distracting the inoperative instrument can become. Since this situation can lead to disorientation and the potential for an unusual attitude, you should teach your students to cover up the inoperative instrument by using a suction cup device, or a piece of paper. If you have taught your students the absolute necessity of a consistent cross-check, you give them the opportunity to discover the loss of one or more instruments before an unusual attitude develops. Although this is the best course of action, you still must teach your students to recover from unusual attitudes using a partial panel.

When recovering from an unusual attitude with partial panel, teach your students to use the turn coordinator to stop a turn, and the pitot-static instruments to arrest an unintended climb or descent. Explain that the correct indication of passing through

OUT OF CONTROL

From the files of the NTSB...

Aircraft: *Piper PA-46-350P, Malibu*

Injuries: *1 Fatal.*

Narrative: During flight, the airplane was cruising at flight level 210 in IFR conditions with turbulence and with the wind from about 255 degrees at 70 knots. The airplane drifted off course at about 1600 CST. At 1610:09, after about ten minutes of unrecognized heading changes, the pilot stated "... I've lost my gyro." At 1610:15, the controller issued a no-gyro vector. At 1611:29, as the airplane was still turning (to a heading that would intercept the original course), the pilot stated "we've lost ALL our instruments... please direct me towards VFR." He was cleared to descend to 14,000 feet. At about that same time, he stated "we're in trouble" and "we've lost all vacuum," then there was no further radio transmission from the airplane. The airplane entered a steep, downward spiraling, right turn. The left outer wing panel separated up and aft (in flight) from overload and impacted the left stabilizer. The airplane crashed, and parts that separated from the airplane were found over a four-mile area. Investigation revealed evidence that the HSI heading card can fail without the HDG flag appearing. Although the pilot had reported the loss of instruments and vacuum, examination of the airplane revealed that the engine, flight controls, electrical system, pitot/static system and vacuum systems exhibited continuity. No malfunction was found that would have led to loss of pressurization or hypoxia.

The airplane's vacuum instruments, which provided pitch and roll information to the pilot, included the pilot's attitude gyro, the copilot's attitude gyro, and the copilot's directional gyro. The cross-check instruments available to the pilot if a vacuum failure occurred were the two electrically powered turn coordinators for roll information. The wet compass was available for heading information. The airspeed indicator, vertical speed indicator, and altimeter were available for pitch information.

The NTSB concluded that the probable cause of this accident was spatial disorientation of the pilot, and his failure to maintain control of the airplane which resulted in his exceeding the design stress limits of the airframe. A factor relating to the accident was turbulence in clouds.

Although it appeared as if all the systems were working properly, this pilot became so disoriented he believed none of his instruments were indicating correctly. A report such as this can clearly illustrate to your students the importance of gaining proficiency in instrument scanning techniques. Point out that one of their responsibilities as pilot in command after they have obtained their instrument rating is to practice and maintain an effective instrument scan. In addition, you must prepare your students to make effective go/no-go decisions based on their amount and recency of experience in IFR conditions.

a level pitch attitude is when the direction of movement of the altimeter and airspeed indicator needles stops and reverses, and when the VSI needle starts moving back toward zero. At this point, stress the use of elevator pressure to maintain this pitch, and teach your students to give the instruments a moment to stabilize before returning to the desired altitude.

MASTERING INSTRUMENT NAVIGATION

As your students progress through their training in basic and advanced instrument flight maneuvers, most likely you have already begun to introduce them to instrument navigation. Competence in instrument navigation is required to be able to safely operate under IFR. How quickly your students gain this competence and become comfortable and proficient in the IFR environment depends in large part on how well they have mastered the important building blocks up to this point. Now you have to teach them more skills, which require additional knowledge and the ability to use VOR, ADF, DME, ILS, and RNAV systems for specific instrument procedures.

VOR NAVIGATION

In earlier flight lessons, it is relatively easy to integrate some **VOR navigation** in each lesson. Your students should be familiar with the principles of the VOR system and how the VOR indicator works. For example, during practice of attitude instrument flight, you may ask them to maintain an altitude, while they track inbound or outbound on a VOR radial. It is also helpful to tune a nearby VOR and have your students determine the aircraft's position in relation to that VOR. Similarly, as your students practice the vertical S and other maneuvers, the VOR can be worked into the scenario. It is a good exercise for your students to be required to navigate to a particular VOR or DME fix while climbing or descending. These are not exercises to be used during the earliest flights, but they should be used as students advance in their training. [Figure 6-37]

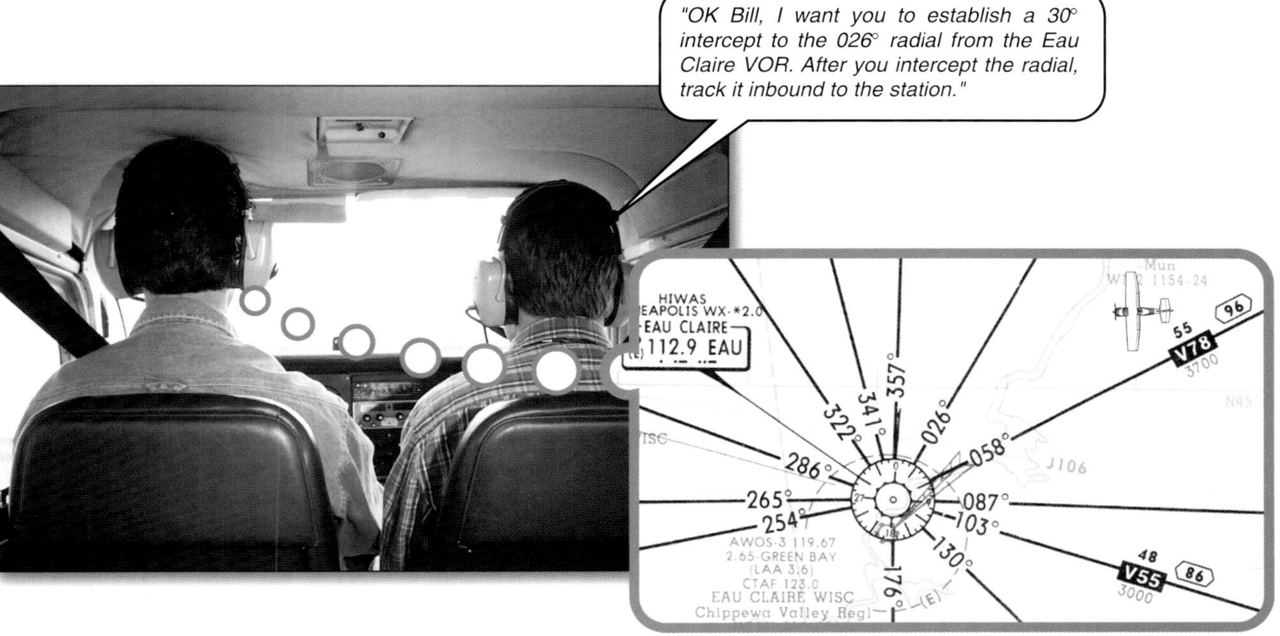

Figure 6-37. The more experience your students have in visualizing their position in relation to navigational aids, the better they will adapt to flying under instrument conditions. This visualization is an essential part of situational awareness.

You also may need to review some of the common features of VOR navaids. For instance, some VORs have a voice transmission capability, and each VOR has a class designation which relates to altitude and reception range. Theses include terminal (T), low altitude (L), and high altitude (H) facilities. In addition, ensure your students are familiar with FAA VOR test facilities, test procedures, and tolerances for both ground and airborne checks.

DISTANCE MEASURING EQUIPMENT (DME)

If your students' training airplane is equipped with **distance measuring equipment (DME)**, you should introduce its use along with VOR tracking and positional awareness exercises. There is a disadvantage if you allow your students to rely heavily on use of DME early in their training. It may diminish their situational awareness when flying without the use of DME. To emphasize that DME measures slant range, you can ask your students to overfly the VOR at varying altitudes. For example, overflying at 10,000 feet AGL can give a DME reading of approximately 2 miles.

ADF NAVIGATION

It is important to ensure that your students understand the limitations and characteristics of **automatic direction finder (ADF)** equipment in their airplane. There are three types of indicators, the fixed card, movable-card, and the radio magnetic indicator, or RMI. With a fixed-card indicator, your students will have to determine magnetic bearing (MB) to the station using magnetic heading (MH) and relative bearing (RB). As an example, on a heading of 020°, with a relative bearing of 020°, the magnetic bearing to the station is 040° — MH (020°) + RB (020°) = MB (040°). A key point to emphasize to your students is that, when properly tuned, the ADF needle always points to the station. While learning ADF navigation can be challenging of students, the movable-card indicator simplifies the process, and the RMI makes learning ADF navigation even easier. Students should be able to accurately track NDB bearings inbound and outbound, and adjust heading to compensate for wind. [Figure 6-38]

GLOBAL POSITIONING SYSTEM (GPS)

As **global positioning systems (GPS)** equipment becomes more common in training aircraft, you must be prepared to teach your students how to use it for navigation. GPS control units and displays include numerous variations from one manufacturer to another, but there are some common characteristics. For example, each unit should have a display, control knobs, function keys, and a slot for the database card. Emphasize to your students that before they use GPS under IFR, they must be sure the database is current. Ensure your students refer to the supplements section of the airplane flight manual (AFM), or the POH, to determine the type and extent of operations approved for their GPS. For IFR operation, a GPS must have been approved in accordance with Technical Standard Order (TSO) C-129, which prescribes the standards for GPS equipment. It must also be installed in accordance with AC 20-138, which provides guidance for airworthiness approval of GPS equipment. Handheld receivers are restricted to VFR flight only. Some panel-mounted receivers are also restricted to VFR flight and must be placarded accordingly in the aircraft. Other receivers may be approved for IFR enroute and terminal operations and should be placarded if not authorized for GPS approaches.

As with ground-based navigation aids, it is extremely important for your students to be aware of any loss of integrity, or position accuracy, of the GPS signals. Many receiver units monitor integrity by use of an internal system referred to as **receiver autonomous integrity monitoring (RAIM)**. If position calculations are not within certain parameters during GPS operations, the GPS unit should provide warning of a loss of integrity. This RAIM failure warning is similar to a traditional VOR warning flag. Some units may be connected with an annunciator panel to provide warning information. [Figure 6-39]

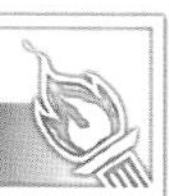

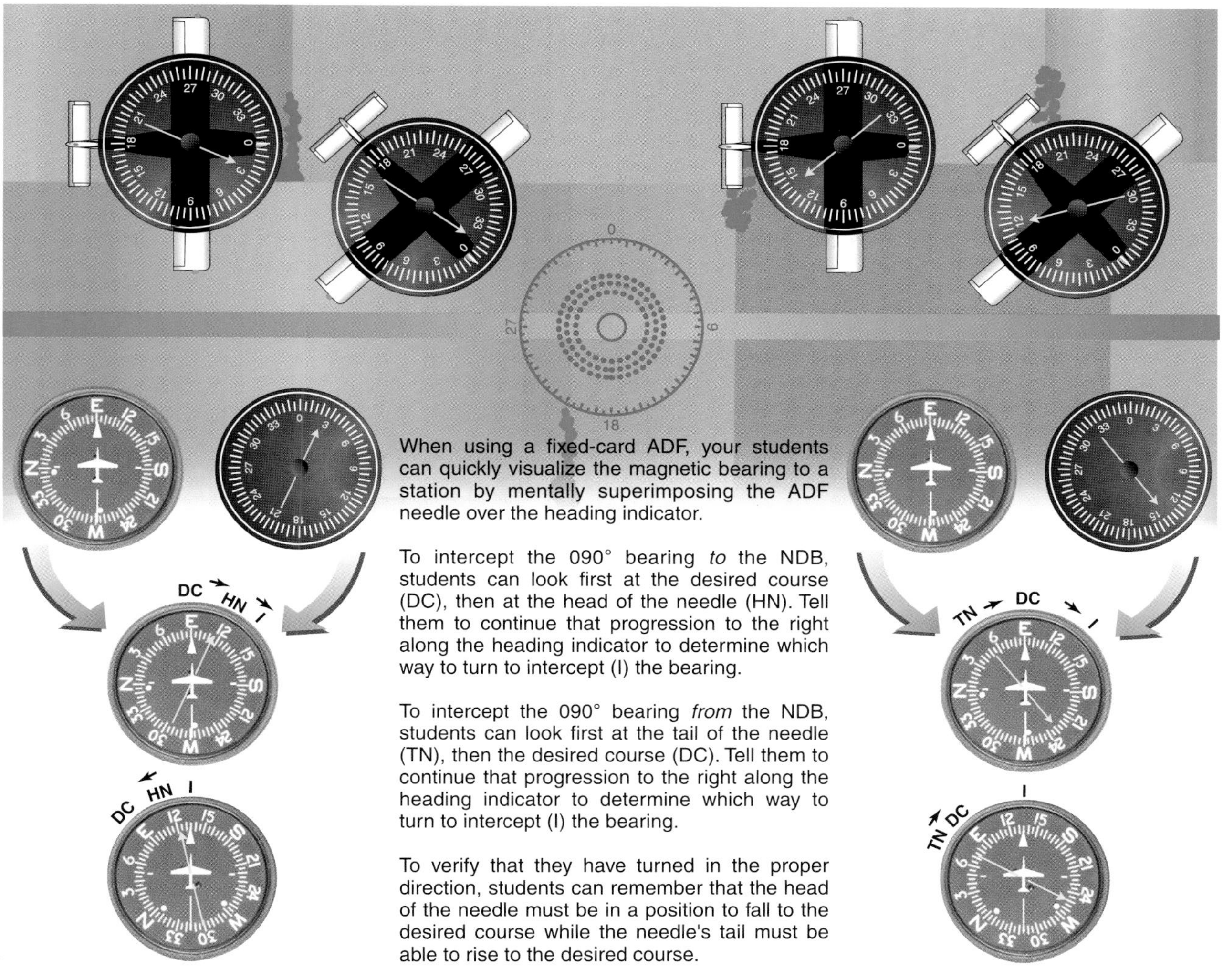

When using a fixed-card ADF, your students can quickly visualize the magnetic bearing to a station by mentally superimposing the ADF needle over the heading indicator.
To intercept the 090° bearing *to* the NDB, students can look first at the desired course (DC), then at the head of the needle (HN). Tell them to continue that progression to the right along the heading indicator to determine which way to turn to intercept (I) the bearing.
To intercept the 090° bearing *from* the NDB, students can look first at the tail of the needle (TN), then the desired course (DC). Tell them to continue that progression to the right along the heading indicator to determine which way to turn to intercept (I) the bearing.
To verify that they have turned in the proper direction, students can remember that the head of the needle must be in a position to fall to the desired course while the needle's tail must be able to rise to the desired course.
DC
HN
I
TN

Figure 6-38. Your students may have difficulty using the ADF to intercept NDB bearings. To help them with orientation, instruct your students to initially turn to a heading parallel to the desired course.

"Piper 45GE, Denver Center, revised routing, proceed direct WILDA, then V-26 to Rapid City VOR, maintain 9,000."
This GPS is great. Once you program your route, it takes you by the hand and leads you home!
Now what? Where is WILDA? Where is my chart?
NEWCASTLE
108.2 ECS
WILDA
PACTO
MRA 9700
ZAMBI
MRA 9300
RULER
MRA 9000
CURSE
MRA 6600
RAPID CITY
S DAK-Regl
KRAP 3202-87
V536
V235
V26
073°
231°
287°

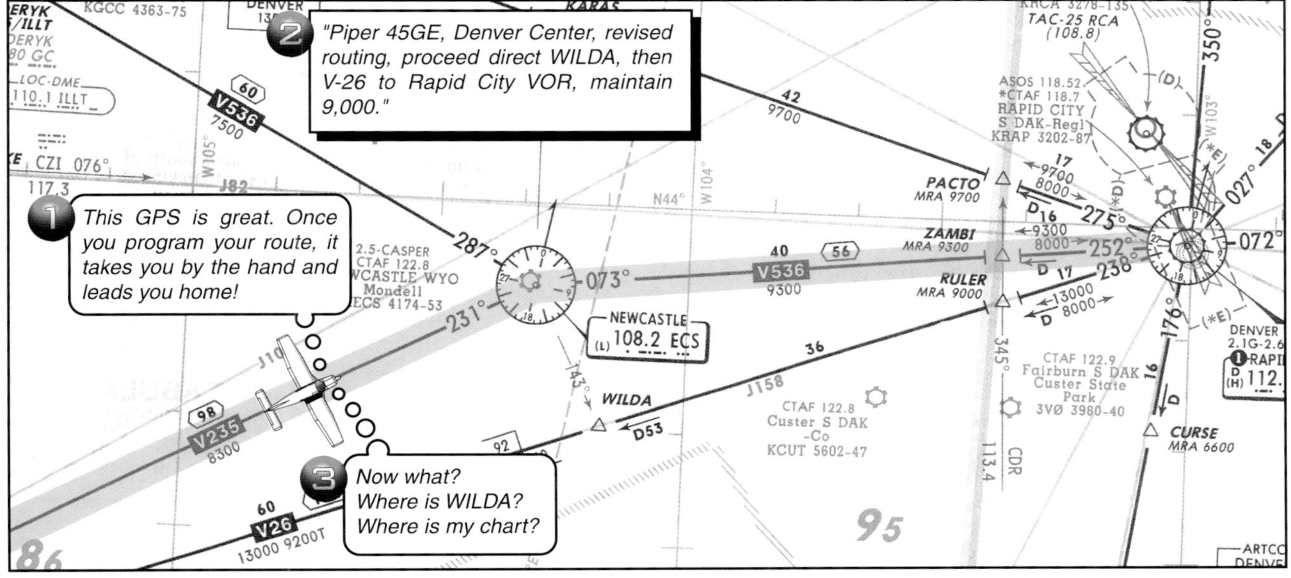

Figure 6-39. Provide an example to your students to illustrate how relying too heavily on GPS equipment for navigation can lead to complacency and loss of situational awareness.

PERFECTING APPROACH PROCEDURES

Since the ILS may be the most challenging of the instrument approaches, it will probably require the most practice for your students. Since flying a precise glide path is the primary difference between an ILS approach and nonprecision approaches, it deserves extra attention. Your students need to learn to estimate a rate of descent that will maintain the glide slope at the proper airspeed and the requisite pitch and power setting which will yield that rate of descent. They can then set the power, adjust the pitch, trim to maintain the attitude, and then fine-tune the configuration as necessary. Make sure your students know where to find rate-of-descent information in approach chart publications. For example, the information on ILS approaches provided by Jeppesen includes glide slope angle and rate of descent for various groundspeeds.

Another area that may be difficult for your students is the increased sensitivity of the localizer course and glide slope as the airplane nears the runway. Though they experienced this phenomenon as they neared the VOR on a VOR approach, the effect is much more pronounced during an ILS approach. You also need to emphasize to your students that on a back course ILS, the localizer is even more sensitive than on a normal ILS due to the location of the localizer transmitter antenna. Your students may have a tendency to overcontrol the airplane and make large corrections during an ILS approach. Have your students watch you perform an approach so they understand how only small adjustments to pitch, power, and heading are necessary to stay on course. [Figure 6-40]

RADAR APPROACHES

Often airports that serve extensive civilian commercial traffic, or joint civil/military traffic are equipped to provide radar approaches. You should make every effort to expose your students to these approaches. If a partial panel approach in IFR conditions must be conducted, a radar approach is recommended. In the absence of actual radar approaches, you can simulate radar approaches for your students with course and glide slope information over the intercom. Normally, you can do this in the practice area or during practice ILS approaches with the student following your guidance rather than the cockpit instruments.

Radar approach facilities can usually provide **no-gyro approaches** for use when gyroscopic instruments are inoperative. The controller determines headings by telling the pilot to *"turn left (right),"* and *"stop turn."* Again, if a radar facility is not available, you can simulate these approaches with your students by using no-gyro phraseology. In some cases, although a full radar approach may not be provided, vectors to the final approach course of an instrument approach are very common. Remind your students that pilots often become complacent when being vectored and fail to maintain awareness of the aircraft position in relation to navigational aids. Maintaining situational awareness can best be taught by giving your students practice vector exercises, and then, suddenly telling them that radar or radio contact has been lost.

CIRCLING AND SIDESTEP MANEUVERS

In most cases, it is easier to teach your students the **sidestep maneuver** before teaching them circling maneuvers. Have your students begin their turn to align with the new runway as soon as possible. This not only helps to facilitate timely alignment with the new runway, but it also allows more time to set up a stabilized approach with better control of airspeed and rate of descent. Airports with parallel runways may provide an opportunity for you to have your students perform sidestep maneuvers in realistic conditions.

ILS APPROACH

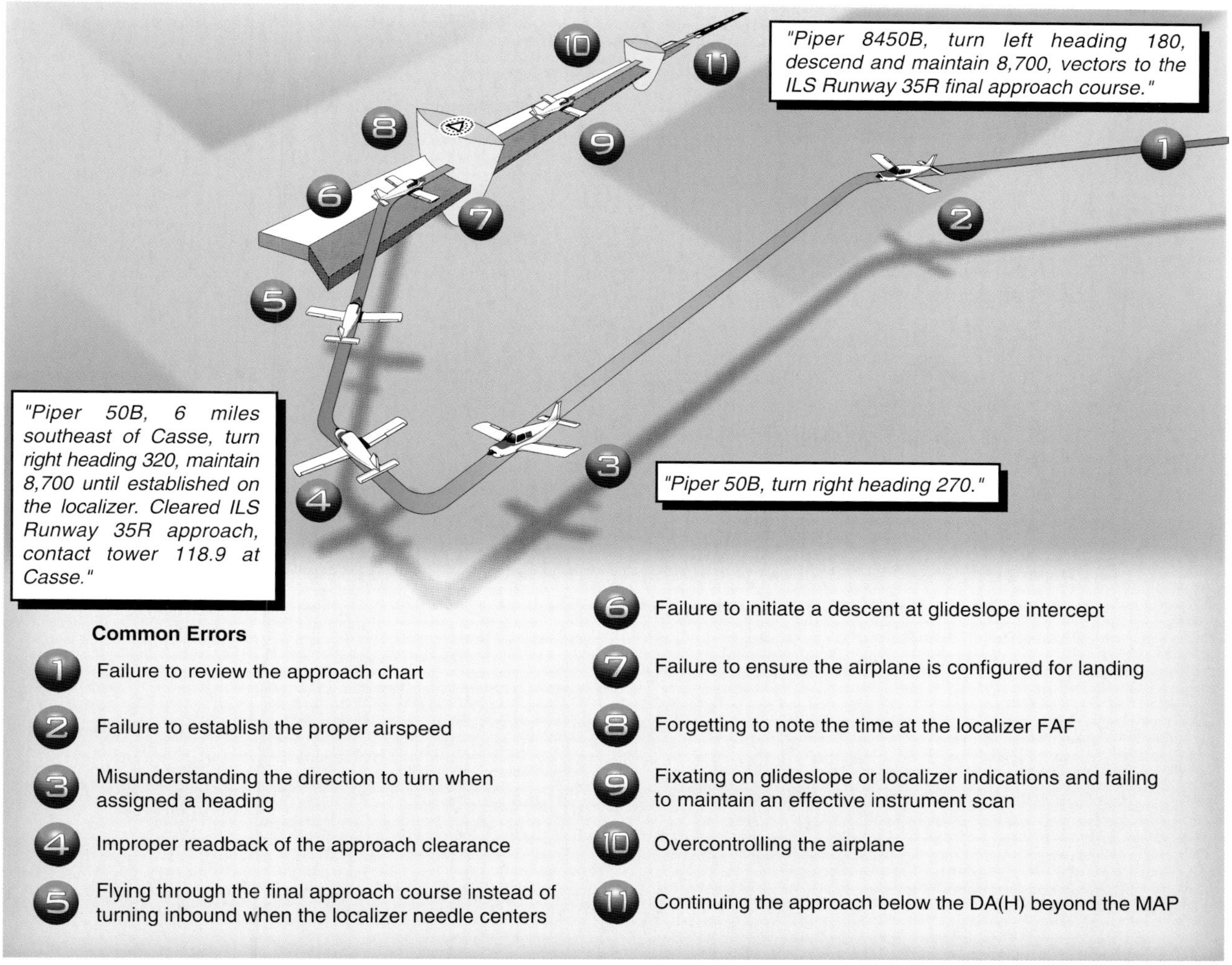

"Piper 8450B, turn left heading 180, descend and maintain 8,700, vectors to the ILS Runway 35R final approach course."

"Piper 50B, turn right heading 270."

"Piper 50B, 6 miles southeast of Casse, turn right heading 320, maintain 8,700 until established on the localizer. Cleared ILS Runway 35R approach, contact tower 118.9 at Casse."

Common Errors

1. Failure to review the approach chart
2. Failure to establish the proper airspeed
3. Misunderstanding the direction to turn when assigned a heading
4. Improper readback of the approach clearance
5. Flying through the final approach course instead of turning inbound when the localizer needle centers
6. Failure to initiate a descent at glideslope intercept
7. Failure to ensure the airplane is configured for landing
8. Forgetting to note the time at the localizer FAF
9. Fixating on glideslope or localizer indications and failing to maintain an effective instrument scan
10. Overcontrolling the airplane
11. Continuing the approach below the DA(H) beyond the MAP

Figure 6-40. Many of these student errors are common to both precision and nonprecision approaches.

Due to traffic conflicts, it may be difficult to practice **circling approaches** often with your students, so it is very important that you cover the procedures in detail on the ground. Take advantage of opportunities to allow your students to conduct circling maneuvers at the conclusion of an actual or practice instrument approach. Your students should fly the circling approach with the least amount of abrupt maneuvering possible, while still keeping the landing environment in sight. Mastery of circling approach procedures requires concentrated effort, practice, and experience. [Figure 6-41 on Page 6-46]

MISSED APPROACH PROCEDURES

Missed approach procedures may be overlooked when practicing instrument flight operations. If you are practicing multiple approaches in a radar environment, your students may simply receive vectors for another approach. Ensure your students have the opportunity to execute a full missed approach procedure which includes holding. Ask your students to describe the missed approach procedure as they are reviewing the approach chart and verify they ensure that navigation equipment is set to fly the procedure. In addition, emphasize that if your students decide to execute a missed approach prior to reaching the MAP, no consideration for an abnormally early turn is given in the procedure design. [Figure 6-42 on Page 6-46]

CIRCLING APPROACH

Common Errors
1 Descending below the MDA before a normal descent to the runway can be established
2 Failure to stay within the appropriate distance from the runway
3 Continuing the approach after losing visual contact with the runway
4 Executing the missed approach without properly positioning the airplane at the MAP
5 Failure to establish a stabilized approach to landing
010°
"Cessna 52241, cleared VOR Runway 1 approach, circle to land Runway 28."

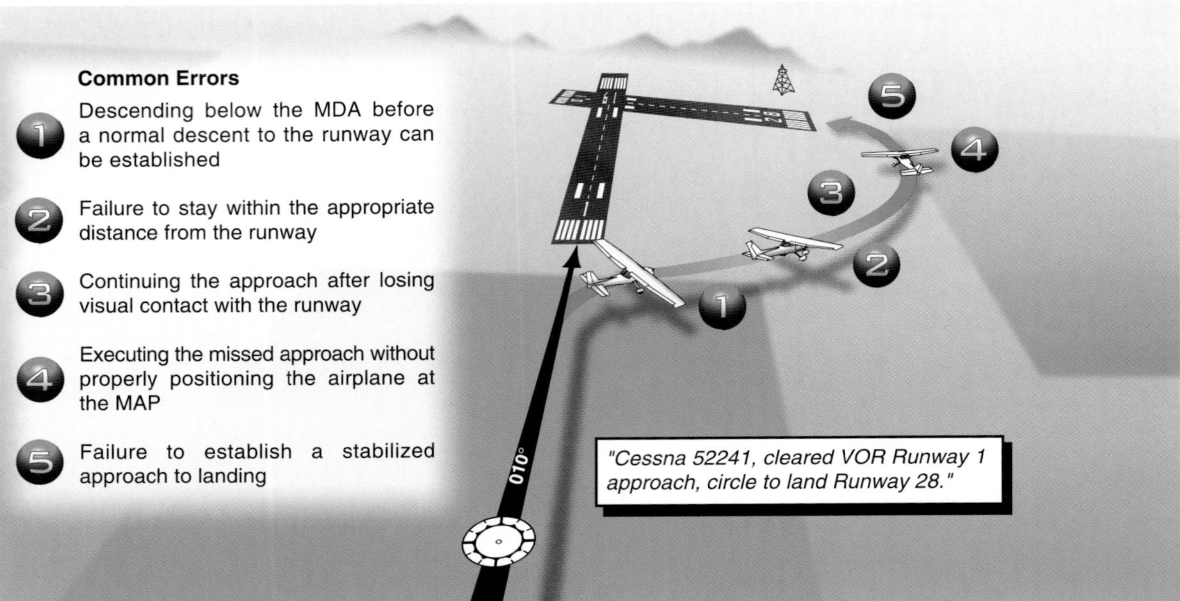

Figure 6-41. Students should understand that maintaining appropriate altitudes during the circling maneuver is critical.

MISSED APPROACH PROCEDURES

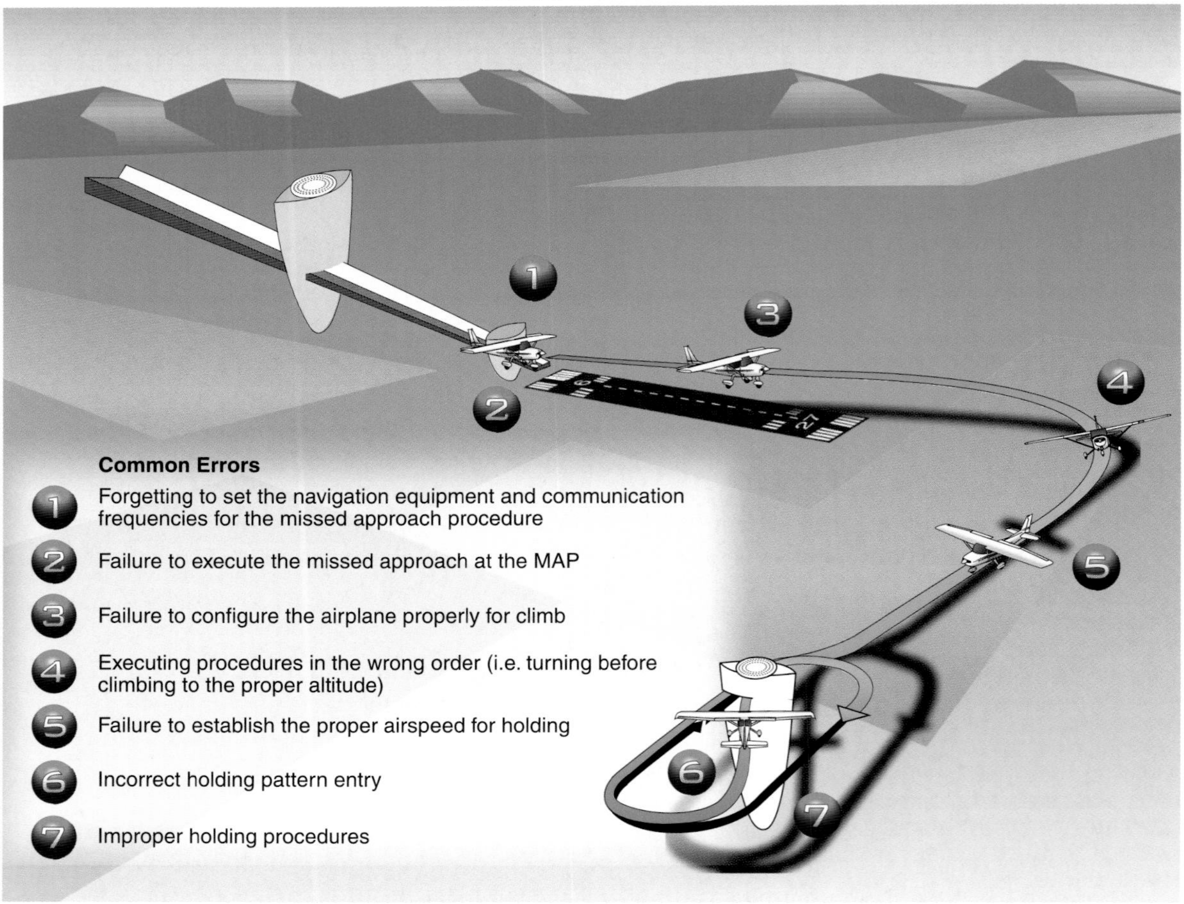

Common Errors
1 Forgetting to set the navigation equipment and communication frequencies for the missed approach procedure
2 Failure to execute the missed approach at the MAP
3 Failure to configure the airplane properly for climb
4 Executing procedures in the wrong order (i.e. turning before climbing to the proper altitude)
5 Failure to establish the proper airspeed for holding
6 Incorrect holding pattern entry
7 Improper holding procedures

Figure 6-42. Explain to your students that if the missed approach procedure requires a turn, they must fly the approach to the MAP before turning. There is no prohibition against climbing early.

SUMMARY CHECKLIST

✓ In addition to traditional ground lessons, you can employ several other methods to help effectively prepare your students for instrument instruction in flight.

✓ The advantages to using a PCATD or FTD include the ability to reposition the airplane, freeze the simulation, conduct safe emergency instruction, control the training environment, and provide more lesson versatility.

✓ By including elements of flight planning into each lesson, you help to instill habit patterns in your students that ensure they are well prepared for each instrument flight.

✓ Beginning with the first instrument training flight, instruct your students to preflight the airplane and perform instrument and equipment checks as if they are about to embark on a flight under IFR.

✓ Your students learn instrument flying skills best when you utilize a building block concept of instruction.

✓ The common instrument scanning errors are fixation, omission, and emphasis.

✓ Since proper use of trim is especially important in instrument flying, you need to teach your students good trimming habits.

✓ Before your students can control an airplane with the precision required for instrument flight, they must be familiar with the pitch and power settings required for certain operations.

✓ Prior to flying with a view-limiting device, have your students operate the airplane with the variety of airspeeds and configurations used for instrument procedures.

✓ Instrument rating applicants must exhibit adequate knowledge of the elements relating to attitude instrument flying, use proper instrument cross-check and interpretation, and apply the appropriate pitch, bank, power, and trim corrections.

✓ Once your students are competent flying straight and level at a constant airspeed, teach them how to perform airspeed transitions and configuration changes.

✓ Failure to adjust the power while leveling off during climbs and descents can result in a failure to maintain the desired airspeed in level flight.

✓ Performing steep turns and vertical S maneuvers helps students to refine their aircraft control skills and perfect their instrument scan.

✓ Practicing stalls and recoveries from unusual attitudes prepares students to recognize potentially hazardous situations in IFR conditions and take the appropriate corrective actions.

✓ Vertical S maneuvers are good exercises to teach your students to transition from one set of flight conditions to another.

✓ You should have your students practice stalls during instrument training to help them recognize the instrument indications associated with an approaching stall and to illustrate that recovery procedures are the same as during VFR conditions.

✓ To effectively teach recovery from unusual flight attitudes, you should instruct your students to close their eyes, and remove their hands and feet from the controls while you maneuver the aircraft in such a way as to induce disorientation. Then, have your students open their eyes, take control of the airplane, and make a proper recovery.

✓ You have a responsibility as an instructor to provide your students with effective training in flying partial panel, from a safety standpoint as well as in preparation for the practical test.

✓ To help with compass turns, teach your students the acronym, OSUN (Overshoot South, Undershoot North).

✓ When recovering from an unusual attitude with partial panel, teach your students to use the turn coordinator to stop a turn, and the pitot-static instruments to arrest an unintended climb or descent.

✓ The more experience your students have in visualizing their position in relation to navigational aids, the better they will adapt to flying under instrument conditions. This visualization is an essential part of situational awareness.

✓ If your students' training airplane is equipped with distance measuring equipment (DME), you should introduce its use along with VOR tracking and positional awareness exercises.

✓ Your students may have difficulty using the ADF to intercept NDB bearings. To help them with orientation, instruct your students to initially turn to a heading parallel to the desired course.

✓ Provide an example to your students to illustrate how relying too heavily on GPS equipment for navigation can lead to complacency and loss of situational awareness.

✓ In most cases, it is easier to teach your students the sidestep maneuver before teaching them circling maneuvers.

✓ Due to traffic conflicts, it may be difficult to practice circling approaches often with your students, so it is very important that you cover the procedures in detail on the ground.

✓ Ensure that your students have the opportunity to execute a full missed approach procedure which includes holding.

KEY TERMS

Personal Computer-Based Aviation Training Device (PCATD)

Flight Training Device (FTD)

Flight Planning

Attitude Instrument Flight

Scanning Errors

Fixation

Omission

Emphasis

Steep Turns

Vertical S Maneuvers

Stalls

Unusual Flight Attitudes

Partial Panel

VOR Navigation

Distance Measuring Equipment (DME)

Automatic Direction Finder (ADF)

Global Positioning System (GPS)

Receiver Autonomous Integrity Monitoring (RAIM)

No-Gyro Approaches

Sidestep Maneuver

Circling Approach

Missed Approach Procedures

QUESTIONS

1. How can a flight training device (FTD) can be utilized for an instrument rating under FAR Parts 61 and 141?

2. True/False. Since your instrument students already know how to inspect an airplane, there is no need for you to discuss preflight procedures with them.

3. True/False. Private pilot certification requires three hours of flight training on the control and maneuvering of an airplane solely by reference to instruments.

4. List the three common instrument scanning errors.

5. At 110 knots, performing a standard-rate turn in a training airplane requires a bank angle of how many degrees?

   A. 11°
   B. 16°
   C. 32°

6. Give an example of a lesson you could use to provide your students with motivation to perfect attitude instrument flight and prepare them to fly instrument approaches.

7. When recovering from an unusual attitude with partial panel, what instruments should be used to stop a turn and which should be used to stop a climb or descent?

8. To emphasize that DME measures slant range, you can ask your students to overfly the VOR at varying altitudes. What would the DME read if overflying at 5,000 feet AGL?

   A. 0.5 miles
   B. 1.0 mile
   C. 5.0 miles

9. True/False. Many GPS units monitor integrity by use of an internal system referred to as receiver autonomous integrity monitoring (RAIM).

SECTION C

INTEGRATING MULTI-ENGINE KNOWLEDGE

Making the transition to flying multi-engine airplanes conjures up an image of professionalism to many pilots. Therefore, instructing students in multi-engine airplanes challenges you to deliver a similarly advanced level of training. The increase in size and performance of multi-engine airplanes lures pilots of all experience levels. These airplanes have distinctive systems and complex aerodynamics compared to single-engine airplanes. The quality of training that you provide has a great impact on the safety of your students' multi-engine operations.

Historically, the way instructors conduct training for multi-engine students is patterned after the training they received. Consequently, this training may not be as standardized as that provided to private and commercial students in single-engine airplanes. This section provides a variety of methods you can use to outline the course of instruction to your students, as well as techniques you may find helpful for teaching advanced concepts such as multi-engine systems, engine-out aerodynamics, performance considerations, and decision making. However, this section does not attempt to cover every aspect of multi-engine knowledge. You should refer to the *Multi-Engine Manual* for additional information on these topics.

INSTRUCTING IN MULTI-ENGINE AIRPLANES

Because of the complex nature of multi-engine airplanes, you are required to have a certain amount of experience before you may instruct a student in pursuit of a certificate. For the particular airplane to be flown, you need to have at least five hours of pilot-in-command time in the specific make and model. Therefore, if you receive your multi-engine instructor rating in one airplane, you may need to gain additional experience before you are able to instruct in another type of multi-engine airplane.

The minimum pilot-in-command time requirement for a flight instructor with multi-engine privileges to give flight training to a student for a multi-engine rating is five hours in the make and model of aircraft in which the training is to be given.

Legend in Its Own Time

In 1933, the Boeing 247 was the most advanced airliner in America, and since Boeing only sold them to constituents of United Airlines, other airlines were at a distinct competitive disadvantage. Progress was rapid in those days, and the following year Douglas introduced the DC-2, which trumped the 247 in performance, payload, and economy. American Airlines went to Douglas Aircraft for an enlarged sleeper version of the DC-2, resulting in the larger, faster Douglas Sleeper Transport (DST). With 21 seats instead of sleeper berths, Douglas called it the DC-3, and by 1940, it is estimated that 90% of the airline passengers in the world were flying in DC-3s!

World War II saw the DC-3 militarized into the C-47. GIs called it the Gooney Bird, but General Eisenhower called it one of the three most important weapons of the war (along with the Jeep and the bazooka).

After the war, the DC-3 continued its role as the world's most popular airliner. Through the 1950s and '60s, each new small airliner was touted as the replacement for the DC-3, but in 1970 more than 200 airlines around the world still relied on the rugged, reliable, 35-year-old design.

Although it is difficult to improve upon its timeless merits, people keep trying. There have been a profusion of different engines, including turboprops and even a trimotor version. It has been flown with no engines at all, as a towed cargo glider. DC-3s have used skis in the arctic and been fitted with enormous floats and flown from the water. At least 10,000 were built in the U.S. by Douglas, more than 2,000 under license in the Soviet Union, and several hundred more in Japan. Every imaginable cargo, both legal and illegal, has seen the inside of a DC-3 at one time or another. At some time or other, almost every conceivable adjective has been used to describe the legendary DC-3 except flimsy, undependable, useless, or impractical.

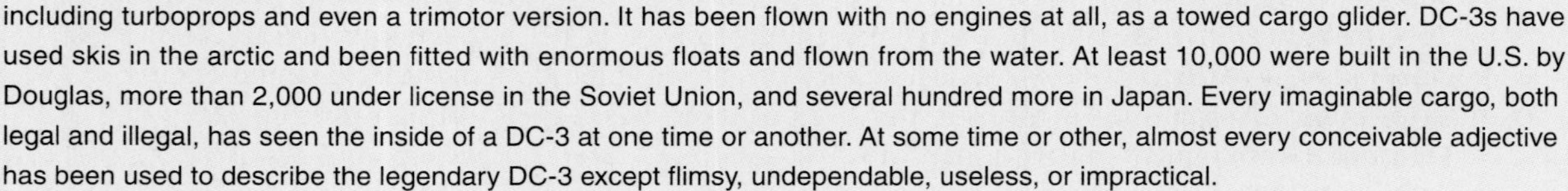

Even today, 65 years after the first flight, hundreds of DC-3s are still in daily use around the world, not as museum pieces or pampered antiques, but as capable, hard-working cargo airplanes. Can there ever be a replacement?

EXPLAINING MULTI-ENGINE SYSTEMS

When introducing **multi-engine systems** to your students, you need to customize the instruction to their experience level. Multi-engine systems vary widely, so it is important that you cover material specific to the airplane used for training. Covering diagrams and illustrations of generic systems is not as effective. The pilot's operating handbook (POH) is a necessary tool when organizing the material you plan to cover with your students. After using the POH to outline various systems, you should sit in the airplane and discuss each of them in detail so that your students have the chance to see the actual components and become familiar with using them. If you are giving classroom instruction, try to use pictures of the aircraft your students are flying, and, if possible, each student should have a copy of the POH. Most multi-engine training is conducted in light, twin-engine airplanes with reciprocating engines. Some of the distinctive features of these airplanes include electrical systems, fuel systems, and propeller systems. Once your students have learned the systems for the training airplane, you can evaluate their depth of knowledge by having them diagram and explain the systems on paper.

ELECTRICAL SYSTEMS

Electrical systems in multi-engine airplanes are similar to those of singles, but there are important differences. With more components to support, multi-engine electrical systems are larger and more complex. Also, multi-engine airplanes have more than one engine to produce the electrical power needed. Because there are additional alternators or generators, you need to familiarize your students with new operational procedures. [Figure 6-43]

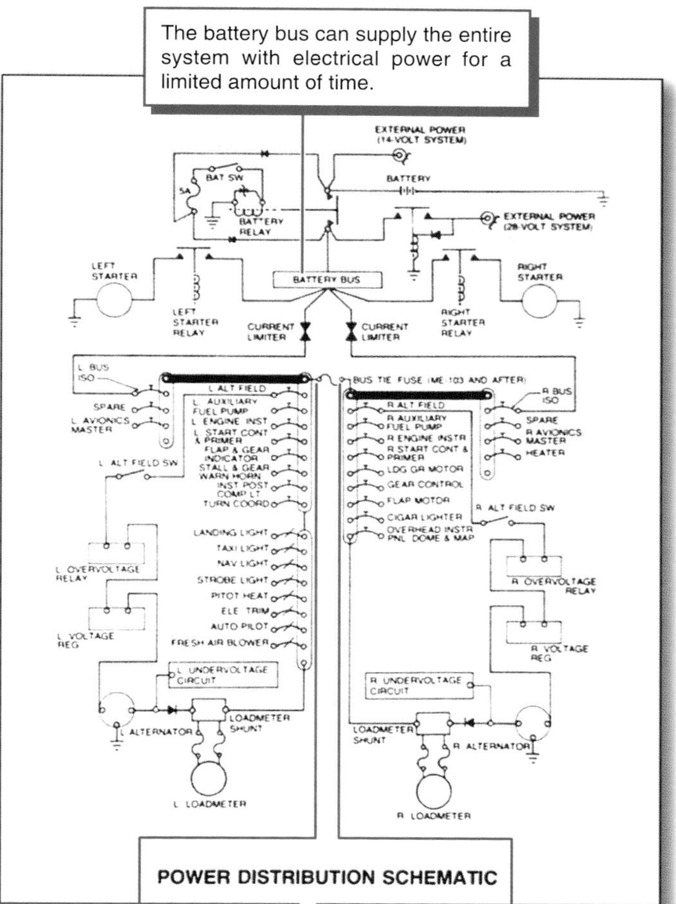

The bus tie fuse will blow if the current between the bus bars reaches a specific amperage.

If one alternator fails, the bus tie fuse allows all electrical equipment to be powered by the functioning alternator.

Figure 6-43. Since each engine provides a source of electrical power, there are some unique characteristics to multi-engine airplane electrical systems you can discuss with your students.

In the event of an alternator or engine failure, your students need to know how the electrical system will be affected. Once your students determine the electrical capacity of the airplane on one engine, ask them to prioritize the equipment needed for safe operation. They should understand which components require the greatest amount of power and which ones are critical to safe flight. [Figure 6-44]

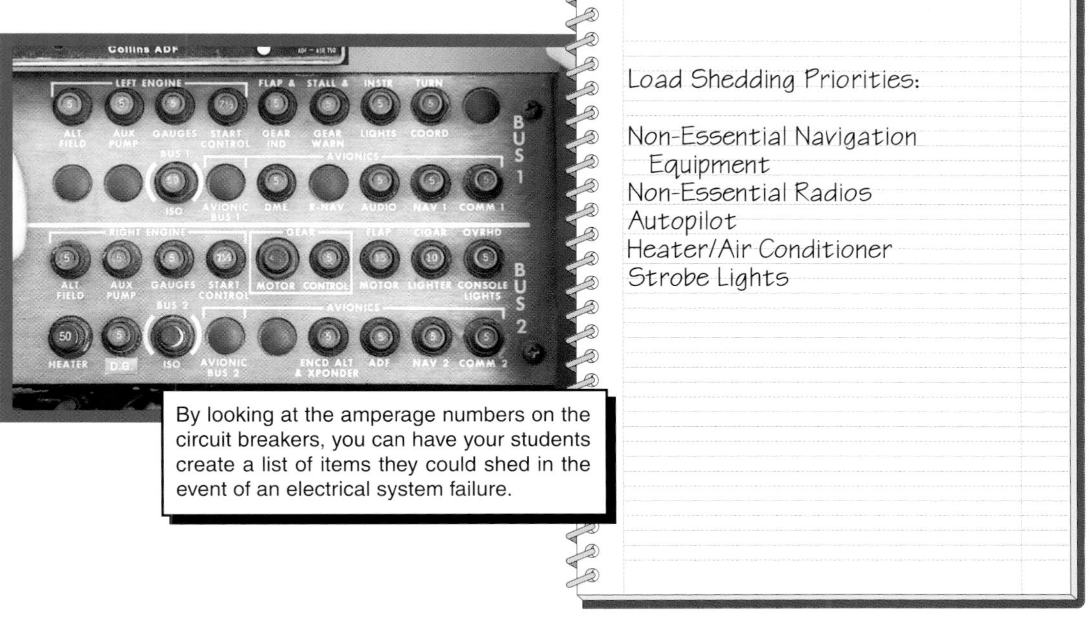

Figure 6-44. Methods for presenting load-shedding exercises to your students include reviewing the circuit breaker panel and constructing a list of non-critical equipment.

FUEL SYSTEMS

Some multi-engine airplanes used in training have complex fuel systems, and the use of multiple tanks and transferring of fuel may be new to your students. Make sure they understand the system they are operating and if possible, know how to crossfeed fuel from one tank to the opposite engine. [Figure 6-45]

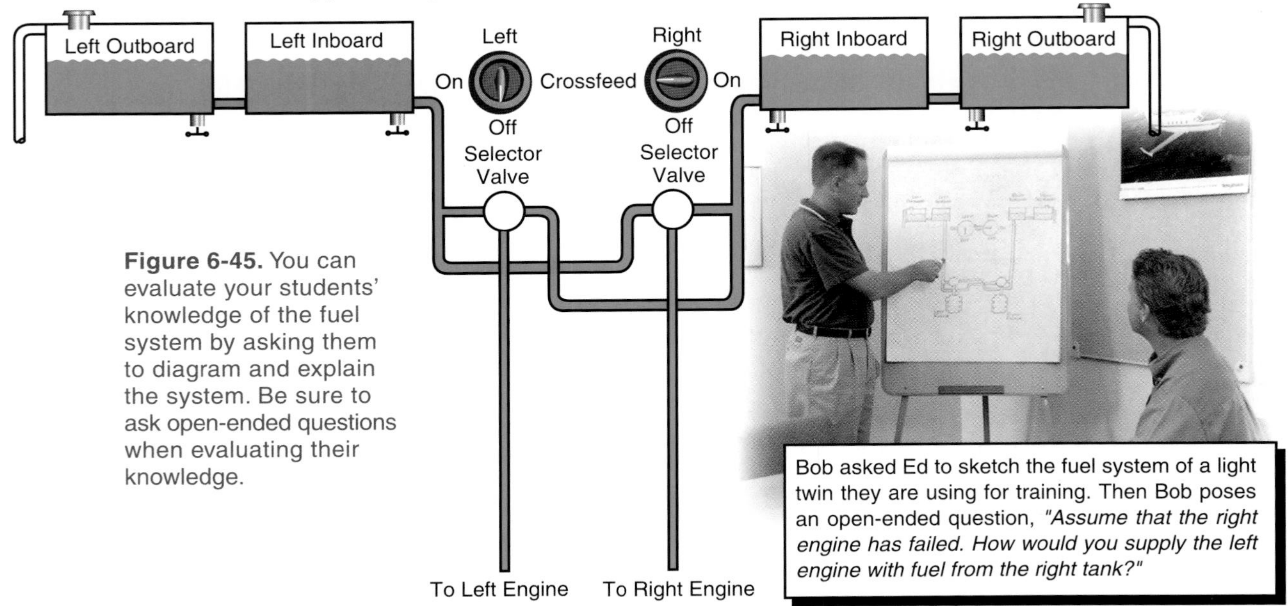

Figure 6-45. You can evaluate your students' knowledge of the fuel system by asking them to diagram and explain the system. Be sure to ask open-ended questions when evaluating their knowledge.

PROPELLERS

You may want to review single-engine propeller systems before moving on to multi-engine propellers. When you are sure your students have a thorough understanding of fixed-pitch and constant-speed propellers, you can build on these principles while explaining the differences in multi-engine systems. Most multi-engine airplanes are equipped with constant-speed, full-feathering propellers. As airplanes increase in size and performance, synchronization and autofeathering systems are common.

SYNCHRONIZATION

In order to reduce the amount of noise within the cabin and provide a better learning environment for your students, you need to cover **propeller synchronization**. This can be achieved manually by adjusting one of the propeller controls or through the use of automatic propeller synchronization systems. When using the manual method, have your students adjust the r.p.m. until the sounds of both propellers merge into one. If you encourage your students to constantly maintain synchronization, this procedure becomes second nature. [Figure 6-46]

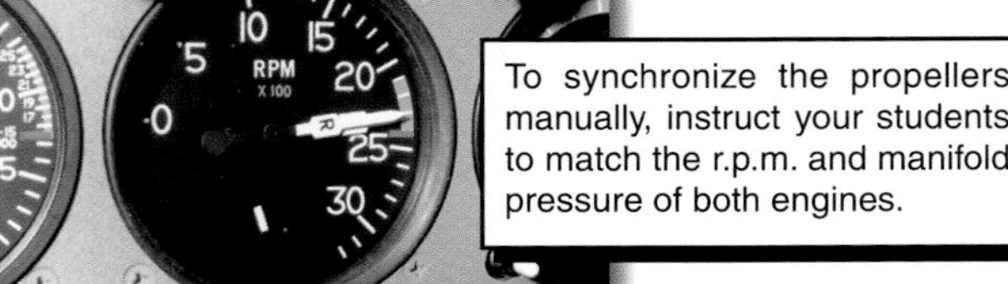

Figure 6-46. Beginning multi-engine students may not notice the pulsating sound of out-of-sync engines. During the first few flights, demonstrate the proper synchronization technique for your training airplane.

On airplanes that have propeller synchronization systems installed, one engine is slaved to the other. Your student should not only know how the system works, but also why the system is operated a certain way. Once the desired r.p.m. has been set on both engines, the system is activated and the slaved engine follows any changes in the other's r.p.m. within a limited range. The system must be deactivated during takeoff, landing, and in the event of an engine failure. Ask your student why this is required. It is reasonable to assume that if the system is activated and the master engine fails, the slaved engine will drop in r.p.m. In fact, as a safety precaution, the system usually disengages automatically if there is a difference of more than 50 r.p.m. between the two engines.

Reversible Propeller Systems

Many of your students will move into more advanced aircraft soon after they attain their multi-engine rating. Many multi-engine turboprop airplanes incorporate reversible propeller systems to decrease the landing roll. Reverse thrust is achieved by increasing the oil pressure in the hub to achieve a negative blade angle.

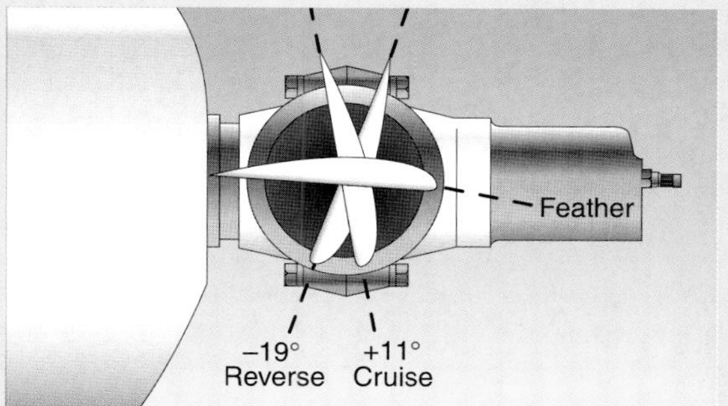

FEATHERING

Your students will be far more motivated to learn how a propeller feathers if they understand why it is necessary for extended engine-out operations. Point out that because of the high drag associated with a windmilling propeller, it becomes very important to feather the propeller of the inoperative engine in order to obtain maximum performance. Since the takeoff and initial climb phases of flight are often critical in terms of single-engine performance, your students must realize the inoperative engine must be promptly identified, verified, and the propeller feathered. Explain to your students that a windmilling propeller can produce an increase in parasite drag that may equal the parasite drag of the entire airplane. Feathering the propeller stops its rotation. Therefore, the parasite drag is significantly reduced. [Figure 6-47]

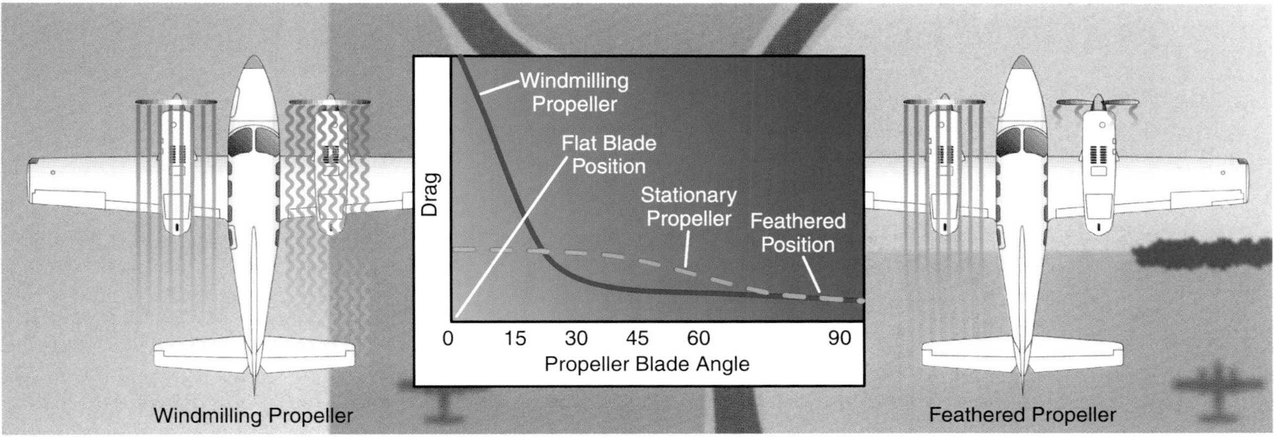

Figure 6-47. You can use the diagram in this illustration to graphically compare the parasite drag of a windmilling and feathered propeller.

As with all constant-speed propellers, a governor varies oil pressure to the hub to keep the rotational speed constant. Your students may already know that this force is applied toward the high pitch, low r.p.m. setting on single-engine airplanes, since the aerodynamic forces of conventional propellers tend to twist the blades to that setting. The propeller automatically changes to a climb setting if oil pressure is lost. This is an undesirable characteristic on multi-engine systems, since this would cause a windmilling condition. In multi-engine propellers, the force of oil pressure is applied in the opposite direction. [Figure 6-48.]

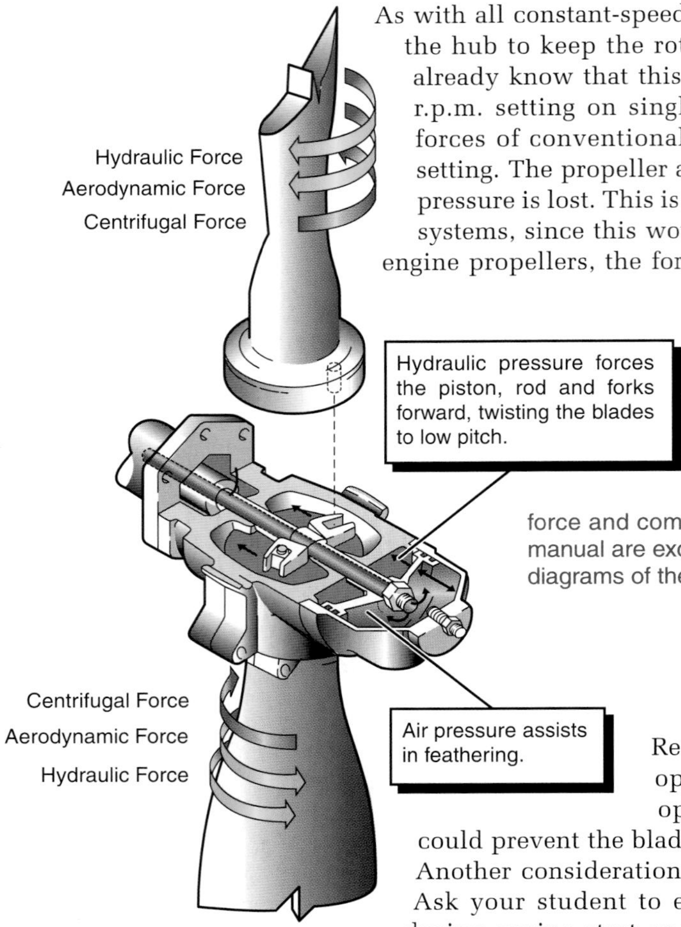

Hydraulic Force
Aerodynamic Force
Centrifugal Force
Hydraulic pressure forces the piston, rod and forks forward, twisting the blades to low pitch.
Centrifugal Force
Aerodynamic Force
Hydraulic Force
Air pressure assists in feathering.

Figure 6-48. Engine oil pressure opposes the feathering forces built into the propeller. In this case, the feathering forces are aerodynamic force and compressed nitrogen. The POH and aircraft service manual are excellent resources for your students to use to locate diagrams of the propeller mechanism.

Remind your students that if the system they are operating uses compressed air or nitrogen to oppose oil pressure, an insufficient charge could prevent the blades from reaching the fully feathered position. Another consideration while feathering the propeller is low r.p.m. Ask your student to explain why the propeller does not feather during engine start and shutdown. They can begin by explaining which position the propeller was in during the preflight inspection and noting that the propellers were not in a feathered position. A locking device is incorporated into the propeller hub, which prevents it from feathering during engine starting or shutdown when oil pressure is very low. Attempting to feather a propeller below a certain r.p.m. (typically 600–800 r.p.m.) could be prevented by the locking device. [Figure 6-49]

Figure 6-49. Engine start and shutdown are excellent times to explain to your students that the feathering lock prevents feathering anytime the engine speed falls below a specific r.p.m.

UNFEATHERING

Before you explain how to bring the propellers out of feather, you need to tell your students why they need to be able to perform this operation. A student might think learning to

Figure 6-50. Begin the propeller unfeathering exercise by asking your students what they might do to get the propeller moving. Logically, using the starter or diving the aircraft, or a combination of both, will usually get the propeller moving.

unfeather a propeller has no value because they are thinking about an actual engine failure rather than engine-out training, but explaining the difference between training maneuvers and actual engine-out procedures will prevent confusion. [Figure 6-50]

Even if your students do not train in airplanes equipped with **accumulators**, they should understand that these devices store a limited amount of oil under pressure after the engine is no longer running. Accumulators assist in bringing the propeller out of the feathered position by providing a burst of oil pressure to the hub as you move the control lever out of the feather position.

If you have any doubt whether an engine will start in the air, do not feather it for training purposes. Bear in mind that air starts can be hard on engines and engine mounts. Also, you should initially keep the power settings low after an air start to allow the engine to gradually warm up.

TEACHING ENGINE-OUT AERODYNAMICS

The largest difference between operating single-engine and multi-engine airplanes lies in engine-out operations. Therefore, you need to emphasize to your students from the beginning the aerodynamic principles that are the basis for these procedures. A good place to start the discussion is with a review of FAR Part 23. According to FAR 23.67, a positive engine-out rate of climb at 5,000 feet density altitude is required only for those multi-engine airplanes weighing more than 6,000 pounds and/or having a stall speed (V_{SO}) greater than 61 knots. If the airplane weighs less than 6,000 pounds and has a stall speed (V_{SO}) of 61 knots or less, a specific, positive engine-out rate of climb is not required. Therefore, your students must not assume that their training airplane is capable of climbing with one engine inoperative.

Impress upon your students that an engine failure in a multi-engine airplane can have profound effects on its aerodynamic characteristics and significantly reduce its controllability and performance. With the loss of an engine in a twin-engine airplane,

your students may easily note the 50% loss of thrust. Make your students aware that climb performance is actually reduced by as much as 80–90% because of the adverse effects that several factors place on the airplane during engine-out flight. [Figure 6-51]

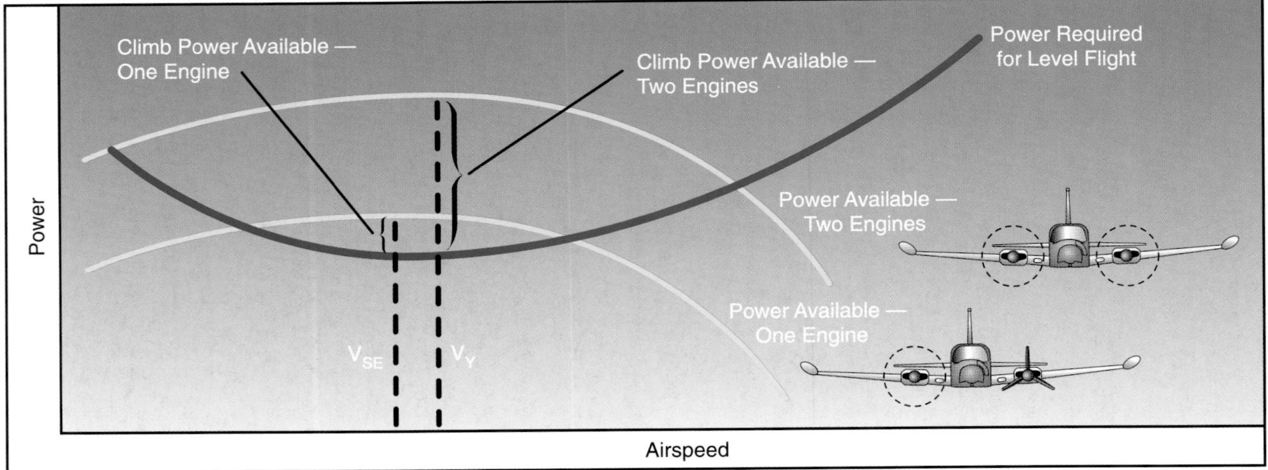

Figure 6-51. A graphic presentation of the loss of climb performance helps your students see the relationship between power available and the power required for single-engine and multi-engine climbs. If power is further reduced as a result of high density altitude, climb capability is diminished even further.

Your students must compensate for the asymmetrical forces due to an engine failure by applying rudder in the opposite direction. Emphasize to your students that this places the airplane in a sideslip, which causes drag because the fuselage is being pushed through the air at an angle. The sideslip also increases the roll and yaw toward the inoperative engine by reducing rudder effectiveness. [Figure 6-52]

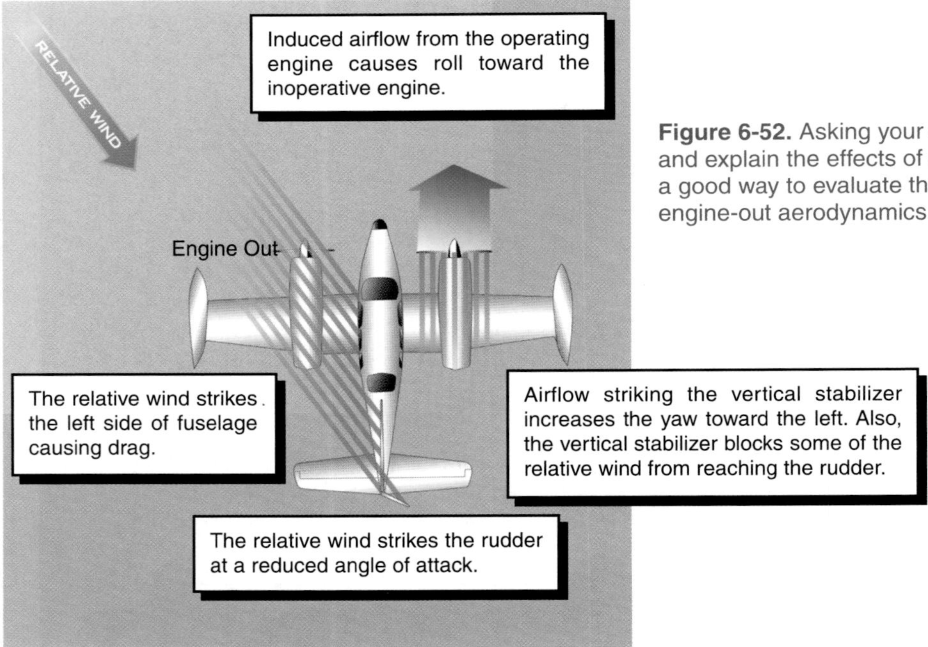

Figure 6-52. Asking your students to diagram and explain the effects of an engine failure is a good way to evaluate their understanding of engine-out aerodynamics.

ZERO SIDESLIP

Traditionally, multi-engine instruction has emphasized maintaining directional control. However, stall/spin awareness and issues of inadequate climb performance should not be overlooked. Also, there are many confusing, incorrect, and misleading concepts pertaining to engine-out procedures. In order to teach your students the proper technique the first time, a complete understanding of **zero sideslip** is required.

IT JUST TAKES YOU TO THE SCENE OF THE CRASH

You may find that many of your students begin their training with the perception that an engine failure in a multi-engine airplane is far safer than one in a single-engine airplane. Present to your students the following scenarios.

The private pilot began the takeoff roll. Just as the airplane approached rotation speed, the left engine lost power. The pilot elected to continue the takeoff, but once airborne, the airplane slowed below V_{MC}. The subsequent roll resulted in a crash just off the departure end of the runway. The pilot had not flown a multi-engine airplane for more than three months prior to the accident.

The commercial pilot was conducting a scenic flight for some friends over mountainous terrain. While flying low through a valley, the right engine began surging, and a few seconds later, it quit completely. Because of the high density altitude, the airplane was above its single-engine service ceiling and unable to maintain level flight. There was no way for the pilot to climb to escape the valley, which was densely forested. The emergency landing destroyed the airplane.

These scenarios illustrate the complex nature of multi-engine operations. Since it would be difficult for you to simulate these types of emergencies with your students, you should provide examples like those above for discussion on the ground. Emphasize that multi-engine emergency operations often require the pilot to make a complicated chain of decisions. Once a course of action is determined, the pilot must practice the necessary procedures often in order to properly execute them in an emergency.

A good place to start when explaining this concept to your students is to look at the historical perspective. Up until about 1980, the general belief was that following an engine failure, the pilot should fly at zero bank angle, or wings level, and keep the ball centered on the inclinometer. In this case, the inclinometer is very misleading and the airplane is actually sideslipping through the air. It is now widely accepted that sideslipping flight leads to an increase in drag and reduces rudder effectiveness. [Figure 6-53]

Figure 6-53. The evolution of engine-out training has progressed throughout the years. Early attempts at single-engine flight were based on trial and error to achieve the best performance. The techniques in use today have greatly benefited from improved aerodynamic modeling.

To alleviate the sideslip of the airplane, you must apply bank in the opposite direction. Most pilots would agree that banking into the operative engine is correct, but the question remains as to how much bank is appropriate. Many pilots believe that holding 5° of bank gives the best performance and directional control. Using 5° of bank stems from FAR Part 23 certification requirements, which are used to determine published V_{MC} and have nothing to do with achieving maximum performance. Research shows that 5° or any other single value does not work in all situations. Instead, the appropriate degree of bank depends on several factors, including weight, the design of the airplane, density altitude, and other elements. Also, as bank angle exceeds the zero sideslip value, there is a sharp loss of climb performance. As obstacle clearance is critical, the margin for error is minimal, and 5° of bank could mean the difference between striking an obstacle or

Figure 6-54. This table can help you explain to your students that zero sideslip angle varies with airplane type. As you gain experience in other aircraft, you can expand this list.

SUMMARY OF ENGINE-OUT FLIGHT TEST RESULTS

Factor	Cessna Crusader	Piper Seminole	Beech Baron
Flight Test Measurements			
Zero Slip Bank	1.5°	2.1°	2.7°
Ball Deflection	0.3	0.4	0.7
Equivalency Calculations (Zero Slip to 5°)			
Weight Penalty	398 lbs.	305 lbs.	296 lbs.
Rate of Climb Change	-91 f.p.m.	-92 f.p.m.	-76 f.p.m.

clearing it. Analysis shows that the zero sideslip angle varies with the airplane type, but optimum performance is achieved at less than 5°. [Figure 6-54]

One way to demonstrate this concept is through the use of a yaw string. Attach a length of string or yarn to the nose of the airplane in a place that is easy to see and has relatively undisturbed air. The zero sideslip bank angle can easily be recognized when the string is parallel to the longitudinal axis of the aircraft. [Figure 6-55]

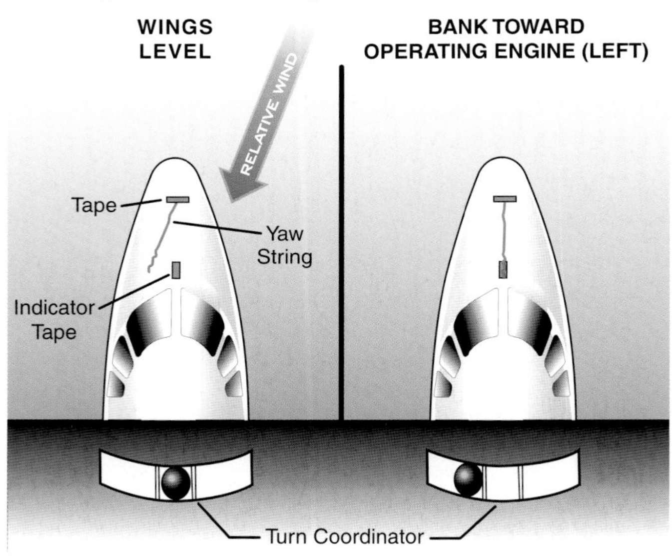

Figure 6-55. Have your students note the bank angle and ball deflection that corresponds with zero sideslip flight. Make sure they understand that bank angle and ball deflection vary from one airplane to another.

Instruct your students that once they have applied rudder to control the yawing moment of the airplane, they should bank into the operative engine as needed to maintain straight-and-level flight. Once aircraft control has been established, configure the airplane for a climb and then reduce the bank angle to establish zero sideslip and best performance. Also, using the inclinometer as a judge of bank angle may be more useful because it is more sensitive than the attitude indicator, and easier to see. Your students should understand that flying at zero sideslip allows adequate directional control with the best possible climb performance.

CRITICAL ENGINE

For multi-engine airplanes, the **critical engine** is the engine that would have the most adverse effect on controllability and climb performance if it were to fail. Even if you are instructing in an airplane with counter-rotating propellers, your students must understand this concept, as they are likely to encounter an airplane with a critical engine at some point in their careers.

Most students remember the effects of P-factor from flying single-engine airplanes. Your students have been previously compensating for this by applying right rudder when climbing, since the descending blade is usually on the right side. Multi-engine airplanes on which the propellers turn in the same direction are constructed so the descending blade of one engine is further from the centerline of the aircraft than the descending blade of the engine mounted on the other side. This makes the failure of one engine more critical than the other, because there is a greater yawing moment created by the engine, which is producing thrust further from the aircraft centerline. [Figure 6-56]

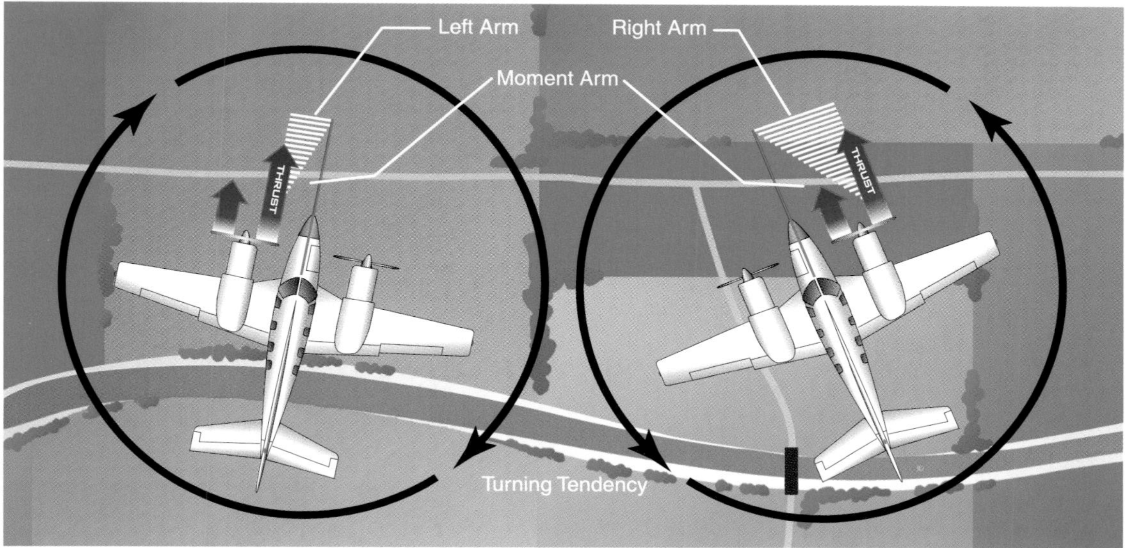

Figure 6-56. A good method to determine whether your students truly understand what causes an airplane to have a critical engine is to ask them to draw a picture of an airplane as viewed from above. Instruct them that both propellers rotate clockwise as viewed from behind and to label the forces creating a critical engine. Then, have them compare the forces and turning moments between the engines, should one fail.

One way to eliminate the critical engine is to design counter-rotating engines. In this case, the descending propeller blades of both engines are the same distance from the aircraft centerline, and neither engine would affect climb performance or controllability more than the other if it were to fail. [Figure 6-57]

Figure 6-57. You should point out that on airplanes with counter-rotating propellers, the descending blades are closest to the centerline.

MINIMUM CONTROL AIRSPEED

An optimum time to cover minimum control airspeed is during the discussion of the critical engine. Your students should understand that there is a minimum airspeed at which directional and lateral control can be maintained if a complete power loss occurs on one engine while the opposite engine is producing maximum thrust. This airspeed is known as **single-engine minimum control airspeed (V_{MC})**. Make sure your students are aware that below V_{MC}, the flight control surfaces cannot generate sufficient aerodynamic forces to counteract the asymmetrical thrust from the operating engine and drag from the windmilling propeller on the opposite engine. For this reason, you should ensure your students know they should not attempt flight at airspeeds below V_{MC}.

CENTERLINE THRUST

A way to eliminate engine-out asymmetrical thrust and asymmetrical drag is the **centerline thrust** design. By mounting the engines along the fuselage centerline, directional control problems of the conventional twin following an engine failure are eliminated. However, the loss of an engine can still reduce climb performance significantly. [Figure 6-58]

When engines are mounted in a fore and aft configuration, identification of the failed engine is more difficult because the yawing and rolling tendency of a conventional twin is not present.

The throttles, propeller controls, and mixture controls are positioned laterally across the quadrant, which can lead to confusion during feathering procedures. Special care needs to be taken to prevent feathering the wrong engine.

Figure 6-58. Caution students that rear-mounted engines might not be visible at all, making it harder to detect an engine failure.

Another consideration for instructing in airplanes incorporating centerline thrust is that they do not have a published V_{MC} speed. This makes the engine-out loss of directional control demonstration impossible. If your students receive a multi-engine rating in an airplane of this type, the restriction, *"Limited to Center Thrust,"* is placed on their pilot certificate. This restriction can be removed if your students subsequently demonstrate the maneuver during a practical exam in a conventional twin.

INTERPRETING PERFORMANCE AND LIMITATIONS

Weight and balance, and performance information for multi-engine airplanes is more extensive and generally more complex than that of single-engine airplanes. For this reason, it important that your students become thoroughly familiar with multi-engine performance and limitations. Students also need to realize that when either weight or balance limitations are exceeded, performance is unpredictable.

DRAG REDUCTION FOLLOWING ENGINE FAILURE

If you can indoctrinate your students with the knowledge that drag is their primary concern in engine-out situations, they are more likely to become safe multi-engine pilots. Any increase in drag, whether parasite or induced, must be balanced by the use of additional thrust. Any use of excess thrust to counteract drag is thrust which cannot be used for single-engine climb. The maximum amount of excess thrust is available in the clean configuration. Typically, drag is reduced by first retracting the flaps and landing gear. Emphasize to your students that the relative amount of drag per component and the specific order of drag reduction may vary between types of twin-engine airplanes, so the manufacturer's specific recommendations should always be followed. [Figure 6-59]

PILOT'S OPERATING HANDBOOK

A good way to present new material to your students is to use the POH. You can sit down and go through the book page by page and point out the differences between various multi-engine airplanes. This helps to organize the material and gives your students a method to review these concepts on their own.

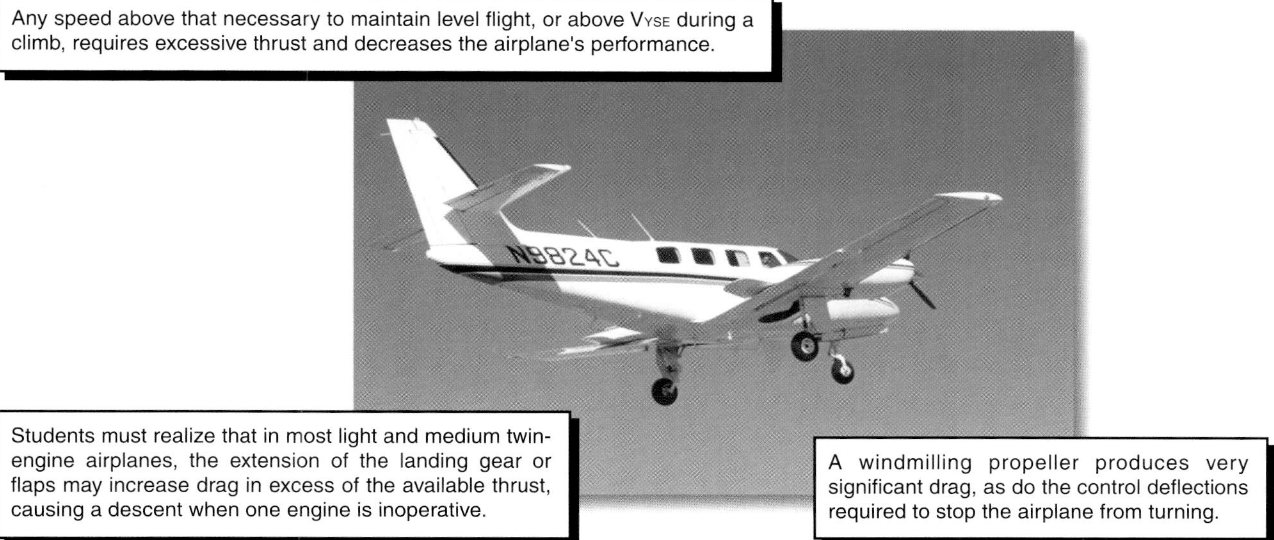

Figure 6-59. During training, it is beneficial to have your students use the vertical speed indicator to compare the relative engine-out performance loss associated with a windmilling propeller, full flaps, and extended landing gear.

AIRSPEED LIMITATIONS

The critical airspeeds used in multi-engine airplanes are listed in figure 6-60 on page 6-64. Your students should be familiar with most of these airspeeds through past experience. It is important that you become familiar with the V-speeds of the particular airplane you are flying. Then, you may properly acquaint your students with the practical applications of all multi-engine V-speeds specific to that airplane.

PUBLISHED V_{MC}

After your students gain an understanding of these airspeeds, you can relate their significance to flight operations. You could begin by covering the first airspeed they should consider on the takeoff roll — V_{MC}. Once the students know the significance of this airspeed, they understand why they should always reject the takeoff if an engine fails below V_{MC}. You should also make sure they are clear that V_{MC} is not a climb performance airspeed, but a minimum speed for maintaining aircraft control with an engine inoperative.

Emphasize to your students that published V_{MC} and actual V_{MC} are seldom the same value. This is because current conditions are rarely identical to the conditions used in certification tests. The certification test is accomplished with the critical engine failed and the operative engine developing takeoff power. The propeller of the failed engine is windmilling, or feathered if the airplane is equipped with an automatic feathering device. The wing and cowl flaps are in the takeoff position and the landing gear is retracted. The aircraft is loaded to maximum takeoff weight (unless a lesser weight is needed to demonstrate V_{MC}) with the most unfavorable center of gravity. [Figure 6-61]

23.149 MINIMUM CONTROL SPEED

(a) V_{MC} is the calibrated airspeed at which, when the critical engine is suddenly made inoperative, it is possible to maintain control of the airplane with that engine still inoperative and thereafter maintain straight flight at the same speed with an angle of bank of not more than 5 degrees. The method used to simulate critical engine failure must represent the most critical mode of powerplant failure expected in service with respect to controllability.

(b) V_{MC} for takeoff must not exceed 1.2 V_{S1}, where V_{S1} is determined at the maximum takeoff weight. V_{MC} must be determined with the most unfavorable weight and center of gravity position and with the airplane airborne and the ground effect negligible, for the takeoff configuration(s) with

(1) Maximum available takeoff power initially on each engine;
(2) The airplane trimmed for takeoff;
(3) Flaps in the takeoff position(s);
(4) Landing gear retracted; and
(5) All propeller controls in the reommended takeoff position throughout.

Figure 6-61. Your discussion should include the Part 23 references for establishing V_{MC}. Point out the conditions under which V_{MC} is established during certification.

Speed	Designation A/S Ind. Marking	Description	Airplane Configuration/ or Significance of Speed
72	V_{SO} Low speed end of white arc	Stalling Speed Landing Configuration	Engines zero thrust, propellers takeoff position, landing gear extended, flaps in landing position, cowl flaps closed
79	V_{S1} Low speed end of green arc	Stalling Speed Specified Configuration	Engines zero thrust, propellers takeoff position, landing gear and flaps retracted
80	V_{MC} * Red radial line ** V_{MCA}	Minimum Control Airspeed (Air Minimum Control Speed)	Takeoff or maximum available power on operating engine, critical engine windmilling (or feathered if auto feather device is installed), landing gear retracted, flaps in takeoff position, and CG at aft limit
92	V_{SSE}	Intentional One Engine Inoperative Speed	Minimum speed for intentionally rendering one engine inoperative in flight for pilot training
85	V_X	Best Angle-of-Climb Speed	Speed which produces most altitude gain over a given distance with both engines operating; obstruction clearance speed
107	V_Y	Best Rate-of-Climb Speed	Speed which produces most altitude gain in a given time with both engines operating
95	V_{XSE}	Best Angle-of-Climb Speed (Single Engine)	Speed which produces most altitude gain over a given distance with one engine inoperative
106	V_{YSE} Blue radial line **	Best Rate-of-Climb Speed (Single Engine)	Speed which produces most altitude gain in a given time with one engine inoperative
138	V_{LO}	Maximum Landing Gear Operating Speed	Maximum speed for safely extending or retracting the landing gear
138	V_{LE}	Maximum Landing Gear Extended Speed	Maximum speed for safe flight with landing gear extended
158	V_{FE} High speed end of white arc	Maximum Flap Extended Speed	Maximum speed with wing flaps in a prescribed extended position
148	V_A	Design Maneuvering Speed	Speed below which structural damage will not occur as a result of full control deflection
181	V_{NO} High speed end of green arc	Maximum Structural Cruising Speed	Maximum speed for normal operation
223	V_{NE}	Never-Exceed Speed	Maximum design speed without structural failure

* The FAA abbreviation V_{MC} is used throughout this section; however, some manufacturers may prefer V_{MCA} in reference to this critical speed.

** Aircraft receiving type certificates under FAR Part 23 after November 11, 1965

Figure 6-60. Your students should memorize all the airspeeds applicable to their training aircraft and be able to explain their significance. This knowledge is essential before you can begin discussing flight procedures and techniques. As a learning exercise, you might consider having your students fill in a V-speed table, similar to this one, for their training airplane.

V_Y

One of the points you should stress from the beginning is the importance of establishing V_Y as soon as possible after takeoff and using that speed to climb to a safe maneuvering altitude. This altitude can vary with airplane performance, local terrain, and obstacles. If you are flying with only one other person in the airplane and less than a full fuel load, this may result in a climb angle that seems uncomfortably steep to your students.

However, you should make sure they understand the desirability of altitude over excess airspeed early in the climbout. By climbing at V_Y, they are already at an airspeed equal to or greater than V_{YSE} in case of an engine failure. They also have reached a greater altitude than if they had used a shallower climb angle. Since performance can deteriorate rapidly with an engine failure, excess altitude is essential to flight safety. [Figure 6-62]

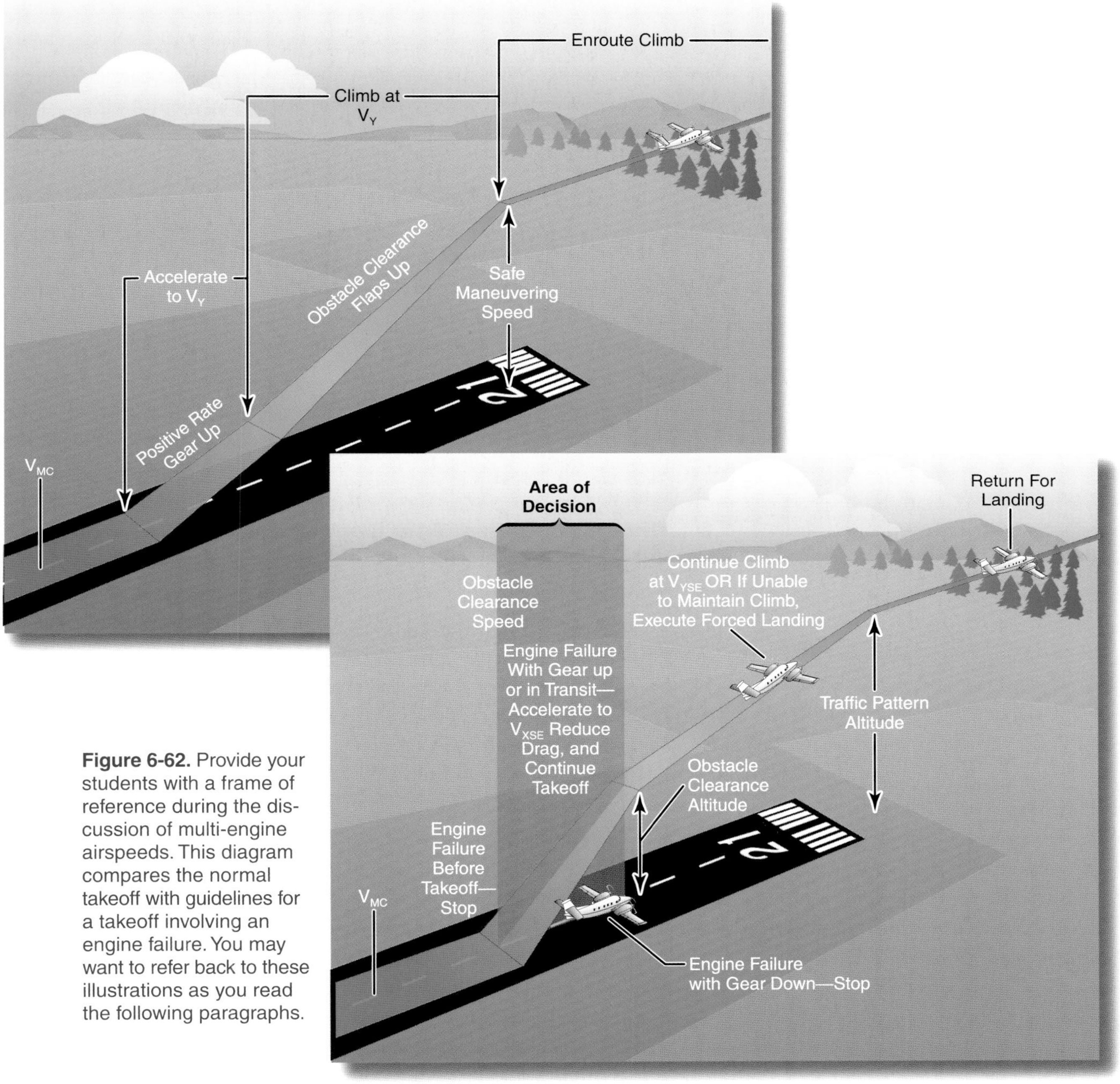

Figure 6-62. Provide your students with a frame of reference during the discussion of multi-engine airspeeds. This diagram compares the normal takeoff with guidelines for a takeoff involving an engine failure. You may want to refer back to these illustrations as you read the following paragraphs.

V_{YSE}

When discussing V_{YSE}, or blue line speed, it is important to make your students understand that this is the airspeed that results in optimum engine-out performance. Of course, they must realize that this may not be a positive rate of climb. For example, if an engine fails above the airplane's engine-out service ceiling, maintaining V_{YSE} will result in the lowest descent rate possible as long as the operating engine is producing maximum continuous power. In addition, make sure your students know that any speed above or below V_{YSE} reduces engine-out performance.

V_{XSE}

Students must also realize that the engine-out best angle of climb speed, V_{XSE}, is appropriate for terrain or obstruction clearance with one engine inoperative. If positive climb performance is possible, this speed results in the greatest altitude gain in a given distance.

V_{SSE}

Some manufacturers designate V_{SSE}, although it is not an airspeed required for certification. This speed is the minimum speed selected by the manufacturer for intentionally rendering one engine inoperative in flight for pilot training. V_{SSE} provides an additional margin of safety, since it is predicated on maintaining conservative controllability margins when one engine is suddenly and intentionally shut down. There is no formula for determining V_{SSE}, since it is based on the characteristics of a particular aircraft type. The only specific limitation is that it must not be lower than 1.05 V_{MC}.

ACCELERATE-STOP DISTANCE

Manufacturers of multi-engine aircraft are required by Part 23 to provide a full range of performance information, including **accelerate-stop distance**. You need to explain to your students that this distance is the amount of runway required under existing conditions to accelerate the airplane to a speed designated by the manufacturer (usually the liftoff speed), experience an engine failure at that point, immediately discontinue the takeoff, and stop the airplane on the remaining runway. [Figure 6-63]

ACCELERATE-GO DISTANCE

Some manufacturers have elected to provide an **accelerate-go distance** chart as well. This performance information tells your students whether or not they can continue the takeoff and climb to clear a 50-foot obstacle following an engine failure at the takeoff decision speed. Most manufacturers recommend against continuing a takeoff following an engine failure at takeoff decision speed. Continuing the takeoff should be based on having achieved the obstacle clearance speed with the gear retracted when the engine fails. These issues are important points for discussion with your students during takeoff planning.

DENSITY ALTITUDE CONSIDERATIONS

As mentioned earlier, an increase in density altitude correspondingly decreases V_{MC}. However, the calibrated airspeed at which the airplane stalls remains the same. This is an important factor when performing stalls with a high density altitude, because the stall speed of the airplane may be higher than V_{MC}. This causes the airplane to stall before reaching V_{MC}. Stalling a twin with power applied to only one engine is extremely dangerous.

According to the multi-engine PTS, when operating in an environment with high density altitude, you may still be able to conduct a V_{MC} demonstration safely by limiting the amount of travel of the rudder. By placing your foot so the student cannot use the full travel of the rudder, you are simulating the maximum travel of rudder has been reached. The student can then demonstrate the maneuver at a speed well above the stall speed of the airplane.

WEIGHT LIMITATIONS

The methods used to calculate the weight and balance of multi-engine airplanes is similar to that of single-engine airplanes. Make sure your students are familiar with methods of calculating and adjusting weight and balance. They should also be aware of how adjusting the center of gravity affects V_{MC}. As the airplane pivots around this point, the distance between the center of gravity and the rudder governs how effective the rudder will be in facilitating directional control. As the center of gravity moves rearward, the rudder's effective moment decreases and V_{MC} is increased. [Figure 6-64]

ACCELERATE-STOP DISTANCE

CONDITIONS:
Flaps 10°
2400 RPM, 32.5 Inches Hg and
Mixtures Set at 160 PPH Prior to Brake Release
Cowl Flaps Open
Throttles Closed at Engine Failure
Maximum Braking During Deceleration
Paved, Level, Dry Runway
Zero Wind

NOTE:
Decrease distances 10% for each 11 knots headwind. For operation with tailwinds up to 10 knots, increase distances by 10% for each 2.5 knots.

WEIGHT LBS	ENGINE FAILURE SPEED KIAS	PRESS ALT FT	ACCELERATE - STOP DISTANCE - FEET				
			0°C	10°C	20°C	30°C	40°C
5150	77	S.L.	2965	3110	3260	3420	3595
		1000	3085	3235	3395	3570	3755
		2000	3210	3370	3540	3725	3925
		3000	3345	3515	3695	3895	4105
		4000	3490	3670	3865	4075	4305
		5000	3645	3840	4050	4275	4515
		6000	3815	4020	4245	4485	4745
		7000	3990	4210	4450	4710	4990
		8000	4180	4415	4670	4950	5250
4800	74	S.L.	2725	2845	2975		
		1000	2830	2955	3095		
		2000	2940	3075	3220		
		3000	3055	3200	3355		
		4000	3185	3340	3505		
		5000	3320	3485	3660		
		6000	3465	3640	3830		
		7000	3620	3805	4010		
		8000	3785	3985	4200		
4400	71	S.L.	2475	2575	2680		
		1000	2560	2670	2780		
		2000	2655	2770	2890		
		3000	2760	2875	3005		
		4000	2865	2995	3130		
		5000	2980	3120	3260		
		6000	3105	3250	3400		
		7000	3235	3390	3555		
		8000	3375	3540	3715	3905	4110

Figure 6-63. This chart uses tabular data to arrive at the accelerate-stop distance under existing conditions.

In the example shown in the inset, the runway length would be considered marginal since variations in the tailwind, braking conditions, or reaction time could easily prevent the aircraft from achieving a full stop on the existing runway.

Takeoff Weight.........................5,150 lbs.
Existing Runway.........................5,600 ft.
Pressure Altitude........................5,000 ft.
Temperature..................................35° C
Tailwind Component.......................5 kts.
Accelerate-Stop Distance...........5,274 ft.

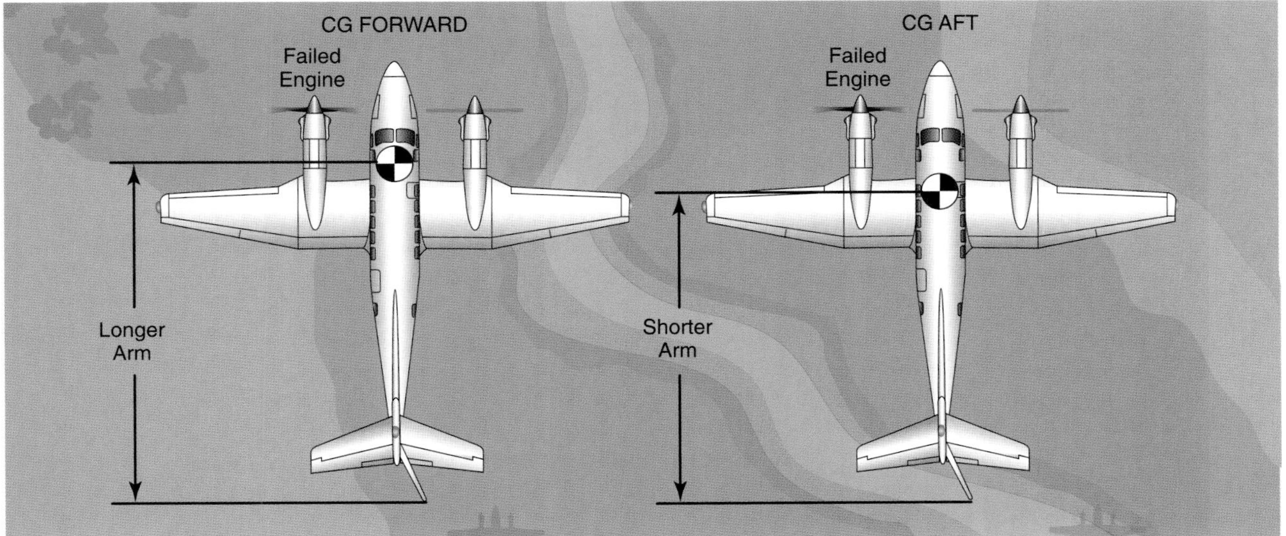

Figure 6-64. By asking your student to diagram the influence that CG location has on V_{MC}, you are able to evaluate their understanding of this concept.

ZERO FUEL WEIGHT

On some airplanes, a **zero fuel weight** is established to limit the ratio of loads between the fuselage and wings. This is a concept that your students may not have encountered in their single-engine experience. It may be difficult for them to grasp the idea that the airplane cabin can be overloaded even though the overall weight of the aircraft is below certification limits. The purpose of zero fuel weight is to prevent this type of situation from happening.

One way to explain this concept to students is to point out that the bending moment on the wings increases as the load carried in the fuselage increases. This means that the distribution of the load also may limit the total load the airplane can carry. For example, 2,000 pounds may be a safe load if 1,400 were carried in the fuselage and 600 pounds were carried in the wings. However, a distribution with 1,600 pounds in the fuselage and 400 pounds in the wings might exceed zero fuel weight. Make sure your students understand that the total of the basic empty weight and the payload, including passengers, baggage, and cargo, must not exceed the zero fuel weight. Any weight in excess of this amount must be usable fuel. [Figure 6-65]

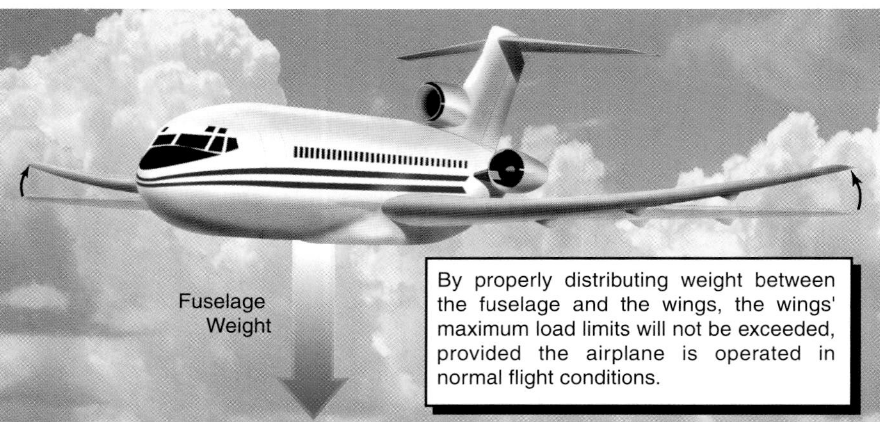

Figure 6-65. Some multi-engine students transition into aircraft with established zero fuel weights. An explanation of this concept helps them make the upgrade more easily.

SINGLE-ENGINE CEILINGS

Your students may not realize how much the operating altitudes of multi-engine airplanes are lowered during single-engine flight. The engine loss reduces total thrust available, resulting in corresponding reductions of service ceiling and absolute ceiling. [Figure 6-66]

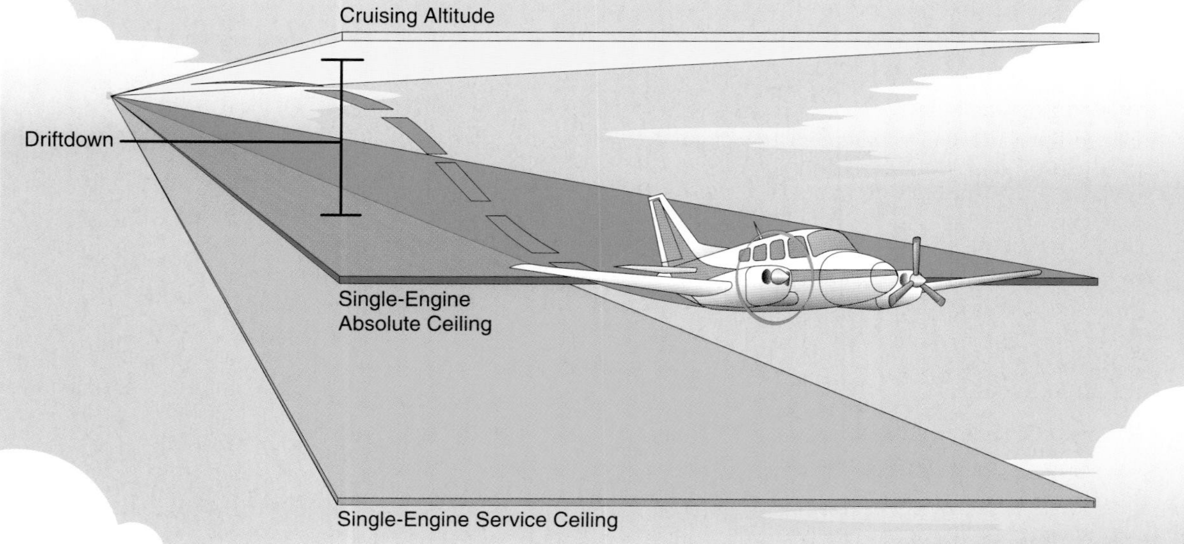

Figure 6-66. A term some multi-engine students may not be familiar with is driftdown. This concept can be used to help explain the single-engine absolute ceiling and single-engine service ceiling.

SINGLE-ENGINE SERVICE CEILING

The **single-engine service ceiling** is the maximum density altitude at which the single-engine best rate-of-climb airspeed (V_{YSE}) produces a 50 f.p.m. rate of climb. You can explain to your students that the ability to climb 50 f.p.m. in calm air is necessary simply to maintain level flight for long periods in turbulent air. This ceiling assumes the airplane is at maximum certificated weight in the clean configuration, the critical engine (if appropriate) is inoperative, and the propeller is feathered. In comparison, the multi-engine service ceiling is the density altitude at which the best rate-of-climb airspeed (V_Y) will produce a 100 f.p.m. rate of climb at maximum certificated weight in the clean configuration.

SINGLE-ENGINE ABSOLUTE CEILING

The **single-engine absolute ceiling** is the density altitude that the airplane is capable of reaching and maintaining with the critical engine feathered and the other at maximum power. This assumes that the airplane is at maximum weight and in the clean configuration, flying in smooth air. This is also the density altitude at which V_{XSE} and V_{YSE} are the same airspeed. Students should understand that if you are above this altitude and the engine fails, you will inevitably descend until you reach the equivalent density altitude conditions. Also, if you are in turbulent conditions, you may continue to descend until you reach the single-engine service ceiling because you will need the capability of climbing 50 f.p.m. in order to sustain level flight.

INTEGRATING DECISION MAKING IN MULTI-ENGINE TRAINING

One of the things you can do to develop better decision-making skills with your multi-engine students is to discuss and analyze accident statistics, so they can better assess the risks of multi-engine flight operations. According to the National Transportation Safety Board, the fatal accident rate for multi-engine airplanes has consistently declined since 1978. This encouraging trend indicates that multi-engine instructors and their students are achieving higher levels of proficiency. However, there is still room for improvement, especially regarding engine-out flight operations.

ACCIDENT STATISTICS

A number of studies have been conducted which analyze accidents caused by engine failure. One such study concluded that engine failure or malfunction accounted for 8% of all fatal accidents in single-engine airplanes. On the other hand, engine failure accounted for 25% of all twin-engine fatal accidents, or more than 3 times the rate for single-engine airplanes.

Another study analyzed 1,768 accidents involving piston- and turboprop-powered twins over a 5-year period. Some 69% of these accidents involved pilot error. As a flight instructor, there is little you can do to improve the operational reliability of aircraft engines. However, you can affect the safety of twin-engine flying through better decision-making training, particularly in regard to engine-out situations.

PREFLIGHT AND TAKEOFF BRIEFINGS

One of the most effective things you can do to enhance the safety of engine-out operations is to always start with a thorough preflight briefing with your students. One of the areas you should emphasize involves the decision-making process you want the student to follow in the event of an actual engine-out emergency. You should thoroughly brief your students as to what role they will play and what functions they will be expected to perform in this situation.

Multi-engine training operations also can be made safer by conducting a **takeoff briefing** covering both normal and emergency procedures just prior to taxiing onto the runway. Among other things, this enables your students to be better prepared to handle engine failures during the various phases of the takeoff profile. This takeoff briefing should review appropriate actions for an engine failure prior to V_{MC}, before the landing gear is retracted, and after the airplane is climbing in the clean configuration. Insist that your students complete this review during every lesson so it becomes a permanent part of their pretakeoff routine. Emphasize that this is not just a training procedure; your students should accomplish this review prior to every multi-engine flight.

As you know, it is possible to have a combination of aircraft loading and temperature conditions which results in the engine-out service ceiling being lower than the airport's density altitude. It's interesting to note that Part 91 does not prohibit takeoff under these conditions. However, students should realize that if an engine failure occurs after takeoff, they have lost virtually all of the flexibility that a twin offers. In this case, they may not be much better off than the single-engine pilot with an engine failure on takeoff. Under these extreme conditions, it is wise to either delay the takeoff until conditions improve, or reduce their payload. [Figure 6-67]

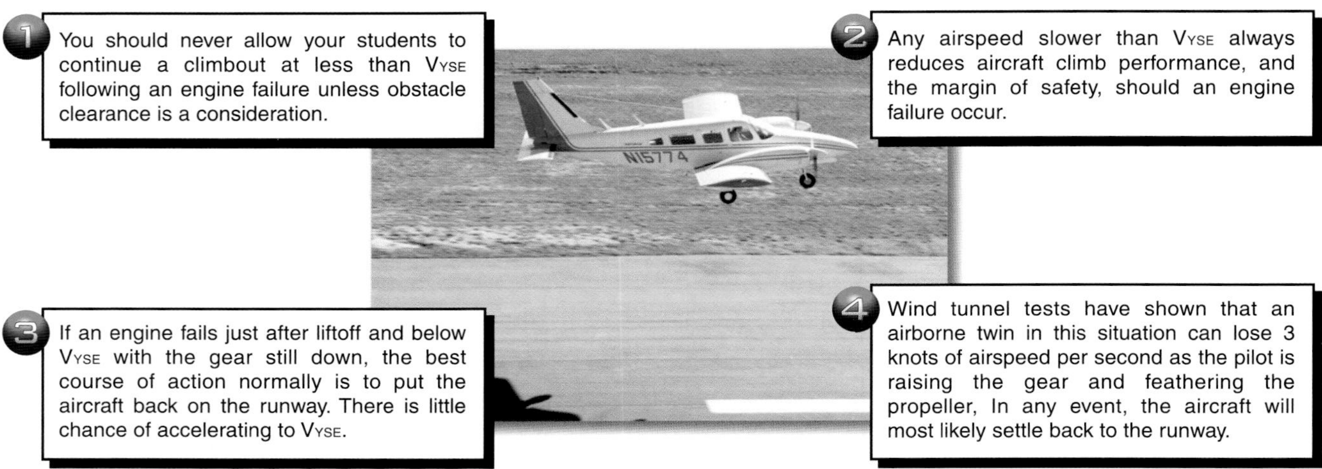

Figure 6-67. Using their knowledge and understanding of engine-out performance, your students should develop a definite plan of action for every takeoff, especially for the decisions they must make in the event of an engine failure.

INSTRUMENT-RATED MULTI-ENGINE APPLICANTS

If your instrument-rated students want to be able to fly under IFR in a twin, they must demonstrate proficiency in this area during the practical test. Specifically, the PTS requires that certain tasks be accomplished using instrument references. [Figure 6-68]

Figure 6-68. An important point for your students to understand is that if they perform any of the instrument maneuvers unsatisfactorily, they fail the entire practical test. They cannot revert to the "VFR only" option once they decide to test for instrument privileges. On the other hand, if they elect not to do these maneuvers prior to the test, their multi-engine privileges will be limited to VFR only.

One of the problems you may encounter is that many of your multi-engine students have not maintained their instrument proficiency. In this case, you should help them regain their skills before attempting to instruct them in multi-engine instrument flight. If possible, begin with a ground trainer, and then move to a high-performance, single-engine aircraft. This keeps the cost of their training down, while avoiding the frustration of trying to accomplish neglected tasks in an unfamiliar type of airplane. As their proficiency improves, gradually increase the airspeeds for various maneuvers, especially instrument approaches, as close as practical to those of the multi-engine airplane they will use.

SUMMARY CHECKLIST

✓ For the particular airplane to be flown, you need to have at least five hours of pilot-in-command time in the specific make and model.

✓ Multi-engine systems vary widely, so it is important that you cover material specific to the airplane used for training. Referring to the POH helps to organize this portion of ground training.

✓ With more components to support, multi-engine electrical systems are larger and more complex than those of single-engine airplanes. Also, multi-engine airplanes have more than one engine to produce the electrical power needed.

✓ Some multi-engine airplanes used in training have complex fuel systems, and the use of multiple tanks and transferring of fuel may be new to your students.

✓ In order to reduce the amount of noise within the cabin and provide a better learning environment for your students, you need to cover propeller synchronization.

✓ Since the takeoff and initial climb phases of flight are often critical in terms of single-engine performance, your students must realize the inoperative engine must be promptly identified, verified, and the propeller feathered.

✓ Even if your students do not train in airplanes equipped with accumulators, they should understand that these devices store a limited amount of oil under pressure after the engine is no longer running.

✓ Impress upon your students that an engine failure in a multi-engine airplane can have profound effects on its aerodynamic characteristics and significantly reduce its controllability and performance.

✓ To alleviate the sideslip of the airplane, your students must apply bank in the opposite direction. This creates a condition known as zero sideslip.

✓ For multi-engine airplanes, the critical engine is the engine that would have the most adverse affect on controllability and climb performance if it were to fail. Your students need to understand this concept even if their training airplane has counter-rotating propellers.

✓ A way to eliminate engine-out asymmetrical thrust and asymmetrical drag is the centerline thrust design. By mounting the engines along the fuselage centerline, directional control problems of the conventional twin following an engine failure are eliminated.

✓ If you can indoctrinate your students with the knowledge that drag is their primary concern in engine-out situations, they are more likely to become safe multi-engine pilots.

- ✓ Emphasize to your students that published V_{MC} and actual V_{MC} are seldom the same value. This is because current conditions are rarely identical to the conditions used in certification tests.
- ✓ When discussing V_{YSE}, or blue line speed, it is important to make your students understand that this is the airspeed that results in optimum engine-out performance.
- ✓ Accelerate-stop distance is the amount of runway required under existing conditions to accelerate the airplane to a speed designated by the manufacturer, experience an engine failure at that point, immediately discontinue the takeoff, and stop the airplane on the remaining runway.
- ✓ The accelerate-go distance chart tells your students whether or not they can continue the takeoff and climb to clear a 50-foot obstacle following an engine failure at the takeoff decision speed.
- ✓ Your students should be aware of how adjusting the center of gravity affects V_{MC}. As the airplane pivots around this point, the distance between the center of gravity and the rudder governs how effective the rudder will be in facilitating directional control.
- ✓ On some airplanes, a zero fuel weight is established to limit the ratio of loads between the fuselage and wings.
- ✓ The single-engine service ceiling is the maximum density altitude at which V_{YSE} produces a 50 f.p.m. rate of climb. The single-engine absolute ceiling is the density altitude that the airplane is capable of reaching and maintaining with the critical engine feathered and the other at maximum power.
- ✓ Multi-engine training operations also can be made safer by conducting a takeoff briefing covering both normal and emergency procedures just prior to taxiing onto the runway.
- ✓ If your instrument-rated students want to be able to fly under IFR in a twin, they must demonstrate proficiency in this area during the practical test.

KEY TERMS

Multi-Engine Systems

Propeller Synchronization

Accumulators

Zero Sideslip

Critical Engine

Single-Engine Minimum Control Airspeed (V_{MC})

Centerline Thrust

V_{YSE}

V_{XSE}

V_{SSE}

Accelerate-Stop Distance

Accelerate-Go Distance

Zero Fuel Weight

Single-Engine Service Ceiling

Single-Engine Absolute Ceiling

Takeoff Briefing

QUESTIONS

1. How much time do you need in a multi-engine airplane in order to give instruction for a rating?

   A. 5 hours in multi-engine airplanes
   B. 5 hours in the particular make and model
   C. 15 hours in the particular make and model

2. True/False. Since there are two engines to support the electrical systems on multi-engine airplanes, these systems tend to be less complex than those on single-engine airplanes.

3. What technique may be used to reduce noise levels and vibration during multi-engine flight?

4. Describe as you would to your students the operation of an accumulator.

5. Select the type of control input your students must make to produce a zero sideslip condition.

   A. 5° of bank into the good engine
   B. Less than 5° of bank into the good engine, in most situations
   C. Zero bank angle, or wings level, with the ball centered on the inclinometer

6. Define the critical engine as you would to your students.

7. Select the aerodynamic issues that are resolved through the use of the centerline thrust design.

   A. Asymmetrical lift
   B. Engine overheating
   C. Asymmetrical thrust and drag

8. When is actual V_{MC} in a given situation equal to published V_{MC}?

   A. Never
   B. All the time
   C. When conditions are the same as those modeled during certification

9. How would you explain to your students the difference between an accelerate-stop distance chart and an accelerate-go distance chart?

10. True/False. On some airplanes, a zero fuel weight is established to limit the ratio of loads between the fuselage and wings.

11. Select the definition of the single-engine service ceiling.

    A. The maximum density altitude at which V_{YSE} produces a 50 f.p.m. rate of climb.
    B. The maximum density altitude at which V_{YSE} produces a 100 f.p.m. rate of climb.
    C. The density altitude an airplane is capable of reaching and maintaining with the critical engine feathered and the other at maximum power.

12. Your student wants to gain instrument privileges along with his multi-engine rating, so he plans to perform the appropriate tasks during the checkride. However, he fails to demonstrate adequately a single-engine instrument approach. May he elect to continue the checkride in pursuit of a VFR-only multi-engine rating?

SECTION D

MASTERING MULTI-ENGINE SKILLS

Working with pilots to master multi-engine flying requires an added level of skill from you, as a flight instructor. Although some of the techniques you have used teaching single-engine operations may carry over to these maneuvers, the multi-engine flight environment presents its own complexities and challenges. You need to remain vigilant while conducting multi-engine flight instruction, even though you generally mentor experienced pilots during this transition. It is up to you to convey the professionalism required to your students, so they may learn to operate multi-engine airplanes with confidence and precision.

This section is not intended to cover the multi-engine ground and flight operations to the depth required for a pilot to master each maneuver and procedure. Instead, you should use the following information primarily as a guideline for instructing multi-engine pilots. This section provides examples of specific teaching techniques, common student errors, and tips to aid you in making your students' flying experience a positive one. For detailed descriptions of multi-engine knowledge and maneuvers, you may refer your students to the *Multi-Engine Manual.*

AIRCRAFT FAMILIARIZATION

You should familiarize your students with the aircraft instruments, systems, and controls as soon as possible. Include both the exterior and interior components of the aircraft in your instruction. **In-cockpit ground training** allows your students to become acquainted with the location of instruments, switches, and controls which may be unfamiliar. Emphasize the propeller feather control, auto synchronization, induction air, de-icing and anti-icing equipment, oxygen and pressurization, and many other systems. Also, have your student physically move the fuel selectors, and point out any safety features that prevent improper fuel operations. [Figure 6-69]

Figure 6-69. You can have your students simulate various procedures in the cockpit while you are on the ground to help them gain familiarity with the airplane.

Centerline Thrust

One way to eliminate the hazards of engine-out operations with conventional twins is to fly multi-engine airplanes designed with centerline thrust. Since the engines are not displaced from the centerline, there is no velocity for minimum control (V_{MC}) but these aircraft have their own set of hazards.

Taxiing is usually accomplished with the front engine at idle. This reduces the chance of debris being thrown into the rear propeller when the front engine is under power. Teaching your student good operating habits can increase safety and reduce the possibility of damage to the aircraft. Also, power should be given to the rear engine first when initiating the takeoff roll. Once acceleration is noted, takeoff power should be applied to both engines and monitoring engine instruments should continue, so as to prevent an engine failure from going unnoticed at a critical phase of takeoff. Accident statistics show that loss of the rear engine has gone undetected by a number of pilots, resulting in the aircraft running out of runway before becoming airborne. Asymmetrical thrust and drag following engine failure with a conventional twin is not present with centerline thrust. In addition, the rear engine provides more than 50% of the thrust. The rear engine usually produces more power because it is placed in a position that has better induction air intake, making it the critical engine as far as performance is concerned.

PREFLIGHT

The preflight inspection is a good time to point out the unique characteristics of multi-engine airplanes. Be sure to allow yourself plenty of time to do a thorough preflight with your students. Obviously, this is a good opportunity to emphasize use of the checklist for all multi-engine operations, including preflight. During the preflight, you may point out to your students items specific to their training airplane. For example, if the airplane you are flying has counter-rotating propellers, the engine accessories, such as oil dipsticks and other inspection items, are not in the same location on the left and right engines.

STARTING ENGINES

It is easy for students who are adjusting to a new cockpit to fixate inside the aircraft when performing the engine start. Make sure they maintain awareness of what is going on outside the airplane, and ensure that the personnel and equipment on the ramp are well clear. Your students may not realize the increased prop blast generated by multi-engine aircraft, so caution them about this hazard from the start of their training.

TAXIING

During initial taxi operations, coach your students to use equal power on both engines and rely on the steerable nosewheel for directional control. This is important from the first power application through the entire taxi phase. Typically, your students may attempt to maintain equal power between the engines by throttle position. Instead, you should encourage them to use the engine tachometers, and emphasize that the use of asymmetrical power is a taxi technique to be used only during crosswind conditions or as an aid in reducing the turning radius. Point out that the disadvantages of using differential power include tire wear and side loading on the landing gear. The least desirable method of directional control is differential braking. Your students should understand that this technique also increases side loads and wear on both tires and brakes, and can easily result in brake overheating and subsequent failure.

TAKEOFF CONSIDERATIONS

As discussed in Chapter 6, Section C, multi-engine departures can be made safer by conducting a takeoff briefing, covering both normal and emergency procedures, just prior to taxiing onto the runway. Among other things, this enables your students to be better prepared to handle engine failures during the various phases of the takeoff profile.

When teaching your students to take off, make sure they bring the throttles up with a smooth and even motion. If an engine falters due to a rapid power application, directional control is difficult to maintain. A common error for many students is to allow the airplane to achieve an excessive amount of speed on the takeoff roll and departure climb. This may result from overconcentrating on engine instruments, improper trim control, or an inaccurate assessment of acceleration by your students. You need to take immediate action to prevent the formation of bad habits and emphasize the importance of precise airspeed control. From the beginning, inform your students that takeoff and climb is the most vulnerable phase of multi-engine operation and they should always be prepared for an engine failure. You may point out that the best indicators of engine trouble are the fuel flow meter and the EGT gauge. Manifold pressure gauges and tachometers are not as suitable for detecting engine trouble quickly. The possibility of an engine failure is another good reason to use all of the available runway, so emphasize this to your students.

You can demonstrate that the takeoff and climb is an orderly progression of events dependent upon precise airspeed control. Single-engine airplane pilots may not place enough importance on accurate airspeed control immediately following liftoff. Your multi-engine students must understand that the proper airspeed is critical, particularly in the event one engine loses power. Figure 6-70 shows the succession of critical airspeeds for the multi-engine takeoff and climb profile.

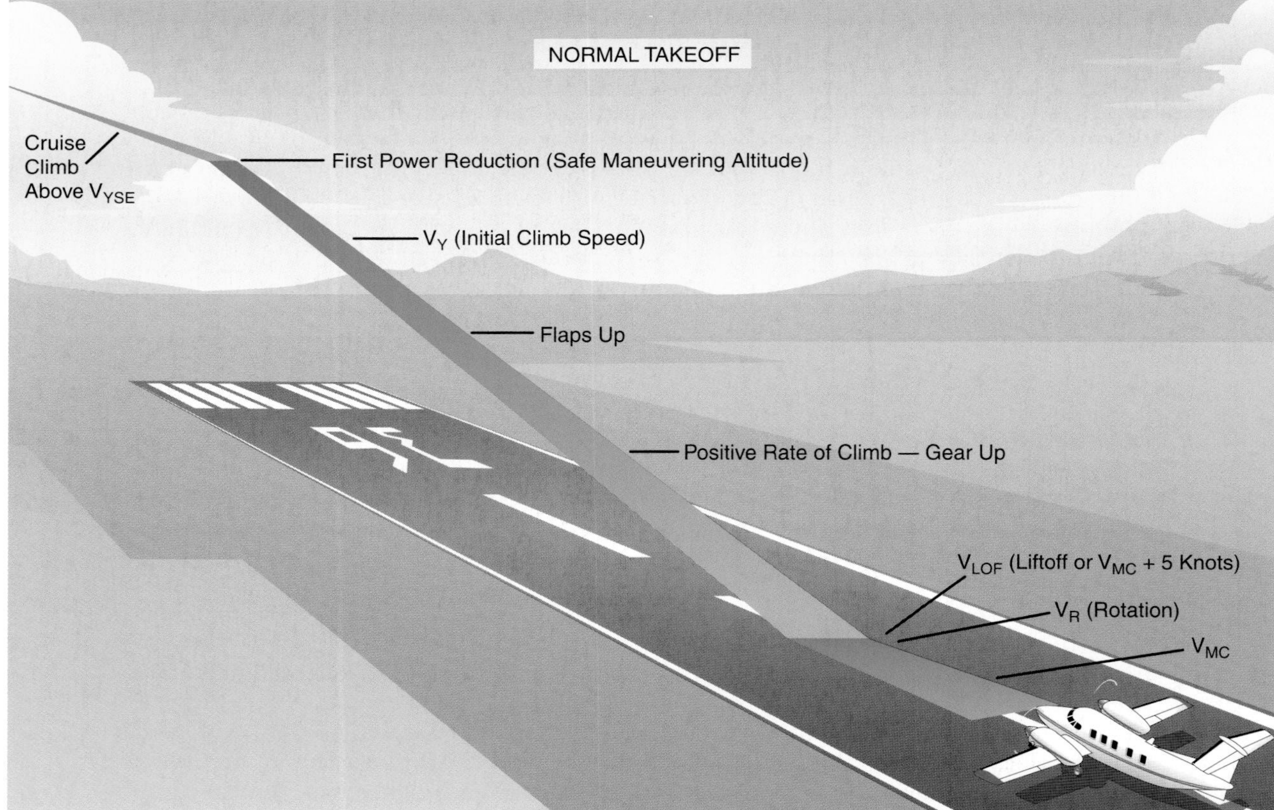

Figure 6-70. Explain to your students that the airspeed for rotation on takeoff must be appropriate to the individual airplane. The FAA recommends liftoff at V_{MC} + 5 knots, or the manufacturer's recommended liftoff airspeed.

Direct your students to retract the landing gear after a positive rate of climb has been established, or when it is no longer practical to land on the remaining runway. After the flaps are raised, the pitch attitude should allow the airplane to accelerate to the best all-engine rate-of-climb speed, V_Y. Your students should maintain their speed with takeoff power until a safe maneuvering attitude is attained.

MAXIMUM PERFORMANCE TAKEOFF

Your students should be fairly proficient with normal multi-engine takeoff procedures and have a good feel for the airplane before you demonstrate a **maximum performance takeoff**. They should also understand that precise airspeed control is imperative to their success. Have your students determine the speed for rotation and liftoff from the POH. If the manufacturer recommends speeds below V_{MC} for this maneuver, your students need to understand that the gain in performance is traded for controllability in the event of an engine failure.

Instruct your students to lift off at the recommended airspeed and allow the airplane to accelerate in ground effect until they have reached V_X or the recommended obstacle clearance speed, whichever is greater. Once clear of the obstacles, or if simulating an obstacle of 50 feet, aim for V_Y. Students typically accelerate beyond the proper airspeed when learning this maneuver. A helpful technique is to start applying back pressure 5 knots prior to rotation speed and stressing pitch attitude reference. [Figure 6-71]

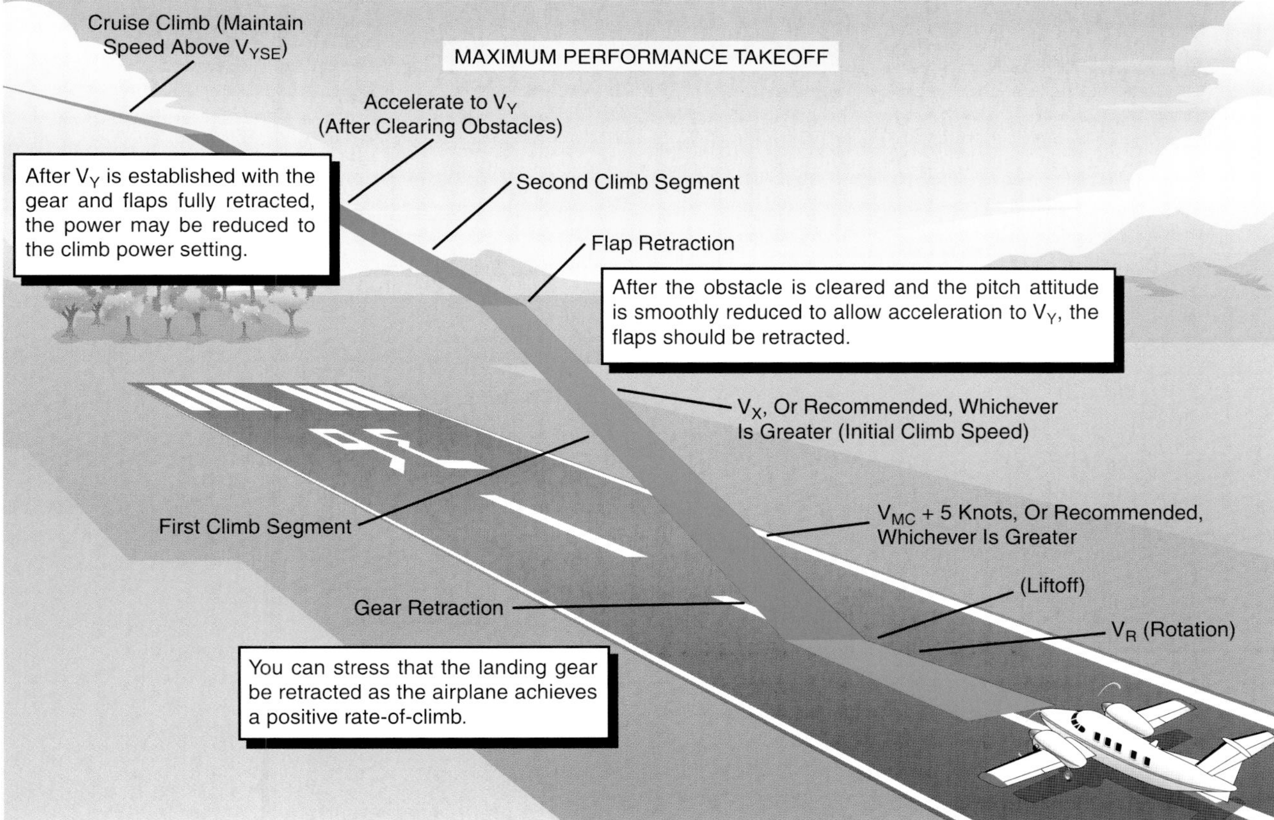

Figure 6-71. As a general rule, you can teach students that power should not be reduced for climb before the landing gear and flaps are fully retracted. This is based on the fact that maximum power should be available until the drag is eliminated, in the event one engine loses power.

Maximum performance takeoffs are subject to some other distinctive errors. Students commonly fail to position the airplane for maximum utilization of the available runway area. In addition, they frequently use the brakes improperly. [Figure 6-72]

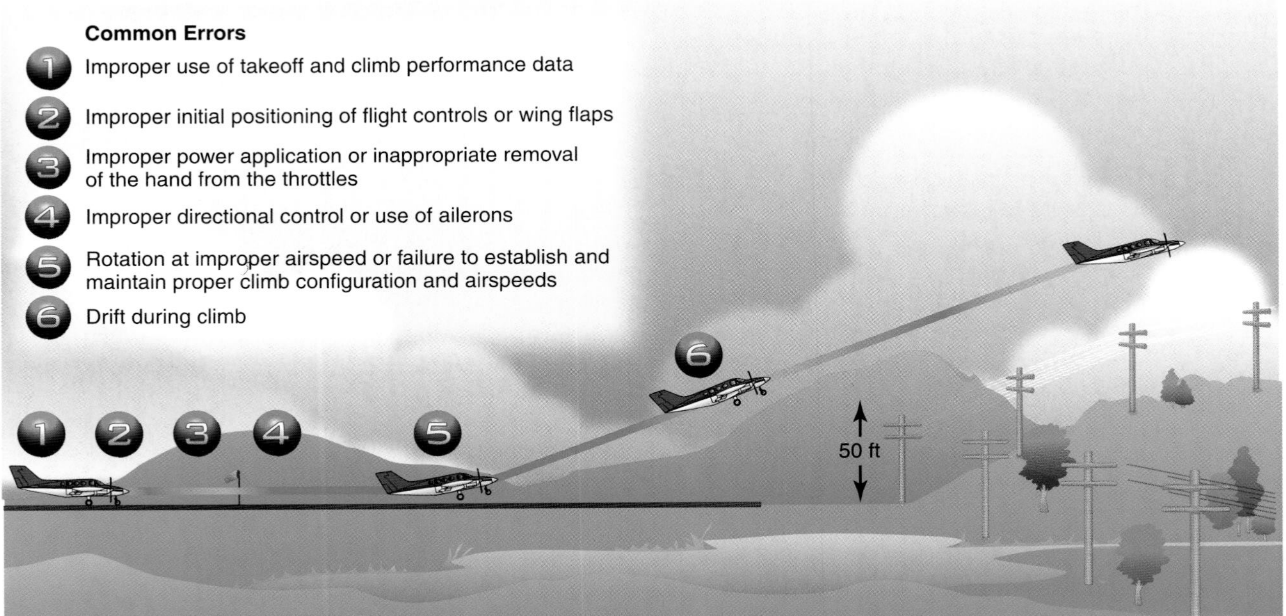

Figure 6-72. These are some of the most common student errors that apply to both normal and maximum performance takeoffs and climbs.

APPROACH AND LANDING

Emphasize the importance of establishing a stabilized power approach when students begin concentrated work with landings. The technique is most easily introduced at altitude where prolonged descents at different power settings and configurations can be established.

Your students should understand that, during a stabilized power approach, the power remains nearly constant and the drag created by the landing gear and flap extension produces the necessary rate of descent. Once the approach is established, minor power adjustments may be made, as necessary, to maintain the approach profile. Your students should realize that a power-off approach in the landing configuration results in a very steep approach attitude and an extremely high rate of descent. Following the exercise in stabilized power approaches, you may want to demonstrate a normal approach and landing. [Figure 6-73]

Some of the common student errors during traffic patterns include those that apply to both normal and maximum performance approaches and landings. The majority of difficulties your students may have are the product of not planning their entry into the traffic pattern. This makes it difficult for them to slow the airplane to the approach airspeed. If your students inadvertently use too high an airspeed in the pattern, they may be tempted to make large and erratic power changes. The excessive airspeed prevents the flaps and gear from being extended on schedule, and the final approach becomes too high, creating a steep approach angle, excessive rate of descent, and a high probability of a go-around. [Figure 6-74]

TEACHING SAFE GO-AROUND PROCEDURES

If you introduce the landing sequence at altitude, you may want to cover **go-arounds** at the same time. The advantage of practicing at altitude is that it gives your students more time to configure the airplane for an approach and landing and establish a stabilized

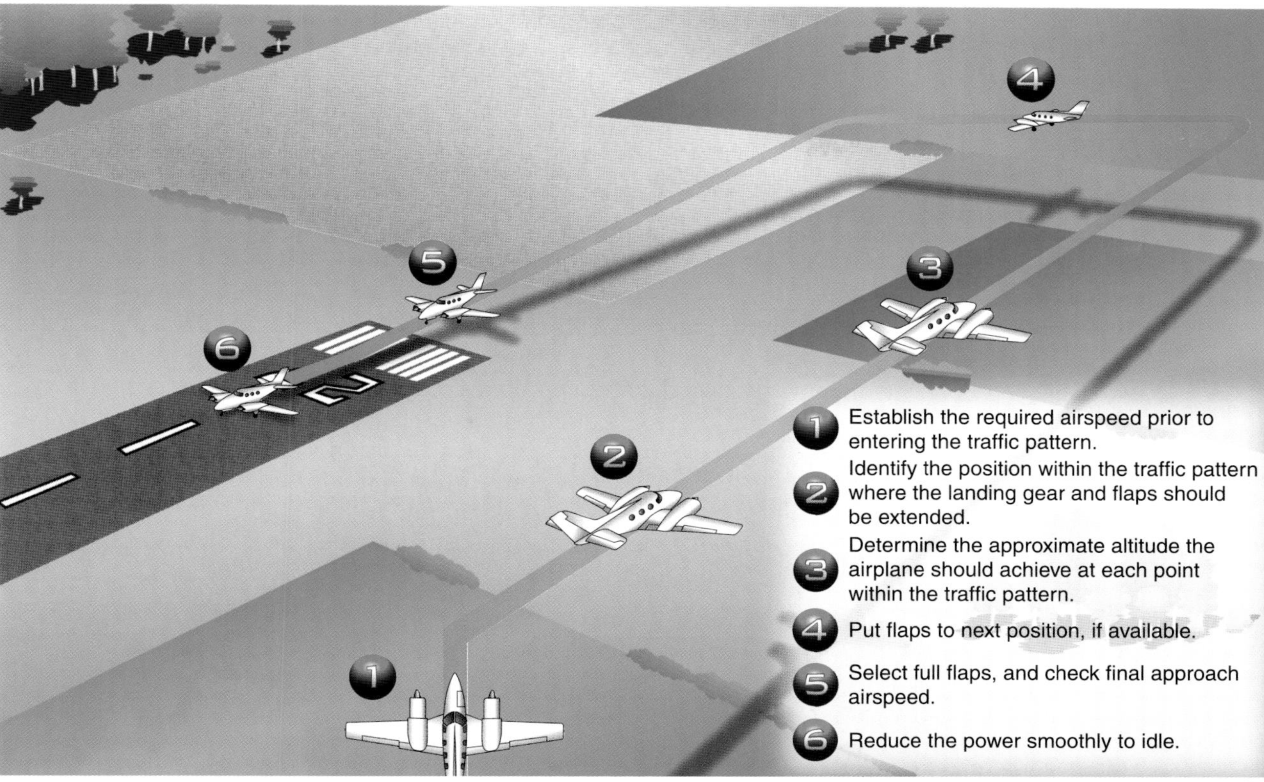

Figure 6-73. The approach and landing demonstration is designed to provide students with a plan of action to accomplish a stabilized approach. Students must fully understand that the landing approach actually begins prior to traffic pattern entry.

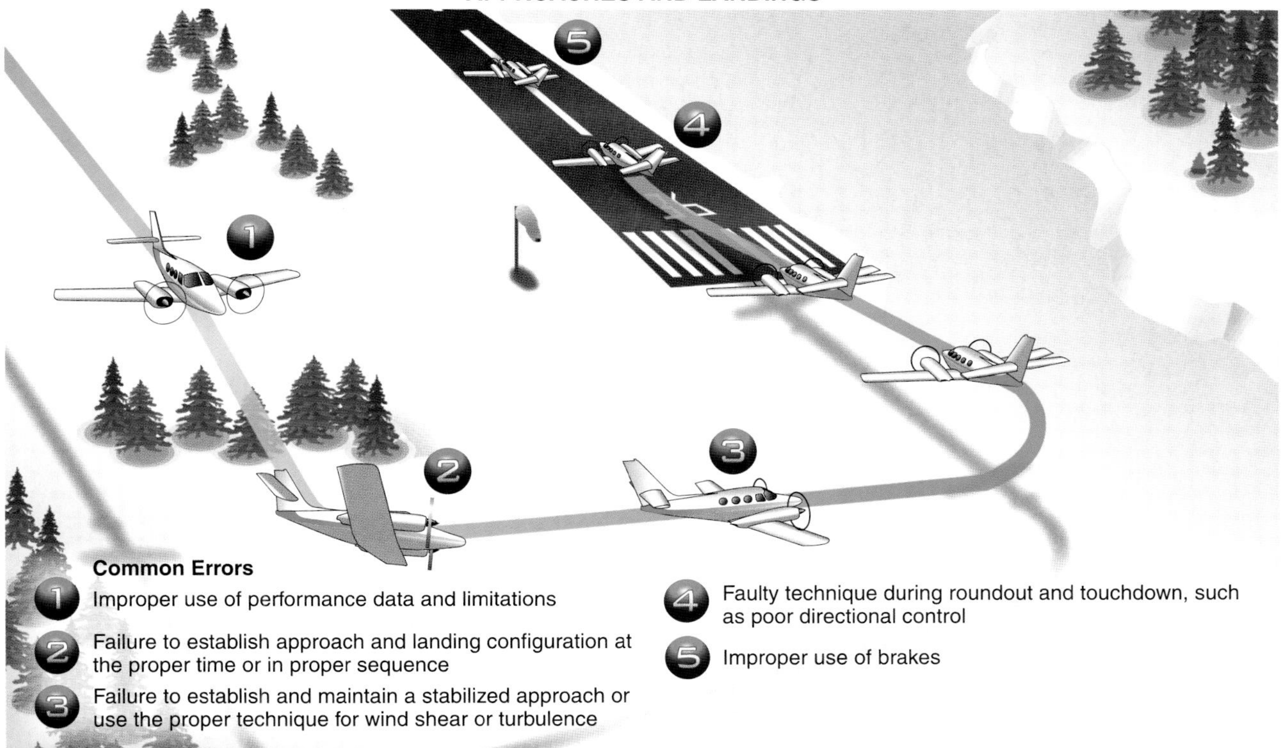

Figure 6-74. During maximum performance approaches and landings, students commonly display faulty technique in the use of power, wing flaps, and trim. Although these problems are typical, they are corrected easily through conscientious preflight and postflight briefings and student practice.

descent. Then, you can have your students initiate a go-around and reconfigure the airplane free from the distractions of the runway environment and conflicting traffic in the pattern. Normally, it is beneficial to your students to practice the sequence several times at altitude before doing it in the pattern. Make sure you discuss the go-around procedure outlined in the POH for the training airplane during the preflight briefing. This way, your students know the correct sequence for drag cleanup when initiating the go-around. You can tell them that most procedures require maximum power to be applied, followed by retracting the flaps to the takeoff setting. After a positive rate-of-climb is established, your students should retract the landing gear and the remaining flaps. If climb performance is not critical, you may advise them to leave the landing gear extended and retract the remaining flaps after a positive rate-of-climb is established. During the entire maneuver, your students should monitor the airplane's speed to ensure acceleration to the best rate-of-climb airspeed as rapidly as practical.

Discuss with your students the situations when a go-around is necessary in a multi-engine airplane. Generally, if the airplane has not touched down in the first third of the runway, you should advise your students to execute a go-around, and set up for another landing. The go-around also may be necessary when other aircraft are on the runway or when they feel uncomfortable with the approach due to incorrect procedures or unsafe conditions. [Figure 6-75]

GO-AROUNDS

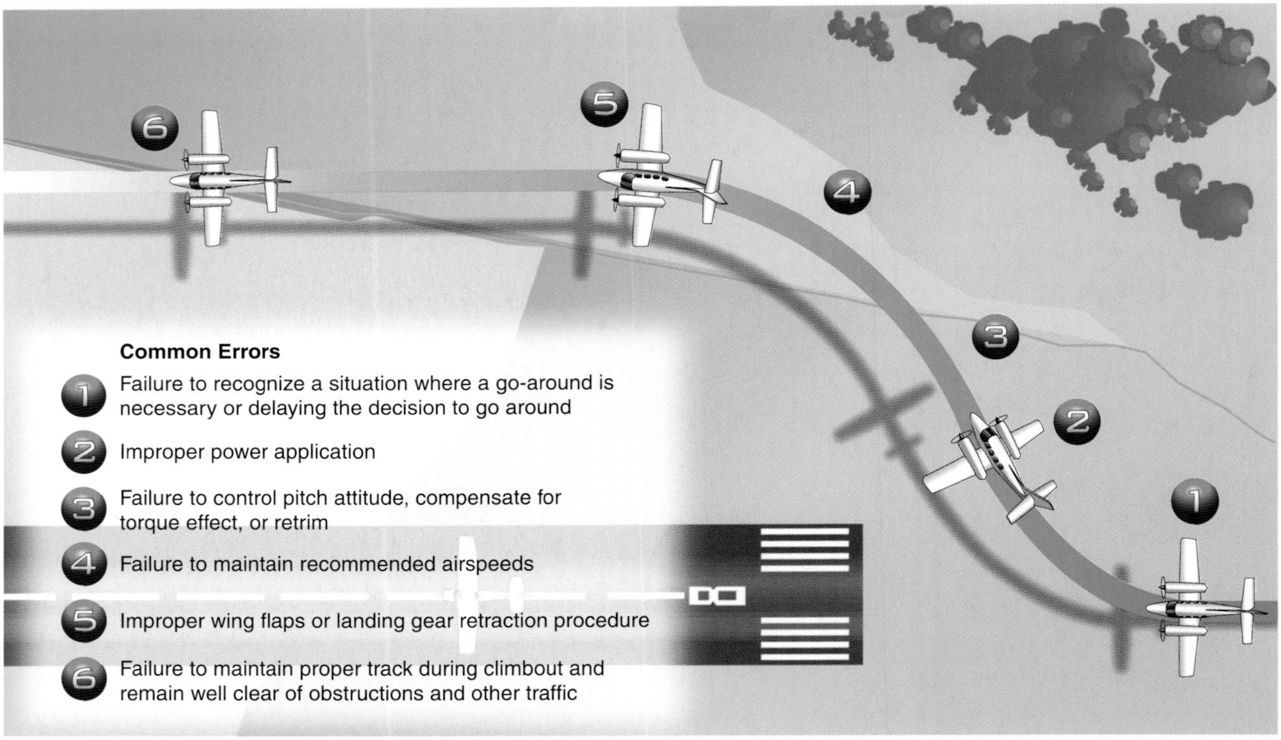

Common Errors

1. Failure to recognize a situation where a go-around is necessary or delaying the decision to go around
2. Improper power application
3. Failure to control pitch attitude, compensate for torque effect, or retrim
4. Failure to maintain recommended airspeeds
5. Improper wing flaps or landing gear retraction procedure
6. Failure to maintain proper track during climbout and remain well clear of obstructions and other traffic

Figure 6-75. The decision to make a go-around should be positive, and you should coach your students to make that decision before a critical situation develops. Once the decision has been made, it should be implemented without hesitation.

TEACHING MULTI-ENGINE MANEUVERS

When you review the private and the commercial multi-engine PTS with your students, you can go through all of the tasks you need to cover during the course of multi-engine instruction. You may notice that certain maneuvers are unique to this transition or require additional instructional knowledge when conducted in multi-engine airplanes.

STEEP TURNS

Practicing **steep turns** helps your students develop a feel for the airplane's heavy control response and an appreciation for proper trim technique. A well-executed steep turn is a smooth, coordinated, visual maneuver that requires an occasional cross-check of the instruments. The use of power is necessary to maintain a constant airspeed. Because of the load factors involved, this maneuver should not be performed above maneuvering speed.

Instruct your students to begin the maneuver on a cardinal heading at a constant airspeed and altitude. It may be helpful to identify a prominent reference point on the horizon that corresponds to your heading. Smoothly initiate a coordinated turn to the desired bank angle of 45° (±5°) for private pilot applicants, or at least 50° (±5°) for commercial training. Once the bank angle has been established, point out that a moderate amount of back pressure is required to maintain a constant altitude. You should encourage your students to use elevator trim to relieve control pressure. If they do not trim the airplane during the maneuver, the back pressure needed to maintain altitude is excessive. If your students trim the airplane for hands-off flight during a steep bank, an excessive amount of forward pressure is required to prevent a climb during the rollout. A good method to determine the proper amount of trim is to first trim the airplane for level flight at a 30° bank. Using the 30° trim setting during the steep bank should provide adequate control pressure relief throughout all phases of the maneuver.

Make your students aware that airspeed decreases as bank angle increases, and power is required to maintain a constant airspeed. You must emphasize that this is a visual maneuver, and primary focus should be outside the airplane. However, some airplanes lack adequate reference points to compare to the horizon, and brief glances at the instruments can help. [Figure 6-76]

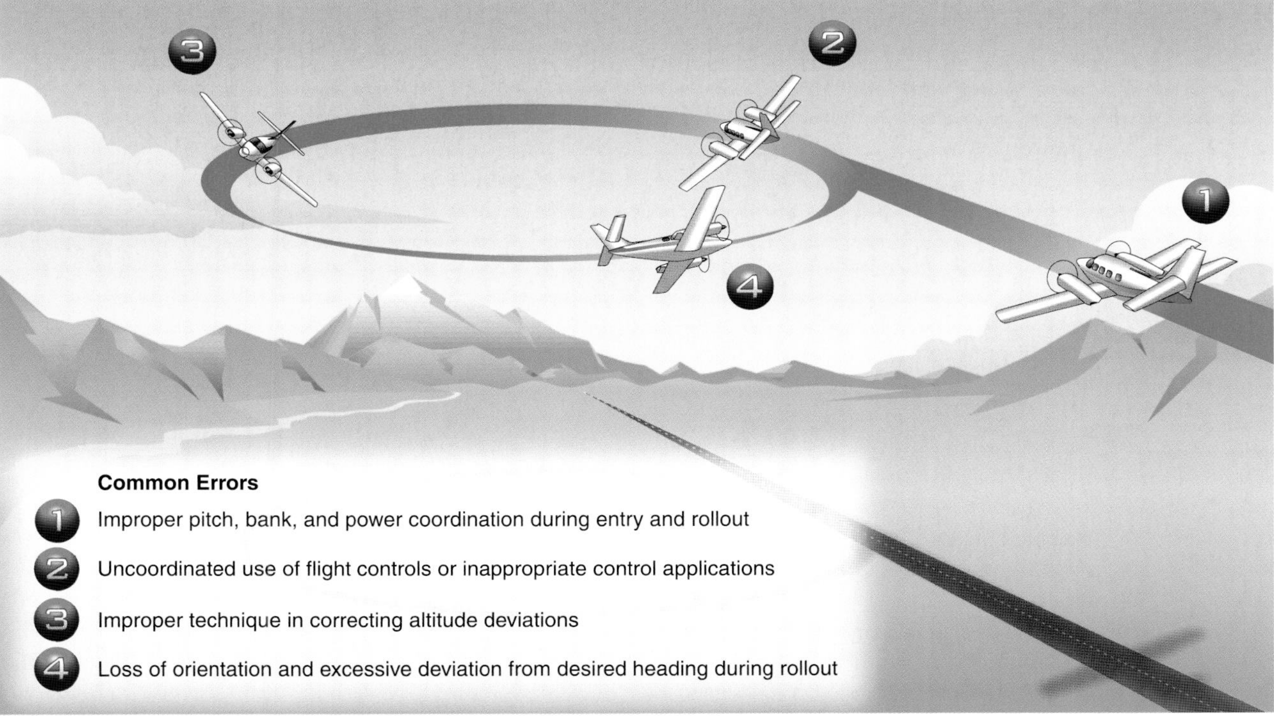

Figure 6-76. If the airplane starts to descend during the turn, make sure your students understand how to make the correction. Simply applying more back pressure only increases wing loading and stall speed, and ultimately tightens the turn. The proper method is to shallow the bank angle, adjust the altitude, and then reestablish the right bank angle.

As the airplane nears the predetermined heading, your students should initiate a smooth rollout to a wings-level attitude. A good general rule for them to follow is to lead the rollout by half of the bank angle. An example for a 50° bank would be to start the rollout 25° prior to the desired heading. As your students gain proficiency, they can practice a turn in one direction followed by a turn in the opposite direction as one continuous maneuver.

MANEUVERING DURING SLOW FLIGHT

Your students should understand how slow flight relates directly to critical flight situations, such as go-arounds and landings, and provides the opportunity to explore multi-engine handling at slow airspeeds. Your students develop airspeed control through practicing this maneuver, and they learn the effects that flaps and the landing gear extension have on performance. You can point out that flight characteristics and controllability during slow flight are directly affected by configuration, weight, CG, maneuvering loads, angle of bank, and power. Your students should learn to perform the maneuver at an airspeed of 1.2 V_{S1}, with an airspeed tolerance of ±5 knots. They should be able to execute the maneuver in straight-and-level flight and during level turns. In addition, the maneuver should be performed with various flap settings in both cruising and landing configurations.

To begin the maneuver, have your students reduce the airspeed by retarding the throttle, leaving the landing gear and flaps retracted. To prevent a descent, they should gradually increase back pressure on the yoke to maintain altitude. As the desired airspeed approaches, they need to add enough power to stabilize the airspeed and altitude. Once stabilized and trimmed, have your students practice medium banked turns in both directions.

Prior to introducing the flaps and landing gear, you should emphasize how the additional drag affects airspeed: the flaps increase induced drag and the landing gear increases parasite drag. Therefore, more power is required to maintain altitude and airspeed. Have your students introduce the first increment of flaps, and note that additional power needs to be added and the airplane should be retrimmed. Introduce the next increment of flaps, followed by the landing gear. Have your students note the power required to maintain altitude and airspeed with each component extended. To complete the maneuver, have your students reverse the process and make power reductions to maintain a constant airspeed and altitude until you are back at slow flight in the clean configuration. Since larger and heavier airplanes respond more slowly while maneuvering during slow flight, this maneuver should be performed at altitudes sufficiently high to allow recoveries to be completed at least 3,000 feet above the ground. [Figure 6-77]

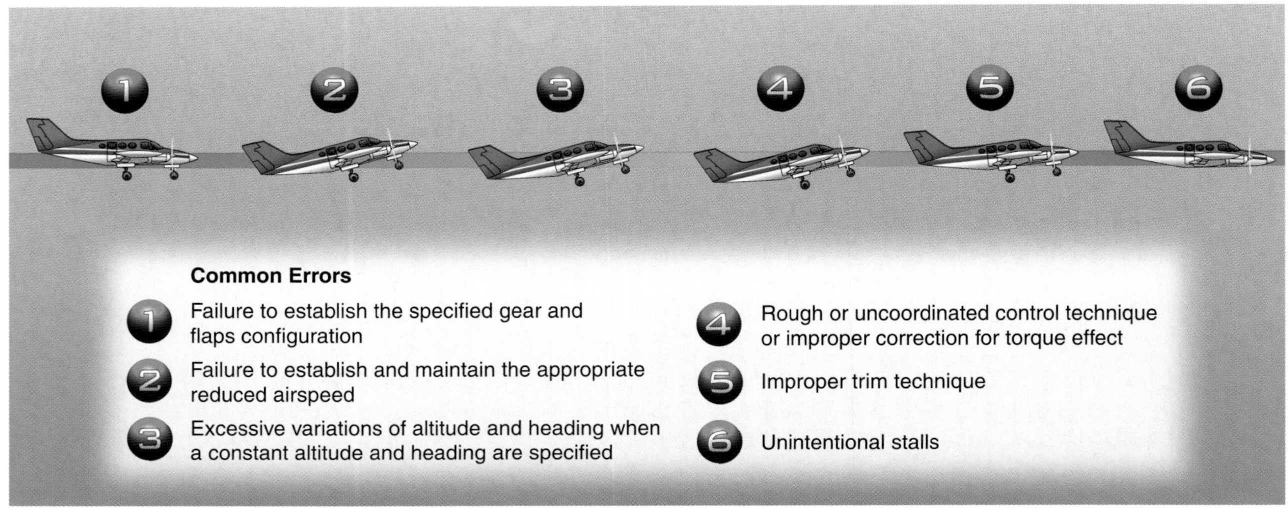

Figure 6-77. Your students should perform the entire exercise with minimal changes in altitude and airspeed as proficiency is gained.

STALLS

The PTS have eliminated full **stalls** in multi-engine airplanes using high power settings, because the high angles of attack required to induce a stall can result in a loss of controlled flight. This practice also stresses the airframe because of the gyroscopic principles acting on the propellers. Abrupt pitch attitude changes produce stress on the airplane's engines and wings, because the propellers resist the rapid transition in pitch attitude. For these reasons, you may need to instruct your students to initiate the maneuver at a reduced power setting that is uniform between both engines. [Figure 6-78]

Figure 6-78. For the practical test, your students will be expected to perform power-on and power-off stalls in multi-engine airplanes in these configurations.

The entry altitude should allow recoveries to be completed no lower than 3,000 feet AGL. The recovery should be initiated at the first indication of buffeting or degradation of control effectiveness by applying slight forward pressure to increase airspeed and reduce the wing's angle of attack. Multi-engine airplanes can produce high sink rates, so recoveries should be made within 50 feet of entry altitude. Inducing a stall with one engine inoperative and the other developing working power is very dangerous. This is because a spin will most likely develop. [Figure 6-79]

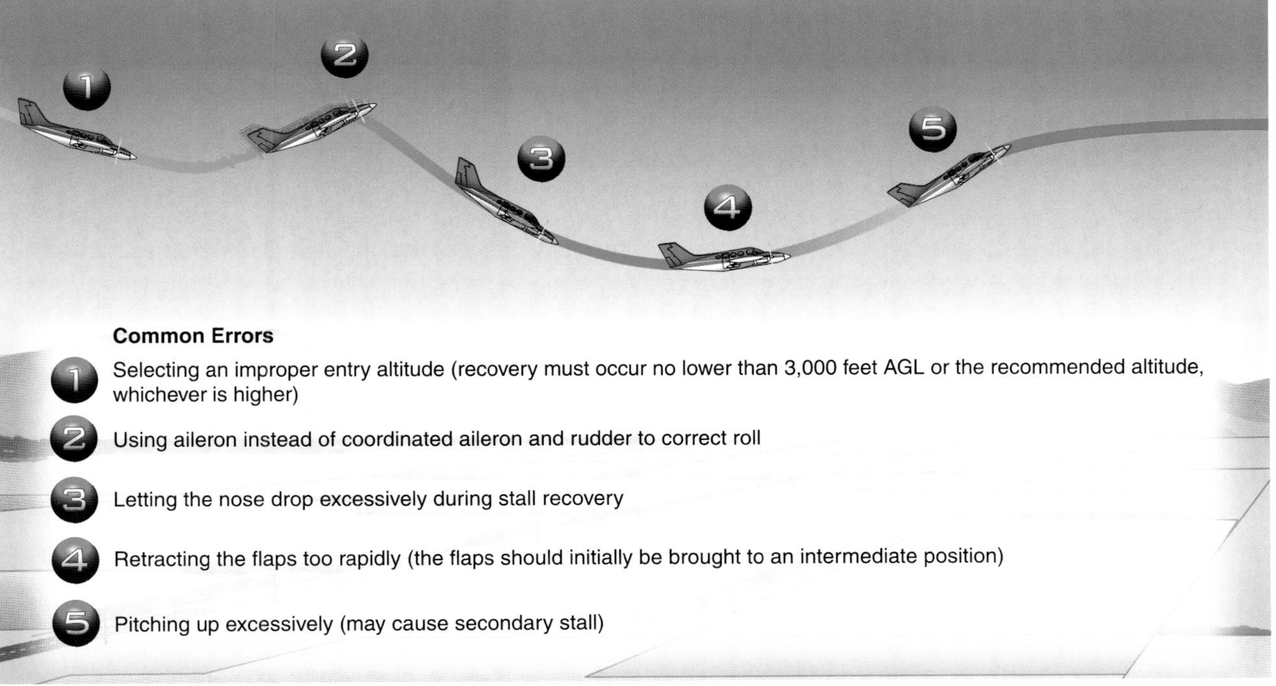

Figure 6-79. You should take extra time to caution your students on the differences between performing stalls in single-engine and multi-engine airplanes.

To make the training as realistic as possible, you can give your students a ground track to fly that simulates a traffic pattern while executing approach to landing stalls. Direct your students to extend the flaps and landing gear, while slowing the airplane to V_{YSE} on the downwind leg of the simulated traffic pattern. [Figure 6-80]

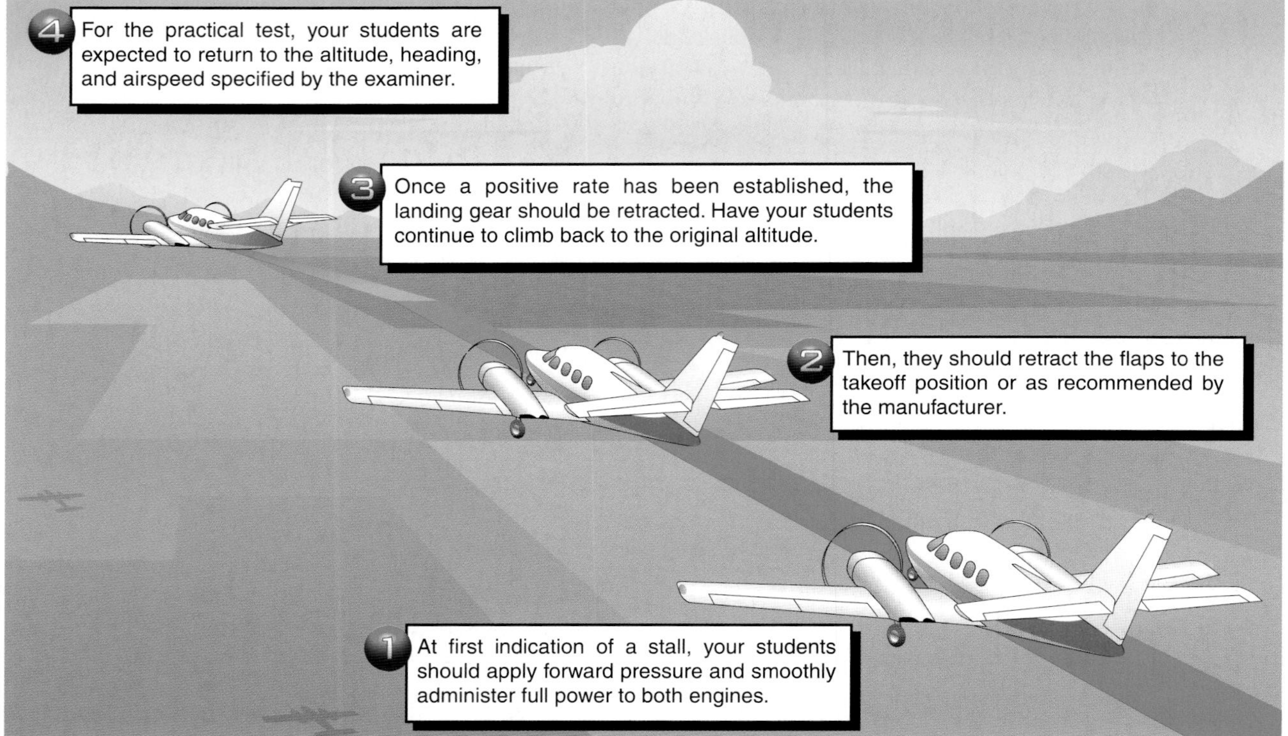

Figure 6-80. Simulate an approach to the base leg of the traffic pattern. Instruct your student to reduce the power and establish a medium bank. Rather than allowing the airplane to descend as normal, have your student apply steady back pressure to maintain altitude as the airspeed decreases.

EMERGENCY OPERATIONS

Before you begin emergency operations, your students should have mastered multi-engine airwork and traffic pattern procedures and be completely familiar with the handling characteristics of the airplane. The emergency operations associated with the multi-engine rating normally focus on engine-out operations.

Prior to introducing **engine-out procedures** and **maneuvers**, you need to conduct a thorough ground training session on the techniques and theories of flight with one engine inoperative. It should be obvious that your student's success is totally dependent on an understanding of the material prior to the flight lesson. The briefing should include the subject matter of the lesson as well as the aerodynamics of engine-out operations, the handling characteristics of the airplane, and engine-out performance considerations.

INTRODUCTION TO ENGINE-OUT OPERATIONS

It is important that your student's first experience with engine-out flight does not contain an element of surprise, since surprise very commonly creates anxiety and tension that continues throughout the remaining lessons, retarding the learning process. Specifically, your student should understand that the first indication of an engine failure is the resultant yaw and roll, which is always in the direction of the inoperative engine. In addition, the control application necessary to stop yaw provides a second method of determining the inoperative engine because the foot which is not applying rudder pressure is on the same side as the inoperative engine. [Figure 6-81]

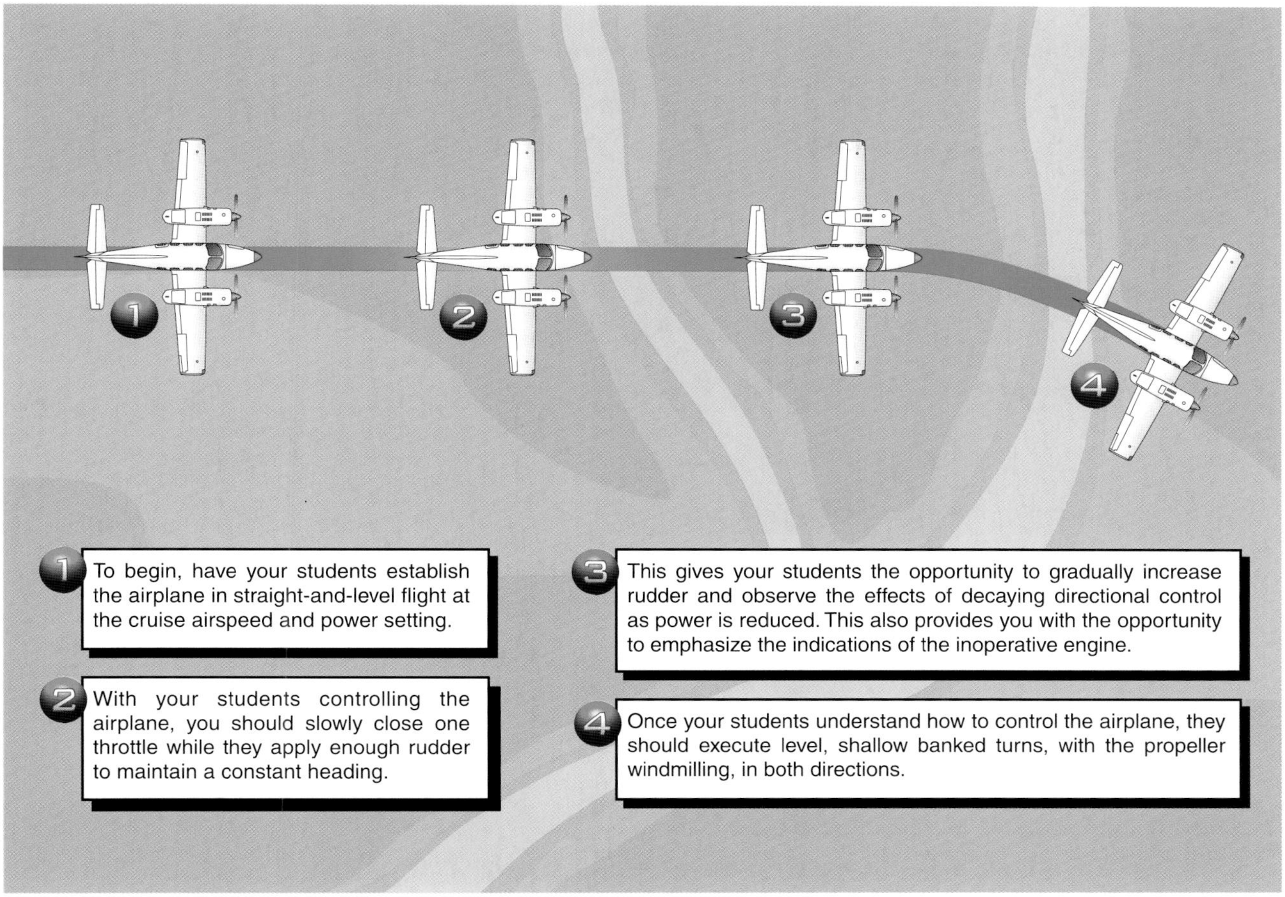

1 To begin, have your students establish the airplane in straight-and-level flight at the cruise airspeed and power setting.

2 With your students controlling the airplane, you should slowly close one throttle while they apply enough rudder to maintain a constant heading.

3 This gives your students the opportunity to gradually increase rudder and observe the effects of decaying directional control as power is reduced. This also provides you with the opportunity to emphasize the indications of the inoperative engine.

4 Once your students understand how to control the airplane, they should execute level, shallow banked turns, with the propeller windmilling, in both directions.

Figure 6-81. This demonstration familiarizes your students with the control pressure required, and with the airplane's handling characteristics when one engine is inoperative.

SIMULATED ENGINE-OUT MANEUVERING

Give your students the opportunity to maneuver the airplane with only one engine producing power. This is most easily accomplished by requiring your students to retract the landing gear and flaps and establish the zero-thrust power setting published by the airplane manufacturer. In this configuration, they should practice engine-out climbs, descents, and climbing and descending turns, using appropriate trim. Through this demonstration, your students should learn the significance of V_{YSE}, specifically that any airspeed above or below V_{YSE} reduces engine-out climb performance. In addition, if the airplane is not capable of maintaining altitude with one engine inoperative, the use of V_{YSE} produces the minimum rate of descent.

You should encourage the use of a predetermined rate of descent, not to exceed 500 f.p.m., at a constant airspeed during the instruction of engine-out descents. This technique requires your student to reduce power on the operating engine rather than simply lowering the pitch altitude. In addition, it is beneficial for your student to extend the landing gear using various increments of flaps during the descent, to demonstrate the effect on power requirements during level-off.

ENGINE-OUT PROCEDURES

When your students are able to control the airplane on one engine, you can introduce engine-out emergency procedures. It is important that the procedures be executed in strict accordance with the manufacturer's recommendations published in the POH. In addition, emphasize that the procedure should be executed in an unhurried, methodical, and accurate manner, as hasty decisions are likely to result in a serious compromise of safety. To ensure the procedures are correctly executed, require your students to commit the initial steps of the engine failure checklist to memory prior to the flight lesson. Emphasize to your students that the checklist procedures to be followed after an engine failure depend upon where the engine failure occurs. For example, during cruise flight, your students may attempt to restart the engine, while immediately after takeoff, checklists normally require the inoperative engine to be feathered immediately. [Figure 6-82]

ENGINE FAILURE AND SECURING PROCEDURES

1. Maintain directional control with rudder and aileron.
2. **Maintain V_{YSE} as a minimum speed.**
3. Apply maximum power by moving the mixtures, props, and throttles full forward.
4. Reduce the drag by retracting the gear and flaps. **Maintain V_{YSE}.**
5. Check auxiliary fuel boost pumps — ON.
6. Check that the fuel selector is in the proper position. **Maintain V_{YSE}.**
7. Identify the inoperative engine by using the *"idle foot, idle engine"* test.
8. Verify the inoperative engine by closing the appropriate throttle.
9. Feather the propeller by moving the propeller lever to the feather position.
10. Move the mixture control to idle cutoff.
11. Trim to relieve excess control pressures. **Maintain V_{YSE}.**
12. Secure the inoperative engine by using the following steps:
    A. Fuel selector — OFF
    B. Auxiliary boost pump — OFF
    C. Magneto switches — OFF
    D. Alternator — OFF
    E. Cowl flaps — CLOSED
13. Review checklist. **Maintain V_{YSE}.**

Figure 6-82. You should stress that the engine-out emergency checklist ultimately provides for maximum available power, elimination of drag, and securing the inoperative engine. You can analyze the manufacturer's checklist with your students in order to teach the correct sequence for completing the items.

Be sure your students understand that the first priority following an engine failure is to maintain control of the airplane at V_{YSE}. At the same time control of the airplane is being maintained, the mixtures should be advanced to full rich, the propellers moved to high r.p.m., and both throttles increased to maximum power. This procedure ensures maximum power from the operating engine, regardless of which engine is inoperative. Next, your students should increase the performance of the airplane by retracting the landing gear and flaps to eliminate drag. Now, your students can devote attention to first identifying, then verifying, and finally feathering the inoperative engine. During most training exercises, your students will retard the propeller control to the detent and you will establish a zero thrust power setting to simulate a feathered condition.

Although your students should have an accurate indication of which engine has failed by the direction of yaw and rudder displacement, you should emphasize the need for verifying which engine is inoperative. Generally, this is accomplished by retarding the throttle of the suspected failed engine. Your students should understand that, if the correct engine has been selected and has completely failed, there is no change in performance or in the amount of rudder pressure needed to counteract yaw. However, if the engine is developing partial power, the asymmetrical thrust condition increases. If the incorrect engine is selected, the asymmetrical thrust decreases. After this final confirmation, your students may feather the propeller, and shut down and secure the engine. This normally entails placing the propeller lever in the feather position and the mixture control in idle-cut-off. Once the checklist is complete, you should advise your students that they should plan to land as soon as practical.

AFTER ENGINE SHUTDOWN

Remind your students to pay close attention to the operating engine. The combination of reduced airspeed and additional power demanded from the engine may cause overheating problems. Therefore, the oil temperature, oil pressure, and cylinder head temperature

must be monitored and kept in the normal operating ranges. Explain to your students that single-engine flight also means you are relying on a single alternator, which may require you to reduce the electrical load. In addition, your students must understand fully that other systems, such as hydraulics and pneumatics, may have greatly reduced capabilities or become completely inoperative.

ENGINE RESTART

You need to carefully cover the procedures for unfeathering the propeller and restarting the engine. Your students should be cautioned that, once the engine starts, they need to keep the power setting at a minimum until the cylinder head and oil temperatures are within normal operating ranges. This is important because the use of high power settings can result in engine damage. In-flight engine restarting should follow the manufacturer's checklist. [Figure 6-83]

RESTARTING PROCEDURES

1. Magneto switches — ON
2. Fuel selector — ON
3. Throttle — FORWARD approximately one inch
4. Mixture — AS REQUIRED for flight altitude
5. Propeller — FORWARD of detent
6. Starter button — PRESS and RELEASE when engine fires
7. Mixture — ADJUST
8. Power — INCREASE after cylinder head temperature is adequate
9. Cowl flaps — AS REQUIRED
10. Alternator — ON

Figure 6-83. Explain to your students why it is necessary to start propeller rotation with the engine starter. This builds oil pressure in the propeller governor, which begins to move the propeller blades from high pitch (feather) to low pitch. The starter can be disengaged as the blades move out of the feather position, because the airflow passing over the blades keeps them turning.

ENGINE-OUT MANEUVERS

When your students understand engine-out emergency procedures, you can introduce unannounced simulated engine failures at altitude. As your students gain proficiency, simulated engine failure during takeoffs, approaches, and landings can be introduced.

SIMULATED ENGINE-OUT TAKEOFF

Simulated engine failures during takeoff require a great deal of discretion and judgment on your part, because your students' reactions may be totally unpredictable. You must carefully plan how and when you simulate an engine failure, and notify your students precisely how the procedure will be accomplished. Once they gain proficiency, unannounced engine failures may be appropriate, but your judgment remains critical. For example, an engine failure that occurs 20 knots below rotation speed has the same instructional value as one demonstrated at rotation speed, yet it provides an extra margin of safety by reducing the distance necessary to stop the airplane and increasing directional control. Therefore, there is no reason to compromise safety for instructional purposes.

You should also use the same level of caution when simulating a power loss after the airplane is airborne during the departure climb. You should first inform your students of the point where the simulated power loss will occur. After they demonstrate the ability to safely control the airplane, you can introduce unannounced simulated power losses. The point at which the power loss occurs must be selected with discretion. For example, you should not reduce power on any engine until the landing gear is in transit and the airplane has reached V_{YSE}. If it is necessary to practice engine-out procedures below V_{YSE}, the maneuver should be taught at a safe altitude rather than in the traffic pattern.

Your students must realize that the specific procedure to follow after an engine failure depends on the situation. Any indication of engine power loss while the airplane is still on the ground requires you to reject the takeoff. If airborne when the failure occurs, the factors affecting the pilot's decision to continue flight are many. Some manufacturers use a concept called the **area of decision** for takeoff planning in light multi-engine airplanes. [Figure 6-84]

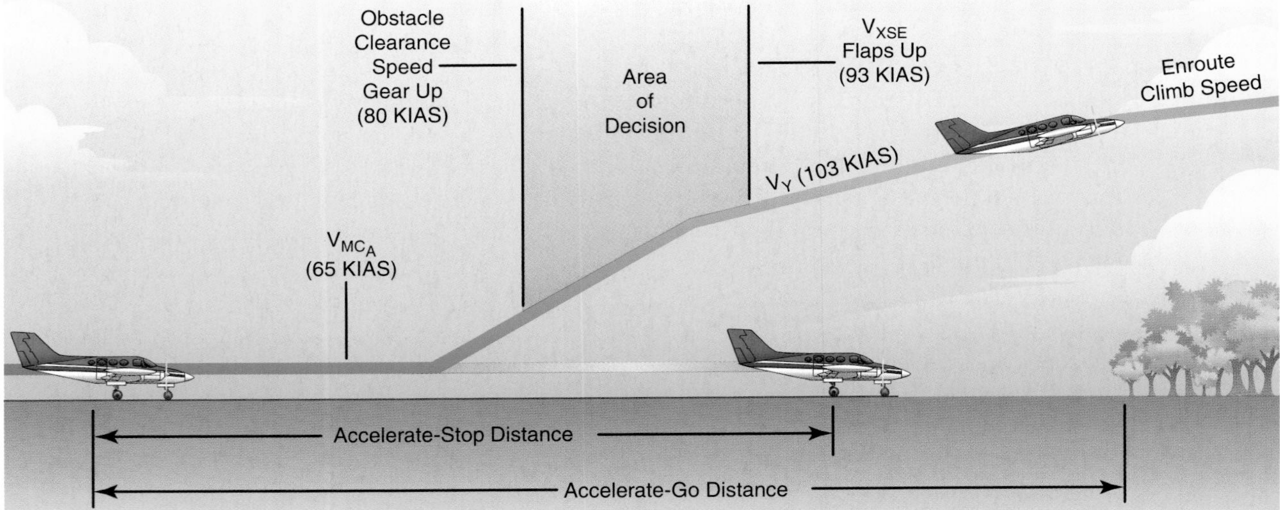

Figure 6-84. In this example, the area of decision begins where obstacle clearance speed is reached and continues until V_{YSE} is reached. Although the aircraft passes through the area of decision in a few seconds, your student must be prepared to decide whether to continue or discontinue the takeoff should an engine fail.

Experienced multi-engine pilots usually make the decision about where to reject the takeoff in case of an engine failure by considering such variables as runway length and gradient, accelerate-stop distance, obstacle height in the area, takeoff weight, single-engine performance, density altitude, and their own level of proficiency. With an awareness of the variables, your student should be taught to formulate a takeoff plan appropriate to the conditions so immediate action can be taken if an engine fails during the takeoff process. [Figure 6-85]

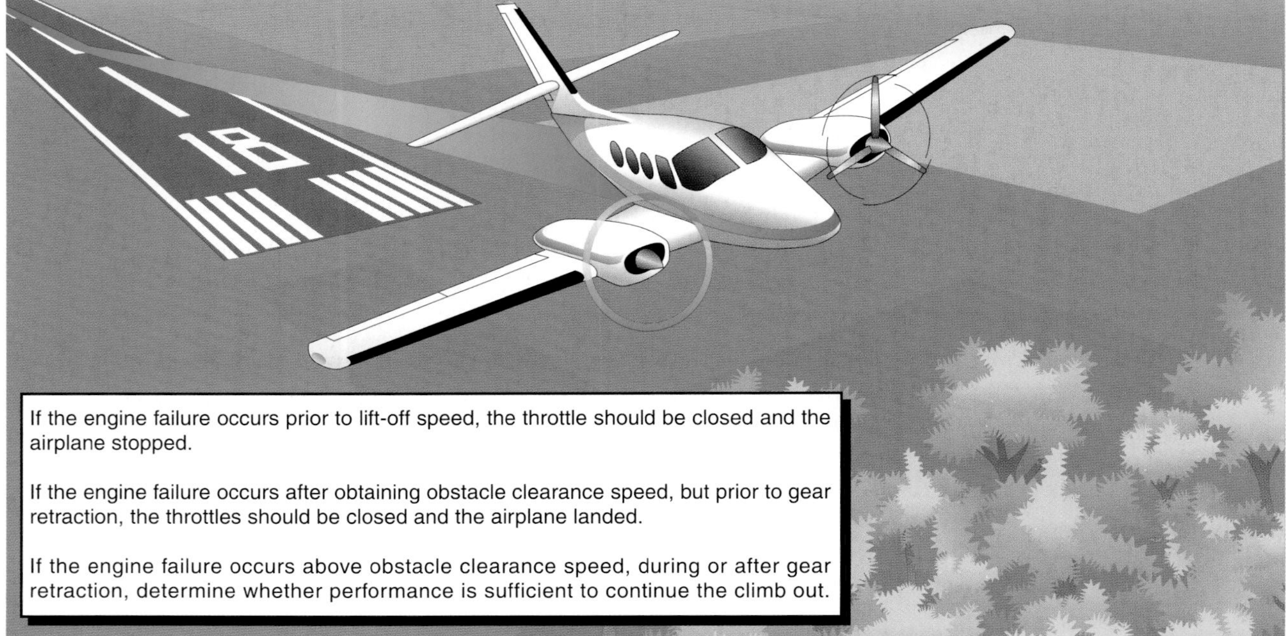

Figure 6-85. Your students should complete this procedure for each takeoff. This example cannot be applied to every situation, however, since conditions may vary significantly.

FLY THE AIRPLANE

From the files of NTSB...

Aircraft: *Aero Commander 500S*

Narrative: *The pilot had the wastegates on the turbochargers adjusted and wanted to test fly the airplane after the work was completed. The airplane departed and had reached an altitude of about 1,000 feet when witnesses heard an engine sputter. The airplane was seen making a left turn and entering a nose low, left spin before impacting the terrain. A tear down of the left engine revealed that the exhaust valves in cylinders #3 and #5 were burnt through at the valve head. The #5 exhaust valve had a mark on the valve system. The failures of both valves were sufficient enough to cause a power failure in the left engine.*

Although the mechanical failure was one of the first items in the chain of events which led to this accident, the pilot's improper emergency procedures and failure to maintain control of the airplane was cited as the probable cause by the NTSB.

This accident underscores the importance of a takeoff briefing as a standard operating procedure. Had the pilot planned for the possibility of an engine failure on departure, the outcome might have been different. At a 1,000-ft maneuvering altitude, continuation under controlled flight with a return to the airport should have been feasible. Surprised by the engine failure, the pilot failed to maintain V_{MC}, causing the airplane to depart controlled flight and spin. Recovery from a spin in a multi-engine airplane is extremely difficult and usually impossible.

SIMULATED ENGINE-OUT APPROACHES AND LANDINGS

The primary objective of simulating engine-out landings is to teach your students to execute well-planned approaches so that it is not necessary to go around on one engine. This is extremely important because density altitude and the performance of most light twins make a single-engine go-around difficult, if not impossible in many situations. You should stress the importance of having a good plan of action that results in an accurate, stabilized approach. It is best to lead any turns in the pattern to avoid steep bank angles. The traffic pattern itself should be flown generally at the same altitude and size as a normal pattern for the airplane you are flying. One exception is that the flaps and landing gear are not extended until the landing is assured.

To begin the maneuver, consult the POH for the recommended engine-out approach speed. However, under no circumstances should the approach be flown at less than the single-engine best rate-of-climb speed. Once you have determined the proper airspeed, have your students enter the pattern at this speed in level flight. [Figure 6-86]

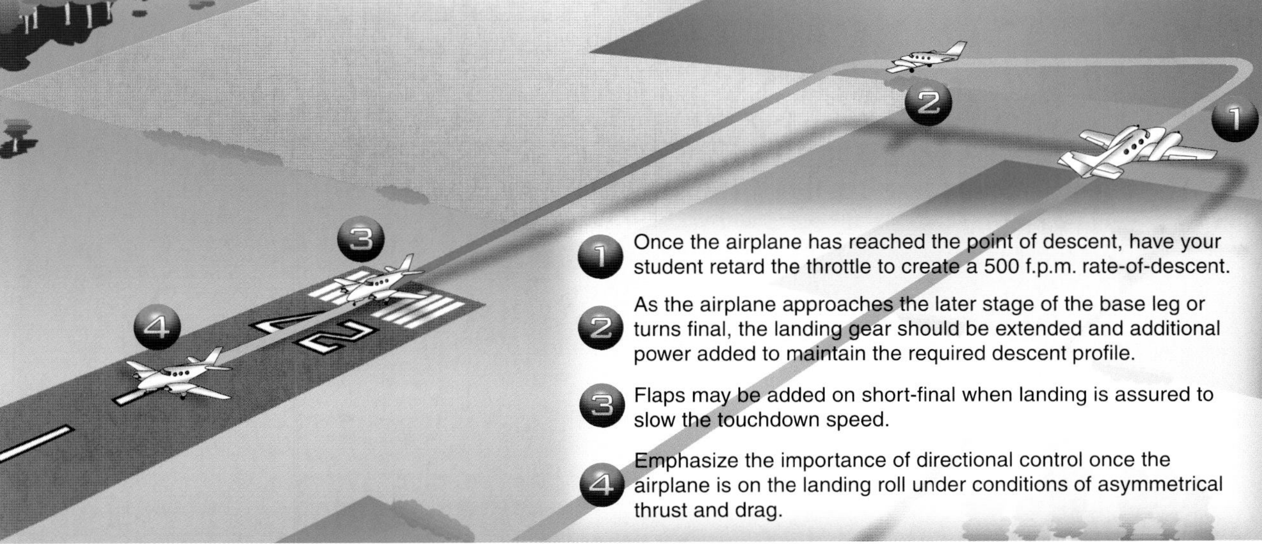

Figure 6-86. It is important that your students know the approximate power setting that results in the desired descent rate. This prevents radical power changes later in the pattern and promotes a stabilized approach.

LOSS OF DIRECTIONAL CONTROL DEMONSTRATION

In the past, multi-engine applicants were required to actually demonstrate V_{MC} both in training and on the checkride. The demonstration was often carried to the point where the airplane suddenly began to roll toward the dead engine. This greatly increased the probability of an accident. When the PTS were developed in the eighties, the procedure was modified to the *"engine inoperative loss of directional control demonstration"* that is still in use today.

When your students are ready to demonstrate **engine inoperative loss of directional control**, make sure they understand the reason for this maneuver and the necessity for an altitude safety margin of at least 3,000 feet AGL. Remember that the manufacturer determined the published V_{MC} figure for your airplane under very specific conditions, which your students should not try to duplicate. Therefore, you should teach your students to expect loss of directional control at a speed that may be higher than the published V_{MC}. Also, remember that as altitude increases, actual V_{MC} decreases and under some weight and altitude combinations V_{MC} and stall speed are the same. This means the loss of directional control demonstration cannot be accomplished safely. [Figure 6-87]

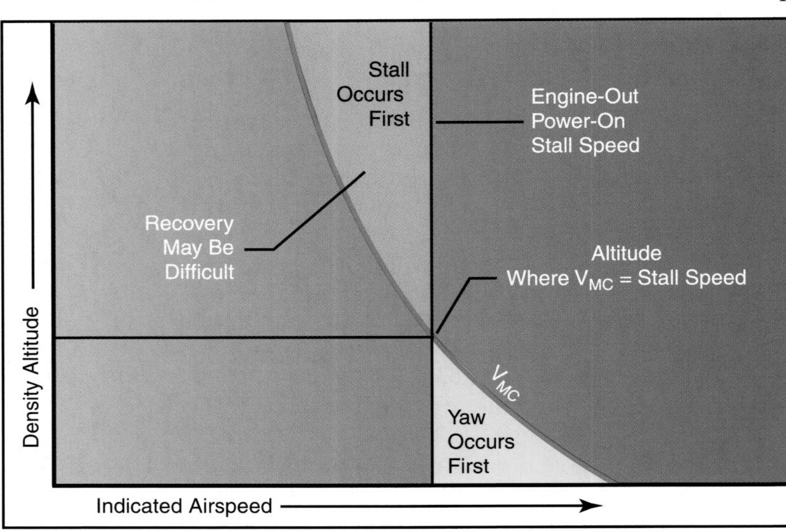

Figure 6-87. You may use this chart to point out the relationship between engine-out stall speed and V_{MC} for normally aspirated, twin-engine airplanes, as plotted against density altitude and KIAS. Note that engine-out stall speed is not significantly affected, as altitude increases until V_{MC} and stall speed are equal.

The crossover point for V_{MC} and the stall speed occurs at about 3,000 feet MSL in many light twin-engine aircraft when they are loaded with half fuel, and the CG is in the middle of the range. You will find these conditions to be typical when you begin multi-engine instruction. Therefore, your students should be prepared to recover at the first indication of stall or loss of directional control, whichever occurs first. The bottom line is that the intent of the engine-out loss of directional control demonstration is to demonstrate the onset of control limits. Normally, this occurs when the nose begins to move, even though full rudder is applied. Conservative technique dictates that you should instruct your students to recover at the earliest signs of stall or loss of directional control. Take the time to review the multi-engine section of the Private or Commercial PTS with your students regarding configuration and procedures for the demonstration prior to the lesson. [Figure 6-88]

C. TASK: ENGINE INOPERATIVE - LOSS OF DIRECTIONAL CONTROL DEMONSTRATION

REFERENCES: AC 61-21; FAA-Approved Airplane Flight Manual, Pilot Operating Handbook.

NOTE: Airplanes with normally aspirated engines will lose power as altitude increases because of the reduced density of the air entering the induction system of the engine. This loss of power will result in a V_{MC} lower than the stall speed at higher altitudes. Also, some airplanes have such an effective rudder that even at sea level V_{MC} is lower than stall speed. For these airplanes, a demonstration of loss of directional control may be safely conducted by limiting travel of the rudder pedal to simulate maximum available rudder. Limiting travel of the rudder pedal should be accomplished at a speed well above the power-off stall speed (approximately 20 knots). This will avoid the hazards of stalling one wing. In the event of any indication of stall prior to loss of directional control, recover to the entry airspeed. The demonstration should then be accomplished with the rudder pedal blocked at a higher airspeed.

Figure 6-88. This excerpt from the Commercial Pilot Airplane Multi-Engine Land PTS explains the limitations of the loss of directional control demonstration for the practical test. You should apply the same limitations during training.

The engine inoperative loss of directional control demonstration should be accomplished within a safe distance of a suitable airport and at an altitude that is appropriate for existing conditions. To begin, have your student set the propellers to high r.p.m., with the landing gear retracted, and the wing flaps, cowl flaps, and trim set to the takeoff position. Then, direct your students to establish a climb attitude with airspeed appropriate to climbout. Excessive nose-high pitch attitudes should be avoided. With both engines developing rated takeoff power, or as recommended, slowly reduce power on the critical engine to idle so it is windmilling but not shut down. You should avoid an abrupt power reduction. After this, have your students establish a bank toward the operating engine, as necessary, for best performance.

From this point, coach your students to slowly reduce airspeed with the elevator, while using rudder pressure to maintain directional control until all available rudder is applied. At this point, recovery should be initiated by simultaneously reducing power on the operating engine and lowering the nose to decrease the angle of attack. Recovery should not be made by increasing power on the simulated inoperative engine. [Figure 6-89]

ENGINE INOPERATIVE LOSS OF DIRECTIONAL CONTROL

Common Errors

1. Inadequate knowledge of the causes of loss of directional control at airspeeds less than V_{MC}, factors affecting V_{MC}, and safe recovery procedures
2. Improper entry procedures, including pitch attitude, bank attitude, and airspeed
3. Failure to recognize imminent loss of directional control
4. Failure to use proper recovery technique
5. Rough and/or uncoordinated control technique

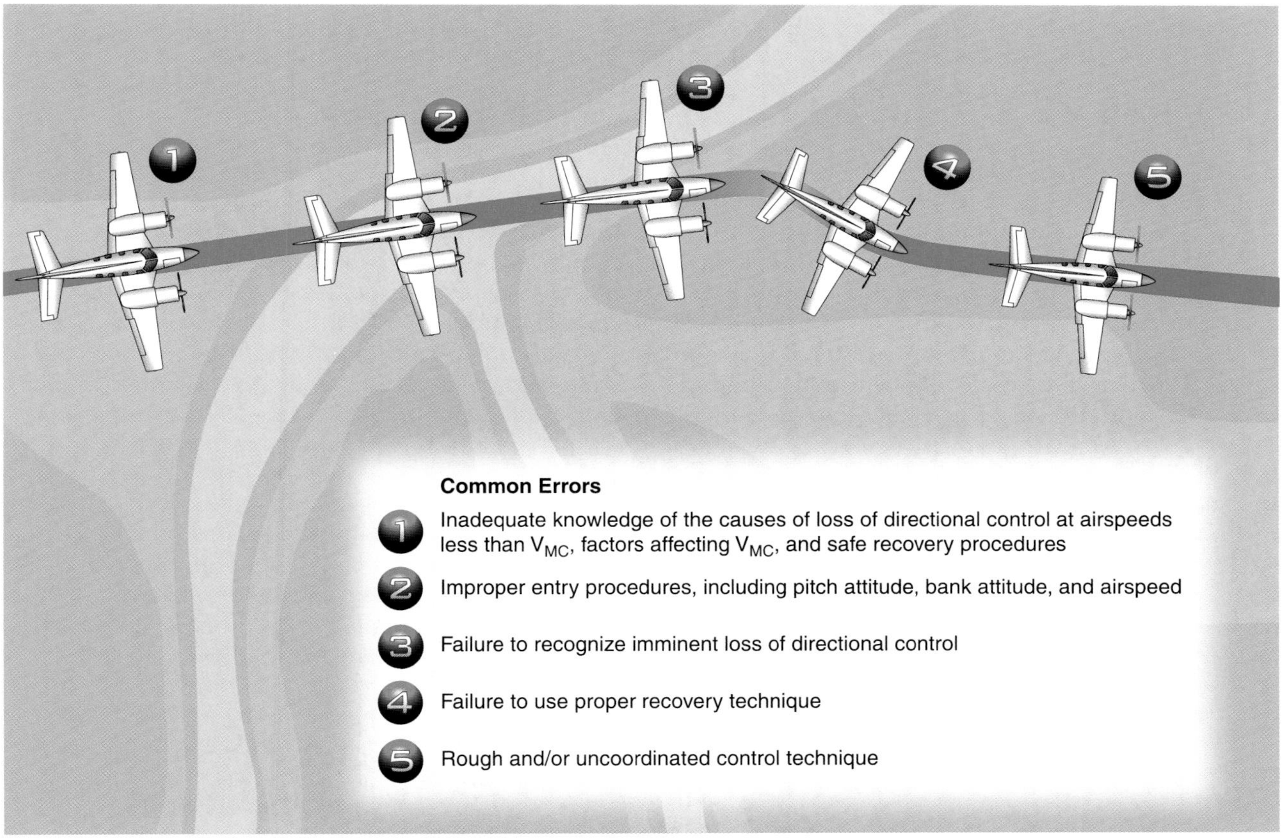

Figure 6-89. You should emphasize the importance of conserving altitude during recovery, but not at the risk of uncontrolled flight. If necessary, power on the operating engine can be reduced to maintain control with minimum loss of altitude.

DRAG DEMONSTRATION

One of the most critical concepts for your students to understand about flying with an inoperative engine is the effect that various aircraft configurations have an overall performance. Specifically, you need to emphasize that, in multi-engine training airplanes, the increase in total drag created by a windmilling propeller exceeds that caused by leaving the gear and flaps extended after the engine has failed. You can illustrate this point by conducting a drag demonstration. [Figure 6-90 on page 6-92]

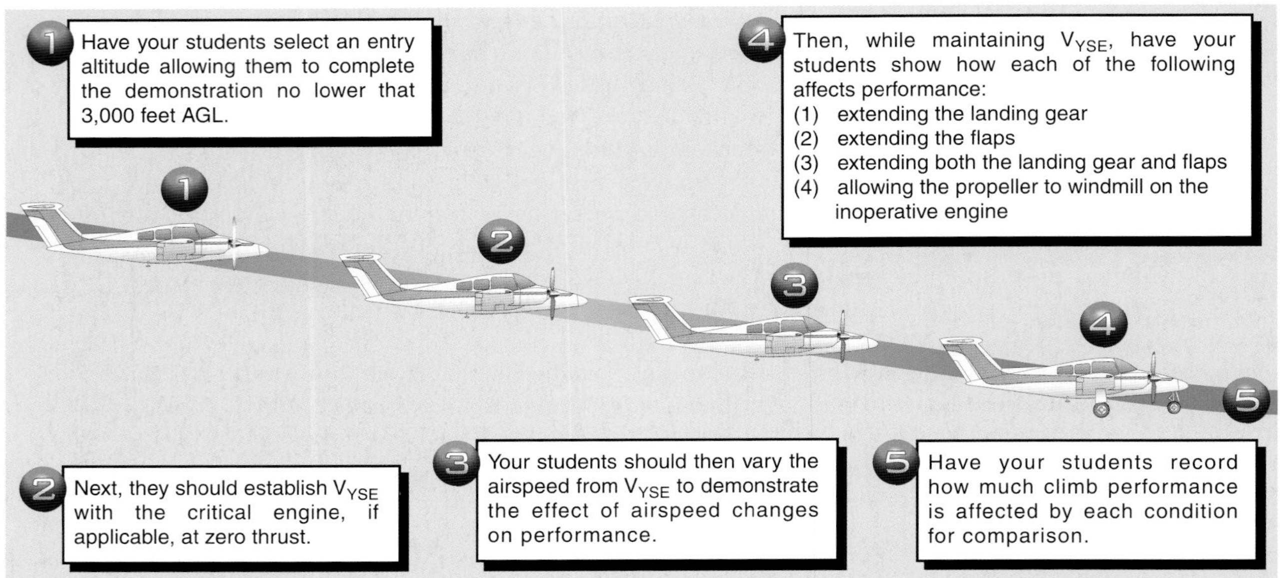

Figure 6-90. Your students may need to perform this maneuver on their practical test.

IMPORTANCE OF ZERO SIDESLIP

The FAA has encouraged multi-engine flight instructors to place more emphasis in training on the importance of maintaining the airplane at zero sideslip after an engine failure. As shown earlier, maintaining a constant heading with wings level and the ball centered causes the airplane to slip into the dead engine with the rudder fully deflected, or nearly so. This resulting high-drag configuration can eliminate any climb or acceleration capability, and causes a marked increase in actual V_{MC}. In an FAA study where an actual flight test was conducted with a light twin, V_{MC} increased from 91 knots to 115 knots with the wings level and the ball centered. It was further noted that decreasing the angle of bank away from the good engine increases actual V_{MC} at the rate of three knots for each degree of bank angle.

This means that you can improve the safety of your engine-out training operations by teaching your students to immediately establish the appropriate bank angle into the operative engine, with the ball deflected toward that engine. Remember, the engine-out performance figures in the POH are based on the zero sideslip. This point also illustrates the importance of being at or above V_{YSE} or V_{SSE}, if applicable, before you deliberately fail an engine during training.

SAFETY CONSIDERATIONS FOR ENGINE-OUT TRAINING

Earlier, it was noted that the most dangerous time to experience an engine-out failure in a multi-engine airplane is immediately after takeoff. Although this statement is hard to debate, engine-out approach and landing accidents actually outnumber engine-out takeoff accidents nearly two to one. Covering certain additional areas in detail can improve multi-engine training safety, as well as better prepare your students for enroute engine-out emergencies. After an engine failure at altitude, instruct your students to apply power to the good engine immediately. As they become preoccupied with troubleshooting, airspeed decay may go unnoticed. The NTSB recorded numerous fatal accidents that were the result of engine-out spins from cruising altitude.

An engine failure after takeoff or in the landing pattern requires prompt responses, and this is how your students become prepared to react to engine failures in general. At altitude,

however, you should instruct your students to take more time to troubleshoot the problem with a checklist. Switching tanks, adjusting the mixture, or turning the boost pump on could restore power to the failed engine. You can reinforce this with your students by restoring power to the failed engine after going through the appropriate checklist. [Figure 6-91]

Figure 6-91. Following an engine failure at altitude when the failed engine has been secured, teach your students to select the nearest suitable airport for landing.

A simulated engine failure in the traffic pattern is excellent training for your students. Simulating engine failure with the throttle rather than the mixture control is the safest procedure in the pattern. Having your students fly a long final allows more time to establish a stabilized engine-out approach. It also gives you more time to critique your students' performance and increases the safety margin if you have to abandon the approach.

SPIN CONSIDERATIONS

During multi-engine flight training, you should give special consideration to the situations where an inadvertent spin may develop. The following information is not designed to review basic spin recovery procedures, but to provide background knowledge regarding multi-engine airplane type certification. In addition, specific situations are described where the post-stall gyration, or the first turn, could develop into a spin.

MULTI-ENGINE AIRPLANE CERTIFICATION

Since the first element of any spin is a fully developed stall, it is important to analyze with your students the required stall characteristics for airplane certification under Part 23. Before the airplane is certified, it must be flight tested and stall recovery must be demonstrated through the normal use of controls. Recovery must not produce more than 15° of roll or yaw.

In addition, Part 23 requires that stalls be performed with the critical engine inoperative. During the test, the airplane must not display any undue spinning tendency and must be safely recoverable without the application of power to the inoperative engine. However, the operating engine(s) may be throttled back during the recovery.

Based on the certification criteria, the airplane should not have adverse or unpredictable characteristics during stall practice. However, Part 23 does not require that any multi-engine airplane be tested for actual spin characteristics. As a result, the airplane's behavior during the post-stall gyration and the spin are unknown. This means that spin recovery techniques are only recommendations and may vary from the recovery techniques required for the individual situation. It is for this reason that, any time a potential spin situation is encountered, you must effect an immediate recovery before the post-stall gyration can develop into a spin. If immediate corrective action is delayed, or if incorrect recovery procedures are applied and a spin develops, recovery is highly improbable and, in some situations, impossible.

SPIN CONDITIONS

Based on the certification criteria for stalls, it is unlikely that a spin will develop during normal stall practice. However, you must be particularly alert in the event your student uses improper recovery techniques. The chances of inadvertent spin entry are greatest during the instruction of engine-out flight maneuvers. These maneuvers are particularly critical considering the relationship between V_{MC} and the single-engine stalling speed. In some density altitude situations, the airplane will stall at an airspeed higher than actual V_{MC} for the current conditions. You and your student must be fully aware of this condition and begin an immediate recovery at the first indication of the stall.

OBTAINING MULTI-ENGINE INSTRUMENT PRIVILEGES

Private and commercial pilots who possess instrument ratings may want to exercise these privileges in multi-engine airplanes. If so, your students are required to demonstrate competency in instrument flight during the checkride. The required procedures include simulated engine failure by reference to instruments, during straight-and-level flight and turns; an instrument approach with all engines operating; and an instrument approach that simulates one engine inoperative. Refer to the multi-engine sections of the Private or Commercial PTS, as appropriate.

TEACHING MULTI-ENGINE INSTRUMENT PROCEDURES

Remember that your students must be able to accomplish all the required actions for an in-flight engine failure solely by reference to instruments. This includes recognizing the situation and determining which engine has failed. As you can probably remember from your own multi-engine training, learning to maintain aircraft control while accomplishing these actions is difficult enough in VFR conditions. This is one of the most challenging aspects of multi-engine instruction, since you must ensure a positive transfer of learning for both instrument flying procedures and previous VFR engine-out practice. You can expect your students to have some trouble maintaining precise flight parameters the first few times you present this situation. Continue to stress the importance of good instrument cross-check and show them how judicious use of trim can help aircraft control once the engine-out situation is stabilized.

Before you have your students fly their first multi-engine instrument approach, make sure they understand that this maneuver requires many tasks to be done in a relatively short time. More detailed checklist procedures, more sophisticated aircraft equipment, and higher airspeeds all combine to increase the workload over a similar operation in a single-engine airplane. You should show them how to accomplish as many tasks as possible early in the approach. For example, have them set the throttles for a stabilized approach prior to the final approach fix. This allows them to control the airspeed and descent rate with configuration changes and keep throttle movements to a minimum. Teaching your students to fly an engine-out approach is a demanding operation because it increases the potential for hazardous situations to develop. Remember, the airplane is relatively close to the ground at a low airspeed with asymmetrical power, and you are in charge of maintaining visual separation while giving instruction. [Figure 6-92]

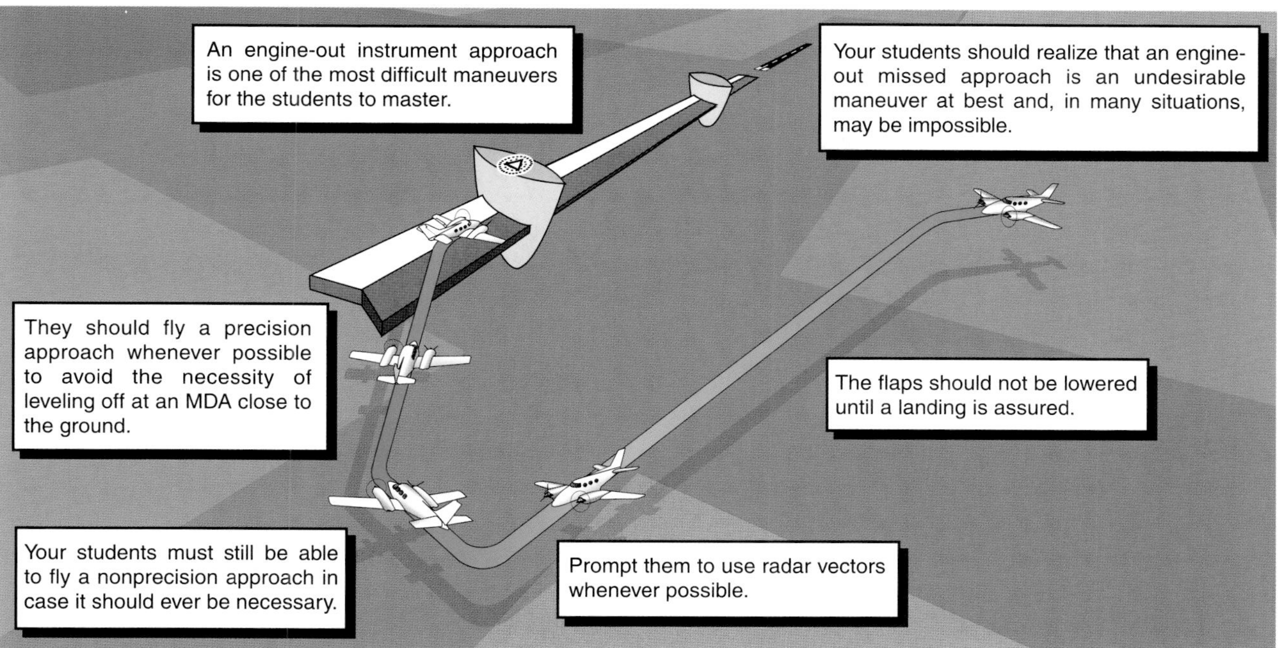

Figure 6-92. You should demonstrate that once the engine-out situation is stabilized, the approach can be flown using nearly the same procedures as with all engines operating. It is important to show students how to reduce the workload so they can concentrate on flying the approach properly. In addition to reducing the navigation workload, attempt to decrease the time required to fly the approach. Techniques such as these are important to help ensure a successful landing on the first attempt.

SUMMARY CHECKLIST

✓ In-cockpit ground training allows your students to become acquainted with the location of instruments, switches, and controls which may be unfamiliar.

✓ The preflight inspection is a good time to point out the unique characteristics of multi-engine airplanes.

✓ It is easy for students who are adjusting to a new cockpit to fixate inside the aircraft when performing engine start.

✓ You should encourage your students to use the engine tachometers, and emphasize that the use of asymmetrical power is a taxi technique to be used only during crosswind conditions or as an aid in reducing the turning radius.

✓ From the beginning, inform your students that takeoff and climb is the most vulnerable phase of multi-engine operation, and they should always be prepared for an engine failure. You can demonstrate that the takeoff and climb is an orderly progression of events dependent upon precise airspeed control.

✓ Emphasize the importance of establishing a stabilized power approach when students begin concentrated work with landings.

✓ Make sure you discuss the go-around procedure outlined in the POH for the training airplane during the preflight briefing.

✓ Practicing steep turns helps your students develop a feel for the airplane's heavy control response and an appreciation for proper trim technique.

- ✓ Your students should understand how maneuvering during slow flight relates directly to critical flight situations, such as go-arounds and landings, and provides the opportunity to explore multi-engine handling at slow airspeeds.
- ✓ The PTS have eliminated full stalls in multi-engine airplanes using high power settings, because the high angles of attack required to induce a stall can result in a loss of controlled flight.
- ✓ Give your students the opportunity to maneuver the airplane with only one engine producing power. This is most easily accomplished by requiring your students to retract the landing gear and flaps, and establish the zero-thrust power setting published by the airplane manufacturer.
- ✓ Before you demonstrate the engine-shutdown procedure, be sure your students understand that the first priority following an engine failure is to maintain control of the airplane at V_{YSE}.
- ✓ You need to carefully cover the procedures for unfeathering the propeller and restarting the engine.
- ✓ You must carefully plan how and when you simulate an engine failure during takeoff, and notify your student precisely how the procedure will be accomplished.
- ✓ Some manufacturers use a concept called the area of decision for takeoff planning in light, multi-engine airplanes. The area of decision begins where obstacle clearance speed is reached and continues until the V_{YSE} is reached.
- ✓ The primary objective of simulating engine-out landings is to teach your students to execute well-planned approaches so that it is not necessary to go-around on one engine.
- ✓ The engine inoperative loss of control demonstration requires an altitude safety margin of at least 3,000 feet AGL. You should teach your students to expect loss of directional control during the demonstration at a speed that may be higher than the published V_{MC}.
- ✓ You can improve the safety of your engine-out training operations by teaching your students to immediately establish the appropriate bank angle into the operative engine, with the ball deflected toward that engine. This produces a zero sideslip condition.
- ✓ The most dangerous time to experience an engine-out failure in a multi-engine airplane appears to be immediately after takeoff. Although this may seem true, engine-out approach and landing accidents actually outnumber engine-out takeoff accidents nearly two to one.
- ✓ Private and commercial pilots who possess instrument ratings are required to demonstrate competency in instrument flight during the checkride if they wish to have instrument privileges in multi-engine airplanes.
- ✓ Remember that your students must be able to accomplish all the required actions for an in-flight engine failure solely by reference to instruments.
- ✓ Teaching your students to fly an engine-out approach is a demanding operation because it increases the potential for hazardous situations to develop.

KEY TERMS

In-Cockpit Ground Training

Preflight Inspection

Engine Start

Maximum Performance Takeoff

Go-Around

Steep Turns

Slow Flight

Stalls

Engine-Out Procedures

Engine-Out Maneuvers

Simulated Engine Failures

Area of Decision

Engine Inoperative Loss of Directional Control Demonstration

QUESTIONS

1. What may your students learn during in-cockpit ground training?

2. When should your students use asymmetrical power during taxi?

   A. Any time
   B. Only when the brakes fail
   C. When necessary to reduce turning radius or during crosswind conditions

3. True/False. Safe multi-engine takeoff profiles are based upon precise airspeed control.

Match the skill developed by the specific maneuver.

4. Steep turns
5. Maneuvering during slow flight
6. Stalls
7. Engine-out climbs, descents, and turns

A. Recovery at the first indication of aerodynamic buffet or loss of lift

B. A feel for the heavy control pressures and the need for trim

C. Maneuvering during go-arounds and landings

D. The significance of V_{YSE}

8. Select the best method to simulate one engine inoperative.

   A. Pull the mixture on the engine you wish to fail
   B. Turn off the fuel on the tank feeding the engine you wish to fail.
   C. Establish the zero-thrust power setting published by the airplane manufacturer.

9. True/False. Your student's first priority in an engine-out emergency situation is to feather the failed engine.

10. List the procedures for securing an inoperative engine.

11. Select the statement that best defines the area of decision.

    A. The segment or final approach when the decision is made to go-around
    B. The area in front of the airplane where most pilots focus their eyes during landing.
    C. The area that begins where obstacle clearance speed is reached and continues until V_{YSE} is reached.

12. Why is it necessary for your students to become proficient at single-engine landings?

13. At what altitude should you perform the engine inoperative loss of control demonstration?

    A. At or above 1,500 feet AGL
    B. At or above 3,000 feet AGL
    C. At or above pattern altitude

14. What maneuvers do your students need to perform on the practical test if they wish to gain instrument privileges with their multi-engine rating?

APPENDIX A
ANSWERS

CHAPTER 1

SECTION A

1. Learning is defined as a persisting change in behavior resulting from experience with the environment, which cannot be attributed to natural growth.
2. *While the following are examples which were stated in the text, any examples which appropriately represent these concepts may be used.*

   Positive Reinforcement — A reward is given for correct behavior. The behavior is strengthened. *In a post-flight debriefing, Steve praises Ann's performance of steep turns.*

   Punishment — A penalty is exacted for incorrect behavior. The behavior is weakened or goes away. *Cheryl shouts at Brian after he forgets to perform clearing turns prior to practicing stalls.*

   Negative Reinforcement — A penalty is removed for correct behavior. The behavior is strengthened. *Eric is constantly criticized for making mistakes during landing practice. He is relieved when he finally performs a landing correctly and Bob does not point out any errors.*

   Extinction — A reward is removed for incorrect behavior. The behavior slowly goes away. *During ground school sessions, Michelle consistently compliments Tanya on her knowledge of the subject areas covered. Tanya knows she didn't prepare well enough for the aerodynamics discussion when she receives no praise.*

   The use of positive reinforcement to help students learn is normally the most successful approach.
3. True
4. *While the following is an example which was stated in the text, any example which appropriately represents this concept may be used.*

   A student is performing with automaticity when rolling into a turn without consciously thinking about rudder pressure or backpressure on the elevator.
5. An example of rehearsing is a student repeating numbers, such as aircraft speeds, over and over while preparing for an aircraft checkout. Although rehearsal will help fix the numbers in the student's long-term memory, coding is normally a more effective way of processing information. Coding is the process of relating incoming information to concepts and ideas already in memory. For example, if the approach speed of the aircraft used for the checkout is the same as another familiar aircraft, it will be easier for the student's working memory to process this information.
6. B
7. Physical organism, basic need, goals and values, self-concept, time and opportunity, element of threat
8. Material that was never successfully processed into long-term memory by working memory, cannot be remembered. The breakdown of neural pathways between the various cells where memories are stored is another reason that things are forgotten. This usually occurs due to disuse of the information over time. Interference occurs when something is forgotten because a certain experience has overshadowed it, or when the learning of similar things has intervened. Interference can arise from competing material learned either before or after the information that the student wishes to remember. Repression can cause forgetting when experiences that are unpleasant or produce anxiety are buried into the subconscious part of the mind.
9. True
10. E. Intensity
11. C. Recency
12. A. Readiness
13. D. Effect
14. F. Exercise
15. B. Primacy

SECTION B

1. Right brain/left brain, reflective/impulsive, holist/serialist, auditory/visual/kinesthetic
2. False
3. C
4. Serialists prefer to start at the beginning and examine material in order. Each piece of information is linked to others to eventually create an overall picture.
5. C
6. The cognitive domain is concerned with knowledge and thought processes. The psychomotor domain encompasses the development of fine and exact physical skills. The affective domain focuses on feelings, attitudes, personal beliefs, and values.
7. True
8. C

SECTION C

1. The three basic elements that comprise the communication process are the source, the symbols used to communicate the message, and the receiver.
2. False
3. Monitoring student feedback provides a way to gauge whether your students are receiving the correct message.
4. Lack of common experience, confusion between the symbol and the symbolized object, overuse of abstractions, interference
5. C
6. B
7. False

8. C
9. C

CHAPTER 2

SECTION A

1. C
2. Preparation, presentation, application, review and evaluation
3. A
4. Description of the skill or behavior, conditions, and criteria
5. True
6. The student will demonstrate how to fly steep turns in the training airplane by use of instrument references. These turns will be accomplished by using a bank of approximately 45°, and the bank will be maintained for either 180° or 360° of turn, both left and right. Altitude will be maintained ± 100 feet, airspeed ± 10 knots, bank angle ± 5°, and roll out will be within 10° of a specified heading. The student will also exhibit proper crosscheck and interpretation, and apply the appropriate pitch, bank, power, and trim corrections.
7. False
8. A

SECTION B

1. A
2. False
3. Performing a problem using a flight computer.
4. The telling and doing technique follows the four steps of the demonstration-performance method, excluding the explanation phase.
5. C
6. Students are able to fly with more precision, which is especially important in high-performance airplanes sensitive to be flown with correct airspeeds and proper power settings.
7. C
8. True
9. A
10. Impatient students fail to understand the need for thorough preliminary training and are more focused on the desired outcome than on the path to achieving it.
11. B
12. You may begin by introducing the aerodynamic principles behind stalls during a ground school session. Then, move into stalls gradually in the airplane by first demonstrating slow flight, and leading into power-off stalls. Save any demonstrated stalls for a subsequent lesson after the student has shown some mastery and confidence in the performance of basic stalls.

SECTION C

1. In education, a course of training may be defined as a complete series of studies leading to attainment of a specific goal. The goal might be a certificate of completion, graduation, or even an academic degree. For example, after completing a specific course of both ground and flight training, a student normally achieves the goal of obtaining a pilot certificate or rating. A course of training also may be limited to something like the additional instruction required for operating high-performance airplanes.
2. C
3. B
4. A
5. A syllabus lesson should contain objectives, content, and completion standards. In addition, it may include the recommended class time, reference or study materials, the sequence of training, and the study assignment for the next lesson.
6. True
7. False
8. False
9. C
10. B
11. *The following is an example of a lesson plan used to conduct an instructional period which introduces a primary student to slow flight. While the details of your lesson plan may be different, it should include similar objectives, content, and completion standards.*

LESSON: Maneuvering During Slow Flight

STUDENT: Kay Jesse

OBJECTIVE: To familiarize the student with the handling characteristics of the airplane during slow flight and introduce stall/spin awareness training.

CONTENT: Preflight discussion
Purpose of Slow Flight
Stall/Spin Awareness Training
Safe Altitudes + 1,500 ft. AGL

Introduce —
Use of Carburetor Heat
Transitions to Slow Flight
Maneuvering During Slow Flight
Slow Flight with Realistic Distractions
Slow Flight with Stall Warning Activated
Slow Flight with the Airspeed Indicator Covered
Transitions from Slow Flight to Cruise

COMPLETION STANDARDS:
The student will understand the purpose of slow flight and demonstrate competency in controlling the airplane in straight-and-level flight and in turns at airspeeds approaching a stall. The student will maintain altitude within ± 100 feet, heading within ±10°, and the specified airspeed within +10/-5 knots.

SECTION D

1. A critique is a step in the learning process, and an evaluation is part of the overall grading process. Critiques should be used to summarize and complete a lesson, as well as to prepare your student for the next lesson. Evaluations measure demonstrated performance against a criteria or standard.

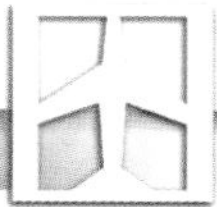

2. False
3. You can devote more time to the critique. You can organize your thoughts more clearly. Your students can keep the critique and use it as a reference.
4. True
5. A.
6. B.
7. True
8. Selection-type tests are objective. You can objectively compare the test results between students. You can test more areas of knowledge.
9. True
10. Avoid the use of absolutes like *"all pilots"* and *"every time"* in the stem. It would be better for the stem to read, *"What action(s) might a pilot take in the event of an emergency?"* Also, the word *"They"* may be eliminated from the responses.

CHAPTER 3

SECTION A

1. Physical — These needs encompass the necessities for survival, which include food, rest, exercise, and protection from the elements. Until these requirements are satisfied, your students cannot fully concentrate on learning, self-expression, or any other tasks.

   Safety — These needs include protection against danger, threats, and deprivation. Sometimes referred to as the security needs, they directly relate to flying. Since safety is a major concern among your students, during the initial stages of training you should avoid accentuating the dangers of flying.

   Social — These are the needs to belong and to associate, as well as to give and receive friendship and love. Since students are usually out of their normal surroundings during flight training, their desire for association and belonging is more pronounced.

   Ego — One type of egoistic need relates to your students' self esteem and are directly linked to their self-confidence, independence, achievement, competence, and knowledge. Another type relates to your students' reputation, such as status, recognition, appreciation, and respect of associates.

   Self-fulfillment — These needs include realizing one's own potential for continued development, and for being creative in the broadest sense. Maslow included various cognitive and aesthetic goals in this echelon.
2. True
3. D
4. C
5. G
6. F
7. E
8. A
9. H
10. B
11. *While the following are examples which were stated in the text, any examples which appropriately represent these concepts may be used.*

    Laurie phones you to cancel yet another lesson due to illness.

    Jim stopped scheduling flights while he "finishes up an important project at work." He promised to return to his training in two weeks, yet it has been over a month and you have not heard from him.

    Karen does not show up for scheduled lessons or is so late that often there is not enough time left during the lesson period to fly.

    When weather conditions are poor, you normally conduct ground school sessions. Jeff consistently ignores marginal weather reports he has received during briefings and tries to convince you conditions are ideal for flying.
12. Choosing a calm, clear day to take a new student on a short introductory flight is one way of minimizing any anxieties that exist about learning to fly. Student anxieties can also be minimized throughout training by emphasizing the benefits and pleasurable experiences that can be derived from flying, rather than by continuously citing any serious consequences. You can explain to your students that safe flying practices are conducive to satisfying, efficient, uninterrupted operations and are not necessary only to prevent catastrophe.

SECTION B

1. Beginning with your students' very first flight lesson, you must emphasize ADM principles.
2. One of the best ways to explain the poor judgement chain to students is to discuss a specific situation which led to an aircraft accident or incident. By discussing the events that led to the incident, you can help students understand how a series of judgmental errors contributed to the final outcome of the flight.
3. False
4. Recognize a Change — You notice a change has occurred or an expected change did not occur.

   Define the Problem — Insight, the senses, and experience, followed by an objective analysis of all available information, are used to determine the exact nature and severity of the problem.

   Choose a Course of Action — You must evaluate the need to react to the problem and determine the actions that may be taken to resolve the situation in the time available. Before you decide on a response the expected outcome of each possible action must be considered and the risks assessed.

   Implement the Decision — Now you must actually take the necessary steps to solve the problem.

   Evaluate the Outcome — Although a decision may be reached and a course of action implemented, the decision-making process is not complete. It is important to think ahead and determine how the decision could affect other phases of the flight. As the flight progresses, you must continue to evaluate the outcome of the decision to ensure that it is producing the desired result.
5. Pilot — Your fitness to fly must be evaluated including competency in the airplane, currency, and flight experience.

Aircraft — The airplane's performance, limitations, equipment, and airworthiness must be determined.

Environment — Factors, such as weather, airport conditions, and the availability of air traffic control services must be examined.

Operation — The purpose of the flight is a factor which influences your decision on undertaking or continuing the flight.

6. C
7. Specifying when refresher training should be accomplished, designating weather minimums which may be higher than those listed in the FARs, and setting limitations regarding the amount of crosswind for takeoffs and landings are examples of elements which your students may include in a personal checklist.
8. Bob typically attributes his poor performance during lessons to "a bad day" and does not put any effort into correcting his mistakes.
9. The sterile cockpit rule specifically prohibits crewmember performance of nonessential duties or activities while the aircraft is involved in taxi, takeoff, landing, and all other flight operations conducted below 10,000 feet MSL, except for cruise flight. Exercising this rule can increase the safety of training flights as well.
10. Some examples of internal and external resources available to your students are — the pilot's operating handbook, ATC, navigation equipment, the autopilot, their instructor, another pilot, passengers, an airport/facility directory, an aviation maintenance technician, a flight service station, various training publications, the Internet, and their ingenuity, knowledge, and skills.
11. Effective workload management ensures that essential operations are accomplished by planning, prioritizing, and sequencing tasks to avoid work overload. One of your primary goals when teaching your students to manage workload is to help them learn to recognize future workload requirements and prepare for high workload periods during times of low workload.

    You can help students manage workload and avoid distractions by teaching them to perform the majority of head-down tasks, such as reviewing charts or navigation logs, during low-workload periods. Set an example for your students by scheduling tasks to minimize conflicts, especially during critical phases of flight.

    If students must perform multiple tasks at the same time, ensure their attention is not focused on one item too long, to the exclusion of others. For example, if your students are performing the before landing checklist when ATC issues a traffic advisory, ensure they take note of the last item completed, locate the traffic, acknowledge the transmission, and promptly return to the checklist.

    You may notice that the first effect of high workload is that your students begin to work faster. As workload increases, their attention cannot be devoted to many tasks at one time, and they may begin to focus on one item. When they become task saturated, there is no awareness of inputs from various sources. Decisions may be made on incomplete information, and the possibility of error increases.
12. False
13. A
14. Duck-under syndrome and descent below the minimum enroute altitude are operational pitfalls common to instrument students.
15. *Any examples which appropriately represent these concepts may be used.* Begin by discussing situational awareness during the preflight briefing. While in flight, your student practices techniques for effectively managing tasks so they can maintain situational awareness, such as prioritizing procedures during a go-around, using checklists, and coping with distractions. When your students are situationally aware, they have an overview of the total operation and are not fixated on one perceived significant factor. For example, during traffic pattern operations, your students are not maintaining situational awareness if they divert too much attention away from operations, such as controlling the airplane or scanning for traffic, when they must perform another task. During the postflight briefing, point out to your students how fatigue, stress, and work overload can cause a loss of situational awareness. Complacency presents another obstacle to maintaining situational awareness. When activities become routine, your students may have a tendency to relax and not put as much effort into performance.
16. C
17. Physical, Physiological, and Psychological

CHAPTER 4

SECTION A

1. False
2. A
3. You need to develop lesson plans for ground and flight instruction sessions. On the ground, you will be asked to explain certain concepts as you would to a student. Your instructor may pose typical student questions and offer suggestions as to how to convey information more effectively. During flight lessons, once you have explained and demonstrated a maneuver, your instructor will play the role of a student and perform this maneuver while making various errors, and you will correct and critique this performance. Your instructor may have you work with students currently pursuing their private or commercial certificates. You may be asked to lead a classroom session of a ground school, or observe dual instruction where you sit in the back seat of an airplane while a CFI gives an actual lesson.
4. Common distractions you can employ include:

    retrieving a dropped pen or pencil;

    determining a heading to an airport using a chart;

    resetting the clock to Coordinated Universal Time (UTC);

    retrieving something from the back seat;

    reading the outside air temperature gauge;

    calling FSS for weather information;

    computing TAS with a flight computer;

    identifying terrain or objects on the ground;

identifying a suitable emergency landing site;

alternately climbing/descending 200 feet and maintaining altitude;

reversing course after a series of S-turns; or

flying at slow airspeeds with the airspeed indicator covered.

5. C

SECTION B

1. C
2. To help students become more aware of fuel quantity issues, ask them to compute a required landing time for each flight. If the flight does not go as planned, your students have already determined at what time it should be terminated.
3. Prior to engine start, your students should look for people or objects around the airplane, especially near the propeller and in the path of propeller blast. Teach them to yell, "Clear" before engaging the starter, and to turn on the anti-collision lights, and, if the flight is at night, the position lights. Discourage students from running the engine for extended periods in a crowded ramp area. They can listen to ATIS and perform other tasks prior to engine start, and promptly taxi from the ramp area once the propeller is moving. They should attend to any remaining checklist items after the airplane is stopped in the runup area. Your students should be prepared for an emergency engine shutdown if anyone ventures close to the aircraft while the engine is running.
4. A runway incursion is any occurrence at an airport involving an aircraft, vehicle, person, or object on the ground that creates a collision hazard or results in loss of separation with an aircraft taking off, intending to take off, landing, or intending to land.
5. False
6. B
7. False
8. Before taxiing onto a runway, check for traffic on final or on the runway.

   During climbout, accelerate to cruise-climb speed upon reaching a safe altitude to improve forward visibility, and perform shallow S-turns if the pitch attitude is too high to see directly ahead.

   Familiarize yourself with special procedures at airports where you intend to operate.

   Check NOTAMs for such items as parachute and glider operations.

   Never overfly an airport where skydivers may be landing, but stay clear and perform a normal 45° downwind entry.

   Use your landing light when near an airport to make your aircraft more visible.

   At uncontrolled airports, report your position on the CTAF or Local Airport Advisory (LAA) frequency. Be alert for aircraft not using a radio.

   Descend to pattern altitude several miles before reaching the airport. Do not descend into the traffic pattern.

   Avoid continuous turns of more than 90 ° while in the traffic pattern.
9. False
10. B
11. False
12. — Explain that an aircraft just reported turning final, and have your student look for the traffic.

    — Ask your student to change the radio frequency, as though the tower requested an alternate frequency.

    — Instruct your student to check and reset the heading indicator to correspond with the magnetic compass.

    — Tell your student to obtain a chart of A/FD from the back seat to verify pattern altitude.

    — Have your students fly at slow airspeeds with the airspeed indicator covered.
13. Fuel exhaustion occurs because of improper preflight planning, or failure to adjust to unexpected conditions during flight. Fuel starvation occurs when the engine stops due to an interruption of the fuel supply to the engine, even though fuel remains available in one or more of the aircraft's fuel tanks.

SECTION C

1. Sincerity is a quality or state of being sincere, honest, and genuine.

   Integrity is the quality or state of being complete. When applied to a person, it usually implies commendable behavioral characteristics, including sound moral principles, forthrightness, honesty, and sincerity.

   When applied to a professional, credibility refers to qualities such as reliability, reputation, trustworthiness, and even appearance.

   Your personal appearance has a significant effect on your image. Many of your students will be successful professionals, and they will expect you to look and act professionally — to be neat, clean, and well dressed.

   Personal habits also have an effect on your professional image. The exercise of common courtesy is perhaps as important as any habit. Be on time for lessons and make sure you answer the phone properly.

   Demeanor refers to your outward behavior or conduct. Your professional image requires development of a calm, thoughtful, and disciplined demeanor that puts your students at ease.
2. False
3. A
4. You can enhance your professional qualifications by: upgrading your pilot certificate or adding a rating to your existing certificate, participating in the Pilot Proficiency Award Program, taking advantage of continuing education courses offered through colleges and universities, becoming an aviation safety counselor, or obtaining a gold seal flight instructor certificate.
5. You can stay informed about various FAA programs and policies by reviewing advisory circulars available through your local Flight Standards District Office, by subscription, or on the FAA web site. You also can obtain current FARs, airworthiness directives, and *The General Aviation Inspector's Handbook* from the Internet. By logging on to the NTSB web site you can review accident statistics and summaries, and by looking up NASA on the Internet you can explore subjects ranging from aircraft design to human factors research.

6. When you participate in the FAA program Operation Raincheck, you can expand your knowledge of ATC services by visiting facilities such as control towers, approach control, or air route traffic control centers. By taking part in Operation Takeoff, you can interact with weather briefers at a local flight service station and learn tips and techniques to get the most out of the services they provide.
7. True
8. C

SECTION D

1. The FAA requires only that you possess a valid third-class medical when acting as pilot-in-command (PIC) in the course of giving instruction. However, it is not necessary for you to possess a current medical to instruct if you do not act as pilot in command.
2. B
3. Part 141 governs the certification of approved pilot schools and sets forth the rules under which they operate. Since approved pilot schools must conduct flight and ground training under specific guidelines and meet rigid operational requirements, graduates of these schools are permitted certification with less total flight experience than that specified in Part 61.
4. False
5. 3 years
6. Your flight instructor certificate is valid for 24 calendar months. You can present the FAA your record of training, and show that at least 5 students were endorsed for a practical test for a certificate and at least 80% of the students passed on their first attempt. You can also show the FAA a satisfactory record as a Part 121 or 135 check pilot, chief flight instructor, check airman, flight instructor or that you are in a position involving the regular evaluation of pilots. Graduation from an approved flight instructor refresher course (FIRC) consisting of at least 16 hours of ground and/or flight training also may be the basis of renewing your certificate at the discretion of the FAA.
7. False
8. A
9. False
10. Your students can fly solo in Class B airspace provided they have a solo endorsement to operate in Class B, and have permission to enter. An operating two-way radio, and an operable mode C transponder, also are required.

    A separate endorsement is required to allow your students to operate solo from or to an airport located within Class B airspace. You must provide ground training on the operations specific to that airport and flight training at the airport. Both the endorsement allowing your students to operate within Class B airspace, and the one enabling them to operate at the airport, must be made within 90 days preceding the date of their intended flight.
11. True
12. A
13. The PTS for aeronautical certificates and ratings include areas of operation and tasks that reflect the requirements of Part 61. Areas of operation define phases of the practical test arranged in a logical sequence within each standard. Tasks are knowledge areas, flight procedures, and/or maneuvers appropriate to an area of operation. Also included within each task are references to the applicable regulations or publications. Areas of operation run the gamut from preflight preparation to postflight procedures.
14. False
15. C
16. To provide initial CFI flight training, you must have held the appropriate flight instructor certificate and rating for at least 24 months and given at least 200 hours of flight training as a CFI. This requirement applies to airplane, rotorcraft, or powered-lift category ratings. If you serve as a CFI in an approved school, there is an alternate requirement. You must have given at least 400 hours of flight training as a CFI, have trained and endorsed at least 5 applicants for a practical test for a pilot certificate, flight instructor certificate, ground instructor certificate, or additional rating, and had at least 80% of the applicants pass the test on the first attempt.

CHAPTER 5

SECTION A

1. Incorporate a visit to the maintenance hanger into a lesson. Sit in the airplane and use the panel and POH as guides. Use some type of visual aid such as a good full-color textbook. Pair a knowledgeable student with a student that has trouble understanding systems during a lesson. Relate certain airplane components to systems and equipment with which your students may already be familiar.
2. In-depth knowledge of systems is a valuable asset when troubleshooting problems that may arise during flight.
3. Wing shapes, flap types, wing planforms, and tail configurations
4. A
5. You can develop a radio phraseology template, suggest your students listen to radio transmissions on the ground, and role-play ATC while your students provide responses.
6. False
7. Asking your students to determine the cause of the accident or incident scenarios illustrates the importance of calculating performance data.
8. Have them routinely practice their judgment skills just as they would maneuvers and procedures. For example, require your students to obtain a weather briefing before each lesson and determine whether the flight can be completed safely. During ground lessons, describe situations to your students they may encounter as pilots and ask them to make choices regarding these scenarios.

SECTION B

1. False
2. B

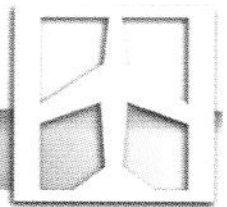

3. B
4. Students may not automatically refer to the horizon as an indicator of aircraft attitude. Interpreting the instrument indications may be unfamiliar. Students may fixate on the flight instruments. Students may have difficulty using the trim correctly.
5. $1.2V_{S1}$
6. The objective of this instruction is for you to learn how to recognize the cues of an impeding stall and initiate proper recovery procedures. If an inadvertent stall occurs. Performing stalls will help prepare you for flying the traffic pattern and landing the airplane.
7. Selecting an improper entry altitude; letting the nose drop excessively during the stall recovery; initially retracting the flaps too rapidly; retracting the remaining flaps prior to reaching V_Y.
8. False
9. B
10. Rectangular course common errors: entering the maneuver improperly, improperly judging wind direction and speed, uncoordinated turns, failure to maintain selected altitude and airspeed, improper wind drift correction

    S-turn common errors: entering the maneuver improperly, using too shallow of a bank angle when the airplane is heading downwind, uncoordinated turns, wings not level when crossing the road, using too steep of a bank angle when the airplane is headed upwind, poor altitude and airspeed control

    Turns around a point common errors: entering the maneuver improperly, too shallow of a bank angle on the downwind leg, insufficient lateral distance from reference point, too steep of a bank angle on the upwind leg, uncoordinated turns
11. Maintaining control of the airplane
12. After simulating an engine failure at a safe altitude in the practice area, you can demonstrate an attempted turn back to the runway. You can also illustrate how much altitude is lost during each stage of the turn by using a diagram.
13. True
14. Full stop-taxi-backs let you observe how well your students maintain directional control of the airplane during the landing roll. As you taxi back to the runway for takeoff, your students have time to relax and collect themselves, and you have an opportunity to effectively critique the landing.
15. True
16. Straight-and-level flight, constant airspeed climbs and descents, turns to headings, recovery from unusual attitudes, radio communication, and the use of navigation systems/facilities and radar services appropriate for instrument flight.

SECTION C

1. False
2. Begin by addressing, in detail, the systems found on the airplane in which your students are training. One way to organize this discussion is to use the POH as an outline. Simply proceed in order through the systems descriptions with your students. Reviewing the POH, studying a schematic, and discussing general operating principles provides your students with a solid foundation in systems knowledge. To create an effective and interesting learning experience, enlist the assistance of an aviation maintenance technician (AMT) to answer student questions.
3. *While the following are examples that were stated in the text, any appropriate questions may be used.*

    Is there more than one reason that a gear indicator light may fail to illuminate?

    What does a flickering gear indicator light signal?

    What signs might indicate a slow leak of hydraulic fluid?

    What will happen to the landing gear if all the hydraulic fluid in the system is lost?

    While on the ground, if you inadvertently move the cockpit gear switch to the retract position, what will happen to the gear?

    If you leave the gear switch in the retract position during takeoff, what can happen?

    What could cause a failure of the gear to retract in flight?
4. Continuous flow, diluter-demand, and pressure-demand
5. The causes, characteristics, and effects of aircraft icing; the difference between de-icing equipment and anti-icing equipment; whether their aircraft is certified for flight in icing conditions; recognizing regions where meteorological conditions are less conducive to ice formation
6. B
7. C
8. False
9. *While the following is an example that was included in this section, any example of an appropriate flight planning scenario may be used.*

    Aircraft: Cessna Pressurized 210

    Payload: 4 Passengers, 450 Pounds of Baggage

    Weather: IFR

    Departure/Destination: Atlanta, Georgia/Ft. Lauderdale, Florida
10. *While the following is an examples which was stated in the text, any example which is appropriate for helping students develop crew coordination skills may be used.*

    You can hold your own line-oriented flight training (LOFT) sessions with your commercial students. Ask one student to play the role of the captain and the other to act as the first officer for a simulator session. If you cannot enlist two students, you can assume one of the roles.

SECTION D

1. An airplane that has an engine with more than 200 horsepower.
2. C
3. True
4. False
5. False
6. Throttle control
7. C
8. True
9. TAS (in M.P.H)^2 ÷ 15
10. B

SECTION E

1. B
2. False
3. Instrument proficiency check.
4. False
5. B
6. A

SECTION F

1. False
2. B
3. Good instructors possess patience and the ability to learn from mistakes, along with a deep desire to impart what they know to others.
4. C
5. A
6. True
7. An altitude sufficient to enable recovery above 1,500 ft. AGL
8. True
9. B
10. True
11. During an uncoordinated stall, the resulting roll and slip of the airplane creates yaw by weathervane effect. The weathervaning produces rotation about the vertical axis of the airplane, and the uncoordinated condition causes the stall of one wing before the other, resulting in roll. The combination of rolling, slipping, and yawing produces the autorotation characteristic of the spin.
12. C
13. A bank of 60 degrees relative to the horizon; or a nose-up or nose-down attitude of 30 degrees relative to the horizon.

CHAPTER 6

SECTION A

1. While the following are examples which were stated in the text, any examples which apply may be used.

   Visit an instrument repair station and examine instruments that have been disassembled. Demonstrate rigidity in space and precession using a spinning bicycle wheel.
2. The three fundamental skills your students must master when learning attitude instrument flying are — instrument cross-check, instrument interpretation, and airplane control.
3. The two generally accepted methods in use for teaching instrument cross-check during attitude instrument training are the primary/support concept and the control and performance concept.
4. Covering instruments in flight does little to prepare your students for the unexpected failure of these instruments. Use of a PCATD, FTD, or simulator allows you to provide your students with unannounced insidious primary flight instrument failures.
5. Operation Takeoff and Operation Raincheck
6. While the following are examples which were stated in the text, any examples which apply may be used.

   Sit in the airplane on the ground and use the heading indicator to teach your students techniques to determine proper holding pattern entries. FTDs and PCATDs are effective for teaching holding procedures. In the classroom, you can have your students follow a holding pattern diagram on the floor
7. C
8. While the following are examples which were stated in the text, any examples which apply may be used.

   You are on an ILS approach past the FAF when you lose glide slope indications. LOC minimums are 600 and 1 mile visibility. Reported ceiling is 500 overcast.

   During the enroute portion of an IFR flight in IMC, you lose communication. Expected clearance time is 1615Z and you arrive at the holding pattern for your destination at 1600Z. Conditions are VMC at your location and the airport is in sight. At what time can you begin the VOR approach into your destination?

   During climbout on an IFR flight, you enter the clouds at 1,000 feet AGL. You notice that the low voltage light is on.

   Headwinds are stronger than forecast. During the enroute portion of an IFR flight, recalculation of your fuel usage shows that you no longer have enough fuel to make it to the alternate after a missed approach at the primary destination. Weather conditions are near minimums at your destination.

SECTION B

1. An FTD that meets the requirements of FAR 141.41(b) allows you to reduce the flight training hour requirements for a Part 141 instrument-rating course by up to 40%. For Part 61 training, up to 20 hours of instrument training accomplished in an FTD can be used to meet instrument flight time requirements.
2. False
3. True
4. Fixation, Omission, and Emphasis
5. B
6. Furnish students with copies of flight patterns which model procedures such as holding and instrument approaches. Create exercises based on published approach procedures. Your students fly the basic ground track and profile of the approach, changing headings, altitudes, and airspeeds based on your directions. This can be accomplished at safe altitudes in the local practice area, with or without the use of navigation aids. As your students practice the pattern, assume the role of ATC and ask them to repeat altitude and heading changes. As proficiency is gained, you can provide distractions by requesting your students change a radio frequency or reset the clock. Finally, this pattern can be flown as your students practice partial panel skills.
7. When recovering from an unusual attitude with partial panel, teach your students to use the turn coordinator to stop a turn, and the pitot-static instruments to arrest an unintended climb or descent.
8. B
9. True

SECTION C

1. B
2. False
3. Propeller synchronization
4. Accumulators assist in bringing the propeller out of the feathered position by providing a burst of oil pressure to the hub as you move the control lever out of the feather position.
5. B
6. For multi-engine airplanes, the critical engine is the engine that would have the most adverse affect on controllability and climb performance if it were to fail.
7. C
8. C
9. Accelerate-stop distance is the amount of runway required under existing conditions to accelerate the airplane to a speed designated by the manufacturer, experience an engine failure at that point, immediately discontinue the takeoff, and stop the airplane on the remaining runway. The accelerate-go distance chart tells whether or not you can continue the takeoff and climb to clear a 50-foot obstacle following an engine failure at the takeoff decision speed.
10. True
11. A
12. No. Once applicants elect to pursue instrument privileges on a multi-engine rating during a checkride, they may not change the course of the checkride once it has begun.

SECTION D

1. In-cockpit ground training allows your students to become acquainted with the location of instruments, switches, and controls which may be unfamiliar.
2. C
3. True
4. B
5. C
6. A
7. D
8. C
9. False
10. Secure the inoperative engine by using the following basic steps: Fuel selector — OFF; Auxiliary boost pump — OFF; Magneto switches — OFF; Alternator — OFF; Cowl flaps — CLOSED
11. C
12. Because in a real emergency situation, performing a go-around on one engine is likely to be difficult, if not impossible.
13. B
14. They must demonstrate instrument competency in the multi-engine airplane. The required procedures include simulated engine-failure by reference to instruments, during straight-and-level flight and turns; and an instrument approach that simulates one engine inoperative.

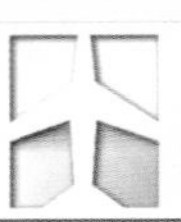

APPENDIX B GLOSSARY

ABSTRACTIONS — Words that are general rather than specific. *Aircraft* is an abstraction; *airplane* is less abstract; *jet* is more specific; and *jet airliner* is still more specific.

ACCELERATE-GO DISTANCE — The distance required to accelerate to lift-off speed, and assuming an engine fails at the instant lift-off speed is attained, to continue takeoff on the remaining engine to a height of 50 feet. Most manufacturers recommend against continuing a takeoff following an engine failure at takeoff decision speed.

ACCELERATE-STOP DISTANCE — The amount of runway required under existing conditions to: accelerate the airplane to a speed designated by the manufacturer (usually the liftoff speed); experience an engine failure at that point; immediately discontinue the takeoff; and stop the airplane on the remaining runway.

ACCOMMODATION — The time required to focus on a distant object after looking at the instrument panel.

ACCUMULATORS — Accumulators assist in bringing the propeller out of the feathered position by providing a burst of oil pressure to the hub when the control lever is moved out of the feather position.

ADVANCED GROUND INSTRUCTOR — A person certificated by the FAA who is authorized to provide: ground training in the aeronautical knowledge areas that are required for issuance of any certificate or rating; ground training required for any flight review; and a recommendation for a knowledge test required for the issuance of any certificate.

AERONAUTICAL DECISION MAKING (ADM) — A systematic approach to the mental process used by aircraft pilots to consistently determine the best course of action in response to a given set of circumstances.

AFFECTIVE DOMAIN — A grouping of learning levels associated with a person's attitudes, personal beliefs, and values, which range from receiving through responding, valuing, and organization to characterization.

AGGRESSION — Because of safety concerns or social structures, students may display the defense mechanism of aggression. They may ask irrelevant questions, refuse to participate in class activities, or disrupt the group.

AIRCRAFT CHECKOUT — An instructional program designed to familiarize and qualify a pilot to act as pilot in command of a particular aircraft type.

AIRCRAFT CONTROL — The third fundamental skill of attitude instrument flying.

AIRCRAFT DAMAGE LIABILITY COVERAGE — A policy that covers any damage to the aircraft, and works much like collision insurance on a car.

ANTIDOTES — A viable alternative to hazardous attitudes in aeronautical decision-making. Each of the five hazardous attitudes has an associated antidote, which should be memorized and employed to minimize their effects.

ANXIETY — Mental discomfort that arises from the fear of anything, real or imagined. May have a potent effect on actions and the ability to learn from perceptions.

APPLICATION — A basic level of learning where the student puts something to use that has been learned and understood.

APPLICATION STEP — The third step of the teaching process, where the student performs the procedure or demonstrates the knowledge required in the lesson. In the telling-and-doing technique of flight instruction, this step consists of the student doing the procedure while explaining it.

APPROVED PARACHUTE — A parachute manufactured under a type certificate or a technical standard order. See FAR 91.307 for further information.

APPROVED PILOT SCHOOL — Pilot schools that are approved by the FAA, must conduct flight and ground training under specific guidelines in FAR Part 141, and meet rigid operational requirements. Graduates of these schools are permitted certification with less total flight experience than that specified in Part 61.

AREA OF DECISION — The most critical time for an engine failure to occur in a multi-engine airplane, which is just after liftoff while the airplane is accelerating and climbing over immediate obstacles. The area of decision exists between the point where obstacle clearance speed is reached and landing gear retracted, and the point where the single-engine best angle-of-climb speed (V_{XSE}) is reached. An engine failure in this area requires an immediate decision to abort takeoff or to continue climbing. To make an intelligent decision in case of a failure within this area of decision, one must consider aircraft performance with the following conditions: runway length, obstruction height, field elevation, density altitude, air temperature, headwind, takeoff weight, and pilot proficiency.

AREAS OF OPERATION — Phases of the practical test arranged in a logical sequence within the PTS. Each area of operation has several task listings to be evaluated during the flight. Areas of operation are based on the corresponding flight proficiency requirements in the FARs.

ASYMMETRICAL THRUST — In single-engine airplanes, left turning tendencies are caused by both asymmetrical propeller loading (P-factor) and torque. Multi-engine airplanes have an even greater tendency to turn during climbs or other high angle-of-attack maneuvers due to the additional engine and propeller. The position of these engines in relation to the airplane's centerline causes asymmetrical propeller loading to exert a more forceful turning moment.

ATTENTION — An element that helps your students gain interest in the lesson.

ATTITUDE — A personal motivational predisposition to respond to persons, situations, or events in a given manner that can, nevertheless, be changed or modified through training as a sort of mental shortcut to decision making.

ATTITUDE MANAGEMENT — The ability to recognize one's own hazardous attitudes and the willingness to modify them as necessary through

the application of an appropriate antidote thought.

AUDITORY LEARNERS — Students who acquire knowledge best by listening.

AUTHORIZED INSTRUCTOR — According to FAR Part 61.3, a person who holds a valid ground instructor certificate issued under Part 61 or Part 143 when conducting ground training in accordance with the privileges and limitations of his or her ground instructor certificate; or a person who holds a current flight instructor certificate issued under Part 1 when conducting ground training or flight training in accordance with the privileges and limitations of his or her flight instructor certificate; or a person authorized by the Administrator to provide ground training or flight training under SFAR No. 58, or Part 61, 121,135, or 142 when conducting ground training or flight training in accordance with that authority.

AVAILABLE LANDING DISTANCE (ALD) — The amount of runway remaining when operating at a controlled airport where land and hold short operations (LAHSO) are in effect. Pilots may accept such a clearance provided that the pilot-in-command determines that the aircraft can safely land and stop within the ALD.

AVIATION SAFETY COUNSELORS — Volunteers within the aviation community who share their technical expertise and professional knowledge as a part of the FAA Aviation Safety Program.

AVIATION SAFETY REPORTING SYSTEM (ASRS) — The ASRS investigates the causes underlying a reported event, and incorporates each report into a database, which provides information for research regarding aviation safety and human factors. Each report is held in strict confidence and the FAA cannot use ASRS information in enforcement actions against those who submit reports.

AVIATION MEDICAL EXAMINER (AME) — A person to whom the FAA delegates authority to examine applicants for, and holders of, airman medical certificates to determine whether or not they meet the medical standards for its issuance. AMEs also issue or deny airman medical certificates based upon whether or not they meet the applicable medical standards. The medical standards are found in Title 14 of the Code of Federal Regulations Part 67.

BARRIERS TO EFFECTIVE COMMUNICATION — Things which impede communication, such as lack of common experience, or confusion between the symbol and the symbolized object. Other examples include overuse of abstractions and interference.

BASIC GROUND INSTRUCTOR — A person authorized by the FAA to provide: ground training in the aeronautical knowledge areas required for issuance of a recreational pilot certificate, private pilot certificate, or associated ratings under Part 61; ground training required for a recreational pilot and private pilot flight review; and recommendation for a knowledge test required for issuance of a recreational pilot certificate or private pilot certificate under Part 61.

BASIC MANEUVERS — Straight-and-level flight, climbs, descents, and turns. These four maneuvers form the foundation of the development of all piloting skills. Each flight maneuver, regardless of its complexity, is composed of combinations of the basic maneuvers.

BASIC NEED — A perception factor that describes a person's ability to maintain and enhance the organized self.

BEHAVIORISM — Theory of learning that stresses the importance of having a particular form of behavior reinforced by someone, other than the student, to shape or control what is learned.

BOUNDARY LAYER — The air next to the surface of an airfoil, which shows reduction of speed due to the air's viscosity or thickness. As air flows from front to back on a wing's upper surface, the boundary layer goes through a transition from smooth airflow to turbulent airflow.

BRANCHING — A programming technique, which allows users of interactive video, multimedia courseware, or online training to choose from several courses of action in moving from one sequence to another.

BRIEFING — An oral presentation where the speaker presents a concise array of facts without inclusion of extensive supporting material.

BUILDING BLOCK CONCEPT/BLOCKS OF LEARNING — Concept of learning that new knowledge and skills are best based on a solid foundation of previous experience and/or old learning. As knowledge and skills increase, the base expands, supporting further learning.

CALIBRATED AIRSPEED (CAS) — Indicated airspeed of an aircraft, corrected for installation and instrument errors.

CENTERLINE THRUST — An aircraft design for multi-engine airplanes that eliminates engine-out asymmetrical thrust and asymmetrical drag. Mounting the engines along the fuselage centerline eliminates directional control problems of the conventional twin following an engine failure. However, the loss of an engine can still reduce climb performance significantly. Airplanes incorporating centerline thrust do not have a published V_{MC} speed. Pilots who receive a multi-engine rating in an airplane of this type have the restriction *"Limited to Center Thrust"* placed on their pilot certificates. This restriction can be removed when they subsequently demonstrate the maneuver during a practical test in a conventional twin.

CFI RENEWAL — A process that allows CFIs to renew their certificates since flight instructor certificates are only valid for 24 months. CFI renewal is not automatic by any means since it requires a specific certificate action by the FAA. Certificate renewal should be in accordance with FAR Part 61.197 by any of the following methods. A CFI can present the FAA with a record of training that shows endorsement of at least 5 students for a practical test for a certificate or rating, and at least 80% of the students passed on their first attempt. A CFI can also show the FAA a satisfactory record as a Part 121 or 135 check pilot, chief flight instructor, check airman or flight instructor, or that he or she is in a position involving the regular evaluation of pilots. Graduation from an approved flight instructor refresher course (FIRC), consisting of at least 16 hours of ground and/or flight training, also may be the basis of renewing certificates at the discretion of the FAA.

CHAINING — Combines behaviors students already know to assemble more complex behaviors.

CHARACTERISTICS OF LEARNING — Effective learning shares several common characteristics. Learning is dynamic and should be purposeful, based on experience, multifaceted, and involve an active process.

CHECKLIST — A systematic list of items and equipment on board an aircraft that are intended for reference, verification, or identification. An essential tool for safely flying the airplane.

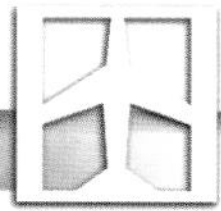

CIRCLING — A maneuver to align the aircraft with a runway for landing when a straight-in landing from an instrument approach is not possible or desirable. This maneuver is made only after ATC authorization and the pilot has established the required visual reference to the airport.

CLIMB GRADIENT — A minimum climb rate expressed in feet per nautical mile. For example, a climb gradient of 400 feet per nautical mile requires a minimum climb performance of 400 feet in a horizontal distance of one n.m. Climb gradient can be converted mathematically (or by use of a table) to feet per minute if groundspeed is known.

CLIMB PROPELLERS — A type of fixed-pitch propeller that provides the aircraft with the best performance during takeoff and climb.

COGNITIVE DOMAIN — A grouping of levels of learning associated with mental activity which range from knowledge through comprehension, application, analysis, and synthesis to evaluation.

COGNITIVE INFORMATION PROCESSING — Describes how information is gathered, processed, and stored by the brain in much the same way as a computer does.

COGNITIVE THEORY — Learning is not just a change in outward behavior but involves changes in thinking, feeling, or understanding. It involves mental processes, such as decision making and problem solving, which are difficult, if not impossible, to observe or measure.

COMMERCIAL MANEUVERS — Consists of maximum performance takeoffs and landings, steep turns, chandelles, lazy eights, and eights-on-pylons

COMMUNICATION PROCESS — Consists of three basic elements: the source, the symbols used to communicate the message, and the receiver. In addition, feedback is essential for effective communication to take place.

COMMUNICATION SKILLS — The skills that an instructor must develop to communicate effectively with students. The ability to communicate effectively as an instructor begins with an understanding of the communication process and is enhanced by experience and training.

COMPASS TURNS — Maintaining heading and making turns with reference to the magnetic compass only.

COMPENSATION — A defense mechanism that attempts to disguise a weak or undesirable quality by emphasizing a more positive one. Students may lower the scope of their goals to avoid possible failure in achieving goals that are more difficult.

COMPLEX AIRPLANE — An airplane that has a retractable landing gear, flaps, and a controllable pitch propeller.

COMPREHENSIVENESS — A characteristic of a measuring instrument when it is based on a liberal sampling of the knowledge or skill to be measured. It must be broad enough to ensure that conclusions are representative of the whole.

COMPUTER-ASSISTED INSTRUCTION (CAI) — Synonymous with computer-based training or instruction, emphasizing the point that the instructor is responsible for the class and uses the computer to assist in the instruction.

COMPUTER-BASED INSTRUCTION (CBI) — Synonymous with computer-based training. The use of the computer as a training device.

COMPUTER-BASED TRAINING (CBT) — The use of the computer as a training device. CBT is sometimes called computer-based instruction (CBI); the terms and acronyms are synonymous and may be used interchangeably.

CONDITIONS — The second part of a performance-based objective, which describes the framework under which the skill or behavior will be demonstrated.

CONFUSION BETWEEN THE SYMBOL AND THE SYMBOLIZED OBJECT — Results when a word is confused with what it is meant to represent. Words and symbols create confusion when they mean different things to different people.

CONSTANT-SPEED PROPELLER — Constant-speed propellers are able to vary the propeller blade angle in flight to provide the most desirable aircraft performance.

CONSTRUCTIVISM — Provides a unique way of thinking about how students learn. Constructivism is based upon the idea that learners construct knowledge through the process of discovery as they experience events and actively seek to understand their environment.

CONTACT APPROACH — An approach where an aircraft on an IFR flight plan, having an air traffic control authorization, operating clear of clouds with at least one mile flight visibility, and a reasonable expectation of continuing to the destination airport in those conditions, may deviate from the instrument approach procedure and proceed to the destination airport by visual reference to the surface. This approach will only be authorized when requested by the pilot and the reported ground visibility at the destination airport is at least one statute mile.

CONTROL AND PERFORMANCE CONCEPT — A method of teaching attitude instrument flying, which focuses on controlling attitude and power as necessary to produce the desired performance. This method divides the instruments into three categories: control, performance, and navigation. It is used predo minantly with high-performance turbine aircraft.

CONTROLLED FLIGHT INTO TERRAIN (CFIT) — A type of accident where an aircraft is flown into terrain or water with no prior awareness by the crew that the crash is imminent.

COOPERATIVE OR GROUP LEARNING — An instructional strategy which organizes students into small groups so that they can work together to maximize their own and each other's learning.

CORRELATION — A basic level of learning where the student can associate what has been learned, understood, and applied with previous or subsequent learning.

COURSE OF TRAINING — A complete series of studies leading to attainment of a specific goal, such as a certificate of completion, graduation, or an academic degree.

COURSE REVERSAL — A method of reversing course, which is depicted on an instrument approach procedure. Some procedures do not provide for straight-in approaches unless the airplane is being radar vectored. In these situations, the pilot is required to complete a course reversal, generally within 10 nautical miles of the primary navaid or fix designated on the approach chart, to establish the aircraft inbound on the intermediate or final approach segments.

CREW RESOURCE MANAGEMENT (CRM) — The application of team management concepts in the flight deck environment. It was initially known as cockpit resource management, but as CRM programs evolved to include cabin crews, maintenance personnel and others, the phrase "crew resource management" has been adopted. This includes single

pilots, as in most general aviation aircraft. Pilots of small aircraft, as well as crews of larger aircraft, must make effective use of all available resources; human resources, hardware, and information. A current definition includes all groups routinely working with the cockpit crew who are involved in decisions required to operate a flight safely. These groups include, but are not limited to: pilots, dispatchers, cabin crewmembers, maintenance personnel, and air traffic controllers. CRM is one way of addressing the challenge of optimizing the human/machine interface and accompanying interpersonal activities.

CRITERIA — The third part of a performance-based objective which describes the standards that will be used to measure the accomplishment of the objective.

CRITERION REFERENCE TESTING (CRT) — System of testing where students are graded against a carefully written, measurable standard or criterion rather than against each other.

CRITICAL ALTITUDE — The maximum altitude at which a turbocharged engine delivers sea level power. If an aircraft climbs above its critical altitude, manifold pressure begins to decrease.

CRITICAL ENGINE — The engine that would have the most adverse effect on controllability and climb performance if it were to fail. Multi-engine airplanes with propellers turning in the same direction are designed so the descending blade of one engine is further from the centerline of the aircraft than the descending blade of the engine mounted on the other side. This makes the failure of one engine more critical than the other because there is a greater yawing moment created by the engine that is producing thrust further from the aircraft centerline. To eliminate the critical engine, manufacturers use counter-rotating engines. In this case, the descending propeller blades of both engines are the same distance from the aircraft centerline, and neither engine would affect climb performance or controllability more than the other if it were to fail.

CRITIQUE — Informal appraisals of student performance, designed to quickly convey feedback. Use critiques to summarize and complete a lesson, as well as to prepare students for the next lesson.

CROSS-CHECK — A systematic way of observing instrument indications during attitude instrument flying. Also called scanning, it requires logical and systematic observation of the instrument panel. It saves time and reduces the workload of instrument flying because the pertinent instruments are observed as needed.

CROSSED-CONTROL STALL — A type of demonstration stall that a flight instructor shows a student pilot. This type of stall can occur during a skidding turn, and is most likely to occur when a pilot tries to compensate for overshooting a runway during a turn from base to final while on landing approach.

CRUISE PROPELLERS — A type of fixed-pitch propeller that provides the aircraft with the best performance during cruise flight.

CURRICULUM — May be defined as a set of courses in an area of specialization offered by an educational institution. A curriculum for a pilot school usually includes courses for the various pilot certificates and ratings.

CUT-AWAY — Model of an object that is built in sections so it can be taken apart to reveal the inner structure.

DECIDE MODEL — To assist in teaching pilots the elements of the decision-making process, a six-step model has been developed using the acronym "DECIDE."

Detect the fact that a change has occurred.

Estimate the need to counter or react to the change.

Choose a desirable outcome for the success of the flight.

Identify actions, which could successfully control the change.

Do the necessary action to adapt to the change.

Evaluate the effect of the action.

DECISION-MAKING PROCESS — Involves an evaluation of risk elements to achieve an accurate perception of the flight situation. The risk elements include the pilot, the aircraft, the environment, the operation, and the situation.

DEDUCTIBLE — The amount that the policyholder is responsible for in the event of a claim.

DEFENSE MECHANISMS — Subconscious ego-protecting reactions to unpleasant situations.

DEMONSTRATION-PERFORMANCE METHOD — An educational presentation where an instructor first shows the student the correct way to perform an activity and then has the student attempt the same activity.

DEMONSTRATION STALLS — Stalls which the instructor demonstrates mainly as an in-flight portion of stall/spin awareness training. The flight instructor PTS lists these stalls, categorizes them, and explains the knowledge and skill associated with successful performance. Advise student pilots that demonstration stalls are not to be practiced in solo flight. Like other flight maneuvers, perform demonstration stalls at an altitude that allows for recovery above 1,500 ft. AGL.

DENIAL OF REALITY — A psychological defense mechanism where students may ignore or refuse to acknowledge disagreeable realities. They may turn away from unpleasant sights, refuse to discuss unpopular topics, or reject criticism.

DESCRIPTION OF THE SKILL OR BEHAVIOR — The first part of a performance-based objective, which explains the desired outcome of instruction in measurable concrete terms.

DESIGNATED EXAMINER — Any person authorized by the Administrator to conduct a pilot proficiency test or a practical test for an airman certificate or rating issued under FAR Part 61. Also, a person authorized to conduct a knowledge test under FAR Part 61.

DETERMINERS — In test items, words which give a clue to the answer. Words such as "always" and "never" are determiners in true-false questions. Since absolutes are rare, such words usually make the statement false.

DEVELOPMENT — The main body of an instructional lesson that contains a detailed listing of the subject matter. Developing material in a structured way speeds up the process and makes it easier to follow a logical progression.

DIFFERENCE BETWEEN THE SYMBOL AND THE SYMBOLIZED OBJECT — The result of a word being confused with an unintended meaning. Words and symbols do not always represent the same thing to every person. Confusion results when the name of an object is not differentiated from the characteristics of the object itself.

DIFFERENCES TRAINING — Training given to pilots who wish to transition between similar makes and

models of a given manufacturer. For example, transitioning from a C-210 to a P-210 would require differences training for pressurization and turbocharging.

DIRECT QUESTION — A question used for follow-up purposes, but directed at a specific individual.

DISCRIMINATION — In a measuring instrument, means being able to detect small differences in understanding of material between individuals.

DISTRACTIONS — During training flights, an instructor should interject realistic distractions to determine if students can maintain aircraft control while their attention is diverted.

DISTRACTORS — Incorrect responses to a multiple-choice test item.

DISUSE — A theory of forgetting that suggests a person forgets those things which are not used.

DOMAINS OF LEARNING — In addition to the four basic levels of learning, psychologists have developed three domains of learning: cognitive, psychomotor, and affective. These domains represent what is to be gained during the learning process, either knowledge, skills, or attitudes.

EFFECT — A principle of learning, which states that learning is strengthened when accompanied by a pleasant or satisfying feeling, and that learning is weakened when associated with an unpleasant feeling.

EGOISTIC NEEDS — Basic personal needs that relate to a student's self-esteem and are directly linked to self-confidence, independence, achievement, competence, and knowledge. Another type relates to a student's reputation, such as status, recognition, appreciation, and respect of associates.

ELEMENT OF THREAT — A perception factor that describes how a person is unlikely to easily comprehend an event if that person is feeling threatened since most of a person's effort is focused on whatever is threatening them.

ELEVATOR TRIM STALL — A type of demonstration stall that a flight instructor shows a student pilot. It simulates the danger zone defined by a rejected landing or go-around, and is demonstrated at altitude with the airplane configured and trimmed for a typical final approach to landing.

EMPTY FIELD MYOPIA — When conditions are hazy, the eyes can relax and focus 10 to 30 feet ahead of the aircraft.

ENGINE INOPERATIVE LOSS OF DIRECTIONAL CONTROL DEMONSTRATION — This demonstration is required during a multi-engine practical test to show the control pressures necessary to maintain directional control with one engine inoperative. This demonstration should be accomplished within a safe distance of a suitable airport, and the entry altitude should allow completion no lower than 3,000 feet AGL. Since actual V_{MC} varies with existing condition, the pilot should not try to duplicate the published V_{MC}, which was established during initial certification. Pilots should expect a loss of directional control at a speed that may be higher than the published V_{MC}. Remember, as altitude increases, actual V_{MC} decreases, and under some weight and altitude combinations, V_{MC} and stall speed are the same. This means that the loss of directional control demonstration cannot be accomplished safely. Pilots should be prepared to recover at the first indication of stall or loss of directional control, whichever occurs first. The bottom line is that the intent of the engine-out loss of directional control demonstration is to demonstrate the onset of control limits. Normally, this occurs when the nose begins to move even though full rudder is applied.

ENHANCED TRAINING MATERIALS — While aviation instructors are expected to be familiar with all regulatory training requirements, use of instructor-oriented training materials, which are enhanced for regulatory compliance, are beneficial for ensuring that required training is accomplished, endorsed, and properly documented. Examples of these materials may include training syllabi, maneuver guides or handbooks, and computer-based training.

EQUIVALENT AIRSPEED (EAS) — Calibrated airspeed corrected for adiabatic compressible flow at a particular altitude.

EVALUATIONS — Measures a demonstrated performance against a criteria or standard, such as a grade of at least 70% to pass a written test. Formal evaluations are typically in the form of written tests, oral quizzing, or check flights, and are used to measure performance and document whether the course objectives have been met.

EXERCISE — A principle of learning, which states that those things most often repeated are best remembered.

EXTERNAL RESOURCES — Many potential resources exist outside the cockpit such as air traffic controllers, maintenance technicians, and flight service personnel.

FAA FORM 8500-8 — Application for airman medical certificate, or airman medical and student pilot certificate.

FAA FORM 8710-1 — Application for an airman certificate and/or rating.

FEEDBACK — Another way to gauge whether students are receiving the correct message. Students must interpret and evaluate the information received and then respond. The transmission of evaluative or corrective information to the original or controlling source about an action, event, or process.

FIRST SOLO — A student pilot may not operate an aircraft in solo flight unless that student has met the requirements of FAR Part 61. "Solo flight," refers to the flight time that a student pilot is the solo occupant of the aircraft, or when the student performs the duties of a pilot in command of a gas balloon or airship requiring more than one pilot flight crewmember. "First solo" refers to the very first time a student embarks on a solo flight.

FIXED BASE OPERATOR (FBO) — An aviation business establishment that may provide pilot training, aircraft rental, fueling, maintenance, parking, and the sale of aircraft and pilot supplies.

FIXED-PITCH PROPELLERS — Fixed-pitch propellers are designed as a climb propeller, a cruise propeller, or a standard propeller.

FLIGHT — To take flight physically, students may develop symptoms or ailments that give them acceptable excuses for avoiding lessons. More frequent than physical flights are mental flights, or daydreaming. Mental flight provides a simple escape from problems.

FLIGHT ASSIST — The help given when the pilot takes the precaution of requesting assistance from air traffic control (ATC). A flight assist report (FAA Form 7230-6) is filed by ATC personnel to help other pilots learn from the incident. This form is not used to initiate enforcement action.

FLIGHT INSTRUCTOR REFRESHER COURSE (FIRC) — An educational seminar for flight instructors, which consists of ground training or flight training or a combination of both. The FIRC must be completed within the 3 calendar months preceding the expiration month of the current flight instructor certificate, and usually consists of at least 16 hours of ground and/or flight training.

FLIGHT REVIEW — An industry-managed, FAA monitored currency program designed to assess and update a pilot's knowledge and skills.

FLIGHT SIMULATORS — A device that is a full-size aircraft cockpit replica of a specific type of aircraft, or make, model, and series of aircraft; includes the hardware and software necessary to represent the aircraft in ground operations and flight operations; uses a force cueing system that provides cues at least equivalent to those cues provided by a 3 degree freedom of motion system; uses a visual system that provides at least a 45 degree horizontal field of view and a 30 degree vertical field of view simultaneously for each pilot; and has been evaluated, qualified, and approved by the Administrator.

FLIGHT STANDARDS DISTRICT OFFICE (FSDO) — An FAA field office serving an assigned geographical area. Its staff of flight standards personnel serve the aviation industry and the general public on matters relating to the certification and operation of air carrier and general aviation aircraft. Activities include general surveillance of operational safety, certification of airmen and aircraft, accident prevention, investigation, and enforcement action, among other duties.

FLIGHT TRAINING DEVICES (FTD) — A full-size replica of the instruments, equipment, panels, and controls of an aircraft, or set of aircraft, in an open flight deck area or in an enclosed cockpit. A force (motion) cueing system or visual system is not required.

FOLLOW-UP QUESTION — In the guided discussion method, a question used by an instructor to get the discussion back on track or to get the students to explain something more thoroughly.

FORMAL LECTURE — An oral presentation where the purpose is to inform, persuade, or entertain with little or no verbal participation by the listeners.

FUNDAMENTALS OF INSTRUCTION — Includes the learning process, elements of effective teaching, student evaluation and testing, course development, lesson planning, and classroom training techniques.

GOALS AND VALUES — A perception factor that describes how a person's perception of an event depends on beliefs. Motivation toward learning is affected by how much value a person puts on education. Instructors who have some idea of the goals and values of their students will be more successful in teaching them.

GOLD SEAL FLIGHT INSTRUCTOR CERTIFICATE — A flight instructor certificate printed with a distinctive gold seal to recognize excellence in flight training based on a CFI's record of performance. To obtain a gold seal certificate, a CFI must have trained and recommended at least 10 students for practical tests within the previous 24 months, and at least 8 of these students must have passed on their first attempt. A CFI must also hold a ground instructor certificate with an advanced or instrument rating.

GROUP TASK — Part of cooperative, or group learning. Each activity your students engage in is known as a group task.

GUIDED DISCUSSION METHOD — An educational presentation typically used in the classroom where the topic to be covered by a group is introduced and the instructor participates only as necessary to keep the group focused on the subject.

HAZARDOUS ATTITUDES — Studies have identified five hazardous attitudes that can interfere with a pilot's ability to make sound decisions and exercise authority properly. The five hazardous attitudes are anti-authority, impulsivity, invulnerability, macho, and resignation.

HEADWORK — Is required to accomplish a conscious, rational thought process when making decisions. Good decision making involves risk identification and assessment, information processing, and problem solving.

HIERARCHY OF HUMAN NEEDS — A listing by Abraham Maslow of needs from the most basic to the most fulfilling. These range from physical through safety, social, and ego to self-fulfillment.

HIGH ALTITUDE CHECKOUT — FAR 61.31(f) requires specific ground and flight training for a pilot to act as PIC of a pressurized airplane that has a service ceiling or maximum operating altitude, whichever is lower, above 25,000 MSL. High-altitude checkouts require both ground and flight training. Included in the ground training is a thorough review of the physiological aspects of high-altitude flight. An overview of these effects is contained in Chapter 8 of the *Aeronautical Information Manual* (AIM) and AC 61-107, *Operations of Aircraft at Altitudes Above 25,000 Feet MSL and/or MACH Numbers (Mmo) Greater Than .75*. AC 61-107 contains a recommended outline for a high-altitude training program. An instructor needs a logbook endorsement for high-altitude operations to give flight instruction in a pressurized airplane that has a service ceiling or maximum operating altitude above 25,000 feet MSL.

HIGH PERFORMANCE AIRPLANE — An airplane with an engine of more than 200 horsepower.

HOLIST — A learning style that focuses on the overall object first and then examines the individual components, using a top to bottom approach.

HOMEBUILT AIRPLANES — An aircraft constructed by an amateur builder. Such builders buy kits and/or plans for the aircraft and assemble the airplane over a period of years in their hangars, garages, and even basements. These airplanes are known as homebuilts. An airplane is considered amateur built if the builder constructs at least 51% of the aircraft. Manufacturers of homebuilt kits may not construct more than 49% of the total airplane.

HOME STUDY COURSE — Under FAR 61.35, a home study course may be used to meet the prerequisites for a knowledge test. Home study curriculums may be developed individually by students from material described in the applicable FAA knowledge test guide. Usually, home study courses are designed by pilot schools, colleges and universities, aviation organizations, publishers, or individual ground or flight instructors. The home study course may feature printed material, video, or computer-based training provided on CDs or accessed over the Internet. Regardless of the medium, students must show that the course has been satisfactorily completed and obtain an endorsement from an authorized instructor. Refer to *Certification: Pilots and Flight Instructors* (AC 61-65), which describes several methods that students can use to show evidence of having satisfactorily completed home study courses.

HUMAN FACTORS — A multidisciplinary field devoted to optimizing human performance and reducing human error. It incorporates the methods and principles of the behavioral and social sciences,

engineering, and physiology. It may be described as the applied science, which studies people working together in concert with machines. Human factors involve variables that influence individual performance, as well as team or crew performance.

HUMAN FACTORS RELATED — The phrase "human factors related" more aptly describes an accident since it is not usually a single decision that leads to an accident, but a chain of events triggered by a number of factors. The poor judgment chain, sometimes referred to as the error chain, is a term used to describe this principle of contributing factors in a human factors related accident.

ILLUSTRATED TALK — An oral presentation where the speaker relies heavily on visual aids to convey ideas to the listeners.

IMPULSIVE — A learning style where a student makes a quick assessment and then decides to take action. Impulsive students may not read each question or all of the answer choices entirely. As a result, they tend to select the first choice that appears correct.

I'M SAFE CHECKLIST — Personal Checklist — I'm physically and mentally safe to fly; not being impaired by:

Illness,

Medication,

Stress,

Alcohol,

Fatigue,

Eating.

INFORMAL LECTURE — A lecture style that lends itself to active student participation.

INITIAL APPROACH FIX (IAF) — The fixes depicted on instrument approach procedure charts that identify the beginning of the initial approach segment(s).

INOPERATIVE COMPONENTS — The lowest landing minimums on an approach are authorized when all components and visual aids are operating. If some components are inoperative, higher landing minimums may be required. If more than one component is inoperative, apply only the greatest increase in altitude and/or visibility required by the failure of a single component.

INSIGHT — The grouping of perceptions into meaningful wholes. Creating insight is one of the instructor's major responsibilities.

INSTRUCTIONAL AIDS — Devices that assist an instructor in the teaching-learning process. They are supplementary training devices and are not self-supporting.

INSTRUMENT GROUND INSTRUCTOR — A person certificated by the FAA who is authorized to provide the following: ground training in the aeronautical knowledge areas required for issuance of an instrument rating under Part 61; ground training required for an instrument proficiency check; and a recommendation for a knowledge test required for issuance of an instrument rating under Part 61.

INSTRUMENT INTERPRETATION — One of the fundamental skills of basic attitude instrument flying. The three fundamental skills include instrument cross-check, instrument interpretation, and aircraft control. Interpretation involves an awareness of the instrument indications that represent the desired pitch and bank attitudes for the aircraft.

INSTRUMENT PROFICIENCY CHECK — An evaluation ride based on the instrument rating practical test standard, which is required to regain instrument flying privileges when the privileges have expired due to lack of currency.

INSTRUMENT TRAINING — That time in which instrument training is received from an authorized instructor under actual or simulated instrument conditions.

INTEGRATED METHOD OF FLIGHT INSTRUCTION — A technique of flight instruction where students are taught to perform flight maneuvers by reference to both the flight instruments and to outside visual references from the time the maneuver is first introduced. Handling of the controls is the same regardless of whether flight instruments or outside references are being used.

INTENSITY — A principle of learning where a dramatic or exciting learning experience is likely to be remembered longer than a boring experience. Students experiencing the real thing will learn more than when they are merely told about the real thing.

INTERACTIVE VIDEO — Software that responds quickly to certain choices and commands by the user. A typical system consists of a compact disc, computer, and video technology.

INTERCOOLERS — A device used to reduce the temperatures of the compressed air before it enters the fuel metering device. The resulting cooler air has a higher density, which permits the engine to be operated with a higher power setting.

INTERFERENCE — (1) A theory of forgetting where a person forgets something because a certain experience overshadows it, or the learning of similar things has intervened. (2) Barriers to effective communication that are caused by physiological, environmental, and psychological factors outside the direct control of the instructor. The instructor must take these factors into account in order to communicate effectively.

INTERIM SUMMARY — An interim summary can be made immediately after each topic to bring ideas together, create an efficient transition to the next topic, divert the discussion to another member of the group, or keep students on track.

INTERNAL RESOURCES — During pilot operations, these are sources of information found within the airplane such as the pilot's operating handbook, checklists, aircraft equiment, aeronautical charts, the instructor, another pilot, and passengers, as well as one's ingenuity, knowledge, and skills.

INTRODUCTION — The first element of an instructional lesson that sets the stage for the rest of the lesson by relating the coverage of the material to the entire course. The introduction itself is typically composed of three elements: attention, motivation, and an overview of what is to be covered.

JUDGMENT — The mental process of recognizing and analyzing all pertinent information in a particular situation, a rational evaluation of alternative actions in response to it, and a timely decision on which action to take.

KINESTHETIC LEARNERS — People who prefer to be doing something and primarily absorb information through actual hands-on experience. Kinesthetic learners ascertain more from performing a preflight inspection than from studying a checklist.

LACK OF COMMON EXPERIENCE — In communication, a difficulty that arises because words have different meanings for the source and the receiver of information due to their differing backgrounds.

LAND AND HOLD SHORT OPERATIONS (LAHSO) — Refers to landing

and then holding short of an intersection runway, taxiway, predetermined point, or an approach/departure flight path. These operations include landing and holding short of an intersecting runway, an intersecting taxiway, or some other designated point on a runway other than an intersecting runway or taxiway.

LEAD-OFF QUESTION — In the guided discussion method, a question used by an instructor to open up an area for discussion and get the discussion started.

LEARNING — A change in behavior as a result of experience.

LEARNING PLATEAU — A learning phenomenon where progress appears to cease or slow down for a significant period of time before once again increasing.

LEARNING STYLE — The concept that how a person learns is dependent on that person's background and personality, as well as the instructional methods used.

LECTURE METHOD — An educational presentation usually delivered by an instructor to a group of students with the use of instructional aids and training devices. Lectures are useful for the presentation of new material, summarizing ideas, and showing relationships between theory and practice.

LEFT BRAIN — A concept that each hemisphere of the brain processes information differently. Students with left-brain dominance are more verbal, analytical, and objective.

LESSON PLAN — An organized outline for a single instructional period. It is a necessary guide for the instructor in that it tells what to do, in what order to do it, and what procedure to use in teaching the material of a lesson.

LISTENING — Hearing your students talk and listening to what they are saying are two different things. Instructors can use a variety of techniques or tools to become better listeners, including: do not interrupt, do not judge, think before answering, be close enough to hear, watch nonverbal behavior, be aware of biases, look for underlying feelings, concentrate, avoid rehearsing answers while listening, do not insist on the last word.

LONG-TERM MEMORY — The portion of the brain that stores information which has been determined to be of sufficient value to be retained. In order for it to be retained in long-term memory, it must have been processed or coded in the working memory.

MACH — The ratio of the aircraft's true airspeed to the speed of sound.

MASLOW'S HIERARCHY OF HUMAN NEEDS — See Hierarchy of Human Needs.

MATCHING — A test item consisting of two lists where the student is asked to match alternatives on one list to related alternatives on the second list. The lists may include a combination of words, terms, illustrations, phrases, or sentences.

MOCK-UP — Three-dimensional working model used where the actual object is either unavailable or too expensive to use. Mock-ups may emphasize some elements while eliminating nonessential elements.

MODEL — A copy of a real object, which can be life-size, smaller, or larger than the original.

MOTIVATION — A need or desire that causes a person to act. Motivation can be positive or negative, tangible or intangible, subtle or obvious.

MULTIMEDIA — A combination of more than one instructional medium. This format can include audio, text, graphics, animations, and video. Recently, multimedia implies a computer-based presentation.

MULTIPLE-CHOICE — A test item consisting of a question or statement followed by a list of alternative answers or responses.

NEGATIVE TRANSFER OF LEARNING — Students interpret new things in terms of what they already know. Some degree of transfer is involved in all learning. Previous learning interferes with students' understanding of the current task.

"NO-GYRO" APPROACH — A radar approach/vector provided in case of malfunctioning gyro-compass or directional gyro. Instead of providing the pilot with headings, the controller observes the radar track and issues control instructions "turn right/left" or "stop turn" as appropriate.

NON-OWNER LIABILITY COVERAGE — An insurance policy against claims arising from bodily injury or damage caused to others or their property while using an aircraft that one does not own.

NORM-REFERENCED TESTING (NRT) — System of testing where students are ranked against the performance of other students.

OBJECTIVITY — Characteristic of a measuring instrument when it is free of any personal bias by the person grading the test.

OPERANT CONDITIONING — Behavior initiated voluntarily by the individual, such as turning on a fuel pump, reading a checklist, or initiating a go-around. Operant behavior is the target of learning and the most important to a flight instructor. It generally consists of three phases: cues are provided to initiate the behavior, the behavior is performed, and consequences associated with that performance are received.

OPERATIONAL PITFALLS — The desire to complete a flight as planned, please passengers, meet schedules, and demonstrate that they have the right stuff can all have an adverse effect on safety by causing pilots to overestimate their piloting skills under stressful conditions. The operational pitfalls are as follows: mind set, scud running, continuing VFR into IMC, operating without adequate fuel reserves, flying outside the envelope, neglect of flight planning, preflight inspections and checklists, getting behind the aircraft, peer pressure, get-there-itis, duck-under syndrome, and descent below minimum enroute altitude.

OPERATION RAINCHECK — A program designed to familiarize pilots with the ATC system, its functions, responsibilities and benefits. Visiting facilities such as control towers, approach control, or air route traffic control centers can expand one's knowledge of ATC services.

OPERATION TAKEOFF — A program that educates pilots on how best to utilize the FSS modernization efforts and services that are available in automated flight service stations (AFSS), as stated in FAA Order 7230.17. One can interact with weather briefers at a local flight service station and learn tips and techniques to get the most out of the services they provide.

ORAL QUIZZING — The most common means of evaluating a student's knowledge. Proper oral quizzing during a lesson promotes active student participation, identifies points that need more emphasis, and reveals the effectiveness of training procedures.

OVERBOOST — Excessive manifold pressure, which can cause damage to internal engine components.

OVERHEAD QUESTION — In the guided discussion method, a question

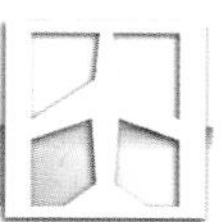

directed to the entire group to stimulate thought and discussion. An overhead question may be used by an instructor as the lead-off question.

OVERSHOOT — Overshoot is caused by rapid increase in throttle, which causes the controller to overshoot the requirement for the engine boost, resulting in overboost.

OVERSPEEDING — Exceeding the maximum r.p.m. limits of the engine. Adjusting pitch stops in the prop governor allow r.p.m. limits to be set.

OVERVIEW — A concise presentation of the objective and key ideas, supplemented with appropriate visual aids, to give students a clear picture of what is to come.

PARALLAX — Apparent displacement of an object if first viewed from one position and then from another.

PARTIAL PANEL — Controlling the airplane without the benefit of all instrumentation due to failure of one or more instruments in flight. Pilots are required to demonstrate basic attitude instrument flying on partial panel and are also required to fly a partial panel instrument approach during the practical test for the instrument rating.

PASSIVE VIDEO — Refers to segments of video that are simply watched by the students.

PERCEPTIONS — The basis of all learning. Perceptions result when a person gives meaning to external stimuli or sensations. Meanings, which are derived from perceptions, are influenced by an individual's experience and many other factors.

PERFORMANCE-BASED OBJECTIVES — A statement of purpose for a lesson or instructional period that includes three elements: a description of the skill or behavior desired of the student, a set of conditions under which the measurement will be taken, and a set of criteria describing the standard used to measure accomplishment of the objective.

PERSONAL CHECKLISTS — To help students determine if they are prepared for a particular flight, encourage them to create personal checklists that state their limitations based on such factors as experience, currency, and comfort level in certain flight conditions.

PERSONAL COMPUTER-BASED AVIATION TRAINING DEVICE (PCATD) — A device which uses software which can be displayed on a personal computer to replicate the instrument panel of an airplane. A PCATD must replicate a type of airplane or family of airplanes and meet the virtual control requirements specified in AC 61-126.

PERSONALITY — The embodiment of personal traits and characteristics of an individual that are set at a very early age and are extremely resistant to change.

PHYSICAL NEEDS — These needs encompass the necessities for survival, which include food, rest, exercise, and protection from the elements. Until these requirements are satisfied, students cannot fully concentrate on learning.

PHYSICAL ORGANISM — A perception factor that describes a person's ability to sense the world around them.

PILOT ERROR — Means that an action or decision made by the pilot was the cause of, or contributing factor, which led to an accident or incident. This definition also includes failure of the pilot to make a decision or take action.

PILOT-IN-COMMAND RESPONSIBILITY — The person who has final authority and responsibility for the operation and safety of the flight; has been designated as pilot in command before or during the flight; and holds the appropriate category, class, and type rating, if appropriate, for the conduct of the flight.

PILOT PROFICIENCY AWARD PROGRAM — WINGS is the FAA Pilot Proficiency Award Program designed to encourage general aviation pilots to continue their training. The objective is to provide pilots with the opportunity to establish and participate in a personal recurrent training program. WINGS is an excellent opportunity for pilots to reevaluate their flight proficiency and knowledge. WINGS is open to all pilots holding a recreational certificate or higher with a current medical certificate, when required. After pilots log three hours of dual instruction under the program and attend at least one FAA sanctioned safety seminar, they are eligible to receive and wear a distinctive set of WINGS. They will also receive a certificate of completion. Each twelve-month interval after earning the first set of WINGS, the pilot will be eligible for more WINGS. CFIs can substitute completion of a flight instructor refresher clinic or renewal program for the safety seminar. In addition, they can satisfy the flying portion of the first three phases by providing the instruction for three WINGS candidates — a minimum of nine hours of instruction.

POOR JUDGMENT CHAIN — A series of mistakes that may lead to an accident or incident. Two basic principles generally associated with the creation of a poor judgment chain are: (1) one bad decision often leads to another; and (2) as a string of bad decisions grows, it reduces the number of subsequent alternatives for continued safe flight. Aeronautical decision making is intended to break the poor judgment chain before it can cause an accident or incident.

POSITIVE TRANSFER OF LEARNING — Since students interpret new things in terms of what they already know, some degree of transfer is involved in all learning. During a learning experience, knowledge or skills they have gained in the past may aid students.

PRACTICAL TEST STANDARDS (PTS) — An FAA published list of standards which must be met for the issuance of a particular pilot certificate or rating. FAA inspectors and designated pilot examiners use these standards when conducting pilot practical tests and flight instructors should use the PTS while preparing applicants for practical tests.

PREPARATION — The first step of the teaching process, which consists of determining the scope of the lesson, the objectives, and the goals to be attained. This portion also includes making certain all necessary supplies are on hand. When using the telling-and-doing technique of flight instruction, this step is accomplished prior to the flight lesson.

PRESENTATION — The second step of the teaching process, which consists of delivering information or demonstrating the skills which make up the lesson. The delivery could be by either the lecture method or demonstration-performance method. In the telling-and-doing technique of flight instruction, this is where the instructor both talks about and performs the procedure.

PRETEST — A test used to determine whether a student has the necessary qualifications to begin a course of study. Also used to determine the level of knowledge a student has in relation to the material that will be presented in the course.

PRIMACY — A principle of learning where the first experience of something often creates a strong, almost unshakable impression. The importance to an instructor is that the first time something is demonstrated, it must be shown correctly since that experience is the one most likely to be remembered by the student.

PRIMARY INSTRUMENTS — Those instruments that provide the most essential information during a given flight condition.

PRIMARY/SUPPORT CONCEPT — A method for teaching attitude instrument flying, which divides the panel into pitch instruments, bank instruments, and power instruments. For a given maneuver, there are specific instruments used to control the airplane and obtain the desired performance.

PRINCIPLES OF LEARNING — Concepts that provide insight into effective learning and can provide a foundation for basic instructional techniques. These principles are derived from the work of E. L. Thorndike, who first proposed the principles of effect, exercise, and readiness. Three later principles were added: primacy, recency, and intensity.

PROFESSIONAL — Characterized by or conforming to the technical or ethical standards of a profession. Exhibiting a courteous, conscientious, and generally businesslike manner in the workplace.

PROJECTION — A defense mechanism used by students to relegate blame for their own shortcomings, mistakes, and transgressions to others, or to attribute their motives, desires, characteristics, and impulses to other people.

PSYCHOMOTOR DOMAIN — A grouping of levels of learning associated with physical skill levels which range from perception through set, guided response, mechanism, complex overt response, and adaptation to origination.

RATIONALIZATION — A defense mechanism that students employ when they cannot accept the real reason for their behavior. This permits them to substitute excuses for reasons; moreover, they can make those excuses plausible and acceptable to themselves. A subconscious technique for justifying actions that otherwise would be unacceptable.

REACTION FORMATION — A defense mechanism where students protect themselves from dangerous desires by not only repressing them, but by actually developing conscious attitudes and behavior patterns that are just the opposite. A student may develop a who-cares-what-other-people-think attitude to cover up feelings of loneliness and a hunger for acceptance.

READINESS — A principle of learning where the eagerness and single-mindedness of a person toward learning affect the outcome of the learning experience.

RECEIVER — In communication, the listener, reader, or student who takes in a message containing information from a source, processes it, reacts with understanding, and changes behavior in accordance with the message.

RECENCY — A principle of learning that things learned today are remembered better than things that were learned some time ago. The longer time passes, the less will be remembered. Instructors use this principle when summarizing the important points at the end of a lecture in order for students to better remember them.

REFLECTIVE — A reflective student considers all possibilities or alternatives before making a decision.

REGIONAL CHECKOUT — A checkout which goes beyond learning about a particular airplane and encompasses learning how to fly in a specific region. Before flying or giving flight instruction in any unfamiliar environment, obtain a regional checkout from a qualified CFI who is experienced in that geographical area. For example, mountain flying offers some breathtaking scenery and wonderful experiences, but it also has some unique challenges and can be extremely dangerous to inexperienced pilots.

RELAY QUESTION — Used in response to a student's question, the question is redirected to the group in order to stimulate discussion.

RELIABILITY — The use of a measuring instrument, including a written test that yields consistent results.

REPRESSION — Theory of forgetting where a person is more likely to forget information which is unpleasant or produces anxiety.

RESIGNATION — A negative self-concept is the factor that contributes most to a student's failure to a remain receptive to new experience, and which creates a tendency to reject additional training.

RESPONSES — Possible answers to a multiple-choice test item. The correct response is often called the keyed response, and incorrect responses are called distractors.

RETENTION — There are five principles that promote deep learning and enhance your student's retention of course material. The principles are: praise stimulates remembering, recall is promoted by association, favorable attitudes aid retention, learning with all the senses is most effective, and meaningful repetition aids recall.

REVERSE QUESTION — Used in response to a student's question. Rather than give a direct answer to the student's query, the instructor can redirect the question to another student to provide the answer.

REVIEW AND EVALUATION — The fourth and last step in the teaching process, which consists of a review of all material and an evaluation of the students. In the telling-and-doing technique of flight instruction, this step consists of the instructor evaluating the student's performance while the student performs the required procedure.

RESOURCE USE — An essential part of ADM training. Since useful tools and sources of information may not always be readily apparent, it is important to teach students how to recognize appropriate resources. Resources must not only be identified, but students must develop the skills to evaluate whether they have the time to use a particular resource and the impact its use will have upon the safety of flight.

RHETORICAL QUESTION — A question asked to stimulate group thought. Normally answered by the instructor, it is more commonly used in lecturing rather than in guided discussions.

RIGHT BRAIN — A concept that each hemisphere of the brain processes information differently. Students with right-brain dominance are characterized as being spatially oriented, creative, intuitive, and emotional. They may be very good with art or music and can easily put together the big picture.

RISK ELEMENTS IN ADM — Take into consideration the four fundamental risk elements: the pilot, the aircraft, the environment, and the type of operation that comprise any given aviation situation.

RISK ELEMENTS — How to assess risk is a skill that students need to learn to make effective decisions. When students are faced with making a decision regarding a flight, ask them to evaluate the status of the four risk elements: the pilot in command, the

aircraft, the environment, and the operation.

RISK MANAGEMENT — The part of the decision making process which relies on situational awareness, problem recognition, and good judgment to reduce risks associated with each flight.

ROLE MODEL — A person whose behavior in a particular role is imitated by others.

ROTE LEARNING — A basic level of learning where the student has the ability to repeat back something learned, with no understanding or ability to apply what was learned.

RUNWAY INCURSION — Any occurrence at an airport involving an aircraft, vehicle, person, or object on the ground that creates a collision hazard or results in loss of separation with an aircraft taking off, intending to takeoff, landing, or intending to land.

SAFETY NEEDS — A level of Maslow's Hierarchy of human needs, which includes protection against danger, threats, and deprivation.

SAFETY PROGRAM MANAGER — An FAA employee who designs, implements, and evaluates the Aviation Safety Program within the FAA Flight Standards District Office (FSDO) area of responsibility.

SECONDARY STALL — A type of demonstration that a flight instructor shows a student pilot. It is normally caused by poor stall recovery technique, such as attempting to climb prior to attaining sufficient flying speed. A secondary stall may occur as a result of increasing angle of attack beyond the critical angle during recovery from a preceding stall.

SELECTION-TYPE TEST ITEMS — Questions where the student chooses from two or more alternatives provided. True-false, matching, and multiple-choice type questions are examples of selection-type test items.

SELF-CONCEPT — A perception factor that ties together how people feel about themselves with how well they will receive further experiences.

SELF-FULFILLMENT NEEDS — Occupy the highest level of Maslow's pyramid. They include realizing one's own potential for continued development, and for being creative in the broadest sense. Maslow included various cognitive and aesthetic goals in this echelon.

SENSORY REGISTER — That portion of the brain which receives input from the five senses. The individual's preconceived concept of what is important will determine how much priority the register will give in passing the information on to the rest of the brain for action.

SERIALISTS — A learning style that starts with the components and pieces them together to understand the whole. Serialists prefer to start at the beginning and examine the material in order.

SHAPING — A primary method of teaching that involves the use of carefully designed stimuli and the correct reinforcers for appropriate behavior. An instructor should decide what behavior is desired from the students. Each time they demonstrate the correct behavior, provide positive reinforcement to help shape or develop this behavior.

SIDESTEP MANEUVER — A visual maneuver accomplished by a pilot at the completion of an instrument approach. It permits a straight-in landing on a parallel runway, which must not be more than 1200 feet to either side of the approach runway.

SINGLE-ENGINE ABSOLUTE CEILING — The density altitude that the airplane is capable of reaching and maintaining with the critical engine feathered and the other at maximum power. This assumes that the airplane is at maximum weight and in the clean configuration, flying in smooth air. This is also the density altitude at which V_{XSE} and V_{YSE} are the same airspeed. If flying above this altitude and the engine fails, the plane will inevitably descend until it reaches the equivalent density altitude conditions.

SINGLE-ENGINE SERVICE CEILING — The maximum density altitude at which the single-engine best rate-of-climb airspeed (V_{YSE}) produces a 50 f.p.m. rate of climb. The ability to climb 50 f.p.m. in calm air is necessary simply to maintain level flight for long periods in turbulent air. This ceiling assumes the airplane is at maximum gross weight in the clean configuration, the critical engine (if appropriate) is inoperative, and the propeller is feathered. In comparison, the multi-engine service ceiling is the density altitude at which the best rate-of-climb airspeed (V_Y) will produce a 100 f.p.m. rate of climb at maximum gross weight in the clean configuration.

SITUATIONAL AWARENESS — The accurate perception and understanding of all the factors and conditions within the four fundamental risk elements that affect safety before, during, and after the flight.

SKILLS AND PROCEDURES — The procedural, psychomotor, and perceptual skills used to control a specific aircraft or its systems. They are the stick and rudder or airmanship abilities that are gained through conventional training, are perfected, and become almost automatic through experience.

SOCIAL NEEDS — A level of Maslow's hierarchy of needs. After physical and safety needs are met, it becomes possible for students to satisfy their social needs. The need to belong and to associate, as well as to give and receive friendship and love.

SOURCE — In communication, the sender, speaker, transmitter, or instructor who composes and transmits a message made up of symbols, which are meaningful to listeners and readers.

SPECIALIZED INSTRUCTIONAL SERVICES — Ground or flight instruction that is oriented to building knowledge and skills in areas other than training pilots for specific certificates or ratings. Some examples include flight reviews, instrument proficiency checks, and transition training. Others involve aircraft checkouts for tailwheel, complex, high-performance, and high-altitude airplanes. In addition, a flight instructor may help experienced military pilots transition to general aviation aircraft or have an opportunity to provide instruction in homebuilt airplanes. Regional or local checkouts are additional areas where specialized instruction can benefit pilots and increase safety.

SPIN CERTIFICATION — To be eligible for the flight instructor-airplane or flight instructor-glider practical test, an applicant must present a logbook endorsement from an appropriately certificated and rated flight instructor certifying spin competency.

SPIN TRAINING — When applying for an initial flight instructor certificate, CFI students need to accomplish specific spin training in accordance with FAR Part 61.183.

STALL/SPIN AWARENESS — The objective of stall/spin awareness training should be to instill in the students' minds a trigger or early warning that causes pilots to react to potential stall/spin situations in an immediate, positive way. This training is required by the FARs, and AC 61-67 offers CFIs guidance in providing this instruction. The intention of the regulations is for instructors to emphasize the recognition of situations that could lead to inadvertent stalls and spins. Many stall/spin accidents occur as a result of pilot distraction while maneuvering at slow speeds close to the ground.

STANDARD TERMINAL ARRIVAL ROUTES (STARs) — A preplanned instrument flight rule (IFR) air traffic control arrival procedure published for pilot use in graphic and/or textual form. STARs provide transition from the enroute structure to an outer fix or an instrument approach fix/arrival waypoint in the terminal area.

STATEMENT OF DEMONSTRATED ABILITY (SODA) — The official term for a waiver. This is a form that may be issued in conjunction with a student's medical exam. SODAs can only be issued by the FAA's federal air surgeon and are granted for a condition normally requiring a denial that is not necessarily a safety factor.

STEM — The part of a multiple-choice test item consisting of the question, statement, or problem.

STERILE COCKPIT — A crew resource management concept that specifically prohibits crewmember performance of nonessential duties or activities while the aircraft is involved in taxi, takeoff, landing, and all other flight operations conducted below 10,000 feet MSL, except for cruise flight.

STRESS MANAGEMENT — The personal analysis of the kinds of stress experienced while flying, the application of appropriate stress assessment tools, and other coping mechanisms.

SUBROGATE — A legal term, which means to pursue action against a third party determined to be responsible for an accident, and attempt to recover damages from them over the amount of the deductible.

SUBJECT MATTER KNOWLEDGE CODES — When taking a knowledge test, incorrect answers are represented on the test results in subject matter knowledge codes. The subject matter knowledge codes represent a broad area of airman knowledge, not specific test questions, and they do not identify the correct answers.

SUPPLY-TYPE TEST ITEMS — Questions where the student supplies answers as opposed to selecting from choices provided. Essay or fill-in-the-blank type questions are examples of supply-type test items.

SYLLABUS — See Training Syllabus.

SYMBOLS — In communication, simple oral and visual codes such as words, gestures, and facial expressions, which are formed into sentences, paragraphs, lectures, or chapters to compose and transmit a message that means something to the receiver of the information.

TAILWHEEL CHECKOUT — To act as PIC of a tailwheel airplane, FAR 61.31(g) requires a demonstration of competency in normal and crosswind takeoffs and landings, wheel landings (unless the manufacturer has recommended against such landings), and go-around procedures. Seek a comprehensive tailwheel checkout from a qualified instructor for each make and model of tailwheel airplane that will be used for instruction. If one has logged PIC time in a tailwheel airplane prior to April 15, 1991, then a tailwheel endorsement is not required in one's logbook.

TAKEOFF BRIEFING — A tool that pilots can use for takeoff planning where they verbally rehearse the entire takeoff and departure prior to taking the active runway. By conducting a takeoff briefing, multiengine operations can be performed safer. The briefing should include both normal and emergency procedures just prior to taxiing onto the runway. Among other things, this enables pilots to be better prepared to handle engine failures during the various phases of the takeoff profile. This takeoff briefing should review appropriate actions for an engine failure prior to V_{MC}, before the landing gear is retracted, and after the airplane is climbing in the clean configuration.

TASKS — Knowledge areas, flight procedures, or maneuvers within an area of operation in a practical test standard. Each task includes a list of the type of aircraft category or class to which it applies with a reference to the applicable regulation or publication.

TAXONOMY OF EDUCATIONAL OBJECTIVES — A systematic classification scheme for sorting learning outcomes into three broad categories (cognitive, affective, and psychomotor) and ranking the desired outcomes in a developmental hierarchy from least complex to most complex.

TEACHING — The systematic and deliberate creation of practical instructional events (experiences) that are conducive to learning.

TEACHING LECTURE — An oral presentation that is directed toward desired learning outcomes. Some student participation is allowed.

TELLING-AND-DOING TECHNIQUE — A technique of flight instruction that consists of the instructor first telling the student about a new procedure and then demonstrating it. This is followed by the student telling and the instructor doing. Third, the student explains the new procedure while doing it. Last, the instructor evaluates while the student performs the procedure.

TEST — A set of questions, problems, or exercises for determining whether a person has a particular knowledge or skill.

TEST ITEM — A question, problem, or exercise that measures a single objective and calls for a single response.

TIME AND OPPORTUNITY — A perception factor where learning something is dependent on the student having the time to sense and relate current experiences in context with previous events.

TIMED TURN — The most accurate way to turn to a specific heading without the heading indicator. Use the clock instead of the compass card to determine when to roll out.

TRAINING COURSE OUTLINE (TCO) — Within a curriculum, describes the content of a particular course by statement of objectives, descriptions of teaching aids, definition of evaluation criteria, and indication of desired outcome.

TRAINING MEDIA — Any physical means that communicates an instructional message to students.

TRAINING SYLLABUS — A step-by-step, building block progression of learning with provisions for regular review and evaluations at prescribed stages of learning. The syllabus defines the unit of training, states by objective what the student is expected to accomplish during the unit of training, shows an organized plan for instruction, and dictates the evaluation process for either the unit or stages of learning.

TRANSITION TRAINING — An instructional program designed to familiarize and qualify a pilot to fly types of aircraft not previously flown such as tailwheel aircraft, high-performance aircraft, and aircraft capable of flying at high altitudes.

TRUE-FALSE TEST ITEMS — Consist of a statement followed by an opportunity for the student to determine whether the statement is true or false.

UNDERSTANDING — A basic level of learning where a student com prehends or grasps the nature or meaning of something.

U.S. STANDARDS FOR INSTRUMENT PROCEDURES (TERPs) — An official FAA publication that prescribes standardized methods for use in designing instrument approach procedures.

USABILITY — Functional characteristic of a measuring instrument when it is easy to read and clear in the use of directions, figures, and illustrations.

USEFUL LOAD — The difference between the empty weight of the airplane and the maximum weight allowed by the manufacturer's specification.

VALIDITY — Characteristic of a measuring instrument that actually measures what it is supposed to measure and nothing else.

VERTICAL S — The basic vertical S begins with a climb at a constant airspeed and rate. Once a particular cardinal altitude is reached, the climb is reversed and a constant rate, constant airspeed descent is begun. The amount of altitude between reversals can be varied. Once students become proficient with the straight-ahead vertical S, add turns to the problem. The vertical S is a good exercise to use in teaching students to transition from one set of conditions to another. These maneuvers are designed to improve students' cross-check and aircraft control.

VIRTUAL REALITY (VR) — A form of computer-based technology that creates a sensory experience that allows a participant to believe and barely distinguish a virtual experience from a real one. VR uses graphics with animation systems, sounds, and images to reproduce electronic versions of real life experience.

VISUAL APPROACH — An approach conducted on an instrument flight rules (IFR) flight plan which authorizes the pilot to proceed visually and clear of clouds to the airport. The pilot must, at all times, have either the airport or the preceding aircraft in sight. This approach must be authorized and under the control of the appropriate air traffic control facility. Reported weather at the airport must have a ceiling at or above 1,000 feet and visibility of three miles or greater.

VISUAL LEARNERS — Students who learn best with their sense of sight. They prefer to absorb the big picture first, then break the information down into individual parts.

VORTEX GENERATORS — Vortex generators are small airfoil-like surfaces on the wing, which project vertically into the airstream. Vortices are formed at the tip of these generators just as they are on ordinary wingtips. These vortices add energy to the boundary layer (the layer of air next to the surface of the wing) to prevent airflow separation. This reduces stall speed and can increase takeoff and landing performance.

WINGLETS — A design that nearly blocks or diffuses wing tip vortices. Winglets are nearly vertical extensions on the wingtips, which are actually carefully designed, proportioned, and positioned airfoils with their camber toward the fuselage, and with span, taper, and aspect ratio optimized to provide maximum benefit at a specific speed and angle of attack.

WORKING MEMORY (SHORT TERM MEMORY) — The portion of the brain that receives information from the sensory register. This portion of the brain can store information in memory for only a short period of time. If the information is determined by an individual to be important enough to remember, it must be coded in some way for transmittal to long-term memory.

WORKLOAD MANAGEMENT — Ensures that essential operations are accomplished by planning, prioritizing, and sequencing tasks to avoid work overload.

WRITTEN TESTS — Often used as an evaluation device. They include computerized tests as well as paper-and-pencil tests, and are often referred to as knowledge tests. A test is a set of questions, problems, or exercises used to determine whether your students have a particular knowledge or skill.

ZERO FUEL WEIGHT — Limits the ratio of loads between the fuselage and wings. The maximum load that an airplane can carry also depends on the way the load is distributed. The weight of an airplane in flight is supported largely by the wings; therefore, as the load carried in the fuselage is increased, the bending moment on the wings is increased.

ZERO SIDESLIP — A control technique used following an engine failure in a multi-engine aircraft where the pilot maintains an attitude which minimizes drag to alleviate the sideslip of the airplane. Many pilots believe that holding 5° of bank into the operating engine (opposite the failed engine) gives the best performance and directional control. Research shows that 5° or any other single value does not work in all situations. Instead, it depends on several factors, including weight, the design of the airplane, density altitude, and other elements. Also, as bank angle exceeds the zero sideslip value, there is a sharp loss of climb performance. As obstacle clearance is critical, the margin for error is minimal, and 5° of bank could mean the difference between striking an obstacle or clearing it. Analysis shows that the zero sideslip angle varies with the airplane type, but optimum performance is less than 5°. Flying at zero sideslip allows adequate directional control with the best climb performance possible.

APPENDIX C
INSTRUCTOR ENDORSEMENTS

The following examples from AC 61-65 are recommended sample endorsements for use by authorized instructors. Refer to these samples when endorsing logbooks for airmen applying for a knowledge or practical test, or when certifying accomplishment of requirements for pilot operating privileges. Each endorsement must be legible and include your signature, date of signature, certificated flight instructor (CFI) or certificated ground instructor (CGI) certificate number, and certificate expiration date, if applicable. All of these endorsements contain the essential elements, but it is not necessary for endorsements to be worded exactly as those in the AC. For example, changes to regulatory requirements may affect the wording, or you may customize the endorsement for any special circumstances of your student. In addition, FAR Part 61.189 requires that you sign the logbook of each person to whom you give ground or flight training.

STUDENT PILOT ENDORSEMENTS

1. Presolo aeronautical knowledge: § 61.87(b)

I certify that (First name, MI, Last name) has satisfactorily completed the presolo knowledge exam of § 61.87(b) for the (make and model aircraft).

S/S [date] J.J. Jones 987654321CFI Exp. 12-31-00

2. Presolo flight training: § 61.87(c)

I certify that (First name, MI, Last name) has received the required presolo training in a (make and model aircraft). I have determined he/she has demonstrated the proficiency of § 61.87(d) and is proficient to make solo flights in (make and model aircraft).

S/S [date] J.J. Jones 987654321CFI Exp. 12-31-00

3. Presolo flight training at night: § 61.87(c) and (m)

I certify that (First name, MI, Last name) has received the required presolo training in a (make and model aircraft). I have determined he/she has demonstrated the proficiency of § 61.87(m) and is proficient to make solo flights at night in a (make and model aircraft).

S/S [date] J.J. Jones 987654321CFI Exp. 12-31-00

4. Solo flight (each additional 90-day period): § 61.87(n)

I certify that (First name, MI, Last name) has received the required training to qualify for solo flying. I have determined he/she meets the applicable requirements of § 61.87(n) and is proficient to make solo flights in (make and model).

S/S [date] J.J. Jones 987654321CFI Exp. 12-31-00

5. Solo takeoffs and landings at another airport within 25 NM: § 61.93(b)(1)

I certify that (First name, MI, Last name) has received the required training of § 61.93(b)(1). I have determined that he/she is proficient to practice solo takeoffs and landings at (airport name). The takeoffs and landings at (airport name) are subject to the following conditions: (List any applicable conditions or limitations.)

S/S [date] J.J. Jones 987654321CFI Exp. 12-31-00

6. Initial solo cross-country flight: § 61.93(c)(1)

I certify that (First name, MI, Last name) has received the required solo cross-country training. I find he/she has met the applicable requirements of § 61.93, and is proficient to make solo cross-country flights in a (make and model aircraft).

S/S [date] J.J. Jones 987654321CFI Exp. 12-31-00

7. Solo cross-country flight: § 61.93(c)(2)

I have reviewed the cross-country planning of (First name, MI, Last name). I find the planning and preparation to be correct to make the solo flight from (location) to (destination) via (route of flight) with landings at (name the airports) in a (make and model aircraft) on (date). (List any applicable conditions or limitations.)

S/S [date] J.J. Jones 987654321CFI Exp. 12-31-00

8. Repeated solo cross-country flights not more than 50NM from the point of departure: § 61.93(b)(2)

I certify that (First name, MI, Last name) has received the required training in both directions between and at both (airport names). I have determined that he/she is proficient of § 61.93(b)(2) to conduct repeated solo cross-country flights over that route, subject to the following conditions: (List any applicable conditions or limitations.)

S/S [date] J.J. Jones 987654321CFI Exp. 12-31-00

9. Solo flight in Class B airspace: § 61.95(a)

I certify that (First name, MI, Last name) has received the required training of § 61.95(a). I have determined he/she is proficient to conduct solo flights in (name of Class B) airspace. (List any applicable conditions or limitations.)

S/S [date] J.J. Jones 987654321CFI Exp. 12-31-00

10. Solo flight to, from, or at an airport located in Class B airspace: §§ 61.95(a) and 91.131(b)(1)

I certify that (First name, MI, Last name) has received the required training of § 61.95(a)(1). I have determined that he/she is proficient to conduct solo flight operations at (name of airport). (List any applicable conditions or limitations.)

S/S [date] J.J. Jones 987654321CFI Exp. 12-31-00

RECREATIONAL PILOT ENDORSEMENTS

11. Aeronautical knowledge test: §§ 61.35(a)(1) and 61.96(b)(3)

I certify that (First name, MI, Last name) has received the required training of § 61.97(b). I have determined that he/she is prepared for the (name the knowledge test).

S/S [date] J.J. Jones 987654321CFI Exp. 12-31-00

12. Flight proficiency/practical test: §§ 61.96(b)(5), 61.98(a) and (b), and 61.99

I certify that (First name, MI, Last name) has received the required training of §§ 61.98(b) and 61.99. I have determined that he/she is prepared for the (name the practical test).

S/S [date] J.J. Jones 987654321CFI Exp. 12-31-00

13. Recreational pilot to operate within 50 NM of the airport where training was received: § 61.101(b)

I certify that (First name, MI, Last name) has received the required training of § 61.101(b). I have determined he/she is competent to operate at the (name of airport).

S/S [date] J.J. Jones 987654321CFI Exp. 12-31-00

14. Recreational pilot to act as PIC on a flight that exceeds 50 NM of the departure airport: § 61.101(c)

I certify that (First name, MI, Last name) has received the required cross-country training of § 61.101(c). I have determined that he/she is proficient in cross-country flying of Part 61, Subpart E.

S/S [date] J.J. Jones 987654321CFI Exp. 12-31-00

15. Recreational pilot with less than 400 flight hours and not logged PIC time within the preceding 180 days: § 61.101(f)

I certify that (First name, MI, Last name) has received the required 180-day recurrent training of § 61.101(f) in a (make and model aircraft). I have determined him/her proficient to act as PIC of that aircraft.

S/S [date] J.J. Jones 987654321CFI Exp. 12-31-00

16. Recreational pilot to conduct solo flights for the purpose of obtaining an additional certificate or rating while under the supervision of an authorized flight instructor: § 61.101(i)

I certify that (First name, MI, Last name) has received the required training of § 61.87 in a (make and model aircraft). I have determined he/she is prepared to conduct a solo flight on (date) under the following conditions: (List all conditions which require endorsement, e.g., flight which requires communication with ATC, flight in an aircraft for which the pilot does not hold a category/class rating, etc.).

S/S [date] J.J. Jones 987654321CFI Exp. 12-31-00

PRIVATE PILOT ENDORSEMENTS

17. Aeronautical knowledge test: §§ 61.35(a)(1), 61.103(d), and 61.105

I certify that (First name, MI, Last name) has received the required training of § 61.105. I have determined he/she is prepared for the (name the knowledge test).

S/S [date] J.J. Jones 987654321CFI Exp. 12-31-00

18. Flight proficiency/practical test: §§ 61.103(f), 61.107(b), and 61.109

I certify that (First name, MI, Last name) has received the required training of §§ 61.107 and 61.109. I have determined he/she is prepared for the (name the practical test).

S/S [date] J.J. Jones 987654321CFI Exp. 12-31-00

COMMERCIAL PILOT ENDORSEMENTS

19. Aeronautical knowledge test: §§ 61.35(a)(1) and 61.123(c)

I certify that (First name, MI, Last name) has received the required training of § 61.125. I have determined that he/she is prepared for the (name the knowledge test).

S/S [date] J.J. Jones 987654321CFI Exp. 12-31-00

20. Flight proficiency/practical test: §§ 61.123(e) and 61.127

I certify that (First name, MI, Last name) has received the required training of §§ 61.127 and 61.129. I have determined he/she is prepared for the (name the practical test).

S/S [date] J.J. Jones 987654321CFI Exp. 12-31-00

INSTRUMENT RATING ENDORSEMENTS

21. Aeronautical knowledge test: §§ 61.35(a)(1) and 61.65(a) and (b)

I certify that (First name, MI, Last name) has received the required training of § 61.65(b). I have determined that he/she is prepared for the (name the knowledge test).

S/S [date] J.J. Jones 987654321CFI Exp. 12-31-00

22. Flight proficiency/practical test: § 61.65(a)(6)

I certify that (First name, MI, Last name) has received the required training of § 61.65(c) and (d). I have determined he/she is prepared for the Instrument - (*Airplane, Helicopter, or Powered-lift*) practical test.

S/S [date] J. J. Jones 987654321CFI Exp. 12-31-00

FLIGHT INSTRUCTOR ENDORSEMENTS

23. Fundamentals of instructing knowledge test: §§ 61.183(d) and 61.185(a)(1)

I certify that (First name, MI, Last name) has received the required fundamentals of instruction training of § 61.185(a)(1).

S/S [date] J.J. Jones 987654321CFI Exp. 12-31-00

24. Flight instructor ground and flight proficiency/practical test: §§ 61.183(g) and 61.187(a) and (b)

I certify that (First name, MI, Last name) has received the required training of § 61.187(b). I have determined he/she is prepared for the CFI - (*aircraft category and class*) practical test.

S/S [date] J.J. Jones 987654321CFI Exp. 12-31-00

25. Flight instructor certificate with instrument - (category/class) rating/practical test: §§ 61.183(g) and 61.187(a) and (b)(7)

I certify that (First name, MI, Last name) has received the required CFII training of § 61.187(b)(7). I have determined he/she is prepared for the CFII - (*airplane, helicopter, or powered-lift*) practical test.

S/S [date] J.J. Jones 987654321CFI Exp. 12-31-00

26. Spin training: § 61.183(i)(1)

I certify that (First name, MI, Last name) has received the required training of § 61.183(i). I have determined that he/she is competent and proficient in instructional skills for training stall awareness, spin entry, spins, and spin recovery procedures.

S/S [date] J.J. Jones 987654321CFI Exp. 12-31-00

NOTE: The above spin training endorsement is required of flight instructor applicants for the airplane and glider ratings only.

GROUND INSTRUCTOR ENDORSEMENT

27. Ground instructor who does not meet the recent experience requirements: § 61.217(b)

I certify that (First name, MI, Last name) has demonstrated satisfactory proficiency on the appropriate ground instructor knowledge and training subjects of § 61.213(a)(3) and (a)(4).

S/S [date] J.J. Jones 987654321CFI Exp. 12-31-00 [*or CGI, as appropriate]
(*The expiration date would apply only to a CFI.*)

ADDITIONAL ENDORSEMENTS

28. Completion of a flight review: § 61.56(a) and (c)

I certify that (First name, MI, Last name), (pilot certificate), (certificate number), has satisfactorily completed a flight review of § 61.56(a) on (date).

S/S [date] J.J. Jones 987654321CFI Exp. 12-31-00

NOTE: No logbook entry reflecting unsatisfactory performance on a flight review is required.

29. Completion of a phase of an FAA-sponsored pilot proficiency award program (WINGS): § 61.56(e)

I certify that (First name, MI, Last name), (pilot certificate), (certificate number), has satisfactorily completed Phase No. ___ of a WINGS program on (date).

S/S [date] J.J. Jones 987654321CFI Exp. 12-31-00

30. Completion of an instrument proficiency check: § 61.57(d)

I certify that (First name, MI, Last name), (pilot certificate), (certificate number), has satisfactorily completed the instrument proficiency check of § 61.57(d) in a (list make and model of aircraft) on (date).

S/S [date] J. J. Jones 987654321CFI Exp. 12-31-00

NOTE: No logbook entry reflecting unsatisfactory performance on an instrument proficiency check is required.

31. To act as PIC in a complex airplane: § 61.31(e)

I certify that (First name, MI, Last name), (pilot certificate), (certificate number), has received the required training of § 61.31(e) in a (make and model of complex airplane). I have determined that he/she is proficient in the operation and systems of a complex airplane.

S/S [date] J.J. Jones 987654321CFI Exp. 12-31-00

32. To act as PIC in a high performance airplane: § 61.31(f)

I certify that (First name, MI, Last name), (pilot certificate), (certificate number), has received the required training of § 61.31(f) in a (make and model of high performance airplane). I have determined that he/she is proficient in the operation and systems of a high performance airplane.

S/S [date] J.J. Jones 987654321CFI Exp. 12-31-00

33. To act as PIC in a pressurized aircraft capable of high-altitude operations: § 61.31(g)

I certify that (First name, MI, Last name), (pilot certificate), (certificate number), has received the required training of § 61.31(g) in a (make and model of pressurized aircraft). I have determined that he/she is proficient in the operation and systems of a pressurized aircraft.

S/S [date] J.J. Jones 987654321CFI Exp. 12-31-00

34. To act as PIC in a tailwheel airplane: § 61.31(i)

I certify that (First name, MI, Last name), (pilot certificate), (certificate number), has received the required training of § 61.31(i) in a (make and model of tailwheel airplane). I have determined that he/she is proficient in the operation of a tailwheel airplane.

S/S [date] J.J. Jones 987654321CFI Exp. 12-31-00

35. To act as PIC of an aircraft in solo operations when the pilot who does not hold an appropriate category/class rating: § 61.31(d)(3)

I certify that (First name, MI, Last name) has received the training as required by § 61.31(d)(3) to serve as a PIC in a (category and class of aircraft). I have determined that he/she is prepared to serve as PIC in that (make and model of aircraft).

S/S [date] J.J. Jones 987654321CFI Exp. 12-31-00

36. Retesting after failure of a knowledge or practical test: § 61.49.

I certify that (First name, MI, Last name) has received the additional (flight and/or ground) training as required by § 61.49. I have determined that he/she is prepared for the (name the knowledge/practical test).

S/S [date] J.J. Jones 987654321CFI Exp. 12-31-00

NOTE: In the case of a failed knowledge test, the instructor may complete the endorsement in the space provided at the bottom of the applicant's airman knowledge test report. The instructor must sign the block provided for the instructor's recommendation on the reverse side of FAA Form 8710-1 application for each retake of a practical test.

37. Additional aircraft category or class rating (other than ATP): § 61.63(b) or (c)

I certify that (First name, MI, Last name), (pilot certificate), (certificate number), has received the required training for an additional (name the aircraft category/class rating). I have determined that he/she is prepared for the (name the practical test) for the addition of a (name the aircraft category/class rating).

S/S [date] J.J. Jones 987654321CFI Exp. 12-31-00

38. Type rating only, already holds the appropriate category or class rating (other than ATP): § 61.63(d)(2) and (3)

I certify that (First name, MI, Last name) has received the required training of § 61.63(d)(2) and (3) for an addition of a (name the type rating).

S/S [date] J.J. Jones 987654321CFI Exp. 12-31-00

39. Type rating concurrently with an additional category or class rating (other than ATP): § 61.63(d)(2) and (3)

I certify that (First name, MI, Last name) has received the required training of § 61.63(d)(2) and (3) for an addition of a (name the category/class/type rating). I have determined that he/she is prepared for the (name the practical test) for the addition of a (name the aircraft category/class/type rating).

S/S [date] J.J. Jones 987654321CFI Exp. 12-31-00

40. Type rating only, already holds the appropriate category or class rating (at the ATP level): § 61.157(b)(1)

I certify that (First name, MI, Last name) has received the required training of § 61.157(b)(1) for an addition of a (name the type rating).

S/S [date] J.J. Jones 987654321CFI Exp. 12-31-00

41. Type rating concurrently with an additional category or class rating (at the ATP level): § 61.157(b)(1)

I certify that (First name, MI, Last name) has received the required training of § 61.157(b)(1) for an addition of a (name the category/class/type rating).

S/S [date] J.J. Jones 987654321CFI Exp. 12-31-00

42. Launch procedures for operating a glider: § 61.31(j)

I certify that (First name, MI, Last name), (pilot certificate), (certificate number), has received the required training in a (list the glider make and model) for (list the launch procedure). I have determined that he/she is proficient in (list the launch procedure).

S/S [date] J.J. Jones 987654321CFI Exp. 12-31-00

43. Review of a home study curriculum: § 61.35(a)(1)

I certify I have reviewed the home study curriculum of (First name, MI, Last name). I have determined he/she is prepared for the (name the knowledge test).

S/S [date] J.J. Jones 987654321CFI Exp. 12-31-00

Name: ______________________________

CHAPTER 1
ANSWER SHEET

SECTION A

1. ______________________________

2. ______________________________

3. ____________

4. ______________________________

5. ______________________________

6. ________

7. ______________________________

8. ______________________________

____
____
____

9. ________
10. ______
11. ______
12. ______
13. ______
14. ______
15. ______

SECTION B

1. ______________________________
____
2. ________
3. ______
4. ______________________________
____
____
5. ______
6. ______________________________
____
____
____
7. ________
8. ______

SECTION C

1. ______________________________
____
____
2. ________
3. ______________________________
____
4. ______________________________
____
5. ______
6. ______
7. ________
8. ______
9. ______

Name: ____________________

CHAPTER 2
ANSWER SHEET

SECTION A

1. ______
2. ____________________
3. ______
4. ____________________
5. __________
6. ____________________
7. __________
8. ______

SECTION B

1. ______
2. __________
3. ____________________
4. ____________________
5. ______
6. ____________________
7. ______
8. __________
9. ______
10. ____________________
11. ______
12. ____________________

SECTION C

1. ______________________________
____
____
____
____
2. ______
3. ______
4. ______
5. ______________________________
____
____
____
6. __________
7. __________
8. __________
9. ______
10. ______

SECTION D

1. ______________________________
____
____
____
____
2. __________
3. ______________________________
____
____
4. __________
5. ______
6. ______
7. __________
8. ______________________________
____
9. __________
10. ______________________________
____
____
____

Name: ____________________

CHAPTER 3
ANSWER SHEET

SECTION A

1. ____________________
2. ________
3. ____
4. ____
5. ____
6. ____
7. ____
8. ____
9. ____
10. ____
11. ____________________
12. ____________________

SECTION B

1. ____________________
2. ____________________

3. ____________

4. ______________________________

____

____

____

5. ______________________________

____

____

____

6. ______

7. ______________________________

____

____

8. ______________________________

____

9. ______________________________

____

____

____

10. ______________________________

____

____

____

11. ______________________________

____

____

____

____

12. ____________

13. ______

14. ______________________________

____

15. ______________________________

____

____

____

____

____

____

16. ______

17. ______________________________

____

Name: ______________________________

CHAPTER 4
ANSWER SHEET

SECTION A

1. __________
2. _____
3. ______________________________
4. ______________________________
5. _____

SECTION B

1. _____
2. ______________________________
3. ______________________________
4. ______________________________
5. __________
6. _____
7. __________
8. ______________________________
9. __________
10. _____
11. __________
12. ______________________________
13. ______________________________

SECTION C

1. ______________________________

2. ______________
3. ________
4. ____

____

____
5. ____

____

____
6. ____

____

____
7. ______________
8. ________

SECTION D

1. ____

____

____
2. ________
3. ____

____

____
4. ______________
5. ______________
6. ____

____

____
7. ______________
8. ________
9. ______________
10. ____

____

____
11. ______________
12. ________
13. ____

____

____
14. ______________
15. ________
16. ____

____

Name: ____________________

CHAPTER 5
ANSWER SHEET

SECTION A

1. ____________________
2. ____________________
3. ____________________
4. ________
5. ____________________
6. ____________
7. ____________________
8. ____________________

SECTION B

1. ____________
2. ________
13. ________
4. ____________________
5. ______________
6. ____________________
7. ____________________
8. ______________
9. ________
10. ____________________
11. ____________________
12. ____________________
13. ______________
14. ____________________
15. ______________
16. ____________________

SECTION C

1. ______________

2. ____________________

3. ____________________

4. ____________________
5. ____________________

6. ________
7. ________
8. ________
9. ____________________

10. ____________________

SECTION D

1. ____________________
2. ________
3. ________
4. ________
5. ________
6. ________
7. ________
8. ________
9. ________
10. ________

SECTION E

1. ________
2. ________
3. ________
4. ________
5. ________
6. ________

SECTION F

1. ________
2. ________
3. ____________________

4. ________
5. ________
6. ________
7. ____________________
8. ________
9. ________
10. ________
11. ____________________

12. ________
13. ____________________

Name: ______________________________

CHAPTER 6
ANSWER SHEET

SECTION A

1. ______________________________

2. ______________________________

3. ______________________________

4. ______________________________

5. ______________________________

6. ______________________________

7. ______

8. ______________________________

SECTION B

1. ______________________________

2. ______________

3. ______________

4. ______________________________

5. ______

6. ______________________________

7. ______________________________

8. ______

9. ______________

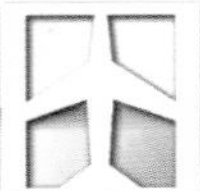

SECTION C

1. __________
2. ______________
3. ____
4. ____

   ____
5. __________
6. ____

   ____

   ____
7. __________
8. __________
9. ____

   ____

   ____
10. ______________
11. ________
12. ____

    ____

    ____

SECTION D

1. ____

   ____

   ____
2. ________
3. ______________
4. ________
5. ________
6. ________
7. ________
8. ________
9. ______________
10. ____

    ____
11. ________
12. ____

    ____

    ____
13. ________
14. ____

    ____

INDEX

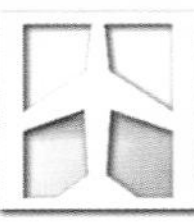

JEPPESEN REFERENCE MATERIALS

AVIATION WEATHER 2ND EDITION

The most compehensive, award-winning aviation weather book just got better. New 480-page hard cover edition is extensively updated with the latest METAR, TAF, and Graphic Weather Products from AC00-45E, Aviation Weather Services. Full-color illustrations and photographs present detailed material in an uncomplicated way. International weather considerations are included as well as accident/incident information to add relevance to the weather data. Expanded coverage of icing, weather hazards, and flight planning. Review questions with answers at the end of the book. All new expanded appendices cover common conversions, weather reports, forecasts, and charts, as well as domestic and international METAR, TAF and graphic weather products. Completely revised Instructor's Guide available on CD-ROM (for flight school use only.)

ITEM NUMBER JS319010 $54.95

JEPPPREP

Now students can prepare for their FAA knowledge exams on the internet. With the purchase of JeppPrep, you will receive a 60-day period of unlimited study for a particular FAA knowledge exam. A renewal can be purchased for each additional 30-day period for an additional charge. JeppPrep contains the latest FAA questions taken from the FAA database, so it is always current. Pilots can take practice FAA exams and review their performance once the exams are scored

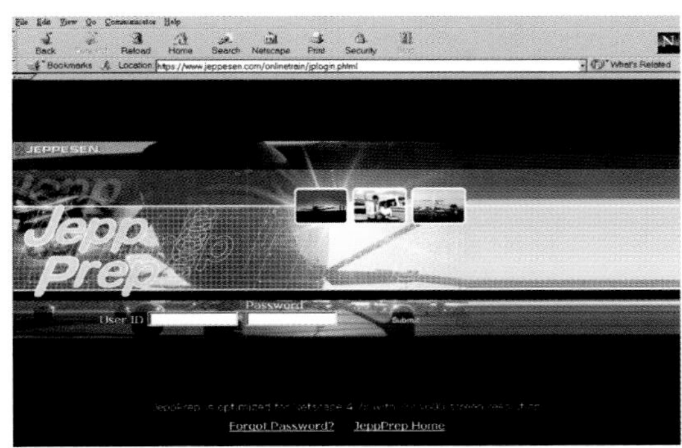

ITEM NUMBER WB100500 JEPPPREP INITIAL ORDER $49.95
ITEM NUMBER WB100543 JEPPPREP 30-DAY RENEWAL $19.95

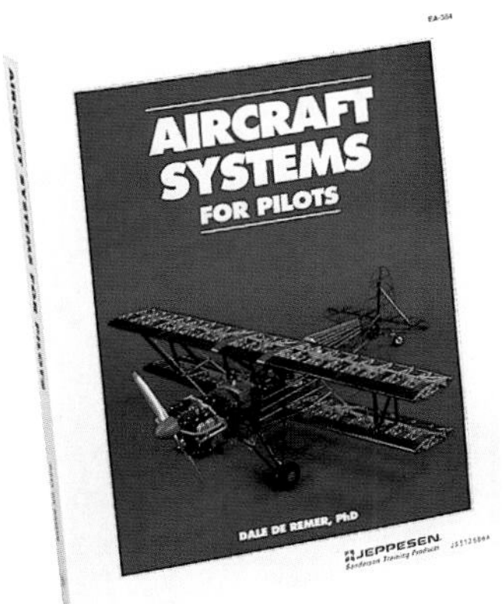

AIRCRAFT SYSTEMS FOR PILOTS

The most comprehensive book available on aircraft systems as they relate to pilots and pilot training. All systems types are covered in detail. Contains excellent descriptions of aircraft systems for all pilots. ISBN#0-8487-214-9. 450 pages.

ITEM NUMBER JS312686 $26.95

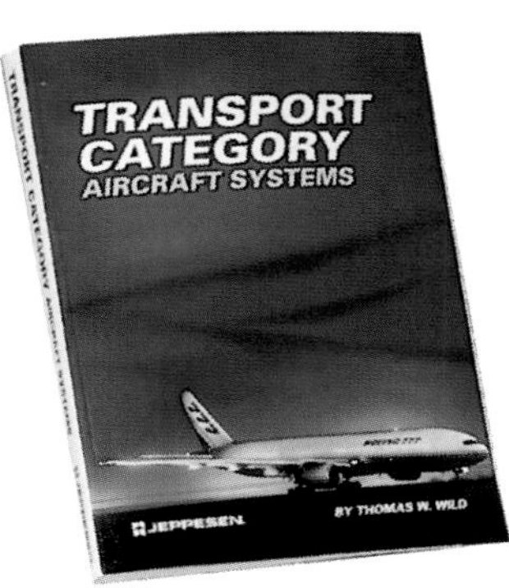

TRANSPORT CATEGORY AIRCRAFT SYSTEMS

The only text available that covers FAR part 121 aircraft. A system-by-system approach to understanding jet transports. Includes systems coverage on the B-777 aircraft. Necessary for A&P students and pilots seeking at ATP license. ISBN#0-88487-232-7. 396 pages.

ITEM NUMBER JS312631 $28.95

Individual Training Books

Aviation History by Jeppesen

Announcing an exciting new full-color book that gives both new and experienced pilots a unique perspective on international aviation history. Each of the ten chapters is packed with information, containing over 950 photographs and color illustrations to guide you through the birth of aviation in the 1700s to the recent record-setting flight of the Breitling Orbiter 3.

Item Number JS319008 $68.00

FAR's Explained

Jeppesen *FAR's Explained* has quickly become an industry standard. It helps answer the question, " I know what it says, but what does it mean?" Includes FAR Parts 1, 61, 91, 141, and NTSB 830. Recently updated and expanded.

Item Number JS319012 $29.95

FAA Reference Handbooks

Aviation Instructor's Handbook

Supercedes AC 60-14. Contains fundamentals of instructing and extensive details on how to pass along aeronautical knowledge and skills to students.

Item Number JS312802 $17.95

Airplane Flying Handbook

Supercedes AC 61-21A. Introduces basic pilot skills and aeronautical knowledge to student pilots. It is beneficial for students and flight instructors who wish to improve their flying proficiency and aeronautical knowledge.

Item Number JS312801 $22.95

Rotorcraft Flying Handbook

Supercedes AC 60-13B. Includes complete illustrated coverage of how to fly helicopters and gyroplanes. It provides authoritative technical information for applicants preparing for private, commercial and flight instructor pilot certificates with helicopter or gyroplane class ratings.

Item Number JS312806 $24.00

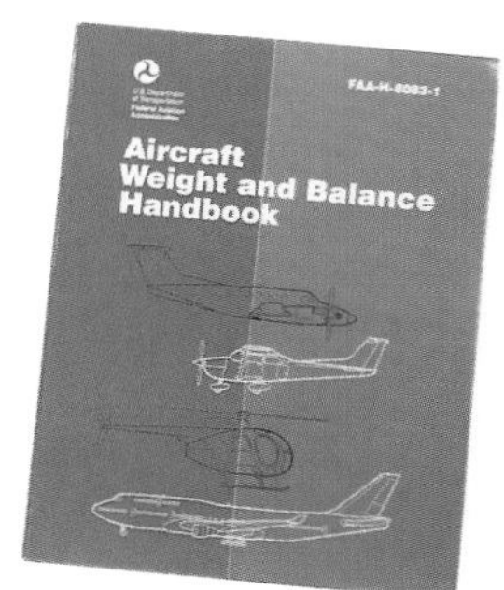

Aircraft Weight & Balance Handbook

Supercedes AC 91-23A. Provides AMT's with a method of determining the empty weight and empty-weight center of gravity (EWCG) of an aircraft and to furnish the basic crew with information on loading the aircraft within allowable limits.

Item Number JS312800 $12.95

Visit Your Jeppesen Dealer or Call 1-800-621-5377
Make sure to check out our web page at HTTP://WWW.JEPPESEN.COM
Prices subject to change.

Pilot Supplies

TechStar Pro and DataLink

Jeppesen's "Next Generation" Aviation Computer

Jeppesen's innovative TechStar Pro is the first handheld flight computer and personal organizer. Combining the latest technology and ease of use, TechStar Pro gives you a 7-function aviation computer and an 8-function personal organizer. All-in-one compact handheld unit. Students to Airline Transport Pilots, use it in the cockpit, home, office or classroom.

TechStar Pro
Item Number JS505000 $149.95

Datalink sold separately.

TechStar Pro DataLink Software and Cable

- Simple to use - Windows 3.1 or higher
- Backup data on your Techstar Pro
- Edit, add and delete records from your PC and then download the records
- Save time when inputting data

DataLink Item Number JS505050 $16.95

Fuel Tester

The last fuel tester you'll ever need! Strong, clear butyrate plastic resists cracking, breaking and yellowing. Works with both pin and petcock actuators. Removable splash guard prevents fuel spillage and attaches to side for flat, slimline storage. Solid bronze rod actuator prevents breaking and pushing down. Measures 8.25″ x 3.25″ x 1″.

Fuel Tester Item Number JS628855 $12.95

JeppShades

IFR Flip-Up Training Glasses

- Replaces bulky, hard-to-use instrument training hoods
- Improved design allows better student/instructor interaction
- Cockpit proven design works conveniently under headsets
- Universal adjusting strap reduces pressure on ears and temple
- Velcro™ strap fits comfortably under headsets • Flip-Up lens allows convenient IFR/VFR flight transition • High quality polycarbonate lens is impact resistant

JeppShades Item Number JS404311 $24.95

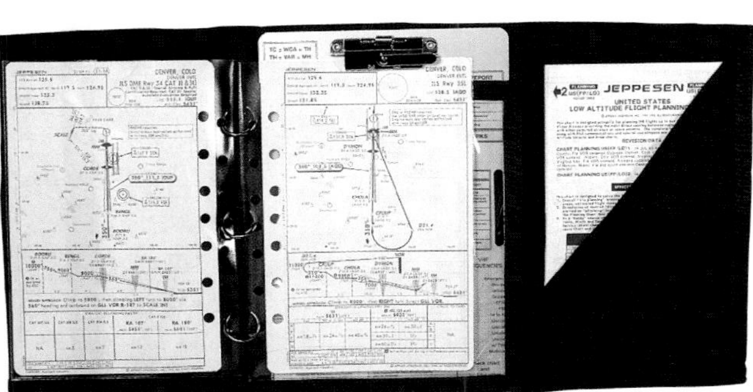

Three-Ring Trifold Kneeboard

• Great for holding approach charts • Valuable IFR flight information on clipboard (also available separately) • Includes three approach chart pockets • Features collapsible rings • Elastic, pen/pencil and penlight holder • Includes Free U.S. Low Flight Planning Chart!
• Measures 10" x 20" open

Kneeboard/Clipboard
Item Number JS626010 $39.95

Clipboard Only
Item Number JS626011 $15.95

Visit Your Jeppesen Dealer or Call 1-800-621-5377
Make sure to check out our web page at http://www.jeppesen.com
Prices subject to change.

Introducing Jeppesen Flight Bags

The Captain Flight Bag

The Jeppesen *Captain Flight Bag* is the most versatile bag available. The headset bags can be removed and attached together to form a dual headset bag. The removable Transceiver/GPS bag can be worn on your belt. The flexible design allows you to add or subtract components to match your flying needs. The roomy interior has a 4-way custom divider that can hold four Jeppesen binders. An exterior zippered pocket provides a convenient storage space to help pilots organize their supplies. Two large zippered storage pockets can hold glasses, charts, pilot operating handbooks and other miscellaneous accessories. Carry your supplies in comfort with a wide cushioned shoulder strap. 12″x22 1/2″x8″

The Captain Flight Bag (Black or Blue)
Item Number JS621214 (Black) $139.95
Item Number JS621251 (Blue) $139.95

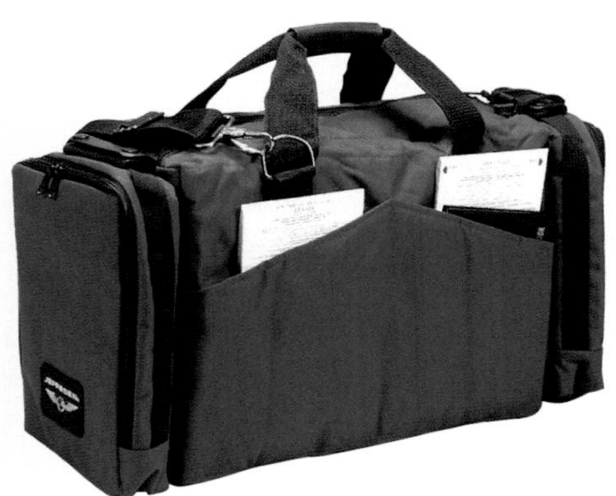

The Navigator Flight Bag

The *Navigator Flight Bag* includes all of the features and benefits of the Captain Flight Bag, except the removable Transceiver/GPS bag and the two zippered exterior storage pockets. Instead, it includes two exterior pockets for easy access to sectional and world aeronautical charts. 12″x22 1/2″x8″

The Navigator Flight Bag (Black or Blue)
Item Number JS621213 (Black) $99.95
Item Number JS621250 (Blue) $99.95

The Protector Headset Bags

The *Protector Headset Bags* are constructed of fully padded 600 denier poly for extra protection. Each bag comes with its own snap-on handle grip for comfort. Large enough to fit the ANR headsets (12″x2 3/4″x8″). Offered in both a single and dual configuration. Designed to fit the Core Captain Flight Bag.

The Protector Headset Bags (Black)
Single JS621220 $17.95
Dual JS621219 $34.95

The Student Pilot Flight Bag

The *Student Pilot Flight Bag* is designed for new student pilots. Numerous outside pockets will organize charts, flight computer, fuel tester, plotter, pens and pencils, flashlight and much more. Additional features include a wide removable shoulder strap for comfort and a reinforced bottom. 10″x5 1/2″x17″

The Student Pilot Flight Bag (Black)
Item Number JS621212 $39.95

New! The Aviator Bag

The *Aviator Bag* is constructed of fully padded vynlon for extra durability. Each bag includes one headset bag and one Transceiver/GPS bag. The interior has a 2-way divider that can be used to separate your pilot accessories.

The Aviator Bag (Black)
Item Number JS621252 $79.95

Visit Your Jeppesen Dealer or Call 1-800-621-5377
Make sure to check out our web page at http://www.jeppesen.com
Prices subject to change.